The Earthscan Reader on NGO Management

Edited by

Michael Edwards
and
Alan Fowler

publishing for a sustainable future

London • Sterling, VA

First published in the UK and USA in 2002 by
Earthscan Publications Ltd
Reprinted 2004, 2006, 2008

ISBN: 978-1-85383-848-4 paperback

Typesetting by Composition and Design Services (www.cdsca.com)
Printed and bound by The Cromwell Press Ltd, Trowbridge, Wiltshire
Cover design by Andrew Corbett

For a full list of publications please contact:

Earthscan
Dunstan House, 14a St Cross Street
London, EC1N 8XA, UK
Tel: +44 (0)20 7841 1930
Fax: +44 (0)20 7242 1474
Email: earthinfo@earthscan.co.uk
Web: www.earthscan.co.uk

22883 Quicksilver Drive, Sterling, VA 20166–2012, USA

A catalogue record for this book is available from the British Library

Library of Congress Cataloging in Publication data applied for

Earthscan publishes in association with the International Institute for Environment
and Development

The paper used for the text pages of this book is FSC
certified. FSC (the Forest Stewardship Council) is an
international network to promote responsible management of the world's forests.

Mixed Sources
Product group from well-managed
forests and other controlled sources
www.fsc.org Cert no. TT-TOC-2082
© 1996 Forest Stewardship Council

This book is printed on totally chlorine-free paper

Contents

Part 4   Strengthening Governance and Accountability

Part 5   Organizing for Good Development Practice: Participation, Empowerment, Partnering and Capacity-building

Part 6   Measuring Achievement: Approaches and Methods

Part 7   Becoming a Learning Organization

Part 8   Mobilizing Resources and Sustaining the Organization

Part 9   Dealing with Gender

Part 10   Human Resources: Their Management, Development and Leadership

List of Tables, Figures and Boxes

Tables

Figures

Boxes

List of Contributors

Jeffrey Avina is the UN resident coordinator and the UNDP resident representative for Honduras.

Lisa Cannon is an author and international consultant specializing in organizational sustainability work with NGOs in Africa, Asia, Latin America and Eastern Europe.

Frances Cleaver works at the Bradford Centre for International Development at the University of Bradford.

Michael Edwards is director of the Ford Foundation's Governance and Civil Society Unit in New York.

Julie Fisher is a programme officer at the Kettering Foundation in Dayton, Ohio, specializing in NGOs and microfinance development.

Alan Fowler is an independent development adviser, co-founder of the International NGO Training and Research Centre and vice president of the International Society for Third Sector Research.

John Gaventa is a fellow at the Institute of Development Studies at the University of Sussex.

Anne Marie Goetz is a fellow at the Institute of Development Studies at the University of Sussex.

David Hulme is professor of development studies at the Institute for Development Policy and Management of the University of Manchester.

Lisa Jordan is programme officer on global civil society in the Ford Foundation's Governance and Civil Society Unit in New York.

Allan Kaplan is a director and consultant with the Community Development Resource Association in South Africa.

Bonnie L Koenig is president of Going International, an organization working on international programme development and strategic planning services for nonprofit organizations in the US.

Adil Najam is an assistant professor in the Department of International Relations at Boston University.

Peter Raynard is an independent researcher whose work covers the social, ethical, environmental and financial performance of private non-profit organizations.

Marion Ritchey-Vance served as representative for Colombia, regional director for the Andean region and learning coordinator for the Inter-American Foundation over a span of 21 years.

Gita Sen is a professor specializing in population and international health at the Indian Institute of Management in Bangalore.

Ellen Sprenger is coordinator of the Oxfam International Gender and Diversity Working Group.

Rajesh Tandon is founder and president of the Society for Participatory Research in Asia (PRIA) based in Delhi.

James Taylor works as a consultant for the Community Development Resource Association in South Africa.

Davine Thaw has been a leader in the South African NGO sector for over 21 years and currently works as an independent OD practitioner, frequently in association with Olive (OD and Training).

Peter van Tuijl is adviser on governance for the United Nations Development Programme in Indonesia.

Dennis R Young is a professor specializing in nonprofit management and the economics of nonprofit organizations at the Case Western Reserve University in Cleveland, Ohio.

Simon Zadek is the chief executive of the Institute of Social and Ethical AccountAbility in London.

List of Sources

The editors and publisher would like to acknowledge, with thanks, permission to reproduce the following chapters:

Chapter 1: Alan Fowler, 'NGO Futures – Beyond Aid: NGDO Values and the Fourth Position', in Alan Fowler (ed), *Third World Quarterly*, Special Issue, Vol 21, No 4, pp589–603, August. © Carfax Publishing, 2000.

Chapter 2: Michael Edwards, 'International Development NGOs: Agents of Foreign Aid or Vehicles for International Cooperation?', *Nonprofit and Voluntary Sector Quaterly*, Special Issue, Vol 28, No 4, Supplement 1999, pp25–37, reprinted by permission of Sage Publications. © Sage Publications, Inc., 1999.

Chapter 3: Michael Edwards and Gita Sen, 'NGOs, Social Change and the Transformation of Human Relationships: A 21st Century Civic Agenda', in Alan Fowler (ed), *Third World Quarterly*, Special Issue, Vol 21, No 4, pp605–616, August. © Carfax Publishing, 2000.

Chapter 4: Michael Edwards and David Hulme, 'Making a Difference: Scaling-up the Developmental Impact of NGOs – Concepts and Experiences', in Michael Edwards and David Hulme (eds), *Making a Difference: NGOs and Development in a Changing World*. © Earthscan Publications Limited, 1992.

Chapter 5: Alan Fowler, 'Organizing Non-profits for Development', in Alan Fowler, *Striking a Balance: A Guide to Enhancing the Effectiveness of Non-Governmental Organisations in International Development*. © Earthscan Publications Limited, 1997.

Chapter 6: Michael Edwards, '"Does the Doormat Influence the Boot?" Critical Thoughts on UK NGOs and International Advocacy', *Development in Practice*, Vol 3, No 3, pp163–175, reproduced with permission of Oxfam Publishing, 274 Banbury Road, Oxford, OX2 7DZ. © Oxfam Publishing, 1993.

Chapter 7: Lisa Jordan and Peter van Tuijl, 'Political Responsibility in Transnational NGO Advocacy', *World Development*, Vol 28, No 12, pp2051–2065, reprinted with permission of Elsevier Science. © Elsevier Science Limited, 2000.

Chapter 8: Jeffrey Avina, 'The Evolutionary Life-cycles of Non-governmental Development Organizations', *Public Administration and Development*, Vol 13, No 5,

Chapter 9: Davine Thaw, 'Stepping into the River of Change', *Ideas for a Change*, Part 3, July 1998. © Olive Publications, Durban, SA, 1998.

Chapter 10: Dennis R Young, Bonnie L Koenig, Adil Najam and Julie Fisher, 'Strategy and Structure in Managing Global Associations', *Voluntas: International Journal of Voluntary and Nonprofit Organizations*, Vol 10, No 4, pp323–344. © International Society for Third-Sector Research/The Johns Hopkins University/Kluwer Academic Pulishers, 1999.

Chapter 11: Michael Edwards and David Hulme, 'NGO Performance and Accountability: Introduction and Overview', in Michael Edwards and David Hulme (eds), *NGOs – Performance and Accountability: Beyond the Magic Bullet.* © Earthscan Publications Limited, 1995.

Chapter 12: Michael Edwards and David Hulme, 'Beyond the Magic Bullet: Lessons and Conclusions', in Michael Edwards and David Hulme (eds), *NGOs – Performance and Accountability: Beyond the Magic Bullet.* © Earthscan Publications Limited, 1995.

Chapter 13: Rajesh Tandon, '"Board Games": Governance and Accountability in NGOs', in Michael Edwards and David Hulme (eds), *NGOs – Performance and Accountability: Beyond the Magic Bullet.* © Earthscan Publications Limited, 1995.

Chapter 14: Frances Cleaver, 'Paradoxes of Participation: Questioning Participatory Approaches to Development', *Journal of International Development*, Vol 11, No 4, pp597–612. © DSA/John Wiley & Sons, Ltd, 1999.

Chapter 15: Alan Fowler, 'Beyond Partnership: Getting Real about NGO Relationships in the Aid System', in Alan Fowler (ed), *IDS Bulletin: Questioning Partnership – The Reality of Aid and NGO Relations*, Vol 31, No 3, pp1–13. © Institute of Development Studies, 2000.

Chapter 16: John Gaventa, 'Crossing the Great Divide: Building Links and Learning between NGOs and Community-based Organizations in the North and South', in David Lewis (ed), *International Perspectives on Voluntary Action.* © Earthscan Publications Limited, 1999.

Chapter 17: Michael Edwards, 'NGO Performance: What Breeds Success? New Evidence from South Asia', *World Development*, Vol 27, No 2, pp361–374, reprinted with permission of Elsevier Science. © Elsevier Science Ltd, 1999.

Chapter 18: Alan Fowler, 'Assessing NGO Performance: Difficulties, Dilemmas and a Way Ahead', in Michael Edwards and David Hulme (eds), *NGOs – Performance and Accountability: Beyond the Magic Bullet.* © Earthscan Publications Limited, 1995.

Chapter 19: Marion Ritchey-Vance, 'Social Capital, Sustainability and Working Democracy: New Yardsticks for Grassroots Development', *Grassroots Development*, Vol 20, No 1. © Inter-American Foundation, 1996.

Chapter 20: Simon Zadek and Peter Raynard, 'Accounting for Change: The Practice of Social Auditing', *Accounting Forum*, Vol 19, Nos 2–3, December 1995. © New Economics Foundation, 1995.

Chapter 21: Michael Edwards, 'Organizational Learning in Non-governmental Organizations: What Have We Learned?', *Public Administration and Development*, Vol 17, No 2, pp235–250. © John Wiley & Sons, 1999.

Chapter 22: James Taylor, 'On the Road to Becoming a Learning Organization', *OD Debate*, Vol 5, No 5, pp3–7, October 1998. © Olive Publications, Durban, SA, 1998.

Chapter 23: Alan Fowler, 'An NGDO Strategy: Learning for Leverage', in Alan Fowler, *Striking a Balance: A Guide to Enhancing the Effectiveness of Non-governmental Organisations in International Development.* © Earthscan Publictions Limited, 1997.

Chapter 24: Lisa Cannon, 'Defining Sustainability', *OD Debate*, Vol 6, No 1, pp12–13, February 1999. © Olive Publictions, Durban, SA, 1999.

Chapter 25: Alan Fowler, 'Options, Strategies and Trade-offs in Resource Mobilization', in Alan Fowler, *The Virtuous Spiral: A Guide to Sustainability for NGOs in International Development.* © Earthscan Publications Limited, 2000.

Chapter 26: Anne Marie Goetz, 'Getting Institutions Right for Women in Development', in Anne Marie Goetz (ed), *Getting Institutions Right for Women in Development.* © Zed Books, 1997.

Chapter 27: Alan Fowler, 'The Role of Gender in NGDOs', in Alan Fowler, *Striking a Balance: A Guide to Enhancing the Effectiveness of Non-governmental Organizations in International Development.* © Earthscan Publications Limited, 1997.

Chapter 28: Ellen Sprenger, 'Organizational Gender Diagnosis', *OD Debate*, Vol 5, No 1, pp17–19. © Olive Publications, Durban, SA, 1998.

Chapter 29: Allan Kaplan, 'Leadership and Management', AVOCADO Series, No 1(98). © Olive Publications, Durban, SA, 1998.

Chapter 30: Alan Fowler, 'Human Resource Management', in Alan Fowler, *Striking a Balance: A Guide to Enhancing the Effectiveness of Non-governmental Organizations in International Development.* © Earthscan Publications Limited, 1997.

List of Acronyms and Abbreviations

ABB	Asea Brown Boveri
BAS	beyond-aid scenarios
BOAG	British Overseas Aid Group
BRAC	Bangladesh Rural Advancement Committee
BWI	Bretton Woods Institution
CA	change agent
CBO	community-based organization
CEO	Chief Executive Officer
CEPES	Centro Peru de Estudios Sociales (Peruvian Centre for Social Studies)
Cida	Canadian International Development Agency
CITES	Convention on International Trade in Endangered Species
DAC	Development Assistance Committee
DESCO	Centro de Estudio y Promoción del Desarollo
EU	European Union
FAO	Food and Agriculture Organization
FDI	foreign direct investment
FONCAP	Fondo de Capital Social (Social Capital Fiduciary Fund of Argentina)
GAD	gender in development
GMO	genetically modified organism
GNP	gross national product
GRO	grassroots organization
HRD	human resource development
HRM	human resource management
IAF	Inter-American Foundation
IAVE	International Association for Volunteer Effort
ICDS	Integrated Child Development Services
ICS	In-Country Support
IES	Income Enhancement Scheme
IMF	International Monetary Fund
IRED	Innovations et Research pour le Developpement
LFA	Logical Framework Analysis
NAFTA	North American Free Trade Agreement
NGDO	non-governmental development organization
NGO	non-governmental organization
NICS	Newly Industrialized Countries
NIE	New Institutional Economics
NNGO	Northern non-governmental organization

ODA	Overseas Development Administration
OECD	Organisation for Economic Co-operation and Development
OOIP	Objective Oriented Intervention Planning
PAIR	Program for Integrated Use of Natural Resources
PEC	Primary Environmental Care
PO	People's Organization
PR	participatory research
PRA	participatory rural appraisal
PREM	People's Rural Education Movement
PRIA	participatory research in India
SCF	Save the Children Fund
SEWA	Self-Employed Women's Association
Sida	Swedish International Development Agency
SNGO	Southern non-governmental organization
TA	transactional analysis
TIRN	Tennessee Industrial Renewal Network
UNCED	United Nations Conference on Environment and Development
UNDP	United Nations Development Programme
UNICEF	United Nations (International) Children's (Emergency) Fund
USAID	United States Agency for International Development
WHO	World Health Organization
WID	women in development
WTO	World Trade Organization

Introduction: Changing Challenges for NGDO Management

Michael Edwards and Alan Fowler

Background and Overview

In 1992, when the earliest contribution in this book was published, non-governmental organizations (NGOs) and 'NGO management' were scarcely a topic of public debate. To be sure, the beginnings of a literature on NGOs and development already existed, and the humanitarian emergencies that hit Africa so hard during the 1980s brought some NGOs to worldwide attention. For the most part, however, NGOs were a marginal force in world affairs, and although their leaders confronted new and complex management challenges on a daily basis, there was little by way of advice or analysis to support them.

Ten years later, the scene has changed completely. NGOs have moved from 'ladles in the global soup kitchen' (Fowler, 2000, p60) to a force for transformation in global politics and economics. This shift has been buoyed up by the democratic openings of the post-Cold War world, the popularity of non-state actors with donors, and rising discontent with conventional politics. They now disburse between US$12 and US$15 billion per annum (Fowler, 2000a), and their numbers and size have grown dramatically – to over 1 million in India, for example, 210,000 in Brazil (Salamon and Anheier, 1999) and at least 35,000 working internationally (Edwards, 2000).

The NGO literature has exploded, and with it has come an increasing body of knowledge and expertise devoted to the distinctive tasks and challenges that face NGO managers. This knowledge, however, is widely dispersed across books, journal articles and agency publications, so that anyone who is interested in finding advice will have to search long and hard to locate it – something that busy NGO staff rarely have the time to do. In this book, therefore, we have brought together a range of key readings in the NGO management literature and organized them according to the major challenges that NGOs face in their work.

Undoubtedly, these challenges have become larger and more complicated as a result of the changing global context. Globalization generates shifting patterns of poverty and insecurity within and between countries that call for more sophisticated strategies and interventions, increasingly connected across the boundaries of geography and sector, causes and effects. The basis of the international system is shifting from subsidized resource transfers (that is, foreign aid) to rules-based cooperation, with the real value of aid from the North falling by 21 per cent between 1991 and 1998, although high levels of funding through NGOs persist (Fowler, 2000a). NGOs have important roles to play in disbursing the aid that remains, but more broadly, in helping to ensure that new global rules – for trade, human movement, finance and environmental governance – are both fair and effective in combating injustice.

Intrastate conflict has replaced war between nations, with NGOs not just the prime providers of relief, humanitarian assistance and specialized services, but increasingly acting as mediators between civilians, governments and the military in 'complex political emergencies'. Overall, the focus of NGO activity has expanded and shifted from 'development as delivery to development as leverage', building outwards from concrete innovations at the grassroots level to connect with the structural forces that influence patterns of poverty, prejudice and violence: exclusionary economics, discriminatory politics, selfish and violent personal behaviour and the capture of knowledge and ideas by elites (Edwards, Hulme and Wallace, 1999; Fowlen, 2000c).

These changes have significant implications for NGO roles, relationships, capacities and accountabilities, and therefore pose new dilemmas for managers and other staff. Clearly, NGOs operate in so many contexts and at so many levels that generalization is hazardous. Some are oriented primarily towards advocacy and others towards operational work on the ground, with philosophies that range from welfare to empowerment, and from the political organizing principles of civil society to the economic principles of the market. Some are specialized providers of relief and humanitarian assistance, while others combine such work with broad-based development activities.

Most NGOs are 'intermediaries' in the sense that they work between the grassroots or community level and other levels and sectors of society (such as governments, the general public, businesses and other institutions of the market), providing a range of support services that connect these different institutions with each other and with groups that are poor or socially excluded. Membership-based groups are rare in the world of international development whose modus operandi has been the provision of foreign aid, although in other areas (like human rights and the environment) they are more common – Friends of the Earth, for example, or Amnesty International. And there are many other potential fault-lines and sources of difference within the development NGO community – North and South, large and small, local and global, and those who accept government funding and those who don't. Increasingly, NGOs are combining elements of these different roles, functions and levels of action in order to achieve their goals. This creates a particular set of management challenges that many chapters in this book address.

This Reader focuses attention on a sub-set of NGOs that we call 'non-governmental development organizations', or NGDOs. These organizations, which are intermediaries working primarily on issues of poverty and injustice within 'developing' countries and at the global level, form the majority of the groups that have grown so dramatically over the last ten years. We have chosen not to include the specific management challenges faced by humanitarian assistance NGOs or NGOs doing anti-poverty and social justice work in Europe and North America, because these groups face different contexts and specific dilemmas that deserve attention in and of themselves. However, we are confident that the chapters in this volume will be of general use to all NGOs, wherever they work.

Despite the diversity that characterizes even this sub-sector of the NGO universe, NGDOs do face a common core of challenges for management and organizational development, around which this book is organized. We employ a definition of 'management' that is broader than the mere 'technics' of decision-making, finance and human resources. Effective management requires the articulation of a clear and common vision for the organization and a set of strategies to achieve it; the mobilization of all the necessary human, financial and intellectual resources, and external contacts and connections that are required to operate these strategies effectively; and the continuous readjustment of strategy and structure in a changing context, implying an intimate relationship between organizational processes and a dynamic internal and external environment.

'Organizational development' implies a conscious process of acquiring and strengthening the characteristics required by an NGDO to position itself for maximum impact and effectiveness. Hence, the Reader opens with general sections on vision, roles and strategy, and then progresses through the management dilemmas that face NGDOs as they grow and change – the dilemmas of governance and accountability, participation and partnership, measuring achievements, organizational learning, resource mobilization and sustainability, gender equity and human resources. Constraints of space mean that we have had to exclude many excellent contributions, but the collection that remains contains a cross-section of the best work published on these themes in the last ten years. They capture and reflect the particular characteristics of NGDOs as a distinct type of organization that are discussed below.

The Distinctive Nature of NGDO Management and Organizational Development

At the most general level, all organizations have to deal with the same basic issues. For example, they all have to set a direction or identify goals, mobilize resources for what they do and find ways of getting employees to behave in ways that are consistent with the goals that have been chosen. On its own, this generic level of analysis is not particularly useful – a more detailed understanding is needed. Consequently, management thinking and analysis disaggregate and focus attention on different organizational types in order to determine and compare how they behave and why. A common first disaggregation is between public administration (the government), private for-profit (businesses) and non-profit organizations (NGOs) – crudely distinguished as the 'first', 'second' and 'third' sectors.

As a subset of non-profit organizations, NGDOs deal with a particular mix of factors that distinguishes them from other NGOs and from governments and businesses. As a result, they face a distinct set of management tasks and approaches to organizational change, distinctions that call for caution when applying lessons learned elsewhere. This warning applies even more strongly when diverse cultural settings and national contexts come into play (Moris, 1976; Hofstede, 1989; Lessem, 1989; Lewis, 1996). What then, is the typical mix of factors that NGDO managers must deal with and how do they compare with management challenges in other types of organization?

First, although like governments they deal with issues in the public domain such as poverty, injustice, exclusion or degradation of the natural world, NGDOs have no statutory authority to act. Their calling is voluntary and self-chosen, so NGDOs must continually justify their presence in, and value to society.

Second, an NGDO's power and influence is based on civic engagement, social mobilization and reliance on social capital, not the political mandate and 'strong arm' of governments, or the financial capital and influence of businesses. The quality of NGDO engagement with citizens is therefore a key determinant of organizational legitimacy and effectiveness.

In terms of their activities, NGDOs have organizational and wider development goals whose achievement relies on forces beyond their control – in the constituencies they work with or try to influence at home and abroad. Consequently, organizational outputs are no real guide to achievement. A manager must look further – to external impact across and in consort with an array of actors with no clear-cut 'bottom lines' of profit and loss or electoral success to rely on (Fowler, 1997). Instead, NGDOs must (re)construct their performance measures continually from a variety of claimants or users (Kanter, 1979).

As for many other non-profit organizations, a third distinctive quality of NGDOs derives from their position as intermediaries, wherein the resources required for their work do not come from those they serve, either as taxpayers or customers. NGDOs sit between, and must negotiate with, resource providers and the populations that justify their existence. For the organizations of concern to us in this book, this position ties them more or less directly to the policies, priorities, fashions and procedures of official aid and to the political economy of foreign relations of the donor countries that drive and direct the aid system. In other words, aid usually exerts an influence on an NGDO's direction and identity that is allied to (inter)national relations, forces and interests.

In addition, NGDOs often work in conditions of instability, conflict, poor infrastructure and poverty. Their constituencies reflect the lower, if not the lowest, strata of society economically, politically and culturally. They have too little purchasing power to be of interest to businesses, but may constitute a potentially destabilizing force of concern to governments, leading to distrust of NGDOs as 'allies of the poor'.

Depending on the politics of a country, the combination of foreign aid and alliances with the poor can lead the ruling regime to place NGDOs in the 'opposition' camp, leading to open or covert constraints on their work, or even on their existence. Unlike businesses that exist to make money, NGDO agendas are more likely to invite official suspicion and control. It cannot be assumed that ruling regimes and those that contend for political power perceive an NGDO as 'neutral'.

Finally, in keeping with other non-profit organizations, NGDOs cannot rely on hierarchy and coercion, or financial rewards and material incentives as the means to obtain the compliance of staff towards organizational goals. Rather, the route to compliance lies in satisfying the self-motivation of staff and volunteers – in other words, responding to the personal value base that persuades an individual to work in and for the third sector (Etzioni, in Lewis, 2001). This values-demand also applies to the processes of organizational change. If the NGDO is to be true to its calling, change must be negotiated and not simply imposed.

So, from an NGDO leader or manager's perspective, what does this combination of factors mean? Typically, it implies that:

1   The processes of external engagement and constituency 'ownership' of development are often more important than tangible outputs or direct 'products' of organizational action.
2   Organizational boundaries are essentially indeterminate. While control may stop at the organization's formal limits, a manager's span of influence must reach beyond.
3   Performance is a dynamic, organization-specific, complex and 'socially constructed' parameter that embraces contending interpretations depending on who is passing judgement and what power they possess.
4   Values count. Managers must create and sustain conditions that allow adequate values-achievement among staff and volunteers, both day-to-day and especially when organizational change is required.
5   NGDOs are 'political', irrespective of what they might say or do, demanding political awareness and sensitivity in decision-making.
6   Civic legitimacy and public trust must be continually invested in and worked for – good intentions are not enough.
7   Resources have a steering effect that must be factored into issues of organizational identity, civic position and rootedness.

Challenges for NGO Management and Organizational Development

The distinctive nature of NGDO management and organizational development set out above creates a particular set of challenges. Six are especially important. The first three relate to the fact that NGDOs are, or would claim to be, 'values-based' organizations, a characteristic that complicates the nature of goals, incentives and management structures in a number of important ways. The second three challenges relate to the complexity and uncertainty of the environment in which NGDOs tend to operate, calling for approaches that recognize and respond to the need to manage multiple relationships, shifting combinations of roles and funding sources, and new connections across old or unfamiliar boundaries.

Social change as a goal

NGDOs see social change as the ultimate goal of their activities, defined very broadly to mean a world without poverty, violence, injustice and discrimination. At root, social change is a question of values, and values pose a constant dilemma for NGDOs who want to link their mission with their management style and organizational development. What is the connection between 'social change' outside the NGDO and social change inside? Can the organization be an effective catalyst for social change unless it practices what it preaches in terms of participation, democracy, non-discrimination and empowerment? On the other hand, can the organization be effective at all unless it imposes a set of management structures and decision-making processes that cut across these values? All NGDOs face a tension between these 'developmental and institutional imperatives' when choices must be made about strategy and structure, partnership and accountability, funding and human resources (Edwards, 1999a). Much of the art of NGDO management lies in reconciling, or at least accommodating, these competing perspectives.

In addition, below this level of generality there are many differences and conflicts of opinion about how best to achieve the goal of social change, and all NGDOs must struggle with the extreme complexity and highly value-laden nature of the processes that underlie the problems they seek to address. Of course, all institutions face complexity: businesses must produce goods and services that make a profit in the marketplace, and governments must perform and communicate sufficiently well to be re-elected. But NGDOs must achieve elements of both these sets of goals – efficiency, effectiveness and public support – *and* use them to transform the worlds of economics, politics and social relationships through the prism of a different set of values. This is a much more difficult task. The first two parts of this Reader provide general guidance on how NGDOs can tailor their roles and strategies to the value base that motivates them.

The nature of incentives

As a result of their values base and mission for social change, staff in NGDOs are unlikely to respond effectively to conventional command-and-control management hierarchies or incentives based solely on material rewards. Of course, these things are not irrelevant (even a modest increase can be significant at the low levels of salary paid in most NGDOs), but in general, personal commitment and satisfaction, a shared ideology and a feeling that staff have a meaningful stake in the mission and direction of the organization are more important incentives to performance.

This means that managers in NGDOs may have fewer levers for influence than in business or government, or at least that the levers are more difficult and complex to operate. Staff must be brought into the processes of organizational change and decision-making on a less hierarchical basis, and change may have to be slower and more incremental in order to secure the necessary internal base of support. Changing or moving the boxes on the NGDO's organagram is a popular option for managers in this sector, as in others, but it is rarely effective without much deeper changes in culture and attitudes that rely on support from staff. Part 10 provides important advice on how to approach the issues of human resources and leadership from a values-based perspective.

Participation and empowerment

An internal commitment to values-based management complicates traditional structures and processes in any organization but most of all in NGDOs, since concepts of participation and empowerment lie at the heart of the paradigm they promote for social change. In theory at least, NGDOs must pay even more explicit attention to diversity, gender equity and other issues of difference, the empowerment of staff so that they can live and work to their full potential, and participatory processes that allow everyone a say in matters that affect them. But these innovations must be organized and managed with great care lest they overly impede decision-making – creating 'participation paralysis' – and introducing tensions that impede responsiveness, flexibility and impact. As intermediaries (especially those based in the North), NGDOs face the added complication that values must be reflected in external relationships if legitimacy is to be maintained – a problem that has led to much debate about the theory and practice of 'partnership' (Fowler, 2000b).

Fortunately, the changing global context opens up a world of possibilities for NGDOs to relate to each other through alliances between equals and networks based on synergy (not competition), replacing the asymmetries of power and voice that have characterized North–South relationships for so many years. Information technology helps this process along by enabling less hierarchical modes of organization and communication – advantages already well-exploited by the business community, but not yet by many NGDOs.

Peter Senge (1998) argues that the most successful organizations of the 21st century will look more like 'democratic societies than conventional corporations'. Rather than trying to impose order on a chaotic world (and complicating matters even further in the process), they will try to generate order *out of* chaos through non-authoritarian relationships between groups who are genuinely interested in helping one another to develop new learning and capacities. Jonathan Kotter (1998) likens this model to a 'smaller mother ship with many more satellites and fewer organizational boundaries'. In respect of non-authoritarian modes of management and operating processes with porous boundaries, NGDOs may already be ahead of many for-profit organizations. Part 5 (Organizing for Good Development Practice) and Part 9 (Dealing with Gender) contain a range of chapters that shed light on these difficult issues.

Multiple accountabilities and shifting relationships

The fact that NGDOs locate their work in the spaces that exist between communities and institutions of different kinds complicates the management of legitimacy, accountability and other external relationships. NGDOs must demonstrate accountability to a wide range of stakeholder groups who may have different information needs, priorities for the organization, visions of success and definitions of legitimacy, including their boards of trustees, their donors (individual and institutional), partners, staff and external critics. As noted above, unlike governments (which must face elections) and businesses (which must face their shareholders), NGDOs have no single 'bottom line' to measure their performance, and they work in situations where attribution and causality are much more complex and dynamic.

The changing global environment also challenges NGDOs to develop ways of working that are less focused on promoting their own profile and more concerned with building alliances, working with others, and dividing up roles and responsibilities in a collaborative way. More openness to new ideas and a greater willingness to learn are essential in the context of new problems and new actors, fast-moving and unpredictable change, the entry of corporations, churches and trade unions into development debates, and the increasing sophistication of information technology (Edwards, Hulme and Wallace, 1999).

Learning is the key to a more sophisticated understanding of the changing context for development work, the implications of these changes for NGDO practice, and the ability of managers to select the most effective alliances and strategies to reach their goals on a continuous basis. Innovations in markets and economics demand much greater detail from NGOs in their analysis and proposals, without losing the power of grassroots testimony and straightforward protest. Finely nuanced judgements in complex political emergencies require more highly developed information-gathering and analytical skills. Yet learning continues to be something of a 'Holy Grail' for NGDOs and their staff (Edwards, 1997). Parts 4, 6 and 7 look in turn at governance and accountability, how to measure performance and systems for organizational learning.

Diverse and unpredictable funding sources

Despite the relative decline of foreign aid, NGDOs are still favoured by the donor community and – in low-income economies – local funds are usually hard to find. As a result, many continue to be funded more from public than private sources, something that may compromise developmental imperatives by shifting account- ability 'upwards', reorienting roles to areas prioritized by donors and inducing a creeping sense of self-censorship (Hulme and Edwards, 1997).

Sources of funds are also volatile, vulnerable to 'donor fatigue' among the gen- eral public, shifts in fashion and relationships among governments and international agencies and the quirks and personalities of corporate philanthropy. Inevitably, therefore, many of the management challenges faced by NGDOs revolve around fund- raising and financial sustainability and how to preserve identity and continuity in core programmes when income is difficult to predict from one year to the next. Keeping overheads low while preserving quality, managing phases of expansion and retrenchment to take advantage of fund-raising opportunities without overexpos- ing the organization, and forging a team composed of permanent staff, short-term assignments and consultants, are all familiar dilemmas for NGDO managers.

In selecting from fund-raising options, a critical challenge for managers is how to avoid funding sources or modalities that lead to 'mission creep', compromise values and lead to cooptation. Another is the need to distinguish between the size and profile of an individual NGDO and structural reform or systemic change as indica- tors of success. This is important, not only because structural reform is the key role for NGDOs in the 21st century, but also because it reduces managerial anxiety about the size of the organization relative to others – a problem that takes energy and commitment away from more important tasks (Fowler, 2000a). What will 'make a difference' to global poverty in the years to come will not be the number of villages that are served or children that are sponsored, but how grassroots action is con- nected to markets and politics at multiple levels of the world system, a collective task in which the ability of NGDOs to work together – not individual competitive- ness – will be critical. Parts 3 and 8 provide advice on the management of growth and the perennial issue of sustainability.

NGDOs as 'connectors'

In many ways, connectivity is the theme that ties all these management challenges together. As we noted earlier in this Introduction, NGDOs belong 'in' civil society, but they are not solely 'of' civil society because they purposefully work in the spaces between civil society, state and market (Edwards, 1999; Fowler, 2000c). They may have a particular geographical focus but recognize that social change requires increasingly integrated action at the local, national and global levels. To be effective, NGDO campaigns need to build broad-based constituencies for implementation as well as policy change among governments and international agencies, so they must develop strong links with the media and with the public, churches, labour unions and NGDOs in other movements (Edwards and Gaventa, 2001). Stronger organizational learning requires an active partnership with universities and think-tanks, consultants and researchers.

In sum, NGDOs constitute a crucial part of the 'connective tissue' of a vigorous civil society, so making and sustaining the right connections lies at the heart of effective NGDO management. The strength of NGDOs lies in their ability to act as bridges, facilitators, brokers and translators, linking together the institutions, interventions, capacities and levels of action that are required to lever broader structural changes from discrete or small-scale actions.

For managers, this is an immensely challenging task because it requires a degree of human and organizational flexibility and responsiveness that is difficult to achieve even in predictable environments, conditions of financial stability and agencies of small to medium scale. Since none of these conditions apply to NGDOs, their task is even harder. Vaill's (1996) image of the 'white-water raft' comes immediately to mind, constantly moving between the rocks and currents of the river, reshaping itself to fit the contours of context and crew, and 'light' enough to survive even the most dangerous of rapids. The mirror image of the white-water raft is the ageing super tanker, an analogy that will not be lost on managers in large, foreign-aid dependent NGDOs.

These challenges require managerial skills of the highest order, tailored specifically to the context and values base of the NGDO world, not the borrowing of second-hand advice from business schools or bureaucracies. The development of an NGDO management framework that can sit confidently alongside management and organizational development theories from other sectors remains an important task for the future. In the meantime, the papers collected together in this Reader give more than a glimpse of what such a framework might contain. We hope that they will help all NGDO managers and staff to fulfil their potential as agents of global social change in the century to come.

References

Edwards, M (1997) 'Organizational learning in NGOs: what have we learned?', *Public Administration and Development*, Vol 17, No 2, pp235–50.

Edwards, M (1999a) 'International development NGOs: Agents of foreign aid or vehicles for international co-operation?', *Non Profit and Voluntary Sector Quarterly*, Vol 28, No 4, pp25–37.

Edwards, M (1999b) *Future Positive: International Cooperation in the 21st Century*, Earthscan, London.

Edwards, M (2000) *NGO Rights and Responsibilities: A New Deal for Global Governance*, Foreign Policy Centre, London.

Edwards, M, and Gaventa, J (eds) (2001) *Global Citizen Action*, Boulder, Colorado, Lynne Rienner, and Earthscan, London.

Edwards, M, Hulme, D and Wallace, T (1999) 'NGOs in a global future: Marrying local delivery to worldwide leverage', *Public Administration and Development*, Vol 19, pp17–36.

Etzioni, A (2001) 'A comparative analysis of complex organizations: on power, involvement and their correlation', in D Lewis, *The Management of Non-governmental Development Organizations: An Introduction*, Rontiedge, London.

Fowler, A (1997) *Striking a Balance: A Guide to Enhancing the Effectiveness of Non-Governmental Organizations in International Development*, Earthscan, London.

Fowler, A (2000a) 'NGOs, civil society and social development: changing the rules of the game', *Geneva 2000*, Occasional Paper, No 1, United Nations Research Institute for Social Development, Geneva.

Fowler, A (ed) (2000b) 'Questioning Partnership: The Reality of Aid and NGO Relations' *IDS Bulletin*, Vol 31, No 3, July.

Fowler, A (2000c) 'Introduction: NDGO Values and The Fourth Position', in Fowler, A (ed), *NGO Futures: Beyond Aid, Third World Quarterly Special Issue*, Vol 21, No 4, pp589–603, August.

Fowler, A (2000d) *The Virtuous Spiral: A Guide to Sustainability for NGOs in International Development*, Earthscan, London.

Hofstede, G (1991) *Cultures and Organisations: Software of the Mind*, McGraw-Hill, Maidenhead.

Hulme, D and Edwards, M (eds) (1997) *Too Close for Comfort? NGOs, States and Donors*, Macmillan, London, and St Martin's Press, New York.

Kanter, R (1979) *The Measurement of Organizational Effectiveness, Productivity, Performance and Success: Issues and Dilemmas in Service and Non-Profit Organizations*, PONPO Working Paper, No 8, Institute of Development Research, Yale University, Boston.

Kotter, J (1998) 'Cultures and Coalitions', in Gibson, R (ed), *Rethinking the Future: Rethinking Business Principles, Competition, Control, Leadership, Markets and the World*, Nicholas Brearley, London.

Lessem, R (1989) *Global Management Principles*, Prentice Hall, London.

Lewis, D (2001) *The Management of Non-Governmental Development Organisations: An Introduction*, Routledge, London.

Lewis, R (1996) *When Cultures Collide: Managing Successfully Across Cultures*, Nicholas Brealey, London.

Moris, J (1976) 'The transferability of the Western management tradition to the non-Western public service sector', in Stifel, L et al (eds) *Education and Training for Public Sector Management in Developing Countries*, pp73–83, Rockefeller Foundation, New York.

Salamon, L and Anheier, H (1999) *Global Civil Society: Dimensions of the Non-Profit Sector*, Johns Hopkins Center for Civil Society, Baltimore.

Senge, P (1998) 'Through the eye of a needle', in Gibson, R (ed), *Rethinking the Future: Rethinking Business, Principles, Competition, Control and Complexity, Leadership, Markets and the World*, Nicholas Brearley, London.

Vaill, P (1996) *Learning as a Way of Being: Strategies for Survival in a World of Permanent White Water*, Jossey Bass, San Francisco.

Part 1

Visions, Values and Roles

NGO Futures – Beyond Aid: NGDO Values and the Fourth Position

Alan Fowler

This chapter rests, for some, on a speculative proposition. The proposition is that non-governmental organizations (NGOs) associated with international development (non-governmental development organizations – NGDOs) face a future scenario where they can no longer rely on a system of international concessional aid as a reference point for their role, work and continuity.[1] Depending on where you live in the world, this scenario is actual, as in Chile, or it may still appear to be far distant, as in Nepal. Whatever the case, this chapter offers reflections on alternative NGDO thinking, practice and financing in the 21st century that are not premised on aid as a redistributive system providing international economic and social subsidy.[2]

This chapter has two purposes.[3] First, to set the scene, so to speak, by examining the rationale for considering NGDOs in beyond-aid scenarios (BAS), in terms of both superficial and deeper-lying causes affecting NGDOs in tomorrow's world. Second, to offer a provisional future-orientated synthesis of perspectives, the crux of which is for NGDOs to adopt a fourth, value-based position between state, market and civil society.

Why Beyond Aid?

Superficially, the urgent and practical reason why NGDOs must consider life in a beyond-aid scenario results from the decreasing volume and redistribution of aid finance. While amounting to US$51.5 billion in 1998, since 1991 the real value of aid from the North has dropped by some 21 per cent (DI, 1999). In addition, there has been inflationary 'definition creep' in terms of what donor governments are now reporting as aid (Raffer, 1999). What you see in such figures is not what you get as aid in the South.[4] However, even definitional sleights of hand cannot obscure the fact that donor countries have become both richer and meaner. Per capita incomes of Organization for Economic Co-operation and Development (OECD) countries grew from an average of US$11,575 in 1960 to US$27,789 in 1997 – that is, by 140 per cent. In, the same period, per capita aid from OECD countries grew from US$47 to US$59 – ie, by 25 per cent (DI, 1999).

Attending this decline is greater pressure from parliaments and taxpayers for aid to 'show results'. This is necessary because of past poor performance and loss of credibility, discussed below. Consequently, donors have set an ambitious goal of reducing absolute poverty by half by the year 2015. Twenty-one indicators have been selected to chart progress, to show achievement and, hopefully, value for money.[5] NGDOs are regarded as an important mechanism for helping to reach this objective. Their contribution is seen to lie in an ostensibly distinct practice in terms of direct operations and policy contribution, as well as in terms of persuading (tax-paying) domestic constituencies (and free-market economic critics) that 'aid works' and that the system is worth keeping and supporting.

Logically, a numerical target and finite date are pushing aid givers to concentrate their efforts on and within countries where poverty is most acute and where they can make most difference most quickly. The Netherlands, for example, has decided recently to concentrate on 20 countries, rather than on around 60. Inevitably, redistributing aid creates winners and losers – with South Asia and sub-Saharan Africa gaining most thanks to higher absolute numbers and higher relative proportion of people in poverty, respectively. Moreover, in concentration countries, such as Bangladesh and Nepal, donor finance is itself being reconcentrated through a Sector Wide Approach or to geographic areas of poverty concentration.[6]

In parallel, Latin America and the Newly Industrialized Countries (NICs) have seen their aid share reduced, supposedly to be replaced by foreign direct investment (FDI). Moreover, it is this latter aspect of economic globalization that signals a shift in the implicit aid agenda. It is a move away from serving old Cold War interests to one of accelerating market penetration by engendering the social stability required for this to happen.

Put another way, replacing Cold War political ideological rivalry as the organizing foundation for world development is the promotion of a rule-based pattern of interaction premised on capitalist market economics and liberal democracy. Two types of rules are supposed to form the pillars of this new type of world order. One set derives from international political and social conventions and laws, negotiated at the United Nations (UN), but yet to be adequately applied and policed (inter)nationally. The other pillar is founded on economic agreements negotiated and enforced by, or alongside, the World Trade Organization (WTO).[7] However, there is an ongoing dispute, or 'backlash', in the construction of both pillars. The major point of contention is the degree to which such negotiation and enforcement are the task, responsibility and mandate of governments alone, as opposed to civil society and other non-state actors (Bond, 2000).

It is this shift in global organizing pattern and agenda that penetrates beyond the superficial aspects of changing aid levels and flows. It takes us into deeper issues of NGDO identity and relevance. In other words, it reaches into the way that NGDOs understand who they are, define their allies and decide what they should do in an emerging New World Order, or Disorder (Malhotra, 2000). It also forces us to consider how growing NGDO interaction with official aid and other 'partners' is affecting their position, nature, public trust, image and effectiveness. In other words, the speculations addressed in this collection go beyond responses to trends in aid levels and distribution to address the heart of NGDO origins, assumptions, roles and the concepts they employ.

Although perhaps not their intention, it is a role that has characterized the 15 years of majority growth of NGDOs as deliverers of placatory (socio-) economic services. This NGDO task results inter alia from donor 'privatization' policies consistent with 'right-sizing' governments and opening countries to market forces. It also reflects the origins, motivation and thinking of many NGDOs as sources of *charitas*. Their recent evolution also reflects an addition to aid policy, which is to treat and fund NGDOs as a democratizing element of civil society (Fowler, 2000a; van Rooy, 1997),

Despite declining aid, all these 'uses' currently favour NGDOs in terms of official aid allocations. This fact is leading to a situation where, in one way or another, over 50 per cent of their disbursements today are derived from taxes.[8] Unless an NGDO's funding comes substantially from non-public sources – like private giving, enterprise or foundations – the picture is one of growing dependency on and vulnerability to shifts in public policy in the North and South. Over-reliance on public funds can and does alter NGDO nature and behaviour by, for example, shifting accountability from the civic to the public domain and inducing self-censorship (Fowler, 2000d; Hulme and Edwards, 1997).

These two examples of change in NGDO behaviour because of a greater reliance on official aid are, in fact, the tip of a more substantial iceberg of the danger of public mistrust by association. By tying themselves more closely to official aid and its excessive, dysfunctionally 'projectized' way of working (Fowler, 1997, pp16–18), NGDOs embrace the risk of being tarred with the same brush of poor performance and of being smitten by the same pathologies. A recent estimate is that aid-funded interventions are only sustainable in some 15 per cent of cases (Cox and Healy, 1998).[9] Moreover, the number of poor people in the world has not diminished, but increased. After 30 years of effort, this result does not inspire public confidence.

What, one might naturally ask, has caused this disappointing level of achievement? One answer is that the aid system has evolved to embody a number of deep-seated illnesses or pathological traits that create perverse incentives, debilitating and corrupt behaviours and a 'suspended' layer of Southern NGDOs. These factors combine to work against best practice, a high level of achievement and gaining public trust. For example, in Russia and countries newly independent of the Soviet Union, NGDOs are too often perceived as covers for organized crime (see, for example CAF, 1999). In Pakistan and Bangladesh some NGDOs are seen to serve as fronts for externally funded fundamentalist causes, while in Central Asia they are utilized as platforms for failed politicians. Simply put, nowhere in the world can the growth of NGDOs be equated with public recognition or trust in who they are or what they do. However, the structural nature of aid pathology is actually more worrying for NGDOs than such 'transitional' problems of post-Soviet Europe and public scepticism elsewhere.

From the outset, alongside overt objectives of accelerating economic growth, the covert purpose of aid was to help win the Cold War. This not so hidden agenda effectively uncoupled a link between actual development achievement – be it growth or poverty reduction – and the level and distribution of aid allocation. In other words, in the last analysis it was not what development finance did for economic growth or poor people that was important, but what it did for geopolitics. Substantial Western aid to countries run by civilian dictators and brutal military rulers was fine as long as they were 'ours'. This 'realpolitics' undermined the moral grounding that aid could have had in the beginning. Instead, it sent a clear message that Northern domestic interests were the issue, not poverty as a moral imperative to act.[10] In a more modem form, this illness continues to express itself. For example, it emerges when donor countries use promises of aid to buy Southern votes for their candidate to run a UN agency; or when aid is offered as an inducement to vote a particular way in international bodies – for example, in the Convention on International Trade in Endangered Species (CITES).[11]

From this corrupting origin flowed a system and institutional culture driven by matching achievement with (annual) disbursement, not development performance. It also fostered short-termism and a system of aid as a tool for shaping and cementing bilateral relations (especially with ex-colonies) and the promotion of business back home in the name of maintaining domestic support – manifest in 'tied aid'.[12] It has caused lack of coordination, consistency and continuity, exacerbated by continuous changes in development 'fashion' and the inability to learn and reform (Edwards, 1999).

Correspondingly, with externally dictated – and more expensive – donor-bonded consultants, goods and services, came disempowerment and loss of ownership of the development process for many recipient governments and their populations.[13] Despite explicit donor rhetoric throughout the 1990s for recipients to be 'in the driving seat', continuing nationalistic behaviour by funders simply took away 'choice' as a vital dimension of recipient empowerment and concomitant responsibility of the South as 'chooser'. Concealed by politically correct, but yet to be practised, calls for 'partnership', this illness continues today.

Moreover, because of deep human psychological imprints, aid as a grant or concessional loan from governments or NGDOs preconditions towards a paternal attitude in 'givers' and a reciprocal dependency or victim syndrome in recipients (Sida, 1996). With some justification, much of the South may argue that aid is a right – that is, a repayment for past injustice and the ongoing exploitation and economic imperialism of the North (McLaughlin, 1998). This argument does not appear to cut much, if any, ice. In practice, the rules of today's aid game are premised on benevolent self-interest rather than on an historical duty or obligation. Recipients should be 'thankful'. In other words, aid reflects patrimony not justice.

In response to experiencing the real rules, the South often exhibits forms of resistance that are common to the powerless. Typical are misappropriation, foot dragging, obstructiveness, delayed approvals, downright bloody-mindedness born of frustration, demands for per diems to be a Southern 'legitimizing presence' at donor-driven meetings, lack of commitment and hence sustainability and 'funging' government budgets (World Bank, 1998) – that is, reallocation of income away from what was agreed, and so on.

In short, over 40 years, the system has both created and institutionalized itself around a set of perverse attitudes, incentives and behaviours: an historical legacy that donor agencies say they are trying to shed.[14] It remains to be seen if the vital and deep institutional reforms – which means more than flurries of defensive poverty reorientation by institutions like the International Monetary Fund[15] – can and will occur before the whole edifice loses it credibility with Northern taxpayers and Southern recipients alike.

While not without their own distinct problems (see, for example, Carroll, 1992; Edwards and Hulme, 1992; 1995; Sogge, 1996; Smillie, 1995; Suzuki, 1998) NGDOs were not originally encumbered by the specific pathologies of the official system. Unfortunately, by growing association with official aid, again under the questionable mantle of 'partnership' (Fowler, 2000b; Malhotra, 2000), NGDOs risk contamination by association. In other words, from donor 'extensions' they become embedded parts of a diseased, underperforming system suffering from a diminishing reputation and public trust.

The usual counter-argument is that, with their better practice, deeper NGDO interaction with official donors will reform the aid system. In other words, NGDOs will be better at coopting donors than the other way around (Najam, 1999). Emerging evidence suggests both opposite as well as contrary outcomes to this expectation. A review of British NGDO interactions with their domestic government development agency concluded that their practice was becoming standardized and sectoralized along official lines (Wallace et al, 1998). In other words, NGDOs' supposed comparative advantages – which is precisely why donors say they want to fund them – were being whittled away. Meanwhile, a recent conference examined how official adoption of NGDO-promoted 'participation' was evolving into a homogenizing 'tyranny' around demands for the use of specific tools and techniques, irrespective of the NGDOs' own competences and context.[16] At its core, the weakness in the counter-argument revolves around the structural power asymmetry of being resource-dependent on those you seek to influence or educate.

In sum, vulnerability to aid trends, reduced autonomy, pathological contamination by association, loss of public trust and civic roots, creeping self-censorship and the erosion of comparative advantages all add up to substantive reasons for NGDOs to look at conceptual and financial alternatives. Hence the question posed to conference panellists: what options are there for NGDOs in a theory and practice beyond aid?

What are Possible Alternatives?

In terms of answers to the question framed above, Edwards and Sen (2000), van Tuijl (2000), Cameron (2000) and Fowler (2000d) offer alternative conceptual foundations for future NGDO roles and related contributions to society. They are not 'solutions' but 'options' – that is, they argue for different ways in which NGDOs can perceive themselves and understand what they are trying to do and why. While distinctive in terms of the ideas employed, they all shift the perspective away from an historically evolved and dominant contemporary role of many, if not most, NGDOs as part of a global redistribution chain.

Edwards and Sen (2000) delve deep into ethics and values; the processes and institutional arrangements that underpin the social system; and an individual's personal state of feelings, intuitions and experiences that give meaning to the world. From these foundations, the core development task, in their view, is to rebalance the competitive and cooperative rationalities that motivate human agency. At the core, achieving such a balance requires a personal transformation of a complacent or selfish heart that feeds and is fed by the 'I'm all right Jack' contentment of the better off and the intensifying global pressure to 'compete to the bottom'.

Consequently, their emphasis is on the role of NGDOs as explicitly value-based agents of personal change whose major task is one of fostering cooperation and collaborative spirit as the basis of human relations in an increasingly interdependent world. They argue that this NGDO role is a vital answer to global trends that are shifting power from the public to private domains and hence demanding a responsible use of private power for the self-development of all. How NGDOs can play such a role is explained in terms of their programmes, constituency building and organizational praxis.

Reflecting a shift to a rule-based order, van Tuijl (2000) helps NGDOs to consider human rights as a framework to guide their self-understanding, language, standards, goals, relationships and activities. Such an approach rests on the proposition that, to be human, all people have an inalienable right to fundamental entitlements, codified in (an unhealthy inflation of) international human rights and humanitarian law.[17] This perspective is incompatible with the concept of NGDOs as agents of philanthropy, charity and welfare. From a rights perspective, the NGDO role is to enable people – specifically the poor, marginalized and powerless – to better act as claimants of entitlements towards duty holders – that is, the state and 'responsible' market institutions. Indeed, some businesses are already adopting Codes of Conduct and other social and environmental self-regulatory mechanisms that NGDOs can help to design and use in their role as validatory 'watchdogs'.

A confounding issue is one of NGDO behaviour in situations where those carrying the duty to provide entitlements – typically the state – do not have adequate resources to do so. How can NGDOs simply not be drawn into a role of surrogate or substitute for failed duty holders? One answer I put forward is for NGDOs to pursue roles of social entrepreneurs and civic innovators, rather than users and distributors of subsidy. These notions can be extended in a 'traditional' NGDO direction of finding, testing and demonstrating different and improved ways in which states and markets can fulfil their obligations. Topical examples are innovations in (non-formal) basic education being pioneered by BRAC in Bangladesh, and by ActionAid, with its ACCESS approach which, through adoption by (local) government, is taken to a larger scale – better fulfilling one 'children's right' or entitlement. At best, NGDOs reach some 20 per cent of the world's poor (Fowler, 2000a). Innovation that can be scaled up, coupled to accountable advocacy, is the only realistic way to make a difference for the majority that NGDOs will not directly reach. It is a vital 'niche competency' for NGDOs to develop further.

Notwithstanding the dilemma of substitution, van Tuijl (2000) argues that the slow, sure but uneven adoption of human rights conventions across the world provides a 'universal' source of language and principles that NGDOs can use as tools not dogmas. For example, they may employ such a perspective as a globally acknowledged – though not undisputed – framework for finding common ground in a linkage and convergence between human rights, governance and development. To play this role requires NGDOs to locate themselves in a way that keeps them bonded and accountable to civil society (see Fowler, 2000d), while occupying a space between civil society, state and market. In this 'fourth position', the NGDO role is one of multisector negotiation, as well as of promoting and exacting compliance of duty holders to deliver people's rights.

This 'positional' perspective also arises in Cameron's (2000) contribution. He suggests that NGDOs see their future role as one of redistributing risk in society away from those – the poor – who carry it most. Against the historical backdrop of development economics, he shows the way in which New Institutional Economics (NIE) can assist NGDOs in shaping their contribution to development in terms of reducing uncertainty and the costs of transition for specific social groups. If risk is expressed as a non-fulfilment of agreed 'rights' – that is, with entitlements for specific social groups, a direct link emerges with Peter van Tuijl's proposition.

NIE also explains why NGDOs are driven to sustain themselves and why forces pull them into ambiguous ground between other sectors of society, in effect creating a fourth position in relation to the three-sector analytic ideal. His framework is particularly apposite if a not unrealistic assumption is made that the New World Order is going to be less stable and less predictable. Instability and turbulence are fed by, among other things, subnational self-determination, 'instantaneous' international (re-)deployment of capital, erosion of state sovereignty, rapid development in global communications, genetically based science, growing environmental stress that knows no borders, accelerating inequality and poorly globally regulated but more powerful international corporations. Cameron's framework argues that the NGDO role in a world of increasing uncertainty is to act as an intermediary agent whose value-base informs and directs risk distribution in pro-poor ways. NIE also enables international NGDOs to understand their role in the 'global South' (Malhotra, 2000) – that is, in their contribution to dealing with the losers from world-inspired domestic turbulence.

My thinking on social entrepreneurship (Fowler, 2000d) focuses on how NGDOs can counter a slide from being civic to being publicly accountable entities, while simultaneously diversifying their resource base. This framework describes how and why the civic rootedness of NGDOs has been eroded in the North and has yet to establish itself firmly in the South. It also offers an alternative strategy for NGDOs to embrace the future beyond aid in ways that, to different degrees, enable them to regain their original imperatives and social base. The strategic options are either to evolve as (hybrid) social entrepreneurs or as more unambiguous civic innovators. My expressed preference for the latter option can be understood in Cameron's terms because it mitigates the problem of identity associated with sectoral ambiguity. It does so by fulfilling van Tuijl's (2000) requirement for NGDOs to retain civic accountability if they are to be seen as legitimate interlocutors with all other sectors.

Despite apparently starkly different options to consider, all these authors are united in that they do not presuppose the existence of the old North–South divide as a basis for their conceptual approach. If anything, the opposite is the case. Implicitly or explicitly, they presume that a way ahead for NGDOs is equally applicable in the North and the South, domestically and internationally – poverty and exclusion are an expression of selfishness and powerlessness everywhere.

Towards a Synthesis

Beyond-aid scenarios can be regarded more as opportunities than threats. Less security in the availability of aid can provoke healthy, more critical questioning. It can stimulate self-reflection and give necessary urgency to organizational reform – all of which are vital for NGDO relevance and continuity under new conditions. In a more complex, interdependent world, NGDOs would do well to draw on features from these ideas and responses to form a coherent set of values, principles, strategy, capacity and practices for their reform into a new era. What might such an arrangement look like?

A common theme in the current discourse is that NGDOs must locate themselves consciously between other actors in society. For example, if NIE does explain why NGDOs are inevitably drawn towards such an intermediary position more than states and markets, it seems more sensible for them to capitalize fully and effectively on this fact than to fight it. In doing so, they become entities that today's management science would regard as complex, purposeful systems.[18] In this case, they contain characteristics commonly associated with each of the 'traditional' three sectors, but cannot be fully understood or analysed from within the framework of any one of them. For example, in this position their behaviour: 1) resembles the state in terms of pursuing public agendas; 2) is associated with markets in terms of surplus generation and self-financing; but 3) expresses a civic identity in terms of roots, a values-based and propagating role and agenda and the (participatory) methods they apply. In short, this type of NGDO 'belongs in' and is anchored to civil society, but is not solely 'of' civil society because it purposefully inhabits and works in the space and interaction between civil society, state and market.[19]

Figure 1.1 provides a schematic presentation of such a place for a 21st-century NGDO with attention to goals, roles and tasks. The essential idea is to draw on but move beyond a too-simple three-sector view of society, to a more complex understanding of an NGDO's grounding, principles of operation, roles and embedding in society, a 'fourth position'. In other words, while bonded to civil society, they use

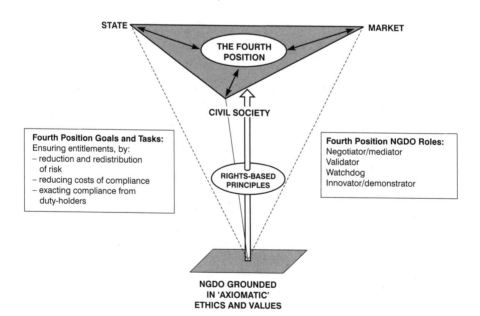

Figure 1.1 *Synthesis–NGDOs in the Fourth Position*

their value-base as a 'springboard' to interact with state, market and civil society itself – which is far from homogeneous and is not inherently 'civil' or conflict free. They would have the competence to speak different 'sector languages' and to engage across diverse institutional boundaries and foster interorganizational linkages.[20] In doing so, the challenge is to help others to see how NGDO values, expressed through human rights, are relevant to everyone in terms of responsible global change, long-term institutional viability and local to global stability and sustainability.

The inspiration and motivational foundation for a 21st-century NGDO is provided by what Edwards and Sen (2000, p606) refer to as 'axiomatic values or ethics' – that is, a humane understanding of and personal commitment towards a particular type of social order and human relationships. While remaining subject to debate, these are inevitably, unashamedly and openly normative. They are an ethics which recognize that personal power relations create and are able to reform inhumane conditions in the world order.

Grounded in a clear set of values and ethics, NGDOs then employ the 'universal' principles and language of human rights to define the goals and tasks required to achieve them. With a focus on people who are poor and excluded, at first sight such goals and tasks would be:

- ensuring human rights entitlements; by
- exacting compliance from duty bearers; and
- undertaking activities that reduce overall risk in society or redistribute risk to those more capable of bearing it.

In their turn, these tasks call for NGDOs to play a set of roles within society, but specifically as entities positioned between and dealing with all other 'sectors'. At least four important roles are:

- (re-)negotiators and trusted mediators between actors and sectors;
- trusted validators of a duty bearer's compliance with rights;
- respected watchdogs of behaviour of duty bearers and of claimants, including themselves;
- acknowledged innovators in the public interest, with a constant eye on adoption by bigger and more powerful actors and on enhancing the capacity of claimants.

Each of the NGDO linkages shown – to state, market and civil society – is bidirectional. In terms of the state, NGDOs seek policy influence and reform, act as a watchdog and push for compliance in satisfying people's entitlements, and demonstrate examples of how the state can better fulfil its obligations. In return, governments demand legitimacy and accountability of NGDOs themselves.

Towards markets NGDOs can seek to influence corporate behaviour; independently validate business compliance with their own codes of conduct; and act as social entrepreneurs in terms of development and non-development enterprise as a source of income. What businesses expect is that NGDOs bring a credible reputation – that is, public trust in what NGDO validation means, as well as expertise.

From civil society NGDOs gain legitimacy, accountability and resources. What they offer are innovations within civil society, articulation of interests to other players, mediation and negotiation expertise and, when mandated, representation of a civic voice.

Linkages to other sectors offer many opportunities to generate domestic resources of different quality – that is, with different effects on NGDO behaviour (see also Holloway, 1999). In the Fourth Position, a critical challenge in selecting resource options is to avoid sources that compromise values or civic embeddedness and lead to unwarranted cooptation (Fowler, 2000c). Unfortunately, NGDO vulnerability in these areas is to be expected because discussions about significant organizational change or repositioning are typically overshadowed by worries about income and size.

The dominance of financial concerns in NGDO reactions to their reform is not to be underestimated. Nor do the authors do so. They recognize that the fear of probably being smaller – while being more effective, with greater impact through altering the behaviour of others – creates anxiety. Such anxiety reflects a history of charitable motivation and thinking, management practice and norm setting under conditions of unlimited demand. The more you spend the better you must have done. Bigger must mean more impact and hence equals actual achievement. In such thinking, concern for size inexorably feeds on itself. However, experience shows that, in terms of poverty reduction, the amount of NGDO spending will be a proxy for an ameliorative, not for a sustained, end result (Fowler, 1997; 2000a). In the 21st century, structural reform in how state, market, civil society and global rules of the game and governing institutions behave, will be a better proxy for NGDOs' enduring impact. In short, in future, insightful NGDOs will look beyond size to systemic change as their measure of achievement.

Many NGDOs will probably choose to remain 'ladles in the global soup kitchen' as the path of least resistance. However, this is not inevitable, nor is it necessary. Moreover, it is likely to be a short-lived choice for most. Long-term viability is more likely if NGDOs systematically reduce their growing dependency on declining aid and privatized compassion, which are past their sell-by date in terms of offering structural solutions to inhumane development in an increasingly interdependent world order.[21] However, we acknowledge that, as big as the challenge of income diversification may be, it is dwarfed by the task of deeply altering the way that NGDOs see themselves as agents of change.

I argue that adopting 'fourth position' thinking and practice would help NGDOs to draw on their original motivations and place them firmly in a pivotal position to accelerate and direct change in the 21st century – a change that really makes a positive, structural and systemic difference to people who are poor, excluded and risk-prone.

As a concluding observation, not to decide consciously about the desired future path beyond aid is itself a decision, one which the authors believe will not further what NGDOs originally stood for in terms of solidarity with and justice for those whose daily life is one of impoverishment, insecurity and marginalization. Responsibility for NGDO choice towards the future cannot be delegated. It cannot be abdicated to circumstance, chance, the media, political expediency or the aid system. NGDOs' future must be grasped actively and self-constructed. Our shared hope is that this publication will help them to do this.

Notes

1   There is no commonly accepted definition of NGDOs. For the purpose of this chapter, they can be regarded as third-party, serving non-profit-based, legally constituted non-state organizations, directly or indirectly reliant on the system of international aid. In most cases they function as intermediaries to promote sustainable development, social justice and enduring improvement in the circumstances of poor and excluded groups. They number in the tens of thousand worldwide. In this volume, the acronyms NGO and NGDO are equivalent and simply reflect authors' preferences.

2   The panel and the authors did not consider NGDOs in relation to emergency and humanitarian assistance. Consequently, this is not an NGDO role addressed in this chapter. This is not to question the significance of this function for the future of NGDOs. Indeed, for some, this may be the area of specialization they end up in, especially if conflict and climatic vulnerability are going to characterize the 21st century. Perhaps another chapter is merited, one which looks at the humanitarian role of NGDOs and the interplay between relief and development. The latter applies mostly to Northern NGDOs, but this role is increasingly challenged by the Southern NGOS – for example, in Ethiopia.

3   I am grateful to Mike Edwards and Ian Smillie for comments on a draft of this chapter.

4   The North is understood as those countries donating aid. The South as countries receiving aid.

5   See OECD website for details and indicators of performance: www.oecd.org/dac/htm/goals and www.oecd.org/dac/indicators.

6   My thanks to Ian Smillie for this information.

7   For example, the recently concluded agreement on trade in genetically modified organisms (GMOS) will be regulated and enforced on a par with the WTO, not as part of it.

8   It is very difficult to obtain sound data on the amount of funds that NGDOs disburse and where they come from. My own estimate is that NGDOs currently disburse between US$12 and $15 billion per annum, with some 50 per cent plus directly from official sources in the North, in the South and through loans to government with NGDOs as implementers (Fowler, 2000a). Official aid to and through NGOs currently amounts to some 12 per cent of the total of annual official disbursements.

9   Of course, it could be argued that aid has been very successful in terms of supporting the covert goal of Cold War victory for the West.

10 A recent study of past criteria for allocating aid from the European Union (EU) demonstrates how the interests of the EU countries came first (Wolf and Spoden, cited in Kenety, 2000).

11 This 'bribery' is alleged to be the case in relation to Japanese government lobbying for the appointment of Dr Nakajima as Head of the World Health Organization. It was also alleged in relation to Japan and Norway with respect to removing the ban on hunting minke whales.

12 It is estimated that tied aid causes a 15 per cent increase in costs of goods and services above international market rates.

13 The degree of a country's dependence on aid usually determines the degree to which this statement applies. India and The People's Republic of China are in a much better position to determine and own their development process than are Chad or Nepal.

14 The World Bank Comprehensive Development Framework (CDF) and its collaboration with the IMF in the promotion of Poverty Reduction Strategy Papers (PRSP) are both justified in terms of the centrality of borrower ownership and commitment.

15 For a recent critique of the self-proposed IMF repositioning and poverty roles, see ODC, 2000.

16 'Participation – The New Tyranny?' conference held at the Institute of Development Policy Management, Manchester, 3–4 November 1998.

17 The most referred to sets of rights approved by the United Nations General Assembly are Civil and Political Rights (CPR) and Social and Economic and Cultural Rights (SECR). International Humanitarian Law, applied in situations of conflict, is codified in the Geneva Conventions and associated Protocols.

18 The idea that there are three clearly delineated sectors with associated social roles and distinctive behaviours has been a useful simplification for analytic purposes. However, it is increasingly regarded as a distorting lens through which to see and understand organizations as they really are. In three-sector terminology, many organizations are becoming less 'pure' types. Rather than 'let this happen to them', NGDOs can grasp the opportunity to be, indeed, a consciously different complex fourth type actively located between the others.

19 I am grateful to Mike Edwards for this formulation.

20 David Brown (1990) has usefully described this type of NGDO as a 'bridging organization'. The idea of a Fourth Force, however, moves beyond the passive notion of a bridge to an active connotation that reflects the nature of the power that NGDOs possess (Mathews, 1997) and power differences in the relationships they are dealing with.

21 Outside organized religion, child sponsorship funding is by far the largest motivation for, and source of, current NGDO private income.

References

Bond, M (2000) 'Special report: the backlash against NGOs', *Prospect*, April, pp1–5.

Brown, D (1990) *Bridging Organizations and Sustainable Development*, Working Paper 8, Boston, Institute of Development Research.

CAF (1999) 'Improving the pubic image of Russian NGOs', *Bulletin*, London, Charities Aid Foundation, September.

Cameron, J (2000) 'Development economics , the New Institutional Economics and NGOs', *Third World Quaterly*, Vol 21, No 4, pp627–636.

Carroll, T (1992), *Intermediary NGOs: The Supporting Link in Grassroots Development*, West Hartford, Kumarian Press.

Cox, A and Healey, J (1998) 'Promises to the poor: the record of European development agencies', *Poverty Briefing*, Vol 1, London, Overseas Development Institute.

DI (1999) 'Poverty, aid and the 2015 targets', *Development Information Update*, Vol 2, p1.

Edwards, M (1999) *Future Positive: International Co-operation in the 21st Century*, London, Earthscan.

Edwards, M and Hulme, D (eds) (1992) *Making a Difference: NGOs and Development in a Changing World*, London, Earthscan.

Edwards, M and Hulme, D (eds) (1995) *Non-Governmental Organizations Performance and Accountability: Beyond the Magic Bullet*, London, Earthscan.

Edwards, M and Sen, G (2000) 'NGOs, social change and the transformation of human relationships', *Third World Quarterly*, Vol 21, No 4, pp605–616.

Fowler, A (1997) *Striking a Balance: A Guide to Enhancing the Effectiveness of Non-Governmental Organizations in International Development*, London, Earthscan.

Fowler, A (2000a) 'NGOs, civil society and social development: changing the rules of the game', *Geneva 2000*, Occasional Paper 1, Geneva, United Nations Research Institute for Social Development.

Fowler, A (2000b) *Partnerships: Negotiating Relationships –A Resource for Non-governmental Development Organizations*, Occasional Paper 32, Oxford, International NGO Training and Research Centre.

Fowler, A (2000c) *The Virtuous Spiral: A Guide to Sustainability for NGOs in International Development*, London, Earthscan.

Fowler, A (2000d) 'NGDOs as a moment in history: beyond aid to social entrepreneurship or civic innovation?', *Third World Quarterly*, Vol 21, No 4, pp637–654.

Holloway, R (1999) *Towards Financial Self-Reliance: A Handbook of Approaches to Resource Mobilization for Citizens' Organizations in the South*, Beta Edition, Geneva, Aga Khan Foundation.

Hulme, D and Edwards, M (eds) (1997) *NGOs, States and Donors: Too Close for Comfort?*, London, Macmillan.

Kenety, B (2000) 'Development – EU/ACP: study criticizes past criteria for allocating EU aid', InterPress Service, Brussels, 9 April.

Malhorta, K (2000) 'NGOs without aid: beyond the global soup kitchen', *Third World Quaterly*, Vol 21, No 4, pp655–668.

Mathews, J (1997) 'Power shift', *Foreign Affairs*, Vol 76, No 1, pp50–66.

McLaughlin, A (1998) 'End of development', *Resurgence*, Vol 189, pp20–22.

Najam, A (1999) 'Citizens' organizations as policy entrepreneurs', in D Lewis (ed), *International Perspectives on Voluntary Action*, London, Earthscan, pp142–181.

ODC (2000) *ODC Task Force Report: The Future Role of the IMF in Development*, Washington, DC, Overseas Development Council.

Raffer, K (1999) 'More conditions and less money: shifts in aid policies during the 1990s', paper presented at the Development Studies Association Conference, University of Bath, September.

Sida (1996) *Aid Dependency: Causes, Symptoms and Remedies*, Stockholm, Swedish International Development Agency.

Smillie, I (1995) *The Alms Bazaar: Altruism under Fire – Non-profit Organizations and International Development*, London, IT Publications.

Sogge, D (ed) (1996) *Compassion and Calculation: The Business of Private Aid Agencies*, London, Pluto Press.

Suzuki, N (1998) *Inside NGOs: Learning to Manage Conflicts between Headquarters and Field Offices*, London, IT Publications.

van Rooy, A (ed) (1998) *Civil Society and the Aid Industry*, London, Earthscan.

van Tuijl, P (2000) 'Entering the global dealing room: reflections on a rights-based framework for NGOs in international development', *Third World Quaterly*, Vol 21, No 4, pp617–626.

Wallace, T, Crowther, S and Shephard, A (1998) *The Standardization of Development: Influences on UK NGOs' Policies and Procedures*, Oxford, Worldview Press.

World Bank (1998) *Assessing Aid: What Works, What Doesn't and Why*, Washington, DC, World Bank.

2

International Development NGOs: Agents of Foreign Aid or Vehicles for International Cooperation?

Michael Edwards

What is the future for development non-government organizations (NGOs) who work internationally but are based in and governed from the industrialized world? Are they destined for redundancy as NGOs and other organizations rooted in Southern societies take over their roles and replace their expertise, or will they retain a legitimate place on the world stage in the 21st century? This chapter looks at the changing context for international NGOs and lays out three alternative routes into the future: incremental change (which is probably unsustainable), global market brands and international social movements. The implications of each strategy are presented and some overall conclusions drawn. The fundamental question facing all NGOs is how to move from their current position – as agents of a foreign aid system in decline – to vehicles for international cooperation in the emerging global arena.

As a long-time student and staff member of NGOs like Oxfam and Save the, Children, I am often asked what future there is for organizations like these – they call themselves international, but are governed from a single country in Europe or North America; they talk constantly about partnership, but rarely practice it in their relationships with NGOs in other parts of the world; and their non-governmental status sits uneasily with the large grants that most of them receive from official aid agencies and their unwillingness to confront deep-rooted questions of politics and power. Increasingly, questions are being raised about the impact, governance and accountability of such organizations – in the academic literature, the news media and among NGOs themselves – and this has led to a flurry of strategic planning exercises, restructurings, new mission statements, and the like as agencies struggle to find a viable route into the future (Edwards and Hulme, 1995; Fowler, 1997; Hulme and Edwards, 1997; Smillie, 1995; Sogge, 1996). In this chapter, I spell out why this has happened, how NGOs are responding, and what challenges lie ahead. Profound changes in the global operating environment for international NGOs and a series of internal pressures are coming together to produce a new range of strategic issues. NGOs are responding to these challenges in two ways: incremental changes, which achieve more security in the short term but are probably unsustainable in the longer term; and more far-reaching reforms, which lead the organization in conflicting directions – further into the global services-providing marketplace and deeper into global social movements. The decisions that NGOs make on these questions will determine their future. So what will it be – a footnote on the history of the 20th century or a central role in shaping the 21st century?

A Changing Global Context

International development NGOs are being challenged by three interrelated sets of changes in the external environment: economic globalization, the reform of foreign aid and the evolution of Southern NGOs as major actors in their own right (Edwards, Hulme and Wallace, 1999). Globalization challenges public authority to influence events and increases the relative importance of private capital flows over official aid. As states are retrenched, more space opens up for civil society actors, and the reach of market processes and values is extended ever deeper into the way we organize to meet our non-market responsibilities, such as health, education, culture and caring. Globalization integrates patterns of wealth creation, social exclusion and environmental degradation around the globe, making traditional North–South, donor-recipient relationships increasingly redundant. Increasingly, NGOs will confront a patchwork quilt of poverty, inequality and violence both within and between societies, rather than solid and geographically distinct blocs of rich and poor – a radically different picture from the one that greeted the architects of the post-World War II system in 1945. In the 21st century, social and economic change will be driven by the interplay between markets and citizen action, regulated but not controlled by states and international authorities.

In this context, the focus of political attention is turning away from foreign aid and towards a wider agenda of international cooperation designed to fit the realities of a globalizing world (Edwards, 1999b). The widespread decline in official aid budgets is one symptom of this shift, even in Japan which had previously been immune from this trend. Post-Cold War, there is no real political constituency for foreign aid in the industrialized world and – although public opinion is generally sympathetic to humanitarian assistance – there is no sign that public pressure will be sufficient to reverse this trend. Governments in the industrialized countries are moving to a different understanding of development that revolves around global security and there is increasing concern for the software of change where the traditional instruments of foreign aid are demonstrably less effective – in building capacities, strengthening institutions and supporting improvements in governance. The intellectual failings of the case for foreign aid are well known (there are simply insufficient examples of a positive causal relationship between aid, growth, poverty reduction and peace), and these failings have been further exposed by international economic trends which suggest that aid will be a marginal influence over growth in all but a handful of the poorest countries – mostly in sub-Saharan Africa – which are not integrated into global trading regimes (World Bank, 1998). As aid declines, new forms of international cooperation become increasingly important in managing the costs and benefits of integrated markets – like social chapters in trading agreements or the proposed Multilateral Agreement on Investment – heralding the arrival of an international system built around negotiated rules and standards rather than subsidized resource transfers. In this system, there will be less emphasis on NGOs as deliverers of foreign aid and more interest in their potential role as vehicles for operationalizing this broader agenda of international cooperation.

For development NGOs based in the industrialized world, there is a third set of changes that are exacerbating the impact of these trends. Although aid budgets are declining everywhere (bar a small recent increase in the United Kingdom), the pro-

portion of foreign aid allocated to NGOs is still rising (ActionAid, 1998; Organisation for Economic Co-operation and Development [OECD], 1998). Increasingly,
however, aid is flowing directly to NGOs in Africa, Asia and Latin America rather
than passing through traditional Northern NGO intermediaries. This is the inevitable result of the development of NGO capacity in the South, but it has been
accelerated by the desire of bilateral and multilateral aid agencies to decentralize
their operations, and by increasing question marks about the value added by Northern NGOs in the transfer of funds (Bebbington and Riddell, 1997; Development
Assistance Committee [DAC], 1997). Because the use of Northern intermediaries
raises the transactions costs of aid delivery, why pay their overheads when the money
could be channelled more cost-effectively directly to the South? For example, NGOs
like the Bangladesh Rural Advancement Committee (BRAC) already have leading-
edge expertise in areas like microfinance and possess a larger research capacity than
all the Save the Children Funds added together. In addition, aid delivery and management are being penetrated increasingly by commercial private-sector companies
and specialist non-profit consultancies which have the skills and critical mass to
put together winning bids in competitive tendering (something that NGOs find very
difficult to do). Overall, there is a much more critical atmosphere for development
NGOs now than there was even five years ago. The widely praised multidonor evaluation of relief operations in Rwanda broke new ground in holding NGOs up for
public scrutiny and there is a steady stream of critical coverage in the mainstream
press – most recently, a series of articles in the *Chicago Tribune* that alleged mal-
practice in child sponsorship NGOs. Calls for more transparency and accountability
are widespread and proposals are afoot for an ombudsman to arbitrate in disputes
between Northern and Southern NGOs in Asia – an idea that would have been
unthinkable in the much more NGO-friendly atmosphere of the past. In short, the
future role and legitimacy of Northern NGOs operating internationally has been
called into question and placed in the public arena as a justifiable topic for debate
(Hulme and Edwards, 1997).

Internal Pressures

International NGOs will be deeply affected by these trends in the external environment, but even in a more stable world they would be facing serious question marks
about roles and relationships as a result of internal dilemmas. In part, these dilemmas stem from the normal life-cycle of organizations that are 40 or 50 years old.
Founded mostly in the afterglow of post-World War II internationalism, they have
passed through a phase of fresh-faced youth (small, dynamic and open to change
and challenge) and have entered a period of mid-life crisis when anxiety about the
future is commonplace and bureaucratization sets in. At a deeper level, most NGOs
are still confused about their identity. They have always been both market-based
actors, providing services at a lower price than the commercial sector, and social
actors, representing particular non-market values and interests in the political process.
These two identities have radically different implications and although they can be
successfully contained within the same organization for a while, this becomes
increasingly difficult as the agency grows and external pressure to perform effectively

in each of these roles increases. A major part of the discomfort that NGOs are experiencing stems from trying to be competitive in both the commercial marketplace and the political process at the same time. These are inherently problematic organizations because they were never designed for the roles and relationships which are now demanded of them. Founded as charities to channel money from rich countries to poor countries, it is hardly surprising that NGOs find it difficult to adapt to a world of more equal partnerships and non-financial relationships.

To an extent, these tensions are inevitable, but international NGOs are facing other internal problems that could have been mitigated with clearer foresight and better management. Careful research over the past five years has cast doubt on many of the cherished assumptions about NGO comparative advantage – closeness to poor people, cost-effectiveness, high levels of innovation and flexibility, and so forth (Carroll, 1992; Fisher, 1998). Independent evaluations have questioned the scale and sustainability of NGO impacts and pointed to accountability procedures that are both weak overall and distorted towards the needs of donors rather than partners or beneficiaries (DAC, 1997; Edwards and Hulme, 1992, 1995; Fowler, 1997). The record of international NGOs in capacity building – promoting strong and financially independent organizations in the South – is generally poor, despite the fashionable nature of this kind of work (Brown, 1998). And many so-called North–South NGO partnerships have been shown to be highly unequal and paternalistic – a continuation of old patterns of dominance in new clothing (Fowler 1998; Malhotra 1996).

Because NGOs have underinvested in learning and research they have had little influence over mainstream thinking, although the microcredit movement has bucked this trend and international NGOs can claim some influence over official aid policy in areas such as popular participation and gender. Generally, however, they have been followers and not leaders in the great political and intellectual movements of the past 20 years. In contrast to the environmental or women's movements, development NGOs have not been able to forge the global alliances and constituencies required to place their issues on the political agenda. Indeed, they find it increasingly difficult to cooperate even with each other (never mind other groups in civil society), because the marketplace in which they operate is increasingly competitive – private income has reached a plateau in most industrialized countries and government grants are being switched to other institutions. In this context, the institutional imperatives of growth, size and market share tend to outweigh the developmental imperatives of partnership and cooperation, especially in winning contracts for the provision of humanitarian assistance, which are central to the continued survival of most international NGOs in their current form (Edwards, 1996). These contracts pay for the infrastructure of the organization as a whole, but reduce the amount of room for manoeuvre in the agency's strategic choices. NGOs tend to import the philosophy of the market uncritically, treating development as a commodity, measuring market share as success and equating being professional in their work with being businesslike. Many seem to have forgotten that they have much to teach the corporate sector as value-based organizations in and of themselves.

This list could be extended further – there is no shortage of criticism these days about NGOs and their work – but the point they all make is the same: international NGOs have been found wanting in key areas of their work and their relationships with others.

Strategic Issues

The coming together of a changing context with these internal weaknesses has produced a range of strategic challenges for international NGOs. Some of these challenges concern the need for new roles in a world of economic globalization and declining foreign aid, and others revolve around the need for different relationships between institutions in different parts of that changing world:

- Globalization makes it imperative for NGOs to influence the shape and pattern of economic growth by mainstreaming the social virtues into market processes—trust, cooperation, equity and the preservation of the environment. Few are prepared for this task on the scale that will be required. They are stuck in project-delivery mode and beyond a few small-scale contacts with corporations, they have little idea about how to reshape the costs and benefits of integrated markets (Zadek, 1998).
- The emergence of rules-based international cooperation (like the World Trade Organization or the Kyoto Declaration on Global Warming) opens up new avenues for NGOs to be involved in negotiating and monitoring international standards and regulations in more pluralistic systems of governance (Archibugi and Held, 1995; Held, 1995). Some NGOs are gaining valuable experience in this field, but because they do not formally represent a constituency they face question marks over the legitimacy of any expanded role in this area. Few are membership organizations and even fewer have genuinely international systems of governance and accountability (Edwards and Hulme, 1995).
- International cooperation requires a domestic constituency in the industrialized world to support global regimes and their application – pollution targets, for example, imply that consumers in the North will eventually reduce their energy use. International NGOs have always talked of the need to build constituencies, but have focused on foreign aid instead of lifestyle change and problems in developing countries rather than responsibilities at home. In any case, most are actually disinvesting in this task by cutting back their development education budgets (Foy and Helmich, 1996).
- Constituency building means creating an agenda for concern using diffuse channels over the long term, but NGOs tend to concentrate on narrow policy lobbying within the international aid system on issues of current but passing concern (such as more and better aid and critiques of the World Bank). These things are important, but they are too detached from ordinary people's experience to be of much use in building public support for international cooperation. In any case, the rapid and unpredictable nature of change in the modern world implies a different sort of advocacy – with less emphasis on converting people to a preset point of view and more stress on engaging with them in a joint search for answers to questions over which no NGO has a monopoly of wisdom – how to secure sustainable development, for example, or how to interpret universal rights in the context of diverse cultures and contexts.
- To be effective in these tasks, NGOs must be good civic actors themselves, otherwise, they will be unable to encourage trust, cooperation and accountability in others – whether businesses or international institutions. These are rarely

the defining characteriztics of the present NGO sector. NGOs cannot fulfil any of their new roles unless they agree to work together, both with other NGOs in other parts of the world and with other allies in civil society. They need to integrate themselves into wider civil society coalitions and cross-sectoral alliances that can reach further into the economic and political arena. Yet rising competition sets them further apart and there are few examples of genuine global alliances in which the large, aid-dependent international NGOs are active. Those that do exist – around the North American Free Trade Agreement (NAFTA), for example – tend to eschew financial relationships between members because of the distortions that money introduces into the dynamics of the alliance (Gaventa, 1998).

These questions pose huge challenges for international NGOs and, not surprisingly, many organizations tend to see them as a threat. Yet they also provide an opportunity for NGOs to reposition themselves as relevant institutions for the next century. For example, they provide a framework to move away from unequal North–South relationships towards genuine multinational partnerships and alliances; a chance to engage with the forces that really will make a difference, instead of being marginalized as 'ladles in the global soup kitchen' (Fowler, 1997); and a rationale for a coherent and exciting mission instead of an increasingly fractious and grasping foreign aid lobby. If NGOs are prepared to put their house in order and to be creative and courageous about the future, they can use these challenges as a platform on which to build a new set of roles and relationships, answering their critics in the process and demonstrating that they have the right to be treated as key players in an emerging global civil society. The question is, will they?

Ways Forward

Incremental change

A number of reactions are already visible among international NGOs as they struggle to come to terms with their internal problems and a changing external context. The most common reaction is incremental change – or tinkering around the edges of current practice – to address some of the most pressing issues while not destabilizing the organization as a whole. Examples of this response include codes of conduct to strengthen accountability, more involvement of partners in evaluation and policy debates, and increased investment in institutional learning. For NGO managers these strategies make obvious sense, but they may be too little, too late. The context for international NGOs is changing very quickly and probably quicker than most can react. As Chris Roche of OXFAM-Great Britain has said, 'We can't change a super-tanker into a whitewater raft.' When there are thousands of jobs and millions of dollars at stake, change will be slow, if it comes at all.

Second, the potential for competition from the commercial sector and from NGOs in the South, may be even greater than currently appears. All bilateral and multilateral donor agencies are committed in principle to shifting resources away from Northern NGOs and into these other institutions. Not many have done so yet (they still need CARE and the others to deliver foreign aid), but as and when they do, the impact will be dramatic. In any case, the potential for reform in many industrialized countries will quickly come up against what is possible within the limits of charity or non-profit legislation (especially in the United Kingdom and United States, where the law is highly restrictive). If they really want to change, Northern NGOs may have to accept the loss of their current status and become a wholly different sort of institution able to adopt a more flexible range of roles in the commercial and political spheres. Finally, incremental change will produce a patchwork quilt of activities and competences among generalist NGOs constantly chasing grants and contracts, but this is unlikely to be attractive to most donors and it will certainly be ineffective in leveraging change where it matters most. For the large, unwieldy, generalist NGOs who are heavily dependent on official aid, the future looks bleak.

Global marketing

The alternative to incremental change is to accept the logic of more fundamental change now, so that the necessary reforms can be phased in over the medium term – with less pain and more gain for the organization and its staff. However, it is already possible to discern two very different directions for international NGOs who want to embark on a more far-reaching change process of this kind. The first is more aggressive global marketing of the NGO's own brand, in which the agency becomes an openly market-oriented institution intent on building its own position vis-à-vis competitors. Separate franchises or business units are spun off under the broad umbrella of the global brand, some of which may be charities and others not – OXFAM research consultants (to take a hypothetical example) or CARE-Emergency Incorporated. Finding agencies in Southern countries to act as franchisees is an essential part of creating a genuine global reach in this strategy – just as McDonalds must open restaurants in Bogota and Bangkok if it is to retain its dominant position in the global marketplace. Their products may be tailored to the local market, but all the business units share a common name and subscribe to a central set of quality standards.

In this scenario, the NGO searches constantly for new business (usually in the form of aid-funded contracts for the provision of humanitarian assistance and project implementation) and new sources of fund-raising, starting with markets – like Brazil or India – which seem to hold out more promise of success because they have a burgeoning middle class. Impact is measured in terms of size and deliverables, such as numbers of beneficiaries or sponsors. Legitimacy is based on transparency in achieving results and legal compliance in each of the markets in which the NGO operates. The focus of attention, as in any market institution, is the organization and its affiliates, not the capacity of other organizations outside the network. These agencies may invest in learning and lobbying, but this is driven as much by the search for profile and competitive edge as by a spirit of cooperation.

Is this a viable route into the future for international NGOs? It can certainly create a clearer focus for the organization and a real bottom line against which decisions can be made, but there are dangers in becoming wedded to the market in this way. For one thing, the international aid business is a business in decline, so even if NGOs are successful they may not be able to guarantee their survival if the supply of foreign aid continues to fall. For another, a marketplace is a marketplace and once the playing-field for competitive tendering is levelled, then NGOs may find themselves relatively disadvantaged against alternative suppliers in the commercial sector and among NGOs with a lower cost base. As in all markets, there will be a tendency towards monopoly (or oligopoly at least) as the largest agencies take business from – and eventually take over – the smaller ones. Market competition requires corners to be cut, producing decisions over fund-raising and operations which may conflict with core values and quality standards. Most important, however large the organization becomes, it is unlikely to make much of an impact on the structural factors that cause poverty and injustice, because attacking these things is not something that can be organized according to market principles.

New social movements, linking the local with the global

There is, however, a second route to more fundamental change. In this scenario, Northern NGOs become equal members of emerging international movements, coalescing around common goals and values but working synergistically to achieve and advance them. The priority goes to work in one's own society and working from it to support the efforts of others – building capacity in different parts of the movement, making space for weaker members to become strong, coming together and breaking apart according to context and circumstance. This is the traditional role of international NGOs, played out much more forcefully and strategically in the context of globalization and shifting North–South relations. Each member of the movement concentrates on its area of comparative advantage and has an equal voice in negotiating solutions to the dilemmas of governance, accountability, management and communications in multilayered international alliances (Brown and Fox, 1998; Keck and Sikkink, 1998).

In this approach, impact comes not from the size or market share of individual NGOs, but from the multiplier effect of working together and leveraging change in much larger structures – markets, businesses, politics, ideas and attitudes. Legitimacy is derived from the NGO's social roots (its domestic constituency) and from demonstrable adherence to the values that hold the movement together. There is no intention of building up ever-larger NGOs because the overall objective is to build support for the cause, not the institutions that promote it.

This strategy has a number of attractions for international NGOs. By sinking roots deeper into their own societies, they can generate a reliable, independent supporter base for their changing roles and relationships, and legitimize their position in an emerging international civil society. They no longer speak on behalf of poor people in other countries – only for their own constituency. And they generate the potential to be much more influential because of the multiplier effect that comes from activating a concerned citizenry to work for change in a wide range of settings. Grassroots projects and financial support to partners are not abandoned in this model. If there is a problem with village food security it would be odd to start by lobbying Western supermarket chains. The real question is who does what best and how different parts of the problem are addressed by different parts of the movement in a coordinated fashion. In that respect there is no logic to a continued operational role in other people's societies for NGOs that are based in and governed from the industrialized world. However, because this implies a less central role for Northern NGOs overall, it is not a strategy that will promote their own institutional growth – mergers, strategic alliances and joint activities are more likely. Thus far, few have taken place (and, in contrast to domestic non-profits organizations in industrialized countries, NGOs rarely consider these options seriously).

Conclusion

The different strategies mapped out above are not, of course, mutually exclusive. Most international NGOs do not fall conveniently into one category or another – they constantly try to combine elements of both in an echo of the confusion they have always faced about their roles and identity as market-based or social actors. Those in between these two identities end up by managing a muddle in the middle, desperately trying to be innovative in tackling fundamental problems while holding on to traditional ways of raising and spending their money. This is an attractive strategy for those who do not want to rock the boat too much (which means most charity trustees and directors), but is unlikely to remain viable beyond the next 10 or 20 years. We cannot fudge our way into the 21st century.

My contention is that this balancing act is insufficient to guarantee a secure and effective future in a rapidly changing world, so all NGOs will be forced, sooner or later, to make a clearer choice about what they are and where they want to go. At present, international NGOs sense the need for radical change but are wary of the institutional consequences, so they try to defend the values-based approach of a social movement inside a framework that drives the organization further into the marketplace (Edwards, 1998). It may be that these organizations are already so large and cumbersome that radical changes are beyond them, in which case new organizations (both NGOs and others) will emerge to replace them over time. This is already happening with the rise of more flexible forms of organization that use electronic communication to achieve economies of cooperation without building up a large bureaucracy – many new think-tanks and knowledge-based networks work in this way (Kotter, 1998; Senge, 1998). In any case, each NGO's response to the changing context will be different, dependent on history and tradition, the character of its supporter base, and its own particular strengths and weaknesses. There are going to be many routes into the future for NGOs and in a sense this does not matter – as long as all NGOs are transparent and accountable for the routes they do choose. Those that cannot justify their decisions to a sceptical public will eventually go to the wall.

The global market approach described above offers the prospect of organizational growth with little impact, but only while the supply of foreign aid lasts and NGOs remain competitive against alternative providers. The second approach – global social movements – promises more impact but little growth because constituency building is less attractive to donors and the focus is on building capacities and relationships with others, not the organization itself. This poses an acute dilemma for NGO staff and trustees, none of whom wants to be the first to see their organization shrink, cede control over governance to more democratic structures, or risk the wrath of charity regulators in becoming more active, both socially and politically. Nevertheless, the decisions they make on these questions will determine whether international NGOs are able to translate the gains of the past ten years into a movement of global civic significance.

There is no reason why international NGOs should come to a consensus on the answers to these questions – the diversity of contexts and organizational characteristics makes uniformity of direction very unlikely. However, the responsibility to make strategic choices in favour of greater impact does remain as a challenge for the sector as a whole. The problem is – with a few exceptions – that NGOs lack the analytical capacity to make these choices. They have a tradition of underinvestment in learning and weak links with the research community (Edwards, 1997). Conversely, international NGOs have been poorly served by academics, especially those who specialize in third-sector studies. Most lack the broad grounding in international development theory and practice that is required to situate organizational questions in the proper context. As I have argued elsewhere (Edwards, 1999a), there is an urgent need to mainstream cross-boundary work in two areas: first, between development studies and third-sector studies; and second, between theory and practice in both (Fowler, 1998; Lewis, 1998). This is a challenge to all concerned. There is no need to suspend critical judgement to facilitate collaboration – alliances between different disciplines and between researchers and practitioners add value to what each already has to offer. However, it does require more openness to working in unfamiliar territory, different institutional structures and incentives, and more humility all round. Combining action and understanding in this way is the key to achieving the NGO mission for social transformation and to the training of a new generation of reflective practitioners who will carry those transformations into the future.

References

ActionAid / ICVA / Eurostep (1998) *The Reality of Aid 1998*, London, Earthscan.

Archibugi, D and Held, D (1995) *Cosmopolitan Democracy*, Cambridge, MA, Polity.

Bebbington, A and Riddell, R (1997) 'Heavy hands, hidden hands, holding hands? Donors, intermediary NGOs and civil society organizations', in D Hulme and M Edwards (eds), *Too Close for Comfort: NGOs, States and Donors*, London, Macmillan, pp107–127.

Brown, L D (1998) 'Capacity-building for civil society', *Institutional Development*, Vol 5, No 2, pp5–15.

Brown, L D and Fox, J (eds) (1998) *The Struggle for Accountability*, Cambridge, MA, MIT Press.

Carroll, T (1992), *Intermediary NGOs: The Supporting Link in Grassroots Development*, West Hartford, CT, Kumarian.

Development Assistance Committee (1997) *Searching for Methods and Impact: An Overview of NGO Evaluation Studies*, Paris, OECD.

Edwards, M (1996) *International Development NGOs: Legitimacy, Accountability, Regulation and Roles*, London, Commission on the Future of the Voluntary Sector.

Edwards, M (1997) 'Organizational learning in NGOs: what have we learned?' *Public Administration and Development*, Vol 17, No 2, pp235–250.

Edwards, M (1998) 'NGOs as value-based organizations: does the reality fit the rhetoric?', in D Lewis (ed), *International Perspectives on Voluntary Action*, London, Earthscan, pp107–127.

Edwards, M (1999a) *The Emerging Sector Revisited ... Again, Alliance*, London, Charities Aid Foundation/CIVICUS.

Edwards, M (1999b) *Future Positive: International Co-operation in the 21st Century*, London, Earthscan.

Edwards, M and Hulme, D (eds) (1992) *Making a Difference: NGOs and Development in a Changing World*, London, Earthscan.

Edwards, M and Hulme, D (eds) (1995) *Beyond the Magic Bullet: NGO Performance and Accountability in the Post-Cold War World*, London, Earthscan.

Edwards, M, Hulme, D and Wallace, T (1999) 'NGOs in a global future: marrying local delivery to worldwide leverage', *Public Administration and Development*, Vol 19, No 1.

Fisher, J (1998) *Non-governments: NGOs and the Political Development of the Third World*, West Hartford, CT, Kumarian.

Fowler, A (1997) *Striking a Balance: A Guide to Enhancing the Effectiveness of NGOs in International Development*, London, Earthscan.

Fowler, A (1998) 'Authentic NGO partnerships in the new policy agenda or international aid: dead end or light ahead?' *Development and Change*, Vol 29, No 1, pp137-159.

Foy, C and Helmich, H (1996) *Public Support for International Development*, Paris, OECD.

Gaventa, J (1998) 'Crossing the great divide: building links between NGOs and CBOs in North and South', in D Lewis (ed) *International Perspectives on Voluntary Action: Re-thinking the Third Sector*, London, Earthscan, pp25–40.

Held, D (1995) *Democracy and the Global Order*, Cambridge, MA, Polity.

Hulme, D and Edwards, M (eds) (1997) *Too Close for Comfort: NGOs, States and Donors*, London, Macmillan.

Keck, M and Sikkink, K (1998) *Activists Beyond Borders: Transnational Advocacy Networks in International Politics*, Ithaca, NY, Cornell University Press.

Kotter, J (1998) 'Cultures and coalitions', in R Gibson (ed), *Rethinking the Future*, London, Nicholas Brearley.

Lewis, D (ed) (1998) *International Perspectives on Voluntary Action: Re-thinking the Third Sector*, London, Earthscan.

Malhotra, K (1996) *A Southern Perspective on Partnership*, Ottawa, Ontario, Canada, IDRC.

Organisation for Economic Co-operation and Development (1998) *Development Co-operation Report 1997*, Paris.

Senge, P (1998) 'Through the eye of a needle', in R Gibson (ed) *Rethinking the Future*, London, Nicholas Brearley.

Smillie, I (1995) *The Alms Bazaar*, London, IT Publications.

Sogge, D (1996) *Compassion and Calculation: The Politics of Private Foreign Aid*, London, Pluto

World Bank (1998) *Assessing Aid: What Works, What Doesn't, and Why*, Washington, DC.

Zadek, S (ed) (1998) 'Consumption', (special issue), *Development*, Vol 41, No 1.

NGOs, Social Change and the Transformation of Human Relationships: A 21st-century Civic Agenda

Michael Edwards and Gita Sen

Globalization shifts the balance of power from public to private interests, including NGOs. However, sustainable development requires a change in power relations that runs much deeper than this: a shift from using power over others to advance our selfish interests, to using power to facilitate the self-development of all. This demands constant attention to personal changes and a series of reversals in attitudes and behaviour. In this chapter we argue that NGOs – as explicitly values-based organizations – have a crucial role to play in supporting these changes through their programme activities, constituency-building work and organizational praxis. The decline of paternalistic foreign aid and the rise of more genuine international co-operation provide an excellent opportunity to advance this agenda. The chapter provides a detailed rationale for these claims and a set of examples that show how power relations could be transformed by civic-led approaches in economics, politics and the structures of social power.

Changes in the distribution of power and authority are characteriztic of the processes we call globalization (Edwards, 1999). The erosion of state sovereignty and the weakening of workers' rights are two obvious examples, but globalizing capitalism also reshapes relations between women and men, adults and children, people of different cultures and those with varying levels of technological competence. This is not just a 'power shift' from public to private/civic interests as Jessica Mathews (1997) has claimed, but a deeper and more complex process in which large numbers of people see their position systematically eroded by economic, social and political forces which work to the benefit of a small proportion of the world's population. Left unchecked, these forces will create an unprecedented degree of inequality and insecurity within and between societies which will never be sustainable. NGOs who wish to promote 'sustainable development' must decide therefore how they are going to address this situation.

At one level, the answers to this question are already apparent: those who are marginalized by global processes must have a 'fairer deal' in economics, politics and social policy. However, at another level this is clearly insufficient without much deeper changes which encourage people to conserve scarce resources, share their wealth and opportunities, protect each other's rights, and cooperate to advance the 'common good' – namely, the long-term health and welfare of the planet and its social fabric on which all our futures depend. Making people 'more competitive' and increasing their voice on the political stage will not promote the changes we seek unless we all learn to use the power we gain in less selfish and self-centred ways.

The individualism and materialism that characterize globalizing capitalism make this exceptionally difficult, for they undermine the cooperative solidarities and institutions we will need to confront the collective problems that will shape the 21st century – transboundary pollution, global trade and capital flows, conflict and the mass movement of refugees and displaced persons. It is one of the paradoxes of globalization that the more we succeed as individuals in the global marketplace, the more we may fail in other areas of our lives and our relationships with others, a failure which destroys the possibilities of similar success for millions of people now and many more in generations still to come. We cannot compete ourselves into a cooperative future, and if the future of the world depends on cooperation, then clearly we must try something different.

Our argument in this chapter is simple:

- 'something different' requires a fundamental shift in values;
- to be sustainable that shift must be freely chosen;
- that choice is more likely to be made by human beings who have experienced a transformation of the heart; and
- NGOs have a crucial role to play in fostering those transformations in the 21st century.

The core of our argument is that personal or inner change, and social or outer change, are inseparably linked. This is as obvious as it is neglected in development thinking, including the praxis of most NGOs. We know that this is difficult and sensitive ground on which to tread and we realize that our arguments are preliminary. However, we are convinced that any realistic vision of sustainable development must tackle head-on the question of personal power relations.

How Does Change Occur?

From the perspective of change, all social systems rest on three bases: a set of principles that form an axiomatic basis of ethics and values; a set of processes – the functioning mechanisms and institutions that undergird the system; and the subjective states that constitute our inner being – our personal feelings and intuitions in the deepest sense.[1] The first of these bases of change describes how we understand and rationalize the workings of the social order, while the third describes how we understand ourselves. Some of this understanding revolves around our own place in the social order, but it also concerns the deeper questions we ask ourselves about the meaning of human existence and the nature of reality.

When we explore any episode of historical change, we can identify how these three bases of change have worked together to produce a particular set of power relations. For example, the evolution of capitalism was built on the axiomatic basis that individual self-interest leads, by the large, to collective welfare. Its institutional structures are rooted in private property and market-based incentives. And the subjective state of being most compatible with capitalism is a commitment to individual advancement and competitive behaviour.

The interaction of these three bases of change determines how different forms of power are exercised in society. Economic power is expressed in the distribution of productive assets and the workings of markets and firms; social power is expressed in the status and position awarded to different social groups; and political power defines each person's voice in decision-making in both the private sphere and public affairs. These systems of power combine to produce a 'social order', and transforming this social order is the task of social change. The social order that is emerging under globalizing capitalism is one which excludes or oppresses certain groups of people, especially those already on the margins, women in labour-rich economies, and those with less access to skills and education wherever they live.

However, the linkages that develop between these different bases of change are not immutable. Considerable room to manoeuvre exists to alter the ways in which they interact in order to produce a different framework of power relations, a better set of outcomes and a new social order. It is this room to manoeuvre that NGOs are trying to exploit in their work, although, as we shall argue later, they rarely do so consciously. For example, people may rebel against the subjective state that is promoted by a particular set of social transformations, as they have always done in relation to capitalism and the selfish values it breeds. Or, working from a different subjective or axiomatic base, they may experiment with new processes and institutions that try to produce the same economic outcomes with fewer social and political costs – much as NGOs are doing today in their work with multinational corporations and corporate codes of conduct. The point about these experiments is not that they generate ready-made answers to questions of economic and social life, but that they consolidate a new bottom line of values, principles and/or personal behaviour from which better models may evolve in different ways in different contexts. Any relationship that is truly principled will lead towards a more fulfilling conclusion, even though we can never be sure what it will look like at any level of detail.

In summary, social change requires a recognition – and conscious integration – of all three bases of change and each of these systems of power. The problem is that few theoretical systems acknowledge this and even fewer institutions use it as a framework to guide their practice. Social theories generally emphasize the axiomatic and institutional aspects of change, assuming that the related subjective states are simply universal descriptions of human nature, or that changes in subjective states follow automatically from changes in institutions and incentives. At the opposite extreme, many of the world's religions focus on the subjective states of persons and their transformation and attach less importance to the institutional basis of social change. Of course, not all religions are identical in this regard. Some assign more importance to outer behaviour; others to the inner motivations that lie behind it. But the tendency to privilege one category over another remains, condemning both social theories and religious teachings to a partial approach that downgrades the links between social change and personal transformation.[2] A fresh look at the links between value systems, institutional processes and subjective states is therefore essential, especially at a time when the processes of globalization are altering each of these things and their relationships with each other.

The Importance of Integration

Against this background, it is clear that social change requires us to adopt an integrated approach that looks for positive synergies between different bases of change and different systems of power. When change in one area supports change in another, there is more of a chance that the outcome will be sustainable, as when ethics of cooperation are matched by institutions through which they can be expressed and the deeper personal commitment required to put those ethics into practice. Such self-reinforcing cycles of cooperation, sharing and stewardship are the key to a social order that enables all people to meet their basic needs for security, voice and equality of rights, with less of a risk that in doing so they will deny others the same opportunities for a fulfilling life.

It is important to recognize that integration is an exercise in rebalancing, not the wholesale replacement of one rationality by another. Not all competition generates overweening selfishness, nor do markets always exploit the poor or powerless. There are many examples that show how well regulated markets and open trade can benefit the poor, and how economic growth can contribute to poverty eradication, the improved provision of social goods and the conservation of natural and social capital (Edwards, 1999). If it is unrealistic to focus on economic systems to the exclusion of personal change, it is equally unacceptable to call for inner transformation unless we can show how material needs will be met in less damaging ways.

However, the general point we wish to make remains valid. The emergence of a new social order requires those who gain power to make room for those with less; and all to use the power they gain in more responsible ways – not submerging their own self-interest entirely, but modulating it so that individual advancement is not bought at the cost of the broader conditions required for a secure and prosperous world. This may sound highly abstract, but as we shall see below, there are already concrete examples to draw on.

History offers us at least some examples of such an integrated approach to social change, notably the Indian nationalist movement under Mahatma Gandhi. There, a powerful underpinning of personal belief in the power of universal love and non-violence energized and sustained large numbers of ordinary Indians in the movement's tumultuous struggle for political independence. The testimony of those who participated in this movement suggests that ordinary people not only behaved and believed differently, but that they *were* different in a more fundamental sense. The failure of Indian politics and society to sustain these transformations in the post-Independence era suggests that the process of integration was far from complete, but it does not invalidate the basic principles involved.

Indeed, there are many more examples of incomplete integration which show why social change is so hard to achieve, even when many of its component parts are in place. We have chosen the example of 'development-as-empowerment' because such strategies are central to current NGO practice. By doing so we are not suggesting that NGOs are worse offenders in this respect than other institutions, merely that even the socially committed will be unsuccessful if they ignore the inner basis of change.

Democratizing the ownership of productive assets, capacities and opportunities continues to be a priority under globalization, even if the nature of these things is changing (Edwards et al, 1999). NGOs have been enthusiastic advocates of this form of empowerment for a decade and more, yet rarely do they question how people use the power they gain. The assumption is that greater material security, organizational capacity and political voice will be used to promote the common interest as well as the advancement of those individuals who benefit directly. Is this true?

In industrial societies, we know that rising wealth and democratic strength tend to produce a 'culture of contentment' or the ebbing away of the 'habits of the heart' (Galbraith, 1992; Bellah, 1985). In these circumstances, rising incomes may act as a block against more fundamental changes that are necessary for the rest of the population to attain the same level of satisfaction of their basic needs. The same pattern is evident from many communities in developing countries, although it is often mediated by cultures that encourage sharing and cooperation, especially in times of crisis. All over the world, broader economic participation breeds selfish and competitive behaviour unless it is accompanied by a deeper shift in values and by new institutions which allow these values to be expressed in collective action. This is especially true in a world of integrated markets, where the temptation to cut costs and 'race each other to the bottom' is particularly strong (Korten, 1995).

Even when successful, economic empowerment may leave the structures of social power untouched, or even reinforce them, especially discrimination based on gender and age. Equally, social advancement may be unsustainable unless political power is also redistributed to the benefit of those who have less voice. Rarely do empowerment strategies make the links that could generate shifts in inner values strong enough to ensure that improvements in one area are not bought at the cost of damage done elsewhere.

Why is Personal Change Imperative?

Generalizing from a theoretical situation like this is clearly dangerous, but the problem it describes is familiar: change at the subjective level is exceptionally difficult to achieve. It is rarely possible to generate sustainable changes in human behaviour simply by altering the rules and institutions that govern our lives. The missing ingredient is personal change, which acts as the well-spring of change in all other areas. Why?

A common lesson of experience is that processes of social change can easily lose touch with the values and principles that originally motivated and sustained them in the rough and tumble of the struggle. As a result, attempts to generate a new social order can unwittingly be poisoned by the 'thieves of the heart' – the negative feelings of personal ego, jealousy and fear that destroy one's inner tranquillity. If people are not caring and compassionate in their personal behaviour, they are unlikely to work effectively for a caring and compassionate society. Resisting these feelings and developing the inner security required for a lifetime of cooperative endeavour requires a disciplined process of self-reflection and contemplation about the values and purposes of our lives, and the desire and willingness to change ourselves. Undertaking this inner journey with courage can reward one with inner peace, greater energy and more effectiveness in one's actions, an expansive compassion in our attitudes towards others and a tenderness of the heart that, on a mass scale, can have profound social implications.

We are not so naive as to believe that a simple recognition of such things will change people's behaviour. Nevertheless, acknowledging the fact that the absence of personal change can impede the social transformations we are searching for can be salutary in the search for a more integrated approach. Nor are we speaking of social indoctrination under duress, as exemplified by the Chinese Cultural Revolution or Maoist self-criticism sessions. Inner change cannot be forced by the self-righteous; when hearts and minds are brutalized into submission or silence there will be little energy left for social engagement. Our vision is a positive one: the energies unleashed by serious and deep-rooted personal transformation can fuel the search for more humane social and economic systems as little else can.

What kind of personal changes could energize the move towards an economic order which rebalances competitive and cooperative rationalities, a politics of dialogue rather than unrepresentative democracy, and a social policy that works against marginalization and values the care and nurture of all human beings? The first principles for such change lie at the heart of the teachings of all the great religions – 'Love thy neighbour as thyself' in the Judaeo-Christian tradition, 'See God in each other' in Sanskrit.[3] It is fascinating to recognize that the core of religious teaching concerns our feelings towards each other – a deeply social statement as much as it is profoundly personal. But to love our neighbours as ourselves, we must come to understand our own inner being, to recognize that in our deepest essence we are compassionate, capable of giving love, and worthy of receiving it.

Even when imperfectly established in this positive self-knowledge, we can identify more easily with the same inner being in other people – what the Hindu *Vedanta* calls 'unity-consciousness'. It then becomes easier to empathize with what it means to be the 'other' from whom we usually distance ourselves in subtle or overt ways. That shift is crucial because it provides the foundation for personal behaviour which is more expansive and less damaging to others – for why would we damage the life-chances of someone who is as much a part of our selves? The irony of today's globalized world is that, as knowledge about each other grows, so do the criteria of 'otherness' that breed selfishness, greed, anger and hatred – the fault-lines of race, ethnicity, gender, sexual orientation, caste, class, nationality, region and economic blocs.[4] We will return to this theme when we come to the role of NGOs in constituency building.

One question that often comes up in this context is whether more attention to inner transformation will divert one's energy away from social change. A related question is whether greater personal tranquillity will sap the angry energy needed to struggle against injustice. Anger is certainly a powerful form of energy that can be harnessed, particularly in the struggles of the socially oppressed. But over time it can be corrosive of those who use it, becoming a deadly and increasingly uncontrolled weapon. Inner centredness, on the other hand, can take more controllable but no less powerful forms. Those who have espoused non-violence, in India, South Africa, the USA and elsewhere, have not been weak. Their courage and energy have often been startling, and their example has sometimes and unexpectedly catalysed a process of transformation in their opponents. Inner-centredness can release enormous energy for the struggle against social injustice without having to draw upon the destructive legacy of anger or hatred.

Are there other dangers in the call to link social to personal change? Throughout the ages organized religions have often spawned fundamentalist bigotry and a narrowing of the realm of personal beliefs to accord with what is considered by some to be 'moral' conduct. Our own age shows us the dangers that religious fundamentalism brings to social institutions when it spills over from the private to the public realm. Social conservatism is rarely more dangerous than when it cloaks itself in religious garb that cannot adequately be challenged by rationalist arguments for social justice because it assumes an other-worldly authority. The rising tide of religious bigotry across the world in recent decades is one of the reasons why space for serious discussion of the links between social and personal change has been so narrow. The other is a woolly-headed and self-indulgent 'new ageism' that confuses material detachment with a wholesale retreat from social engagement.

However, disciplined self-enquiry of the kind we have described provides a way out of this impasse, by constantly exposing attitudes and behaviours that masquerade as compassionate or detached. Paradoxically, the expansive compassion and tenderness of heart of which we speak calls for all the toughness of mind, courage and flexibility that are also required in the outer struggle for social change. Our conclusion, then, is clear: personal transformation is essential if we are to see society change in the directions we espouse. Confronting this challenge squarely and with honesty is the need of the hour.

What Can NGOs Do to Foster Personal Change?

NGOs are unlikely vehicles for the direct transformation of the individual, although the best traditions of the sectors – like selfless service among volunteers and the courage to undertake the seemingly impossible – sometimes generate experiences that come close to the spiritual realm. However, the model of social change we have described makes it clear that there are many indirect ways to encourage the transformation of people's subjective states, as long as our approach to processes and institutions is properly integrated. In other words, the goal of personal change must be a conscious and explicit element in all that we do. Most of us know that our true Self is loving and compassionate, but feel we must disguise it in the street-fighting of everyday life. However, when we consciously create more institutional spaces for inner transformation, we can begin to exercise our economic, social and political responsibilities in ways that both draw from and encourage the personal changes we are looking for. It may sound romantic to call for an economics or politics that is loving and compassionate, but this is exactly what we can shape through conscious action.

We want to look briefly at three areas in which NGOs have a crucial role to play in fostering these integrated changes: first, in their programme activities (the work they support in the field, directly or through others); second, in their fund-raising and constituency-building work; and third in their own organizational praxis – the ways in which values are expressed in structures, systems and management. Constraints of space mean that we can only mention a small number of examples.

Programme activities

As we see it, the overriding challenge for NGOs in the 21st century will be to help rebalance the competitive and cooperative forces that motivate each one of us, whether in economics, politics or social life. They can do this by regulating – and ultimately reconstructing – all systems of power in ways which achieve three things: a more equal distribution of what they deliver, less costly ways of producing it, and more cooperative values and behaviour among those involved as producers or consumers. When we talk of 'costs', we explicitly include damage done to ourselves, the social fabric that sustains us fully as human beings and the environment we all depend on for our future.

Although NGOs rarely see their work in this way, there are plenty of experiments already underway which show how such integrated transformations might work on a much larger scale (Edwards, 1999):

- In economics, for example, new forms of enterprise are competing effectively in open markets but distributing work and profits with a social purpose, backed up by codes of conduct to level up working conditions and supported by a growing movement for 'ethical consumption'. The links that are developing between peasant production systems in Latin America and supermarket campaigns in industrialized countries provide a good example of this wave of the future. The best NGO credit schemes provide another.
- In politics, Latin American municipalities are inventing new forms of 'dialogic democracy' in which representatives from civil society and business share in decision-making with local government. Similar experiments are underway in other parts of the world – like India's 'Panchayati Raj' system of decentralized governance – and around Agenda 21 planning, post-conflict reconstruction and the elaboration of national development strategies. These innovations give everyone a voice in decision-making and reduce the dangers of 'elected dictatorships' which favour the interests of the rich. At the same time, they build new capacities for dialogue and cooperation across old institutional boundaries.
- In the area of social policy, organizations like India's Self Employed Women's Association (SEWA) and the Grameen Bank in Bangladesh are promoting different ways of sharing the costs, risks and responsibilities of child care so that women can increase their incomes and assets without sacrificing their own health and welfare to the interests of their children. These innovations achieve a better set of trade-offs between social and economic outcomes, challenging the structures of social power in the process and building the material security that people need to participate in dialogic politics.

Although personal change is rarely an explicit element in these experiments, there is a clear linkage between the processes and institutions they foster and the subjective states they grow from and reinforce. Ethical production systems are not viable without ethical consumers, for example; equitable social policies are impossible if men and women are unwilling to share the burden of paid and unpaid work. Such experiments can consolidate their gains by making personal change a more explicit part of their agenda, so that new, more cooperative institutions can be backed up by corresponding innovations in values and behaviour.

Taking these experiences into the mainstream will require pioneers in all walks of life, but government and business are unlikely to spearhead moves for radical changes which involve reduced consumption or the ceding of authority to non-state actors. The major pressure must come from those parts of civil society who are committed to new social and economic models. It is NGOs and other civic groups that are already lobbying corporations to be more responsible, organizing collective approaches to welfare and acting as a counterweight to vested interests in decentralized politics (van Tuijl, 2000). We believe that these activities will dominate civic action in the next 50 years.

Constituency building

Although there are many interesting experiments like these to report on, they do not add up to much when compared with the forces that really drive change in the contemporary world. What are missing are scale, depth and sustainability – to make these innovations the norm rather than the exception. Achieving those goals requires a mass base to support radical change, and that in turn requires an inner transformation on a scale not realized in any period in history. Motivating large numbers of people to shift to more cooperative behaviour and persuade those in power to create more inclusive institutions goes against the heart of the current socioeconomic order. Without personal change towards more caring and compassionate ways of being and dealing with each other, it will be very hard to generate the momentum to bring about such a shift.

At first sight this might appear to be the job of the churches and other faith-based groups in civil society, not of development NGOs. It is no accident that dissatisfaction with current models of development and foreign aid has coincided with a resurgence of interest in the developmental role of the faiths, even in such non-spiritual organizations as the World Bank.[5] However, there are a number of reasons for thinking that development NGOs also have a crucial role to play, not least because the established religions so often fail to live up to their theology. More broadly, it is the secular world of environmental and social activism that forms at least as powerful a connection in most people's lives between the 'personal and the political'. We no longer reserve our moral expressions for church on Sunday; indeed, the increasing diffusion of moral action through civil society and beyond has been one of the most heartening developments of the late 20th century.

Development NGOs have been an important part of this expanding moral space, but they have never fulfilled their potential as constituency builders on the wider stage. In contrast to environmental NGOs, they rarely use their high, but fragile, levels of public trust and extended fund-raising networks as channels for personal transformation and lifestyle change, while their membership of civil society (both domestic and international) is increasingly called into question. Consequently, we still lack institutional expression for the exercise of conscience on the scale that would be necessary to resolve world poverty or intervene against fundamental abuses of human rights. Without such mass-based institutional pressure, there *will* be another Rwanda, and then another.

One of the key problems here takes us back to the discussion of 'unity-consciousness'. This is the fact that traditional fund-raising images – and the paternalistic cloak of foreign aid – elicit sympathy, but not solidarity. Under the guise of bringing people closer together, they force them further apart, increasing the psychological distance between donor and receipt, and reinforcing the conviction of separateness that lies at the root of our failure to act. 'Caught in the models of the limited self, we end up by diminishing one another. The more you think of yourself as a philanthropist, the more someone else feels compelled to be a supplicant' and the less inclination they both have to cooperate together as equal partners (Dass and Gorman, 1988). Fifty years of foreign aid have left us ill-prepared to face a cooperative future.

Paradoxicaly, therefore, the decline of foreign aid provides a window of opportunity to advance a transformative agenda, by refocusing attention on international cooperation and the values that make cooperation work. There won't be a constituency for international cooperation unless there is a commitment to cooperative living generally, for why should people cooperate with distant strangers if they do not do so with their neighbours? Global regimes impose clear limitations on personal autonomy, so it won't be the United Nations that will solve global warming, but you and us – by reducing the energy we use in our homes, cars and factories. Cooperation requires the constant exercise of cooperative values, rather than the peddling of stereotypes about other people who need a 'sponsor' to 'save' them. This implies relationships among equals and the acceptance of responsibility to put our own house in order. And at root, that is always a matter of personal change.

Organizational praxis

The claim that development NGOs are explicitly 'values-based' organizations is something of an article of faith these days. However, there is less evidence that NGOs put these values into practice in their organizational structures and behaviour, or even that they are clear about what their core values are (Edwards, 1998). This is a major weakness because it is the link between values and actions that is crucial in generating legitimacy when arguing the case for change. Institutions must be seen to implement values as the bottom line in their own practice if they are to build a coalition in support of those values on the wider stage. The best way that NGOs can help to foster the mass movement that has been missing from the field of international development since the end of the Cold War is for them to be exemplars of the society they want to create. In other words, to show that it is possible to be an effective organization which values its employees as it does its partners, fights discrimination, practices internal democracy and always uses the organizational power it has in liberating ways.

Unfortunately, few development NGOs have done this. For one thing, high levels of dependence on foreign aid and the limitations of contractual relationships make it very difficult to expand into real values-based action – there are simply too many compromises that must be made. For another, NGOs are not immune from class, race and gender problems, nor from the oppression and sexual exploitation they breed. Behind the screen of progressive attitudes towards social change in the world outside, the world inside the organization can be an ethical morass. Such organizations cannot be the basis of far-reaching social change.

Fortunately, this point is beginning to be taken to heart in many NGOs. The link between personal change and organizational effectiveness is increasingly being recognized (Kaplan, 1997; Chambers, 1996), even though its practical application remains weak. These pioneers emphasize that it is certainly possible to help others effectively, but only if we realize that in doing so they help us to grow to a fuller, more independent knowledge of ourselves – closing the circle once more between personal change and change in the wider world. If our own practice is autocratic, closed and chauvinist, it is unlikely that we will be able to encourage others to be democratic, open and egalitarian.

What remains is for NGOs to experiment more seriously with management practices, organizational structures and personnel polices that create the feedback loops we are looking for between personal change, institutional performance and wider impact. A start has been made in this direction, but a huge area remains unexplored (Fowler, 1997). Perhaps a revisioning of NGO strategy around values-based action in programme work, constituency building and organizational praxis would be a useful place to start.

Conclusion

This paper is only a beginning in our exploration of what are clearly some complex and personally demanding questions. However, we are convinced that the journey is the right one and that the responsibility to undertake it is inescapable. Although questions of personal transformation and spirituality may appear threatening to mainstream NGO activity, the roles and relationships we have sketched out above constitute an exciting agenda for civic action in the 21st century. Transforming systems of power is the key to a sustainable future in which all people can live in dignity and fulfilment, but it is impossible unless we ourselves are also transformed. Such an agenda would simultaneously help NGOs to make a reality of their stated mission for social change; provide a clear focus for civic action in a world where foreign aid looks set to decline still further; and to establish a genuine leadership role in society at large. It would therefore meet both the 'institutional and the developmental imperatives' that all NGOs must manage (Edwards, 1996).

In a profession that talks constantly about results, the importance of personal accountability is often forgotten. Yet, as we have argued in this chapter, the willingness to confront the shadow of the Self is the secret of all sustainable progress.

Notes

1   We are not trying here to put forward a theory of social systems or of social change, but simply to find a way of talking about the links between inner and outer change.

2   A sharp literary intuition of the importance of all three bases of change is present in George Orwell's *1984*, in which the rebellious protagonist is forced to submit not only outwardly but in his inmost sense of himself through a subtle use of terror.

3   '*Paraspara devo bhava*'.

4   We are referring here not to the struggles of the oppressed against their 'otherness' (although this may take the form of fierce identity politics), but to the creation of 'otherness' as a way of establishing dominance or justifying social inequality or injustice.

5   For example, the 'World Faiths Development Dialogue' initiated by James Wolfensohn and the Archbishop of Canterbury in 1997 (WFDD, 1998).

References

Bellah, R (1985) *Habits of the Heart: Individualism and Commitment in American Life*, Berkeley, CA, University of California Press.

Chambers, R (1996) *Challenging the Professions*, London, Intermediate Technology Publications.

Dass, R and Gorman P (1988) *How Can I Help? Stories and Reflections on Service*, New York, Knopf.

Edwards, M (1996) *International Development NGOs: Legitimacy, Accountability, Regulation and Roles*, London, Commission on the Future of the Voluntary Sector.

Edwards, M (1998) 'NGOs as values-based organizations', in D Lewis (ed) *International Perspectives on Voluntary Action: Rethinking the Third Sector*, London, Earthscan, pp258–267.

Edwards, M (1999) *Future Positive: International Co-operation in the 21st Century*, London, Earthscan.

Edwards, M, Hulme, D and Wallace, T (1999) 'NGOs in a global future: marrying local delivery to worldwide leverage', *Public Administration and Development*, Vol 19 , No 2, pp117–36.

Fowler, A (1997) *Striking a Balance: A Guide to Enhancing the Effectiveness of Non-Governmental Organizations in International Development*, London, Earthscan.

Galbraith, J K (1992) *The Culture of Contentment*, London, Sinclair-Stevenson.

Kaplan, A (1997) *The Development Practitioners' Handbook*, London, Pluto Press.

Korten, D (1995) *When Corporations Rule the World*, West Hartford, CT, Kumarian Press.

Mathews, J (1997) 'Power shift', *Foreign Affairs*, Vol 76, No 1, pp50–66.

van Tuijl (2000) 'Entering the global dealing room: Reflections on a rights-based framework for NGOs in international development', *Third World Quarterly*, Vol 21, No 4, pp617–626.

WFDD (1998) *Key Issues for Development*, Occasional Paper 1, World Faiths Development Dialogue (available from: email wfdd@btinternet.com)

Part 2

Strategy, Scaling-up and Advocacy

Making a Difference: Scaling-up the Developmental Impact of NGOs – Concepts and Experiences

Michael Edwards and David Hulme

Introduction

There are now some 4000 development non-governmental organizations (NGOs) in Organisation for Economic Co-operation and Development (OECD) member countries alone (OECD, 1989), dispersing almost three billion US dollars' worth of assistance every year (Clark, 1991, p47). They work with around 10,000 to 20,000 Southern NGOs who assist up to 100 million people (ibid, p51). Yet despite the increasing scale of this sector and the growing reputation that NGOs have won for themselves and for their work over the last ten years, their contribution to development on a global level remains limited. Many small-scale successes have been secured, but the systems and structures which determine the distribution of power and resources within and between societies remain largely unchanged. As a result, the impact of NGOs on the lives of poor people is highly localized and often transitory. In contrast to NGO programmes, which tend to be good but limited in scope, governmental development efforts are often large in scale but limited in their impact. Effective development work on a sustainable and significant scale is a goal which has eluded both governments and NGOs.

One of the most important factors underlying this situation is the failure of NGOs to make the right linkages between their work at micro-level and the wider systems and structures of which they form a small part. For example, village cooperatives are undermined by deficiencies in national agricultural extension and marketing systems; 'social-action groups' can be overwhelmed by more powerful political interests within the state or local economic elites; successful experiments in primary healthcare cannot be replicated because government structures lack the ability or willingness to adopt new ideas; effective NGO projects (and not all are) remain 'islands of success' in an all-too-hostile ocean. 'If you see a baby drowning you jump in to save it; and if you see a second and a third, you do the same. Soon you are so busy saving drowning babies that you never look up to see that there is someone there throwing these babies in the river' (Ellwood, quoted in Korten, 1990). Or, as an Indian development worker once asked us in Rajasthan: 'Why help trees to grow if the forest is going to be consumed by fire?' In other words, small-scale NGO projects *by themselves* will never be enough to secure lasting improvements in the lives of poor people. Yet what else can NGOs do and how can they increase their developmental impact without losing their traditional flexibility, value-base and effectiveness at the local level? Resolving this dilemma is the central question facing NGOs of all kinds as they move towards a new millennium.

Of course, an emphasis on *quality* in NGO work is never misplaced. Good development work is not insignificant just because it is limited in scale, and some might disagree with Clark's (1992) statement that 'maximizing impact is the paramount objective of NGOs'. As Alan Fowler (1990, p11) rightly points out, the roots of NGO comparative advantage lie in the quality of relationships they can create, not in the size of resources they can command. Some NGOs appear to have lost sight of this fact in a headlong rush for growth, influence and status, forgetting that 'voluntarism and values are their most precious asset' (Brown and Korten, 1989). Simple, human concern for other people as individuals and in very practical ways is one of the hallmarks of NGO work. There is a danger that these qualities will go 'out of fashion' because of mounting concerns for strategy and impact, but in so doing the voluntary sector will lose its most important defining characteristic.

Nevertheless, all serious NGOs want to increase their impact and effectiveness, ensure that they spend their limited resources in the best way possible and thereby maximize their own particular contribution to the development of people around the world. The question is, how are these goals to be achieved? We believe that there are many possible answers, but none which ignore the importance of macro-level influences in determining the success of people's development efforts at grassroots level. We find it inconceivable that NGOs will achieve their objectives in isolation from the national and international political process and its constituent parts. It is this interaction, this search for greater impact, that forms the central theme of the debate on 'scaling-up'. It should be noted at the outset that this term does *not* imply expanding the size of NGO operations. There are many different ways in which impact can be achieved, and the contributions to this book have been chosen deliberately to reflect the wide diversity of approaches chosen by different NGOs at different stages in their development. There is no attempt to identify the 'best' strategy for achieving greater impact, still less to impose a consensus where none exists.

The term 'NGO' also embraces a huge diversity of institutions. International NGOs such as Save the Children and Christian Aid (commonly referred to as Northern NGOs or NNGOs); 'intermediary' NGOs in the South (SNGOs) who support grassroots work through funding, technical advice and advocacy; grassroots movements of various kinds (grassroots organizations or GROs and community-based organizations or CBOs) which are controlled by their own members; and networks and federations composed of any or all of the above. Clearly, each of these NGOs plays a distinctive role in development and faces a different range of choices and strategies when considering the question of impact. Added to this is the obvious importance of *context* in determining which strategies are chosen and how effective they are in practice, and the observation that 'scaling-up' is often a spontaneous process rather than the result of a pre-planned strategy. These complications make generalization difficult and dangerous.

Nonetheless, a conceptual framework is needed if any sense is to be made of such a wide range of case studies. There are at least five models of scaling-up we have considered in writing this chapter. The first comes from Clark (1991) who differentiates between 'project replication', 'building grassroots movements' and 'influencing policy reform'. These distinctions are echoed by Howes and Sattar (1992), who separate organizational or programme growth (the 'additive' strategy) from achieving impact via transfers to, or catalysing other organizations (the 'muliplicative' strategy). Mitlin and Satterthwaite (1992) comment that successful NGOs concentrate on 'pulling in' resources rather than expanding the scale of their own service provision, while Robert Myers (1992, p379) makes the opposing case, defining scaling-up as 'reaching as many people as possible with services or programmes'. This is a limiting definition, but Myers goes on to make a useful distinction between 'expansion, explosion and association'. 'Explosive' strategies begin with NGO operations on a large scale and adapt programmes to local circumstances afterwards. In contrast, 'associational' strategies 'achieve scale by piecing together coverage obtained in several district (and not necessarily coordinated) projects and programmes, each responding to the needs of a distinct part of the total population served' (Myers, 1992, p380). In Myers' model the most obvious form of scaling-up is direct programme expansion. Robert Chambers (1992) adds a further important dimension to the debate by highlighting what he calls 'self-spreading and self-improving strategies' – 'to develop, spread and improve new approaches and methods', gradually extending good practice through NGO and government bureaucracies until their entire approach is transformed, and rejuvenating the NGO sector by stimulating the formation of new, independent NGOs.

From all this it seems to us that the most important distinction to be made lies between *additive* strategies, which imply an increase in the size of the programme or organization; *multiplicative* strategies, which do not imply growth but achieve impact through deliberate influence, networking, policy and legal reform, or training; and *diffusive* strategies, where spread is informal and spontaneous. These distinctions are important because each group of strategies has different costs and benefits, strengths and weaknesses, and implications for the NGO concerned. Different strategies may be more, or less, effective according to circumstance, and it may not be possible to combine elements of each one in the same organization. We make some preliminary observations about these trade-offs in the second part of this chapter. The value of a strong conceptual framework is that it can clarify the strategic choices available to different NGOs and help them to make the decisions appropriate for the specific realities they face.

For the sake of clarity, we have divided the first part of this chapter into four sections, each representing a particular approach to scaling-up. Three of these approaches fall into the 'multiplicative' and 'diffusive' categories: working with government, linking the grassroots with lobbying and advocacy, and advocacy in the North. The fourth strategy – increasing impact by organizational growth – falls under the 'additive' approach. These categories are not intended to be wholly self-contained, and there is a good deal of overlap between them.

Working with Government

Traditionally, most NGOs have been suspicious of governments, their relationships varying between benign neglect and outright hostility. Governments often share a similarly suspicious view of NGOs, national and international, and their relationship, at least in Africa, has been likened to cat and mouse (Bratton, 1990). It is not hard to see why this should be the case. Government structures are often rigid, hierarchical and autocratic. Power and control rest at the topmost level where programmes are designed and resources allocated. All governments are encumbered with authoritarian relationships with their citizens, for they are collectors of taxes, enforcers of the peace and protectors of the social order (Copestake, 1990). They have a natural tendency to centralization, bureaucracy and control. NGOs, on the other hand, are (or should be?) distinguished by their flexibility, willingness to innovate and emphasis on the non-hierarchical values and relationships required to promote true partnership and participation.

Nonetheless, there are sound reasons for NGOs to enter into a positive and creative relationship with the institutions of both state and government. Governments remain largely responsible for providing the health, education, agricultural and other services on which people rely, although this is changing under the impact of the 'new conditionality' and its attempts to expand the role of the private sector at governments' expense. The state remains the ultimate arbiter and determinant of the wider political changes on which sustainable development depends. Some would argue that *only* governments can do these things effectively and equitably – that any attempt, for example, to privatize services is bound to result in declining access to quality care for the poor. Whether or not this is true, it remains a fact that (in most countries) government controls the wider frameworks within which people and their organizations have to operate. While this remains true, NGOs ignore government structures at their peril. An increasing number of NGOs have acknowledged this and are working actively to foster change at various levels. International NGOs tend to restrict themselves to the institutions of government, working within ministries to promote changes in policy and practice. National NGOs, on the other hand, can take a more active role in the political process and the wider institutions of the state. Usually, this takes the form of subjecting these institutions to various forms of external pressure and protest, as in the case of social action groups in India lobbying the local Forest Department or Block Development Officer (a strategy covered under 'Linking the Grassroots with Lobbying and Advocacy' below).

A more direct approach is to work *within* the structures of government in an explicit attempt to foster more appropriate and effective policies and practices which will eventually be of benefit to poorer and less powerful people as they filter through into action by civil servants lower down the system. The aim here is to ensure that governments adopt policies which are genuinely developmental at national level – policies which ultimately will enable poor people to achieve greater control over their lives in health, education, production, and so on. NGOs have attempted to do this via direct funding, high-level policy advice, 'technical assistance', the provision of 'volunteer' workers, or (usually) a mixture of these things. Many NGOs provide government with a 'package' of inputs which includes material support as well as people and ideas. It is important to remember that these strategies are *not* an attempt to replace the state, but rather to *influence* the direction of government policy or to support existing policies. 'NGOs cannot seek to replace the state, for they have no legitimacy, authority or sovereignty, and, crucially, are self-selected and thus not accountable' (Palmer and Rossiter, 1990).

A number of conclusions occur from studies of NGO – government interaction. First, when the decision is taken to work within government, the constraints and difficulties of the government system have to be accepted as a starting point. Unlike in NGO programmes, good staff cannot be hand-picked and supported with high salaries or generous benefits; systems and structures cannot be changed at will and resources are always in short supply. Motivation is often lacking because salaries are low and conditions poor. Public services are suspicious of change and often officers at lower levels in the hierarchy have been actively discouraged to experiment, innovate or take the initiative. Inevitably, progress, if it is achieved, will be slow, and agencies must commit themselves to partnership for long periods of time. The chances of succeeding in this approach are increased if NGOs agree to work within the government system, right from the start. This increases the likelihood of sustainable reforms and enables the NGO to understand and deal with the constraints faced by the official system.

Second, personalities and relationships between individuals are a vital element in successful government – NGO partnerships. If these relationships do not exist, no amount of money or advice will make a difference. In addition, conflicting interests and agendas within government ministries may make dialogue and consensus impossible, undermining the efficacy of even the strongest NGO inputs. The whole notion of 'counterpart training' needs to be closely examined to ensure that NGO expatriate inputs really do have a lasting impact when faced with such a range of constraints. Even when good relationships do exist, this is no guarantee of success. This is partly because individuals are moved around the government system with alarming regularity (making influence through individual training and advice difficult to achieve), and partly because there is often a barrier between the 'pilot project' stage of cooperation (which is heavily dependent on a small number of like-minded officials) and the acceptance and diffusion of new approaches throughout the government hierarchy. The case of special education in Bangkok (Ireland and Klinmahorm, 1992) provides a graphic illustration of this problem. VSO has also had some success in making this transition by using what Mackie (1992) calls 'the planned multiplication of micro-level inputs' – the slow and careful evolution of different forms of support which are small in themselves but significant in the aggregate. Such approaches appear most likely to make an impact in smaller countries where NGOs have better access to key decision-makers.

Third, NGOs are generally 'small players' when it comes to influencing governments, as compared with bilateral and multilateral donors such as the World Bank. It is these much larger agencies that tend to determine the ideological context in which policies are formed, a classic case in point being the 'new conditionality' of good governance and free markets which NGOs have thus far largely failed to influence (Edwards, 1991). In addition, in a situation where donor funds abound and government needs are acute, NGOs which insist on detailed assessment of programmes and on long-term, low-input strategies may be labelled as 'unhelpful' and 'obstructive', a case in point being SCF's work at provincial level in Mozambique (Thomas, 1992). There are many official donors (and NGOs?) who are willing to commit large-scale resources for immediate consumption or ill-thought out interventions, with little acknowledgement of the longer term implications of their actions. The impossible recurrent cost burdens imposed by vertical programmes in basic services are a good example of this problem.[2]

Certainly, greater success may be achieved if NGOs allow governments to take credit for progress in programme and policy development, regardless of their own influence in these areas (for an example of reforms in primary healthcare in Indonesia, see Morley et al, 1983, p13). Something similar may be happening in the much vaunted District Development Programme supported by Britain's Overseas Development Administration (ODA) in Zambia (Goldman et al, 1988). There is also evidence that concentration at central ministry level and coalitions of NGOs reinforcing each other's influence, can help to combat the impact of the larger donors (Edwards, 1989).

The relative influence of NGOs and official agencies on Southern governments is a useful reminder that this strategy needs to be approached with care. The decision to work with (but not for) government must be based on an assessment of the 'reformability' of the structures under consideration, the relationship between government and its citizens, the level at which influence can be exerted most effectively and (for international NGOs) the strength of the local voluntary sector. NGOs *must* also calculate the costs and benefits of this strategy in relation to others. For example, it may be difficult to operate simultaneously as a conduit for government and an agent of social mobilization, or to work both within government and as an advocate for fundamental change in social and political structures. There are also dangers in identifying too closely with governments which may be overthrown or voted out (as in the case of well-known health activists in Bangladesh). Nonetheless, even under the most authoritarian governments there are often opportunities for progressive change. For example, the Ministry of Health in Pinochet's Chile developed a strong policy on breastmilk substitutes with help from NGOs. OXFAM worked alongside rigid government structures in Malawi to foster reforms in primary health care (Clark, 1992). There are certainly enough examples of NGO impact on government policy and practice to give hope for the future, as long as the conditions for influence are right.

The Direct Approach: Increasing Impact by Organizational Growth

For many NGOs the obvious strategy for increasing impact is to expand projects or programmes that are judged to be successful. Over the 1980s this approach has been pursued in the South, where it has led to the evolution of a set of big NGOs in Asia (Howes and Sattar, 1992), and in the North where many NGOs have dramatically expanded their operational budgets and staffing. Expansion can take several forms. It may be *geographical* (moving into new areas or countries); by *horizontal function* (adding additional sectoral activities to existing programmes – for example, adding a housing component to an income-generating programme); by *vertical function* (adding 'upstream' or 'downstream' activities to existing programmes – for example, adding an agricultural processing project to an agricultural production scheme); or by a combination of these forms.

Apart from the strong common-sense appeal, there is a logic in supporting direct operational expansion. At its foundation is the argument that any agency capable of alleviating poverty has a moral obligation to help as many poor people as it can. Added to this are the claims that, in a resource-scarce situation, NGOs can use existing resources more efficiently than other agencies and can mobilize additional resources. Successful past experience means that NGOs have already learned what to do, so that they can tackle development problems with comparatively short 'start-up' times. For the NGO itself, large-scale operational successes enhance credibility for other scaling-up strategies – for example, lobbying domestic governments or international agencies is more effective for organizations that demonstrate a considerable operational capacity in the field. Finally, one can draw upon institutional theories arguing that organizational pluralism in service delivery creates choice and efficiency that makes poverty alleviation more probable (Leonard, 1982).

Those who espouse the direct expansion approach recognize that difficulties will be encountered, particularly in terms of how to manage organizational change. The characteriztics that are presumed to explain NGOs' comparative advantage in local-level poverty alleviation – the quality of relationships with beneficiaries, their flexible and experimental stance and their small size (Fowler, 1988; Tendler, 1987) – all require modification or compromise as expansion occurs. If we conceptualize the internal features of an organization in terms of its systems or procedures, its structure and its culture (values and norms), then we can identify the nature of these problems. Commonly, expanding NGOs assume that the systems or procedures developed in a locally 'successful' project or programme can be used on a wider scale, provided that internal structures are suitably modified. These modifications usually require: (1) the extension of the hierarchy that separates those who manage the organization from those who manage field operations; (2) increased functional specialization between parts of the organization; and (3) increased capacity to raise resources, both material and human. The need to raise significant additional finance almost invariably requires 'Southern' (and often 'Northern') NGOs to take grants from official aid agencies. This fosters upward accountability and may lead to NGOs being increasingly '... driven by the procedures ...' (Fowler, 1991).

The impact of these changes on organizational culture can be dramatic, as Billis and MacKeith (1992) demonstrate. There is a shift from a task-orientation to a role-orientation; control from higher up the hierarchy grows in significance; and professionalism subordinates commitment and 'mission'-related values. As Dichter (1989, p2) warns, many NGOs encounter severe problems as they expand because they retain '... cultural predispositions to non-hierarchical structures and are often anti-management'. The NGOs that seem best able to avoid partial paralysis during such transitions are those directed by charismatic, and often autocratic, founder-leaders.

As expansion occurs, these changes in culture, structure and accountability may accumulate to change the organization from a voluntary organization (based upon the pursuit of a developmental mission) trying to shape events, to a public service contractor oriented towards servicing needs as defined by donors and national governments. Korten (1990) has provided examples of NGOs foundering with expansion and, in particular, has charted the evolution of the International Planned Parenthood Foundation (IPPF) from a path-breaking crusader on a forbidden topic to '... an expensive and lethargic international bureaucracy ...' (ibid, p126).

For observers who adopt a more explicitly political form of analysis, the cooptation of expansionist NGOs by the status quo (both domestic and international) is not simply the result of changes in organizational characteristics. Rather, it is an outcome that is consciously sought by those who hold power as they respond to the growing popularity of NGOs. At the level of local and national power structures, it can be argued that a strategy of service-delivery expansion permits the alleviation of the symptoms of poverty without challenging the causes. From this radical perspective, NGOs are seen as eroding the power of progressive political formations by preaching change without a clear analysis of how that change is to be achieved; by encouraging income-generating projects that favour the advancement of a few poor individuals but not 'the poor' as a class; and by competing with political groups for personal and popular action.

A focus on international relations yields a different but equally distressing scenario. NGO expansion is seen as complementing the counter-revolution in development theory (Toye, 1987) that underpins the policies of liberalization, state withdrawal and structural adjustment favoured by official donors. NGOs are viewed as the 'private non-profit' sector, the performance of which advances the 'public-bad, private-good' ideology of the new orthodoxy.

It is no surprise to such radical commentators that strategies of operational expansion emasculate NGO attempts to serve as catalysts and advocates for the poor and lead to a focus on delivering healthcare, credit, family planning and housing, while issues such as land reform, access to public services, civic and human rights, the judicial system and economic exploitation lose significance.

Given the strength of these counter-arguments in some contexts, the strategic decision to scale-up by additive mechanisms should never be seen as incontestable 'common sense'. At the very least, NGOs that are considering operational expansion need to plan for the stresses of organizational restructuring and cultural change; examine how dependent they will become financially on official donors and consider the consequences of this for accountability; study the trade-offs and complementarities with other strategies for enhancing impact; and analyse the implications of such a choice for the poor majority who are not beneficiaries of their projects or programmes.

Advocacy in the North

Rather than working directly *within* the structures they intend to influence, NGOs may choose to increase their impact by lobbying government and other structures from the outside. This is a time-honoured activity for NGOs around the world, particularly for Northern NGOs, some of whom focus exclusively on advocacy and have no 'practice base' overseas. The rationale for this approach is simple: many of the causes of underdevelopment lie in the political and economic structures of an unequal world – in trade, commodity prices, debt and macro-economic policy; in the distribution of land and other productive assets among different social groups; and in the misguided policies of governments and the multilateral institutions (such as the World Bank and the International Monetary Fund) which they control. It is extremely difficult, if not impossible, to address these issues in the context of the traditional NGO project. Other forms of action are necessary, particularly on the international level where the biggest decisions are made.

However, success at this level has proved elusive. There are, for sure, some signs of impact, and Clark (1992) provides examples such as the international baby milk campaign, increasing environmental awareness and better systems for food aid, to illustrate how effective and sophisticated NGO advocacy has become. One commentator goes as far as to claim that 'non-governmental groups managed by half a dozen professionals have shown that they can change the course of decision-making about a country they may never have seen' (Jha, 1989). Northern NGOs have made some progress on the debt issue (playing a major part in lobbying for successive improvements in the terms on offer for debt relief); on 'structural adjustment' (though here the influence of another multilateral agency – UNICEF – was more important than that of the NGOs); on international refugee issues (with NGO consortia persuading international agencies to adopt improved food regimes for refugees); and in primary healthcare (Save the Children Fund-UK in particular being a constant thorn in the flesh of UNICEF and the World Health Organization (WHO) on the issue of sustainability in health-sector development).

NGO strategies in this field range from direct lobbying of key individuals within bilateral and multilateral agencies, through staff exchanges and working together in the field, to publications, conferences and participation in joint committees (such as the World Bank – NGO Committee). One of the most controversial issues here is the choice all NGOs must make between 'constructive dialogue' (the incrementalist or reformist approach) and 'shouting from the sidelines' (the abolitionist approach). Opinion differs widely among NGOs as to the usefulness of these opposing approaches, the choice resting on the degree to which the NGO concerned feels its 'target agency' is reformable over time. This debate has been fuelled by the increasing profile given to NGOs by neo-liberal thinking on 'governance and democratization'. Most NGOs see their relationship with bilateral and multilateral agencies as a dialogue on policy, but the donors themselves are increasingly enthusiastic about NGOs as *implementers* of projects. This is true of both Northern and Southern NGOs, and indeed, some NGOs are perfectly happy with this trend. It gives them vastly increased resources and enables them to 'scale-up' their work directly as never before. The international NGO community is deeply divided over this issue. 'NGOs have generally been used for the ends of the borrowing governments or the [World] Bank, and not as partner institutions with their own unique development purposes' (Salmen and Eaves, 1989). The same internal World Bank report states that only 11 per cent of NGOs with whom the Bank cooperated in 1988–1989 were used in the design phase of projects (Salmen and Eaves, 1989). If this remains the case, it is difficult to see how NGOs will be able to take advantage of the wider windows for international advocacy which Clark claims are opening up to them in the wake of the 'new conditionality', environmentalism, the end of the Cold War and the increasing scale of NGO operations (Clark, 1992).

It is probably true to say that, while NGOs have succeeded in influencing official donor agencies on individual projects (such as the Narmada Dam in India and the Polnoreste Project in Brazil) and even on some programme themes (such as participation and the environment), they have failed to bring about more fundamental changes in attitudes and ideology, on which all else depends. Nagle and Ghose

(1990) make the telling comment that, while operational guidelines on participation in project design will be useful to World Bank staff, many do not actually see the connection between 'participation' and 'development' that NGOs take as axiomatic. They do not see, in other words, *why* people should be placed at the centre of the planning process. Clark's (1992) optimistic assessment of the future of NGO advocacy needs to be tempered by an acknowledgement of the limited gains made thus far. Lobbying, alongside the other strategies for scaling-up, has to be carefully planned and evaluated to establish what really works and why. The importance of advocacy cannot simply be taken for granted. It is worth reminding ourselves that decades of NGO lobbying have not dented the structure of the world economy and the ideology of its ruling institutions, nor has it brought about the alternative vision of development that most NGOs ascribe to, albeit poorly articulated in practical terms. Indeed, one of the criticisms often made to NGOs by official donor agencies is that insufficient work has gone into developing workable alternatives to the policies that NGOs oppose: alternatives which will guarantee rising living standards without the social and environmental costs imposed by current systems.

NGO contact with the wider structures they seek to influence is often too limited to effect any real change. By definition, NGOs are peripheral to the systems they are trying to change and lack the leverage necessary to maintain their influence when there are other, more powerful interests at work (World Bank, 1991). Although NGO lobbying networks do exist (organized, for example, around debt and environmental issues), they have yet to make a concerted effort to work together on a common agenda. In addition, the sheer size and complexity of international institutions is often overwhelming, even to large NGOs such as Oxfam and Save the Children Fund. Many NGOs do not understand the way in which multilateral agencies operate, although the specialist advocacy groups have developed a good knowledge of their targets. Even if the agency's structure and procedures are known, these organizations remain hierarchical, technocratic and often unwilling to listen. Multilateral and bilateral donors have been keen to set up internal 'NGO liaison units' in recent years, but it remains to be seen whether these are to facilitate communication or merely to keep NGOs away from the departments that take significant decisions. The fundamental requirement for successful influencing is a degree of openness on the part of the organization that is being lobbied; if this is not present, no amount of information or experience-sharing will induce changes in the system.

Many NGOs maintain that a practice base overseas is essential for successful influencing. There are organizations (such as the World Development Movement) in the UK which have no involvement in development practice, but they are not registered as charities; there are also charities outside the UK (such as Bread for the World in the USA) which are purely advocacy based. For the majority of British development charities, however, there is no escaping the linkage between practical experience and influencing, for it is their practice base which generates the themes and the evidence (and therefore the legitimacy) for their related, but subsidiary, information and educational work. In his presentation to the Manchester workshop on scaling-up, Ahmed Sa'di of the Galilee Society for Health Research and Services made a powerful plea that NGOs put much more effort into research and information work based on grassroots views and experiences, in order to counter the 'knowledge produced by the official institutions which reflects the interests of the powerful' (Sa'di, 1992). Clark (1992) takes this one step further by admonishing NGOs for their failure to capitalize on their knowledge of grassroots realities in their dialogue with governments and donor agencies. As the role of Northern NGOs changes in response to the growing strength and range of Southern development institutions, they will have to develop new attitudes, skills and partnerships as they move from 'operational' work overseas to international advocacy in support of local NGO efforts – from 'projects' to 'information', as Clark puts it. How many NGOs recognize the need for such a transition, let alone are equipped to manage it successfully?

A consistent theme here is the need for much stronger links between development efforts at micro-level, and NGO advocacy at meso- and macro-levels. Only when these activities are mutually supportive can lasting change occur. For example, the success of the Voluntary Health Association of India in influencing government policy comes only partly from its sophisticated use of the Indian media and parliamentary process, but also because it maintains very strong links with thousands of voluntary health workers and organizations around the country. In this way, advocacy is anchored in real experience and the messages transmitted to government have a power and legitimacy which is difficult to ignore. NGO agendas for advocacy must grow out of grassroots experience if they are to claim to 'speak for the poor.' Similar themes are raised by Hall, who shows how progress in particular cases was achieved in Brazil through a combination of pressure 'from above' (national and international advocacy) and 'from below' (strengthening grassroots organization and concrete initiatives), acting towards the same goal. In this analysis, development at local level and advocacy at other levels form complementary components of the same overall strategy. The key question then becomes how to strengthen these complementarities so that action at each level informs and supports the other. Few agencies have achieved this, either in their own work or in the partnerships they have formed with other organizations working for the same objectives.

If it is true that advocacy will become a more important strategy for NGOs in the future, then legitimizing this activity in the eyes of governments, official donor agencies and the general public (whose financial and moral support is vital) is going to be a vital task in the years ahead. Development education among the countries of the rich North will play a key role in generating widespread support for changing NGO roles, just as official donors will have to see NGOs as valuable, independent actors with something different and positive to offer. Unless this happens, it is difficult to see how the NGO voice will be heard, let alone acted on, fatally undermining the credibility of this approach to achieving greater impact.

Linking the Grassroots with Lobbying and Advocacy

Grassroots organizations (GROs) or community-based organizations (CBOs) that are managed by members on behalf of members, have been central to the activities of many NGOs. Such organizations can originate spontaneously from local initiative but '... while isolated instances of local institutional development can be impressive their cumulative effect is negligible ... what counts are systems of networks of organizations, both vertically and horizontally' (Uphoff, 1986, p213). As a consequence of this, many Southern and Northern NGOs have recognized and adopted an intermediary role to accelerate the creation of local organizations (sometimes referred to as catalysis), to provide assistance in strengthening and expanding such organizations, and fostering linkages between them. This, it is believed, will lead to the proliferation of grassroots organizations that, as a 'people's movement', can have a beneficial impact on development policies and wider political processes.

The main emphasis for NGOs involved in such efforts is usually held to be the 'process' involved in supporting local initiative – awareness raising, conscientization, group formation, leadership, training in management skills – rather than the 'content' of the programmes and activities which local organizations pursue. This is because such a strategy seeks the 'empowerment' of people – a much used and abused term that we take to mean the process of assisting disadvantaged individuals and groups to gain greater control than they presently have over local and national decision-making and resources, and of their ability and right to define collective goals, make decisions and learn from experience. While in its pure form such an approach would mean that NGOs should not influence GRO activities, many intermediaries mix catalysis with their other programmes and provide members with loans and services. Mitlin and Satterthwaite (1992) present a number of examples of such mixes. The relative weightings in such mixes – that is, whether catalysis or service delivery is paramount – are usually very difficult to determine.

Many different ideas underpin strategies of grassroots organization but all have in common the notions that disadvantaged individuals need to be stimulated into taking group action, that groups of the disadvantaged can have a discernible impact on the local situation, and that the combined efforts of grassroots organizations can coalesce into movements that have the potential to influence policies and politics at the national level. The conceptual bases for these ideas range from liberal-democratic notions of pluralism (for example, Esman and Uphoff, 1984) to radical formulations that see grassroots organizations as confronting (sometimes violently) oppressive social forces. Paulo Freire's ideas have been particularly influential on those agencies adopting the radical perspective, arguing the need to 'conscientize' the poor as an initial step in the process of identifying and ultimately challenging the social and political structures that oppress them.

Differences in the conceptual roots which intermediary NGOs recognize, along with local contextual factors, mean that approaches to supporting local level initiative vary considerably. Among agencies that seek to serve as catalysts for group formation, there is a vast analytical gulf between those who believe that membership should be open to all in a 'community' (that is, inclusive) and those who opt for exclusive organizational forms in which membership is open only to the disadvantaged. Depending on the ideas that guide an approach, the work of the promoter (facilitator, change agent, catalyst) may initially focus on the advantages of group action and the management of group activities or alternatively, concentrate on an analysis of the social and political causes of poverty in a locality and the need for groups to see themselves as political actors. Group formation is usually recognized as a slow process (at least in public statements if not in practice) and one in which non-governmental intermediaries have a significant comparative advantage over state intermediaries because of the quality of their non-directive, 'participatory' interaction with intended beneficiaries.

While a vast number of GROs can be seen as having the potential to achieve locally beneficial results, intermediary organizations are usually keen to create linkages between GROs. In part this is to promote more effective local action (through exchanges of knowledge and access to pooled and external resources). Even more significantly, however, such linkages are seen as making it possible to take actions that are beyond the capacity of local associations. Constantino-David (1992) examines the highly sophisticated networking and federating of NGOs that has occurred in the Philippines in an attempt to challenge national policies and establish new institutions. Linkages may be horizontal (that is, networking between GROs so that they can exchange information and negotiate collective action) or vertical (that is, federating GROs into a regional or national level organizational structure, in the direction of which all member organizations have a say and a vote).

From the foregoing arguments, a strong case can be made for supporting and linking GROs: they 'empower', relate knowledge with action, are sensitive to local contexts, flexible and, when collectivities take collective action, can tackle regional and national level issues. In addition, and in contrast to other NGO activities, this approach may permit a degree of downward accountability so that NGOs which claim to represent the 'voice of the poor' may add some legitimacy to the image they seek to portray.

There is, however, a potential 'downside'. From a programme management perspective, there are difficulties in maintaining the interests of poor people in conscientization, mobilization and empowerment when they have pressing short-term needs. Hence, many intermediary NGOs incorporate a 'service' element, such as savings and credit schemes, in their approaches. BRAC provides an illustration in Bangladesh (Howes and Sattar, 1992). This helps to maintain member interest, but it can also be seen as contradicting the logic of empowerment and group autonomy. In some cases it leads to the beneficiaries of NGO mobilization strategies reporting to independent researchers that they are recipients of service delivery programmes (Hashemi, 1995). There is also the practical problem of 'who' does the catalysis. Few NGOs have been able to tap into volunteers on a significant scale, so they rely on paid staff. This places them in a position, not dissimilar to government mobilization efforts, of having to maintain the commitment of change agents for whom mobilization is a means to a livelihood.

From a political perspective a number of objections can be raised. For some, the assumptions of pluralism that underpin liberal configurations of mobilization are misplaced. Genuine empowerment will generate responses from local and national elites and the state that range from intimidation to violence (as in the case of Thailand in the mid-1970s when more than 20 organizers of agricultural labourers' associations were murdered). There is thus an ethical dilemma for NGOs about exposing staff and intended beneficiaries to violence, and a practical dilemma as to whether entrenched local and national elites need to be confronted more radically. For those who adopt a radical view (for Bangladesh this position is examined in Wood and Palmer-Jones, 1991, pp220–224), NGO mobilizations are seen as supporting the status quo. They are 'diversionary' in that they take resources (finance, leadership, popular action) away from political parties and underground movements dedicated to fundamental political change, and they create false impressions of pluralism and change.

Have the results of mobilizing strategies been as negative as the radical critics suggest? Much depends on the cases and regions one examines. In terms of the 'narrow' goal of providing tangible benefits to members, Uphoff (1986, p208) provides considerable evidence of success in South and South-East Asia. In terms of broader political change, claims have been made that networks of local organizations significantly helped the push for democracy in the Philippines (the fall of Marcos) and Bangladesh (the fall of Ershad). However, these have only been weakly substantiated. In Latin America, the evidence of local organizations working together to promote political change is clearer (Hirschmann, 1984) in no small part because such organizations saw the local and national political arena as a major focus for their actions. Hall's study (1992) of Itaparica provides a clear example of the way in which well-supported local initiative has influenced national and multilateral development policies in Latin America, and the complementarities that can be found between strengthening local level organizations and advocating policy reform. The involvement of groupings of grassroots organizations in African development would appear, from the literature available, to be much more limited than in Asia or Latin America. The reasons for this are complex (Fowler, 1991) but clearly a major factor in many countries has been the desire and ability of the state to control or eliminate any non-official mobilization of the populace. Clearly, contextual factors are of great significance in determining the feasibility and results of such approaches.

Commentators on the future role that NGOs should play in development are presently highlighting strategies for catalysing and federating local-level organizations. Clark (1991, pp102–119) sees such movements as reshaping national politics, redefining and ultimately 'democratising development'. Hirschmann (1984) sees 'collective action' as the means by which the economic and political well-being of the masses is most likely to be attained in Latin America. For Korten (1990, p127) the key to future effectiveness is '... to coalesce and energise self-managing networks over which it [the NGO] has no control whatever' and '... involve themselves in the broader movement of which they are a part as social and political activist'. Developmental NGOs will not only forge linkages between grassroots organizations, but they will also forge linkages with other movements that have related missions – peace, environment, women, human rights and consumer affairs. In this grand vision NGOs become a force for dramatic social change that restructures class relationships and reforms global economic processes by non-violent, non-revolutionary means.

Making a Difference? Concluding Comments

What, then, are we to conclude from the diversity of experiences presented in this chapter? The most obvious point to note is that there are no straightforward answers to the question of how to enhance the developmental impact of NGOs. There are strong arguments for adopting all, or any, of the strategies represented. But each strategy faces significant obstacles that must be overcome if it is to be effective, and the efficacy of each can be challenged by critical counter-arguments. There is, therefore, no such thing as an 'optimal' strategy for all NGOs, even given similarity in context and background. This does not imply that all choices are equally valid, for NGOs have considerable 'room for manoeuvre' in their decisions and there will be more and less effective approaches for achieving impact in particular situations.

A summary of the lessons which we feel can be drawn from experience thus far, and a listing of the key issues that must be considered when a choice is being made, is presented in Table 4.1. This list is not comprehensive, and it only partly illuminates the costs and benefits of the three approaches identified in our Introduction: additive, multiplicative and diffusive. It is not yet possible to produce definitive judgements about these approaches, but the following conclusions can be inferred from the evidence currently available.

First, whatever strategy is chosen to increase impact must be subjected to rigorous analysis before and during implementation, to ensure that decisions are based on the strongest possible foundation and that effectiveness is measured over time. NGOs will have to be much more systematic about appraisal, monitoring and evaluation. More emphasis will need to be placed on research and the documentation and dissemination of experience. The need for these changes will increase as agencies move towards multiplicative and diffusive strategies in their work. As Chambers (1992) stresses in relation to 'self-spreading and self-improving', NGOs who are successful in this respect will have to develop the openness, self-criticism and cooperative spirit that is characteristic of a learning organization. Developing these attitudes and approaches will help NGOs to build credible alternatives at micro- and macro-levels to conventional economic thinking, surely one of the major tasks of the next ten years. Claims to NGO 'success', 'comparative advantage' and 'impact' must be demonstrated in a systematic way to those outside the NGO community.

Second, all strategies for scaling-up have implications for the linkages (to 'the poor', 'partners', supporters or volunteers) through which NGOs base their claim to legitimacy – that is, their right to intervene in the development process. Indeed, NGOs should not attempt to scale-up anything before identifying what role or roles are legitimate for them as international NGOs, national NGOs or grassroots movements, in different contexts. The degree to which a strategy or mix of strategies compromises the logic by which legitimacy is claimed needs to be considered carefully and can provide a useful means of testing whether organizational self-interest is subordinating mission when a choice is being made. International NGOs need to be particularly careful here, given the increasing scale of resources available to them and the opportunities they have for influencing Northern donors and governments. The choice to work directly (that is, operationally) at grassroots level in other people's countries, or to work within or alongside their governments, needs to be based on a clear analysis of the strength and role of local institutions and the comparative advantages of local and international agencies in promoting positive change. Similarly, NGOs who claim to represent the 'voice of the poor' in Washington or Brussels must specify how this authority is derived and ensure that grassroots experience is not misrepresented or distorted by intermediaries. In this respect, multiplicative and diffusive strategies for scaling-up may be easier for international NGOs to justify than the additive approach (this theme is taken up below). One clear conclusion to emerge across contexts is that *institution-building* is the critical task

Table **4.1** *Scaling-up NGO Impact: Some Lessons of Experience and Key Issues*

---

1 Scaling-up via working with government

Lessons

- NGOs must work within the constraints of government systems – poorly-resourced, poorly-motivated usually bureaucratic agencies that are resistant to change.
- Personal relationships with key staff are crucial.
- The problems of employing expatriate staff – unsustainability, problems of hand-over – must be thought through in advance.
- High mobility of government staff reduces the impact of advice and training – tackle this issue directly if feasible.
- Allow government to take the credit for success.
- Plan for very long time-horizons.
- Concentrate on policy reform at central government level.
- Recognize that larger donor influence on policy reform outweighs that of NGOs and select a complementary strategy to lobby donors.

Key issues

- Can governments be reformed? If so, which types should one focus on?
- How should Northern NGOs relate to Southern governments?
- How should NGOs cope with the practical difficulties of working within government systems?

2 Scaling-up via operational expansion

Lessons

- NGOs adopting this approach must anticipate dramatic strains as organizational culture is changed and they restructure.
- Sustainability should be planned from the start in financial, manpower and legal terms.
- Extensively pursuing donor preferences for service delivery is likely to convert NGOs from agencies with a 'mission' into public-service contractors.
- This strategy may require trade-offs from other strategies – the tone of advocacy work and the nature of support for local initiatives may be compromised.

Key issues

- Does operational expansion automatically reinforce existing power structures?
- Does the 'donor view' of NGOs define a narrow role for them in terms of strategies and activities? Does it reduce accountability to intended beneficiaries and supporters?
- Can NGOs expand operations without becoming bureaucracies?
- Does operational expansion by NGOs displace the state and strengthen the policies of liberalization and unfettered markets?
- Are there some services that *only* NGOs can provide, so that operational expansion is the only option?

3 Scaling-up via lobbying and advocacy

Lessons

- To date, NGO influence has been confined to projects rather than fundamental attitudes and ideology.

Table 4.1 *Continued*

- Donors are keen to see NGOs as project implementers, not as actors in a policy dialogue.
- NGO knowledge of donors is partial and this limits their impact.
- A practice base is important for UK NGOs to legitimize their lobbying work with charitable status.
- UK charity law will significantly determine the future influencing work of UK NGOs with charitable status.

Key issues
- How to carry out successful influencing while remaining within charity law?
- How to balance programme work with influencing and link the two more closely together?
- Which issues and targets are most important for influencing?
- Should NGOs seek to influence symptoms or causes, programme design or underlying ideology?
- How can Northern and Southern NGOs combine to influence donors more effectively?

4 Scaling-up via supporting local level initiative

Lessons
- The opportunity for effective involvement in such work is very dependent on state sanctioning. Where such approval is denied, NGOs must carefully analyse their options for becoming 'apolitical' or partisan.
- Official aid agencies are unwilling to support serious initiatives to mobilize and empower disadvantaged groups.
- Many NGOs are happy to obfuscate the extents to which their social mobilization programmes are intended to empower or deliver services. At times this may be a tactical device (to hide intentions from the state), but commonly it is based on an unwillingness to make this key decision.

Key issues
- Should strategies of social mobilization be the major role for Southern and Northern NGOs in the future?
- What steps can be taken to ensure that grassroots organizations are member-controlled and do not merely follow the dictats of their 'parent' NGO?
- Are the regional patterns of social mobilization very different? If so, what might Africa or Asia learn from Latin America?
- Should networks of local organizations remain politically unaffiliated or should they openly ally with political parties?
- What are the trade-offs between empowerment and welfare when 'parent' NGOs become heavily involved in mounting donor-financed service-delivery activites?
- How can cadres of professional social mobilizers be developed without a reduction in the quality of relationships with intended beneficiaries?

facing all NGOs in their search for sustainable development. This applies as much to the institutions of government and civil society as it does to themselves. Building effective, representative and sustainable institutions at different levels implies a much longer time-horizon in funding and other support than many NGOs are used to.

Third, the roles of different types of NGO are changing rapidly in response to forces and trends within and outside the voluntary sector. As grassroots movements and national NGOs become stronger and more confident in their work, international NGOs can concentrate more and more on supportive advocacy at the level of their own governments, public opinion in the North and global institutions, a development articulated very clearly in many of the chapters in this book. But such a move poses considerable challenges for NGOs, particularly those based in the North. They will have to develop new skills (in information and communication) and new partnerships – both with each other (to forge more powerful alliances on common themes) and with their 'partners' in the South (on whom they will rely for information, experience and their claim to legitimacy). This will be a particular challenge to international NGOs who see a 'practice base' (that is, concrete initiatives controlled by them in the South) as a prerequisite for institutional learning, legitimacy (in the eyes of their donors and supporters) and credibility in lobbying. Clearly, no strategy for scaling-up can be effective without concrete improvements in people's lives at grassroots level. The question that NGOs must ask themselves is who carries responsibility for direct support of such initiatives and for those organizations that do not or cannot be directly involved, how to link grassroots experience more powerfully with their own activities on the national and international stage? However, it is not just the NGOs themselves who will need to be convinced of the need for such changes, but also, and perhaps more importantly, the individual and institutional donors on whom they depend for financial support. At present it is difficult to see mass public or government support for a move away from concrete intervention 'overseas' to advocacy and education in the countries of the North. This transition, if transition it is, will need to be very carefully managed and will require considerable work by international NGOs to legitimize their changing roles in the eyes of their own supporters and governments. Few NGOs (at least in the UK) are prepared for this challenge.

In addition, increasing interest and support for NGOs among official donor agencies may foster a predisposition towards operational and organizational expansion. While NGOs themselves may see a logical progression from additive to multiplicative and diffusive strategies, pressures from the donor community may force them in the opposite direction. A fundamental choice all NGOs will face is whether to scale-up along the lines that aid donors and host governments prefer, or whether to keep some distances and accept the reduced access to official funding that this will entail. Donor incentives need to be treated cautiously because the decision to expand with official finance may foreclose potential courses of future action, orient accountability upwards (redefining the relationship between an NGO and its intended beneficiaries) and support policies for wholesale economic liberalization, which may not be in the longer-term interests of the poor. The increasing dependence of many development NGOs in the USA on US government funding is not unrelated to the decline of the voluntary sector there as an independent and critical influence on official policy.

Fourth, the interactions of different strategy mixes need to be considered carefully. Combinations of strategy offer the possibility of mutual reinforcement, as many authors show in relation to policy lobbying and the strengthening of local initiative. This mutual reinforcement of strategies seems to be especially significant where NGOs have a particular sectoral specialization (for example, health, housing, forestry). NGOs need to investigate more systematically ways in which such 'complementarities' can be strengthened and exploited. Equally, certain combinations of strategy within the same NGO can generate internal conflict and reduce effectiveness significantly – as when advocacy annoys the state or donors so much that permission to mount field operations or future access to funds are denied. Experience shows that it is difficult (though not impossible) to combine additive, multiplicative and diffusive strategies in the same organization because of the very different implications of each of these approaches for internal systems, structure, management, attitudes and priorities.

Finally, the biggest challenge facing all NGOs is how to achieve greater impact (with all that this implies in the way of evaluation, strategic thinking and improved systems) while maintaining their traditional strengths such as flexibility, innovation and attachment to values and principles. The processes described by Constantino-David (1992) in relation to NGOs in the Philippines are mirrored very closely on the international NGO scene: with greater access to resources comes a preoccupation with growth, a tendency towards bureaucratization and an increasing danger of becoming 'contractors for the international system and its agenda'. These pressures are well known to NGOs in the UK who have seen their income grow dramatically over the last ten years. The recruitment of professional accountants, computer experts, fundraisers and other 'managers' to support organizational growth comes as something of a shock to NGO staff who are used to working on a smaller and more informal basis, and this induces tensions explored by Billis and MacKeith (1992). Sooner or later, calls for performance-related pay' and other attributes of the commercial sector rear their head and internal organizational issues, rather than mission, may begin to determine decisions. Of course, such trends are not inevitable, but they do need much more careful planning and consideration than most NGOs have thus far been able or willing to give them. There is a particular danger that multiplicative and diffusive approaches to scaling-up will be frustrated by organizational growth because they depend so much on openness, innovation, flexibility and learning. Yet it is clear that no approach will be successful in organizations which cannot be self-critical, creative and open to change. The NGO of the future may look very different from the NGO of the present, but in all cases a fundamental requirement will be how to retain a sense of humility while celebrating and building on what is successful. NGOs need to be careful that the increasing resources and attention they are receiving from the international community do not lure them into a sense of complacency or self-delusion, when their real impact on world poverty still remains very limited.

Clearly, scaling-up NGO impact is not synonymous with expanding the staff and budgets of NGOs. The choices facing NGOs are complex, since all options seem certain to generate internal difficulties and all require careful analysis to gain an insight into 'who gains and who loses' when a particular option is selected. Either by design or default, all NGOs will have to make these strategic choices in the coming years. Whether or not they 'make a difference' will be determined by the quality of the choices they make.

References

Arnold, S H (1988) 'Constrained crusaders? British charities and development education', *Development Policy Review*, Vol 6, No 3, pp183–209.

Billis, D and MacKeith, J (1992) 'Growth and change in NGOs: concepts and comparative experience', in M Edwards and D Hulme (eds), *Making a Difference: NGOs and Development in a Changing World*, Earthscan Publications, London.

Bratton, M (1990) 'Non-governmental organizations in Africa: can they influence public policy?', *Development and Change*, Vol 21, pp87–118.

Brown, D and Korten, D (1989) *Understanding Voluntary Organizations: Guidelines for Donors*, Policy, Planning and Research Working Papers, No WPS 258, World Bank, Washington, DC.

Chambers R (1992) 'Spreading and self-improving: a strategy for scaling up', in M Edwards and D Hulme, op cit.

Charity Commission (1991) 'OXFAM: Report of an inquiry submitted to the Charity Commissioners', 8 April, London.

Clark, J (1991) *Democratizing Development: The Role of Voluntary Organizations*, Earthscan, London.

Clark, J (1992) 'Policy influence, lobbying and advocacy', in M Edwards and D Hulme, op cit

Constantino-David, K (1992) 'The Philippine experience in scaling-up', in M Edwards and D Hulme, op cit.

Copestake, J (1990) 'The scope for collaboration between government and PVOs over agricultural technology development: the case of Zambia', Overseas Development Institute, London, (mimeo).

Dichter, T W (1989) 'NGOs and the replication trap', *Findings '89*, Technoserve.

Drabek, A G (ed) (1987) 'Development alternatives: the challenge for NGOs', *World Development*, No 15 (supplement).

Edwards, M (1989) *Learning from Experience in Africa*, OXFAM, Oxford.

Edwards, M (1991) 'Strengthening government capacity for national development and international negotiation: the work of Save the Children Fund in Mozambique', paper presented to the Annual Conference of the Development Studies Association, Swansea.

Esman, M and Uphoff, N (1984) *Local Organizations: Intermediaries in Rural Development*, Cornell University Press, Ithaca , New York.

Fowler, A (1988) *NGOS in Africa: Achieving Comparative Advantage in Relief and Microdevelopment*, IDS Discussion Paper, No 249, Institute for Development Studies, University of Sussex.

Fowler, A (1990) 'Doing it better? Where and how NGOs have a comparative advantage in facilitating development', *AERDD Bulletin* No 28.

Fowler, A (1991) 'The role of NGOs in changing state-society relations: perspectives from East and Southern Africa', *Development Policy Review*, Vol 9, No 1, pp53–84.

Gladstone, F (1989) 'Towards a plentiful planet', report on development education in Britain, National Council for Voluntary Organisations, London.

Goldman, I, Mellors, R and Pudsey, D (1989) 'Facilitating sustainable rural development – an experience from Zambia', *Journal of International Development*, Vol 1, No 2, pp217–230.

Hashemi, S (1995) 'NGO accountability in Bangladesh', in M Edwards and D Hulme (eds), *NGOs – Performance and Accountability*, Earthscan, London.

Hall, A (1992) 'From victim to victors: NGOs and empowerment at Itaparica', in M Edwards and D Hulme, op cit.

Hirschmann, A O (1984) *Getting Ahead Collectively: Grassroot Experiences in Latin America*, Pergamon Press, Oxford.

Hyden, G (1983) *No Shortcuts to Progress: African Development Management in Perspective*, Heinemann, London.

Howes, M and Sattar, M (1992) 'Bigger and better? Scaling up strategies pursued by BRAC 1972–91', in M Edwards and D Hulme, op cit.

International Freedom Foundation (1989) 'A multitude of sins' and accompanying letter, 22 March, London, IFF.

Ireland, K and Klinmahorm, S (1992) 'Special education in Bangkok', in M Edwards and D Hulme, op cit.

Jha, S (1989) 'Internationalizing national decisions', *Mainstream*, 8 July, Delhi.

Korten, D (1980) 'Community organizations and rural development: a learning process approach', *Public Administration Review*, No 40, pp480–511.

Korten, D (1987) 'Third generation strategies: a key to people-centred development', in Drabek, 1987.

Korten, D (1989) 'Global realities: issues for the 1990s', draft for review and comment, Institute for Development Research, Massachusetts, Boston.

Korten, D (1990) *Getting to the 21st Century: Voluntary Action and the Global Agenda*, Kumarian Press, West Hartford.

Leonard, D (1982) 'Choosing among forms of decentralization and linkage' in D Leonard and D Marshall (eds), *Institutions of Rural Development for the Poor*, University of California, Berkeley.

Mackie J (1992) 'Multiplying micro-level inputs to government structures', in M Edwards and D Hulme, op cit.

Morley, D, Rhode, J and Williams, G (1983) *Practising Health for All*, Oxford University Press, Oxford.

Mitlin, D and Satterthwaite, D (1992) 'Scaling up in urban areas', in M Edwards and D Hulme, op cit.

Myers, R (1992) *The Twelve Who Survive*, Routledge, London.

Nagle, W and Ghose, S (1990) *Community Participation in World Bank-supported Projects*, SPRIE Discussion Paper, No 8, World Bank, Washington, DC.

National Council for Voluntary Organisations (1989) *NCVO Response to the White Paper 'Charities: A Framework for the Future'*, National Council for Voluntary Organisations, London.

OECD (1989) *Voluntary Aid for Development – The Role of NGOs*, OECD, Paris.

Palmer, R and Rossiter, J (1990) 'Northern NGOs in Southern Africa: some heretical thoughts', paper presented to the Conference on Critical Choices for the NGO Community, African Development in the 1990s, University of Edinburgh.

Sa'di, A H (1992) 'The role of research in NGOs', paper presented at the workshop on 'Scaling-up NGO Impact' at the University of Manchester.

Salmen, L and Eaves, A (1989) *World Bank Work with Non-governmental Organisations*, Policy, Planning and Research Working Paper, No WPS 305, World Bank, Washington, DC.

Tendler, J (1987) *Livelihood, Employment and Income Generating Activities*, Ford Foundation, New York.

Thomas, S (1992) 'Sustainability in relief and development work: further thoughts from Mozambique', *Development in Practice*, Vol 2, No 1, OXFAM, Oxford.

Toye, J (1987) *Dilemmas of Development*, Blackwell, Oxford

Uphoff, N (1986) *Local Institutional Development*, Kumarian Press, West Hartford

Wood, D and Palmer-Jones, J (1991) *The Watersellers*, ITDG, London

World Bank (1990) *World Development Report 1990*, Oxford University Press, Oxford

World Bank (1991) *Co-operation between the Bank and NGOs: 1990 Progress Report*, International Economic Relations Division, World Bank, Washington, DC.

Organizing Non-profits for Development

Alan Fowler

The Capacities Framework

There are almost as many ways of describing organizations as there are writers about them. The model applied here, shown in Figure 5.1, has evolved from the concerns of non-governmental development organizations (NGDOs) themselves. While not pretending to be 'the' model, the framework reflects NGDOs' key characteristics: it concentrates on areas which are critical to their work and their role in society. To do development well, NGDOs must have adequate capacity in five areas; each must be consistent with the other. The first two relate to an organizational design and systems which link vision to action through appropriate development strategies, programmes and projects; these are carried out by competent and well-managed people. The next three capacities link the NGDO to the outside world by mobilizing necessary resources; maintaining a variety of external relationships; and producing results consistent with the mission. This chapter looks at the first type of capacity, which is the ability to define activities and create the right organizational set-up to do them effectively. To begin, both capacity and effectiveness require a short explanation.

Organizational capacity

What is organizational capacity? The simplest definition of capacity is the capability of an organization to achieve what it sets out to do: to realize its mission. In this sense, capacity measures an organization's performance in relation to those it is set up to benefit.[1] While we can look at the many factors which contribute to capacity – people, finances, physical facilities, procedures, and so on – these ingredients are not the same as seeing capacity itself; this must be viewed according to an organization's results. Therefore, efforts at capacity building must not be separated from assessing external change.

The problem for NGDOs is that results are seldom clear-cut. Moreover, the role of NGDOs must be to dissatisfy' some stakeholders, such as governments or development banks, when exerting policy influence in favour of people who are poor or disadvantaged. Whatever the mix of specific goals and stakeholders an NGDO has, it is vitally important to be consistent about which one is the most significant – who is the NGDO's primary stakeholder – because the values and expectations in

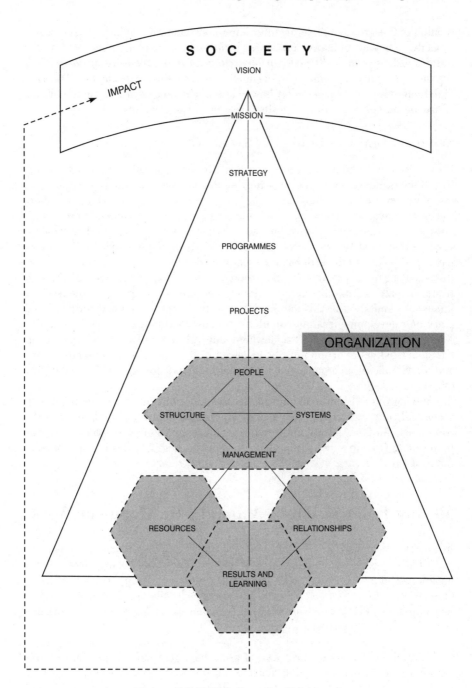

Figure 5.1 *NGDO Capacity Framework*

relation to this group provide the most important standards against which to assess capacity. The dualism between satisfying some and dissatisfying others leads to the following definition of NGDO capacity: *capacity is the measure of an NGDO's capability to satisfy or influence stakeholders consistent with its mission.* This type of definition has consequences for how to approach and evaluate capacity-building efforts because it requires asking the question: capacity-building for what?

What is organizational effectiveness?

If capacity is the ability to achieve an impact in terms of satisfying or influencing stakeholders, effectiveness means achieving this impact at an appropriate level of effort and cost. It means only doing the things that are necessary and doing them well within available resources. The starting point for effectiveness, therefore, is knowing what tasks to do, why, and how they must relate to each other. This involves a reasonably logical set of steps that move from the organization's vision of a changed society to the actions or activities needed to reach it. In technical terms, this is moving from reaffirmation of mission to ensure that it is still relevant, through strategic analysis, into operational planning and then development activities. The immediate limitation of this approach is that the planet is not a readily ordered place and development is too complex a process to anticipate every eventuality. Nevertheless, you have to start somewhere, but with the understanding that action based on (shaky) prediction must be balanced with an ability to continuously learn and adapt. Building an organization which can do this is a prerequisite for an NGDO's effectiveness.

Moving from vision to action calls for two types of consistency: first, between vision and concrete development activities with stakeholders; second, between the chosen activities, organizational structure and principles of participation and empowerment. How this looks in practice for development NGDOs is the subject of the next two sections.

Moving From Vision to Action in Development Work[2]

Inconsistency between an NGDO's vision of the world, what it says it wants to be and what it does is a common source of ineffectiveness. Staff, supporters and the outside world get confused, actions do not combine and support each other in optimal ways, there is a loss of focus and energies become dissipated. It is therefore important that the path from vision to action hangs together. Achieving this condition has three essential stages:

- re-examination and confirmation of what the organization stands for in terms of coherence between vision, mission, identity and role in society;
- linking these to longer-term strategic choices that give it overall direction and maximize impact on society; and
- translating choices into tangible actions and tasks to be carried out by staff, volunteers and others in collaboration, or perhaps in opposition, to some stakeholders.

Going through each stage properly should ensure consistency throughout the organization.

What makes the whole affair complicated is the knowledge that, to be relevant and sustainable, this cannot be worked out by the organization on its own. This top-down approach must be matched by a bottom-up process of dialogue and negotiation with the external stakeholders that eventually determines if there are lasting social changes and benefits from the NGDO's efforts. Matching these two directions is one of the most difficult problems facing NGDOs. It crops up in virtually everything they do and is a constant tension which must be managed. Managing the tension is made easier if there is consistency between what an NGDO says it wants to be and what it does.

Ensuring coherence between vision, mission, identity and role

Vision and mission are concepts and statements which tie NGDOs to processes of desired social change. But they are not enough to 'position' an organization and give it a clear identity and role which is understood both by insiders and outsiders. The degree of clarity and shared ownership of vision, mission and identity differs widely between NGDOs; however, as a rule-of-thumb, this is likely to be clearer and stronger for organizations founded on ideological motivations and activist roots, as in much of Latin America and parts of South and East Asia. But the post-Cold War era continues to challenge the founding ideologies of existing NGDOs – so how are they redefining their identity and role in society?

The following examples suggest that there is no single answer, but a variety of options are available, depending on the system of governance and mechanisms existing for internal dialogue. For example, DESCO in Peru has been a think-tank for the political Left. With over 100 staff, most located in field programmes, mechanisms for extensive dialogue were not in place. DESCO therefore utilized a strategic planning process to redefine what it stood for – a method also chosen to engage the whole organization in debate and to 'objectify' the findings. This latter dimension was necessary because staff representatives formed a majority in the governing assembly and were effectively being asked to put aside personal interests to adjudicate on the organization's, and hence their own, future.[3]

For CEPES, a Peruvian NGDO known for its activism on behalf of peasants, the search for new values based on the original principle of solidarity has taken place in a weekly meeting of all (16) professionals and a tradition of working lunches where issues affecting the organization are discussed. This tradition provided a recognized forum for debate; no new mechanism was needed to address the fundamental issue of 'Who do we want to be in the new context?'. Overall, without recognized fora for wide internal dialogue and a mediating input by independent outsiders, the path to redefining position and values in ideological NGDOs is likely to be rocky. The departure of staff who cannot reconcile themselves with new perspectives is not uncommon.

A different situation arises when an NGDO without any particular ideological position sets out to (re)define identity by clarifying beliefs and values. One operational Northern NGDO organized a workshop for staff at various levels from all countries of operation with the aim of defining organizational beliefs and values and making them explicit. An immediate difficulty in this exercise was to move

through cultural differences, particularly regarding gender. The deliberations eventually focused on basic human aspirations, such as mutual respect, appreciation of
the equal value of individual lives and the rights that reflect this belief.[4]

A common bottleneck with defining organizational values as a way of clarifying
identity is that the task is not taken seriously enough because it is not recognized
as building the foundations for effectiveness. Instead, it is perceived to be an abstract, academic luxury which unnecessarily depletes hard-won overheads. A lesson
when defining values that underpin vision, mission and identity is therefore that:

- it must be seen and treated as an organization-wide priority endeavour; and
- allocating time and resources to dissemination must be built in; the human process of grappling with values is more important in the long run than the actual
  wording of value statements.

Value statements are not an optional extra for professional NGDO's; together with
beliefs, they are the most fundamental expression of what the organization stands
for – its identity. Clarifying vision and mission, which are usually framed as broad
aspirations, provide the necessary initial orientation for choosing paths and goals
for action.

Using strategic planning to move from a social role to development goals

A consistent vision, mission, identity and social role are preconditions for effective
actions; however, they only reside in people's minds, hearts and on paper. Linking
these aspirations and intentions to the right activities means understanding what is
going on in the outside world and then 'fitting' the organization's work into the
environment in a way which maximizes impact. This task is sometimes called 'positioning' the organization. A common way of working out the best fit or position is
through strategic planning.

The objective of strategic planning is to make long-term choices in terms of
concrete goals and resource allocations that are likely to maximize impact without
compromising identity, autonomy and viability. Strategic planning has been relatively neglected by NGDOs during the period when resources were expanding with
few questions being asked about effectiveness. Those days are over and strategic
planning is now a common way of rationalizing and prioritizing resource allocations. But this process can only be carried out properly if vision, mission and identity
are in place, consistent with each other, widely understood and internalized by staff.[5]
A strategic planning process can also help in creating and spreading consistency.

Many NGDOs have grown haphazardly or opportunistically. Strategic planning
is a useful way to sort themselves out and focus their skills and energies on what
they can do best and where. However, one problem in the way NGDOs are going
about this is that they confuse strategic planning with strategic management.[6] Some
NGDOs believe that through strategic planning they have laid out a railway track
which will then carry them smoothly along for five years or so. But people-centred
development is not a known track. Given the high degree of uncertainty, complexity and open-endedness involved, the assumptions which underlie planning systems

make them a risky tool to rely on. Their principal benefit is the rigour of thinking and argument they introduce.

Nevertheless, strategic planning can benefit NGDOs in adapting to the new world order if it helps them to get their house in order, ensures a (re)orientation towards what they are good at, establishes a common framework for responding to the unexpected and ensures that third-sector principles inspire people to move in the same direction. But a plan is not a substitute for managers who must manage with a strategic perspective; managers must have an ability to judge correctly the long-term implications of short-term events, in relation to the strategic direction, and respond accordingly. Hopefully, NGDOs will move quickly through the phase of investing in strategic planning to concentrating on building competencies in strategic management.[7] For the moment, strategic planning in NGDOs is a necessary 'waste' of time, which still needs to be done well – but how?

Figure 5.2 describes a strategic planning process framework for large or international NGOs. This flow, together with reflections on an exercise carried out by an international NGO provided by Hans Hoyer, and my own experience, are drawn on to offer pointers about how this activity can contribute to better organizational functioning, as well as making programme and project choices.

Starting points for carrying out a strategic planning exercise
Strategic planning is commonly assumed to be a linear process which starts at the apex of the organization and then moves logically out to the periphery. This is not the case. Why? Because the nature of sustainable development processes means that they cannot impose and have to be negotiated. So, for NGDOs, any plan has to be arrived at through a process of consultation. If done properly, strategic planning is a down-up-down-up, inside-outside-inside process between the organization and its key stakeholders.[8] Figure 5.2 illustrates this process, which eventually leads to choices about direction, priorities for action and indications for expected resource allocations that can be applied throughout the organization, but then tailored to context.

The balancing act in strategic planning is to create sufficient firmness to ensure organizational coherence and maximum impact, and then to match this with sufficient flexibility to allow for local interpretation and application. It is not just the technical content of planning in terms of analysis, activities and budgets which must give this balance, but also the method used, which should include as many different perspectives as possible. The starting point for strategy formulation, however, must be at the top because this is the only place able to generate an overview of the whole organization and its surroundings. For example, this is the vantage point for seeing trends in financing which determine possibilities for growth. In addition, it is where the final accountability for legitimacy rests. And, assuming that internal systems are generating the right information, this is the place where an assessment can and must be made of how well the organization performs in terms of its mission, as opposed to individual activities or projects. For small NGDOs, these functions may all be within two or three people; for large NGDOs they can involve dozens.

The importance of first setting strategic parameters
In addition to a restatement of identity and desired position, strategic planning must start with decisions about a few basic parameters; these may carry the heavy name

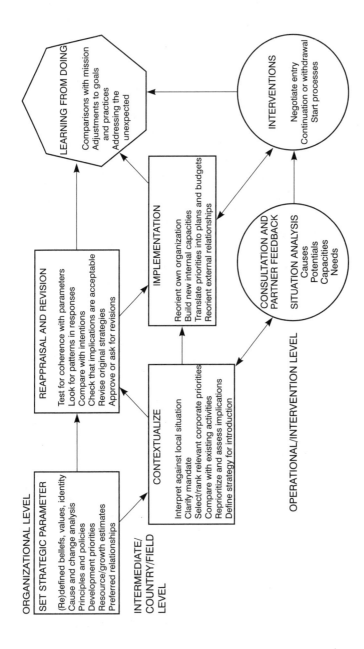

Figure 5.2 *Strategic Planning Flow*

of 'corporate policies': principles and choices that are the governors' responsibility and which should be adhered to throughout the organization. One key policy is about financial growth and mobilization. Other corporate policies could deal with gender, relations with other organizations, mandates to different levels of authority and decision-making.

There is no universal name for the framework of organizational policies and priorities which an NGDO's leadership must set at the beginning of a strategic planning exercise. The term 'strategic intent' was used by Oxfam UK/I for this step in its process; other NGDOs call the same thing a vision statement, or a corporate vision. Whatever the title, the formulation process tends to be similar in that necessary background materials and preliminary ideas are gathered by staff, either as part of their normal work or as members of a task force. To incorporate governors' perspectives, board members or constituency representatives are commonly involved.

The degree to which field staff are asked to submit their ideas, situation analyses and preliminary priorities, or other inputs to strategic planning, varies between NGDOs. However, experience indicates, that if no basic parameters are made available when such requests for input are sent out, responses may be incoherent. In drafting their inputs, field staff may have consulted with their key stakeholders. Unless they do this with extreme care, unwarranted expectations can be created which have to be renegotiated later, causing frustration all round.

BOX 5.1 EXPERIENCE WITH INTRODUCING A STRATEGIC PLANNING EXERCISE SUGGESTS THE FOLLOWING TIPS

Initial data collection should draw on existing internal and external sources, rather than soliciting draft plans from field staff unless there is an initial orienting framework. The starting point should be a board-approved framework which includes:

- A restatement of organizational identity: beliefs, values, and mission.
- A restatement of the cause and change analysis which justifies the overall approach to development work and provides the basis for the interpretation of events.
- A restatement of key principles to be applied throughout the organization – for example, on relations with government, participation, gender, organizational and individual accountability.
- A statement of intentions with respect to qualitative and quantitative growth.
- A statement of organization-wide thematic priorities for development – for example, environment or income generation or human rights.
- An indication of any desired changes in relationships that significantly affect the organization's position in society – for example, working more (or less) with civic actors, such as trade unions, informal sector organization, or with governments and official aid agencies.

Lessons from strategic planning in practice

A successful strategic planning exercise will ensure consistency between the NGDO's vision and the practical directions it will take in the environment in which it lives. There are, however, a number of reasons why strategic planning may not go well. Box 5.2 provides one example of what happens when corporate intentions are translated into strategic plans. As the lessons indicate, where strategic planning is introduced for the first time, leaders and managers have a pivotal role to play in creating conditions necessary for staff (and outsiders) to critically question existing ways of working and to re-evaluate the organization's role. In this situation, the attitude, styles and competencies of those guiding strategic planning has a strong influence on the degree to which the planning process becomes a form of staff development.

BOX 5.2 LESSONS FROM STRATEGIC PLANNING IN A TRANSNATIONAL NGDO

Background
PLAN International is an NGDO founded in 1937. Using funds raised from some 800,000 child sponsors in the North, it carries out development work in 35 countries, managed through 6 regional offices. A corporate strategic planning task force – composed of seconded field managers, a board member and headquarters staff – was established in 1993. The task force respecified vision and mission, indicated preferred levels and locations for growth, and initiated a further process which subsequently identified five priority 'domains' for PLAN's work: child learning; economic participation and well-being; growing up healthy; child protection and participation; and habitat.

The Regional Strategic Planning Process
PLAN Region for South Asia (ROSA) comprises Bangladesh, India, Nepal, Pakistan, and Sri Lanka. Like other regions, ROSA was engaged in the corporate planning process, providing senior level responses to draft plans and other documents and approving of the final board submission. Translation of corporate intent to regional action was the task of a special group drawn from a cross-section of regional and country staff. The drawback of so many levels was balanced by the multiple perspectives which enriched data selection, collection and interpretation. The approach involved a down-up-down process between the group and country staff, with time built in for sharing and feedback. The steps adopted were:

- Undoing the historical conditioning of group members to create a common understanding, bolstered by a spirit of enquiry, entrepreneurship and risk-taking.
- Redefining vision and values from a regional perspective, by awakening, sharing and exploring innermost feelings.
- Defining mission, particularly by sorting out the contending stakeholders and defining a model of sustainable development which calls for cause analysis and provides progress measures.

Box 5.2 Continued

- Formulating strategic questions which guide the collection of information.
- Undertaking analysis which answers the strategic questions and leads to specific actions.
- Converting mission into objectives in each of the themes, which correspond to priority areas within PLAN's corporate domains.
- Assessing organizational implications and strategizing implementation.

Lessons: blockages and how to deal with them

Strategic planning was a new process for staff which also demanded reflection. The following lessons emerged about blockages and how to deal with them:

- *Functional myopia:* staff prioritize their own functions and underplay the significance of the work and links to other units. A solution is patience, placing stress on shared values, creating a common vocabulary and criticizing ideas which are myopic.
- *Command-and-control orientation:* staff are regarded as hands to be directed, rather than heads to be tapped and hearts to be engaged, leading to their passivity and risk avoidance. A solution is to foster and guide dissatisfaction actively by exploiting the difference between the actual and the desired organizational culture.
- *Preoccupation with daily routines:* people cannot balance their work with plans for the future. A solution is to create space, not to underplay the magnitude of the task, and to stress that crafting a strategy is an exercise in entrepreneurship which entails a degree of risk.
- *Excessive formalization:* too strict adherence to systems constrains innovation, induces a fear of straying over the line, and produces apathy which is not conducive to the inquisitiveness and exploration that strategic planning calls for. A solution is to agree that mistakes are a natural and valuable source of human learning and to create space to do so by allowing selective relaxation of rules and procedures.
- *Insufficient external orientation:* internal preoccupations filter out signs of external changes which have a direct bearing on relevance and effectiveness. Paying attention to what is outside, however, requires a capacity to absorb and process what is seen and heard. A solution is to build up and retain an analytic capacity because sheer effort and creativity are not sufficient for correct organizational positioning, which must be grounded in an assessment of the external environment.
- *Lack of will to change:* conforming with authority, limited mobility across functional areas and excessive job security all conspire to make any change seem threatening. A solution is to create triggers against the status quo which link external forces for change with internal dissatisfactions – for example, by raising questions about staff perception and assumptions.

Source: Adapted from a contribution by Dr Hans J Hoyer, Regional Director, PLAN International South Asia

The origin of a strategic planning initiative influences how the process runs and its impact on the relationship with partner NGDOs. Occasionally, strategic planning is prompted by internal reflection, but more frequently results from external pressure as the aid system shifts into a post-Cold War mode. Today, in pursuit of greater accountability, a concern for cost effectiveness and demonstration of impact, donors are calling for a better specification of what NGDOs intend to do with their funds, why and the measures they will use to prove their performance. Strategic planning is the tool usually chosen by Northern NGDOs to come up with a response. As the next link in the aid chain, Southern and Eastern partners are on the receiving end of this process. They must decide how to respond.

All too often weak, dependent Southern NGDOs respond by embarking on a strategic planning exercise which simply reorients their priorities towards those of their Northern partners. In other words, they do not look for options which will make them less dependent and then negotiate an uncoupling from the existing relationship based on a well-thought through strategy. This is an important issue because three lessons from strategic planning by Northern NGDOs give cause for concern:

- Strategic plans, particularly at the country level, seldom include an analysis of their consequences, especially for existing partner relationships and staff competencies. A rough calculation for those I know about suggest that some 15–30 per cent of partners and 10–15 per cent of staff would no longer fit into the strategic priorities being chosen by Northern NGOs.[9]
- Strategic plans must themselves make provision for resource allocations for the plan's implementation, including a process for withdrawal from existing relations and entry into new ones.
- A third shortcoming is the highly unlikely idea that a strategic plan is operational in its first year. A more realistic assumption is that it will take the duration of a new strategic plan to introduce it. In other words, the pattern of priorities envisaged in the plan will only be in place by the end.

Notes

1 There are cases where an NGDO's existence is itself a desired result. This can occur where political regimes are authoritarian.
2 See Lessem, 1989, pp556–574.
3 The reorientation of DESCO cost 30 staff positions.
4 There is obviously a danger of Western ethnocentric values being pushed and this type of exercise is a minefield of absolutism versus relativism. But to ignore these difficulties does not make them go away, as any international NGDO will tell you – be it in dealing with salary differences between local and expatriate staff or 'imposing' gender as an issue. In fact, one sign of a professional NGDO is that they have worked through such areas of contention and found

their own, often uneasy, solutions which become part and parcel of organizational culture.

5   The planning exercise can and should be used to clarify, share, reaffirm and internalize identity.

6   I advise NGDO managers to read Mintzberg (1994).

7   Bouwman, 1990.

8   Further readings contain examples of the recently published NGDO strategic planning guides.

9   An extreme case I came across was where only 3 out of 11 existing Southern partners would qualify within the strategy chosen by a Northern NGDO.

References

Blankenberg, F (1993) *The Institutional Support Model: A Reflection on the Experiment in Three Latin American Countries, 1989–1992*, Policy Support Unit, NOVIB, The Hague.

Bowman, C (1990) *The Essence of Stragetic Management*, Prentice Hall, London.

Brinkerhoff, D and Ingle, M (1989) 'Integrating blueprint and process: a structured flexibility approach to development management', *Public Administration and Development*, Vol 9, pp487–503.

CDRA (1996) *Annual Report (1995–96)*, Community Development Resource Association, Cape Town.

Fowler, A (1992) 'Decentralization for international NGOs', *Development in Practice*, Vol 2, No 2, pp121–124.

Leach, M (1995) 'Models of inter-organizational collaboration in development', *Institutional Development*, Vol 2, No 1, pp27–49.

Lessem, R (1989) *Global Management Principles*, Prentice Hall, London.

Mintzburg, H (1979) *The Structuring of Organizations*, Prentice Hall, Englewood Cliffs.

Mintzberg, H (1994) *The Rise and Fall of Strategic Planning*, Prentice Hall, New York.

'Does the Doormat Influence the Boot?' Critical Thoughts on UK NGOs and International Advocacy

Michael Edwards

Most UK development non-governmental organizations (NGOs) engage in advocacy work at the international level in an attempt to reduce the constraints imposed on grassroots development by global economics and the actions of the official aid agencies. Thus far, their record has been disappointing and this chapter explores some of the reasons which lie behind the failure of NGOs to fulfil their potential in this field. Four strategic weaknesses are identified: an overall absence of clear strategy, a failure to build strong alliances, a failure to develop alternatives to current orthodoxies and the dilemma of relations with donors. Each weakness is analysed with reference to practical examples and appropriate conclusions are drawn.

Most UK development NGOs accept that significant improvements in the lives of poor people around the globe are unlikely to be achieved solely by funding 'projects' at grassroots level. This is because local initiatives can easily be blocked, undermined or coopted by more powerful forces, whether economic or political. Development work which fails to address these forces can expect to have an impact only on the short-term welfare of a small number of poor people. Those forces which emanate from the national or subnational political economy must be addressed by indigenous institutions; others are international in character and include the structure of the world trading system, financial and investment flows, energy consumption, technological innovation and intellectual property, and the policies of multilateral and bilateral donor agencies. The increasing internationalization of decision-making in economic and political fields, and the limited accountability of global institutions have increased the power of these interests.

Northern NGOs have tried to influence these international forces in order to create a more favourable climate for development in the South. They have largely failed to do this and this chapter presents a personal view of some of the reasons which might underlie this failure. I have no wish to attack NGO attempts to exert greater influence at the international level. Rather, as a passionate believer in the importance of NGO advocacy, I am concerned by our collective failure to fulfil our potential in this field and want to see how we can improve the effectiveness of our advocacy work.

A Simple Conceptual Framework for NGO Advocacy

The basic rationale for Northern NGO advocacy is identified as an attempt to alter the ways in which power, resources and ideas are created, consumed and distributed at global level, so that people and their organizations in the South have a more realistic chance of controlling their own development. It is useful to distinguish between two different forms of NGO advocacy:

- *Attempts to influence global-level processes, structures or ideologies:* for example, reform of the GATT and the world trading system or attempts to overturn the 'neo-liberal orthodoxy' of market-led economic growth. These issues raise major questions for powerful interest groups and, in the absence of countervailing public pressure, mere dialogue is unlikely to induce significant change. Successful advocacy on such issues requires a mass base, so that sufficient pressure is exerted on Northern governments and consequently on international institutions and multinational capital. Advocacy is likely to be confrontational or at least publicly critical of existing orthodoxies. The stakes are high, not least because of the tendency in the UK of this kind of advocacy to fall foul of charity law. Logically, NGOs must call for lifestyle changes among their constituents. The aim is fundamental change.
- *Attempts to influence specific policies, programmes or projects:* for example, UNICEF health policy or World Bank lending to resettlement schemes. These may be issues where the institution or government is under less pressure from interest groups and therefore accepts, or even welcomes, a dialogue with NGOs on alternative ways of operating, – although on 'problem projects', such as the Narmada Dam in India, this is less true. Successful advocacy on such issues requires a high level of technical knowledge, information-exchange and practical experience. This kind of advocacy often takes place behind closed doors and the NGO concerned will probably not broadcast any success it may have in inducing changes, lest avenues for future influence be closed off. Such advocacy is likely to be based on cooperation rather than confrontation. The aim is incremental reform.

Clearly, this model is an abstraction and in reality the two forms of advocacy often merge into each other, so that NGO strategies contain elements of both. Some authors argue that UK NGOs will opt for piecemeal reform rather than a more fundamental challenge because of the financial, legal and other constraints that face them (Dolan, 1992). In my view, these approaches to advocacy are complementary and mutually supportive. They share a common goal in the long term (system change), but adopt different strategies to reach it because the short-term issues they address come from different levels in the system which they wish to change. Indeed, it can be argued that one kind of advocacy cannot succeed *unless* it is supported by the other. Hence, detailed policy work is unlikely to generate significant change unless it is backed up by public and media pressure in the long run: NGOs can easily be coopted and the targets of their advocacy may adopt superficial reforms which fail to address more fundamental issues. For example, official donors or multilateral agencies may adopt the vocabulary of the NGOs ('empowerment', 'primary environmental care', and so on), while meaning and acting on a completely different understanding of what they imply. The title of this chapter – 'Does the doormat influence the boot?' – is a quotation from an SCF Adviser working with government within the context of a World Bank loan for health and population programmes who is rightly sceptical about the possibility of influencing Bank policy through cooperation in the field alone.

On the other hand, calls for global change are more likely to be heeded if they are backed up by a detailed, rigorous presentation of issues and a credible set of alternative options. It is not enough to present a critique of policy without also demonstrating what might have worked in its place. Rather than posing a dichotomy between 'gradual reform' and 'paradigm shifts', it may be more helpful to see the one slowly leading into the other or to see the two approaches as complementary. For example, the extension or markets in health and education is a particular manifestation of a more general principle of the neo-liberal orthodoxy. By providing evidence of the impact of markets in particular situations, it may be possible to illumine, step-by-step, the weaknesses of the orthodoxy itself and to do so more effectively than by mounting a full-frontal attack on the underlying ideology. Linking action and experience at the 'micro' (grassroots) and 'macro' (global) levels is perhaps the single most important element in successful advocacy, a theme to which I return later.

In spite of this, the distinction is relevant because the two approaches to advocacy *do* have different implications for the NGO concerned, in terms of organizational structure and styles of work. One of the reasons underlying the relative weakness of NGO advocacy has been a failure to recognize this and make maximum use of the benefits which come from '*synergy*' – combining different forms and levels of action in mutually supportive and mutually reinforcing ways, within a single strategy for change. In this case, synergy means working simultaneously and in a coordinated fashion at local, national and international levels, both in detailed policy work, and public campaigning, educational and media activity.

There is in any case a wide spectrum of styles of advocacy, stretching between full-scale public campaigns and informal chats with civil servants in the corridor. It is no exaggeration to say that every staff member in an NGO is an advocate for the agency and its mandate, and plays some role in advocacy somewhere along this spectrum. Rather than seeing advocacy as a distinct activity separate from 'programme work', NGOs need to build all their activities into a single system in which each activity supports and draws from the others. To an extent, this is a requirement in the UK in any case because charity law demands that international advocacy is rooted in direct experience. But there is much more potential synergy here. 'Advocacy' is not the same as 'public campaigns', although campaigns may form one component of an advocacy strategy. Advocacy relates to all the activities of the NGO which aim to influence actors, systems, structures and ideas – at many different levels and in many different ways. The failure of NGOs to grasp the implications of this constitutes a significant weakness and is explored in more detail below.

Finally, the real strength of Northern NGOs lies in their simultaneous access to grassroots experience in the South and to decision-makers in the North. This puts them in a unique position in terms of communicating what is actually happening to people in the South, to institutions in the North, and vice versa. This is not without its difficulties, not least in ensuring that the 'voice of the poor' is not distorted. But the potential for Northern NGOs to act in this way is clear. Providing an effective channel for real experience is more important than trying to compete with the World Bank and others in terms of theoretical research, although, of course, the two are not mutually exclusive. Experience has to be analysed and ordered if it is to have any wider significance. However, there will always be counter-arguments to NGO critiques; and with their hugely greater resources, agencies like the World Bank can develop these at a speed and a level of sophistication which no NGO can match. But what the Bank and others do not have (or are unwilling to develop) is access to accurate information on the consequences of their actions among real, living people. Neither do the official agencies have the same popular appeal, credibility and access to the media which NGOs have developed over the last ten years. Potentially, this puts NGOs in a position of great power.

What has International Advocacy by UK NGOs Achieved?

Most UK NGOs have increased their expenditure on international advocacy over the last five to ten years, although to varying levels and at different times. But what have we achieved? In his review of advocacy in the North, John Clark (1992, p197) provides the following list of examples to illustrate some of the achievements of NGOs in this field:

- a code of conduct for the marketing of baby milks;
- the drafting of an essential drugs list;
- removing restrictions on the importation of certain clothing manufactured in the South (such as shirts from Bangladesh);
- establishing an emergency reserve so that EC food surpluses become more readily available for famine relief;
- concerted action on international environmental issues such as global warming and rainforest destruction;
- affording special debt relief to the poorest countries;
- the imposition of sanctions to combat apartheid.

To this rather mixed bag of 'successes' one might add:

- developments in World Bank policy in the areas of gender, participation, poverty and the environment;
- reversal or modification of some 'problem projects' funded by the World Bank (mostly large dams and associated resettlement schemes);
- a move away from vertical interventions in health-sector investment, especially immunization (although the 1993 World Development Report – *Investing in Health* – may reverse this trend);
- improvements in the food regime of refugees and displaced persons;
- modifications in 'structural adjustment' packages to take more account of social impact;

- country-specific initiatives such as reconstruction aid for Cambodia or joint action (by Oxfam and Christian Aid) to promote access to EC markets for banana producers in the Windward Islands.

According to Clark (1992, p197), 'if it were possible to assess the value of all such reforms, they might be worth more than the financial contribution made by NGOs'. This might well be true, but also begs many questions. What have the achievements of NGOs really been worth? Can even these successes be attributed to NGO advocacy? And is this a cause for satisfaction or for circumspection? Perhaps it is unfair to seek answers to these questions, given the very long timescales involved, the dimensions and complexity of the issues, the power of the targets of their advocacy, the relatively small resources devoted to advocacy and the obvious point that UK NGOs cannot and do not expect to alter international policies or systems *by themselves*. NGOs expect their advocacy to work like a 'dripping tap', with policy changes coming about over the long term through the actions of many different agencies and individuals. Nevertheless, if we cannot begin to find some answers, strategic planning for advocacy becomes very difficult. Real success will always be hard to achieve when the issues are so broad. But there is always more chance of success when strategy is as strong as it can be. It seems to me that the following conclusions can be drawn from experience to date:

- Most achievements have been at the level of detailed policy and/or on issues where NGOs have not come up against strong interest-group pressures (although the adoption of the international code on the marketing of breast-milk substitutes is a notable exception here). Least progress has been made at the level of ideology and global systems – trade, financial flows and 'conditionality' (the growing insistence of Western donors on progress towards multiparty 'democracy' and guarantees of human rights). This may not be surprising; but it does reinforce the need to link the two forms of advocacy described above, so that the one supports the other.
- Progress on more fundamental issues, such as the conservation of the environment and the impact of structural adjustment on the poor, appears less impressive the more one delves into the details. There have been superficial reforms, but basic ideology and structure remain intact. There has, for sure, been an increasing uptake in the official aid community of the traditional NGO agenda in areas like popular participation, sustainable development, poverty-focus, human rights, gender and the 'learning process' approach to development work (Korten, 1980). The 1993 *Human Development Report* from the United Nations Developing Programme (UNDP) is a case in point. Even the International Monetary Fund (IMF), in its *World Economic Outlook*, has moved to the use of 'Purchasing Power Parity' rather than gross national product (GNP) per capita, a move long recommended by NGOs. However, these moves have yet to feed through into practice at the field level.
- NGOs may overestimate their own impact on some issues (such as 'sanctions to combat apartheid' in Clark's list), where hindsight reveals other forces at work which were more influential. Structural adjustment is a case in point, with at least two other factors – pressure from other multilateral agencies (especially

UNICEF) and the political unsustainability of the original package in countries being 'adjusted' – being crucial.

NGOs have failed to build an international movement for development, in contrast to the worldwide environmental or women's movements. While the latter are very different in character, genesis and history, both have found successful ways of strategizing across national boundaries and interest groups, in ways which seem to have escaped development NGOs thus far.

Whether the UK NGOs' record on international advocacy is seen as 'disappointing' depends on one's initial expectations, but we should at least register a concern that results have been modest. Is this inevitable, simply a reflection of doing advocacy work in a complex and hostile world, or are there steps which could be taken to improve our chances of success?

Barriers to Successful International Advocacy by UK NGOs

Clearly, the scale and complexity of advocacy issues facing NGOs and the relatively small resources devoted currently by NGOs to international advocacy, need to be borne in mind in the discussion which follows. It would be simplistic to assume that better results would be achieved solely by increasing the scale of resources devoted to international advocacy. However, I identify four strategic weaknesses in our current approach which require attention:

*   an overall absence of clear strategy;
*   a failure to build strong alliances;
*   a failure to develop credible alternatives to current orthodoxies; and
*   the dilemma of relations with donor agencies.

Strategy

NGOs are increasingly concerned with strategic planning, evaluation, institutional learning and 'distinctive competence'. But how have these concerns been applied to international advocacy work? Of course, evaluation is difficult where there are other forces at work, but it sometimes seems that the disciplines adopted in programme development are neglected in advocacy. The only indicator of success that seems to be used is the number of meetings attended as the same individuals jet frantically from one part of the globe to another! This is not helped by the tendency in some NGOs to separate 'advocacy' from 'programme management' and develop semi-independent advocacy units. Rather than seeing advocacy as an integral part of everyone's job at all levels, advocacy can become divorced from the concerns and priorities of people directly involved in development or relief work (whether staff or local counterparts). This produces a tendency to concentrate on general issues (systems and ideology) rather than on detailed policy lobbying tied to specific circumstances. Consequently, themes for advocacy then tend to be determined by the international debate – even fashion – instead of by the work of the NGO and its local counterparts. This makes it more likely that the NGO will either be coopted into the concerns of the wider system or retreat into ideology. Advocacy becomes market-driven rather than programme-driven. Information flows between field and head office are weakened because field staff do not feel part of one system with common objectives, driven by and supportive of their own work. Without a continuous supply of good-quality information, successful advocacy is impossible. NGOs need to develop a planning process which ensures that themes for international advocacy emerge from genuine priorities in the field. This does not mean that advocacy should be driven exclusively by field concerns, since there will always be trends and initiatives in the international environment which demand a response. However, there must be a clear link between an NGO's advocacy and direct practical experience, so that influence can be exercised with some degree of authority, legitimacy and credibility.

The rationale for separating 'advocacy' from other responsibilities seems to be two fold. First, to be effective, advocacy requires special skills, access to decision-makers and time. Second, senior managers may see international advocacy as a particularly attractive area of work because of its high-profile nature, and so attempt to control it. Neither argument stands up to scrutiny: special skills or access may be required for particular styles of advocacy or for advocacy on particular issues, but there are many other aspects of advocacy where the skills and experience of people throughout the organization (programme managers, researchers, fund-raisers and communicators) are decisive. Programme staff have the knowledge of local realities and access to decision-makers required to influence the details of policy, while fund-raisers and other communicators have the ability and opportunity to enlist wider public support by conveying complex messages in a straightforward way. NGO directors and other senior managers can gain access to high-level bureaucrats and so help to expand the 'political space' within which more detailed work can expand. The rationale for large and separate advocacy units is less convincing once an organization sees advocacy as a corporate responsibility in which everyone plays a different but complementary role. This does not remove, of course, the need for overall coordination of these different efforts. A degree of centralization is essential to achieve coordination, generate economies of scale (with regard to particular target agencies and themes) and develop a global overview; but if centralization is achieved at the cost of wider commitment throughout the organization, advocacy can be undermined by the absence of a shared vision and understanding.

UK NGOs have generally failed to find the right balance between the two forms of advocacy described above – mass-based advocacy on global systems and ideology and specialized or technical advocacy on specific policies and projects. Instead, individual NGOs tend to concentrate on one to the exclusion of the other. This might not be a problem if UK NGOs were to work more closely together, each contributing something distinctive to an overall advocacy strategy; but at present no such alliance exists. As a result, neither approach fulfils its potential. In Save the Children Fund (SCF), for example, a huge amount of detailed work goes on to influence the policies of the official aid establishment, not only at the international level but also in the field (through joint missions with donors, staff exchanges, meetings with local aid representatives, information exchange, and so on). However, this is not yet backed by a similar attempt to enlist the support of SCF's huge UK constituency in a general movement for change. On the other hand, concentration on global systems alone is dangerous, partly because the issues at stake are well outside any possible influence the NGO can hope to exert. A mass of general material on debt, trade and the environment is constantly being produced, but is read only by the converted and makes little impact on its ultimate targets in the policy-making sphere because, quite literally, it is 'speaking another language'. A great deal of heat may be generated, but not much light.

UK NGOs face a real dilemma here: on the one hand, if they try to 'speak the same language' as the targets of their advocacy and go about their work quietly and constructively, they risk being coopted or generating a superficial response, there being no wider pressures for more fundamental change. On the other hand, if NGOs opt for a more radical path, they risk being marginalized because their recommendations are so far outside the intellectual and ideological framework of the prevailing orthodoxy that they are simply ignored. The logical conclusion is to combine the two approaches.

Finally, UK NGOs have failed to pay sufficient attention to building capacity in the South for advocacy work, either to strengthen the ability of local institutions to advocate change at national level or to assist them in playing a more active role in international advocacy. SCF has made some attempts to strengthen the capacity of Southern governments to negotiate more effectively in discussions with donors (Edwards, 1991, 1993), while other UK NGOs, especially Oxfam, have tried to help Southern NGOs to develop their own advocacy work. A great deal of effective advocacy takes place within the countries of the South, both directly – such as with the national offices of donor agencies – or indirectly (that is, strengthening the part played by Southern actors and institutions in a multilayered strategy for international advocacy). It is in this area – developing alliances for advocacy between NGOs in the North and South – that some Southern NGOs have shown increasing disappointment with their Northern counterparts (Clark, 1991). We cannot allow international advocacy to become a self-contained process among Northern institutions.

In summary, what is needed is a proper, multilayered and multifaceted strategy for NGO advocacy which relates themes, targets, objectives, activities, roles and responsibilities together in a coherent way; which is monitored carefully and evaluated at regular intervals; which integrates detailed policy work with public campaigning; which is rooted in real experience, and which embraces the whole organization in pursuit of a common cause. Table 6.1 provides an illustration of how such a strategy might look in theory in relation to one current theme: structural adjustment. The importance of advocacy cannot simply be assumed. Its structure must be planned and its impact evaluated in relation to other strategies to achieve impact. This requires much closer and more sophisticated monitoring, engagement and follow-through, and the development of better indicators (or proxy indicators) of change in policies and attitudes.

Alliances

Although individual NGOs can hope to exert influence on detailed policy issues in which they have a distinctive competence (for instance, SCF in health-systems

Table 6.1 *A Model Framework for International Advocacy*

NB This framework is intended to give a 'flavour' of strategy; it is not intended to be comprehensive. It assumes that the organization's aim is to replace existing approaches to adjustment with alternatives which generate equitable and sustainable development.

Objectives: to increase understanding of the impact and weaknesses of current approaches; to develop credible alternative approaches; to have these approaches adopted by the World Bank and bilateral donor agencies.

Levels of action	Types of action
Grassroots (programme staff and partners)	• Building concrete alternatives • Action research to generate information • Capacity-building among local NGOs and government (research, information advocacy)
National (country office)	• Strengthen government capacity to negotiate with donors • Support to NGO federations/networks in developing policy critiques and alternatives • Join World Bank Missions in the field (take Bank staff into the field, work with them on individual loans) • Monitor the implementation of agreed World Bank policy (for example, Operational Directives)
Regional (regional office)	• Lobby regional development banks (IDB, ADB, and so on) • Lobby regional offices of the World Bank • Support to regional alliance – for example, South Asia Association for Regional Co-operation
International (headquarters: overseas department)	• Lobby task managers for specific loans and policy staff on general issues (maximize ongoing information flows) • work through World Bank/NGO Committee • Work through UK Executive Director and ODA in London • Participate in conferences and meetings (for example, World Development Report) • Research/publications on macro-level alternatives (including in academic journals and internal bank publications) • Staff exchanges and secondments • Contribute to World Bank evaluation methodologies – for example, participatory poverty assessments • Strengthen global NGO alliances
(communications and fund-raising departments)	• Development education among supporters/schools • Information to UK Parliament/MPs • Increase links with other movements (for example, the environment)

development), more fundamental issues require a joint approach in order to achieve any impact. Are UK development NGOs prepared to form the kinds of alliance that will be necessary if international advocacy work is to be strengthened? Are they prepared to enter into a 'grander coalition' of development, environment and other groups to work on the very broad but common issues of global systems and life-style changes? There are some NGO networks (such as the British Overseas Aid Group (BOAG), the Aid and Environment Group, Debt Crisis Network, EC-NGO Liaison Committee, and others), but until now their function has been to share information and/or to organize joint events at donor meetings, rather than to coordinate interagency action on global campaigns over the longer term. However, there are some encouraging signs – for example, development and environmental groups worked with some success to shift the UK Government's position on 'sustainable development' in the run-up to the United Nations Conference on Environment and Development (UNCED), and ran a powerful campaign against proposed cuts in the UK aid budget. Does this herald a new way of working or is it the exception that proves the rule? The mood of UK NGOs and some international NGOs (and of churches, environmental groups and even some political activists) may be changing towards a more positive stance on the value of cooperation, but this commitment is yet to be tested in practice.

There are some obvious reasons for the traditional reluctance of UK NGOs to work together: competition (for funds, but stretching into general agency profile), disagreements on ideology and policy, lack of a common vocabulary, differing priorities, and so on – and some authors believe that these constraints are insurmountable (Dolan, 1992). If this is true, the impact of NGO advocacy at the broader 'systemic' level is likely to be dissipated in a mass of individual approaches. It is a truism that 'the whole is greater than the sum of its parts'; in addition, we need to recognize that alliances could help NGOs to make more creative use of their different competencies and experience. For example, agencies like SCF have a much deeper involvement in the technical details of policy because they have their own staff in the field and have tended to specialize in certain areas (such as health-systems development or humanitarian assistance) and in certain approaches (working within line ministries, for example) which give them access to considerable information and experience about what is actually happening as a result of particular donor policies (Edwards, 1993). For example, SCF is currently engaged in a programme with the Food and Agriculture Organization (FAO) to develop a new and much more accurate early-warning system for predicting food crises, based on the integration of quantitative and qualitative data in the form of 'vulnerability maps', the potential benefits of which are immense.

On the other hand, other NGOs (or non-charitable trusts like the World Development Movement) may lack this sort of access but be able to engage more effectively in public campaigns. If, for whatever reason, the two cannot be combined in the same agency, then at least different agencies can pool their expertise in pursuit of a common set of objectives. Rather than arriving at a consensus based on the lowest common denominator, a more creative approach to alliances would be to recognize and build on the differences which exist among the NGO 'community'. The aim should be synergy (working individually but in a mutually supportive way), not standardization (all doing the same thing). UK development NGOs do not yet seem to have learned the lessons of the women's and environmental movements which have succeeded to a far greater extent precisely because they are movements (not organizations funding projects), able to spread their influence through networks and coalitions of different groups sharing a broadly similar agenda.

Alternatives

Among official donor agencies, a common criticism of NGOs is that, while strong on criticism, they are short on credible alternatives – or at least on alternatives which are credible to the donors. Advocacy is probably likely to be more effective if positive suggestions are included alongside NGO critiques. This is particularly true in the economic field, where we need to demonstrate that living standards among poor people in the South can be increased without the social and environmental costs associated with existing policies. In essence, this means developing alternatives to the current orthodoxy of global economic growth based on an ever-expanding trading system and 'free markets'. Because alternatives may involve choices about consumption in the North, the supporters of UK NGOs also need to be convinced of their validity. We do not seem to be making very much progress in this direction.

Of course, it is much easier to criticize the impact of policies which are clearly misconceived than it is to wrestle with the complexities of alternatives. There is no shortage of critiques of the existing system, but people faced with daily choices and decisions need much more than this if they are to make progress. The tendency of NGOs to focus on global-level issues may also reflect a reluctance to look critically at their own practice at the grassroots level. Yet NGOs need to consider very carefully whether they really do have any 'distinctive competence' in global-level research. They can certainly innovate and think creatively about alternatives, but real alternatives must grow from action and practical development experience, not from the minds of thinkers in the North. However, NGOs have failed to integrate the work they *have* undertaken on alternative development models at grassroots and global levels. There has been some work on 'Primary Environmental Care' (PEC) at local level and some work on alternative trading systems and energy strategies at global level, but little that ties the two together in a convincing fashion. One of the major weaknesses of PEC is its localism and consequent failure to address issues of policy and power at other levels. Perhaps this is why PEC has been embraced so enthusiastically by the official aid community.

Strengthening links between global and grassroots activity is fundamental if NGOs wish to improve the effectiveness of their advocacy work, since only when these activities are mutually supportive can lasting change occur. NGO advocacy must grow out of and be informed by grassroots experience if it is to claim to speak on behalf of the poor. However, this is extremely difficult to do. I know of no NGO that has in place systems to collect, channel, analyse, synthesize, generalize and disseminate information of this sort. In addition, UK NGOs usually base their advocacy work on what their 'partners' or 'counterparts' say, but of course these are a small group whom we select because they agree with us (and we with them) in terms of basic philosophy and objectives. They do not 'represent the poor' in any general sense, nor would they necessarily claim to do so. Northern NGOs must be careful not to use the groups with which they choose to work to legitimize a view of the world in which they believe, but which may not be shared by the broad mass of people in the South. Of course we should not be ashamed of voicing our own opinions (or even those of our partners), as long as we are explicit about 'who' it is that is speaking. However, genuine, credible, and sustainable alternatives must emerge from local debate and action in both North and South, even if the results are more complex and less comfortable than we expect. This is particularly true where the alternatives have a direct impact on people's living standards. In this respect, it is vital to promote the development of wider networks in the South which can be more truly representative of different shades of opinion than is possible if we listen only to 'our' (narrowly defined) partners. The same goes for the North – hence the importance of alliances and coalitions.

Donors

While most UK NGOs see their relations with official donor agencies as involving a dialogue about policy, the donors by and large see NGOs as implementers of projects. There is certainly an increasing openness to working with *or* through NGOs, but to what end? Part of the neo-liberal orthodoxy is the privatization of welfare functions previously provided by the State, but the impact of increasing NGOs' role in service provision seems to be negative in terms of their advocacy. After all, we cannot bite the hands that feed us and hope to find a meal waiting for more than a week or so! This is less of a problem for detailed influence on policy of the 'behind closed doors' variety, but 'a fundamental choice all NGOs will face is whether to scale-up along the lines that aid donors and host governments prefer, or whether to keep some distance and accept the reduced access to official funding that this will entail' (Edwards and Hulme, 1992, p214). The likelihood is that UK NGOs will make different choices in this respect, something that hangs over the future of alliances between them. Increasing competition for funds may press NGOs into accepting ever more money from official donors and so bring about a creeping compromise in their advocacy agendas.

Some Key Issues for Discussion

This brief survey of UK NGOs and international advocacy reveals four key issues:

1   We need to develop a clearer sense of strategy, to evaluate our efforts and learn from experience, so that advocacy work can be refined on a continuous basis. We need to exchange ideas on what seems to work best in different situations or with different targets and themes. We should evaluate how organizational structures and planning systems affect the impact of advocacy. We need to analyse the compromises and complementarities between detailed policy work and public campaigning and explore how the potential synergy between the two can be maximized. We should embark on a systematic effort to learn from the experience of more successful international movements.

2   We need to find better ways of linking local-level action and analysis with international advocacy. How can the necessary information flows be developed in ways which do not compromise the legitimacy of grassroots views? How can

the voices of real people best be combined with the sophisticated conceptual framework, detailed policy work and wider public pressure required to induce significant change at the highest levels? The implications of moving into the 'information age', as Clark (1992) puts it, are significant, since NGOs will require people, systems, structures and capacities to play an effective role in an emerging international movement, rather than a series of country programmes alone. How can we best contribute to the development of wider networks and a stronger capacity to enable institutions in the South to play more of a role in international advocacy, both directly and indirectly?

3   We need to devote resources to developing viable alternatives to accepted orthodoxies, particularly in the field of economics. This is a particularly good candidate for interagency work because the issues are so complex and no single NGO can claim a distinctive competence in all of them. The UK NGO group which is currently trying to harmonize research on structural adjustment might provide a basis for this sort of dialogue on wider alternatives. We certainly need in any case to develop stronger alliances among UK NGOs within this country, linking into broader international networks. Which other issues are suitable for developing such alliances? And how do we persuade UK NGOs to commit themselves to joint strategies?

4   We must bring our supporters with us as our international advocacy work develops and our agencies change to accommodate new styles of work. This is even more important if lifestyle changes are part of the strategy for change, otherwise our independent support base will gradually be eroded. The implications of UK charity law need to be considered carefully, as does the likely reaction of institutional donors. These factors may slow the pace of change in organizational development, since the choices involved are complex and require careful thought and analysis.

This is a formidable list, but not an insurmountable one. UK NGOs, as part of a wider movement for change, do have the ability and potential to 'make a difference', but not unless they adopt a much more critical, creative and cooperative approach towards advocacy at the international level. Do we want to be the 'doormat' or the 'boot'? The choice is up to us.

References

Clark, J (1991) *Democratizing Development: The Role of Voluntary Organizations*, London, Earthscan.

Clark, J (1992) 'Policy influence, lobbying and advocacy', in M Edwards and D Hulme (eds), *Making a Difference: NGOs and Development in a Changing World*, London, Earthscan.

Dolan, C (1992) 'British development NGOs and advocacy in the 1990s', in M Edwards and D Hulme (eds), op cit.

Edwards, M (1991) 'Strengthening government capacity for national development and international negotiation: the work of SCF in Mozambique', paper presented to the DSA annual conference, Swansea.

Edwards, M (1993) 'International NGOs and Southern governments in the New World Order: lessons of experience at the programme level', paper presented to the INTRAC Workshop on 'Governance, Democracy and Conditionality: What Role for NGOs?', Amersfoort, the Netherlands.

Korten, D (1980) 'Community organization and rural development: a learning process approach', *Public Administration Review*, No 40, pp480–510.

Oxfam (UK and Ireland) (1992) *Lobbying Methodology*, Briefing Paper, Oxford, Oxfam (UK).

Spray, P (1992) 'Advocacy in the North', London, Christian Aid (mimeo).

Political Responsibility in Transnational NGO Advocacy

Lisa Jordan and Peter Van Tuijl

Non-governmental organizations (NGOs) manifest a new political reality in the global realm. NGOs have come to mobilize, articulate and represent people's interests or concerns at different levels of decision-making – locally, nationally and internationally. The central argument of this paper is that the relationships that emerge among transnational NGO networks are highly problematic. The dynamics in these relationships determine the quality of NGO advocacy, both in terms of its function as a channel to articulate different development aspirations and in terms of effectively embracing their responsibilities to other actors in the network. This chapter introduces a concept of political responsibility to clarify representation and accountability in transnational NGO networks. Based on different case studies of NGO advocacy campaigns, the chapter also introduces four typologies of relationships which may develop among networks, leading to a varying degree of political responsibility.

Introduction

NGOs are widely considered to be one of the most dynamic phenomena in international relations today. Most of the literature on NGOs is exceedingly optimistic about the roles that NGOs play in the international, national and local arenas. The academic literature has addressed NGOs as the citizen sector (Najam, 1999), NGOs as agents of accountability (Brown and Fox, 1998), NGOs as the magic development bullet (Edwards and Hulme, 1996) and the expanding role of NGOs in global governance (Williams and Young, 1994).

This chapter contributes to the critical literature on what Keck and Sikkink (1998) refer to as the 'most interesting' dimension of transnational NGO advocacy networks – namely the management of risks and tensions in international advocacy campaigns. Keck and Sikkink (1998), Nelson (1997) and others have discussed inherent tensions within these networks. For example, Keck and Sikkink (1998) note:

> Because transnational advocacy networks normally involve people and organizations in structurally unequal positions, networks can become sites for negotiating over which goals, strategies, and ethical understandings are compatible (Keck and Sikkink, 1998, p121).

Nelson writes:

Although NGO networks have often united northern and southern NGOs in opposition to a government policy, North–South differences have extended in part, to the
NGO activists network (Nelson, 1997, p427).

Keck and Sikkink (1998) while touching upon this topic do not elaborate on how
tensions in transitional advocacy networks are resolved. Nelson argues that some
tensions are structural features of the networks. In this chapter, we postulate that
tensions arise when NGOs active in campaigns fail to understand the political responsibilities that arise in a campaign process. When political responsibilities are
not embraced, NGOs are left open to criticism about their legitimacy and accountability. After presenting some key concepts, we introduce the concept of political
responsibility. We then outline four typologies of transnational advocacy campaigns.
Based on the typologies, we conclude with questions about existing literature on
transnational advocacy, accountability and representation.

The political responsibilities inherent to transnational advocacy campaigns reflect
a healthy debate about the role of NGOs, their legitimacy and accountability. The
role of NGOs continues to be contested between a narrow service delivery role and
an advocacy role. The service delivery role is perpetuated by the World Bank, some
United Nations agencies and national governments, while some NGOs prefer to
describe themselves in terms of advocacy. Furthermore, the legitimacy and accountability of NGO advocacy is increasingly questioned not only in the academic literature
(Edwards and Hulme, 1996) but also by international financial institutions such as
the International Monetary Fund and the World Bank, generally in an attempt to
divert attention from the pressure of NGOs on their activities (Bain, 1999). If NGOs
are to respond successfully to these challenges, they will need to deal with the political
responsibilities inherent to promoting issues such as the rights of the poor, poverty
alleviation, natural resource conservation, human rights and sustainable development.

The definition of NGOs is not commonly agreed upon. NGOs are certainly part
of the citizen sector and as such 'concerned with the articulation and actualization
of particular social visions' as noted by Najam (1999, p146). We adopt Anna Vakil's
definition of NGOs as 'self-governing, private, not-for-profit organizations that are
geared toward improving the quality of life of disadvantaged people' (Vakil, 1997,
p2060). As we discuss predominantly transnational advocacy campaigns, Vakil's
definition with its emphasis on NGOs striving towards a normative change, 'improving
the quality of life of disadvantaged people' is rooted in the experience of the networks we will discuss.

NGOs have come to be a force in many societies or are at least so perceived.[1]
As NGOs have gained experience and credibility, they have recognized that national
and international policies as well as commercial market forces often undermine
sustainable development efforts and limit the ability of people at the grassroots level
from participating in public or private policy decisions that will affect them.
Informed by the needs and experiences of the poorer or disadvantaged sectors in
their or other societies, NGOs have come to mobilize, articulate and represent people's interests or concerns at different levels of decision-making – locally, nationally
and internationally. This advocacy work is increasingly seen by NGOs as an integral part of the role they play in civil society. Using information as a key tool, it

entails the ambition to change the course of human development by promoting equal power relationships in national and international arenas.

NGO advocacy is an act of organizing the strategic use of information to democratize unequal power relations. This definition differs from others that tend to emphasize actions related to influencing policy, especially public policy (Tandon, 1994; Edwards and Hulme, 1996). Others tend to outline advocacy relatively unspecified, simply as 'communication for change'. In our view, these definitions are too limited in expressing what advocacy stands for, as they assume too much unity in objectives and value systems among the NGOs involved. Furthermore, they often emphasize impact on formal political systems, while disregarding other functions of advocacy. NGO advocacy can very well be aimed at directly influencing reality rather than policy.

The act of advocacy to empower weaker sectors of society is not limited to helping people to access information or giving them tools to reach out to decision-makers. The underlying function of advocacy is often to enhance the self-respect of weaker communities, to improve their self-confidence, constitute integrity and promote mutual trust – all essential ingredients to develop a healthy community. It is often overlooked that NGO advocacy also entails a fight against cynicism and despair to which powerless communities tend to fall victim, in the face of massive political and practical obstacles impairing them to improve their lot.

Grounding NGO advocacy in democratizing power relations rightly puts upfront the fact that NGOs challenge the status quo. In general, advocacy NGOs reveal truths that are not liked by vested interests and power holders. Being involved in NGO advocacy therefore entails taking risks – politically, legally, mentally and physically in the South as well as in the North. Managing these risks invokes a political responsibility towards other groups active in the campaign.

Advocacy is often the key activity of transnational NGO networks, operating in global campaigns. We define transnational advocacy networks as a set of relationships between NGOs and other organizations that simultaneously pursue activities in different political arenas to challenge the status quo. Political arenas are spaces within which decisions are made. Most are geographically bound, such as Washington or Nairobi, but they can also be institutionally bound such as the process of establishing a biodiversity convention. The definition of transnational advocacy networks does not lead us into the sticky territory of assuming shared values among NGOs engaged in advocacy. Transnational advocacy networks are often led by activists, a concept elegantly defined by Keck and Sikkink (1998) as 'people who care enough about some issue that they are prepared to incur significant costs and act to achieve their goals' (Keck and Sikkink, 1998, p14).

Transnational advocacy networks often form around global campaigns. A transnational NGO advocacy campaign (global NGO campaign) as described herein is the pursuit of loosely linked political objectives carried out by transnational advocacy networks. Campaigns are often named after the dominant concern or after the targeted object. For example, the Land Mine Campaign is commonly understood to describe a global campaign against the use of land mines and the Toxics Trade Campaign is the common reference for a decade-old campaign against the trade in toxic waste.

Introducing Political Responsibility

Global campaigns challenge development projects, economic policies and political forces that threaten to marginalize local communities further or ruin pristine ecosystems. There are political responsibilities that are inherent to taking part in these advocacy campaigns. Political responsibility is a commitment to embrace not only goals in a campaign but to conduct the campaign with democratic principles foremost in the process. Political responsibility is a normative concept that differs slightly from accountability in that accountability has formal obligations embedded within its definition. Within transnational advocacy networks there are no formal mechanisms to enforce obligations. Thus, to discuss accountability within these networks would be to suggest something that is not yet existent.

Many NGOs deny the concept of representation, pointing out that local communities, be they in the North or South, are able to represent themselves adequately. This position belies the fact that in global NGO campaigns, NGO networks are often formed to allow for the expertise and experience of multiple NGOs to be heard in varying political arenas. While it is true that local communities are often able to present adequately their own interests, spokespersons are often tied to the local geographical space within which they live and are reluctant or unable to leave the area under threat. They do not have daily access to other political arenas, nor have they invested the time which is required to understand the mechanics of investment banks, the United Nations, and so on. Thus there is a need for networks to engage in multiple political arenas. With the globalization of decision-making on the increase, we can only expect that the need to articulate concerns in more than one political arena will continue to grow. A democracy deficit is on the rise precisely because of the dispersed nature of decision-making across national borders. NGOs, by organizing advocacy campaigns in different political arenas at the same time, try to address this democracy deficit, either implicitly or explicitly.

While cooperation in a global advocacy campaign does not compare itself easily to academic concepts of representation, it cannot be denied that NGOs are, in fact, representing interests when they operate with an expertise in a specific political arena and use that knowledge to carry a campaign concern to a new level of decision-making. The sheer fact of participation in a global campaign embodies a political responsibility towards others engaged in the campaign but operating in a different political arena.

We introduce the notion of political responsibility to respond to the problem that 'representation' does not provide a sufficiently viable conceptual or practical approach to come to terms with power relations and responsibilities as they emerge in the context of transnational NGO advocacy campaigns. Transnational NGO advocacy usually works in and around systems of formal representation and established forms of international governance, but does not replace them. A member of parliament in a Northern country has no resources to conduct effectively a certain level of control over a bilateral aid programme. A local community in the South equally has no means, no knowledge and no established avenue to articulate its interest in Washington. An authoritarian government may actively repress the voice of its citizens calling on international human rights standards, who subsequently resort to their NGO friends abroad. These are the gaps in which the democratizing contribution of transnational NGO advocacy networks has to be framed. A network requires a different approach to qualify simultaneously the responsibility for the actions of both the individual players in the network and the aggregate results of the network as a whole.

An additional advantage of introducing political responsibility is that 'accountability', as having a political connotation in conjunction with 'representation', is extremely difficult to translate effectively into any other language and for that reason alone provides a major problem in a conceptual framework about transnational NGO advocacy.[2]

Political responsibility in NGO advocacy manifests itself in the following seven areas:

- dividing political arenas;
- agenda setting and strategy building;
- raising and allocating financial resources;
- information flow;
- information frequency and format;
- information translation into useful forms;
- the formalization of relationships.

In each area there are parameters by which political responsibility can be assessed. The sum of all variables combined can help NGOs to measure the extent to which they have successfully managed political risks and embraced their political responsibilities. While in the case materials below, we have predominantly used examples of environmental campaigns to illustrate our arguments further, these areas of political responsibility arise in any development action that utilizes more than one political arena. In any action whereby an international and a locally based organization are engaged, be it a food delivery service in an emergency situation or an agriculture extension service, these responsibilities arise, regardless of the nature of the partnership between beneficiaries and NGOs.

Dividing political arenas

It is typical for a global NGO campaign to grow from the need to engage more than one political arena. In addition, no one NGO generally has the understanding of each arena that needs to be engaged. For example, it cannot be expected that a grassroots social movement organization in the hinterland of India will know all the politically important people in Washington, DC, will understand the protocol associated with contacting relevant decision-makers, or will have the resources to bring pressure to bear in that political arena. The opposite is true as well. Organizations based in Washington, New York or Geneva may be intimately familiar with the way in which those arenas work and how decisions are made, but will not be able to understand the pace, the mechanisms or the reality of a local situation in Africa. Many readers may interpret our division of arenas to be a North–South division. That is not the case. Expertise in a political arena is based on a long-term presence in that arena. Thus, FAVDO, which is an African-based organization, maintains a presence in Washington, DC, and has expertise in the Washington arena that we would argue should be respected by partner organizations when practising advocacy. Recognizing who has expertise and knowledge in which political arena and respecting the boundaries established by that expertise is the first necessary act of accountability in a joint NGO advocacy effort. By recognizing the boundaries within which each NGO prevails, NGOs networks go a long way towards recognizing the political responsibility in advocacy.

Agenda setting and strategy building

The second major issue that NGOs need to engage is the question of agenda setting and strategy building. Questions that require engagement include: what are the substantive priorities?; for whose benefit?; using which time frame and with what level of antagonism are authorities or power holders approached in which political arena? These questions point at the fact that agenda setting and strategy building are closely related to the management of risks. Tactics and strategies decided upon can have major consequences for all actors involved. Agendas in advocacy will vary, depending on the objectives of each NGO. It is essential, therefore, to find a format to lay out explicitly what one's objectives are and then to develop a strategy with transparent goals. Among the issues that need to be recognized is who bears the risks associated with campaign positions. Not surprisingly, specific attention is often needed for the NGO in the campaign who has fewer resources or has to deal with a repressive government.

Allocation of available financial resources

The need for financial resources varies from arena to arena. The availability of financial resources is a major factor contributing to the risk of lopsided relationships among NGOs around the globe, as the bulk of financial resources is in the hands of a relatively small group of NGOs in the North.[3] Prioritizing expenses is an issue that can cause tension among organizations. Determining who has money and can pay for activities, who has access to other sources of financing and who cannot contribute financially to the activities agreed on is one step towards recognizing the relationships of power which money generates among NGOs. A rough review of a number of NGO networks and relationships with which we have been involved has taught us that it helps for more powerful – that is, financially resourceful – organizations to separate clearly the responsibility for raising and appropriating money from advocacy. Financial accountability and political responsibility are different and should not be confused.

Information flow

In advocacy, information is the most powerful tool: the direction in which the information flows in networks, whether all participants in an advocacy campaign have equal access to the same information, the density of the flow of information and the quality of available information will all have an impact on how and whether political responsibility is embraced. The ability actually to analyse, process or generate information is equally important.

Information frequency and format

The frequency with which NGOs relay information to one another is not only important in the context of the management of political responsibilities, but also in the effectiveness of the campaign. Significant events can erupt at any given moment and can either positively or adversely affect any member of a campaign. Getting information out can help other partners in the campaign to be prepared and/or protected. Equally important is determining an appropriate mix of communication formats. The necessary trust to discuss seriously agenda setting, strategies and risk-management cannot be developed by email alone (if it is available). Again, certain participants in the advocacy effort at hand may prefer to speak rather than write, which requires using the telephone, while a certain frequency of meetings in person will also be inevitable, preferably including meetings in the political arena(s) where the most urgent problems occur.

Articulating information into useful forms

Information by itself is not enough to pursue effective advocacy. Often the available information needs interpretation in accordance with the political arena in which it is being articulated. For example, World Bank documents and Indian newspaper articles are equally difficult to understand unless they are translated for the reader who is not familiar with the institution or the political arena. Pointing out the critical statements or aspects of the documentation to fellow activists in other political arenas and translating the important pieces of information (either from the local language into English or vice versa), are critical responsibilities. In many situations, oral communication is the only method of communication that is effective at a local level. A key indicator of the quality of a campaign is the length to which NGOs will go to break through communication and language barriers.

The formalization of relationships

In global campaigns, networks are often fluid. Global campaigns require time to determine who is going to be involved in the issue. As campaigns develop, relationships tend to become more formalized. They can even get to the point where they have statutes such as in the case of World Rainforest Movement (WRM) or the International NGO Forum on Indonesian Development (INFID). Action committees, a memorandum of understanding, the production of joint newsletters, and so on represent varying levels of formalization of mutual relationships in NGO advocacy. Formalization can help to establish transparency, which is another key issue in advocacy. Transparency is a very valuable tool in that it often highlights the lack of transparency in counter forces.

Recognizing and clearly establishing the parameters of networks involved in global campaigns can help in defining political responsibilities, certainly if the relationships in question are expected to be productive over a longer period. The more parameters that are defined, the more explicit the level of responsibility toward partners in the network and the better that risks can be managed.[4]

Typologies of NGO Relationships in Transnational Advocacy

The seven areas above are intended to help recognize different aspects of political responsibility in global NGO campaigns. Below, we take one step further and suggest four overall typologies of transnational NGO relationships. The typologies are highlighted by campaign case studies meant to illuminate the above areas of political responsibility in practice (see Table 7.1). They are not meant to be the definitive historical description of what happened in each of these cases, nor do we fully explore the success or failures of these campaigns vis-à-vis their ultimate goals or objectives. The sole purpose of suggesting these typologies is to elaborate further our argument and to propose an additional tool to better understand political responsibility in transnational NGO advocacy.

In our typologies we match the commensurability of different objectives of an advocacy campaign in different political arenas with a qualification of what happens with information and how strategies, risks and funds are managed. The level of political responsibility that is attained in each typology is an outcome of these indicators. An overview of the four typologies is given at the end of this section.

The cooperative campaign

We call our first typology of relationships among NGOs engaged in advocacy a 'cooperative campaign'. In a cooperative campaign, the level of political responsibility towards the most vulnerable actors is optimal. For the most part, advocacy agendas and strategies are set in close consultation with the groups who are supposed to benefit from the campaign and risks are assumed only in regard to the burden that can be borne by the most vulnerable. There are four dynamics that frame the typology:

- a pursuit of interlocking objectives by different NGOs in multiple political arenas is intertwined;
- a very fluid and continuous flow of information among all NGOs involved;
- a continuous review of strategies and joint management of political responsibilities by all NGOs involved. Risk management is purely based on local realities in the political arena where participants in the campaign are most vulnerable;
- a high level of political responsibility.

To highlight the parameters of political responsibility in a cooperative campaign, we take the relatively well-known case of the Sardar Sarovar Dam in the Narmada River in India as an example (Alvarez and Billorey, 1988; Fisher, 1995; Morse, 1992).[5] The Narmada campaign had a high level of political responsibility among campaigners because the above four factors were achieved. The objectives of each set of actors in their own political arena were clearly defined, understood and eventually intertwined. There was a fluid and continuous flow of information among all the actors involved. There was a continuous review of strategies and joint management of political responsibilities by all the actors involved. Risk management was based on the strength of the most politically exposed.

Table 7.1 *Overview of Campaign Typologies*

Title Objectives	*Cooperative* Interlocking	*Concurrent* Compatible	*Disassociated* Conflicting	*Competitive* Opposing
Information	High frequency, global distribution, easily accessible, freely shared	Regular, multiphased, more tightly directed, freely shared	Infrequent, lopsided, difficult to access, shared with reservation	Minimal, no direct flow, inaccessible, not shared
Strategy	Continuous review, joint management, risks based on most vulnerable	Frequent review, coexisting management, risks based upon national arena	Occasional review, management and risks exclusive to varying arenas	No review, single arena management, no recognition of risks
Level of political responsibility achieved	High	Medium	Low	None

By way of providing the reader with a very brief history, the Sardar Sarovar Dam in India provoked controversy from its inception in the early 1980s. The project became controversial because in its original formulation it would have resulted in the flooding of the traditional lands of over 250,000 tribal people living on the banks of the Narmada River in Gujarat, Madhya Pradesh and Maharashtra. In total, over 1 million people are expected to be affected. The NGO campaign to stop the dam became an international campaign when the World Bank agreed to finance the construction of the Sardar Sarovar Dam.

On the local level, the objectives of the tribal people were first limited to obtaining proper resettlement compensation. On the international level, the destruction of pristine wildlife areas motivated the first campaigners in countries other than India to raise their voice. The concern for the environment, however, was quickly blurred by a concern for the rights of the tribals. Once it became clear that the authorities involved would not be able to properly compensate 'oustees', the campaign on the local level became an anti-dam campaign. Gradually the anti-dam message filtered through to the international campaign.

The targets of the various actors in the campaign differed from the outset. The tribals targeted the national state of India and the three states involved in the project. The tribals employed national NGOs in India, based in New Delhi, to help to influence both national level ministries and, as the campaign developed, the national court system. International actors targeted national bilateral aid programmes and the World Bank. Each actor in the campaign concentrated on their own political arena, developing dialogues and tactics specific to those arenas. But there were many instances where shows of mutual solidarity worked best and thus there were many instances when actors visited political arenas other than their own. The purposes of these visits were either to tell their own stories, as in the case of the tribals coming to Washington, or to understand better the realities and threats at the local level and to provide protection to those who were politically exposed, as was the case when international actors went to the Narmada Valley. While the varying political arenas were shared, the strength of each set of actors in specific arenas was recognized and respected. Overlap was by invitation only.

In the Narmada campaign, advocacy agendas of different NGOs were varied: to seek proper compensation for the tribals; to get the Bank out of the project; to stop other governments from supporting the project; to expose the Bank's failure to be able to abide by its own policies; to expose the State governments' failures to abide by their policies and ultimately to stop the construction of the dam. Not all of these agendas were shared on the tactical level. But, all agendas were repeatedly discussed among the various actors involved and agreed on. Different tactics were developed in the different political arenas and regularly shared.

A Narmada Action Committee (NAC) was established on the international level to keep communication flowing and to highlight new events and decisions taken in the Narmada Valley. The NAC fulfilled not only information needs but also established a level of responsibility to the tribals from many centres around the world. The tribals knew they could call Amsterdam or Washington and their requests would be heard all over the world within a matter of hours. The NAC also helped people to share in decision-making. Generally, once a year, actors would meet to compare notes; to reaffirm their interest in the case; and to hear from someone who may have just arrived from the Valley. In this way, the global relationships among international campaigners who were active in the Narmada case was somewhat formalized. The lines of communication were relatively clear; the frequency of communication was substantial; the responsibility of each actor to the local arena and to one another was articulated and transparent.

Similar mechanisms were employed between the national level in India and the local arenas. Information generated on the international level was translated into tribal languages while the Narmada Bachao Andolan produced updates of local facts and events for the international NGO community on a regular basis. These were often handwritten bulletins faxed to Washington and then distributed globally.

When particular activists might be tempted to go too far with a strategy, the threat of being cut off from the primary sources of information and the threat of being ostracized by the movement in the Narmada Valley were used. Furthermore, decisions made in the most politically vulnerable arena were respected by all players. When the actors in the local arena chose not to participate in an academic study about the movement, all international actors abided by that decision and did not cooperate.

The Narmada case was special in that money did not flow between various arenas. Money from the international arena was considered to be more harmful than helpful for the tribals, although resources were shared. For example, faxes were paid for by the international organizations, telephone calls were made with charges being paid by wealthier NGOs, and so on. Money hardly ever crossed from one political arena to another. This dissipated any unhealthy power relationships that might have developed in the campaign.

The concurrent campaign

Our second typology of relationships among NGOs that are engaged in advocacy is the 'concurrent campaign'. Which has coinciding representation of different but compatible objectives. It does not achieve a high level of political responsibility given that the objectives in various political arenas are different. Thus, information loops are not as tight as they would be in a cooperative campaign where everything is intertwined and direction is taken from the most politically exposed. The dynamics of a concurrent campaign can be qualified as follows:

*   a coinciding representation of different but compatible objectives by NGOs operating in their own political arena;
*   a regular but multiphased flow of information among the NGOs involved;
*   a frequent review of strategies and coexisting management of political responsibilities by varying combinations of the NGOs involved at different levels;
*   a medium level of political responsibility.

We present the Arun Dam campaign as an example of a concurrent campaign.[6] The Arun III was a Japanese-conceived run-of-the-river hydroelectric dam project scheduled to be built in a remote area of Nepal, the Arun Valley (*Bank Check Quarterly*, 1992-1995; Brown and Fox, 1998; *World Rivers Review*). The valley, while relatively sparsely populated, contained an ecosystem rich in biodiversity. The dam was meant to supply energy to two major city centres in Nepal and the rest to India. The total cost of the project (over a decide) was estimated at US$764 million, about the size of Nepal's annual national budget.

In the Arun case the objectives of NGOs in different political arenas varied. On the national level in Nepal, the Arun case was an anti-dam campaign from the outset. The issues advocated upon were purely environmental and economic. At the international level, the case was also anti-dam, predominantly because of its environmental impact. The case in part, however, became an international one because it arose at a time that coincided with the creation of the World Bank's Inspection Panel. The planned participation of the World Bank in the financing of the Arun Dam thus provided an opportunity to test the new inspection mechanism. These objectives were well understood by all the actors and were not in conflict with one another. In fact, it was the national-level actors who chose to use the Inspection Mechanism as an additional advocacy tool. Nevertheless, the possibility of using the mechanism generated interest in the case at international levels to a greater extent than before. Overlap in the objectives occurred in the writing of the inspection claim, where the economic arguments favoured by the local people were predominant, next to alleging violations of environmental assessment, resettlement and other World Bank policies. After the Inspection Panel had completed a review of the project, newly appointed World Balk President Wolfensohn announced in August 1995 that the Bank would no longer support Arun III, thereby effectively killing the project.

The flow of information in the Arun case was specific as opposed to all-encompassing in the Narmada case. Information flowed between various actors but not across, so that the Nepalese were responsible for communicating with each and every contact made at international level (as opposed to contacts flowing between and among international players). Relationships between campaigners internationally were less formal than in the Narmada case. On the national level in Nepal, however, relationships were formalized by establishing two NGO coalitions, the Alliance for Energy and the Arun Concerned Group. The connections to the local arena were weak in the Arun case, so theories about the needs and desires of the local people were not very well tested. This was the greatest weakness of the campaign. There was a low level of maintaining political responsibility with respect to the local region. As a result, when the World Bank's decision to withdraw from the project was announced, the Nepalese NGOs initially were afraid to show their satisfaction openly as they feared a backlash from some local interest groups that had anticipated benefits from the project. At the same time, international NGOs released a press statement declaring victory on the assumption that Nepalese people were dancing in the streets.

The disassociated campaign

We call the third typology to qualify the relationships among NGOs engaged in transnational advocacy the 'disassociated campaign'. This type of campaign takes us one step further away from truly interwoven relationships among NGOs, to a situation where – based on the same issue – advocacy objectives represented by various NGOs in different political arenas begin to clash. The dynamics of the typology are:

- a parallel representation of conflicting objectives by different NGOs in their own political arena;
- a regular but lopsided flow of information among the NGOs involved, usually more information flows from the South to the North rather than vice versa;
- occasional and unaffiliated review of strategies and the management of political responsibilities among the different NGOs involved, predominantly exclusive to their own political arena;
- a low level of political responsibility.

The example we use to illustrate the typology of a disassociated campaign is the intended investment of the US Scott Paper Company in a pulp and paper plantation in Irian Jaya, East Indonesia (Cleary, 1997; Stern, 1991). Like the previous cases, environmental concerns and issues of people's participation were at the forefront of the NGO agenda(s). Next to national and provincial authorities, however, the main target of the campaign was a private company rather than the World Bank.

In October 1988, the US-based Scott Paper Company announced a US$653.8 million investment in a tree farm and pulp mill project in the south-east part of Irian Jaya. The project was to be realized by means of a joint venture between Scott Paper and PT Astra, a large Indonesian conglomerate, well connected to the Indonesian Suharto regime. The aim of the project was to establish gradually a eucalyptus plantation of up to 200,000 hectares to provide logs for a pulp and wood factory in nearby Merauke.

Soon after the public announcement of the project, local and national NGOs began to put forward criticisms and demands. The Indonesian Network for Forest Conservation (Skephi) led a coalition with nine other Indonesian Jakarta-based NGOs who began to raise concerns. Skephi questioned how a forest concession could have been granted to PT Astra Scott Cellulosa without the implementation of an Environmental Impact Assessment in conformity with Indonesian Environmental Law. Other issues raised by Indonesian NGOs were: how Scott and Astral planned to involve local communities in the project, especially with respect to the use of tribal land; the impact on customary land ownership; the selection of pristine tropical rain forest (which would lead to the destruction of genetic resources, while the resulting deforestation could lead to the drying up of natural rivers); the composition of the necessary labour force and how it would be recruited; and whether upstream and downstream wastes would be handled appropriately. NGOs in the United States adopted these demands.

In response to initial NGO criticism, Scott promised an environmental as well as a social impact assessment, and explained that there would be an extended test period for the project to review its environmental and social soundness. The company stated that the intention was to approach the project carefully. The relationship with the local communities was described as a 'win–win' situation with promises being made as to the creation of 6000 jobs, training for local people, as well as the provision of schools and medical facilities.

Subsequently, communication between Scott and NGOs developed on various levels, primarily in Irian Jaya and the United States. A group of five local NGOs got together and established fairly regular communication with representatives of PT Astra Scott Cellulosa. The local NGOs obtained a copy of the project plans, which they translated into Indonesian and circulated among local communities. NGOs were assigned to help to explain and discuss the documents and the project in general with the local communities, in a series of meetings that were organized by the NGOs. The local district authorities also became involved in these meetings.

In the course of 1989, an agenda for local NGOs emerged, in which they basically accepted the establishment of the plantation, trying to gain training and employment opportunities, fair compensation for tribal land and proper control over environmental, social and cultural impacts. The discussions with Scott went as far as the establishment of an agreement to keep prostitution and bars away from the project area. With respect to the important question of land ownership, Scott started to make a map of the project area using village maps, as opposed to using official maps that did not properly reflect traditional land ownership. The local communities also expressed a preference to lease – rather than sell – their land, which Scott was willing to discuss. Part of the financing of the local level negotiations and capacity building efforts was provided for by United States Agency for International Development (USAID) and the Asia Foundation.

Meanwhile, at the international level, an NGO campaign with a different character had emerged. The project in Irian Jaya was framed by linking Scott Paper to their responsibility for environmental damage in the United States and Canada. Scott Paper in the United States and its subsidiaries in Europe were vigorously targeted by a number of NGOs, like the Rainforest Action Network (RAN) and Survival International. NGOs threatened a consumers' boycott of Scott Products if Scott would not leave pristine rain forest and the areas of tribal people untouched. These NGOs cooperated in particular with the Skephi-led coalition in Indonesia. Some Jakarta-based NGOs and international groups, such as the Indonesian Environmental Forum (WALHI) and the Environmental Defence Fund (EDF), tried to follow a road in between. They communicated in a less aggressive way with the Scott Paper Company and stated their willingness to accept the project, as long as a number of demands were met.

While NGOs at the international level communicated intensively with each other, there was little communication between the local and international levels of the NGO campaign. International groups suspected that local people were in fact not well informed and were already worn out by years of Indonesian oppression and intimidation in this remote region of Irian Jaya. This perception was strengthened by the decision of the Indonesian authorities virtually to close of the area to outsiders.

The situation reached a climax in the second half of 1989. The Scott Paper project was one of the cases highlighted by RAN in a full-page advertisement in the *New York Times*, pointing at the destruction of tropical rainforest. On 13 October, Scott announced its withdrawal from the project, apparently to the surprise of PT Astra and the Indonesian authorities who had already boosted the overall data of foreign investment in Indonesia in 1989 by including the project in Irian Jaya. The reason for the withdrawal given by Scott was that 'extensive studies now indicate the Company can meet its anticipated needs for pulp from other sources'. In interviews, however, Scott agreed that NGO pressure played an important role in the considerations of the company to withdraw.

The differences between NGOs operating at different levels in appreciating the outcome of the campaign were best summed up in a letter from a local NGO to

Survival International after Scott's withdrawal. The local NGO agreed that it would be best if the project was stopped altogether. But PT Astra and the Indonesian authorities had already announced that negotiations with various new potential foreign counterparts for the project were on the way. The question from East Irian Jaya was what would the international NGOs do if a new company from Japan, Taiwan or Korea entered the local arena, most likely much less willing to negotiate with the local communities or NGOs as compared with Scott Paper? To date there has been no new investment of this kind.

The competitive campaign

Our fourth typology provides the worst case scenario, the 'competitive campaign'. In this situation, advocacy on one level may actually have an adverse or counter-productive impact at another level. There is a serious lack of information exchange and coordination among the NGOs involved, resulting in an absence of account-ability and a failure to embrace political responsibilities. The dynamics of the competitive campaign are:

- a parallel representation of opposing objectives by different NGOs in different political arenas;
- no direct flow of information among different NGOs at different levels;
- no joint review of strategies or management of political responsibilities which may result in human rights violations or other negative impacts on the interests of local communities;
- no political responsibility.

As an example of a competitive campaign we take the case of the Huaorani fighting against US oil interests in Ecuador (Kane, 1995). Since 1967 US oil companies have exploited oil resources in Ecuador with impunity. Leaking pipelines, oil fires, violence and intimidation have all been part of the operational realities in search for the black gold. Rainforests and thriving tribal communities have been destroyed by the practices of Texaco and Petroecuador. In the battle to keep Texaco or any other oil interests out of the Huaorani territory, some international activists fought to save the rainforests while the battle on the local and national level concentrated on protecting the lives and rights of the indigenous peoples. While these two interests did not necessarily compete at all stages of the campaign, at various points in the campaign the differing interests did result in competition. The international campaign against Conoco ran from the late 1980s to the mid-1990s.

In the case against Conoco drilling in Huaorani territory, many US and European-based environmental and human rights groups had taken up the issue and staked out political positions which ran the gamut from opposition to Conoco to support for the company as the best option in a bad situation. For the most part, these positions were taken without consultation with the Huaorani (who were deep in the forest) and at best using information provided by a variety of national level actors in Ecuador, but sometimes with no in-country contacts at all. According to one source, the only thing the European and US groups had in common was that the Huaorani people did not recognize any of them.

There was very little information flowing between the different actors in the campaign. Strategies were adopted based on what was considered to be politically feasible, as opposed to what was requested by the affected communities. Deals were agreed which undercut the rights of indigenous peoples to manage their own territories. In some cases environmental and human rights organizations raised money in the name of the campaign but did not share those resources in any way with the people on whose behalf they had raised the funds. In fact, activists close to the indigenous people operated on shoestring budgets while those operating in the United States or Europe had plenty of money. At one point, a US-based environmental organization attempted to cut a deal with Conoco which would have allowed the company to build a road straight through the Huaorani territory. While decisions taken in the international political arena did not immediately jeopardize the safety of the people on the ground in Ecuador, those decisions in effect cut off the negotiating abilities of the indigenous communities and destroyed a fledgling alliance between the local arena (indigenous peoples) and the national arena (Ecuadorian environmentalists). The struggle of the Huaorani continues. The campaign against Conoco in Ecuador provides an example of the worst kind of campaign when measuring political responsibility.

Managing Relationships in Transnational NGO Advocacy

The central argument of this article is that the relationships that emerge among NGOs engaged in global campaigns are highly problematic. If not handled with care, they may reflect as much inequality as they are trying to undo. The inability of national and international bureaucracies and powerful sections of the private sector to include and respect a variety of development aspirations is perhaps the main driving force behind NGO advocacy across borders. But it is difficult to deal with multiple desires for change that can only be realized by engaging many organizations in complex relationships. This is true at a practical level as well as for theory construction.

Many observers like to reduce the fundamental plurality which is expressed in NGO advocacy to a format which is easier to grasp and allows for picking up on what is seen as hopeful signs of a vaguely homogeneous 'globalization from below' (Falk, 1995). But if it is possible still to distinguish an 'above' and a 'below' in globalizing political realities, changes concerning specific issues need to be – and are – advocated by NGOs in different arenas simultaneously. This creates a variety of patterns and dynamics in networks which are not necessarily homogeneous or coherent. To an important extent the dynamics in these relationships determine the quality of NGO advocacy, both in terms of its communicative functions as well as effectively shaping new forms of democracy.

There is no empirical evidence which allows for generalizing about transnational advocacy networks as 'those relevant actors working internationally on an issue, who are bound together by shared values, a common discourse, and dense exchanges of information and services' (Keck and Sikkink, 1998, pp2, 200). Nor can an NGO campaign be defined as 'a set of strategically linked activities in which members of a diffuse principled network develop explicit, visible ties and mutually recognized rules in pursuit of common goals (and generally against a common target)' (Keck and Sikkink, 1998, p6). There is a discourse in NGO networks, but the common elements are often only partly shared. Advocacy agendas, targets and strategies can vary in different political arenas. The exchange of information or services may be dense, but irregular and unbalanced. The quality of the ties between different members of a network is hardly ever constant and mutually recognized rules in a campaign are far from common.

We are also uncomfortable with attributing too big a role to the binding function of common values in transnational NGO advocacy networks. As a matter of fact, most networks start with a campaign concern and not by determining shared values among the network-participants. Particular values may very well motivate the individual NGO activist, but provide a disproportionate approach to explain the communality in transnational networks. The one cross-cutting principle standard in transnational NGO advocacy is the international system of human rights. But this is a well-defined and institutionally enshrined normative framework, as opposed to a much less distinct value-orientation (Van Tuijl, 1999). Moreover, human rights provide an essential practical foundation for NGO advocacy strategies as well.

The ideal form of cooperation and interaction in transnational advocacy networks, which we have labelled a 'cooperative campaign', is the exception rather than the rule. In that sense, the success of the Nannada campaign has perhaps set an example to strive for, but at the same time has misinformed the debate on NGO advocacy, precisely because the case is not representative of what often happens in transnational networks.

We believe that NGOs will set themselves a more feasible and still very useful target if they begin with trying to manage their relationships minimally at the level of what we have called a 'concurrent campaign'. The concurrent campaign leaves more room for a variety of objectives in different political arenas, however, with care taken to respect the interests or aspirations of the most vulnerable groups involved in the campaign. The overlap between different players at different levels in a concurrent campaign is dispersed and far from complete. That is what most transnational NGO advocacy efforts will look like when the participants try to embrace their political responsibilities but take into account the limitations in their capacities.

What deserves to be highlighted is the extreme difficulty of pursuing NGO advocacy effectively and responsibly outside one's own political arena. There are three reasons for this and they are among the most important factors that help to explain why some of our typologies are enacted in practice.

First, people and NGOs primarily act on incentives which emerge in their own space, certainly not on a notion of 'planetary risks' (Sogge, Biekart and Saxby, 1996, pp169–170). In this respect, the popular slogan 'Think globally, act locally' is highly confusing because it suggests an inherent link between local actions and an aggregate global political clout of local actions which is far from evident. Moreover, it assumes the capacity to 'Think global', but what does that exactly mean? For sure, no transnational NGO network has a mechanism to check whether all network participants have the same thing in mind if they start to 'think globally'. At the end of the day, connecting activities from a global to a local level and vice versa in a way which is both strategic and meaningful for all network participants involved is a long road full of potholes. The frontiers of nation states may be crumbling as an obstacle for the physical movement of information, capital or people. Regardless, NGO activists do have borders in terms of who they are and what they possibly can do when considering their legitimacy, language, culture, education and ways of communication.

Second, the expansion of NGO relationships to overcome the limitations of one's own specialization in one political arena and create more effective alliances with other types of social or civil actors within and across national borders is often not a feasible solution. There are numerous ideas for human rights NGOs to work with environmental NGOs, for private aid agencies to work with knowledge-based NGOs, for development NGOs to work more with trade unions or local governments, for intermediary NGOs to work with grassroots organizations and social movements, and so on. This is related to NGOs playing a role in concepts such as the 'thickening' of civil society or the development of 'social capital' (Fox, 1997, p963). But what NGO is capable of managing such a multitude of relationships effectively? Even at the basic level of information exchange, the maintenance of every relationship requires resources.

In addition to the question of resources, there is the related danger of becoming entangled in conflicting alliances if NGOs continue to expand their relationships. The more relationships an NGO is involved in, the more it becomes possible that one alliance will at a certain moment articulate a position which contradicts another alliance in which the same NGO is involved. We are aware of NGOs who are simultaneously affiliated with the International Union of Conservation (IUCN), with World Wide Fund For Nature (WWF), with Friends of the Earth (FoE) and Greenpeace, even though these four entities have very different global strategies and visions.

For an NGO to engage effectively in transnational advocacy requires hard choices about resource allocation: which issue to take up, which networks to join, which research to participate in, which meeting(s) to attend? It is difficult for NGOs to deal with their political responsibilities because necessary choices about resource allocation are avoided or made in a haphazard way. For example, NGOs often give in to the expectations of donors, to the urgency of a problem or to the desire to be perceived as a courageous actor on the cutting-edge of important change. Resource allocation and priority setting for transnational advocacy within NGOs are usually not the result of a clear planning and decision-making process. As a result, there is a risk for NGOs and their networks to become overburdened and spread their resources too thin. This in turn exposes them to superficiality, and insignificance can ultimately backfire when targeted parties turn the table and start to question the accountability and representational aspects of the NGOs' actions.

Some authors have argued that networks which include NGOs concerned about multiple issues (such as the environment and human rights) will be more accountable (Covey, 1996). This argument misses the point. The composition of an NGO network, in terms of the variety of backgrounds and specializations of the NGOs involved, does not say anything imperative about the political dynamics between these organizations or about the impact of their advocacy work. As we argued in the previous section one level of action in a particular political arena may be very effective in itself, but could be counterproductive in another arena. Likewise, looking at different sources of legitimacy invoked by individual NGOs to support their advocacy role, such as specific expertise or a strong bond with a particular constituency, does not provide much insight into the dynamics between these organizations or the impact of their advocacy (Nelson, 1996).

A third reason for NGOs to be careful in operating outside their own political arena is that it may lead to an erosion of relationships in the local arena. The difficulties of engaging effectively and responsibly in NGO advocacy away from home rapidly increase if one loses touch with a place of origin because working the global arena can easily be all-consuming but does not provide a self-standing legitimacy. The iron law of transnational advocacy is that a firm relationship with one's own political arena is an essential condition for working in one or more other political arenas. This approach to transnational NGO advocacy equates the importance of advocacy in the local arena with that in the global arena.

Our vision is related to those who have tried to frame global NGO campaigns in the language of universal human rights in which development policies should be formulated, including the actions of NGOs themselves (McCormack and Mendonca, 1997). The hallmark of an NGO which fully embraces the concept of political responsibility is its capacity to sustain coherence and consistency between the goals it professes and the manner in which it pursues them. In NGO advocacy decisions about what to do, or not to do, with a certain piece of information are often made in a split second. In that sense, the exercise of political responsibility in NGO advocacy is foremost an operational problem.

The democratic quality of NGO advocacy depends to an important extent on how NGOs manage their mutual relationships. Being rooted in one political arena, NGOs are setting out to seek each other's cooperation and partnership to overcome the democracy deficit which is being created by the globalizing processes of decision-making. Somewhere in between a competitive campaign and a cooperative campaign, transnational NGO advocacy may very well help to open up space to articulate strategically a plurality of development aspirations, at people's own conditions and risks, using their own timeframes, speaking their own language and applying their own design of political expression or association.

Notes

1   The power attributed to NGOs in popular perceptions is sometimes astonishing: 'Once relegated to the do-good fringes of traditional diplomacy, NGOs have moved front and center on the world stage ... There is a basic re-sorting of power from nation-states to non-governmental entities ... The century is ending with state power in decline throughout most of the world. And without many people having clearly noticed, NGOs are rushing in where soldiers and bureaucrats no longer tread.' *Newsweek*, 1 August 1994.

2   Accountability in a context of finances stands as a translatable term. In fact, the dominant connotation of accountability with finances is one of the reasons leading to difficulties in translating the word as being related to political relationships.

3   This is not always the case. Advocacy NGOs in the North often either cannot or do not avail themselves of funds from government sources and thus can have fewer resources than large NGOs in the South.

4   There is an argument against formalizing relationships which is applicable to situations, whereby NGOs may not want to identify themselves explicitly because of threats to their security. This is a valid argument. There is, however, often the further counter-argument that safety lies in numbers.

5   Events now under way in this campaign have not been taken under consideration in this discussion.

6   An elaborate description of another case which we would qualify as a concurrent campaign can be found in Rumansara in Brown and Fox (1998, p123).

References

Alvares, C and Billorey, R (1988) *Damming the Narmada: India's Greatest Planned Environmental Disaster*, Penang, Malaysia, Third World Network, APPEN.

Bain, K (1999) 'Building or burning bridges? The accountability of transnational NGO networks in policy alliances with the World Bank', paper prepared for the conference 'NGOs in Global Future: Marrying Local Delivery to Worldwide Leverage', Birmingham, England.

Bank Check Quarterly (1992–1995) Berkeley, CA, International Rivers Network.

Brown, D L and Fox, J (eds) (1998) *Assessing the Impact of NGO Advocacy Campaigns on World Bank Projects and Policies: The Struggle for Accountability. The World Bank, NGOs and Grassroots Movements*, Boston, MIT Press.

Cleary, S (1997) *The Role of NGOs under Authoritarian Political Systems*, London, Macmillan Press.

Covey, J (1996) 'Accountability and effectiveness in NGO policy alliances', in M Edwards and D Hulme (eds) *Beyond the Magic Bullet: NGO Performance and Accountability in the Post-Cold War World*, West Hartford, CT, Kumarian Press, pp198–214.

Edwards, M and Hulme, D (eds) (1996) *Nongovernmental Organisations – Performance and Accountability: Beyond the Magic Bullet*, West Hartford, CT, Kumarian Press.

Falk, R (1995) *On Human Governance, Towards a New Global Politics: World Order Models Project*, Cambridge, Polity Press.

Fisher, W F (ed) (1995) *Toward Sustainable Development? Struggling Over India's Narmada River*, New York, M E Sharp, Columbia University Seminar Series.

Fox, J (1997) 'The World Bank and social capital: contesting the concept in practice', *Journal of International Development*, Vol 9, No 7, pp963–971.

Kane, J (1995) *Savages*, NewYork, Vintage Books.

Keck, M and Sikkink, K (1998) *Activists Beyond Borders: Advocacy Networks in International Politics*, Ithaca, NY, Cornell University Press.

McCormack, M and Mendonca, M (1997) 'Human rights capacity-building and advocacy work with nongovernmental organizations: Ethiopia, Eritrea, Djibouti, Somaliland', unpublished paper prepared for the human rights programme of the fund for peace, Caribbean initiative on equality and non-discrimination, Georgetown, Guyana.

Morse, B (1992) *Sardar Sarovar: Report of the Independent Review*, Resources Futures International, Vancouver, Canada.

Najam, A (1999) 'Citizens' organizations as policy entrepreneurs', in D Lewis (ed) *International Perspectives on Voluntary Action: Reshaping the Third Sector*, London, Earthscan.

Nelson, P (1996) 'Transnational NGO networks in global governance: promoting 'participation' at the World Bank', paper prepared for the International Studies Association Annual Meetings, San Diego, California.

Nelson, P (1997) 'Conflict, legitimacy, and effectiveness: who speaks for whom in transnational NGO networks lobbying the World Bank?', *Nonprofit and Voluntary Sector Quarterly*, Vol 26, No 4, pp421–441.

Rumansara, A (1998) 'Indonesia: the struggle of the people of Kedung Ombo', in D L Brown, J Fox (eds) *Assessing the Impact of NGO Advocacy Campaigns on World Bank Projects and Policies: The Struggle for Accountability: The World Bank, NGOs and Grassroots Movements*, Boston, MIT Press, pp123–150.

Sogge, D, Biekart, K L and Saxby J (1996) *Compassion and Calculation: The Business of Private Foreign Aid*, London, Pluto Press.

Stern, A J (1991) 'The case of the environmental impasse: how can companies and activists find common ground?', *Harvard Business Review*, May–June, pp14–29.

Tandon, R (1994) 'Influencing public policy', *Bureau of Adult Education (ASPBAE) Courier*, No 59. Colombo, Sri Lanka.

Vakil, A C (1997) 'Confronting the classification problem: toward a taxonomy of NGOs', *World Development*, Vol 25, No12, pp2057–2070.

van Tuijl, P (1999) 'NGOs and human rights: sources of justice and democracy', *Journal of International Affairs*, Vol 52, No 2, pp493–512.

World Rivers Review, Berkeley, CA, International Rivers Network.

Williams, D and Young, T (1994) 'Governance, the World Bank and liberal theory', *Political Studies*, Vol 42.

Part 3

Developing the Organization: Managing Growth, Change and Structure

8

The Evolutionary Life-cycles of Non-governmental Development Organizations

Jeffrey Avina

Introduction: NGOs Worldwide

This chapter argues that non-governmental organizations (NGOs) active in community development exhibit different organizational characteristics at different phases of their evolution. Being able to recognize the characteristic descriptive elements of the different phases of organizational development better positions one to understand the nature of an NGO's relationship with donors, beneficiaries and the world around it. Perhaps more importantly, recognizing what phase of its organizational development cycle an NGO is in will assist the practitioner to understand the types of problems the NGO may be facing, their cause and the range of options available for problem resolution.

No reliable database has been created to record NGO development worldwide. It is safe to say, however, that there are thousands of NGOs in addition to the 2200 represented from the Development Assistance Committee (DAC) member countries. Some NGOs are affiliated with international organizations which may or may not have originally sponsored them. CARE, Save the Children, World Wide Fund For Nature and the credit institutions Solidarios and FINCA are examples of organizations which have founded affiliates throughout the world. Other NGOs, whether externally supported or not, have participated in the establishment of federal structures which group NGOs on a local, regional, national or even international basis.

The implementational methodologies applied by NGOs are also quite varied. Figure 8.1 indicates that the range of approaches extends from the very traditional relief model followed by some NGOs since World War II to a more social movement-oriented strategy. Korten (1991) notes that, as a general rule, donors and governments are more interested in supporting NGOs involved in relief and welfare interventions than those aimed at fundamental structural change.

The difference between the illustrated methodological extremes is most clearly manifest in terms of outcomes. NGOs generally share a concern for the immediate needs of beneficiaries. NGOs further to the right on the continuum, however, have an additional agenda. Broadhead (1987) argues that no authentic development organization can operate without a 'theory' directed at the underlying causes of development. To do so relegates the organization to that of a relief agency focused

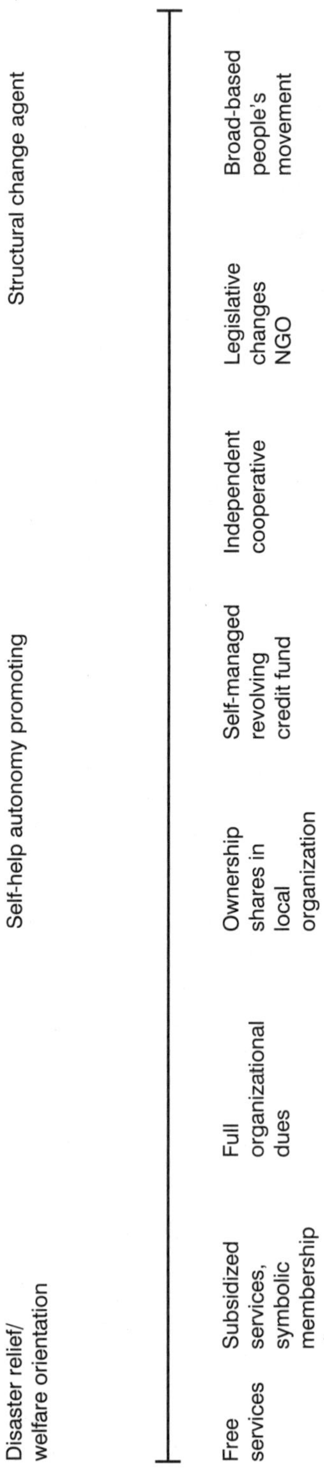

Figure 8.1 *An Indicative Continuum of NGO Methodologies*

Disaster relief/welfare orientation

Self-help autonomy promoting

Structural change agent

Free services

Subsidized services, symbolic membership dues

Full organizational dues

Ownership shares in local organization

Self-managed revolving credit fund

Independent cooperative

Legislative changes NGO

Broad-based people's movement

on the symptoms of underdevelopment rather than its root causes. Korten (1991, p114) adds that, without a theory, an organization cannot establish a meaningful development strategy. The concept of strategy implies a systematic vision as to how resources will be used to address the problem at hand. Organizations without a strategy often scatter their resources in response to immediately visible needs. For example, 'self-help' NGOs can be distinguished from welfare-oriented NGOs by their stress on ensuring that project gains will be maintained after their assistance ends (Tandon, 1989). Likewise, NGOs further to the right on the continuum in Figure 8.1 often attempt to expand their impact beyond individual communities by promoting organizational networks which can catalyse social movements and promote structural change. This schematic can also be viewed as a time continuum. Some NGOs which begin with a welfare-oriented approach adjust their methodology over time in a more progressive fashion. Save the Children USA provides one example of this evolution.

An introduction to the NGO life-cycle

NGOs undergo a variety of experiences which, to an important degree, reflect their level of maturity and development. The NGO life-cycle can be loosely divided into four organizational stages:

- Start-up
- Expansion
- Consolidation
- Close-out.

The remainder of this chapter explains each life-cycle phase and the characteristics which generally describe organizations found within them. It includes a general description of NGOs within a specified level of evolution, the motivation pushing them to evolve, the issues likely to arise during that phase of development as well as the potential outcomes which can result.

For the sake of simplicity, the analysis will present the life-cycle model in the above-indicated sequential order. It must be understood from the start, however, that organizational evolution is neither static nor unidirectional and, as a result, this analytical method cannot be applied mechanistically. Some organizations follow the four-step life-cycle in its most mechanistic form. The majority of organizations, however, follow less predictable courses. Some may skip stages, while others may start down the four-step path only to reverse at various times before possibly rereversing direction. For example, as indicated in the figure, an NGO which consolidates successfully may expand again at a later date or it may be forced to close out because of additional considerations which were not known at the time of the consolidation. Start-ups which fail may immediately close out. An organization which fully closes may reinitiate operations at a more propitious moment or in a more suitable location. Finally, an NGO which closes out operations in one area may be spinning off new programmes elsewhere and thus be closing out and starting up simultaneously.

Surprisingly, the fact that there is only a limited capacity to chart a uniform process of organizational evolution is relatively unimportant. What is critical, however, is knowing that there are definable phases of organizational evolution and that each has its own set of distinguishable characteristics. Thus, the key for development practitioners is to:

1   determine what stage an NGO is in at any particular moment;
2   know the potential set of issues the NGO is likely to face within that evolutionary stage; and
3   develop a strategy which takes these issues into account in order to make the appropriate management decisions.

Without further commentary, the four phases of organizational development are presented below.

Phase 1: Organizational Start-up

New NGOs generally can be placed into one of two categories: those which are organic or self-generating in origin and internally financed (at least initially) and those established with external financial, conceptual or technical support. Briefly, an internally initiated NGO as defined here is likely to be small in size and to pursue very moderate goals related to the immediate needs and resource capacity of the surrounding community. An externally initiated NGO may build around locally perceived needs or may promote an externally designed development approach. It may build on existing local institutions and capacity or import a new organizational model into the site. It is likely to be larger or have the capacity to expand rapidly and to have broader goals.

Because of the distinctive character of these two categories of start-up NGOs they are described separately below.

Self-generating start-ups

As stated above, self-financed grassroots start-ups are generally small in nature and the breadth of their impact is very localized. They are often born from the initiative of a 'catalytic agent', either a single motivated leader or a small cadre. The leader(s) are generally respected community members, quite possibly with higher educational levels and greater relative exposure to the world outside the community. The group founder(s) are often teacher(s), local political or religious leader(s), business person(s), or community members recently returned from schooling or an urban work experience.

The range of potential activities to which a local start-up can commit itself are as broad as community needs. The reason for group formation, the institutional *raison d'être*, could stem from a gap in public services made available to the community. It may also reflect a desire to improve local income-generating capacity. Group membership will closely reflect the organization's interest and resource capacity. Logically, a local service-providing agency such as a crèche, sanitation or education group will target membership differently from an association of farmers or an artisan cooperative.

The NGO's institutional purpose also plays a large role in determining the new NGO's organizational character. We have seen that most NGOs can be loosely characterized as either community-service oriented or income-generating. These distinctive pursuits may involve the use of separate methodological modalities which engender distinguishable organizational structures and a differing set of issues and complexities. For example, a community-service NGO can promote broad community participation. This is because socioeconomic and educational differences rarely constrain participation in these types of activities.

In contrast, market-oriented pursuits can exacerbate existing economic disparities and thus limit access and participation. This is because an organization whose principal *raison d'être* is economic is likely to distribute its benefits to a more limited set of members based on their proportional economic contribution.

Relatively limited exposure to modern managerial practices often means that the structure of a localized start-up follows traditional or only semi-formalized institutionalized patterns characterized by a low level of administrative and managerial sophistication and formal accountability. More than likely, accounting and monitoring are rudimentary and largely informal. This may not pose any great constraint to a small, resource-poor organization, however, since informal communication networks and strong local participation may offset the lack of more formal monitoring procedures. Poor auditing and financial management will be more problematic for a fledgling income-generating NGO since the success of its performance will relate to how well it manages capital flows, billing procedures, marketing and inventory stock.

Since, by this definition, local start-ups are largely unassisted at inception, links to the external environment are still in the formative stages. However, the level of external contact with private or governmentally assisted agencies will vary widely, depending on a number of factors, including leadership, location (urban, rural), organizational mandate, governmental disposition and the priority given to the area where the NGO was established. New NGOs may be actively courting outside assistance from any number of sources (that is, church, government, private, bilateral or multilateral donors). Many, however, are unaware of how to initiate or formalize this procedure.

Thus, a small resource base is perhaps one of the more indicative aspects of an internally financed NGO during its start-up phase. A service-oriented organization may be financed solely by modest contributions from members. In instances where these groups assist with the development initiatives of government or private development agencies, they may at some point receive some level of external financial or infrastructural input. Income-generating NGOs are often internally financed, by a portion of the earnings of their members. Following the demonstration of their potential value, they may receive some support (individually or as a group) from private distributors and other intermediaries who purchase and market their goods. Conversely, if the new NGO is viewed as a threat, these same intermediaries may seek to undercut it.

Externally assisted intermediary or grassroots level organizations

New externally assisted initiatives often begin operations on a small-to-medium scale. Some external assisting agents experiment with 'clustering' organizational start-ups to set the stage for potential future federal linkages. When a donor is the initiator of the local NGO, its programme is usually based on a model pretested elsewhere and, ideally, pilot tested *in situ.*

Externally financed organizations vary as widely as their funders and thus resist definite typology. In some instances, they will mirror their parent organizations in most, if not all regards. In others, they will have developed their aims, objectives and development methodologies independently. Some funders prefer to support innovative local initiatives and project concepts that they believe will best assist the local populace, and this itself has potential replication value. However, the recipient organization is generally beholden, in some form, to the funder. While this may only be in terms of standard reporting and accounting procedures, it often involves significantly more.

The range of programme structures employed by externally assisted NGOs is also quite broad. They may use centralized service institutions, intermediary service organizations or promote grassroots groups. An equally important factor is the methodological approach to be utilized by the new NGO. Some NGOs favour a 'welfare approach' wherein the NGO provides all the services without any charge (either cash or in kind). Others opt for a more contributory approach which requires an escalating level of material input (symbolic or real) and individual responsibility from the beneficiaries. The purpose of this approach is to encourage local participation and a sense of 'community ownership'. Still others may have political or religious motivations. Quite logically, each method engenders a different organizational result.

The organizational leadership of an externally financed NGO will vary, depending on the level of external influence and input. It is likely, however, to be more professional than the leadership found in unassisted grassroots organizations. Many job posts will be remunerated. There may be full-time international staff or some arrangement to provide technical assistance from a professional consulting agency. Technical assistance may take the form of a 'counterpart' arrangement wherein the expert may also function as a trainer until he or she is no longer required.

Externally assisted organizations are more likely to use a formalized administrative and managerial approach than are unassisted grassroots organizations. In some instances, an institutional model complete with prefabricated administrative and managerial procedures may have been imported to reflect a funder's requirements.

One can expect to find higher levels of institutional accounability in an externally financed agency, if only because it will probably be a condition for external support. Heightened accountability will often include a systematic accounting procedure (if not an actual project accountant) and annual external audit of all project expenses. In addition, there are likely to be pre-established mechanisms for project monitoring. Whether or not the appropriate personnel will be in place to carry out these functions is, of course, an independent question. The nature and calibre of project monitoring can vary widely, depending on the interest of the NGO staff and the rigorousness of the donor's requirements.

Why NGOs start up

The impetus for group formation is quite broad. As mentioned above, it may stem from discontent with the status of government service provision (such as basic health, education, water, sanitation, credit and agricultural subsidies). The motivation may also relate to some catalytic event which inspires local action. An example would be where market prices given to local producers by middlemen fall to unacceptable levels without due cause or where state services are suddenly withdrawn for macroeconomic or political reasons. Conversely, a local NGO may begin activities in response to governmental or private development initiatives. The impetus for organizing may reflect a local desire to influence the direction, methodology or content of a governmental or non-governmental development effort as well as its impact on the local community.

More specifically in the case of externally assisted NGO start-ups, there may be additional reasons which cause an NGO to be formed. The developmental initiative can be the product of an established plan or the recognition of a local need. For example, occasionally governments will promote local NGOs to enhance the performance of large-scale state development efforts. Some NGOs are developed in response to local calamities such as earthquakes or floods. Whether or not such relief assistance leads to the creation of sustainable organizations will depend on the degree, purpose and nature of the assistance package.

Group formation may be largely 'donor driven'. Donors partly evaluate their institutional performance by their disbursement levels. Thus, some donors finance new NGO start-ups in order to target selected priority areas and increase their own disbursement levels. The project or organizational concept may have been developed by an outsider who is familiar with donor operations and procedures of funding agencies. Such persons design projects in exchange for compensation which can vary from direct employment to a percentage commission fee. It should be noted that many large donors are not set up to target small NGOs. Instead they prefer to work with government agencies or other agencies who can absorb larger disbursements and development projects. Increasingly, however, more large donors are recognizing the value of NGOs as effective microtargeting disbursement vehicles.

Lastly, local organizational initiatives may be the direct offshoot of organizing efforts by legally recognized or unrecognized political or religious elements. Such NGOs often focus on local needs fulfilment, but they often retain their political or religious character, and rely on their sponsors for continued financial and political support.

Issues to consider

The principal concern for a new self-generating NGO is to establish an institutional environment within which the organization can flourish. This will include determining the organizational and managerial structure, organizational goals and mandate, output targets, securing adequate financing, determining the role and obligations of beneficiaries and determining if and when to formally incorporate. In many countries in Latin America, for example, new organizations are required to obtain juridical status before they can qualify for state or any assistance from foreign aid agencies.

Unlike self-generated NGOs, externally financed NGOs will experience a stronger push to establish a formal executive structure with clear oversight powers. This type of organization is also more likely to be legally incorporated and to have a clear charter complete with rules governing the terms and mandates of officers and employees.

New organizations must be concerned with building up (and ultimately expanding) their human and financial resource base. While an externally initiated start-up should be more financially secure than a locally initiated one, it too must exercise restraint and judgement with regard to project expenditures and make strong efforts to maintain or expand its resource base. The search for new resources should take the organization eventually beyond the greater organizational self-determination. A weakly led NGO, however, may find itself shackled with yet another set of donor expectations and restrictions.

A less certain but no less critical factor associated with the establishment of a new NGO is its methodological vision. The new NGOs must make decisions on how to manage relations with beneficiaries participants and with the other public and private organizations operating within their impact area. Will the organization be participatory or top-down in style? Does it coordinate with other agencies or is it isolationist or competitive?

For example, where an organization has been formed to resist an unfair private interest or to replace or lobby for additional governmental services, determining organizational strategies and alliances is a critical aspect of strategic planning. These and similar issues may ultimately have a greater impact on project outcomes than the NGO's resource base or institutional structure.

An externally initiated development organization is susceptible to all the constraints that can affect an internally initiated one. The organization is likely to be more resilient, however, because of its stronger resource base and the external leverage to withstand outside pressures.

The viability and ultimate sustainability of any initiative is highly dependent on local interest and participation. This combination can engender a sense of 'community ownership' which will help to sustain an organization even during difficult periods. An externally financed NGO might attract broad local interest because of its resource profile. Its resource attributes, however, cannot preserve an organization which ultimately fails to meet local needs and interests. While an externally financed operation can continue to function even without strong local enthusiasm, the organization is unlikely to survive much beyond the duration of its external funding. One advantage, however, that an externally financed type of organization may have over an internally financed start-up is that external financing provides it with a buffer period in which it can attract local interest or modify its operations to conform with local needs.

Thus, the need remains to monitor closely project activities and local responses to them. Too often this follow-up does not occur or is poorly orchestrated and important adaptations in methodological approach are missed. By failing to adapt, a new NGO risks programme failure, a curtailment of external assistance (where it exists) or an externally imposed remake of project content or methodological orientation. The actual timeframe in which this will occur will vary greatly, depending on the diligence of the funder. Some donors are quite lax in their follow-up, which provides the NGO with an extended window in which to continue status quo operations.

The situation described above may differ for NGOs financed by religious or political bodies who may not allow any adaptation to their organizational methodology. Such organizations may continue to finance relatively unsuccessful activities in order to maintain an active presence in the targeted community. Any NGO must recognize its limits. Thus, the NGO should define explicitly its programme agenda within the parameters set by its resource capacity.

Finally, local, regional or national resistance of a political or economic nature can quickly undermine a local organizational initiative. This is all the more likely if the group has no outside source of support to counteract whatever hostility it may encounter. Indifference can have a similarly negative albeit less dramatic impact on a local NGO.

Possible outcomes

While success and failure define the realm of possible outcomes, there are substantial gradations within those categorizations which NGOs can experience.

Success may mean that the organization achieves its limited ends and either sustains itself by maintaining past achievements or closes out. It is equally likely, however, that the NGO will take on new project activities or expand the area of coverage, perhaps with new sources of internally or externally generated resources. Some groups may align themselves with like-minded agencies and form federations.

Success, however, is not always that clear-cut. The organization may achieve some but not all of its goals. Conversely, the organization may realize that it does not have the resources that are necessary to do all that it originally set out to do. A mid-project modification could delay or foreclose upon the realization of some predetermined goals. The NGO is still successful in the sense that it has adjusted to its prevailing reality.

A new group may fail for a number of reasons previously mentioned. In the worst case, group failure may lower community interest in future initiatives and badly discredit the organization's founders. Perhaps the most promising outcome of a failed effort is local reflection on the causes of failure and a subsequent group commitment to avoid similar pitfalls in the future.

Perhaps the four factors which best distinguish the externally initiate NGO from a self-generated one are:

1   the availability of outside technical assistance;
2   the experience of the founding organization;
3   the political and/or economic leverage the founding organization can provide; and
4   the extra financial cushion it can give to help the new NGO to accept higher levels of risk and/or to recover from past mistakes.

While it is not certain that externally assisted NGO start-ups make fewer fundamental mistakes, they are better positioned, however, to weather crises. While there are clear advantages to learning lessons the hard way, one bad slip by a resource-poor organization can spell disaster.

Phase 2: Organizational Expansion

NGOs expand at various times and for various reasons. Organizational expansion may result from conscious planning. It is just as likely, however, to be a spontaneous response to initial success, local need or prodding from donors, government or other actors.

Organizational expansion can manifest in various forms. It may result from an increase in beneficiary coverage within the established project area. Organizations also expand when they increase the number of services they provide to their existing beneficiary set. Finally, organizations expand as they enlarge their current project area or target an entirely new location to initiate project activities.

Planned expansions generally occur in conjunction with an increase in available financial resources (such as donor grants, credit, service fees, beneficiary contributions). In the best of cases, these will fully finance the project expansion including administrative support and the technical assistance needed to manage it.

In cases where the expansion is spontaneous, new resources are not always forthcoming. When they are not, existing financial resources will be depleted more quickly and NGO staff may be placed under greater strain. When new resources are expected, managers must time their expansions in a manner which takes into the account the largely inevitable time lag between application and actual receipt of funds. Failure to do so will place the organization under unnecessary stress.

The institutional structure of an NGO undergoing a planned expansion often becomes more sophisticated. Such a formalization may be required to handle the growth of project responsibilities. An NGO which expands on the basis of external financing can also expect a commensurate increase in accounting and monitoring responsibilities. This is certainly the case where the NGO has attracted a new donor which has its own accounting standards to which the NGO must conform. Most donors still require their aid recipients to adhere to their own standard of accounting and monitoring procedures. There is a slowly growing trend on the part of sophisticated aid recipients, however, to demand the right to develop their own accounting and monitoring procedures and provide this information to the donors. The clear advantage of this approach when it is done well is that it enables the NGO to devise monitoring structures which better support their project endeavours. Some NGOs are experimenting with participatory evaluations which involve the beneficiaries as part of the evaluation team.

Organizations undergoing more spontaneous growth may experience a gradual, less formalized institutional adjustment. For example, when a locally initiated grassroots NGO finds that traditional methods of organizational management, such as broad community oversight and participation in decision-making, become less tenable, it may opt for a more structured venue which includes designated officers and limited participation in decision-making, such as annual or biannual membership meetings.

It should be noted that the further an organization removes participation in decision-making from individual beneficiaries, the greater is the need for a separation of powers and a system of checks and balances. Without such controls, the opportunity for individual actors to appropriate power or resources is too strong. Some NGOs which expand spontaneously, however, fail to adjust their organizational structures at all.

A growing organization will require either an expansion in key personnel concomitant with programme growth or an increase in the systematic delegation of administrative and managerial responsibilities to junior staff, volunteers or more senior project beneficiaries. Where the NGO expands into a different region, the attention of key leadership personnel will be diverted towards the new start-up activity. This will make an increase in staff size and task delegation even more critical.

An important danger associated with rapid expansion is that it may jeopardize the organization's value consensus. Since NGOs are defined, in large part, by the values they espouse, a rapid expansion may lead to the integration of staff with different visions which undermine the organizational consensus. Such a development is not always bad. It is often unsettling, however, especially to an organization in the process of testing its capacity to take on larger tasks.

Many organizations attempt to expand without increasing their staff at all. Others prioritize the deployment of additional programme staff while increases in administrative staff lag behind. This is because administration-oriented work is perceived as less relevant to expanding programme delivery. A well-financed and planned expansion, however, may require the recruitment of additional administrative staff to support programme operations and lessen the load on NGO leadership.

Organizational expansion without an increase in paid or voluntary administrative and programme staff can be problematic. Failure to respond to resulting staffing constraints may overtax the NGO and presage a decline in staff morale, increased turnover and a decline in programme quality, administrative capacity and managerial responsiveness. An expanding NGO which maintains its staff constant will probably find that its capacity to manage and account for project expenditures and monitor project activities decline as a result of the thinning of its labour force.

In short, the preceding paragraphs illustrate the importance of a flexible, responsive and far-sighted leadership. Once an NGO reaches the phase of organizational expansion, leadership must be involved intricately in redefining organizational management procedures. A principal component of the adjustment is the development of an institutionalized system of administration and decision-making so that mundane tasks can be handled by lower level officers.

This development frees leaders to focus on strategic planning both in the sense of current project management as well as assessing future needs and likely sources of support or conflict. Leaders must be intimately involved with monitoring and evaluation activities within the context of programme operations. They must be equally concerned with keeping a pulse upon the external environment, whether local, national or international (such as donor perceptions), which may impact upon organizational success.

Why NGOs expand

Below is a partial list of events which may induce an organization to expand.

Some organizations expand as part of a scheduled 'phase-up' in operations. This may be a transition, for example, from a pilot test to full-scale programme operations. Occasionally two or more nearby community organizations may choose to join together into a larger agency or, even more rarely, to establish some type of federal structure.

An NGO may expand upon recognizing a gap in locally available services that it can fill. By doing so, it probably believes that providing the new service will make its initial intervention more effective. Unexpected programme success can also induce an NGO to assume greater challenges than initially envisaged. This may result from an initial underestimation of local interest or demand. NGOs also expand in line with a general broadening of organizational goals.

Some organizations expand thanks to propitious economic circumstances. For example, a dairy processing group or an agricultural export cooperative may need new members in order to pursue a larger market share or acquire greater certainty of meeting production targets.

Working within an environment of scarcity requires both sensitivity as well as a certain hard-edged managerial discipline. Some organizations expand because their leaders simply cannot justify turning away the needy. Unfortunately, this action can be irresponsible if available resources are spread too thinly and the quality of the output or the integrity of the organization is jeopardized.

Some NGOs expand under pressure from donors or other external agents. Donors, for example, just like NGOs, are under pressure to perform. To maintain institutional credibility to their funders, they must demonstrate a record of orderly disbursements and quantifiable outputs which are (preferably) directly associated with their financial contribution. Donors strongly prefer to finance new project activities (rather than administrative overhead) precisely because they are easily sourced and quantifiable. Thus, donors seek out organizations with a proven developmental track record who are willing to initiate new project activities directly linked to their contribution.

It follows that a particular donor may not be interested in either the specific region where an NGO is currently operating or the type of assistance it provides. Rather the donor's attraction may relate to the NGO's performance record. Many donors use their financial clout to coax NGOs to take up activities elsewhere or to implement a project which the donor has designed. An NGO may rightly fear that it will lose the offer if it balks at a donor siting request or relays less optimistic estimates of the start-up time and the pace of the programme expansion. It is no surprise that in today's world of financial scarcity few NGOs can resist such an attractive lure.

It is equally common for NGOs which are familiar with donor motivations to design programmes which they know will attract donor support. At the bottom of this performance for payment syndrome – whether donor or NGO initiated – lie the remains of many NGOs which have overcommitted themselves and paid the price in terms of their effectiveness and institutional longevity. A failure to maintain institutional integrity *vis-à-vis* donor demands can precede organizational disaster.

Some NGOs intentionally extend themselves beyond their carrying capacity in the belief that their funders will bail them out. As indicated above, there is a certain logic which supports this strategy. After all, a donor would rather provide a modest financial amendment and leave behind a project success than an organization in desperation and disarray. This strategy may work once or twice. By pursuing this approach, however, the NGO risks long-term damage to its reputation, which may keep other donors from supporting it in the future.

Issues to consider

The ultimate success of an organizational expansion will depend upon a wide array of intraorganizational considerations. The feasibility, scope, content, pace and character of the programme expansion are all-important decisional indicators. External factors, such as the NGO's relation with its donors and other political and economic actors which influence organizational performance, also have a determinative impact on the consequences of an attempted programme expansion.

With regard to the issue of feasibility: is the NGO in a position to manage a new project activity? If so, according to what parameters? By comparing resource availability with projected needs, for example, the NGO can begin to determine the level of expansion it can manage effectively. Related to this, the NGO must assess its institutional capacity to manage an expansion. This will involve an assessment of its leadership capacity, administrative and programme structure, additional manpower requirements and the professional competence of available labour.

With regard to scope: if the expansion is geographic, how broad an area should be covered? Are there natural boundaries which help to define the expanded programme's reach? What impacts will result from expanding into areas where different ethnic groups dominate, or where different social, economic, cultural, political, religious and geographic conditions exist? The manager must consider these issues both broadly as well as in relation to the capacity of his or her NGO.

An NGO's capacity to manage organizational growth will also depend on the pace and character of the expansion *vis-à-vis* prior experience. Where the organization is expanding existing services to new beneficiaries in the demarcated project area or to a similar area or providing new services to existing beneficiaries, the NGO's historical performance record provides an important indicator of a realistic pace and necessary resource requirements.

Conversely, even a resource-rich NGO will be hard-pressed to manage fluidly a rapid expansion where the target area is culturally, ethnically, geographically or politically distinct. Instead, significant efforts will be required to modify the programme to suit local conditions. This will include a disproportionate amount of time from key leaders and should include programme pilot testing with major attention placed on monitoring the results and adapting the methodology accordingly. Where cultural or ethnic differences prevail, it may also involve hiring and training an entirely new set of project staff. Thus, an NGO can expect its programme expansion to be relatively slower and more costly than that achieved during its prior experiences.

It should also be noted that, where an expansion has occurred spontaneously, leaders can still attempt to manage the pace of the expansion and thereby regain some control over organizational development.

External influences can also strongly affect organizational expansion. As mentioned above, the nature and pace of an expansion should reflect the NGO's prior experience and implementation capacity. This unfortunately does not always occur. Donors may attempt to influence siting decisions or programme content or modify aspects of the NGO's programme methodology as the price of their contributions. Political actors may precondition their approval or support with a series of conditions or demands. Even private-sector actors may attempt to influence the nature, content or size of a cooperative sector expansion.

Where NGOs incorporate new project activities or modify existing ones, they must consider fully the impact of external influences. Is the proposed activity still sufficiently linked to existing initiatives? Is there sufficient familiarity within the organization or easily accessible external assistance to ensure effective implementation? What is the potential benefit that is expected to result from a change in programme content? What is the likelihood of achieving it? How sustainable is the outcome? Is this the type of activity the NGO wishes to pursue? If the activity is not suitable, what alternative does the NGO have (such as other donors, protective political alliances or rejecting expansion outright).

Potential outcomes

There is no recipe which lists all the elements of a successful expansion. Success in this sphere is as varied as the NGOs and the conditions facing them. In general, however, an expansion is successful if the organization has evolved institutionally to the point where it can manage the augmented level of activities effectively, can finance itself into the foreseeable future, has retained a necessary level of programme autonomy from external actors and is providing desired and sustainable services to its target beneficiaries.

Not all programme expansions are successful. Improper motivation, insufficient planning, inappropriate programme design, an inadequate human or financial resource base, managerial incompetence or external pressure may cause an expansion drive to fail. The repercussions of such a failure often reverberate throughout the organization, producing lower staff morale and higher turnover and jeopardizing the NGO's credibility. Failed expansion is the reason for the collapse of many NGOs. Conversely, the failure may provoke an organizational restructuring which could induce a much needed turnaround in management or approach.

The biggest losers of a failed expansion drive are the beneficiaries. Beneficiaries in the expansion area lose their tangible and intangible contributions (such as time, resources, faith and commitment). They are likely to be more hesitant to engage in future development initiatives as a result. Beneficiaries from the initial target area may be better positioned to withstand the NGO's new failure. They will still suffer, however, from the resulting organizational repercussions, such as a decline in resources.

Phase 3: Organizational Consolidation

All organizations undergo planned or unintended consolidations at various times in their evolution. During a consolidation, an NGO analyses its performance to better align its operative capacity to its external reality. This may involve a reconsideration of its development methodology, organizational structure, programme focus, operational procedures and/or development priorities. Consolidation may occur as the result of an established management plan. It may also be the direct outcome of an internally or externally generated crisis, such as a failed expansion, as discussed in the preceding section.

The methods employed during an organizational consolidation may be rigid and formalistic. They may also involve a multidisciplinary or participatory methodology incorporating the input of project beneficiaries. The desired end result is an institution with a clear set of programme priorities and the means to achieve them.

Where consolidation occurs as a scheduled activity, the NGO is likely to have an established procedure to manage the process. This may involve an analysis of administrative, managerial and programme performance by an evaluation unit within the NGO. Many NGOs, however, do not have this internal capacity. Instead, they rely upon periodic assessments by external evaluators, including those contracted by donors or, less commonly, by the NGO's executive board (if one exists) to assess programme status.

External evaluations are often very useful because project staff may lack the objectivity which is necessary to ascertain the appropriateness of their organizational direction. External evaluators, however, may have insufficient time to isolate more than superficially the cause of organizational difficulties. Moreover, they may lack the clout to force a reticent management to follow through with their recommendations.

Where a consolidation occurs in response to a crisis, the NGO may be in varying degrees of institutional disarray. If the crisis is resource related, the NGO may be forced to lay off staff and curtail programme activities. If it is programme related, the NGO will need to reconsider its institutional purpose and/or its developmental methodology. If the crisis is politically induced, the NGO's response may need to be even more severe. This issue will be dealt with in greater detail below.

Why organizations consolidate

The causes of organizational consolidation vary widely. As mentioned above, a periodic internal organizational review may lead actors to realize that their NGO is overextended and in need of streamlining. Consolidations may also occur upon the completion of a developmental phase or activity on a project-wide basis or within a specific project area.

Additionally, organizational consolidation may occur following the realization that project performance is unacceptably low. Poor performance may be marked by low beneficiary participation, disinterest or even hostility. Inappropriate project design may be the culprit. This frequently results when a project model is imported without pilot testing or sufficient efforts to familiarize the NGO staff. An adept project monitoring unit could quickly pick up on a failing of this type and trigger an organizational evaluation. Organizations which are not strong in this particular area, however, miss a golden opportunity to adapt their programmes and generally await more serious developments before responding. A weakness in project monitoring could be reason enough for an organizational assessment. In most instances, however, weakness in project monitoring will go unnoticed until the initial difficulty has become a more institutionally menacing dilemma.

External actors can play a dynamic role in promoting NGO consolidations. The preceding section intimated, for example, that donors' self-interest can push NGOs into untenable situations. Still, most donors condition assistance on a schedule of project performance assessments. The United Nations Development Programme (UNDP), for example, requires biannual internal project reviews with local UNDP participation as well as external evaluations at the project mid-term and upon completion. Finally, potential new donors may require an external evaluation and, when deemed necessary, an organizational consolidation as a precondition to financial assistance. It is important to note that donor leverage can thus be used to pressure an NGO to restructure its activities to better reflect the funder's own priorities to the detriment of the NGO's original intent. NGOs can lessen the risk of this eventuality by avoiding dependence on too few donors whenever possible. Careful donors may structure the resulting aid package in tranches which condition disbursements on the outcome of periodic reviews by external evaluators or donor agency staff or on the attainment of predesignated performance criteria.

Unscheduled consolidation pressure will occur if donors become aware of specific programme failings. For example, inconsistencies in administrative and financial record-keeping will increase donor scrutiny and can lead to active external pressure for an organizational reassessment. If the NGO resists, it may jeopardize current and future donor assistance.

Unintended consolidations commonly occur when an NGO leadership suddenly realizes that resource reserves are insufficient to cover continued expansion or even to sustain current operations. Such a crisis can result from poor budget management, the underestimation of project expenses, unexpectedly high inflation or the failure of a specific project activity such as a revolving credit fund or an income-generating scheme. It can also result from an NGO's failure to set realistic limits on its programme size and expenditure. Financially induced consolidations most commonly occur near the end of a project-funding cycle when management has failed to locate new sources of financing. As mentioned earlier, donor-funding cycles are not always in synchronization with project implementation schedules. Thus the danger of financing gaps must also be addressed by NGO management. In some instances this problem can be alleviated by a sympathetic donor who will provide for early fund disbursement. The International Fund for Agricultural Development (IFAD), for example, has been known to release a small percentage of future project loans prior to the actual start-up date of project activities.

Since staff morale has an important impact on the quality of programme delivery, it is not surprising that consolidations also occur when morale declines and turnover rises. Staff morale may plummet for a number of reasons. These include a change in administrative policy, management insensitivity, lack of performance incentives, personality clashes, low wages or exorbitant workloads.

Pressure to consolidate or to close out may originate in the economic or political condition of the country in which the NGO works. In the debt-ridden Latin American context of the 1980s, for example, severe national fiscal crises provoked deep economic and social imbalances. Many governments retrenched on social service provision, placing unbearable pressure on NGOs and other development agencies to fill the service gap.

Macroeconomic crisis also engenders instability that severely distorts day-to-day economic relations at all levels. Cumulative hyperinflation of 24,000 per cent in Bolivia in 1984–1986, for example, forced many public and private entities into bankruptcy in spite of their efforts to consolidate. The resulting vacuum in the provision of basic services caused widespread political tumult, including violent demonstrations in many Bolivian cities.

Managing a consolidation is a difficult task. To do so effectively, the leadership must have a strategic orientation to NGO management. To assume this posture effectively, the NGO leadership must necessarily maintain an active role in the monitoring and evaluation of NGO performance. In addition, it must pay great attention to events within its project area as well as to those occurring in the surrounding community and the nation at large. NGO leaders must also be able to disassociate themselves from the mundane managerial and administrative tasks associated with NGO operations. If they are unable to do so, they will be unable to view objectively the conditions which have arisen that have generated the need for a consolidation.

NGOs which have established a strategic and decentralized management system are structurally more capable of seeing the cause of organizational problems and responding accordingly. In many instances, since the events precipitating consolidation are generally evolutionary in nature they are even able to foresee difficulties before they manifest themselves and make preventative adjustments in time to limit any negative effects. On the other hand, NGOs bereft of a strategic and decentralized approach to management tend to trip blindly from one crisis to another until they learn their lesson or fail.

Issues to consider

A principal managerial concern during organizational consolidation is to keep operations functioning smoothly. We have seen, however, that in many instances, this is simply not possible. Consolidation may require the NGO to suspend some or all project activities in particular areas. It may also lead to the application of unpopular managerial innovations, such as increased oversight of daily operations, a cutback in access to office resources or establishing increasing beneficiary service charges for programme activities.

Whatever the cause of an organizational consolidation, the timing of the response to the crisis is a critical indicator of how well the NGO can shield itself and its beneficiaries from any related consequences. However, many NGOs respond very late in the game. As mentioned earlier, many NGOs lack a responsive programme monitoring system. Others are weak in terms of administrative accuracy. Others still are so absorbed in their internal programme performance that they lose perspective on the external environment and how changes within it may affect their initiatives. As a result they are not in tune with the principal signalling sources of impending difficulties.

Timing notwithstanding, in certain instances, all efforts at consolidation are likely to be futile. The most common examples of such a circumstance are when the crisis occurs outside the NGO's direct operative realm. A national fiscal emergency, an ideologically unfavourable political development or a determined attack from a strong economic rival may undermine even a well-planned and well-timed consolidation.

Certain types of NGOs, however, are more resistant to macroeconomic and, to a lesser extent, political crises. For example, those active in income generation will be less directly affected by a reduction of state-provided social services than would an NGO social service provider who will probably face a demand influx. The same income-generating organization's capacity to withstand an attack from a private-sector adversary, however, will depend on the type of attack and the strength of the NGO in terms of resource base, market reach, diversification of output, etc. Related to this, an NGO which bases its programme on leveraging government resources will suffer appreciably more from a national fiscal crisis than would an NGO which operates without any direct governmental inputs or subsidies.

One should not underestimate the difficulty in carrying out even a planned consolidation. A certain institutional will is required as it may be necessary to counteract resistance from NGO staff and/or beneficiaries to potentially unpopular decisions. The heavy workloads many NGOs face can also make a programme evaluation appear as an optional luxury; when the push for consolidation is caused by unfavourable events, institutional resistance is likely to diminish. In a non-crisis scenario, however, consistent and sincere efforts are required by the NGO leaders to ensure that far-ranging periodic evaluations do occur.

Potential outcomes

The chances for an NGO to reconstitute effectively depend on a broad range of internal and external factors. If the NGO does survive, it will probably pay greater attention to the issue which provoked the consolidation or the lessons which were learned during the exercise. The evaluation process itself may bear important fruit. It may produce a more systematic approach towards programme management as well as greater attention to monitoring and evaluation, fund-raising, resource management, prefeasibility work, beneficiary participation and other important matters.

During the course of organizational evolution, an NGO that has undergone a successful consolidation will probably expand operations again in the future. The expansion – consolidation – expansion cycle could repeat several times within the life-cycle of a healthy organization.

Based on the above discussion, it should come as no surprise that not all organizational consolidations succeed. While the 'failed' NGO may not immediately

Table 8.1 *Some Factors Which Help to Define Successful Consolidation*

Planned consolidations
- Systematic evaluation
- Timely incorporation of lessons learned
- Strengthening of administration and monitoring and evaluation capacity as required

Internally induced consolidations
- Early recognition of the problem(s)
- Institutional will to face the cause of consolidation
- Dynamic leadership
- Willingness to make unpopular decisions
- Access to necessary resources
- Luck
- Relative autonomy from donors

Externally induced consolidations
- Financial security
- External allies
- Well-established organization
- Committed membership
- Capacity to delink from the government and other causes of the crisis
- Luck
- Programme niche

disappear, it may fragment or be forced to wind down quickly service provision. Even in cases where an NGO fragments and closes out, dedicated ex-staff may make informal efforts to support the beneficiaries in the short to medium term.

Phase 4: Organizational Close-out

A close-out can be defined as either a full-scale termination or a partial reduction of project activities. Thus, while one imagines a close-out to entail a gross reduction in aggregate operations, this may not always be the case. For example, an NGO closing-out in one area may be expanding elsewhere such that the net effect is an aggregate growth in programme size. Another NGO may replace one particular activity with a new array of follow-up programmes of greater immediate relevance.

As in the case of organizational consolidation, close-outs may occur according to plan or in response to an internally or externally generated crisis. A well-orchestrated close-out will probably occur in phases. Thus, an NGO may gradually diminish in size (whether in a specific area or overall) as its beneficiaries assume a greater proportion of project responsibilities. In other instances, however, a close-out is a 'damage control' device resigned to cut the losses associated with a badly designed project or a failed consolidation attempt.

Why NGOs close-out

The explanations as to why NGOs fully or partially close-out vary widely. A full or partial close-out can be the natural result of a successful termination of planned project activities. NGOs can close-out failed operations in a similarly orderly fashion. To the extent that these closures are induced by programme failure, however, they are considered to be 'forced close-outs'. Project success in this sense is broadly defined. It may mean that the NGO's goals have been met and no additional inputs are required. It could also be that the NGO has 'graduated' the beneficiaries on to a different donor or introduced them into the formal economy (such as private banks, commercial input suppliers or marketing links).

From a community empowerment perspective, success could imply that local beneficiaries have been sufficiently well organized and trained in order to operate autonomously. In some instances, new beneficiary organization may self-finance future managerial and organizational technical assistance from the NGO or elsewhere.

An NGO which closes-out in accordance with an organizational plan may find it earns greater esteem from donors and other development agencies, particularly when it has achieved its goals and left some type of sustainable operation in its wake. Its success may interest new or existing donors to start new initiatives elsewhere. As mentioned previously, donors may wish for changes in programme content or methodology in spite of past proven success. In essence, the evolutionary organizational cycle renews itself, perhaps with new actors, new donors and new dilemmas. Sadly, there is no guarantee that past achievements will guarantee future success.

NGOs can be forced to close for a variety of reasons which, as we have seen, include faulty start-ups, foolhardy expansions and badly managed or belated consolidations. In addition, many organizations are overly dependent on individual charismatic and visionary leaders. Their sudden departure may cause an NGO to founder. Similarly, organizations fail if they are overly dependent on external technical assistance. This failing highlights the importance of external advisers investing a significant portion of their time in on-site training of NGO counterparts. Some groups simply fall prey to internal corruption or managerial incompetence. Finally, a bad management decision or even bad luck can push a credit- or revenue-generating organization into untenable financial straits.

The preceding section highlighted the fact that external factors such as a severe economic downturn can also force an NGO to close-out. An overvalued currency can make the production of an export-oriented cooperative uncompetitive. Likewise, spiralling inflation can bankrupt a credit organization if it fails to develop an appropriate response mechanism.

A change in the political climate can also compel an organization to cease operations. This may result from a reshuffling of leadership at the local, regional and/or national level, especially when the transition involves a shift in political ideology and, thus, governmental receptivity to a particular style of NGO activities. An NGO may also fall from political grace as a result of a controversial stance it may take in support of its beneficiaries. Some NGOs, for example, enter directly into oppositional politics to great effect. This approach, however, can leave them vulnerable if the strategy fails and the government feels particularly retributive. Undesired pressure from donors may lead an NGO to shut down rather than bend to external will. We have already seen that some donors attempt to precondition financial assistance to changes in project target areas, methodology or monitoring procedures. Fortunately, there are NGOs with enough conviction to refuse in spite of the potential repercussions on their own institutional longevity.

Issues to consider

An NGO's primary concern during a close-out should be the impact that a close-out will have on its beneficiaries. Thus the process and timing of the close-out acquire great importance. Organizational close-outs are most effective when they occur in phases and at a pace which gives beneficiaries ample time to prepare for full autonomy. Quite logically, NGOs which use self-help developmental methodologies have a clear advantage in promoting autonomous beneficiary organizations. NGO management should assess whether or not follow-up services are required and whether there is local capacity to provide them. If not, can such capacity be created locally or are there other alternatives? For example, has the NGO helped beneficiaries to find new sources of technical and financial assistance? Can they now generate their own resources to pay for outside help or has some other arrangement been made?

In instances where organizational closure is involuntary, NGOs will have less capacity to ensure that a beneficiary-supportive close-out process occurs. Thus, closure under these circumstances more directly threatens the sustainability of project activities. Once again, however, NGOs that promote self-reliance in their programmes are more likely to leave behind a stronger beneficiary group than are organizations with a more paternalistic bent.

It should be noted, however, that in spite of methodological orientation, even during forced closures, some resourceful NGOs are able to find the means to lessen the blow of their sudden departure. For example, NGO management may be able to delay a shut-down or leverage some form of political or economic support for its project beneficiaries prior to its departure. Such assistance will help determined beneficiaries to withstand the shock of the NGO's inevitable disappearance.

During a fall or partial close-out, management should also be concerned about the impact the closure will have on its staff. An NGO forced to fully close, however, may not be in a position to assist them. Some staff may stay behind to work under less formal arrangements with the beneficiaries. Others may find new posts with like-minded development agencies.

An NGO which shuts down only certain programmes or in specific areas will have more staff placement options. It can transfer them to new areas or phase them into a new organization established by the beneficiaries themselves. The transfer of personnel to new project areas, however, will be problematic if the new site is ethnically, culturally or linguistically distinctive. In this circumstance, veteran programme staff may no longer be appropriate as field operatives. They may be used, however, as local trainers in the NGO's working methodology and as support officers. Over time, some may become sufficiently familiar to operate effectively in the new project venue.

An NGO's capacity to monitor and maintain institutional accountability is a function of managerial priorities and the solidity of its structure. As an organization weakens, its accounting and monitoring capacity is likely to decline. The actual state of institutional integrity of all organization undergoing a close-out will depend on two factors: first, whether the close-out is voluntary and, second, whether it is partial or complete. Organizations undergoing an involuntary close-out are more likely to suffer administrative lapses and their performance in this area may be sporadic at best. Groups fully or partially closing-out on a planned basis are more likely to maintain orderly procedures throughout.

It is relatively common to find NGOs that periodically close-out a portion of their operations. It is all too rare, however, to find NGOs (excluding emergency relief agencies) which voluntarily and fully close-out following successful performance. Many NGOs never intend to close-out. Social service providers, including many of those sponsored by religious and political organizations often consider their presence to be permanent.

Others, however, by the logic of their own community-empowerment methodologies, can be presumed, at least in theory, to be pursuing this end. Theory aside, even community-empowered NGOs develop an institutional will which resists just such an event. Large, mobile and resource-rich NGOs justifiably opt to take their programmes and their lessons learned elsewhere rather than shelving them.

Smaller, site-bound NGOs may have less justification for their refusal to close-out or at least to develop new areas of programme expertise. Instead of releasing

Table 8.2 *Close-out's Organizational Outcomes*

	Crisis induced	Planned
Close-out	Organizational decline	Orderly
Partial close-out	Organizational setback	Orderly

veteran beneficiaries, some site-bound NGOs maintain them. This action is often rationalized by the claim that the beneficiaries still need significant support. In some cases, this may be true, as, for example, when an NGO is assisting the beneficiaries to handle increasingly sophisticated production or marketing operations. Even then, however, the NGO can choose to nudge beneficiaries towards greater self-reliance by, for example, instigating fees for services in spite of beneficiary resistance. In the end, it is the character of the leaders and their determination to remain true to their original institutional purpose which will determine whether an NGO of this type ever fully and voluntarily closes-out.

Potential outcome

It is overly simplistic to suggest that an intended close-out always signals success while unintended ones imply NGO failure. It has been shown that many factors are involved in determining the success of an intended close-out, such as the timing of a close-out and the close-out process itself. Is the close-out occurring in phases which enable the beneficiaries to accustom themselves to the NGO's departure? Has the NGO determined what links might be necessary to maintain with the project area to support the sustainability of a locally run initiative? Has it helped to determine the strengths and weaknesses of the local initiative and assist in a planning process which takes these factors into account? Is there an alternative system in place which can provide necessary support (such as credit, technical assistance or marketing)? Where the answer to these and similar questions is no, then the long-term sustainability of the local endeavour may be threatened and the close-out must be judged accordingly.

Some NGOs that are forced to close still leave potentially sustainable initiatives behind. This 'staying power' is generally an indication of the institutional mettle of the NGO and its beneficiaries. This often occurs where the initial project idea is a good one, the methodology well suited to local conditions and local interest is high enough to overcome internally or externally generated setbacks. It may take significant organizational will and beneficiary commitment to resist externally induced crises. Fortunately, external political or economic factors which make a particular activity non-viable in the immediate term may reverse themselves and operations may be resumed with or without the direct support of the NGO. In these circumstances, however, the evolution of the local initiative will often have been stunted by the same events which forced the sponsoring NGO to depart initially.

For this and other reasons, unintended close-outs are more likely to have a detrimental effect on project beneficiaries. Project closure may produce significant financial losses, unmanageable debts or political disfavour which may make exbeneficiaries very wary about future participation with development agencies. NGOs would do well to remember that the legacy of such outcomes are very long-lasting for the resource poor. While they may have little control over many external events, there is much they can do in terms of management, planning and strategic understanding of the external environment that their activities impact in order to support the welfare of the beneficiaries in a very broad sense.

Conclusion

This chapter has presented the NGO organizational life-cycle in four stages. Its purpose has been to assist development practitioners and especially those active in the NGO community to better understand the evolutionary process of organizational development and the incumbent set of relations, issues and problems which are generally characteristic of each separate development stage.

No model can cover the full range of potential issues affecting evolving organizations. It is the author's hope, however, that an understanding of the NGO life-cycle as it is presented here will assist NGO development practitioners to better understand and manage their own process of institutional development.

References

Broadhead, T (1987) 'NGOs: In one year, out the other?', *World Development*, Vol 15, pp1–6, (supplement).

Korten, D (1991) *Getting to the 21st Century*, W Hartford, Kumarian Press.

Tandon, R (1989) 'The state and voluntary agencies in Asia', in R Holloway (ed) *Doing Development: Government, NGOs and the Rural Poor in Asia*, Earthscan, London.

9

Stepping into the River of Change

Davine Thaw

This chapter begins from the premise that there are different ways of seeing and approaching organizational change. We consider the ways in which a range of authors have made sense of change, the assumptions underlying different approaches and the forms of intervening in organizations as a consequence of different approaches. We then provide some ideas and exercises that we hope will assist you in approaching change with greater clarity and less trepidation.

There is no one way of seeing. We have, however, all learned particular ways through our families, schooling, peers and through the dominant thinking and behaviour patterns of the culture or cultures that pervade our society.

How Do I See Change?

Before reading on, we invite you to consider the questions below (Table 9.1), which aim to help you to reflect on how you see and think about change in organizations.

Table 9.1 *How Do I See Change?*

Statement	My comment
Conflict is a sure sign that some change is needed in an organization.	
Leaders can control most of what happens in their organizations.	
If we need to change, we'll see it.	
Change happens all the time.	
If we need to change, the director will see to it – it's not another's problem.	
If you want to change, call in an outsider to help.	
Change is frightening.	
People are basically resistant to change.	
I can control most of what happens to me.	
If change is needed, develop a vision for the future and go for it.	
I know more about what change is needed in my life than anyone else.	

Statement	*My comment*
We know change is needed all the time; we simply need to be aware of this.	
Change is a response to opportunities.	
There is a solution out there for most organizational problems.	
Organizations don't plan for change; they simply adapt on the way.	
Organizations have to respond to changes in the broader environment.	
Change is a response to a threat.	
If one doesn't change, one stagnates.	
Finding stability and equilibrium is the most important task in an organization.	
Change is the result of different people's interaction in an organization.	
We create change – in ourselves and in our organizations.	

Three Views on Change

Change happens all the time. It is constant and can move in any direction. By this we mean that:

- It can have a positive or negative impact; or it can have little impact at all.
- The extent of the impact depends on the situation and the group.

We live in a world of constant flux – everything is dynamic, often turbulent. Thus we need to learn to live with uncertainty and have the courage to respond constantly to changing circumstances and dynamics.

In this chapter we offer the views of three groups of writers, each of whom offers new insights. All three have, as their point of reference, how people see change in organizations.

Robert Marshak (1993) explores change through *Kurt Lewin's* contributions to Organizational Development (1947, 1951) and a *Confucian* orientation. George Binney and Colin Williams (1995) explore the interplay of opposites between a *mechanistic view* and a *living systems* perspective of organizations. They develop a framework that draws elements from both. Felkins, Chakiris and Chakiris (1994) offer four perspectives on change and argue that each can contribute to and deepen our understanding of change.

Lewin and Confucius

Marshak (1993) proposes that the views of Lewin and Confucius emerge from two different cultural settings. First we look at Lewin, an American social scientist (1890–1947), who proposed a three-stage change process.

Simply put, the present state needs to be unfrozen – through confrontation – and altered by a planned intervention. The desired state, when reached, is frozen and holds in a state of equilibrium.

The assumptions underpinning this approach are as follows:

- A change process can be planned through a designed intervention.
- This is achieved by creating disequilibrium – deliberately stirring things up.
- Change is linear or one-directional from the past, to the present and into the future.
- Change occurs progressively (current to future) and is goal-oriented – the planned intervention has an envisaged end point.
- Things are usually in a fairly static state and need to be disrupted. The disruption is instigated and managed by people who regard themselves as separate or independent of the process. The intervener is an 'outsider'.

Second, a look at the Confucian or Taoist approach to change.

The Confucian (551–479 BC) approach is cyclical rather than linear.[1] The images drawn on are the yin and yang and the five agents of cyclical change. Yin and yang are understood as the two polarities of one unity which are interdependent and give each other definition or meaning. They are in a constant process of 'becoming the other in an endless cycle' (Marshak, 1993, p399). The universe is in constant flux.

The other image reveals continual cyclical movement between the elements comprising the universe. Each depends on the other, and harmony and balance is maintained. If imbalance occurs, it will be restored.

Some assumptions here are that:

- Change is cyclical: 'No matter what begins, it always ends. No matter what ends, it always begins.'
- Change moves in an orderly sequence and is 'journey-oriented' rather than goal-oriented.
- Change is based on maintaining equilibrium rather than disrupting it. One acts only to restore harmony.
- Change is normal as everything is in a constantly changing, dynamic state.
- Change is 'observed and followed by people who are one with everything' and act to maintain balance.

Marshak argues that these two approaches lead to quite different ways of working with change. He offers a number of comparisons.

Linear-progressive versus Cyclical-processional

If change is seen as linear and progressive it is future-oriented – one does not go back or repeat the same thing again. This would be regarded as getting nowhere. His example of group development is useful. It is assumed that the objective is a high level of performance and once there, the group is challenged to maintain this level. Anything else is viewed as retrogressive.

The Confucian, cyclical approach assumes a constant renewal, a constant motion. One stage is not considered as better than any other. They are all needed. A person working in this way would engage with a group from 'where they are' and support them in renewing any stage. To deform allows new purpose, new norms and new ways of doing.

Destination-oriented versus Journey-oriented

In the destination or goal-oriented approach, the emphasis is on setting objectives in order to reach the desired end state. One would gather data to inform how one moves from the present to the future state and then monitor to see how change is progressing. The first step would be to identify the goal.

In the cyclical model, the change agent would start with the values and orientation of the organization and support people in finding ways of improving how they work now and continuously, not in terms of an objective, but in terms of the principles and values that inform the group.

Create disequilibrium versus Maintain equilibrium

In the Lewin model, change results from an intervention; a breaking up of the equilibrium, leaving the past and taking steps into the future. Thus the change agent would focus on disrupting the current state, working with resistance and encouraging movement towards a new end state.

In the Confucian approach, change *is*. It is initiated naturally in the ebb and flow of life. The role of the change agent is not to disrupt, but to restore balance and equilibrium in the organization. For example:

*   Rapid growth may need more systems to carry it.
*   Emphasis on one activity or product for too long may call for increased innovation.

A key goal is to enable the organization to realize the present fully before moving on – to come to terms, for example, with its authoritarianism, distance from its 'customers' or the erosion of its values, and to work through this stage in order to move to the next. In this awareness, harmony can be restored.

Separate from versus One with the client system

The change agent with a goal-oriented approach stands apart from the client organization (or system); she is neutral and focuses on what needs to be done in order to intervene and disrupt the equilibrium in the system 'out there'.

The Confucian-oriented change agent serves as a role model in an interdependent relationship and in alignment with the organization and its journey. The emphasis is on finding harmony with principles and values on the path of change.

Static versus Dynamic universe

For the Lewin orientation, constant change is regarded as chaotic and dangerous. The task is to stop change, restore order and 'refreeze' the new situation.

For the Confucian change agent, change is natural, constant and normal. To stop it would be seen as dangerous. The aim is to restore balance by removing blockages to the natural flow of change.

Marshak suggests that different situations call for different responses, not one *or* the other. Table 9.2 summarizes his ideas on this point.

Table 9.2 *The Usefulness of Contending Views about Change*

Assumption	More effective when	Less effective when
Linear progressive	The current situation can be contrasted unfavourably with some future condition	It is hard to prove there is something wrong with current conditions
Cyclical–processional	Required to move from a current unsatisfactory situation to a different one	Need to secure 'gains' and/or maintain a specific plateau or condition
Destination-oriented	A specific achievable goal can be articulated	A specific goal is absent, unclear and/or cannot be provided
Journey-oriented	Continuous enhancements are needed without a given problem or goal	Need to focus more on the goals than the means
Create disequilibrium	Need to challenge the status quo or marshal forces to create change	Need to accept things as they are and harmonize with them
Maintain equilibrium	Need to harmonize while waiting for the appropriate moment of change	Challenging or disrupting the (natural) order of things
Planned and managed	Need analysis of what to do to modify or change existing factors and forces	Required to 'go with the flow' against one's wishes and desires
Observed and followed	Observing natural 'rhythm' of change and aligning oneself and others with it	Need to act in opposition to flow of events (for example, 'swim against the tide').
Change is unusual	Dealing with stuck or static situations	Facing continual change without the chance to stop and plan
Change is usual	Adapting to constantly changing conditions while maintaining equilibrium	Need to plan ways to defend and/or stabilize a particular situation.

Source: Marshak, Robert J 1993 'Lewin Meets Confucius: A review of the OD model of change' in the *Journal of Applied Behavioural Science*, Vol 29, No 4, NTL Institute, p409

Leaning into the Future

Binney and Williams (1995) offer an interesting comparison between organizations as machines and as living systems. Again, they suggest not an either/or decision, but the need to draw from each orientation. If one sees organizations as machines, one is probably making the following assumptions:

- *Change needs to be driven* Energy needs to come from the outside and change needs to be made to happen. People are usually resistant and fearful of change and will defend their interests and position. Consequently, intervention is needed.

- *Changes start with visioning* Create a beacon ahead to inspire people and to draw them into and towards a change process. All programmes and activities are developed in terms of this vision.
- *The answer is out there* Change has happened in many organizations. Smart people exist who can guide us or find a solution. The answer exists; we simply have to find it.
- *You have to start afresh* For change to take place, one must break with the past. The rise in 're-engineering' – essentially, starting over – is evidence of this assumption. Let go of conventional wisdom; destroy to build.
- *Everyone is for change – for others* Change is seen as an issue for others – they need it, need to do it and it is the 'change agent's' job to do it to them. It assumes that the change agent has the answer and 'they' (the others) are the blockage.
- *Change can be planned and predicted* If the answer is known, then all we need to do is carefully plan towards it, allocate appropriate resources and monitor our progress. Change is a 'project' so manage it.

* * *

'We are so addicted to looking outside ourselves that we have lost access to our inner being almost completely. We are terrified to look inward, because our culture has given us no idea of what we will find' *Sogyal Rinpoche*

* * *

On the other hand, if you see organizations as living systems, other assumptions apply:

- *Change is natural, but not easy.* Change happens all the time, but adjusting to it can sometimes be painful. Giving up known behaviours, ideas and ways of doing is difficult. So it is not that change is a problem; it is simply difficult to let go of the past.
- *There is an interest in change.* People usually want change, but they fear letting go of the old. So it is not about driving change, but releasing the potential for change, removing obstacles and encouraging people to connect with the process of change.
- *Don't be anxious about change.* Change is inherent in the growth and evolution of living systems. One does not have to force it; rather, allow it. Too rapid and overwhelming change disregards the need for some stability and certainty. Hold what works and allow change when 'the old' stops working.
- *Awareness of current reality.* Look at the now, rather than a vision of the future. To ignore the present may be to ignore the frustrations and difficulties as well as the achievements and value of the current situation. To shape the future is to disregard, perhaps, much of what *is* working. Study the patterns in the present and build on them rather than creating wish lists for an imaginary future.
- *The answer is within.* Each organization is unique, with its own history, purpose and reasons for doing what it does. There is no one formula from outside 'experts'. There are also no 'excellent' organizations to copy. Explore the organization's past and present and identify what is healthy (and build on this) and what is a blockage (and find ways of moving beyond it).

- *Reinforce emerging patterns.* If the organization is there and working, there are reasons it has survived. Study its history. What has it learned? What are the patterns of being, seeing and doing that contribute to the system's functioning? How can these be nurtured and valued rather than washed away in a goal-directed, imposed change effort?
- *We need to change.* All elements in a living system are interlinked – change one element and it will affect the others. This cannot be seen ahead of time. All people in organizations, especially leaders, need to observe and learn from what is happening. All need to change, not only the 'others'. 'Very often the attitudes that top managers complain about are merely the reflection of their own behaviour and thinking' – a classic example of projection. It is critical to be aware of change and of one's experience beyond the organization. Our own life experience outside the workplace is valuable to organizational change.
- *Live with uncertainty.* Living systems are unpredictable and the future is unknowable. Ways of thinking and being that allow an organization to be successful in the future have not yet been discovered. So accepting uncertainty as an element of change enables all to learn together in the process.
- *Feelings and emotions are important.* People are whole – they have a rational and an emotional side; they have a conscious and unconscious element. They are directed by unconscious motivation and feelings as well as logic. Instinct counts. Even though some know what needs to be done, or could be done, they may not be able to explain why. Create space for the intuitive in discussions about change.
- *Managers should try less hard.* The energy is there for change, but has few outlets and consequently can be expressed negatively. Create opportunities for this energy to be used constructively. Tap existing energy and listen to what is already there.

Two pictures of change, or metaphors, emerge from this analysis – leading and learning. Leading is seen as a fundamental value of the machine perspective – the strong sense of intention and clarity for change determined by clear objectives. Learning is the focus of the living systems perspective – change is neither predictable nor containable, so we must learn from our past and the current working patterns in our organization to make a future together.

Together, they create a new concept – 'Leaning into the future' – that recognizes the need for both leading and learning. Learn as far as you can, have a vision, but with your feet on the ground, rooted in the present reality. The framework is captured in the following diagram.

The idea of 'complementary opposites' is a valuable one. The development of Western thought is rooted in the idea of dualities – that is, there is one right way and the task is to choose it. When the choice is made, stay with it, live with it and enact it. We suggest that dogma and stubborn resistance are *the* consequences of defending this position.

There is another way of working with potential choices, and that is to see options not as 'either/or', but 'both ... and' – there is value in one perspective and something to work with and learn from the other. Drawing what is meaningful from both perspectives and exploring them together can give rise to new thoughts, fresh perspectives and often the courage to face the unknown and break new ground.

LEADING *TOP–DOWN PROGRAMMES*	AND	LEARNING *BOTTOM–UP APPROACH*
Leader as Hero → Knows the answer; inspirational; wills others to follow	**Forthright and Listening Leadership** Combines assertive leadership with responsiveness to others	← **Leader as Facilitator** Self-aware; enables others to realize their potential
Vision → Clear and inspiring visions, which explain why clean breaks with the past are needed, energize people to change. The answer is 'out there'	**Seeing Clearly** The energy to change – and to develop existing strengths – comes from seeing clearly where the organization is now and what possibilities are open to it.	← **Awareness** People change as they become more aware of their own needs and their interdependence with the world around them. The answer is 'within'
Drive → Change is driven through by determined individuals who plan carefully and minimize uncertainty	**Working with the Grain** Individuals shape the future by combining clear intention with respect and understanding for people and organizations. They work *with,* not across, people's hopes and fears	← **Release** Effective leaders release the natural potential of people and organizations to adapt to change and are prepared to live with uncertainty
'They' are the Problem → Individuals see the need for change in others	**All Change** Leaders encourage others to change by recognizing that they too need to shift	← **'We Need to Change'** Change starts with me/us
Training → People are taught new ways of working in extensive training programmes	**Learning While Doing** Most learning takes place not in the classroom or training session, but as people perform, as they interact with others and reflect on their experience	← **Reflection** People learn when they step back from day-to-day tasks and reflect deeply on their thoughts and feelings
Organizations as Machines	**Complementary 'Opposites'**	**Organizations as Living Systems**

Source: Binney and Williams, 1995

Figure 9.1 *Learning into the Future*

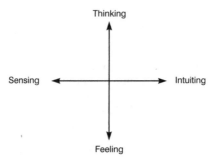

Figure 9.2 *Perspectives on Change from Jung's Psychological Functions*

Subjective and objective approaches

A third approach to change comes from Felkins, Chakiris and Chakiris (1994). They argue that 'ultimately, the organization is created by people through their decisions actions and interpretations of reality'. Therefore, sharing and understanding each other's interpretations is an important starting point. While one might not develop any 'truth' in this process, the organization will have what Senge (1990) calls 'mental models'.

Drawing from Carl Jung's four psychological functions (thinking, feeling, sensation and intuition) they devise a model consisting of four perspectives on change.

This model is based on the assumptions underlying four different perspectives on change:

- Rational/behavioural
- Systems
- Cultural/interpretive
- Critical humanism.

Although change happens all the time and is not in our control, the rational/behavioural perspective does alert us to the need to:

- Think ahead
- Imagine a future beyond current difficulties
- Focus on how we deal with change
- Explore mechanisms together for planning for change.

The systems approach urges us to:

- Recognize the linkages and interdependence in an organization
- See the whole
- Acknowledge that change is fluid, continuous and not in our control
- Recognize uncertainty, but seek to restore some stability in the system since we cannot live permanently in chaos.

The cultural/interpretive alerts us to the idea that each person sees the world differently, based on past experience and her/his own values and cultural experience. Therefore, it is a valuable perspective for exploring how to work with change (rather than the *source* of change). Each person's interpretation of reality and change is valid and it is through interaction and communication that the interests and needs of people facing change can emerge and be discussed.

An additional insight from this perspective is the exploration of organizational culture – what is dominant and what is suppressed?

The critical humanist perspective is useful as we find ourselves in the process of change and need to:

- Check our assumptions
- Critique our present position and confront old patterns
- Bring awareness through reflection on experience and analysis – for example:
  - Why are we where we find ourselves?
  - How can we build consciousness and responsibility for dealing with change?
  - What will the consequences be for the organization as a whole?

The following are some questions to work with:

- What perspective dominates in your organization?
- How is this expressed?
- Might another perspective, if expressed:
  - Bring more balance?
  - Allow more voices to be heard?
  - Bring more critical analysis?
  - Bring more focus to the purpose of the organization?
  - Help people to see the implications of change in the whole organization?

Organizations and the Degree of Change

Change is happening all the time – both inside and beyond the organization. We suggest that there are three ways that organizations respond:

- They *assimilate it*
- They *adapt* to it
- They *transform* as a consequence of it.

All three responses are valid, but when does each occur? We suggest that the following factors are important:

The *health* of the organization. The healthier the organization, the more change it can handle. Some elements for health are:

- Clarity of purpose
- Shared values underpinning the work of the organization
- The ability to deal constructively with conflict
- Open and honest communication and feedback
- Technical capability where it is needed (systems, computers, planning, management, and so on)
- Institutionalized leadership – people are clear on their roles and tasks and take personal responsibility for the authority they have
- All people have an understanding of the whole organization and its work

• Very importantly, there are open channels of communication to get feedback from each other, stakeholders and particularly client or target groups.

The *source* of change. Is change prompted from *within the organization?* (Three staff leave simultaneously; a dramatic conflict of interests explodes; a system crashes). We are often more able to work with these issues, as they are, in a sense, more in our control. Or is it prompted *from the environment?* (Two new organizations start in 'competition' with the work you do; two donors withdraw without warning; legislation on NGOs changes.) These factors are not in our control and organizations would have a difficult task in facing the challenges they create.

The *scale* or *degree* of change. Whether prompted internally or from the external environment, the sheer scale of change will affect how the organization is able to assimilate or adapt. Sometimes change can become a crisis which challenges the organization to transform itself.

Are we *constantly alert* to change? Some organizations tend to 'fall asleep' and fail to be conscious of what is happening, both to themselves and in their wider environment. This can be induced by laziness (long-term, assured funding?), self-righteousness (no feedback systems are in place because 'we know, so we don't need to listen to clients/target group/stakeholders'), or boredom (lost purpose? Doing the same thing and not learning?). If we are not awake, we don't see what is happening to us or around us and change takes us by surprise.

Organizations that remain constantly alert to what is happening around them can see change coming – they ask questions, they notice things, they read, they listen to their clients and beneficiaries, and they adapt and shift on the way.

The healthier an organization and the more alert it is, the greater its capacity to handle change. Healthy organizations can see most change coming and can organize to accommodate or assimilate the effects. Usually, such an organization has policies, systems and the good will of staff that allow it to reorganize quickly and deal with these changes.

Sometimes the change is larger and the organization needs to adapt. This might mean introducing cost-cutting measures, changing policy and finding the resources to comply with legislation, closing down a project, shifting the emphasis from one area of work to another, and so on. Sometimes, however, the demand for change is so great that it induces a crisis.

Typically there are three responses to a crisis:

• *Try to ignore it* But it doesn't go away – it deepens until it overwhelms the organization.
• *Sit in it* People try to project the problem on to others, escape it by working harder in the same way, or collapse into helplessness. Two options follow: the crisis overwhelms the organization or people finally decide to face it.
• *Face it consciously* Consciously go through the painful process of transformation. To transform is to let go of old behaviours and take up the challenges of a new phase in the life of the organization. Letting go is the painful part. Taking up new challenges can be a very joyful experience – as though drinking in fresh cool water.

So, how healthy is your organization? Are you wide awake, paying close attention to both your internal and external environments, or beginning to doze off? The next section contains ideas and exercises that may help you to approach change with greater awareness.

Ideas and Exercises to Work With

The ideas outlined in this section are drawn from our own experience in South Africa. Obviously, they are informed by different theories and approaches, but all have been developed in practice:

* Constructing your own theory of change.
* Exploring value rather than constructing vision.
* Understanding the elements of organizations – a systems approach to change.
* Reflecting on experience – change in organizations.

Constructing our own theory of change

The idea of theory often leaves the average non-academic feeling vulnerable, but we all work with theory every day:

* 'I did that because ...'
* 'Why?'
* 'Well, I think that ...'

Theory: a supposition or system of ideas explaining something, especially one based on general principles independent of the particular things to be explained. *Oxford Concise English Dictionary*

An important source for developing theory is our own experience. Lying within us is theory that is not yet conscious. The following exercise assists people to construct their own theory about change and development.

Turning Points[2]
The following are questions for the exercise:

1 Identify three recent, important turning points in your life. It is sometimes worthwhile not to choose the most recent turning points, as they are often still too painful or euphoric. The greater the emotional distance from the turning point, the more objective a perspective can be attained.
2 Describe each event in detail. Paint a picture of words so that the event becomes visible to you.
3 Explore in depth how you handled the situation. What were your responses, rationalizations, your emotions, your actions, and so on.
4 Characterize the nature of the different aspects of your life after this experience. What has changed, which were sustained? What was different?
5 Once you have done this for each experience, compare your answers. Can you see any patterns emerging, any commonalities across these experiences?

6   What, then, did you learn about yourself? What insights did you gain about the ways in which you learn or develop; the manner in which you respond to change? And what does this tell you about your leadership of others' change now?

Exploring *value* rather than constructing vision

Lewin's approach and the rational/behaviourist perspective argue that developing a vision to guide a change process is fundamental.

In our experience, while this activity is fun, inclusive and useful for exploring the future, it has certain limitations. We have found that:

- Too often the outcome is dreamlike (which many argue is what it should be) and a collection of every person's wishes, rather than a coherent statement that can guide the organization.
- Consequently, it does not provide direction as much as accommodating a range of interests and intentions that reduce the conflict inherent in making values-based choices. This is a weakness which may lead participants to skip over real issues which need to be surfaced.
- The vision statement is published in annual reports and brochures but is rarely reviewed or checked, as it is but 'a dream'.
- Perhaps most importantly, being long term and in the future, it does not challenge current practice or value present patterns of thinking and work.

It could be argued that the above issues arise, not because a vision is developed, but because of the way it is developed; indeed, this can be the case. However, we offer another way of working in this area of organizational life. This is to explore what value the organization produces in the world, closely allied to the notion of impact. If the organization sets out to tackle a particular problem, the measure of its success is whether it does, in fact, resolve, alleviate or have an impact on the problem. This impact can be described in terms of the developmental value it adds to society.

Exploring the value of what the organization contributes keeps us in the present and provides powerful guidelines for what it will continue to contribute in the future. It also helps us to ask the following questions:

- What actually *is* it (the value we produce)?
- Do we *all* know?
- If we do, and we agree, is it enough?
- If it is not enough to justify the resources and energy we put in, what must we do?

The potential for exploring value, rather than vision, includes:

- Being clear about what it is that we do that contributes value.
- How our contribution is *different* from other efforts similar to our own – this helps us think about our own positioning (are we supplementing, complementing; augmenting or challenging the status quo?)
- Holding us in the present and reflecting on what we do now, rather than what we intend to do.

- Links back to the values that guide our work – an important reality test that we practice what we preach.
- Being clear about the values that underlie our work in order to produce the value we want and clarifying the identity of the organization in the process. Each organization is unique and the clearer it is about its identity, the more effective it can be in the world.

Example

The organization claims to enable participatory processes in development efforts, but is itself run as a fairly rigid hierarchy.

The organization sees its value in society as creating innovative alternatives in Adult Basic Education and Training, but follows one ideological thrust.

Organizations that try to be all things to all people and have weak boundaries lose their sense of identity.

- A vision statement is usually described as the vision of society or a community to which we can contribute. It is not something we can achieve alone. The value we claim or aim to produce must be produced by us. This helps to achieve clarity about our specific contribution. This is not described only quantitatively (the number of women, farmers, teachers or policy-makers who benefit), but also qualitatively. One way of seeing value is the qualitative difference we make.
- Often the value that an organization contributes has more to do with how the organization does its work, rather that what it does.
- The value of our contribution to society often relates to people, particularly in the NGO sector. For example, the extent to which people acquire greater economic or political access to power; gain in confidence or awareness, or are enabled to struggle for rights, access or justice.

Example

An example of a vision could be as follows: 'All women in South Africa have access to quality reproductive health services.'

The value added – because of how the organization strategizes to achieve this vision – may be: 'Every woman using our support and services is both healthier and has more confidence and awareness to challenge for a quality service.'

Exploring the value which an organization seeks to produce also assists organizations to clarify which strategy will enable them to do this.

So, we suggest that exploring the value an organization aims to produce can help it to:

- Clarify the organization's values
- Define its identity
- Position the organization in relation to others, and
- Select or develop the most effective strategy.

Understanding the elements of organizations – a systems approach

If one approaches change from a living systems perspective it is useful to have an understanding of some of the elements in the system, how they interrelate and, further, to explore how the organization relates to its environment. This section does not include an exercise, but rather offers ideas on how readers might look at their organization from a systems perspective.

A reminder

The systems perspective assumes:

* The importance of seeing the *whole* system, not only parts of it.
* That the organization is located in an environment and is linked to other systems that both influence and are influenced by them.
* When one element in the system changes, it has a knock-on effect on other parts of the system.

Let us move through a series of steps which focus on:

* Understanding a system
* Seeing an organization as a system
* Developing our core purpose
* Developing strategy

A system

The concept of a system comes from the biological sciences:

* A certain input goes into the system
* It is transformed through the functioning of the system
* It emerges as an output and, critically,
* The output enables a renewal of energy to return into the system – for the continued functioning of the system, a continual renewal of energy is required.

For organizations as systems, inputs (or energy) may take the form of:

* *Money* to attract the right people, purchase equipment, materials, pay for rentals, services, and so on.
* *Feedback*, including new ideas, knowledge, views of the users and beneficiaries, and information about changes and challenges in the environment.

These are processed or organized through the functioning of the organization to produce the outputs sought from the system.

Outputs may include the services or products that are needed or sought by the environment. When they are valued, the 'energy' needed in the system is renewed. The organization becomes aware of the extent to which its outputs are valued through feedback from the environment.

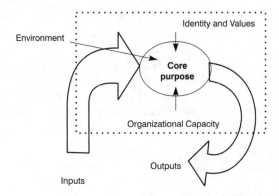

Figure 9.3 *Source and Purpose of Core Values*

Developing our core purpose

A typical challenge for NGOs is to find a core area of work rather than doing a wide range of different things. This is called the 'core purpose' of the organization. Clarifying and defining, a core purpose involves thinking and working at a *strategic* level, rather than at a day-to-day, operational level.

There are at least three areas to think about:

- Who we are (our identity and values)
- What we have (our capacity – resources and capabilities)
- What is needed (what is the problem or demand in society that we are responding to?)

And therefore, because of who we are and with our current capacity, how can we best make an impact on the problem or respond to real demand?

Some challenges we face as we enter this process are as follows:

- Are we setting ourselves up to do more than we realistically can with our current capacity? Is this because we can't let go of some of the work? If so, why is this?
- Are we intending to do some work that is not really our business (that does not fit with who we are and why we exist)? Are we being unnecessarily competitive or fearful to let go of something that does not relate to our core purpose?
- Are we being pushed by some stakeholders (donors, other organizations, our users) to do work that could best be done by others? How do we deal with or argue this?
- Are we taking on work or projects for which we don't really have the expertise and so setting ourselves up for failure and letting down our client groups?

Developing strategy

It is one thing to have a vision (or identified value) and a core purpose which gives coherence and identity to the organization, but 'a specific strategy – or strategies – is required to give effect to vision, to operationalize a general direction' (Kaplan, 1994). Developing strategy is about making a choice; selecting from a range of possible ways to operationalize one's purpose. It is about *how* we go about achieving our purpose.

Distinguishing strategic, operational and organizational areas

In approaching change it is worthwhile exploring which areas in the system will be affected if change in other areas occurs. Looking at change in the whole system, we focus attention first on the strategic area – that is being clear on:

*   Who we are
*   What capacity we have, and
*   What problems we are addressing.

Within this process we are making choices:

*   About which critical issues we respond to
*   Around what we can and cannot do
*   About the scale of our work
*   About how we operationalize our vision and core purpose.

Then we focus on our programmes – the operational area – what we will do to implement our strategy and achieve our purpose. It includes:

*   Planning and establishing systems for monitoring our work
*   Allocating resources
*   Getting the right people for the different elements of the work
*   Developing, supporting and managing people in the implementation process
*   Reviewing how things are progressing.

The third area – the organizational area – contains the things needed to support and carry the strategy and programmes forward. It includes:

*   What systems do we need to support our work (finance, management, communication, and so on)
*   Structure – how we organize power, people and the work in order to be effective and fair.
*   Identification and procurement of the financial and other resources we need.
*   Who and how we administer the 'vehicle' (the organization) which carries our strategy and programme of work forward.
*   Who leads on what and how leadership is developed in the system.

A Word of caution

Function before form. Purpose before structure. It is of little avail to reorganize the chairs if the ship is sinking. Revisit purpose before working with the organizational elements. Revisit the environment before changing the programme.

And a last word ...

At the end of this discussion, it may be interesting to go back to your responses to the questions raised at the outset. Have your views shifted? If so, how? If not, why not? What new thoughts strike you when you think of change?

We hope the ideas in this paper have captured your attention and raised new questions. We welcome feedback: connect with us – we would enjoy opening a conversation around building organizational development practice in the South.

Notes

1 Marshak acknowledges that there is no one model of change drawn from Confucianism and/or East Asian culture. Rather, he presents the culture's 'dominant image' of change.
2 Originally developed by consultants from the Netherlands Pedagogical Institute, this exercise has been used and developed by the Community Development Resource Association (CDRA), Olive and many others. Cited in Kaplan (1998), this is an adapted version of the exercise.

References

Barnard, C I (1938) *The Functions of the Executive*, Cambridge, MA, Harvard University Press.

Berger, W G and Luckmann, T (1966) *The Social Construction of Reality: A Treatise on the Sociology of Knowledge*, Garden City, New York, Doubleday.

Bertalanffy, L (1968) *General System Theory*, New York, George Braziller.

Binney, George and Colin Williams (1995) *Leaning into the Future: Changing the Way People Change Organizations*, London, Nicholas Brearley Publishing.

Chang, W T (trans and ed) (1963) *A Sourcebook in Chinese Philosophy*, Princeton University Press, New Jersey.

Community Development Resource Association, 'A manual of readings', unpublished.

Felkins, Patricia K, Chakiris, B J and Kenneth, N (1994) *Change Management: A Model for Effective Organizational Performance*, New York, Quality Resources.

Kaplan, Allan (1994) 'NGOs, civil society and capacity building: towards the development of strategy', *AVOCADO*, No 5, Durban, Olive Subscription Service.

Kaplan, Allan (1998) 'Leadership and management', *AVOCADO*, No 1, Durban, Olive Publications.

Kets de Vries, M F R and Miller, D (1984) *The Neurotic Organization: Diagnosing and Revitalizing Unhealthy Companies*, New York, Harper Business.

Kotter, John P (1996) *Leading Change*, Boston, MA, Harvard Business School Press.

Leigh, Andrew (1988) *Effective Change: Twenty Ways to Make it Happen*, London, Institute of Personnel Management.

Marshak, Robert J (1993) 'Lewin Meets Confucius: a review of the OD model of change', in *Journal of Applied Behavioural Science*, Vol 29, No 4, NTL Institute.

Moss Kanter, Rosabeth (1983) *The Change Masters: Corporate Entrepreneurs at Work*, New York, Simon & Schuster.

Moss Kanter, Rosabeth (1989) *When Giants Learn to Dance: Mastering the Challenges of Strategy, Management and Careers in the 1990s*, New York, Simon & Schuster.

Parsons, T (1960) *Structure and Process in Modern Societies*, New York, The Free Press.

Senge, Peter M (1990) *The Fifth Discipline*, New York, Doubleday.

Taylor, F W (1911) *Principles of Scientific Management*, New York, Harper & Row.

Weick, K E (1979) *The Social Psychology of Organizing* (2nd ed), New York, Random House.

Weisbord, Marvin R (1987) *Productive Workplaces: Organizing and Managing for Dignity, Meaning and Community*, San Francisco, Jossey Bass Publishers.

10

Strategy and Structure in Managing Global Associations

Dennis R Young, Bonnie L Koenig, Adil Najam and Julie Fisher

A key aspect of civil society worldwide is the emergence of thousands of non-governmental organizations (NGOs) that operate on a global scale. The special challenges of organizing and managing these organizations include massive communications problems and the need to accommodate a wide diversity of interests. In this chapter we ask what kinds of organizational structures and management strategies are utilized by globally oriented NGOs involved in the development of civil society, and we consider the advantages and disadvantages of alternative structures. From 15 case studies, we find that three principal types of structures are utilized: corporate partnerships, federations and membership associations. We also find that management challenges are addressed in various creative ways within these structures, and that the federation form appears to be generally effective and avoids some of the risks associated with other forms.

Introduction

In a recent issue of *Foreign Affairs*, Jessica Mathews (1997) argued persuasively that the world's political economy is fast becoming global and that nations are losing their sovereignty to international business and global manifestations of civil society. In this chapter we focus on one component of the latter – the work of international NGOs concerned with the development of civil society in various parts of the world.

Definitions of civil society vary, but most centre around the concept of citizen interaction and participation in governance through non-governmental institutions. Darcy de Oliveira and Tandon (1994, p1) describe civil society simply as '... men and women, groups and individuals, getting together to do things by themselves in order to change the societies they live in'. Macdonald (1997, p3) asserts that 'civil society constitutes the arena of organized political activity between the private sphere (the household and the firm) and the formal political institutions of governance (the parliament, political parties, the army, the judiciary, etc). Fukuyama (1995, p4) conceives of civil society as '... a complex welter of intermediate institutions, including businesses, voluntary associations, educational institutions, clubs, unions, media, charities, and churches ...'.

At the international level, a key aspect of civil society is the emergence of thousands of NGOs and networks that operate on a global scale (see Fisher, 1993; Edwards and Hulme, 1996; Najam, 1999a). The special challenges of organizing and managing globally oriented NGOs include massive and complex communications problems associated with transacting business worldwide, and the need to accommodate the diversity of interests of constituents from a wide variety of nations, cultures and economic circumstances (see, for example, Fisher, 1994; Koenig, 1996; Najam, 1999b; Smith, Pagnucco and Romeril, 1994; Young, 1992a). With neither the police powers of government nor the economic resources of big business, and the expectation to operate democratically as part of civil society, globally focused NGOs must find creative and flexible ways to organize and manage themselves in order to survive and work effectively.

We address two principal questions in this chapter. First, we ask what kinds of organizational structures are utilized by globally oriented NGOs to cope with their special challenges, and we consider the advantages and disadvantages of alternative structures. Second, we inquire about management strategies, policies and tactics that help NGOs to manage globally within whatever organizational structure they may utilize.

We are specifically interested in global organizations whose missions are to support the development of civil society in some manner.[1] This includes the convening of meetings and conferences for various constituents of civil society to discuss mutual interests and collaborate on common initiatives; the provision of information to keep constituents well informed of current developments, issues, and ideas; the facilitation of networking among various parties with interests in promoting civil society; advocacy of standards and principles of civil society at the international level and support for advocacy at the country level; and serving as an honest broker among parties in the business, government and non-profit sectors in order to solve problems of mutual concern. We recognize that most global organizations promote civil society indirectly. The primary focus of The Nature Conservancy, for example, is to foster sustainable development. Yet the process of supporting and working with NGOs at the national level also strengthens civil society. Other global organizations focus more directly on civil society. Partners of the Americas, for instance, works with five Latin American NGOs that train other NGOs in promoting citizen participation through public deliberation, civic education, voter education and strengthening NGOs and local philanthropic activity.

Earlier work (Young, 1992a) has suggested that global advocacy-oriented NGOs are best organized as decentralized federations. Here we explore whether that same conclusion applies to globally oriented associations which seek to carry out functions such as these.

Literature Review

Organizational structure has long been a subject of intense scholarly interest, although most attention in the literature has focused on organizations in a generic way, with implicit emphasis on businesses and little attention to not-for-profit organizations. Although scholars differ on many questions in this literature, there is reasonable consensus on what is meant by structure itself. Litterer (1969, p11), in his well-known compendium of literature on organizations, writes: 'By structure we mean the identification of the elements in an organization and relations between them.'

Other, more detailed definitions, such as those of Gerwin (1981), Chandler (1962) and Ben-Ner, Montias and Neuberger (1993), identify Litterer's 'elements' in terms of groups of people within organizations and his 'relations' in terms of the patterns of resource allocation, authority, incentives, division of work, and information now that connect and coordinate people within organizations. Chandler specifically focuses on '... the design of organization through which the enterprise is administered'.

There are several schools of thought on what factors determine the choice of organizational structure (Gerwin, 1981). One school posits that the size of an organization and the technology that it uses are key determinants. Mintzberg (1989, p106) argues that choice of structure derives from the influences of 'the age and size of the organization; its technical system of production; various characteristics of its environment, such as stability and complexity, and its power system, for example, whether or not it is tightly controlled by outside influencers'. Another class of models posits that environmental factors such as demographic, economic and technological developments create choices for organizational managers who respond by implementing new organizational *strategies* that ultimately lead to structural changes. Child (1972), for example, emphasizes the element of choice, arguing that structure is not a deterministic result of environmental conditions, technology or size, but that these variables contribute, along with other considerations including decision-maker preferences, to the formulation of organizational strategy and structure. Alternatively, Fligstein (1990) argues that changing forms of business reflect strategic efforts to gain stability in an economic and policy environment that varies over time. Seminal in the strategy-determines-structure approach is Chandler (1962, 1990), who sees the minimization of costs through exploitation of economies of scale and scope as the driving force behind major structural changes in business corporations over time. Relatedly, theorists led by Williamson (1985) argue that 'transactions costs' are the most important determinant of organizational structure. Illustrating this idea for non-profits, Wils (1996) notes the preference of Northern NGOs to partner with local organizations on a contractual basis rather than to expand their own organizations formally.

Chandler's and Williamson's approaches focus on the global architecture of organizations, that is, the degree to which organizations concentrate their operations within centralized operating units or disperse them through decentralized or market-based arrangements among separate operating units. Chandler (1962), for example, chronicles the evolution of the M-form of corporate structure in which operating divisions of the corporation are organized as autonomous entities around particular products or markets and the central headquarters focuses on setting general direction for the corporation as a whole.

The literature on organizational structure in the private, non-profit sector is relatively sparse, but it does illustrate that several different structures are in use and that various factors seem to influence the choice of structure (Jenkins, 1983;

Knoke 1993; Young, 1989). Young, Bailey and Bania (1992) apply Chandler's framework to the structural development of national non-profit associations, postulating various historical, technological, economic, demographic and internally driven scenarios that can influence organizational strategy and structural choice. Gerlach and Hine (1970) explain why fragmented, decentralized organizations work best in highly charged political situations and where rapid adaptation is required. Freeman (1979) shows how a centralized organization may work best where goals are focused on the national level. Oster (1992) demonstrates how national non-profit organizations structure themselves as franchise like systems in order to exploit the benefits of local initiative while maintaining control over quality, fund-raising and membership competition. Young et al (1996) demonstrate how the structures of national non-profit associations affect accountability relationships between national offices and local affiliates. Knoke (1990) cites the tension between democratic decision-making and bureaucratic operations in the structures of trade and professional associations. Drucker (Young, 1992b), McCarthy and Zaid (1987), and Handy (1988) argue that the federal form of organization in non-profit associations provides for both central direction and responsiveness to local needs, and encourages innovation within a framework of shared authority. In a similar manner, Scott, Mitchell and Peery (1981) observed that 'governance systems using democracy and federalism are more decentralized, use participation to achieve substantive due process, and require more self-control by members. Stable environments encourage the use of autocracy and totalitarianism. Turbulent environments encourage use of democracy and federalism because ... such designs facilitate adaptation and performance under turbulent conditions.'

The basic character of global associations as complex, participatory organizations operating in multiple, highly diverse and sometimes turbulent environments suggests a closer look at the federal form, and there are indications in the literature that the federal structure is particularly germane to such associations. Young (1992a), focusing on two case studies, found a decentralized federal structure especially appropriate for international advocacy organizations. A similar result was found by Hudson and Bielefeld (1997) for multinational organizations more broadly. Zaid and Gamer (1987) observed that the effectiveness of an association structure depends on the political environment in which it operates: 'In a highly centralized system local movements can win few victories.' The converse also holds. In a decentralized system, centralized organizations will be ineffective unless they adapt to local circumstances. In the case of international associations, effective action is required at the national level in many countries simultaneously. Wilson (1973) points out, in comparing the US and Britain, that this means different numbers and types of voluntary association involvement in each country. Zaid and Gamer also observe in their study of social movements in Italy and the US that diversity among nations leads to different modes of organization within countries, but also the need for coordinated action at the international level.

Similar observations are made by Suzuki (1998) for Northern-based NGOs in the economic development field: 'The complexity of Northern-based international development NGOs ... is especially profound due to their globally dispersed office locations where different socioeconomic systems, political structures, and religious and ethnic groups prevail.' This author models the Northern NGO as a federated system in which tensions derive from the different sources of accountability faced by local (national) field offices on the one hand and international headquarters on the other. Suzuki offers a series of management strategies for NGO staffs to address the issues stemming from these tensions.

Finally, several recent scholars of international voluntary sector activity have observed the emergence of 'networks' as a prime form of organization. Keck and Sikkink (1998, p8) define networks as '... forms of organization characterized by voluntary, reciprocal and horizontal patterns of communication and exchanger'. Fisher (1998) observes that '... the idea of networking [has] become contagious' in the field of economic development. However, networks are a diffuse form of organization serving somewhat as overarching structures within which formal international NGOs operate. According to Keck and Sikkink (1998, pp1, 6), transnational advocacy networks are '... networks of activists, distinguishable largely by the centrality of principled ideas or values. [I]nternational and domestic... NGOs play a prominent role in these networks'. Given that we are focused on formal organizations in this chapter, we will not give much further attention to the network structure, except as it relates to the efficacy of other structures.

Overall, within the contexts of networks, the federated structure would appear to accommodate the twin demands for national diversity and internationally coordinated action. Hence, we would expect to see this form common and functional among NGOs that cross national boundaries. We also expect to see a wide variety of forms, in keeping with Child's (1972, pp11–12) observation that 'given the widespread prevalence of imperfections in the economics of resource allocation and competition, especially for *non-business organizations* (emphasis added), considerable stack may often be present; [t]herefore... organizational decision-makers may well perceive that they have a substantial element of choice in the planning of organizational structure.' Moreover, we expect to see differences even within the federation category among associations that have reached their particular structural designs from different directions, historically speaking (see McCarthy and Zaid, 1987). For example, in this study we found that Oxfam International has 'federated upward' through the coordination of pre-existing national organizations, whereas Transparency International, established as a central global organization, was 'federating downward'.

Methodology

Through a variety of means, including consultation with a committee of expert advisers,[2] and the inspection of rosters compiled by InterAction (Geohegan and Allen, 1995), the United Nations (1995) and CIVICUS, 15 international NGOs operating on a global scale were selected for study. Criteria for selecting these cases were as follows.

1   They should be working on an international scale with operations in several different countries (although not necessarily all regions of the world).
2   They should be involved with some aspect of the development of civil society in countries where they work.

3   They should be accessible for study on a limited budget. In practical terms, this meant having offices in a major city in the US or Europe. Thus, we were essentially confined to NGOs whose headquarters were in the North but that operated over a substantial portion of the globe. This still allowed inclusion of several organizations that operate primarily in the Southern hemisphere. (Indeed, relatively few global NGOs are actually headquartered in the South.)

No criteria were imposed on how the selected organizations were structured. Rather, we sought to identify and study a variety of structures and to understand how the different structures worked in practice.

The executive director or other high official of each selected NGO was interviewed, and documents were collected on the history, purpose, structure and operations of the organization.[3] In all but four cases, on-site interviews were held in person by one of the four members of our team (the authors); in the remaining cases, inquiries were conducted by telephone and email. Written profiles using a common format were compiled to facilitate comparisons. Each profile documented the history, purpose and background, organizational dimensions (size and scope), structure (including governance and finances), and the particular lessons the organization has learned in managing globally. Table 10.1 summarizes the various NGO missions.

Organizational Structures

Although the 15 NGOs varied considerably in size, shape, and orientation, we found that they could be clustered within three broad categories of organizational structure.

1   Corporate partnerships: a unified corporation executes centrally directed project work or contracts with autonomous regional, national or subnational partner organizations to carry out particular assignments.
2   Federations: an international body oversees or collaborates with a group of affiliates at the regional or national levels, which have comprehensive responsibility for carrying out the work of the association within their domains. This category includes strong federations in which the international organization has substantial authority and weak confederations in which the international organization is subordinate to its affiliates.
3   Membership associations: individual or organizational members belong to a central association and govern its operations, and which may develop chapters at the regional, national or local levels to carry out association work particular to those domains. Membership associations may be highly inclusive or they may restrict the number and types of members they admit.

Some of the NGOs we examined combine features of more than one of these categories. For example, IRED (Innovations et Research pour le Développement) is a membership association of individuals, but these individuals are associated with local NGOs with which IRED collaborates and that are referred to as organizational

Table 10.1 *Profiled International NGOs and Their Missions*

Ashoka: to help social entrepreneurs apply the vision, creativity and extraordinary determination of the business entrepreneur to societal problems.

InterAction: to enhance the effectiveness and professional capacities of NGOs engaged in international humanitarian efforts.

International Association for Volunteer Effort (IAVE): to promote volunteering and to support the development of structures and programmes that help to institutionalize volunteering throughout the world.

International Council of Voluntary Agencies (ICVA): to support NGO movements throughout the world.

International Crisis Group (ICG): to strengthen the capacity and resolve of the international community to anticipate, understand and prevent crises arising from human causes.

Innovations et Research pour le Développement (IRED): to build the NGO movement around the world by promoting networking among 'people's organizations'.

The Nature Conservancy: to preserve plants, animals and natural communities that represent the diversity of life on Earth by protecting the lands and waters they need to survive.

Oxfam International: to work as an international partnership to relieve poverty, combat distress and alleviate suffering in any part of the world regardless of race, gender, creed or political conviction.

Partners of the Americas: to work together as citizen volunteers from Latin America, the Caribbean and the United States and to encourage civic participation, hemispheric cooperation for development, community leadership training and strengthening local NGOs.

International Save the Children Alliance (ISCA): to make a reality of children's rights, by emphasizing three principal programmatic priorities: The UN Convention on the Rights of the Child; Children in Armed Conflict and Displacement; and Children, Poverty and the International Economic System.

Synergos Institute: to develop effective, sustainable solutions to poverty problems worldwide by strengthening the support and cooperation that community-level groups receive from civil society, government and the private business sector.

Transparency International (TI): to curb corruption, internationally and nationally, by building coalitions, creating higher public consciousness to support anti-corruption measures and encouraging parties to international business transactions to operate at the highest level of integrity and transparency.

United Way International (UWI): to develop civil society worldwide by promoting voluntary initiatives and non-profit sector development through community-based philanthropy

World Conservation Union (IUCN): to influence, encourage and assist societies throughout the world to conserve the integrity and diversity of nature and to ensure that any use of natural resources is equitable and ecologically sustainable.

World Neighbors: to strengthen the capacity of marginalized communities to meet their basic needs and to determine and sustain an equitable and inclusive development process.

---

partners. Similarly, IUCN is governed by members but administered in a federal style. Nonetheless, the 15 organizations proved fairly easy to fit into the three broad structural categories.

Table 10.2 provides a summary description of the nominal parameters of each of the three models (corporate, federal and member association), with identification of the profiled associations in each category (see last row). For convenience, we call these models 'NGO Inc.', 'NGO International', and 'NGO Society', respectively. Note that we have not analysed each of the profiled associations in sufficient depth to be able to judge whether their chosen structural forms are actually optimal for each of them, although this is an underlying assumption of our work. Note also that there exists a great deal of flexibility and variation within each of the model categories. Some of this richness can be observed along the dimensions of governance, administration, financing, membership and regional substructure.

Table 10.2 *Alternative Structural Models for Associations Operating on a Global Scale: Nominal Characteristics*

Aspect/Type	Corporation Partnership (NGO Inc)	Federation (NGO international)	Member Association (NGO society)
Governance	Self-selected board	Board of directors selected by affiliates	Membership elects governing board
Administration	Central staff reports to board; regional field offices report to headquarters and articulate with local partners	International secretariat reports to board; regional field staff serves/monitors affiliates; affiliates have own staffs	International secretariat reports to board; regional field staff are accountable to headquarters and serve local chapters and members
Finance	Grants and contributions; government funds; investment income; leveraged partner resources	Affiliate dues; grants and contributions; government grants	Member dues; private grants and contributions; governmental grants
Membership	No formal members; networks of advisers may be treated as members; partner organizations may have members	Affiliates may be considered members; individual or organization members may belong to affiliates	Selected organizations and/or individuals; classes of membership according to type and level of participation
Regional substructure	Multiple, diverse, local autonomous partner organizations	Semi-autonomous affiliates with exclusive use of name, logo, mission	Chapters, regional working groups, or regional or national committees
Examples	ICG, Synergos, Nature Conservancy, World Neighbors	Save the Children, UWI, Oxfam, Partners of Americas	IAVE, ICVA, IUCN, TI, IRED, InterAction, Ashoka

Governance

Under corporate partnership arrangements, boards are generally self-sustaining and corporate partners are not involved in governance of the international organization. Under the federation model, affiliates play a strong role as board members in some organizations, but a much weaker role in others. Federations also vary as to whether all affiliates participate directly in governance of the international federation or whether a smaller board is employed. In most member associations examined, the membership as a whole elects the governing board. However, one association (Ashoka) is governed by a small self-sustaining board that is guided by a member-based advisory committee.

Administration

Corporate partnerships generally feature a central staff and staffed field offices in various parts of the world. Alternatively, one organization (Synergos) organizes headquarters staff into regional teams that travel extensively. Where field operations are utilized, there is a strong emphasis on decentralization and local autonomy. Some corporate organizations are highly decentralized, which requires strong efforts by headquarters to coordinate regional operations. Devices such as management committees of regional directors or international planning conferences are used for this purpose.

The secretariats of federations are generally small (fewer than ten people). International Save the Children is especially interesting because it maintains no central project or programme staff; the secretariat's role is purely coordinative and administrative, and affiliates are expected to staff and execute all the project, programme and task force work. The staffing of membership associations varies greatly, from all-volunteer operations (IAVE) in which the secretariat moves with the elected president and depends on a host agency and local volunteers for administrative support, to very large paid staffs. Most of the studied membership associations employ a paid staff of modest size.

Generally, regional field staff of associations report directly to the central secretariat. However, the degree of autonomy and local discretion of field offices, and the influence of local members on them, can be controversial. Given their modest sizes, the work of member associations is generally carried out by members themselves and by volunteers, organized into commissions, task forces, regional groups or Standing committees, often supported and coordinated by central staff.

Financing

Corporate organizations do not rely on dues, although some leverage resources from local partners. Federations exhibit two different types of dues structures. Some tax their affiliates at a percentage of their budgets, whereas others charge their affiliates flat fees. Dependence on dues revenues varies widely; some federations depend entirely, while other depend minimally, on dues revenues.

Membership associations depend on member financing to widely varying degrees. Associations commonly differentiate their dues structures to accommodate differences between members from Northern countries and those from the South, between organizations and individuals, between NGO and governmental members, and between different levels of participation in the association.

Membership

Corporate partnership arrangements do not feature formal memberships, although some work with advisory networks of various kinds. In federations, the national affiliates may be considered (organizational) members of the international federation, and those affiliates themselves may have (individual or organizational) members.

Some membership associations have large open memberships and others have very limited memberships. Some confine membership to individuals or organizations and others include both. Some make distinctions among types of organizational members and others do not. Some include only a particular type of organizational member (such as NGOs) and others are more inclusive.

Regional Substructure

Globally oriented organizations often feature autonomous or semiautonomous substructures at or below the regional level. For example, corporate organizations commonly enter contractual partnerships with autonomous national or subnational entities. Globally focused federations operate partly through their national-level affiliates, which generally enjoy a high level of autonomy. These federations encompass both long-standing national affiliates and also undertake to create new ones where they do not yet exist.

Membership associations exhibit a considerable variety of regional substructures. Some have formal chapters and others do not. Some associations use regional and national committees or working groups. Sometimes, national-level associations of the same name (such as the Association for Volunteer Effort) form on their own and later seek to affiliate with the international association.

Management Strategies

The selection of a structure depends in part on the specific functions that an internationally focused NGO intends to perform. As noted earlier, five relevant functions were identified for organizations focused on aspects of developing civil society: convening, information provision, networking, advocacy and brokering. Based on the experience of the 15 profiled NGOs, Table 10.3 demonstrates how each of these functions can be carried out within each type of structure. The table suggests that alternative structures have different advantages vis-à-vis each function, yet all structures can carry out each function in some way.

Our case studies illustrate that leaders of globally oriented NGOs work within a variety of structures to meet similar challenges. In doing so, they have developed substantial wisdom about managing on a global scale that often cuts across structural contexts. We found a variety of creative and insightful strategies in use, especially in two broad categories of management practice – human resources and strategy. Just a few of the more innovative strategies are described as follows.

Human Resources

Globally oriented NGOs engage a variety of personnel, including volunteer leaders, staff and members with diverse backgrounds and viewpoints. A number of lessons point to how these personnel can be best managed and utilized. Organizations such as International Save the Children and IAVE demonstrate that enormous accomplishments can be achieved with very small central paid staffs. However, that is only possible if the members of the organization understand the implications of dividing the work and responsibilities for support of services and programmes, between the secretariat and the organization's affiliate members. A very small secretariat means that its tasks are confined to coordination and facilitation, and programmes of the international body must be accomplished by working groups, commissions and task forces in which member organizations take designated leadership roles, raise supporting resources and supply staff.

Several of the studied globally oriented organizations (such as IAVE, International Save the Children) use to advantage the fact that their resources are limited. A very small central budget and staff or dependence on volunteer workers can be highlighted to stress that responsibility for leveraging local resources and getting tasks accomplished lies with the affiliate members. Under these circumstances, there is no central pot of resources for members to fight over, the benefits of giving can be emphasized ('the getting is in the giving'), members can bid for the status and prestige associated with sponsoring international activities and events such as a world assembly, and realistic expectations may be set.

Strategy

Our profiled NGOs have also provided insights into how these organizations set priorities, define their services, and utilize different approaches to mobilizing their resources in the global context. For example, membership associations recognize that members want specific products and services as well as the opportunity to contribute to collective goals. Although such outputs need not be described as the main reason for joining an internationally focused NGO, and although sales of services and products are unlikely to become a major source of revenues, they constitute an important membership benefit.

Corporate partnerships especially are able to cope with the diversity of needs in different regions by contracting with a variety of indigenous organizations and focusing on different issues, problems and needs as appropriate to local conditions. Whatever the structure, the organization must be able to accommodate diverse approaches. For example, federations must define the concept of affiliates broadly enough to encompass the different types of regional organizations appropriate for affiliation, the varied approaches these groups may take to their work, or the different levels of organizational development of potential affiliates that exist in various regions of the world.

Table 10.3 *Functions of Globally Focused NGOs*

Function	Partnership	Federation	Member Association
Convening	World conferences sponsored by NGO Inc with possible local partner; cosponsor local conferences and educational events with partners	National/regional conferences and educational events held by affiliates; world conferences and other global meetings held by NGO International	NGO Society holds biannual world assembly and regional conferences in off years and other local educational events, working with local chapters
Information provision	NGO Inc assembles and distributes reports, newsletter globally; contracts as needed with partners for local dissemination; NGO Inc. runs global internet civil society information service and also engages in grant-funded (research) projects on selected issues	NGO International assembles information from affiliates, distributes global comparative information to affiliates; affiliates develop/distribute information for their own members; NGO International runs internet service for affiliates, oversees commissions on special topics	NGO Society publishes reports, newsletter, journal and runs an internet service for its members; chapters and members contribute information where possible
Networking	NGO Inc sponsors conferences, events and internet service; special projects bring together people from various regions; local events co-sponsored with partners	Affiliate events facilitate national networking; world assembly, commissions and task forces, and internet service provide global networking	World assembly, special commissions and task forces, and internet service offer global networking; chapters facilitate local networking
Advocacy standard bearing	NGO Inc is expert source on civil society matters; called in as authority by national and regional groups worldwide, including its own partners	NGO-International legitimacy as a worldwide federation provides entree to major corporations and international government agencies and multilateral forums; affiliates bring in NGO International as authority for promoting national agendas; NGO International's standards for civil society carry weight in national and international fora	NGO Society's legitimacy as a significant, cross-cutting membership body provides access to major international, national government and business institutions. NGO Society's standards for civil society offer points of reference in national deliberation; local members and chapters call on NGO for help on local issues

Table 10.3 *Continued*

Function	Partnership	Federation	Member Association
Brokering	NGO Inc's stature as an independent organization allows it to mediate national issues and to convene major actors from all sectors in neutral fora	NGO-International's major international federation allows it to sit at the same table with major international government business organizations and to help its affiliates on national issues	NGO Society stature as a major international association representing civil society allows it to convene fora and working groups with major international and national level business and governmental agencies

Some of the NGOs that we examined recognize that they can be instrumental in helping to raise funds in particular regions and nations, but that they need to avoid competing with indigenous organizations and needs. This often means leveraging the NGO's international cache to help partners, affiliates, chapters or members to raise resources, but also ensuring that those resources are targeted for local use and not perceived as supporting the overhead of an overseas organization. Over the long term, it is believed that such a strategy can result in self-sufficient affiliates, partners or chapters that can carry the burden of the NGO's work in their own domains.

Various federations and membership associations have recognized the difficulties of establishing dues structures that accommodate members or affiliates with different abilities to contribute financially to the organization. Various practices have evolved to cope with this issue, including explicit cross-subsidy, policies that attach premiums to dues-paying members in rich countries in order to ease required payments from poorer countries; obtaining grants from foundations and multinational agencies to subsidize the dues structure or pay for memberships from certain parts of the world; and creating arrangements for members to belong to national subunits and pay memberships in local currencies, while these subunits enter financial agreements with the international body to pay for national memberships en masse.

Given the richness of regional NGO networks, several organizations that we studied make a point of viewing their memberships as access nodes to much wider swaths of civil society. For example, associations such as ICVA and InterAction are essentially associations of networks, whereas IRED's individual members are explicitly chosen for their connections to networks and partner organizations. In any case, organizations operating on a global scale are often highly decentralized and diverse, having members, affiliates or field offices in many parts of the globe. Hence they have evolved a number of strategies that appear to be especially helpful in providing integration and fostering a common identity and purpose in the face of this diversity. Organizationwide strategic planning, utilizing strategic planning conferences, is one approach used effectively by World Neighbors. Other strategies include sophisticated electronic communications networks, exchange visits among members from different regions, focusing on common messages and core themes, exchanges of staff among affiliates and with the international office, internships in the international office, cross-attendance of members at regional conferences, and interstaff coordinating bodies such as management committees that bring together executives and programme managers working on issues of mutual interest in different parts of the world.

Finally, we found that NGOs that operate on a global scale undertake a variety of programmatic initiatives that need not all be managed in the same way. Some organizations such as Ashoka pursue multifaceted management strategies. Some tasks are best addressed centrally and hierarchically, others by various local units, others by task forces, and still others by networking and partnership arrangements with other organizations and groups. The task of overall coordination becomes more complex as the number of different approaches multiplies, but with sophisticated management systems, work tasks can be allocated to those organizational entities most capable of carrying them out effectively.

Discussion

As we have observed, NGOs utilize a variety of structures to address the challenges of managing on a global scale, adapting in different ways to carry out the principle functions served by such organizations. Moreover, they have developed a substantial body of common wisdom with which to manage their operations.

Still, organizations have opportunities at critical junctures in their histories to make structural choices or to set a course for evolving from one type of structure to another. Hence, it is relevant to consider the overall merits of alternative forms and what trade-offs are involved in moving from one structure to another. In this context, we considered the experience of our 15 case studies in relation to five general criteria of organizational effectiveness. Although there is no theoretical consensus on the definition of organizational effectiveness, the following criteria were compiled specifically for international NGOs to reflect some general notions of organizational effectiveness (such as the achievement of goals, adaptability over time, cost effectiveness); also included are specific criteria that apply to organizations seeking to strengthen civil society (democratic decision-making, broad participation). (See Herman and Renz, 1999 and Edwards and Hulme, 1996 for further discussions of this subject.)

1   Which structure enables the organization to have the greatest impact? This criterion translates in part into how well each structure enables the five functions in Table 10.3 – convening, information provision, networking, advocacy, and brokering – but it also asks how well the organization can focus its resources on specific goals and priorities.
2   Which structure is most adaptive and flexible responding to changes over time and to differences in the state of civil society from place to place? Some structures allow wider discretion than others for organizational leaders to modify

programme and move resources to suit changing economic and social conditions or adapt to different local circumstances.
3   Which structure embodies favoured values such as democratic decision-making, citizen participation, third-sector solidarity, openness and intrasector and intersector dialogue? Some organizations want to lead by example. It may be important, therefore, for such NGOs themselves to be democratic, inclusive and transparent, and to be able to accommodate conflicts among constituents.
4   Which structure is most economical in the costs it incurs and the expense it imposes on its supporters? Given the scarcity of resources available to support civil society organizations and the challenges of funding a global effort, it is important for internationally focused NGOs to run efficiently and to find reliable sources of funds.
5   Which structure best achieves balanced participation and support from different regions of the world and from a wide cross-section of civil society? Some structures can accommodate sectoral and regional balance better than others. Moreover, the legitimacy of some organizations hinges in part on how well they are able to speak for large segments of the non-profit sector or civil society throughout the world.

Based on our study of the profiled organizations. Table 10.4 projects, in relative terms, how well each of the structures rates against each of the foregoing criteria. The table reveals that each model has different strengths:

1   A corporate partnership model is likely to be the most flexible and adaptive because it can engage a variety of temporary national, regional and local partnerships that can be changed over time. Membership associations are likely to be least flexible because change requires consensus among the largest numbers of constituents.
2   A membership association is likely to be most democratic in its operations and provides the opportunity for a variety of interests to participate directly at the global level. Corporate partnerships are governed by self-selected boards and are least democratic.

Table 10.4 *Rankings of Organizational Models by Alternative Criteria*

Criterion/Model	Corporation partnership	Federation	Member Association
Flexibility	1	2	3
Democratic	3	2	1
Expense	3	1	2
Coverage/ balance	3	2	1
Overall Impact	1	2	3
Networking	3	2	1
Convening	3	1	2
Information provision	1	2	3
Advocacy	3	1	2
Brokering	1	2	3

3   A federation is likely to be the least expensive because much of the work can be done directly by national and regional affiliates. Corporate arrangements require substantial centrally mobilized resources.

4   Member associations promise the widest global coverage and balance because members can be recruited explicity from all parts of the globe and from all non-profit subsectors. Corporate arrangements are selective by design and unlikely to be comprehensive or balanced in their coverage.

5   Because corporate partnerships can most easily set priorities and concentrate their resources. Table 10.4 suggests that a greater overall impact on developing civil society can be achieved under this arrangement. Member associations are least able to set such priorities or concentrate their resources, although as noted above, some (for example, Ashoka) may compensate by adopting multiple management strategies.

6   Member associations have the most widely diverse and extensive participation: hence they may be most effective in providing networking opportunities. Corporate partnerships are the least well equipped to do that.

7   The affiliates of federations are often themselves conveners of their constituencies in their respective countries and regions. As such, the global federation can be seen as a convener of conveners. Hence federations seem best equipped for this function and corporate partnerships least so.

8   Corporate partnerships, with their emphasis on professional staff, are likely to be best equipped to provide information services, whereas member associations are least so. Federations can utilize the information services of their member affiliates and are thus better equipped than associations.

9   Federations, whose affiliates represent segments of civil society in their respective countries, are most likely to be effective in the advocacy role. Corporate partnerships have the least political legitimacy and are least likely to be effective in advocacy.

10 Corporate partnerships can most easily engage powerful, high profile, skilled individuals to their boards and advisory committee, providing them with an edge in bringing civil society to the table with high-level government and business interests. Member associations seem the least well organized to do that.

Admittedly, these are broad generalizations to which many exceptions probably exist. As suggested above, there is substantial room for discretionary behaviour and variance in performance within structural categories. Certainly some of our observations should be qualified. For example, it can be argued that member associations may be more effective than corporations in addressing specific civil society goals if those goals require building trust with local citizenry; or that member associations are more effective information providers than corporations in some circumstances because of their strong networking capacities. Nonetheless, if, overall, the foregoing tendencies that we have identified in Table 10.4 are close to the mark, it is interesting that the federation model seems to offer an attractive middle ground, confirming much of the literature on the prominence of the federated form among national and international non-profit associations. The federation model takes 'first place' in a several categories and is never last. In this sense, it may be the least risky alternative.

It must be re-emphasized, however, that these judgements are based on a qualitative assessment of the general tendencies of the alternative structural models, as
derived from the experience of relatively few case studies. Any specific organizational design, if carefully conceived, may be able to minimize the generic weaknesses
of a given model and function satisfactorily on most of these important dimensions.
Moreover, other important, idiosyncratic factors such as an organization's history
or the size and scope of its operations are also likely to influence its decisions
concerning structure.

Concluding Comment

We hope that this chapter makes a modest contribution to understanding the structural choices and management strategies of NGO charged with addressing aspects of
civil society development on a global scale. Obviously, our conclusions must be appreciated within the limitations of a relatively small sample of organizations selected
for their variety within a given field of activity, rather than for their representative-
ness or comprehensiveness. Moreover, our analysis did not allow delving into each of
our case studies in very great depth. For example, we have generally assumed that the
practices and arrangements observed in the sampled associations were chosen for their
efficacy. A more intensive study would explicitly investigate this assumption.

Still, we have succeeded in demonstrating by this research that international
NGOs involved in supporting civil society around the world employ a variety of
structural forms to carry out their work. This is consistent, at least in the international NGO arena, with Child's (1972) conjecture that non-business organizations
are likely to have a substantial margin of choice in selecting an organizational structure. We have also identified three broad types of structures that these NGOs are
likely to employ. These types reflect and extend into the international arena the
categories identified by Young (1989) for nationally based non-profit umbrella
organizations in the US.

Within the wider array of structural forms identified, our observations here also
echo findings in the literature (such as McCarthy and Zald, 1987) that point to the
overall efficacy of the federated form of organization for coping with the challenges
of broadly based non-profit organizations. In particular, the experiences of the
associations we studied tend to confirm the viability of the federated model in
addressing the various requirements of association governance on an international
scale. This form appears to address a variety of organizational effectiveness criteria
fairly well, with less vulnerability to the particular risks of other (corporate and
membership association) forms.

We hope that our findings, however rudimentary, will enable further theoretical and empirical work to connect the various goals of international associations
with the most desirable structural arrangements for implementing these goals. The
experiences of the 15 global, civil society-oriented NGOs we studied demonstrate
that organizations in this field share a broad swath of common experience, and they
are embedded in emerging networks of global and local organizations. Although
these NGOs tend to choose one of three generic types of formal structure, they adapt

these structures in widely different ways, presumably to emphasize different functional objectives and performance criteria.

Our analysis also suggests that any new internationally focused organization, or one that faces a critical change in direction that requires structural adaptation, must recognize not only that there is substantial choice among structural alternatives, but that also there may be no one best structural type. In particular, the corporate, federation and association-forms accommodate the various functional mandates of internationally oriented NGOs in different ways, and they meet performance criteria such as flexibility, cost, democratic process, global coverage and impact to different degrees. An organization must first be clear about its programmatic objectives and how its performance is to be judged before necessary trade-offs can be made. After that, the collective wisdom of colleague organizations, on how to manage within structural constraints, can be exploited to substantial advantage. Indeed, we have found that the NGOs studied here have accumulated considerable practical management experienced-strategies, tactics and tricks of the trade – that permit them to fine-tune their operations within whatever organizational structures they have chosen.

Notes

1   The study reported here was underwritten by CIVICUS, a worldwide alliance intended to promote civil society around the globe. To CIVICUS, this has meant supporting the development of third sector (non-profit, non-governmental) organizations around the world, although it also includes engaging governmental and business sector organizations in the development and effective functioning of democratic society.

2   The committee consisted of a dozen leading scholars, consultants and chief executives of international NGOs assembled to advise CIVICUS on its organizational and structural issues.

3   We recognize that reliance on single high-level interview sources and written documents, made necessary by time and resource constraints, presents risk of bias and incomplete information. In all cases, however, we encountered full cooperation and took advantage of follow-up email communications to fill in gaps and answer remaining questions.

References

Ben-Ner, A, Montias, J M and Neuberger, E (1993) 'Basic issues in organizations: a comparative perspective', *Journal of Comparative Economics*, Vol. 17, pp207–242.

Chandler, A D (1962) *Strategy and Structure*, Massachusetts Institute of Technology Press, Cambridge, Massachusetts.

Chandler, A D (1990) *Scale and Scope*, Harvard University Press, Cambridge, Massachusetts.

Child, J (1972) 'Organization structure, environment and performance: the role of strategic choice', *Sociology*, Vol 6, January, pp1–22.

Darcy de Oliveira, M and Tandon, R (1994) 'An emerging global civil society', in M Darcy de Oliveira and R Tandon (eds), *Citizens: Strengthening Global Civil Society*, CIVICUS, Washington, DC, pp1–17.

Directory of Non-Governmental Organizations Associated with the Department of Public Information (1995, July), United Nations, New York.

Edwards, M E and Hulme, D (1996) *Beyond the Magic Bullet*, Kumarian Press, West Hartford, Connecticut.

Fisher, J (1993) *The Road from Rio: Sustainable Development and the Nongovernmental Movement in the Third World*, Westport, Connecticut, Praeger.

Fisher, J (1994) 'Is the iron law of oligarchy rusting away in the Third World?', *World Development*, Vol 22, No 2, pp129–143

Fisher, J (1998) *Non-Governments*, West Hartford, Connecticut, Kumarian Press.

Fligstein, N (1990) *The Transformation of Corporate Control*, Harvard University Press, Cambridge, Massachusetts.

Freeman, J (1979) 'Resource mobilization and strategy', in M N Zaid and J D McCarthy (eds), *The Dynamics of Social Movements*, Winthrop Publishers, Cambridge, pp167–189.

Fukuyama, F (1995), *Trust*, The Free Press, New York.

Gerlach, L P and Hine, V H (1970) *People, Power, Change*, Bobbs-Merrill, New York.

Geoghegan, T and Allen, K (eds) (1995) *InterAction Member Profiles: 1995–1996*, InterAction, Washington, DC.

Gerwin, D (1981) 'Relationships between structure and technology', in P C Nystrom and W H Starbuck (eds), *Handbook of Organizational Design*, Vol 2, Oxford University Press, New York, Ch 2.

Handy, C (1988) *Understanding Voluntary Organizations*, Penguin Books, London.

Herman, R D and Renz, D O (1999) 'Theses on non-profit organizational effectiveness', *Nonprofit and Voluntary Sector Quarterly*, Vol 28, No 2, pp107–126.

Hudson, B A and Bielefeld, W (1997) 'Structures of multinational non-profit organizations', *Nonprofit Management and Leadership*, Vol 8, No 1, pp31–49.

Jenkins, C J (1983) 'Resource mobilization theory and the study of social movements', *Annual Review of Sociology*, Vol 9, pp527–533.

Keck, M and Sikkink, K (1998) *Activists Beyond Borders*, Cornell University Press, Ithaca, New York.

Knoke, D (1990) *Organizing for Collective Action*, Aldine de Gruyter, New York.

Knoke, D (1993) 'Trade associations in the American political economy', in D C Hammock and D R Young (eds), *Nonprofit Organizations in a Market Economy*, Jossey-Bass, San Francisco, Ch 5.

Koenig, B (1996) 'The management of international non-governmental organizations in the 1990s', *Transnational Associations*, February, pp66–72.

Litterer, J A (ed) (1969) *Organizations*, Vol I, John Wiley & Sons, Inc, New York.

Macdonald, L (1997) *Supporting Civil Society*, St Martin's Press, New York.

Mathews, J T (1997) 'Power shift', *Foreign Affairs*, January/February, pp50–66.

McCarthy, J D and Zaid, M N (1987) 'Resource mobilization and social movements', in M N Zaid and J D McCarthy (eds), *Social Movements in an Organizational Society*, Transaction Books, New Brunswick, New Jersey, pp15–47.

Mintzberg, H (1989) *Mintzberg on Management*, The Free Press, New York.

Najam, A (1999a) 'Citizen organizations as policy entrepreneurs', in D Lewis (ed), *International Perspectives in Voluntary Action*, Earthscan, London, pp142–181.

Najam, A (1999b) 'The World Business Council for Sustainable Development: the greening of big business or a greenwash?', in H O Bergson, G Parmann, and O B Thommesen (eds),

Yearbook of International Cooperation on Environment and Development 1999/2000, Earthscan, London.

Oster, S M (1992) Nonprofit organizations as franchise operations', *Nonprofit Management and Leadership*, Vol 2, No 3, pp223–238.

Scott, W G, Mitchell, T R and Peery, N S (1981) 'Organizational governance', in P C Nystrom and W H Starbuck (eds), *Handbook of Organizational Design*, Vol 2, Oxford University Press, New York, Ch 6.

Smith, J, Pagnucco, R and Romeril, W (1994) 'Transnational social movement organizations in the global political arena', *Voluntas*, Vol 5, No 5, pp121–134.

Suzuki, N (1988) *Inside NGOs*, Intermediate Technology Publications, London.

Williamson, O E (1985) *The Economic Institutions of Capitalism*, The Free Press, New York.

Wils, F (1996) 'Scaling up, mainstreaming and accountability', in M Edwards and D Hulme (eds), *Beyond the Magic Bullet*, Kumarian Press, West Hartford, CT, pp67–79.

Wilson, J C (1973) *Political Organizations*, Basic Books, New York.

Young, D R (1989) 'Local autonomy in a franchise age', *Nonprofit and Voluntary Sector Quarterly*, Vol 19, pp101–117.

Young, D R (1992a) 'Organizing principles for international advocacy associations', *Voluntas*, Vol 3, No 1, pp1–28.

Young, D R (1992b) 'An interview with Peter F Drucker', Part II, *Nonprofit Management and Leadership*, Vol 2, No 3, pp295–301.

Young, D R, Bailey, D, and Bania, N (1992) '*The Strategy and Structure of National Non-profit Associations: A Conceptual Framework*', Mandel Center Discussion Paper, presented to the Annual Conference of the Association for Research on Nonprofit Organizations and Voluntary Action, New Haven, CT, October.

Young, D R, Bania, N and Bailey, D (1996) 'Structure and accountability: a study of national non-profit associations', *Nonprofit Management and Leadership*, Vol 6, No 4, pp347–365.

Zald, M N and Garner, R A (1987) 'Social movement organizations: growth, decay, and change', in M N Zald and J D McCarthy (eds), *Social Movements in an Organizational Society*, Transaction Books, New Brunswick, NJ, pp161–180.

Part 4

Strengthening Governance and Accountability

NGO Performance and Accountability: Introduction and Overview

Michael Edwards and David Hulme

By any standards, the 1980s and 1990s have seen an explosion in the numbers of non-governmental organizations (NGOs) and grassroots organizations (GROs) active in relief and development.[1] The number of development NGOs registered in countries belonging to the Organisation for Economic Co-operation and Development (OECD) of the industrialized North has grown from 1600 in 1980 to 2970 in 1993 (Smillie and Helmich, 1993), and over the same period the total spending of these NGOs has risen from US$2.8 billion to US$5.7 billion in current prices (OECD, 1994). The 176 'international NGOs' of 1909 had blossomed into 28,900 by 1993 (Commission on Global Governance, 1995). Similar figures have been reported in most countries in the South where political conditions have been favourable, with a particularly rapid increase over the last five years. For example, the number of NGOs registered with the government in Nepal rose from 220 in 1990 to 1210 in 1993 (Rademacher and Tamang, 1993, p4); in Bolivia the figure increased from around 100 in 1980 to 530 12 years later (Arellano-Lopez and Petras, 1994, p362); and in Tunisia there were 5186 NGOs registered in 1991 compared with only 1886 in 1988 (Marzouk, 1995).

Paralleling this increase in overall numbers has been the growth of some individual NGOs to cover the provision of health, education and credit services to millions of people in thousands of communities, especially in South Asia. For example, the Bangladesh Rural Advancement Committee (BRAC) now has more than 12,000 staff and has plans to work with over 3 million people (AKF/Novib, 1993); in India, the Self-Employed Women's Association (SEWA) has over 1 million clients in its credit programmes; while Sarvodaya in Sri Lanka works in 7000 villages (Perera, 1995). The access of NGOs to decision-makers in both North and South is greater than ever before, as their advocacy role continues to expand and they are courted in debates over policy and practice. GROs have a lower public profile, but they have also experienced considerable growth over the last decade and are beginning to organize themselves much more at the international level (Korten, 1990; CIVICUS, 1994). Clearly, something significant is happening in the world of international development. Lester Salamon (1993, p1) goes as far as to say that 'a veritable associational revolution now seems underway at the global level that may constitute as significant a social and political development of the latter twentieth century as the rise of the nation state was of the nineteenth century'.

Whether or not Salamon's conclusion is justified by current trends, the rise of NGOs and GROs on the world scene is an important phenomenon which has implications for the development prospects of poor people, for the future of these organizations themselves and for the wider political economy of which they form a small but growing part. But what lies behind these trends? This chapter takes the view that the rise of NGOs is not an accident; nor is it solely a response to local initiative and voluntary action. Equally important is the increasing popularity of NGOs with governments and official aid agencies,[2] which is itself a response to recent developments in economic and political thinking. Over the last 15 years, and particularly since the end of the Cold War, development policy and aid transfers have come to be dominated by what Robinson (1993) calls a 'New Policy Agenda'. This agenda is not monolithic – its details vary from one official aid agency to another, but in all cases it is driven by two basic sets of beliefs organized around the two poles of neo-liberal economics and liberal democratic theory (Moore, 1993).

First, markets and private initiative are seen as the most efficient mechanisms for achieving economic growth and providing most services to most people (Colclough and Manor, 1991). Governments 'enable' private provision but should minimize their direct role in the economy; because of their supposed cost-effectiveness in reaching the poorest, official agencies support NGOs in providing welfare services to those who cannot be reached through markets (Fowler, 1988; Meyer, 1992). Of course, NGOs have always provided welfare services to poor people in countries where governments lacked the resources to ensure universal coverage in health and education; the difference is that now they are seen as the *preferred channel* for service-provision in *deliberate substitution* for the state.

Second, under the New Policy Agenda, NGOs and GROs are seen as vehicles for 'democratization' and essential components of a thriving 'civil society', which in turn are seen as essential to the success of the agenda's economic dimension (Moore, 1993). NGOs and GROs are supposed to act as a counterweight to state power – protecting human rights, opening up channels of communication and participation, providing training grounds for activists and promoting pluralism. The rise of citizens' movements around the world documented by Korten (1990) and crystallized most recently in the establishment of CIVICUS (1994) (the 'World Alliance for Citizen Participation'), is not just (or perhaps even primarily) a result of developments in official aid, but it cannot be separated entirely from the political ideals of the New Policy Agenda.

As a result of these developments, governments have been prepared to channel increasing amounts of official aid to and through NGOs. Although accurate and comprehensive data are hard to come by, there is a good deal of evidence to suggest that the rise and growth of NGOs (and less so, of GROs) is directly related to the increasing availability of official funding under the New Policy Agenda. NGOs are seen as effective vehicles for the delivery of the agenda's economic and political objectives, although these roles are potentially incompatible, at least within the same organization (a proposition which is explored later in this chapter). The proportion of total aid from OECD countries channelled through NGOs increased from 0.7 per cent in 1975 to 3.6 per cent in 1985, and *at least* 5 per cent in 1993–1994 (some US$2.3 billion in absolute terms). This figure is certainly an underestimate since it omits multilateral agency funding to NGOs and NGO funding from the US Government, which represented over half the DAC (Development Assistance Committee) total in all previous years (OECD, 1988, 1994, 1995). Figures vary greatly between countries, donors and NGOs, but in general bilateral agencies are spending a steadily increasing proportion of their aid budgets through NGOs (including most recently directly through NGOs in the South), and most NGOs (especially the largest ones in both North and South) depend on these donors for an increasing slice of their total budgets, partly as a result of a flattening out in voluntary income over the last year or two.[3] NGOs which are *not* dependent on official aid for the majority of their budgets are now the exception rather than the rule. As Smillie (1995) says, 'when CIDA (the Canadian International Development Agency) sneezes, Canadian NGOs reach for their Vitamin C!'.

Although both the economic and political dimensions of the New Policy Agenda are important to official agencies, aid to NGOs has gone primarily to finance welfare services. Some authors have criticized what they see to be a fundamental change in *the function* of NGOs as a result of official funding, with service-delivery and contracting replacing support to GROs and institutional development (Arellano-Lopez and Petras, 1994). The increasing numbers of NGOs in many countries, a growth in the size of individual NGOs, an increasing concentration on service provision, and rising reliance on official funding, do all seem to be related to each other, but this is not universally true.

The overall picture is one in which NGOs are seen as the 'favoured child' of official agencies and something of a panacea for the problems of development. As Vivian (1994) puts it, official agencies (and the supporters of Northern NGOs) often see NGOs as a 'magic bullet' which can be fired off in any direction and, though often without very much evidence, will still find its target. Clearly, the increasing availability of official funding for NGOs, the popularity they enjoy and the increasing access they are offered to centres of national and international decision-making, represent both an opportunity and a danger. NGOs can scale-up their operations using official funds and use the New Policy Agenda to make their voices heard more loudly and more often through lobbying and advocacy; at the same time, by becoming more dependent on governments, NGOs run the risk of being coopted into the agendas of others and seeing their independent social base eroded. As far back as 1988, Jan Pronk (in Hellinger et al, 1988) warned that 'the corruption of NGOs will be the political game in the years ahead'. Pronk saw 'corruption' not simply in terms of financial scandal, but more broadly as the deviation of NGOs from their mission for social transformation. The only way in which NGOs can avoid 'corruption' in this sense is to develop systems for performance-monitoring, accountability and strategic planning which 'ensure that a line remains drawn between transparent compromise and blind co-option' (Eade, 1993, p161). That is why the central themes of this chapter – performance and accountability – are so important.

Strong accountability systems can help NGOs to take advantage of the opportunities offered by the New Policy Agenda while ensuring that any warning signals are identified, listened to and addressed. Of course, performance and accountability would be crucial subjects for debate whether or not NGOs were growing closer to governments. Performing effectively and accounting transparently are essential components of responsible practice, on which the legitimacy of development intervention ultimately depends. Moving 'beyond the magic bullet' means taking accountability much more seriously than has hitherto been the case among most NGOs, Northern or Southern. But the New Policy Agenda does complicate the issue of accountability considerably; there are real dangers that dependence on official aid and the models of planning and intervention which underlie it will make an already unsatisfactory situation significantly worse.

NGO Performance

For reasons which are explained later in this chapter, assessing NGO performance is a difficult and messy business. In any case, the absence of a large body of reliable evidence on the impact and effectiveness of NGOs and GROs makes it very difficult to generalize about this subject, despite claims that NGOs are 'cost-effective' or that GROs 'are close to the poor' (Fowler, 1988). Most studies of NGO and GRO impact are based on small samples and are often restricted to agencies working in a particular sector (often economic development) or context (usually favourable), which makes measurement easier. Internal evaluations are rarely released and what *is* released comes closer to propaganda than rigorous assessment. Nevertheless, there is increasing evidence that NGOs and GROs do not perform as effectively as had been assumed in terms of poverty-reach, cost-effectiveness, sustainability, popular participation (including gender), flexibility and innovation.[4] In terms of service provision, there is certainly evidence that NGOs are able to provide some services more cost-effectively than governments – for example, the Orangi Pilot Project in Pakistan has developed sanitation systems at less than one-third of the equivalent cost in the commercial or government sectors (Hasan, 1993); similar cost advantages have been claimed for BRAC in primary education and credit provision (AKF/ Novib, 1993). However, evidence from other studies contradicts this conclusion (Tendler, 1989) and there is no empirical study which demonstrates a general case that NGO provision is cheaper than public provision. Even where NGO service provision is 'low cost', it usually fails to reach the poorest people, although it may still reach a wider cross-section of the population than government or commercial agencies (Hashemi and Schuler, 1992; Farrington and Bebbington, 1993; Hulme and Mosley, 1995). The sustainability of large-scale service provision by NGOs has also been called into question by those who cite the large subsidies granted to NGOs (and denied to governments) which make the gap between private and public provision a 'self-perpetuating reality' (Farrington and Lewis, 1993, p333). There are also worries about a 'patchwork quilt' of social services developing in which only certain regions are supplied by well-resourced NGOs, leaving others to fend for themselves under weak central oversight (Robinson, 1993; Edwards and Hulme, 1994). In all cases, very careful management is needed to avoid a fall-off in quality when NGOs scale-up service provision to cover large populations, although as Howes and Sattar (1992) and Wils (1995) show, there is no necessary trade-off.

Evidence on the performance of NGOs and GROs in democratization is more difficult to come by, except in the area of 'micro-policy reform' where a growing number of case studies demonstrate that NGOs and GROs can influence governments and official agencies, especially where they come together to form a united front (Edwards and Hulme, 1992). On occasion (as in Bangladesh with the fall of President Ershad or the Philippines in the case of President Marcos), such united action can exert an influence on the position of governments as a whole. However, there is little evidence that NGOs and even GROs are managing to engage in the formal political process successfully, without becoming embroiled in partisan politics and the distortions that accompany the struggle for state power. In both Latin America and Africa, evidence shows that NGOs have had little impact on political reform, partly because states are adept at containing such a possibility, and partly because NGOs themselves (as non-representative organizations) have failed to develop effective strategies to promote democratization (Lehmann, 1990; Fowler, 1991; Bratton, 1990). The failure of many NGOs, and even GROs, to democratize their own structures makes them less effective in this process and poses a particular problem for 'downward' accountability to members and beneficiaries (Carrol, 1992; Bebbington and Thiele, 1993). Nevertheless, NGOs and GROs can be proud of their achievements in helping to cement human and political rights in many societies, and in democratizing the informal political process by training grass-roots activists, building stronger local institutions, promoting micro-policy reform and undertaking education for citizenship (Friedmann, 1992; Ghai and Vivan, 1992).

A particular area of concern here is the contradiction which may exist between effective performance in the two dimensions of the New Policy Agenda – economic and political – an issue to which little attention has been paid thus far. Large-scale service provision requires standardized delivery mechanisms (to reduce unit costs), structures which can handle large amounts of external funding and systems for speedy, and often hierarchical, decision-making; effective performance as an agent of democratization rests on organizational independence, closeness to the poor, representative structures and a willingness to spend large amounts of time in awareness-raising and dialogue (Edwards and Hulme, 1994). It is difficult to combine these characteristics within the same organization and there is little evidence that alliances of different organizations (which could enable the two to go together) have developed very far. The fear is that, because service delivery tends to attract more official funding, there will be a growing rift between well-resourced service-providers and poorly funded social mobilization agencies, a danger already identified by Pearce (1993) in Chile and Central America.

The tendency of Northern NGOs to base their strategic plans on the easy availability of funding for humanitarian emergencies poses similar problems for their longer-term work in institutional development and development education. Some critics cite the switch from 'conscientization' to 'service delivery' by NGOs such as BRAC in Bangladesh as evidence that they have retreated from any serious role in addressing structural constraints to poverty and injustice. However, recent attacks on BRAC and other large NGOs by religious fundamentalists citing their 'success' in 'empowering women' suggest that such pessimism is misplaced, or at least that the real situation is more complex than is suggested by the supposed dichotomy between service delivery and conscientization.

As NGOs become more involved in large-scale service delivery (or grow for other reasons) and/or become more reliant on official funding, one might expect some fall-off in their flexibility, speed of response and ability to innovate. Although organizational growth can be managed successfully, bureaucratization poses problems for any agency, as do the complex appraisal and reporting requirements which accompany official aid (Edwards and Hulme, 1992, 1994). When official agencies finance service delivery they expect contracted outputs to be achieved and are less interested in a 'learning process' (Voorhies, 1993; Perera, 1995). Time and space for reflection may be reduced and the ability of NGOs to articulate approaches, ideas, language and values which run counter to official orthodoxies may also be compromised. These issues are discussed later in this chapter. A further concern is that the willingness of NGOs to speak out on issues which are unpopular with governments will be diluted by their growing dependence on official aid. There is evidence from Africa that NGOs which depend on external funding (although not just on official funding) are more likely to be ignored as 'illegitimate' by their own governments in policy debates (Bratton, 1989); in the USA, the largest operational NGOs (which are all heavily dependent on USAID) tend to avoid a campaigning role, no doubt fearful of the consequences that would follow if they spoke out too sharply against government policy (Smith, 1990; Salamon and Anheier, 1993; Smith and Lipsky, 1993); and a context in which NGOs compete with each other for government grants seems unlikely to foster the collaborative relationships on which effective policy alliances are built (Fowler, 1992; Edwards, 1993).

Finally, NGOs which depend on official funding often perform poorly in the crucial task of local institutional development' (Esman and Uphoff, 1984), the gradual strengthening of capacities and capabilities among grassroots organizations to enable them to play a more effective and independent role in development. This is because many official agencies are unwilling to support the long-time horizons, slow careful nurturing and gradual qualitative results which characterize successful institutional development (Carroll, 1992; Fowler, 1992). Such work is difficult to 'sell' to the politicians and their constituents on which aid bureaucracies depend for their budgets (LaFond, 1995).

The point of presenting this evidence is not to claim that NGOs perform *less effectively* than other organizations (public or private) in these various tasks; simply that they often perform *less well* than their popular image suggests. A comparative analysis of performance between NGOs, governments and commercial operators is beyond the scope of this book, although there is reason to believe that any differences which do emerge have less to do with inherent traits and more to do with factors which cut across the public–private divide (Tendler, 1983). In any case, comparisons with other types of organization which perform less well (something at which NGOs excel!) do not provide grounds for arguing that current NGO performance is satisfactory: NGOs should always be striving to serve others better.

NGO Accountability

Accountability is generally interpreted as the means by which individuals and organizations report to a recognized authority, or authorities, and are held responsible for their actions (Edwards and Hulme, 1994). Accountability is a complex and abstract concept, however, and relatively little research has been conducted on this topic with regard to NGOs and GROs (Brett, 1993). Although accountability is viewed as a desirable organizational characteristic, empirical studies commonly indicate that both leaders and subordinates in public and private organizations[5] seek to avoid accountability (Fox, 1992). The common perception that, somewhere else, there are organizations that are perfectly accountable must be dismissed. However, there is clearly a level at which the absence of accountability begins to make the likelihood of ineffective or illegitimate actions by an organization much more probable.

Table 11.1 The Accountability Matrix (for a Hypothetical Southern NGO)

Forms of accountability and quality of accountability at different stages in the accountability process

	Functional Accountability¹			Strategic Accountability²		
	Capacity to demand reports and information	Capacity to appraise reports and information	Capacity to operate sanctions	Capacity to demand reports and information	Capacity to appraise reports and information	Capacity to operate sanctions
Beneficiaries/members	Low³	Low	Low	Low	Nil	Nil
Trustees	Medium	Low	Medium	Low	Low	Low
Private contributors	Medium	Low	Low	Medium	Low	Low
NGO network	Low	Low	Low	Low	Low	Nil
National government	Medium	Low	High	Low	Low	Low
Official donors	High	Medium	High	Low	Low	Nil
NNGOs	High	Medium	Medium	Medium	Low	Low

1 Functional accountability = accounting for resources, resource use and immediate impacts.
2 Strategic accountability = accounting for impacts on other organizations and the wider environment on a medium- to long-term basis.
3 Alternatively, the matrix could include short statements on the capacity of different authorities at different stages, rather than nil/low/medium/high.

Effective accountability requires a statement of goals (whether in adherence to certain rules or achievement of identified performance levels), transparency of decision-making and relationships, honest reporting of what resources have been used and what has been achieved, an appraisal process for the overseeing authority(ies) to judge whether results are satisfactory and concrete mechanisms for holding to account (such as, rewarding or penalizing) those responsible for performance. GRO and NGO accountability may be formal (for example, an evaluation of whether agreed objectives in a programme have been met) or informal (for example, ongoing discussions between partners). It may emphasize the honesty and efficiency with which resources are used (commonly referred to as 'probity') or the impact and effectiveness of the work (commonly called 'performance'). Avina (1993) usefully distinguishes between short-term *functional accountability* (accounting for resources, resource use and immediate impacts) and *strategic accountability* (accounting for the impacts that an NGO's actions have on the actions of other organizations and the wider environment).

Crucially, GROs and NGOs have *multiple* accountabilities – 'downwards' to their partners, beneficiaries, staff and supporters; and 'upwards' to their trustees, donors and host governments. Multiple accountability presents any organization with problems, particularly the possibilities of having to 'over-account' (because of multiple demands) or being able to 'under-account', as each overseeing authority assumes that another authority is taking a close look at actions and results. Legally, most NGOs, as non-membership organizations, are accountable to their trustees who often exercise only a very light hand in governance. NGOs cannot be formally accountable to their beneficiaries, however much they may want to be. By contrast, GROs are accountable to their members. Both usually have an obligation to account to the governments of the countries in which they operate, although in practice this often means only brief annual reports and occasional audits. Morally (in accordance with values of participation and empowerment), and in terms of their wider claims to legitimacy, NGOs are accountable to other constituencies, most obviously beneficiaries and contributors. But of course equal accountability to all at all times is an impossibility. Many of the concerns expressed about the weak accountability of NGOs relate to the difficulties they face in prioritizing and reconciling these multiple accountabilities (see Table 11.1).

Although the accountability of GROs (to their members) may seem more straightforward, there is surprisingly little evidence that they perform better than NGOs in this respect. Indeed, Carroll (1992, p89) finds the opposite to be true in Latin America. These conclusions are confirmed by Bebbington and Thiele (1993, p21) who state that 'we cannot say *a priori* that any one type of organization is inherently more or less responsive to, or representative of, the needs of the rural poor'. In GROs, problems of accountability often arise due to social and political factors (such as interest-group manipulation), whereas among NGOs, economic factors, and particularly links to donors, are likely to be more influential (Pearce, 1993). Indeed, it is NGOs, especially those based in the North, that come in for the most damning criticisms. Lehmann (1990, p201) calls their lack of accountability 'extraordinary', while Smillie (1993), finds that 'Northern NGO survival has been almost completely delinked from performance', since they appear under little obligation to tell the truth to their supporters (Edwards, 1994). While NGOs may contest these assertions, we can find no evidence that the contemporary accountability of NGOs is satisfactory.

Measuring impact and effectiveness in an uncertain world: 'interpretative' accountability

A great part of the dilemma faced by GROs and NGOs lies in the nature of the work they do and the messy and complex world in which they do it – measuring performance in relation to the kind of development subscribed to by most NGOs is an extraordinarily difficult task, particularly in relation to 'empowerment' and other qualitative changes. As Drucker (1990) points out, the ultimate objective of 'nonprofit' agencies is 'changed human beings'. There are few agreed performance standards available to NGOs in this realm, beyond probity and some quantifiable impact indicators in certain types of NGO activity such as service provision and economic development. Neither is there any obvious 'bottom line' against which progress can be measured. Unlike businesses (which must make a profit) and governments (which must face elections), the 'bottom line for NGOs shifts according to the situation at hand' (Fowler, 1995). Organizational, as opposed to project, indicators are even more difficult to find, especially given the seeming obsession of many NGO managers with size and growth as indicators of 'success'. Indicators of the *quality* of organizational performance are very rare (with the exception of the 'social audit' described by Zadek and Gatward, 1995) and the general lack of satisfactory evaluative mechanisms is a serious drawback when it comes to GRO/NGO accountability. Because so few fixed, absolute standards exist, NGO evaluation (even more than evaluation in other organizations) is inevitably a matter of judgement and interpretation. This is the line of argument developed by Guba and Lincoln (1989) in their work on 'Fourth Generation Evaluation', and applied specifically to social development by Marsden et al (1994). The same line of reasoning is employed by Uphoff, (1995) and Fowler (1995) to emphasize the non-linear and 'open systems' nature of NGO work and the need to adapt concepts of performance-measurement and accountability accordingly.

In addition, NGOs and GROs are rarely able to control all (or even most) of the factors which influence the outcome of their work – macroeconomic performance, state policy and the actions of other agencies are obvious examples. Handy (1993, p15) lists at least 60 variables which influence the effectiveness of any organization, while Uphoff (1995) points to the 'second- and third-order effects' of NGO actions which are essential for sustainable development but are ignored in most evaluations. When positive long-term results are achieved, this is not because of one organization or project acting in isolation, but because a whole series of forces and actors come together to produce, for example, a sustainable change in agricultural production or the development of a strong grassroots federation. This makes measuring 'strategic' accountability in its most fundamental sense almost impossible – no organization can be held accountable for the impact of forces which are beyond its control, although, of course, NGOs can and should be able to account for the way in which they use their resources within the framework set by these forces. As Rondinelli (1993) puts it in the context of the Canadian International Development Agency (CIDA) the question becomes whether agencies use their resources 'effectively', efficiently and prudently to achieve reasonable progress toward worthwhile development objectives', including how well they learn from experience and judge the costs and benefits of putting resources to different purposes. This still leaves a great deal of room for interpretation, which is why, as laid out in the next section, accountability must be a process of negotiation among stakeholders rather than the imposition of one definition or interpretation of 'effectiveness' over another.

For some NGOs and GROs, however, there is also a political dilemma to accountability. If the organization's overt or covert goal is 'empowerment' – that is, making those who have little power at present more powerful – then transparency on this issue will, at best, make it easier for vested interests to identify what is happening and thus more effectively oppose it or, at worst, lead to the deregistration and closure of the organization for being subversive (and perhaps violence to staff).

Negotiating performance and impact among stakeholders: multiple accountability

Since there are few absolute performance measures in NGO evaluation and no single bottom line, negotiation among stakeholders is the essence of accountability in this area. All NGOs and most GROs have, as mentioned above, multiple accountabilities. Therefore, definitions of objectives, interpretations of results and decisions on what response may be appropriate, all have to be negotiated among a wide range of actors. For example, are higher NGO overheads an indicator of effective performance (since they are essential for improved research, learning, monitoring and dissemination), or a sign of inefficiency? Presumably the answer to this question varies according to circumstance and opinion. As the contributions to this book show, NGOs and GROs in the South are often more interested in the wider questions of where NGOs fit in relation to society and politics, rather than the narrower question of how inputs and outputs are related at the project level, which is of prime concern to donors. Biekart's (1995) analysis of NGO accountability in Central America and Bejar and Oakley's (1995) description of current evaluation trends in Latin America (1995) both show how understandings of performance vary greatly over time and between different partners. The questions posed by Karim (1995) are very relevant here: *who* defines accountability, *for whom* and *why*?

The impact of the New Policy Agenda and official aid: distorting accountability

An already complex situation is made even more difficult by official aid to NGOs and the demands imposed by the New Policy Agenda. Given the financial and political muscle of official agencies, there is an obvious fear that donor funding may reorient accountability upwards, away from the grassroots, and bias performance-measurement towards criteria defined by donors (Edwards and Hulme, 1994; Fisher, 1994; Tandon, 1994). Many studies provide evidence of this problem, although it is difficult to disentangle the influence of official funding from pre-existing weaknesses in 'downward' accountability. Fox and Hernandez (1989) and Fisher (1994) provide some evidence that GRO leaders can be further distanced from their members by foreign influence and assistance, although this can be mitigated by the deliberate encouragement of new generations of leaders from within the organization. Given that GROs are membership organizations, the reorientation of accountability away from the grassroots is a particular threat to them as *de facto* it turns members into customers.

The type of appraisal, monitoring and evaluation procedures insisted on by donors, especially their heavy reliance on 'logical framework' approaches and bureaucratic reporting, may also distort accountability by overemphasising short-term quantitative targets, standardizing indicators, focusing attention exclusively on individual projects or organizations, and favouring hierarchical management structures – a tendency to 'accountancy' rather than 'accountability'; audit rather than learning. This is perhaps an inevitable result of the pressure for short-term visible results in order to keep Parliament or Congress happy. Accountability may focus too much on control functions – 'Is the money being spent properly?' – rather than on learning and sharing, something criticized by Smillie (1995) in relation to NGO evaluation procedures adopted by CIDA in Canada. Compressed project planning cycles often leave very little time to learn the lessons of experience, let alone *use them*. In this process there is a particular danger that women will be penalized as qualitative changes in gender relations are inadequately monitored and women are excluded from senior positions in large, growing, hierarchical institutions.[6] The competitive nature of contracting also fosters an orientation towards treating information as a public relations activity (that is, releasing the good and hiding the bad) and this compromises transparency. The contemporary management of their external image by international NGOs and large NGOs in South Asia provides evidence of this. As Chambers (1995) states, the 'self-deceiving NGO' is already a reality. There is, however, some evidence that donor funding may strengthen some forms of accountability by increasing external pressures for accurate reporting and more sophisticated monitoring (Tendler, 1989; Bebbington and Riddell, 1996).

Second, the sheer volume of donor funds made available to GROs and NGOs may result in problems of probity, especially where internal management and financial systems are originally based on informality and trust. The example of Sarvodaya in Sri Lanka provides a good illustration of this (Perera, 1995). The organization's accounting and reporting systems were adequate for a small and later medium-sized organization, with an energetic leader and a highly personalized management style. However, rapid growth led to the breakdown of these systems and confusion on the part of the organization and donors as to whether functional accounting was simply weak or whether it was hiding improprieties.

Third, closer links with donors (and the suspicion of foreign influence this creates in government) may result in a move away from self-regulation to regulation from above by the state. Self-regulation is not sufficient to ensure accountability, but the informal consultative processes and codes of ethics that characterize the voluntary sector in many countries (North and South) have maintained a balance between 'room for manoeuvre' and regulation (Carroll, 1992; Constantino-David, 1992; ICVA, 1991; InterAction, 1993). Formal accountability procedures may discourage innovation and speed of response, and promote politicization and patronage (Brown and Tandon, 1992; Farrington and Bebbington, 1993; Rademacher and Tamang, 1993). Government coordinating mechanisms may also provide avenues for the state to gain access to NGO funding and information on organizations they consider 'subversive'. Possible avenues for government influence over NGOs include legislation, taxation, public consultation, coordination and official support, with the balance between monitoring, co-optation and outright repression varying according to political context (Bratton, 1989; Clark, 1995; Farrington and Lewis, 1993). Not surprisingly, 'government – NGO relations are likely to be most constructive where a confident and capable government with populist policies meets an NGO that works to pursue mainstream development programmes ... and most conflictual where a weak and defensive government with a limited power base meets an NGO that seeks to promote community mobilization' (Bratton, 1989, p585). Most examples lie somewhere in between these two extremes, and the overall conclusion to be drawn by Brown and Tandon (1992) is that government – NGO coordinating mechanisms would perform best if changed from a hierarchical link to a 'bridge' between the two which can balance necessary accountability with essential independence.

The message that must come out of this section is that little is known about the changing nature of GRO and NGO accountability. This is a serious matter, given that GRO/NGO claims to legitimacy are premised at least in part on the strength of their accountability, particularly to the 'poor'. Indeed, the New Policy Agenda thrusts the question of legitimacy into centre stage, for if NGOs are becoming more responsive to external concerns, what is happening to the links – to their values and mission, and to their supporters and others – through which they claim their right to intervene in development? NGOs do not have to be member-controlled to be legitimate, but they do have to be accountable for what they do if their claims to legitimacy are to be sustained. Recent doubts expressed by Southern NGOs about the advocacy role of NGOs in the North (speaking 'on behalf of the poor') provide one illustration of this difficult issue (Edwards, 1993). Although poorly understood and often ignored, questions of legitimacy and identity are crucial to the future of NGOs and we return to these questions in the second part of this chapter.

Notes

1   Throughout this chapter a distinction is made between NGOs, which are intermediary organizations engaged in funding or offering other forms of support to communities and other organizations; and grassroots organizations (GROs), which are membership organizations of various kinds. Other authors make the same distinction, but use different terms. For example, Carroll (1992) distinguishes between 'grassroots support organizations' (which are NGOs), and 'membership support organizations'; GROs are also sometimes called 'community-based organizations' (CBOs). The most important difference between the two groups lies in their accountability structures: GROs are formally accountable to their members, while NGOs are not. However, many other authors use the term 'NGOs' to cover all forms of non-profit organization.

2   Official aid agencies are those which are funded by Northern governments either directly (bilateral agencies such as the British Overseas Development Administration, or the Swedish International Development Agency (Sida) or indirectly (multilateral agencies such as the World Bank and the European Union).

3   The figures here vary considerably, as do methods of calculating aid transfers to and through NGOs, and NGO dependency on official agencies. For example, the proportion of Sida funds channelled through NGOs increased from 9 per cent in 1990–1991 to 30 per cent in 1994: Sida funds over 2000 NGO projects, while the British Overseas Development Administration (ODA) is already funding over 450 Indian NGOs directly, and a similar number in Bangladesh. All five of the largest NGOs in the UK show a significantly increasing level of financial dependence on ODA, while in other countries (such as Canada, the USA, Germany, the Netherlands and Norway) dependency ratios of between 50 per cent and 90 per cent are common. In the South, the large South Asian NGOs such as BRAC receive most of their funding from external sources, although it is difficult to specify whether more of this is coming from official agencies rather than from traditional Northern NGO sources. The availability of official aid under 'social compensation funds' in adjusting economies, however, has been an important source of support for NGOs in countries such as Bolivia and Uganda (Arellano-Lopez and Petras, 1994). For details of these trends, see Smillie and Helmich (1993), Good (1994), Bebbington and Riddell (1995), Edwards and Hulme (1994) and German and Randel (1994).

4   Early work on this subject was carried out by Judith Tendler (1982, 1983); more recent studies include Fowler (1991, 1993); Lehmann (1990); Carroll (1992); Riddell and Robinson (1992); Farrington and Lewis (1993); Bebbington and Thiele (1993); Wellard and Copestake (1993); Vivian (1994); and Hashemi and Schuler (1992).

5   See *The Economist*, 29 January 1994, 'A Survey of Corporate Governance' for a discussion of the weakness of accountability in private sector corporations.

6   Some participants at the workshop from which this chapter emerged criticized us for not paying explicit attention to gender issues in the discussion of NGO performance and accountability. This remains an important area for further research, as we can locate no specific analysis of the many ways in which the definition of performance and accountability may be male-biased.

References

Aga Khan Foundation Canada/Novib (1993) *Going To Scale: The BRAC Experience 1972–1992 and Beyond*, Aga Khan/Novib, The Hague.

Arellano-Lopez, S and Petras, J (1994) 'NGOs and poverty alleviation in Bolivia', *Development and Change*, Vol 25, No 3, pp555–568.

Avina, J (1993) 'The evolutionary life cycle of non-governmental development organizations', *Public Administration and Development*, Vol 13, No 5 (December), pp453–474.

Bebbington, A and Riddell, R (1995) 'New agendas and old problems: issues, options and challenges in direct funding of Southern NGOs', in D Hulme and M Edwards (eds) *Too Close for Comfort? NGOs, States and Donors*, Macmillan, London.

Bebbington, A, Thiele, G (eds) with Davies, P, Prager, M, Riveros, H (1996) *NGOs and the state in Latin America: Rethinking Roles in Sustainable Agricultural Development*, Routledge, London.

Bratton, M (1989) 'The politics of government – NGO relations in Africa', *World Development*, Vol 17, No 4, pp569–587.

Bratton, M (1990) 'Non-governmental organizations in Africa: can they influence government policy?' *Development and Change*, Vol 21, pp87–118.

Brett, E (1993) 'Voluntary agencies as development organizations: theorizing the problems of efficiency and accountability', *Development and Change*, Vol 24, pp87–118.

Brown, D and Tandon, R (1992) *Public-NGO Financing Institutions in India: An Exploratory Study*, World Bank, Washington, DC.

Carroll, T (1992) *Intermediary NGOs: the Supporting Link in Grass-roots Development*, Kumarian Press, West Hartford.

Chambers, R (1995) 'The Primacy of the Personal', in M Edwards and D Hulme, op cit.

CIVICUS (1994) *Citizens Strengthening Global Civil Society*, CIVICUS, Washington, DC.

Clark, J (1997) 'NGO–state relations: a review of the principal policy issues', in D Hulme and M Edwards (eds), op cit.

Colclough, C and Manor, J (1991) *States or Markets? Neo-liberalism and the Development Policy Debate*, Clarendon Press, Oxford.

Commission on Global Governance (1995) *Our Common Neighbourhood: The Report of the Commission on Global Governance*, Oxford University Press, Oxford

Constantino David, K (1992) 'The Philippine experience in scaling-up', in Edwards, M and Hulme, D (eds) *Making a Difference: NGOs and Development in a Changing World*, Earthscan, London.

Covey, J (1995) 'Accountability and Effectiveness in NGO Policy Alliances', in M Edwards and D Hulme, op cit.

Desai, V and M Howes (1995) 'Accountability and Participation: A Case Study from Bombay', in M Edwards and D Hulme, op cit.

Drucker, P (1990) *Managing the Non-Profit Organization*, Harper Collins, New York.

Eade D (1993) 'Editorial', *Development in Practice*, Vol 3, No 3, pp161–162.

Edwards, M (1993) 'Does the doormat influence the boot? Critical thoughts on UK NGOs and international advocacy', *Development in Practice*, Vol 3, No 3, pp163–175.

Edwards, M (1994) 'NGOs in the age of information', *IDS Bulletin*, Spring 1994, IDS, Sussex.

Edwards, M and Hulme, D (eds) (1992) *Making a Difference: NGOs and Development in a Changing World*, Earthscan, London.

Edwards, M and Hulme, D (eds) (1994) *NGOs and Development; Performance and Accountability in the 'New World Order'*, background paper to the workshop on NGOs and Development, SCF/IDPM, Manchester. 27–29 June 1994

Esman, M and Uphoff, N (1984) *Local Organizations: Intermediaries in Rural Development*, Cornell University Press.

Farrington, J and Bebbington, A with Wells, K and Lewis, D (1993) *Reluctant Partners? NGOs, the State and Sustainable Agricultural Development*, Routledge, London.

Farrington, J and Lewis, D (eds) with Satish, S and Miclat-Teves, A (1993) *NGOs and the State in Asia: Rethinking Roles in Sustainable Agricultural Development*, Routledge, London

Fisher, J (1994) 'Is the iron law of oligarchy rusting away in the Third World?', *World Development*, Vol 22, No 2, pp129–143.

Fowler, A (1995) Assessing NGO Performance: Difficulties, Dilemmas and a Way Ahead, in M Edwards and D Hulme, op cit.

Fowler, A (1988) *NGOs in Africa: Achieving Comparative Advantage in Relief and Micro-development*, IDS Discussion Paper, No 249, IDS, Sussex.

Fowler, A (1991) 'The role of NGOs in changing state–society relations: perspectives from Eastern and Southern Africa', *Development Policy Review*, Vol 9, pp53–84.

Fowler, A (1992) *Distant Obligations: Speculations on NGO Funding and the Global Market*, paper presented to the annual conference of the DSA, Nottingham, September.

Fowler, A (1993) 'NGOs as agents of democratisation: an African perspective', *Journal of International Development*, Vol 5, No 3, pp325–339.

Fox, J (1992) 'Democratic rural development: leadership accountability in regional peasant organizations', *Development and Change*, Vol 23, No 2, pp1–36.

Fox, J and Hemandez, L (1989) 'Offsetting the iron law of oligarchy: the ebb and flow of leadership accountability in a regional peasant organization', *Grassroots Development*, Vol 13, No 2, pp8–15.

Friedmann, J (1992) *Empowerment: The Politics of Alternative Development*, Blackwell, Oxford and Cambridge, Mass.

German, T and Randel, J (1994) 'Trends in official aid and the implications for NGOs', paper presented to the Workshop on NGOs and Development, SCF/IDPM, Manchester, 27–29 June 1994.

Ghai, D and Vivian, J (1992) (eds) *Grassroots Environmental Action: People's Participation in Sustainable Development*, Routledge, London and New York.

Good, A (1994) 'Paying the piper. Calling the tune? Present and future relationships among Northern NGOs, Southern NGOs, and the ODA', paper presented to the SCF/IDPM workshop on NGOs and Development: Performance and Accountability in the 'New World Order', Manchester, 27–29 June.

Guba, E and Lincoln, Y (1989) *Fourth Generation Evaluation*, Sage, London.

Handy, C (1993) *Understanding Organizations*, Penguin (4th edition), Harmondsworth.

Hasan, A (1993) *Scaling-up the OPP's Low-cost Sanitation Programme*, OPP/RTI, Karachi.

Hashemi, S and Schuler, S (1992) *State and NGO Support Networks in Rural Bangladesh: Concepts and Coalitions for Control*, Centre for Development Research, Copenhagen.

Hellinger, D, Hellinger, S and O'Rogan, F (1988) *Aid for Just Development*, Lynn Rienner, Boulder, Colorado, and London.

Howes, M and Sattar, M G (1992) 'Bigger and better? Scaling-up strategies pursued by BRAC 1972–1991', in Edwards, M and Hulme, D (eds) *Making a Difference: NGOs and Development in a Changing World*, Earthscan, London.

Hulme, D and Edwards, M (eds) (1996) *Too Close for Comfort? NGOs, States and Donors*, Macmillan, London.

Hulme, D and Mosley, P (1995) *Finance Against Poverty* (Vols 1 and 2), Routledge, London.

ICVA (1991) *Relations between Southern and Northern NGOs: Policy Guidelines*, ICVA, Geneva.

InterAction (1993) *InterAction Private Voluntary Agencies (PVOs) Standards*, Washington, DC.

Karim, M (1995) 'NGOs in Bangladesh: Issues of Legitimacy and Accountability', in M Edwards and D Hulme, op cit.

Korten, D (1990) *Getting to the 21st Century: Voluntary Action and the Global Agenda*, Kumarian Press, West Hartford.

LaFond, A (1995) *Sustaining Primary Health Care*, Earthscan/SCF, London.

Lehmann, D (1990) *Democracy and Development in Latin America: Economics, Politics and Religion in the Post-War Period*, Polity Press, Cambridge.

Marsden, D, Oakley, P and Pratt, B (1994) *Measuring the Process: Guidelines for Evaluating Social Development*, INTRAC, Oxford.

Marzouk, M (1995) 'The associative phenomenon in the Arab world: engine of democratization or witness to the crisis?', in D Hulme and M Edwards (eds), op cit.

Meyer, C (1992) 'A step back as donors shift institution building from the public to the "private" sector', *World Development*, Vol 20, No 8, pp1115–1126.

Moore, M (1993) 'Good government? Introduction', *IDS Bulletin*, Vol 24, No 1, pp1–6.

OECD (1988) *Development Assistance Committee Report 1987*, OECD, Paris.

OECD (1994) *Development Assistance Committee Report 1993*, OECD, Paris.

OECD (1995) *Development Assistance Committee Report 1994*, OECD, Paris.

Pearce, J (1993) 'NGOs and social change: agents or facilitators?', *Development in Practice*, Vol 3, No 3, pp222–227.

Perera, J (1995) 'Unequal dialogue with donors: the Sarvodaya experience', in D Hulme and M Edwards (eds), op cit.

Rademacher, A and Tamang, D (1993) *Democracy, Development and NGOs*, SEARCH, Kathmandu

Riddell, R and Robinson, M (1992) *The impact of NGO poverty-alleviation projects: results of the case study evaluations*, ODI Working Paper, No 68, ODI, London.

Robinson, M (1993) 'Governance, democracy and conditionality: NGOs and the new policy agenda', in A Clayton (ed) *Governance, Democracy and Conditionally: What Role for NGOs?*, INTRAC, Oxford.

Rondinelli, D (1993) *Strategic and Results-based Management in CIDA: Reflections on the Process*, Canadian International Development Agency, Ottawa.

Salamon, L (1993) *The Global Associational Revolution: The Rise of the Third Sector on the World Scene*, Occasional Paper No 15, Institute for Policy Studies, Johns Hopkins University, Baltimore.

Salamon, L and Anheier, H (1993) *The Third Route: Subsidiarity, Third-Party Government and the Provision of Social Services in the United States and Germany*, report to OECD, Paris

Shah, P and M Shah (1995) 'Participatory methods for Increasing NGO accountability: A case study from India', in M Edwards and D Hulme, op cit.

Smillie, I (1995) 'Painting Canadian Roses Red', in M Edwards and D Hulme, op cit.

Smillie, I and Helmich, H (1993) *Non-Governmental Organizations and Governments: Stakeholders for Development*, OECD, Paris.

Smith, B (1990) *More than Altruism: The Politics of Private Foreign Aid*, Princeton University Press, NJ.

Smith, S and Lipsky, M (1993) *Non Profits for hire: The Welfare State in the Age of Contracting*. Harvard University Press, Mass.

Tandon, R (1994) 'Civil society, the state and the role of NGOs', in I Serrano (ed) *Civil Society in the Asia-Pacific Region*, CIVICUS, Washington, DC.

Tandon, R (1995) 'Board games: Governance and accountability in NGOs', in M Edwards and D Hulme, op cit.

Tendler, J (1982) *Turning Private Voluntary Organizations into Development Agencies: Questions for Evaluation*, Evaluation Discussion Paper No 10, US Agency for International Development, Washington, DC.

Tendler, J (1983) *Ventures in the Informal Sector and How They Worked out in Brazil*, Evaluation Special Study No 12, US Agency for International Development, Washington, DC.

Tendler, J (1989) 'Whatever Happened to Poverty Alleviation?', *World Development*, Vol 17, No 7, pp1033–1044.

Uphoff, N (1995) 'Why NGOs are not a third sector', in M Edwards and D Hulme, op cit.

Vivian, J (1994) 'NGOs and sustainable development in Zimbabwe: no magic bullets', *Development and Change*, Vol 25, pp181–209.

Voorhies, S (1993) *Working with Government using World Bank Funds*, World Vision International Staff, Working Paper, No 16.

Wellard, K and Copestake, J (1993) (eds) *NGOs and the State in Africa: Rethinking Roles in Sustainable Agricultural Development*, Routledge, London.

Wils, F (1995) 'Scaling up, mainstreaming and accountability: The challenge for NGOs', in M Edwards and D Hulme, op cit.

Zadek, S and M Gatward (1995) 'Transforming the transnational NGOs: Social auditing or bust?', in M Edwards and D Hulme, op cit.

Beyond the Magic Bullet?
Lessons and Conclusions

Michael Edwards and David Hulme

Clearly, any attempt to identify common conclusions and implications in this debate runs the risk of overgeneralization, particularly given the difficulty of disentangling the effects of official aid and the New Policy Agenda from pre-existing or other related influences. Non-government organization (NGO) and grassroots organization (GRO) performance, accountability and legitimacy are tremendously complex areas. The situation of Sudanese migrant associations described by Pratten and Ali Baldo (1995) provides a particularly good example of these complexities, with all sorts of 'checks and balances' between GROs and their members mediated by history and culture, and dependent on 'contemporary reconstructions of community identity'. Nevertheless, there are some clear and common threads that do seem to indicate that similar influences are at work. At least five sets of conclusions present themselves.

The Influence of the New Policy Agenda – Real or Imagined?

There is certainly evidence from the NGO literature that official aid to NGOs and the roles adopted by NGOs under the New Policy Agenda can distort accountability upwards and overemphasize linear approaches to performance-measurement, with damaging effects on the ability of NGOs to be effective catalysts for social change. Desai and Howes' (1995) account of Apnalaya in Bombay provides some such evidence, but the influence of official aid and external agendas is only one of many factors at work. With or without the New Policy Agenda, strategic accountability is nearly always weaker than functional accountability and downward accountability nearly always weaker than upward accountability. Even among very large NGOs (Southern or Northern) there is to date only limited empirical evidence of a significant fall-off in quality consequent on the growth of official funding, or of an incompatibility between service-provision, advocacy and 'development-as-empowerment'. Certainly, there are individual examples of negative trade-offs – for example, Perera (1995) – but perhaps as Howes and Sattar (1992, p117) put it for the Bangladesh Rural Advancement Committee (BRAC) in Bangladesh, 'when attention is given to building organizational capacities to support programme expansion, there is no inherent contradiction between quality and scale. Bigger can be better.'[1] Such conclusions may simply reflect the fact that we still have insufficient evidence of the impact of current trends to conclude very much at all, and/or that the New Policy Agenda constitutes a *potential* threat to NGO performance and accountability whose real influence is yet to be fully felt, and/or an indication that it is in other areas, such as broader state-society relations, that the real issues will emerge (Hulme and Edwards, 1995). But the evidence we do have suggests that there are certainly no universal relationships between official funding and the 'corruption of NGOs', nor any necessary correlations between NGO size, growth, function and funding.

Overall, the evidence show that it is the *quality of the relationships* between GROs, NGOs, donors and governments that determines whether patterns of funding and accountability promote or impede the wider goals of all these organizations in development. Issues of quantity and size are less important (Fowler, 1991). A partnership approach, which emphasizes participation, learning, reciprocity and transparency, may permit the problems that accompany organizational growth and donor funding to be managed: GRO/NGO performance, legitimacy and accountability need not be eroded. Donors (whether official or Northern non-government organizations (NNGO)) must therefore be encouraged to move towards funding arrangements which provide stability and predictability in the long term, and timeliness and flexibility in the short term (Van der Heijden, 1987). Long-term institutional support requires a 'continual dialogue about objectives and strategies, rather than simply a specification of outputs and targets' (Carroll, 1992, p164) and hasty evaluations by overseas consultants. This is very different from the cut and thrust of the contract culture which (contrary to current thinking in official agencies) may ultimately disable organizations and compromise long-term quality of impact. It may be better to channel official donor funds to NGOs and GROs via an independent public institution which can protect them from undue donor influence, as recommended for the USA (Hellinger et al, 1988, p114) and in other countries (Smillie, 1993; Baron, 1993), or via local NGO networks which can ensure quality control through self-regulation and peer pressure, as in the Philippines (Constantino-David, 1992). Official donors, such as the European Union, the Canadian International Development Agency (CIDA) and the Overseas Development Administration, who are considering more direct funding of NGOs and GROs in the South, need to reflect on the alternatives available to them in this respect, rather than simply expanding their own offices in Southern capitals (Crombrugghe et al, 1993).

The Importance of Negotiation

One of the most striking conclusions to emerge from the NGO literature is the emphasis placed on *negotiation among stakeholders* as a guiding principle for improving NGO accountability in the future. Indeed, Fowler (1995) makes it clear that there can be no improvements without such negotiations, supporting Marsden et al's (1994, p1) earlier understanding of evaluations as 'negotiating points in the process of development'. Increasing the involvement of grassroots constituencies (beneficiaries and supporters) is the only way to correct the weakness of downward accountability which is such a common characteristic of the NGO world. 'Structured involvement' of a wider range of stakeholders can help to resolve many of the dilemmas facing

NGOs and GROs in performance-assessment and accountability, although it will not make these dilemmas disappear. As Shah and Shah (1995) show, increasing the involvement of grassroots stakeholders also opens up the prospect of major changes in roles, responsibilities and accountabilities, and should not be undertaken by agencies who have no serious commitment to reform in their own institutions and structures. But wherever there are multiple constituencies, negotiation may be the only way to deal with differences over performance standards, 'bottom lines', and evaluation results. Since the short-term objectives of different stakeholders are likely to differ, such negotiations should focus on long-term aims and mission if any consensus is to be generated (Drucker, 1990, p110). The concept of 'stakeholders' is not, of course, uncontroversial. Poor people's development is 'their' process, which they must control; to this extent they are 'shareholders' in development, not 'stakeholders' – a situation analagous to Tandon's (1995) distinction between the legitimate involvement of donors in NGO accountability but not in NGO governance.

A related conclusion concerns the importance of informal mechanisms in maintaining legitimacy and accountability. As Pratten and Ali Baldo (1995), and Uphoff (1995) show, these mechanisms can often be very effective – more so than formal (democratic, representative) mechanisms introduced from the outside. This resonates with Carroll's (1992) conclusion that an open, collegial style, and attitudes which encourage bottom-up participation, can help to build organizations which are responsive and accountable to grassroots constituencies, even when they are not formally membership organizations. The possible erosion of such indigenous and informal systems by foreign aid is therefore very worrying.

As Biggs and Neame (1995) point out, the key issue for NGOs in the New Policy Agenda is not how to preserve a 'mythical autonomy', but how to strengthen multiple accountabilities and 'room for manoeuvre' so that they can negotiate more effectively. The 'social audit' methodology described by Zadek and Gatward (1995); the Aga Khan Foundation's participatory monitoring and evaluation framework presented by Shah and Shah (1995); and the checks and balances analysed by Covey (1995) in her work on policy alliances, are practical mechanisms for promoting stakeholder involvement in performance-assessment and strengthening downward (and sideways) accountability. Their example deserves to be followed by other NGOs, governments and official aid agencies.

The 'Baby and the Bathwater'

It is impossible to take part in this debate without being fully appraised of the sheer complexity of NGO performance-assessment and accountability. Clearly, this is an area which is full of difficulties – the problems of identifying impact when individual NGOs and projects are such a small part of the overall picture; how to measure qualitative changes in the strength of institutions or the awareness of individuals; how to deal with the many and often conflicting pressures for different forms of accountability from different directions, and so on. Faced by such a daunting range of problems, there is sometimes a tendency to abandon completely the search for more rigorous performance measures or to establish more sophisticated systems for tracking impact. In our view, this is a mistake, equivalent to 'throwing the baby out with the bathwater and refusing to take the issue of professionalism seriously' (Smillie, 1995). Despite the complexities and uncertainties involved, all agree that the current state of NGO and GRO accountability is unsatisfactory. The search for improvements must go on, even if, as Rondinelli (1993) concludes, accountability has to be restricted to the ways in which NGOs and others use their resources rather than the long-term impact of resource use on development. This poses particular problems for 'strategic accountability' as defined earlier in this chapter.

Finding accurate links between causes and effects is a problem for all development agencies, not just NGOs, and indeed poses a dilemma for social science as a whole as it struggles to emerge from the limitations of its positivist 'Newtonian paradigm' (Uphoff, 1992). But even if individual NGOs find it impossible, for good reason, to measure the long-term impact of their work on broad development trends, they can still improve significantly on their current performance in evaluating learning, institution-building, levels of participation, gender equity, and so on. As Desai and Howes (1995) conclude, 'it may be very difficult to prove success conclusively, but the easier task of demonstrating that (NGOs) have not failed in key areas would in itself represent a considerable advance on the present state of affairs'. There is certainly no room for complacency. If NGOs do not improve significantly in this area, they run the risk of being 'sidelined to a backwater of carping utopianism ... [to be avoided only if they] ... further develop their capacity to identify concrete steps and achievable targets, and to agree on reasonable ways in which these can be measured' (German and Randel, 1994). Drucker's (1990) advice, 'always ask how can we do what we already do better', is a useful reminder of the need to look for practical and incremental improvements even where 'reality is contingent' and impact is so difficult to establish.[2]

Accounting for What?

Although functional specialization is clearly not essential for efficiency, some of problems concerning NGO performance and accountability do seem to be related to an inability among NGOs to decide what they really want to do, or to a mix of functions and tasks that may conflict with each other. The potential contradiction between the organizational characteristics required to perform effectively as a service-provider and as a catalyst of social change and institutional development was highlighted earlier. Similar conflicts may exist between accountability and effectiveness in policy alliances. Equally, however, the reverse may be true, given the need for 'empowerment' approaches to bring material benefits if people's interest is to be sustained. Hence, different functions must be married together successfully. The same is true for NGOs who need to have solid field experience of the issues on which they lobby if they are to remain authoritative and credible (Edwards and Hulme, 1992). This is the key to what Alan Fowler (1993, pp334–335) calls the 'onion-skin approach' – an 'outer layer of welfare-oriented activity that protects inner layers of material service-delivery that act as nuclei for a core strategy dedicated to transformation'. Whether such an integrated strategy would be openly supported by donors or tolerated by governments is another matter, with important implications for the degree of transparency afforded to different accountabilities.

The Management of Accountability

Because stakeholder perceptions inevitably differ and NGOs are subject to so many conflicting pressures, the dilemmas of accountability identified above cannot be 'solved' – they have to be *managed*. For example, Northern NGOs will always remain accountable to their donors and supporters, as well as to their partners, and, to some extent, to the beneficiaries of their work. As the example of Apnalaya in Bombay shows, managing multiple funding sources and therefore accountabilities is already normal practice in many NGOs (Desai and Howes, 1995). Official aid agencies, while they may move towards less 'linear' approaches to development, will have to satisfy the demand for 'results' which comes from their political paymasters. Many NGOs *choose* to work across national boundaries, sectors of work, service-delivery and other approaches to development; they do not see these choices as mutually exclusive. In other words, these are management issues rather than issues of principle. As Commins (1995) puts it, 'it is possible to remain operationally accountable to governments in terms of use of funds and yet remain accountable to the low-income communities where the NGO is carrying out programmes'. Chief among the factors which enable NGOs to manage these dilemmas effectively are: a strong sense of mission and attachment to values and principles; effective learning and action research (Hasan, 1993; Wils et al, 1993); local-level institution building and high levels of participation (Riddell and Robinson, 1992); effective management, strategic planning and accountability mechanisms; skilled and committed staff; and a favourable external environment (progressive donors, open governments and strong links with other NGOs). This in turn requires organizational structures and cultures which encourage learning, accountability and experimentation – organically structured organizations which are decentralized, problem-solving and task-oriented (Wierdsma and Swieringha, 1992; Fowler, 1988; Edwards, 1994; Beets, Neggers and Wils, 1988). Underlying these characteristics are some deeper traits, which include a willingness by NGO staff to hand over more control to partners and/or beneficiaries, and an ability to live with non-standardised responses and procedures in order to promote flexibility and experimentation – the 'open systems' approach to development work recommended by Chambers (1995), Uphoff and Fowler (1995). With these features in place, NGOs can analyse strategic choices about cooperation with donors or governments, or indeed any decision on programming, and identify those that are likely to weaken their comparative advantages or relations with beneficiaries (Fowler, 1988, p22). They will also be in a better position to prevent a 'law of diminishing returns' from setting in when increasing bureaucracy threatens to reduce the value added by each increment in funding.

The Future of NGOs?

What implications do these findings have for the future of NGOs and their role in development? The first point to make is that without effective performance-assessment and strong, multiple accountability mechanisms, no NGO is likely to be able to find its way through the increasingly complex maze constituted by the world of development assistance, nor to find and maintain the right balance between the opportunities and dangers afforded to NGOs as the 'favoured child' of official aid. Weak or distorted accountability, and an inability to demonstrate impact and effectiveness in a reasonably rigorous manner (where this is possible) are likely to leave NGOs more vulnerable to cooption into the agendas of others, or simply to lead them into areas where they are not doing very much that is useful. Improving performance-assessment and accountability is not an 'optional extra' for NGOs; it is central to their continued existence as independent organizations with a mission to pursue. However, judged by the meagre level of resources devoted to organizational development in these areas and the reluctance of NGOs to innovate, an independent observer would have to conclude that most were not seriously concerned with accountability at all. Despite record increases in income between 1984 and 1994, very few NGOs (North or South) have invested sufficiently in evaluation, learning, research and dissemination; nor have they become more transparent or accountable to their different constituencies. This is despite the fact that their 'continued existence depends on the belief by staff and supporters that they are ethical according to explicit values and principles' (Zadek and Gatward, 1995).

Second, many of the problems facing NGOs in this field (less so GROs) arise because NGOs are *problematic organizations*. By their very nature, NGOs must live and work in situations of necessary ambiguity. Some of these ambiguities are the result of the characteristics of NGOs as a form of organization – accountable to trustees in one country but working with communities in others; committed to fundamental reforms but funded by donors and supporters who (by and large) demand short-term results; wanting to 'democratize development' but forbidden from entering formal politics. Others are a matter of choice, as, for example, when an NGO decides to work across a range of approaches embracing service delivery, institutional development and advocacy, each of which may require different funding mechanisms, organizational structures, skills and timescales. Faced by these potential contradictions, it has become fashionable to conclude that NGOs must choose to be one thing or another–either they are 'public service contractors' or 'citizens' movements' (Korten, 1990); a 'first force' which 'harnesses independent energy for a moral purpose' or a 'third force' acting as sub-contractors to the state (Knight, 1993); organizations which are 'market-led' or 'values-based' (Robinson, 1995).

However, there is good reason to believe that such conclusions are misplaced, although no doubt there will be certain NGOs (as there already are) which do fall clearly and consciously into one category or another. Social justice requires that people be liberated from the conditions of material poverty as well as being able to organize themselves to defend their rights, and different sorts of organization will be more or less effective in promoting these goals according to context and circumstance. The scale of material poverty and the size of gaps in access to basic services in many of the world's poor countries requires that NGOs continue to play a significant role in service provision and 'welfare', although clearly this cannot be in permanent substitution for the state if progress is to be equitable and sustainable. At the same time, it is perfectly possible (although perhaps increasingly difficult) to innovate and to retain a sense of mission, a high level of independence, and an attachment to values and principles. There are many NGOs which play a major role in social organization, awareness-raising and advocacy, just as there are many GROs which aim to support material improvements in their members' lives. Indeed, there are strong arguments (some outlined above) to suggest that these functions are best combined together. If this is true, then the future of NGOs and GROs may be dominated by two developments: the rise of the 'legitimate hybrid', to use Korten's (1990, p105) terms; and the evolution of national and international networks, alliances and federations in which organizations with different roles and characteristics work synergistically to achieve common long-term goals.

In this sense, the future of Northern NGOs may resemble the 'new internationalist conglomerates' envisioned by Zadek and Gatward (1995). The lessons generated by the Institute for Development Research's work on international policy alliances and the importance of the 'bridging role' for NGOs which their research highlights, are extremely relevant here (Covey, 1995). This does not mean that difficult questions of legitimacy and accountability can be ducked – differences in these areas between, for example, membership and non-membership organizations will remain, and the dilemmas of performance and accountability highlighted earlier will still have to be managed. However, variations in needs, context, funding sources, organizational competences, legal and regulatory systems, supporter profiles, donor attitudes, tradition and politics point to a necessary focus on partnership, effectiveness and learning, rather than on particular organizational forms which are deemed 'right or wrong', 'good or bad'. As Nielsen (in Keating, 1994, p73) puts it, 'the landscape of the third sector is untidy but wonderfully exuberant. What counts is not the confusion, but the profusion.'

These observations do not mean that 'all is well' in the world of NGOs, particularly NGOs based in the North. Far from it: criticisms of NNGO performance and accountability surface regularly throughout this book, and they cannot be ignored. The complacency born of ten years of relatively easy fund-raising between 1984 and 1994 must give way to more serious reflection and openness to change. As Southern NGOs grow in number and authority (opening their own offices 'overseas', as BRAC has done in Kenya and as Filipino and African NGOs are doing in Washington), and as an increasingly integrated global economy throws up new challenges to NNGOs in their own 'backyard', Northern NGOs are bound to come under increasing pressure to take partnership and accountability more seriously. As Bebbington and Riddell (1995) put it, the challenge to NNGOs is to 'define a role that can help to enhance the impact of the work of their Southern partners, and define it *with them*'. Joint advocacy, 'fair trading', facilitating access to specific expertise and information, and domestic development work, are examples of what these roles might be, redirecting NNGOs to address those parts of the global problematic of exclusion which they can tackle most effectively. As Bejar and Oakley (1995) put it, the key task is to 'abandon unequal relationships between donors and recipients in favour of an effective South–North dialogue around common and practical tasks: to move from accountability to shared responsibility'. Much more effort must go into support to local fund-raising and other means of promoting the financial independence of NGOs in the South, which Biekart (1995) sees as central if legitimacy and accountability are to be strengthened in the longer term. As in all 'open systems', to achieve real impact NGOs must focus more on changing relationships between people and institutions, and the values on which they are based, and less on shifting small, but growing, amounts of funding from one part of the world to another. The changes implied by such a shift will be slow and difficult, not least because of the need to bring NNGO constituencies along to provide consistent and independent support to this transition. If NNGOs have not already started to do this (and most have not), then they need to do so *now*.

In this process the questions of legitimacy, identity and governance take centre stage; these questions are even more demanding than issues of performance and accountability, for they go right to the heart of the NGO and its mission: most obviously, 'What are NGOs for in the 21st century?' Clearly, there can be no one answer to this question, but thus far few NNGOs have even faced up to the question itself, preferring instead to decentralize their management functions within existing, Northern-controlled, structures of governance. Of course, NGOs will adapt to the demands of a changing world, as they have done in the past, but will they adapt enough? Unless NNGOs begin to face up to the challenges of a new millennium quickly; unless they begin to redefine a role for themselves which recognizes what is happening in the world around them; and unless they begin to take accountability much more seriously, they are likely to be bypassed in the future by governments, official agencies, citizens' movements, and perhaps even by their own supporters. NGOs have spent too much time criticizing others and not enough time 'putting their own house in order'. Despite their rhetoric, no NNGO is seriously trying to 'work itself out of a job', and, sadly, most give the impression that only a financial crisis will be enough to enforce more fundamental changes in this direction. No matter how effective NGOs are technically in monitoring and evaluation, strategic planning, or managing multiple accountabilities, hard decisions will still need to be made about future roles and responsibilities. Moving away from operational work (and the large official grants that come with it) will inevitably mean a reduction in income for NNGOs. But perhaps a recognition of the 'limits to growth' is no bad thing, if it provides NNGOs with the room they seem to need for more profound reflection on their future, a greater commitment to issues of quality in their work, and the courage and vision they need to rethink and reform their roles into the 21st century.

In this task personal accountability is going to be essential, given the inertia which characterizes all large NGOs, the resistance they will put up to change, and the temptations for NGO managers provided by organizational growth and the status of size. All organizations and all individuals within them possess some room for manoeuvre which can be used to promote incremental reform, transparency, learning and sharing. As Chambers (1995) puts it, 'if primacy were accorded to the personal, would the problems of performance and accountability largely be resolved?'. Perhaps not, given the dilemmas which face NGOs and the inherent difficulties of measuring performance and managing multiple accountabilities, but without an acceptance of personal responsibility and the determination to be accountable individually, there will be no resolution of these dilemmas and certainly no improvement in NGO performance. Moves in this direction, towards the 'open systems' mode of thinking and acting would be in the very best NGO tradition – innovation, solidarity and humility.

The focus of this chapter on the New Policy Agenda and the influence of official aid may have led us to underestimate the influence of endogenous factors, and to overestimate the negative impact of donor funding, but it is on this basis that we posit that the modes of programming of NGO and GRO operations, of defining performance indicators, of claiming legitimacy and of accounting for achievements, are being reshaped. From a neo-liberal perspective, the emergence of NGOs and GROs is desirable for its contribution to economic efficiency and political pluralism, although it may only be transitional as the commercial sector evolves and effective interest groups crystallize. From a radical perspective, it may be cooption: the abandonment of a mission for social transformation to become the implementer of the New Policy Agenda. If this *is* what is happening, then perhaps the best that can be hoped for is that the bubble will burst and that NGOs and GROs may then return to their former position – smaller and less lauded, but more independent and effective as agents of social change. The present popularity of NGOs with donors will not last forever: donors move from fad to fad and at some stage NGOs, like flared jeans, will become less fashionable. When this happens, the developmental impact of NGOs, their capacity to attract support and their legitimacy as actors in development, will rest much more clearly on their ability to demonstrate that they can perform effectively and that they are accountable for their actions. It is none too soon for NGOs to get their 'houses in order'; rethinking and reforming accountability – moving 'beyond the magic bullet' – is central to this challenge.

Notes

1   In reality, it is difficult to know whether such conclusions are accurate, since independent empirical evidence is very scarce. There is anecdotal evidence that the credit repayment rates and other impact indicators publicized by large NGOs in South Asia, including BRAC, are exaggerated, but insufficient evidence exists to confirm this view. Independent evidence in this area is urgently needed.
2   The key here is to experiment in practice with as wide a range as possible of different techniques for monitoring and to evaluation, and learn from these experiences. Save the Children-UK has recently published a 'toolkit on assessment, monitoring, review and evaluation which provides a useful foundation for such a process.

References

Baron, B (1993) *Innovation and Future Directions in East Asian Philanthropy: Strengthening the Public/Private Interface*, Asia Foundation, San Francisco.

Beets, N, Neggers, J and Wils, J (1988) *Big and Still Beautiful: Enquiry in the Efficiency and Effectiveness of Three Big NGOs (BINGOs) in South Asia*, Programme Evaluation NR32, DGIS/Novib.

Commins, S (1995) 'Too close for comfort?', in D Hulme and M Edwards (eds), *NGOs – Performance and Accountability: Beyond the Magic Bullet*, Earthscan, London.

Constantino-David, K (1992) 'The Philippine experience in scaling-up', in M Edwards and D Hulme (eds) *Making a Difference: NGOs and Development in a Changing World*, Earthscan/SCF, London.

Crombrugghe, G, Douxchamps, F and Stampa, N (1993) *Evaluation of EC–NGO Co-financing in Relation to Institutional Support for Grassroots Organizations in Developing Countries,* COTA, Brussels.

Keating, M (1994) 'North America's independent sector', in CIVICUS, *Citizens Strengthening Global Civil Society,* Washington, DC.

Knight, B (1993) *Voluntary Action,* CENTRIS, London.

Perera J (1995) 'Unequal dialogue with donors: the Sarvodaya experience', in D Hulme and M Edwards, op cit.

Robinson, M (1995) 'NGOs as public service contractors', in D Hulme and M Edwards (eds), op cit.

Rondinelli, D (1993) *Strategic and Results-based Management in CIDA: Reflections on the Process,* Canadian International Development Agency, Ottawa.

Smillie, I (1993) *From Partners to Stakeholders: The CIDA-NGO Challenge,* Ottawa (mimeo).

Uphoff, N (1992) *Learning from Gal Oya: Possibilities for Participatory Development and Post-Newtonian Social Science,* Cornell University Press, Ithaca, New York.

Wierdsma, A and Swieringha, J (1992) *Becoming a Learning Organization,* Addison-Wesley, London.

Wils, F, Maddin, V, Alexander, K and Sohoni, N (1993) *AWARE and its Work with Tribals and Harijans in Andhra Pradesh,* Institute of Social Studies, The Hague.

Van der Heijden, H (1987) 'The reconciliation of NGO autonomy and operational effectiveness with accountability to donors', *World Development,* Vol 15, supplement, pp103–112.

'Board Games': Governance and Accountability in NGOs

Rajesh Tandon

There has been considerable recent debate among donors and NGOs on the issue of accountability (Edwards and Hulme, 1994). However, there is as yet no agreed definition of accountability for non-government organizations (NGOs). While all parties aspire to a comprehensive view of the subject, in most practical situations NGO accountability boils down to the domain of finance. This narrow operational definition is partly a consequence of the ease of establishing specific and quantifiable criteria for measuring financial accountability. It is also partly due to the fact that donors (and other resource providers) have been the most vocal commentators on the issue. The regulatory dimension of accountability has also been emphasized in many contexts (including India), being narrowly defined in relation to finance (submitting regular financial reports which are externally certified to ensure legitimacy). The regulatory context in which an NGO operates defines the laws, rules and procedures that prescribe parameters and behaviours relevant to NGO accountability. For a detailed analysis of these regulatory aspects in India, see Tandon (1989).

Therefore it is not surprising to find elaborate mechanisms and regulations being proposed and imposed to improve NGO accountability. This has been a recent trend in India where several European NGO donors (most notably EZE of Germany) have started to create formal, local and professional mechanisms for close monitoring and reporting of the financial aspects of the NGOs they support. However, the need to examine this issue from a wider conceptual perspective continues. As actors within civil society, NGOs are autonomous institutions inspired by a particular vision of the society they wish to see develop, pursuing their defined mission in that regard (Tandon, 1991). Thus NGOs find themselves in a web of complex interactions in a particular context. The concept of multiple 'stakeholders' helps to further our understanding of NGO accountability. The constituency which is the focus of NGO interventions could be seen as one such stakeholder. When this constituency comprises of a local community where NGO programmes are carried out, further differentiation arises, creating multiple interests or 'stakes' within the broad category of community stakeholders. Donors and other resource-providers have a stake in the outcomes of NGO performance too. There is often a chain of donors, each being accountable to the next level in their hierarchies, thereby further expanding this aspect of stakeholdership. In this complex web of stakeholders one aspect of NGO accountability that is often neglected is that which relates to the NGO's own governance. There has been considerable discussion, training and codification of practice with respect to NGO governance in many countries in the North (as can be seen from the vast literature that has been produced by institutions such as the National

Centre for Non-Profit Boards in the USA). But this has been a neglected area of attention and debate in most countries of the South (and in particular, in South Asia). Therefore, this chapter elaborates the different forms of NGO governance which exist in South Asia, examines the linkages between them and NGO accountability, and raises a number of questions in relation to the need to strengthen NGO governance from the perspective of performance, accountability and institutional development.

NGO Governance

The governance of NGOs implies the totality of functions that are required to be carried out in relation to the internal functioning and external relations of organizations. It is not the same as NGO management. The governance of NGOs focuses on issues of policy and identity, rather than the issues of day-to-day implementation of programmes. Thus, governance implies addressing the issue of NGO vision, mission and strategy; it focuses on future directions and long-term strategic considerations; it addresses the issues of policy in relation to internal programming, staffing and resources; it defines norms and values that are the basis of institutional functioning; it includes obligations entailed in fulfilling statutory requirements applicable to the NGO; and focuses on defining the external positions that are consistent with the overall thrust of the NGO as an institution in civil society. Most importantly, the governance of an NGO is concerned with its effective functioning and performance in society. This is both a legal and a moral obligation. Therefore, governance requires the creation of structures and processes which enable the NGO to monitor performance and remain accountable to its stakeholders. In the 'for-profit' sector, most criteria for performance are monetary. In the case of NGOs, however, they are based on vision, mission and values. To that extent, creating and sustaining appropriate structures and processes of governance in an NGO is a much more complex and challenging task.

Forms of Governance

In the case of most voluntary development organizations and NGOs in South Asia, certain patterns of governance reoccur regularly. For those NGOs which are legally incorporated, statutory forms of governance provide the basic framework. The two most common statutory forms are the *Society* and the *Trust* (Tandon, 1987), which prescribe mechanisms for the purposes of governance in legal terms. This mechanism is variously called the Executive Council or Committee, Governing Board, and so on. Also included are statutorily identified positions such as Chief Executive Officer (CEO), variously labelled as Secretary, President, Convener, Coordinator, Director or Executive Director. The legal basis of these structures dates back to the colonial period in the Indian subcontinent, and so much of the details of these statutes date back to the 19th century. The present reality of such forms of governance poses serious questions in relation to the efficacy and effectiveness of governing mechanisms. Current practice displays a range of behaviour of what could be called 'board games', described below and concretised, each with a case study from South Asian experience.

Family boards

One of the common characteristics of many NGO boards is their family character. In both composition and style of functioning, these boards operate like a family, with all the necessary informality, affection and trust that a family-held small business demonstrates. At the formative stage, such boards provide support (emotional, physical and material) for the launching and stabilization of the NGO. However, they do have limitations in situations of growth and expansion; they also demonstrate the behaviour characteristic of a patriarch in a family-run business in the face of assertion by his offspring. When new staff or volunteers begin to feel a part of such an organization, family boards are unable to provide a competent governing mechanism.

Case study

Grameen Vikas Samiti in North Bihar was set up as a voluntary organization in 1978 by Sudhanshu Misra. Misra was very active in the student movement inspired by Jayaprakash Narayan. When the Janata government in Delhi failed to deliver, Misra (and many others like him) felt disillusioned by party politics. His commitment to organize and empower the landless rural poor led to the rapid acceptance and growth of Grameen Vikas Samiti. When the Samiti was incorporated, Misra asked some of his family (wife, brother, father) to be cosignatories. Later, his wife's brother and his brother's wife also joined the Managing Committee. When the Samiti undertook an adult education programme in 1979, it recruited a full-time staff of 35 and 300 part-time teachers. The Samiti grew rapidly, but due to a sudden change in government policy, all adult education projects had to be wound up. This created a difficult situation for Misra as he could no longer pay his staff. When he announced the decision that most staff had to leave the Samiti, Misra was abused and demonstrations were mounted against him.

Invisible boards

Many NGOs have a largely invisible board comprising a small coterie of friends and family, assembled by the founder(s), merely for the purposes of meeting statutory requirements on paper. The actual functions of governance are carried out by the founder(s), with or without the help of other staff in the NGO, and the board merely acts as a 'rubber-stamp'. It is not uncommon to come across examples where the board does not meet for many years and the founder(s) merely obtains the thumbprint of board members on the minute book from time to time. Such a situation clearly provides the founder(s) with the ease of pursuing his or her vision with speed and energy, unencumbered by the usual hurdles related to paperwork and bureaucracy. However, in situations where the founder(s) needs advice or support, the invisible board remains both invisible and inaudible. In addition, the absence of a clear separation between governance and management in such organizations reduces the avenues available for internal accountability.

Case study

Abhay Singh was a student activist in Osmania University, Hyderabad, who decided to work with tribal groups, and particularly in strengthening tribal knowledge, culture and art. He set up the Institute for Socio-Cultural Development in Hyderabad to support this work. Since he spent most of his time in the villages, he requested three of his college friends (now teachers in Hyderabad) to join the Governing Council of the Institute. The positive impact of Singh's work resulted in a grant to develop a large three-year project focusing on tribal culture. This grant helped Singh to set up a small residence-cum-office in the tribal area, recruit 10 outside students, and train nearly 30 tribal youths as part-time animators. Nearly two years after the project began, Singh and two of his colleagues were abducted by a militant Naxalite group active in the area. The media coverage of the incident resulted in a number of enquiries from the government about the Institute. When the Commissioner of Police in Hyderabad asked the three teachers (on the Governing Council of the Institute) to bring the Institute's files, documents and minute books to help the police in their search for clues to assist in tracing Singh's abductors, they pleaded complete ignorance of any of the organization's paperwork.

Staff boards

It is quite common for NGOs in South Asia to have a board largely comprised of current staff. Where an NGO has been set up by a group of people in pursuit of a shared vision, they themselves decide to become the board. In other cases, senior staff members are brought on to the board subsequently, similar to the concept of board representation by trade union/worker representatives on the boards of 'for-profit' corporations. Such boards are very effective in ensuring a shared vision and a common perspective on the direction of the NGO; there is also a collective commitment by the board towards the well-being of the organization. These boards also help in the process of building and strengthening the stake which staff feel they hold in the future of the NGO. However, one of the major problems which arises in such cases is the confusion over, and the blurring of, the distinctions between the requirements of governance and the needs of day-to-day management. It is not uncommon to find situations in which staff confuse programmatic accountability to the CEO with shared responsibility for governance. In many such cases, staff representation on the board gets bogged down in issues related to the interests of the staff, sometimes at the expense of larger institutional concerns (a situation not too different from those corporations where workers' representatives were nominated to the board). Also, in situations where serious ideological, programmatic or perceptual disagreements emerge among senior staff in the organization (a situation that is widespread in the functioning of most NGOs), the governing mechanism is unable to deal with disagreements rationally, since the conflict is brought forward and replayed in the board itself.

Such boards are also unable to provide a fresh, objective and balanced perspective on the strategies, programmes and functioning of the organization. The staff develop perceptual blocks and vested interests in pursuing particular strategies and programmes; and these remain unquestioned by such a board because it is comprised mostly of staff themselves.

Case study
*Akriiti Sanathan in Gujarat was set up by five social workers who had worked to-
gether previously in a large rural development agency. They decided to create a new
organization in another district where they worked with women agricultural labourers. The Executive Committee of the Sansthan was made up by the five founding
members. After five years of intensive work, the state government offered the Sansthan
a large grant for integrated rural development in 250 villages in the area. Within the
agency, debates within this 'gang of five' over whether to accept this offer became
polarised around two personalities. An embryonic leadership struggle surfaced and
divided the entire staff. Over the next two months, the Sansthan's fieldwork came to
a standstill while the debate and conflict intensified. One of the five founders was
acting as Secretary of the Sansthan and one day signed a contract with the government to accept their offer. A week later, two of the original founders and 13 other staff
left the Sansthan and created another voluntary organization a few blocks away.*

Professional boards

The composition of these boards is based largely on the shared vision of a set of
like-minded people, but also includes consideration of the professional and strategic requirements of the institution. In such situations, the composition and functioning
of the board exhibits a more formal character: board appointments are made with
careful consideration of the requirements and future direction of the institution.
The board has a formal system of meetings, discussions, decision-making and
recording (agenda papers, minutes and so on); members take individual and collective
responsibility for different aspects of governance (such as subcommittees, and the
roles of Chair, Treasurer and Secretary); the performance audit and review of the
institution as well as that of the CEO and other senior staff is undertaken by the
board on a regular and formal basis; and the institution is represented in external
fora by different members of the board.

Such boards tend to provide ongoing professional direction to the institution and
to help shape its policies and strategies in a more rational and coherent manner. In
situations of stability, they ensure the periodic assessment of mission and strategy,
and its translation into programmes and internal mechanisms. In situations of crisis,
such boards are able to take on the true function of governance, rising above day-to-
day management. However, in many cases it has proven difficult to generate and sustain
a shared vision in such a board, particularly when the board functions merely as a
collection of well-meaning and concerned individuals (and not as a coherent, unified
and effective group acting together). It is also difficult to generate and sustain the
commitment of the board as a stakeholder, particularly when individual board members do not serve on the board for long periods of time. Other studies tend to confirm
these observations for NGOs elsewhere in the world (Billis and Mackeith, 1993).

Case study
*Sita graduated with a Masters degree in social work from the Tata Institute of Social
Studies in 1970. She worked in a voluntary organization outside Bombay among rural women, helping to organize a dairy cooperative. Later, she moved back to Bombay
to set up an NGO called 'Creative Development' to assist women's groups to under-*

take livelihood projects. Sita decided to seek the advice of a few colleagues and in the process insisted that they join the governing board of Creative Development. These board members were: a professor from the National Institute of Bank Management, a scientist from the Indian Council of Agricultural Research, a graduate from the Indian Institute of Management currently working with Lever Brothers in Bombay, the directors of two other rural development NGOs from Maharashtra, and her favourite professor from the Tata Institute. During the first year, the board met three times to elaborate a set of policies which enabled Sita to carry forward the programme.

Even from this brief typology, it is clear that the form and functioning of governance mechanisms in many South Asian NGOs is inadequate from the perspective of accountability. Where the board is 'sleeping' or invisible, the full spectrum of governance functions cannot be performed properly. In many other situations, the style of functioning of the board also results in the curtailment of governance. Weaknesses in governance limit the possibilities of continuous, objective and appropriate feedback to the implementation and management functions of the NGO, including to the CEO.

Other Issues

A key issue in the arena of governance arises in situations where the founder is the leader of the NGO for a substantial period of time. By its very nature the NGO begins to reflect the vision and perspective of its founder; its culture and programmes imbibe the style and background of the founder too. Over a period of time, the NGO's identity becomes very closely linked to the person of the founder-leader. In such situations the board is initially assembled by the founder, and most board members are individually known to and associated with the founder-leader. This has the potential to limit the autonomous identity of the board (even in the case of a professional board) and creates a particular set of dynamics. On the one hand, the founder-leader provides the bulk of the energy and ideas for the NGO, thereby building up 'sweat-equity'; on the other hand, the long-term sustainability of the NGO requires the institutionalization of energy and ideas beyond one person. The conduct of the totality of the functions of governance in such circumstances poses a range of interesting and practical challenges.

The second issue of relevance to this discussion is the fact that *priorities in governance in an NGO change over time.* In the early formative stages, defining the vision and mission, and building a programme, takes precedence; once established, the NGO turns its attention to issues of growth in size, coverage and resources. The life-cycle of an NGO determines the priority which issues take in its governance. Thus, the composition and functioning of the board tend to be more informal and spontaneous at the formative stage; this helps in providing support and space for the founder(s). During the phase of growth and consolidation, the board needs to acquire greater formality and professionalization in its structure and processes. This *temporal* dimension of governance requires understanding and attention if effectiveness and accountability are to be maintained.

Another issue in NGO governance that is gaining increasing currency (particularly with donor agencies) is the active role of different stakeholders. It is being repeatedly argued by some donors that beneficiary-participation and representation on boards is crucial to ensure NGO accountability to their 'clientele'. Some donors even ask for evidence of this at the time of approving a grant. In response, some NGOs provide for a 'token' beneficiary representation on their boards. A similar argument is often made for including donor representatives on the governing structure. Even governmental funding and regulatory agencies sometimes ask for this as a matter of right. For example, some states in India have attempted to incorporate such a requirement in their modified Society Registration Acts. Rather than simply acceding to these demands from donors and regulators, some NGOs have experimented with creative solutions to these demands.

In the case of the (legitimate) need for beneficiary participation in the planning and implementation of NGO programmes, this can be, and is being, carried out through systematic consultation and participation mechanisms on the ground. In the case of (legitimate) donor concerns to make an input into the direction and programmes of the NGOs it supports, regular joint review and planning fora are common practice. However, the demands of regulatory agencies are clearly aimed at strengthening controls over NGOs and should not be seen as legitimate merely for the purposes of regulation.

It is important to distinguish here between the concept of stakeholders and the concept of governance. A stakeholder, by definition, is any party which has a stake in the outcomes of an NGO. In this sense, beneficiaries, donors and regulators are all stakeholders, as are other NGOs and NGO staff. However, their stakes relate to the performance of the institution, not to its governance directly. Hence, their demands for access to the institutional governance of the NGO lies through the requirement that the NGO performs effectively. This is where *critical and regular performance monitoring* by stakeholders is the key to ensuring the accountability of the NGO to them. This situation is somewhat akin to that in 'for-profit' corporations, where consumers of its products or services have a stake and therefore a right to corporate accountability, without needing to be part of the formal governance mechanism of the company. Donors to NGOs are supporters of desirable processes and outcomes, whose interests and concerns must be matched by the performance of the NGO in order for resources to continue to flow. A major cause of ambiguity at present, however, is that undue importance is given to the existence of a shared vision and perspective among NGO and donor, and less emphasis is placed on the performance and results obtained. Accountability to donors needs to be more clearly related to output indicators than is the case in current practice, and not to NGO governance. Innovative practices and ongoing documentation of the best practice are needed to promote better performance accountability. Social audits provide one such approach (Zadek and Gatward, 1995).

Linkages to Accountability

In the light of this discussion, it is important to understand the linkages which exist between NGO governance and accountability. NGO accountability is related to three dimensions:

1 *Accountability vis-à-vis its mission:* as an institution oriented to social change within the framework of civil society, an NGO needs to define, refine and pursue a clear mission.
2 *Accountability vis-à-vis its performance in relation to that mission:* demonstrable performance, both in process and outcome terms, is essential to generate feedback to the programmes and approaches implemented in a given time frame.
3 *Accountability vis-a-vis its role as an actor in the civil society:* norms, rules and styles of functioning that match standards of being a good civic institution.

In all three respects, the governance of an NGO is a critical element. An effective system of governance enables an NGO to formulate, review and reformulate its mission in a changing context. 'Good governance' ensures that programmes follow the requirements of the NGO's mission; promotes a performance orientation and accountability in the institution; and requires that the values (integrity, participation, professionalism, quality, commitment), statutes (reporting and legal standards and procedures) and norms of socially concerned civic institutions are articulated, practised and promoted. An effective structure and process of governance in an NGO is absolutely critical for ensuring accountability in this wider sense.

Even in its narrow sense, financial and statutory accountability requires an active, alert and functioning board which feels both a legal and a moral obligation in these regards. Such a board provides a set of measures needed in the organization to ensure the necessary checks and balances for proper recording and reporting according to agreed targets and rules.

PRIA 's governing board has been conscious of developing standards and procedures of good governance over the years. Programme monitoring and review is carried out at least annually by a group of partners and concerned professionals. The board conducts annual organizational and staff reviews. A separate annual performance review of the Executive Director is carried out by the board. Over the past 14 years, PRIA has had three external evaluations. The board coordinates and facilitates these evaluations. A system of monthly internal audits by an external professional is used to generate feedback on financial management. The treasurer also reviews these reports with the Executive Director. During the years, PRIA's governing board has established high-quality formal policies of human resource management. Many of these policies, systems and procedures have become models of good practice for other NGOs in the region. The norms and procedures for the functioning of the governing board are continuously evolved, upgraded and established.

In recent years, donors and regulators (such as government agencies) have demanded better performance with respect to NGO goals and programmes. In the post-Cold War world, there are going to be even greater demands for 'demonstrable' performance. This will require better documentation of existing performance, as well as the enhanced, transparent and critical functioning of mechanisms for NGO governance. In this sense, performance, accountability and governance are likely to become linked with each other more and more closely. Particular attention needs to be given to improving this linkage in operational terms so that NGOs can face the challenges which are emerging proactively.

Future Challenges

Inadequate attention is being paid to the issue of effective governance in NGOs in many countries of South Asia today. It is of crucial importance that NGOs, their supporters and their donors begin to understand the meaning and significance of effective governance and its contribution to NGO accountability. There is also a need to document, analyse and promote good practice in relation to NGO governance and accountability. Such interventions need to be viewed as part of the fabric of institutional development efforts needed to strengthen an NGO. Strategic planning and capacity-building need to include interventions directed at making its structures and processes of governance more effective. A number of such efforts, studies and manuals developed and used in countries in the North can help to clarify and support this challenge in the South (Conrad and Glenn, 1976).

While a basic understanding of NGO governance already exists in most countries, considerable ambiguity remains with respect to the situation of NGO networks and associations. The considerations discussed in this chapter become even more complex when applied to a body that brings together a set of independent and autonomous institutions. Much of the practical experience with governance in such associations has been unproductive and frustrating. There is much useful experience in other countries from which our current understanding and practices could benefit. There is also a need to develop educational programmes and learning materials on the theme of NGO governance so as to strengthen NGO practice. The growing emphasis on NGO performance and accountability *must* include the challenge of making NGO governance more effective.

References

Billis, D and Mackeith, J (1993) *Organizing NGOs*, Centre for Voluntary Organization, London School of Economics, London.

Conrad, W R and Glenn, W E (1976) *The Effective Voluntary Board of Directors*, Ohio University Press, Athens.

Edwards, M and Hulme, D (1994) *NGOs and Development: Performance and Accountability in the 'New World Order'*, background paper to the international workshop at the University of Manchester, 27–29 June.

Tandon, R (1987) *Forms of Organizations: Square Pegs in Round Holes*, PRIA, New Delhi.

Tandon, R (1989) *Management of Voluntary Organizations*, PRIA, New Delhi.

Tandon, R (1991) *NGOs, the State and the Civil Society*, IDR Occasional Paper Series, Boston, Mass.

Zadek, S and Gatward, M (1995) 'Transforming the transnational NGOs: social auditing or bust?', in M Edwards and D Hulme (eds) *NGOs–Performance and Accountability: Beyond the Magic Bullet*, Earthscan, London.

Part 5

Organizing for Good Development Practice: Participation, Empowerment, Partnering and Capacity-building

Paradoxes of Participation: Questioning Participatory Approaches to Development

Frances Cleaver

Introduction

This chapter suggests that the concepts underlying participatory approaches to development should be subject to greater critical analysis. Drawing on research on water resource management in sub-Saharan Africa and on social theory concerning the recursive relationship between agency and structure, it illustrates the need for a more complex understanding of the issues of efficiency and empowerment in participatory approaches. Particularly, two key concepts are examined: ideas about the nature and role of institutions and models of individual action. The article concludes by identifying the questions such an analysis raises about the relationships between community, social capital and the state.

Participation in Development Discourse

Heroic claims are made for participatory approaches to development, these being justified in terms of ensuring greater efficiency and effectiveness of investment and of contributing to processes of democratization and empowerment. The conundrum of ensuring the sustainability of development interventions is assumed to be solvable by the proper involvement of beneficiaries in the supply and management of resources, services and facilities.

However, despite significant claims to the contrary, there is little evidence of the long-term effectiveness of participation in materially improving the conditions of the most vulnerable people or as a strategy for social change. While the evidence for efficiency receives some support on a small scale, the evidence regarding empowerment and sustainability is more partial, tenuous and reliant on the assertions of the rightness of the approach and process rather than convincing proof of outcomes.

Participation has therefore become an act of faith in development; something we believe in and rarely question. This act of faith is based on three main tenets: that participation is intrinsically a 'good thing' (especially for the participants), that a focus on 'getting the techniques right' is the principal way of ensuring the success of such approaches and that considerations of power and politics on the whole should be avoided as divisive and obstructive.

In questioning these it is not my intention, as some critics have suggested, to deny the usefulness of a people-centred orientation in development, nor to dismiss all attempts at community-based development as well-meaning but ineffectual. Rather I hope to subject such approaches to critical analysis in the belief that this is equally as important as constant assertions of their strengths.

This chapter outlines some of the conceptual underpinnings of participatory approaches and illustrates how the translation of these into policy and practice is not necessarily consistent with the desired impacts. In doing this I have drawn on insights derived from my previous work on the collective management of water resources which is referred to in more detail elsewhere (Cleaver, 1998b; 1998c; Cleaver (ed), 1998).

Efficiency or empowerment?

The theorizing of participatory approaches is often dichotomized into means/ends classifications (Oakley et al, 1991; Nelson and Wright, 1995). These distinguish between the efficiency arguments (participation as a tool for achieving better project outcomes) and equity and empowerment arguments (participation as a process which enhances the capacity of individuals to improve their own lives and facilitates social change to the advantage of disadvantaged or marginalized groups).

While the predominant discourses of development engaged in by development agencies are practical and technical, concerned with project dictated imperatives of efficiency, with visible, manageable manifestations of collective action, they are commonly cloaked in the rhetoric of empowerment, which is implicitly assumed to have a greater moral value. Such a conflation of efficiency and empowerment arguments is not necessarily cynical, or even conscious; indeed participation *in itself* is considered by many as empowering, regardless of the actual activity undertaken.

So, for example, in the water sector women's participation is seen as both efficient and empowering, these factors working in synergy. Thus women's contribution of labour to construct water supplies is deemed practically beneficial, it is empowering in creating a sense of ownership and the related perceptions of responsibility which then efficiently result in the proper maintenance of facilities. The inclusion of women in management roles on water committees and associations is seen to represent a form of female emancipation, representing women's assertion and control over their lives as well as conveniently ensuring the sustainability of facilities. Poor women paying for water services are supposedly 'empowered' as consumers, while the financial efficiency of the project is furthered.

There is an inherent difficulty in incorporating project concerns with participatory discourses. A project is, by definition, a clearly defined set of activities, concerned with quantifiable costs and benefits, with time-limited activities and budgets. The project imperative emphasizes meeting practical rather than strategic needs, instrumentality rather than empowerment. Recent discussions of this issue highlight the limitations of the participants' influence over the wider structural factors shaping the project and the difficulties of trying to further empowerment approaches explicitly within a project framework (Eyburn and Ladbury, 1995; Cleaver and Kaare, 1998).

As 'empowerment' has become a buzzword in development, an essential objective of participation, its radical, challenging and transformatory edge has been lost. The concept of action has become individualized, empowerment depoliticized. Radical empowerment discourse (with its roots in Freirean philosophy) is associated with both individual *and* class action, with the transformation of structures of subordination through radical changes in law, property rights, the institutions of society. The model of 'participation' implied is of development practitioners working with poor people to struggle actively for change (Batliwala, 1994). Such ideas, associated as they are with structural change and with collective action both facilitated by and in opposition to the state, are rather out of fashion in development although within feminist scholarship and within the Latin American participatory tradition the debate continues (for example, Fals-borda, 1998; Jackson and Pearson, 1998).

A number of problems arise when we analyse critically the currently fashionable version of empowerment (the concept is often implicitly rather than explicitly referred to in policy documents). It is often unclear exactly who is to be empowered – the individual, the 'community' or categories of people such as 'women', 'the poor' or the 'socially excluded'. The question of how such categories of people might exercise agency is generally side-stepped. In many policy documents we see an apolitical individualization of the concept; the individual is expected to take opportunities offered by development projects to better themselves and so contribute to the development of the group or community. The mechanisms of such empowerment are either startlingly clear (for example, empowerment of the individual through cash transactions in the market) or conveniently fuzzy (as in the assumed benefits to individuals of participation in management committees). The scope (and limitations) of the empowering effects of any project are little explored; the attribution of causality and impact within the project alone are problematic.

There seems then to be a need to conceptualize participatory processes more broadly, for more complex analyses of the linkages between intervention, participation and empowerment as suggested by Moser and Sollis' (1991) analysis of a participatory slum upgrading project in Ecuador. We need to understand better the non-project nature of people's lives, the complex livelihood interlinkages that make an impact in one area likely to be felt in others and the potential for unintended consequences arising from any intended intervention or act (Giddens, 1984; Long, 1992).

A move away from narrow project approaches may be seen in the current concern with the role of social capital in development. Ideas about overcoming the problem of social exclusion have linked concepts of individual responsibility and citizenship with participation in the institutions of community and democracy. The concept of social inclusion emphasizes involvement in the structures and institutions of society – 'most fundamentally, the participatory and communicative structures, including new forms of social partnership through which a shared sense of the public good is created and debated' (IILS/UNDP, 1997). Although not a major focus of this chapter it will be argued that concepts of social inclusion mistakenly assume automatic linkages between involvement and social responsibility.

The tyranny of techniques

Much of the discourse of participatory approaches is conducted through debate and analysis about the appropriate techniques for uncovering the 'realities' of poor people and ensuring their involvement in decision-making. Any cursory review of the literature on participation in development reveals a huge volume of work on techniques as the 'solution' to locally based development they have the advantage of being tangible, practically achievable and of fitting well with project approaches. This techniques-based participatory orthodoxy is increasingly being subjected to critical analysis (Mosse, 1995; Goebbel, 1998). Biggs (1995) suggests that a techniques-based approach to participation fails to address adequately issues of power, control of information and other resources, and provides an inadequate framework for developing a critical reflective understanding of the deeper determinants of technical and social change. It is not my intention here to deal substantially with this debate except to point out that reviewing and improving participatory techniques cannot substitute for a more fundamental examination of the very concepts which inform such approaches, issues to which I now turn.

Critiquing the Concepts

The place of structure and agency

The following analysis is drawn strongly from ideas about the recursive relationship between agency and structure. I do this because it helps to resolve some of the artificial dichotomies present in our current thinking about development and to accommodate a number of critical paradoxes and apparent conflicts. Considerable attempts have been made to understand the complexities, diversity and regularities of patterns of interaction between individuals and social structure (Giddens, 1984; Douglas, 1987; Granovetter, 1992; Long, 1992; Goetz, 1996, and so on). However, such critical reconceptualization and analysis apparently makes little impact on the development mainstream as articulated through policy and practice. Concepts of 'the individual' underlying participatory approaches swing widely between 'rational choice' and 'social being' models. The former attributes individual behaviour to calculative selfinterest, the latter to culture and social norms. Social structure is variously perceived as opportunity and constraint but little analysed; the linkages between the individual and the structures and institutions of the social world they inhabit are ill-modelled. A convenient and tangible alternative is found in the ubiquitous focus on the *organizations* of collective action; organizing the organizations then becomes a central plank of participatory approaches to development. It is in an attempt to highlight some of these issues that the following discussion will be structured.

Institutionalism

Discourses of participation are strongly influenced by the new institutionalism, theories which suggest that institutions help to formalize mutual expectations of cooperative behaviour, allow the exercise of sanctions for non-cooperation and thereby reduce the costs of individual transactions. Social institutions are perceived as clever solutions to the problems of trust and malfeasance in economic life as they can make cheating and free riding too costly an activity to engage in (Granovetter, 1992). Institutions (mostly commonly conceptualized as organizations) are highly attractive to theorists, development policy-makers and practitioners as they help to render legible community; they translate individual into collective endeavour in a form which is visible, analysable and amenable to intervention and influence (Scott, 1998).

The aim of many development interventions is apparently to establish or support formalized community structures which most clearly mirror bureaucratic structures. (A paradox surely, when part of the justification for participatory approaches is that they avoid the shortcomings of development delivered by state bureaucracies?)

Ideas about social capital and civil society are also strongly institutionalist, although often vague. Visible, often formal, manifestations of association are attributed normative value, denoting initiative, responsibility, good citizenship and political engagement among the community as well as allegedly contributing to a vibrant economic life (IILS/UNDP, 1997; Putnam, 1993).

Institutional inclusion then has become an integral strand of participatory approaches; a process which is assumed to ensure the more efficient delivery of development, the inculcation of desirable characteristics among participants (responsibility, ownership, cooperation, collective endeavour) and therefore empowerment. Exclusion from local institutions is considered undesirable, marginalizing, inefficient.

Such institutional models of participation may be criticized on a number of grounds.

Formalization and functionalism

There is a tendency in the development literature to recognize the importance of social and 'informal' institutions but nevertheless to concentrate on the analysis and building of formal institutions (Uphoff, 1992a; 1992b).[2] Here there is a concentration on contracts, associations, committees and property rights as mechanisms for reducing transaction costs and institutionalizing cooperative interactions (Brett, 1996; Folbre, 1996). Formalized institutional arrangements are considered more likely to be robust and enduring than informal ones; desirable characteristics, for example, include a clearly identified group and boundaries, a system of graduated sanctions imposed on those who offend against collective rules and public conflict resolution mechanisms (Ostrom, 1990). Formalization is strongly linked to evolutionism in these models. A general progression from traditional (implicitly 'weak') forms of management to modern (by inference 'strong') forms is considered desirable and is the focus of much 'local institution building' in development (INTRAC, 1998). Very influential here is Elinor Ostrom's concept of the possibility of 'grafting' institutions to render them more fit for the job in hand. Such grafting generally is seen to involve formalization in the interests of functional ends.

These models have been criticized for an oversimplistic evolutionism (Nelson, 1995) and for a blindness to historical and social context, and the importance of path dependency in shaping institutions. Evidence suggests more complex and fluid processes of institutional evolution – their ebb and flow according to circumstances (season, political intervention, need), the ad hoc use of different institutional arrangements as appropriate, not necessarily conforming to project activities. For example, in the water sector a concern with institutions has been manifested through much work on water committees, water-user groups and associations – that is, with the organizations for water-resources management. Elsewhere I have shown how water resource management may also occur almost entirely outside such structures, through practices embedded in social networks, daily interactions and the application of cultural norms (Cleaver, 1995; Cleaver, 1998c). Drawing on a rural Zimbabwean example, I have illustrated how the institutions for the management of water and grazing land are socially located and critically depend on the maintenance of a degree of ambiguity regarding rights of access and compliance with rules; a continuous process of negotiation between users; the principle of conflict avoidance; and decision-making through the practical adaptation of customs and everyday interactions.

A project focus defines institutions functionally as specific to the project task, but people rarely organize their decision-making solely in this way. In one village in Tanzania, local water management indeed took place through 'formal' organizations, but not those specified by project plans. In this case a narrow project focus on establishing new participatory institutions (Water User Groups) was in danger of obscuring the actual water management activities being undertaken by community members loosely organized through other well-established, familiar and locally adapted channels, such as savings and women's clubs and sub-village administrative structures (Cleaver and Kaare, 1998).

Organizational approaches to institutions contain two strong and conflicting ideas about individual participation. Because of a focus on committee-like institutions there is a strong tendency to emphasize participation through democratic representation, and a concentration on the election of representatives. Paradoxically, there is also a strong assumption that meaningful participation in public meetings is evidenced by individual (verbal) contributions. Neither idea is necessarily in concurrence with local norms and practices, and an insistence on them may both exaggerate and disguise people's actual involvement. For example, research into community decision-making in Tanzania revealed that when women spoke at public village meetings, they were representing other women. When men spoke, they were speaking as individuals. Thus, while fewer women than men spoke at such meetings, this did not imply a lack of participation on the part of the majority of women who were actively engaged in choosing and briefing their representatives. Spokeswomen were chosen on a meeting-by-meeting basis for their knowledge of the particular issue being discussed and their eloquence, and were constantly briefed and prompted by other women (Cleaver and Kaare, 1998).

To strengthen work with institutions in participatory development, a much better understanding is needed of local norms of decision-making and representation, of how these change and are negotiated, of how people may indirectly affect outcomes without direct participation (Cleaver (ed), 1998). How far do the participatory fora that are promoted through development accommodate such complexities? There is a danger that unless they are taken into account, the formal manifestations of community-based approaches to development become mere empty shells, with meaningful decision-making, interaction and collective action taking place elsewhere.

Socially embedded institutions are not necessarily 'better' than formal/organizational ones as they may uphold and reproduce locally specific configurations of inequity and exclusion. However, the mere setting up of formal organizations and the specification of their membership does not necessarily overcome exclusion, subordination or vulnerability. It does not do so because the wider structural factors which shape such conditions and relations are often left untouched. Codifying the rights of the vulnerable must surely involve far more wide-reaching measures than the requirement that they sit on committees or individually speak at meetings?

Myths of community

The 'community' in participatory approaches to development is often conceptualized as some kind of natural, desirable social entity imbued with all sorts of desirable values and the simple manifestation of this in organizational form. This is unsatisfactory for a number of reasons.

The unitary community
There is a strong assumption in development that there is one identifiable community in any location and that there is a coterminosity between natural (resource), social and administrative boundaries. The very definition of community in development projects involves defining those who are 'included' in rights, activities, benefits and those who are excluded because they do not belong to the defined entity. The assumed self-evidence of 'community' persists in our participatory approaches despite considerable evidence of the overlapping, shifting and subjective nature of 'communities' and the permeability of boundaries (Peters, 1987; IASCP, 1998). A concentration on boundaries highlights the need in development for clear administrative arrangements, more to do with the delivery of goods and facilities than a reflection of any social arrangement. Researching community-based water-resource management in Zimbabwe it became clear that the idea of an administratively defined community little reflected the wealth and complexity of local networks of resource use, decision-making and social interaction. Thus, while domestic water resources were largely managed at waterpoint and at village level, decisions about grazing land and water for cattle use involved a wider group of people from three villages. Cultural ceremonies such as rain-making (an occasion for the reinforcing of 'community' norms and resource use regulations) involved a wider and more diverse constituency than that of the village. Moreover, individual households were connected through complex relationships of kin and associational activities (such as church membership) to networks of wider and overlapping 'communities', often physically distant from the household location (Cleaver, 1998a; 1998c).

Power and process
Project approaches to community, where they recognize power, tend to adopt oversimplified approaches to it, little recognizing processes of conflict avoidance negotiation and accommodation between people. A number of writers have illustrated the shifting, historically and socially located nature of community institutions,

the power dimensions of public manifestations of collective action (Mosse, 1997; Peters, 1987; Goebbel, 1998). However, the 'solidarity' models of community, upon which much development intervention is based, find difficulty in reconciling evidence of social stratification and conflict with project goals. There is a strong sense in which, for development policy purposes, the existence of a definable 'community' is desirable, preferably one whose shape is coterminous with administrative boundaries, and for it to be characterized by consensual cooperation (Li, 1996). For example, field workers on a community-based water and sanitation programme in Tanzania were reluctant to publicly refer to, or even admit socioeconomic differences within the communities with which they worked. They had dropped wealth ranking from their exercises in participatory rural appraisal (PRA) fearing that this highlighted inequalities and saw the public acknowledgement of difference as incompatible with the desirable model of solidarity that was necessary for the smooth functioning of the project (Cleaver and Kaare, 1998).

More realistically, we may see the community as the site of both solidarity and conflict, shifting alliances, power and social structures. Much recent work on common property resource management, for example, recognizes the role of communities in managing internal conflicts (IASCP, 1998), and conflict and opposition can be reconceptualized in certain circumstances as evidence of the exercise of individual agency (Alien, 1997).

The resourceful community?

Development practitioners excel in perpetuating the myth that communities are capable of anything, that all that is required is sufficient mobilization and the latent and unlimited capacities of the community will be unleashed in the interests of development. The evidence does little to support such claims. Rather there is significant evidence of very real structural and resource constraints operational on communities, most severely impacting on those which may need development the most. Even where a community appears well motivated, dynamic and well organized, severe limitations are presented by an inadequacy of material resources. The people of one village studied in Zimbabwe were notable for their self-reliance and positive sense of community. They had built their own school, established a variety of income-generating clubs and had high levels of associational activity. In response to severe water shortages, they had established a community fund from household contributions for the purchase of a windmill pump. However, due to drought and low agricultural incomes, the fund was insufficient to buy a windmill. The villagers, constrained by their remote location, were unsuccessful in lobbying the district council and donor agencies for assistance and several years after the first visit they still lacked adequate water supplies and were forced to travel 10km to access water from another village (Cleaver, 1996).

Culture and foundationalism

Contradictory ideas about the nature of 'culture' feature prominently in development discourses about community. Culture is variously perceived as a constraint (for example, restricting the participation of women), the 'glue' which keeps the community together (particularly through the cultural inheritance of habits of solidarity and cooperation from some past golden age) and a resource to be tapped in development (in terms of using the 'authority' of 'traditional' leaders to legitimize development interventions). It has already been seen how institutions are at once supposed to develop from weak 'traditional' forms to strong modern forms, while at the same time remaining culturally embedded (Cleaver, 1998c).

Positive views of culture tend towards a profound foundationalism about local communities and their inhabitants (Sayer and Storper, 1997). For example, in the writings of Robert Chambers, a moral value is attributed to the knowledge, attitudes and practices of the poor, the task of development being to release their potential to live these out (Chambers, 1997). How are situations dealt with where appeals to 'tradition' run contrary to the modernizing impulses of development projects, or where local 'culture' is oppressive to certain people? Why is so little debate about these tensions seen in the development literature? Is it that development practitioners fear criticizing local practices and being seen as the professionals so roundly condemned in Chambers' work? Is there not a danger of swinging from one untenable position ('we know best') to an equally untenable and damaging one ('they know best')?

Model of Individuals

Participatory approaches can be criticized further for their inadequate model of individuals and the links between these and social structure. Despite the strong assumption of the links between individual participation and responsibility, there is little recognition of the varying livelihoods, motivations and impacts of development on individuals over time. Indeed, project approaches which focus strongly on institutions as a development tool often see people as 'inputs', as the 'human resource' (see, for example, Khan and Begum, 1997). Social difference is recognized only through the categorization of general social or occupational roles; 'women', 'farmers', 'leaders' and 'the poor'.

Paradoxically, models of individual motivation and action implicit in participatory approaches swing between the under- and oversocialized (Granovetter, 1992). The concept of the 'rational economic man' is so deeply embedded in development thinking that its influence is strongly felt even where development efforts are concerned with activities which are not directly productive – with community, social action, citizenship. However, there is often a simultaneous and rather vague assumption of the 'social being' whose better nature can be drawn upon in the interests of community and development. In both abstractions the complex positions of real individuals and real groups is lost.

Incentives, rationality and participation

While the participatory literature is often rather vague on the incentives which will persuade people to participate, it is infected by the pervasive functionalism and economism of development thinking. Participation is supposed to depend on a mobilization process, upon the realization among participants that high levels of involvement are for their own good. It is assumed that people will calculate that it is sensible to participate; due to the assurance of individual benefits to ensue (particularly in relation to 'productive' projects) or, to a much lesser extent, because this is socially responsible and in the interests of community development as a whole (particularly in relation to public goods projects). Interestingly, many policy approaches make significant efforts to link participation with social responsibility, to characterize non-participation as irresponsible, and at the same time to define benefits which may, in fact, be long term, cumulative and community wide as of immediate productive advantage to the individual. Such positions are well illustrated in the literature on women's participation in water projects, on the advantages of time savings to be obtained through improved supplies and the supposed economic benefits to individual women of paying for water (see Cleaver and Lomas, 1996, for a critique).

In explaining motivations to participate, social norms are seen to occupy a secondary place to economic rationality. Social relations and participation, while supported by norms of responsibility and community service, are seen ultimately to serve the ends of economic development. Such perceptions allow little place for personal psychological motivations, for the needs of individuals for recognition, respect or purpose, which may be independent of other material benefits. Accounts of the motivations of young men involved in community activities in Zimbabwe and St Vincent illustrate this point (Cleaver (ed), 1998; Jobes, 1998). Nor are the complexities of long-term and diffuse relationships of reciprocity occurring over lifetimes adequately recognized as shaping participation (Adams et al, 1997; Cleaver, 1998c).

The fragility of a conceptual model which directly relates individual motivation and participation to the receipt of benefits can be illustrated with the following example. It is commonly asserted that women should participate more fully in the upgrading and management of water supplies as they are the primary carriers and users of domestic water. It is claimed that because of this role they have great incentives to participate and that the outcomes of such participation (greater sense of ownership and responsibility leading to improved supplies, time savings and economic gains) will directly benefit them. However, analysis of actual water use and decision-making leads us to question such assumptions. Women in a position to do so commonly delegate water fetching to other women and men (often to poorer relatives, kin, hired workers) and to children (Cleaver and Kaare, 1998). Moreover, old women may not fetch water themselves but must be dependent on others to do so for them. The water carrier, decision-maker, manager and beneficiary are not always manifest, then, in one individual. Do children and young people participate in public decision-making about water supply improvement or management? Are those to whom water work is delegated represented institutionally? Do they have strong interests in reducing water-fetching times and improving supplies? Perhaps they supplement their livelihoods through water work, perhaps it is part of a complex web of reciprocal exchange upon which they depend. Are old women not to be included in participatory decision-making processes regarding water supply improvements because they no longer fetch the water directly themselves?

Located identities, differential costs and benefits

Functional project approaches to participation little recognize that in examining motivation it is helpful to see a person positioned in *multiple* ways with social relations conferred by *specific* social identities (Giddens, 1984) and that, in Long's words, individuals are only ever partly enrolled in the projects of others (Long, 1992).

According to Giddens, the actions of human agents should be seen as a process rather than as an aggregate of separate intentions, reasons, motives and acts, and much of our day-to-day contact is not directly motivated. In querying the modelling of action as individual acts, Giddens draws attention to the difference between much routinized day-to-day activity which forms part of 'practical consciousness' and that about which actors may be discursively conscious and can analyse and reflect upon. Critical to such alternative interpretations of motivation and participation is the role of agency in processing experience and shaping action, and the role of structure in both enabling and constraining such choices.

The individual in participatory approaches is usually defined in terms of the functional nature of the project. Little recognition is made of the changing social position of individuals over life-courses, of the variable costs and benefits of participation to differently placed people, of contending and complementary concerns with production and reproduction. But the intersection of age, gender and class and individual agency is crucial in shaping people's perceptions about the desirability of participation. For example, poor young women with small children commonly find it difficult to publicly participate in development projects due to their burden of productive and reproductive activities. However, some individual women actively find ways of participating through engagement with NGOs and new associational activities, while others meet their needs in differing ways – for example, by drawing on kinship relationships for assistance with agricultural activities, educational expenses and basic needs (Cleaver, 1998a).

Contrary to the ubiquitous optimistic assertions about the benefits of public participation, there are numerous documented examples of situations where individuals find it easier, more beneficial or habitually familiar not to participate (Adams et al, 1997; Zwarteveen and Neupane, 1996). Non-participation and non-compliance may be both a 'rational' strategy *and* an unconscious practice embedded in routine, social norms and the acceptance of the status quo. A fascinating study of irrigation management in Nepal shows how some women, constrained by prevailing ideas about proper gender roles, did not participate in the irrigation association but secured their water partly through the participation of male members of their own household and through other kin and neighbour networks, and partly through stealing and cheating. Their absence from the formal user association made it far easier for them to do this without detection or censure (Zwarteveen and Neupane, 1996).

There have been calls recently to recognize both the costs and benefits of participation for individuals (Mayoux, 1995) and yet these are little pursued, the conventional wisdom being that participation is 'a good thing'. If it is accepted that costs and benefits fall differentially and are mediated and perceived by people in differing ways, what does this imply, for example, in terms of policies which target the participation in development of 'the poor' or of 'women'? Also, how is the evaluation of such costs and benefits linked with a model of choice and voluntarism? It seems that where poor people are concerned, their choices may be seriously limited, the scope for variation of action narrow. They may lack the resources for effective participation (Cleaver (ed), 1998) and yet remain vulnerable in their live-lihood strategies based on kin and existing social structures. Participation in water supply projects, where water is scarce and it is difficult to procure enough for basic needs, is less a matter of choice (an expression of agency), and more a matter of necessity imposed by constraint.

Negotiation, inclusion and exclusion

A recognition that community participation may be negotiated and mediated at the household and community, and shaped by prevailing social norms and structures, raises a critical question about whether participation can be empowering to the individuals involved. The example of women irrigators in Nepal (Zwarteveen and Neupane, 1996, cited above) illustrates this. Some women chose not to participate because they saw that in so doing they would be bound by rules and the norms of the Irrigators Association, dominated by prominent men. However, in (consciously and unconsciously) drawing on ideas about the proper role of women as confined to the domestic arena to justify their non-participation, were they exercising agency and some degree of freedom, or simply reinforcing their gendered subordination, or both? Research reveals doubts among many individuals about the merits of being included in development projects, suggesting a sophisticated analysis among people of the structural instruments of their subordination and a blindness among development agencies to this (Long, 1992; Scott, 1985).

The participatory literature is very unclear on the links between inclusion and subordination, largely because it consistently omits an analysis of the structural and political. In development policy and practice it is essential to examine the issues of empowerment and subordination more critically, recognizing that they are not necessarily diametrically opposed conditions (Jackson, 1999). Lessons can be sought in the literature on participation and inclusion outside the development field (Willis, 1977; Allen, 1997; Croft and Beresford, 1996). It is salutary also to remember that 'community' may be used as a definition of exclusion as well as inclusion, that associating concepts of responsibility, ownership and social cohesion with local entities (which may draw on religious, ethnic, locational differences in definition) is not necessarily compatible with the universalizing of quality. Exclusionary tendencies may be increased in locally based participatory development. The introduction of concepts of 'ownership' of water sources through development efforts in Zimbabwe resulted in restrictions on access which most adversely affect the poorest residents who had not made cash or labour contributions and who were therefore not seen as part of the 'rightful' user community (Cleaver, 1996).

Community, Social Capital and the State

There is a need for a radical reassessment of the desirability, practicality and efficacy of development efforts based on community participation. This involves not just rethinking the relationship between differently placed individuals and historically and spatially specific social structures, but also the role of individuals, households, communities, development agencies and the state.

'Participation' has been translated into a managerial exercise based on 'toolboxes' of procedures and techniques – it has been 'domesticated' away from its radical roots; we talk of problem solving, participation and poverty rather than problematization, critical engagement and/or class (Brown, nd). With the emerging reconsideration of the role of the state in development, the time is ripe for a critical analysis of 'participation' (several studies now link meaningful social change to state action prompted by powerful social movements for change; see, for example, Deere and Leon, 1998, on women's land rights in Latin America). This is required both conceptually and in terms of a detailed collection of empirical evidence which, despite nearly two decades of the implementation of participatory approaches, is still surprisingly lacking.

The focus needs to be expanded away from the nuts and bolts of implementing participatory development projects in order to consider the wider dynamics of economic and social change. A more dynamic vision is needed of 'community' and 'institutions' that incorporates social networks and recognizes dispersed and contingent power relations, and the exclusionary as well as inclusionary nature of participation. It is also necessary to develop a more complex modelling of livelihood concerns over life-courses, of the negotiated nature of participation and a more honest assessment of the costs and benefits to individuals of becoming involved in agency and state-directed development processes.

A number of specific areas for further work can be identified from this discussion which may contribute to resolving some of the paradoxes of participation:

1 An analysis of the resources which people need in order to be able to participate in development efforts, and in particular an analysis of which participatory approaches are low cost and high benefit to poor people.
2 An analysis of whether and *how* the structures of participatory projects include/protect/secure the interests of poor people.
3 More data on participatory 'partnerships' which are claimed to work. In particular what is the role of better, more responsive bureaucracy in such partnerships (Jarman and Johnson, 1997; Thompson, 1995).
4 Analyses of 'competent' communities and 'successful' participatory projects that focus on process, and on power dynamics, on patterns of inclusion and exclusion. This would involve more process documentation and analysis of conflict, consensus building and decision-making within communities, not just those activities related to the particular development project in hand.

Notes

1 The terms 'formal' (modern, bureaucratic, organizational) and 'informal' (social, traditional) institutions are convenient but misleading. Traditional and social institutions may indeed be highly formalized although not necessarily in the bureaucratic forms that we recognize. Much literature also exists in organizational studies about the informal dimensions of organizations. An alternative terminology might characterize institutions as 'organizational' and/or 'socially embedded' more nearly representing our actual usage of the terms. Obviously the two terms are not mutually exclusive; the dichotomy is a false one.

References

Adams, W, Watson, E and Mutiso, S (1997) 'Water rules and gender: water rights in an indigenous irrigation system, Marakwet, Kenya', *Development and Change*, Vol 28, pp707–730.

Allen, T (1997) 'Housing renewal – doesn't it make you sick?', paper presented to HSA Conference, York University, 15–16 April.

Batliwala, S (1994) 'The meaning of women's empowerment: new concepts form action', in G Sen, A Germain, and L Chen (eds) *Population Policies Reconsidered: Health, Empowerment and Rights*, Cambridge, Harvard.

Biggs, S (1995) *Participatory Technology Development: A Critique of the New Orthodoxy*, Durban, Olive Information Service, AVOCADO series, June.

Brett, E A (1996) 'The participatory principle in development projects: the costs and benefits of participation', *Public Administration and Development*, Vol 16, pp5–19.

Brown, D (nd) 'Strategies of social development: non-government organization and the limitations of the Frierean approach', The New Bulmershe Papers, Department of Agricultural Extension and Rural Development, University of Reading.

Chambers, R (1997) *Whose Reality Counts? Putting the First Last*. London, IT Publications.

Cleaver, F (1995) 'Water as a weapon: the history of water supply development in Nkayi district, Zimbabwe', *Environment and History*, Vol 1, pp313–333, Cambridge, The White Horse Press.

Cleaver, F (1996) 'Community management of rural water supplies in Zimbabwe', PhD Thesis, University of East Anglia, Norwich.

Cleaver, F (ed) (1998) 'Choice, complexity and change: gendered livelihoods and the management of water', *Journal of Agriculture and Human Values*, Vol 15, No 4, (editorial for special edition).

Cleaver, F (1998a) 'Gendered incentives and institutions: women, men and the management of water', *Journal of Agriculture and Human Values*, Vol 15, No 4.

Cleaver, F (1998b) 'There's a right way to do it – informal arrangements for local resource management', *WATERLINES*, Vol 16, No 4.

Cleaver, F (1998c) 'Moral ecological rationality: institutions and the management of communal water supplies, Nkayi district, Zimbabwe', Seventh Conference of the International Association for the Study of Common Property, Vancouver, 10–14 June 1998

Cleaver, F and Kaare, B (1998) 'Social embeddedness and project practice: a gendered analysis of promotion and participation in the Hesawa programme, Tanzania', University of Bradford for Sida, June.

Cleaver, F and Lomas, I (1996) 'The 5% rule: fact or fiction?', *Development Policy Review*, Vol 14, No 2.

Croft, S and Beresford, P (1996) 'The politics of participation', in D Taylor (ed) *Critical Social Policy: A Reader*, London, Sage.

Deere, C and Leon, M (1998) 'Gender, land and water: from reform to counter reform in Latin America', *Journal of Agriculture and Human Values*, Vol 15, No 4, (special issue).

Douglas, M (1997) *How Institutions Think*, London, Routledge & Kegan Paul.

Eyburn, R and Ladbury, S (1995) 'Popular participation in aid assisted projects: why more in theory than in practice?', in N Nelson and R Wright (eds) *Power and Participatory Development*, London, IT Publications, Ch 17.

Fals-Borda, O (1998) *Peoples Participation: Challenges Ahead*, London, IT Publications.

Folbre, N (1996) 'Engendering economics: new perspectives on women, work and demographic change', in M Bruno and B Pleskovic (eds) *Annual World Bank Conference on Development Economics*, Washington, DC, The World Bank.

Giddens, A (1984) *The Constitution of Society: Outline of the Theory of Structuration*, Cambridge, Polity Press.

Goebbel, A (1998) 'Process, perception and power: notes from "participatory" research in a Zimbabwean resettlement area', *Development and Change*, Vol 29, pp277–305.

Goetz, A-M (1996) *Local Heroes: Patterns of Field Worker Discretion in Implementing GAD Policy in Bangladesh*, IDS Discussion Paper, No 358, University of Sussex.

Granovetter, D (1992) 'Economic action and social structure: the problem of embeddedness', in M Granovetter and R Swedburg (eds) *The Sociology of Economic Life*, Oxford, Westview Press.

IASCP (1998) 'Crossing boundaries', book of abstracts for the Seventh Conference of the International Association for the Study of Common Property, 10–14 June, Simon Fraser University.

ILS/UNDP (1997) 'Social exclusion and anti-poverty strategies: project on the patterns and cases of social exclusion and the design of policies to promote integration. A synthesis of findings', International Institute for Labour Studies/United Nations Development Programme.

INTRAC (1998) *ONTRAC*, the newsletter of the International NGO Training and Research Centre, No 10, August.

Jackson, C (1999) 'Social exclusion and gender: does one size fit all?' *European Journal of Development Research*, Vol 11, No 1.

Jackson, C and Pearson, R (eds) (1998). *Feminists' Vision of Development: Gender Analysis and Policy*, London, Routledge.

Jarman, J and Johnson, C (1997) 'WAMMA: Empowerment in practice', a WaterAid report, London, WaterAid.

Jobes, K (1998) 'PME under the spotlight: a challenging approach in St Vincent', *WATERLINES*, Vol 16, No 4, pp23–25.

Khan, N A and Begum, S A (1997) 'Participation in Social Forestry re-examined: a case study from Bangladesh', *Development in Practice*, Vol 7, No 3.

Li, T M (1996) 'Images of community: discourse and strategy in property relations', *Development and Change*, Vol 27, pp501–527.

Long, N (1992) 'From paradigm lost to paradigm regained?: the case for an actor orientated sociology of development', in N Long and A Long (eds) *Battlefields of Knowledge: The Interlocking of Theory and Practice in Social Research and Development*, London, Routledge, pp16–43.

Mayoux, L (1995) 'Beyond naivety: women, gender inequality and participatory development', *Development and Change*, Vol 26, pp235–258.

Moser, C and Sollis, P (1991) 'Did the project fail? A community perspective on a participatory primary health care project in Ecuador', *Development in Practice*, Vol 1, No 1, pp19–33.

Mosse, D (1995) 'History, ecology and locality in tank-irrigated South India', *Development and Change*, Vol 28, pp505–530.

Mosse, D (1997) 'Social analysis in participatory rural development', *PLA Notes, No 24, Critical Reflections from Practice*, London, IIED, Sustainable Agriculture Programme.

Nelson, N (1995) 'Recent evolutionary theorizing about economic change', *Journal of Economic Literature*, Vol XXXIII, pp48–90.

Nelson, N and Wright, S (1995) *Power and Participatory Development: Theory and Practice*, London, IT Publications.

Oakley, P et al (1991) *Projects with People: The Practice of Participation in Rural Development*, Geneva, ILO.

Ostrom, E (1990) *Governing the Commons: The Evolution of Institutions for Collective Action*, New York, Cambridge University Press.

Peters, P (1987) 'Embedded systems and rooted models', in B McCay and J A Acheson (eds) *The Question of the Commons*, Tucson, University of Arizona Press.

Putnam, R D (1993) *Making Democracy Work: Civic Traditions in Modern Italy*, Princeton, Princeton University Press.

Sayer, A and Storper, M (1994) 'Ethics unbound: for a normative turn in social theory', *Environmental and Planning D: Society and Space*, pp1–17.

Scott, J C (1985) *Weapons of the Weak: Everyday Forms of Peasant Resistance*, London, Yale University Press.

Scott, J (1998) Address to the Seventh Annual Conference of the International Association for the Study of Common Property, Vancouver, 10–14 June.

Thompson, J (1995) 'Participatory approaches in government bureaucracies: facilitating the process of institutional change', *World Development*, Vol 23, No 9, pp1521–1554.

Uphoff, N (1992a) 'Local institutions and participation for sustainable development', *IIED Gatekeeper Series*, No 3, London, IIED.

Uphoff, N (1992b) 'Monitoring and evaluating popular participation in World Bank assisted projects', in B Bhatnagar and A Williams, *Participatory Development and the World Bank*, Discussion Papers Series No 183, Washington, DC, World Bank.

Willis, P (1977) *Learning to Labour: How Working Class Kids Get Working Class Jobs*, Farnborough, Saxon House.

Zwarteveen, M and Neupane, N (1996) *Free Riders or Victims: Women's Nonparticipation in Irrigation Management in Nepal's Chhattis Mauja Irrigation Scheme*, Research Report No 7, Colombo, International Irrigation Management Institute.

Beyond Partnership: Getting Real about NGO Relationships in the Aid System

Alan Fowler

Introduction

In today's official aid system, only one type of relationship seems to count. It is called 'partnership'. This chapter takes a critical look at this relational preference. It does so from the perspective of non-governmental organizations (NGDOs) involved in development of countries in the South that are directly or indirectly related to aid thinking, policy, practice and financing.[1]

This introduction concentrates on the question: why has 'partnership' come to the fore now and does it make sense in terms of effective development work? The answer, in terms of both theory and practice, suggests that adopting partnership as a dominant concept may be doing more harm than good in improving system credibility and performance.

In brief, the story of partnership as pre-eminent model for relationships in the current aid system is one of convergence. This dynamic results from the spill-over into the aid arena of prevailing donor domestic policies – variations on the theme of a reformed 'social contract'. This conceptual underpinning, allied to the post-Cold War impact of globalization on the international political economy, is creating insecurity in the continuation of official aid. A consequence of this interplay is the promotion of 'partnership' as the 'politically correct' mode of relating. It also reflects a defensive institutional strategy against decline in aid levels and its post-Cold War political and instrumental importance, with the eventual replacement of international concessional finance by foreign direct investment (FDI). In addition, it signals the probability of deeper and wider external penetration into the internal processes of developing countries.

Relations and Partnership in Development: A Brief History

Since the 1970s, 'partnership' has been a guiding idea for the quality of relationships that many NGDOs were looking for. In its original expression, partnership was understood as a code word reflecting humanitarian, moral, political, ideological or spiritual *solidarity* between NGDOs in the North and South that joined together to pursue a common cause of social change.[2] It signalled an alliance of a *dependencia* analysis of underdevelopment (Lehmann, 1986), set against the subsequently disproven modernization, 'lift-off and trickle-down' approach adopted by official aid at this time.

This era was characterized by a strong emphasis on government as the principal actor and engine of growth and development. The task of 'nation-building' was governmental, as was the nature of international aid. Hence, intergovernmental relations were paramount. As far as NGOs were involved in development work, they were tolerated as marginal contributors but were not embraced by the official system. Moreover, in the 1970s the NGDO universe, especially in the South, was not densely populated. However, it was gaining ground. One cause of growth was an influx of Northern NGDOs (as role models) in ex-colonies. Another was their emergence as a domestic refuge for intellectuals or others of the political left where military or civilian dictatorships prevailed, as in much of Latin America. The task of business was to contract for aid projects, little more. The role of the private sector as the source of growth was yet to be prioritized. Typically, NGDOs saw (transnational) corporations as part of the problem of exploitation. Consequently, mutual mistrust was a typical stance. In short, until the late 1970s, the relational world of international development was essentially split into self-contained corridors between North and South, each inhabited by government, NGDOs or businesses with little respect or interaction between them.

This situation was set to change in the early 1980s, which marked a rightwards shift in Northern politics – the Reagan–Thatcher era. The domestic policies of these two moved attention from government to the market as the engine of growth and progress. In addition to freeing business from restrictive shackles, a push for 'less government' also meant more responsibility to citizens and their organizations. Hence, the start of the rise in official finance to, and number of, NGOs that continues today. The spill-over of a market perspective into international aid was spearheaded by the Bretton Woods Institutions (BWIs): the International Monetary Fund (IMF), the World Bank and its sister regional development banks.

The instrumental framework for a translation of domestic into international policy became known as 'structural adjustment'. It was the start, through more stringent and similar loan conditions, of a growing domination of these institutions in terms of overly uniform development policy and thinking. Over 100 countries have been subject to donor-led adjustment. In effect, the dominant role of the BWIs in shaping development agendas has stifled choice, a search for situation-specific alternatives and local ownership of development processes.[3] Redefining the motor of development away from government to markets, however, said nothing about the relationship between them. Other events and forces were needed to push towards the adoption of partnership as the desired mode.

A second impetus to relational change arose from the implosion of the Soviet Union and the rise of the concept of civil society as a legitimate and necessary actor in society. Consequently, the third sector came into its own as a recognized player that must be associated with development goals, both as means and ends.[4] For the aid system, greater interaction with and dedicated efforts to enhance the growth of civil society were necessary for two reasons. One, discussed in more detail below, is to help deal with the institutional reconfiguration required by 'privatization' of supposedly over-extended government (social) services. Another is to accelerate the consolidation of democracy as the political agenda of aid, especially in transition economies – those formerly constituting the Soviet Union that are now implementing capitalist, free-market economic systems.

A third cause of expanded relationships with government came from NGDOs themselves. Experience of having their local development efforts undermined by ill-conceived policies and often poor, corrupt national public management, caused them to shift their horizons to policy formulation and its actors at home and abroad. The result has been growing and active NGDO pressure on and engagement with governments, not just about policy implementation, but about policy choices themselves and the right of citizen participation and of rights-based development more generally (Nelson, 1995; van Tuijl, 1999). Substantial citizen presence and lobbying at the Rio Summit on the environment and demonstrations at the recent meeting of the World Trade Organization (WTO) in Seattle are examples of how far things have come.

Finally, alongside this aid picture, as a fourth force, is the growth in relations between NGDOs and market actors. Originally spearheaded by the environmental movement, this enhanced interaction is occurring, among others, under the rubrics of developing corporate citizenship and socially responsible business (Murphy and Bendell, 1997). Where corporations are transnational, they face growing interaction with both Northern and Southern NGDOs working, thanks to the internet, more closely together than ever before. One example of such collaboration was (boycott) pressure on US company Nike to treat its foreign suppliers more fairly, leading to it adopting an international code of conduct, compliance with which is independently monitored. There are increasing examples of these and other forms of NGDO-business collaboration (Bendell, 2000).

The forces sketched above have all contributed to 30 years of relational convergence. Gone are the separate North–South sectoral corridors of the 1970s. They have given way to complex relational arenas of intensive and extensive interaction between governments, business and civic institutions in the North and South around development agendas, where the rules of the game are being made up on the spot. The processes are far from transparent or stable. Also unclear is how interests are played out for whose benefit. Particularly, what does it all mean for people and groups that are poor and marginalized? This issue of the bulletin concentrates on answers related to NGDOs and other parts of the aid system, not with businesses.

To capture this emerging relational complexity, exemplified by policy pronouncements from the Development Assistance Committee (DAC) of the Organization for Economic Co-operation and Development (OECD), the official aid system has resorted to the term 'partnership'. In fact, partnership is now a cornerstone of the new agenda for international aid (OECD, 1996). But what it means, how relations are negotiated, and who wins and who loses, when the nature of power and of power difference between parties is so divergent, is far from clear. Today's rule-of-thumb in international development is that everybody wants to be a partner with everyone else on everything, everywhere. This is so patently and transparently illogical, that it requires a critical analysis typical of development studies, which is to ask: who gains, who loses and why?

Inevitably, and to its detriment, multiple and diverse users mean that the original idea and premise of partnership has been stretched in many directions and interpreted in many ways. In this respect it has become a 'something nothing' word (Malhotra, 1997). Authentic partnership implies *inter alia*, a joint commitment to long-term interaction, shared responsibility for achievement, reciprocal obligation, equality, mutuality and balance of power (Fowler, 1998). This is not a common relational condition in any walk of life. Just why, then, is 'partnership' selected as the appropriate language and modality for bringing together disparate actors under vastly different (national) preconditions and historical trajectories? Why not – depending on the parties, the purpose and the nature of power truly involved (Lister, 2000) – employ terms like counterpart, collaborator, contractor, ally, associate, supporter, backer, benefactor, sponsor, client or patron (Fowler, 2000b)?

Illogical as it may seem at first sight, there are 'good' reasons why this single term has gained currency, if not credibility, in the 'new' aid system. The following section therefore sets out what is probably going on. The final section offers an assessment of partnership as a real relationship for NGDOs.

Why Partnership for Everyone, Everything and Everywhere?

The adoption of partnership as the relational mode of choice in aid thinking and agenda can be understood from at least three perspectives. The first is a deep-lying theory of state–society relations as social contracts. The second is partnership as a practical solution to inadequate aid performance. The third is a self-serving mystification of power asymmetry allied to a cooptation of opposing forces in a system of concessional resource provision that penetrates deeper into recipient society, at the cost of a sovereignly chosen speed of change or of development alternatives. This section deals with each in turn.

From times of Greek and Roman cultural and political prominence, philosophers such as Plato have been concerned about the origin and nature of political power and of its obligations towards citizens. The latter part of the 16th century saw this enquiry framed (by Locke, Hobbes and others) and later refined (Rousseau, Mill), into the liberal democratic doctrine in terms of a 'social contract' between rulers and the ruled. Here the initial argument was that people would accept a common superior power to protect themselves from their own baser instincts and enable them to fulfil human needs and desires. But it was subsequently argued that a necessary legitimizing condition of a social contract was that state power derived from a sovereign citizenry, for which the state acted as trustee and could be legitimately overthrown if it failed to discharge its function to the people. This formulation underpins the theory and principles of liberal democracy to be found in, and now globally propagated by, many donor countries.

Over the past two 200 years or so in continental Europe, struggles between contending religious, social, political, economic and other groups led to sophisticated configurations in terms of how a social contract would be defined and enforced. Germany's workers' representation in business governance; a national Social Eco-

nomic Council in the Netherlands, with a statutory role in public policy formulation and decision-making; joint management by trade unions and employers of social
security funds in France; the tight interlocking of political parties, government, banks
and industry in Japan; the appointment of ombudsmen and women to adjudicate
on transactions between citizen and state in many countries – are but some examples
of the evolution of social contract theory into the complex institutional structures,
norms and practices of non-Anglo-Saxon industrialized societies.[5]

These arrangements reflect the fact that interests can, indeed, be aligned as a
'partnership' between contending groups and the power differences they manifest.
In other words, power realignment is possible, even in a zero sum game, because
more powerful parties see that it is in their overall interest to accommodate others
or face prolonged conflict requiring ongoing repression that is inherently politically unstable and economically costly. Framed another way, such configurations
are a positive product of an apparent paradox that 'social conflict may be necessary
for the stability of a democratic society, and it is a vehicle for oppressed groups to
stimulate social change and to ensure long-term social stability' (Gidron et al, 1999,
p276).

However, it must be remembered that this Western evolution occurred in an era
of closed markets and limited cross-border investment. In other words, a nation-
state was a relatively self-contained entity where stability required negotiation and
accommodation of enclosed diverse interests for the good of everyone. This condition holds less and less true today. For example, capital can now move more freely
and quickly than labour. Government sole control over domestic economic policy
is being eroded. Enhanced communication is allowing citizens to see alternative
ways of doing things and organizing for their common interests across borders.
Subnational ethnic groups are asserting their identity, prevailing against the old
consensus about state formation and state – society relations. Together, these and
other forces are conspiring against the continuation of 'old style' social contracts –
beyond individual rights in a democracy – as the basis of relationship between
European states and their citizens. One obvious consequence for effective development work is to question the sense of propagating such a theoretical foundation in
the South under very different global conditions.

Put another way, Western experience indicates that partnership as social contract is the product – under a specific set of historical conditions – of internal,
iterative processes involving social assertion, contention and resolution that eventually match and balance forces and capacities leading to negotiated, collaborative
and stable power arrangements. It is not something to be 'given' by existing power-
holders or externally constructed by foreign finance.

Despite progress in economic liberalization that often differentially benefits
transnational over local corporations (Korten, 1995), a predisposition towards
redistribution of political power away from existing holders cannot be seen in many
developing countries – China being a foremost example, Zimbabwe another. Without this precondition, to establish effective partnerships, aid must generate positive
sum outcomes in power redistribution. This is a stringent requirement that aid
itself has so far been unable to deliver, even by financing the costs of 'empowerment,
that is, inducing and ameliorating a structural power transition from more to less
powerful groups, especially the poor and marginalized. Instead, aid is often used to

retrench, refine and solidify existing power relationships and structures that maintain poverty and do not foster economic growth (Mosley, 1997, quoted in Abugre, 1999, p3; World Bank, 1998).

In other words, the emphasis on partnership across the aid system rests on a questionable axiom that wilfully ignores donor countries' own history and current conditions. Nevertheless, this eroding paradigm is consciously chosen to inform today's official development goals, priorities and methods. The partnership idea applied to international aid envisages establishing in the South a social contract model of development previously prevailing in many Northern countries. In the model being propagated, state, market and third-sector actors can apparently be persuaded or induced to perform in consort. This is considered to be the best way of overcoming the social and environmental dysfunctions created by the limits to competition in a globally expanding capitalist market economy (Lisbon Group, 1995). The validity of this model rests on the dubious assumption that the long, differentiated evolutionary processes and struggles between contending forces, which the North has undergone to reach contemporary social contract arrangements, can be circumvented by judicious application of foreign funds within a uniform framework and in a different era. Historical analysis of development anywhere offers no confirmation that this assumption holds true. In fact, the opposite appears to be the case – namely, that development models, policies and approaches need to be tailored 'to a country's moment in history. Situational relativism must be accepted by academic development economists as well as by policy-makers, both within developing countries and in the international development policy community' (Adleman and Morris, 1997, p840).

In other words, employing partnership to create social contract arrangements everywhere will not be the most appropriate way of bringing about structural change from the perspective of poverty reduction. Contention is needed just as often as cooperation, if those who are poor and marginalized are to have any hope of being heard and really listened to outside aid inducement. Relying or social contract theory to inform social change is just too simplistic and ahistorical to be useful. In fact, as we will see later, it can be a blinkering impediment to effective and sustainable attainment of aid's overt goals.

Partnership as a practical solution to aid's failings

Charles Abugre provides a succinct summary of the intended role of partnership in redressing the problems and pathologies (Fowler, 2000b) of the aid system:

> The purpose of the 'partnership' framework is to address what recent diagnoses of the aid industry conclude are the critical gaps which accounted in the past for the ineffectiveness of aid. These are identified as: (1) the lack of local 'ownership' of policies and programmes, perceived as the key to good management; (2) inappropriate donor behaviour, including [insufficient] aid co-ordination and the ineffectiveness of conditionality as a surveillance and quality control mechanism and; (3) the underlying environment, including the nature of policies, institutions and the political system. Consequently, partnership seeks to address inclusiveness, complementarity, dialogue and shared responsibility as the basis of managing the multiple relationships among stakeholders in the aid industry (Abugre, 1999, p2).

The role for partnership spelled out above is, to say the least, daunting. As Abugre goes on to point out, 'it is an overstated ascription of what is possible with the best of intentions' (Abugra, 1999, p2). This is even more the case in the light of necessary preconditions that are unlikely to exist in many countries. But one example, common to sub-Saharan Africa, is the lack of trust between rulers of (previously) prebendal and rapacious states (Joseph, 1983) and weak notions of citizenship and political identity beyond ethnic affiliation (Ayode, 1988). Another example is the closed and tightly (corruptly) interlocking economic and political power in many developing countries.

In terms of promoting *inclusiveness*, partnership fostered or forced though aid conditions must deal with an important internal contradiction. On the one hand, aid must respect the sovereignty of the government it is dealing with – that is, its right to determine its own process of public engagement, negotiation and division of roles. On the other hand, the aid system must push, pull, cajole, enable and induce to the negotiating table (disempowered) actors who might otherwise be excluded, potentially undermining sovereign choice, organic political processes and regime mandate. In other words, it will weaken rather than reinforce local ownership of and commitment to development action, which is now considered to be a *sine qua non* for aid effectiveness and sustainability of change (Wolfensohn, 1999; World Bank, 1998). Moreover, not all parties will have equal competence to engage, which often calls for prior 'capacity-building' investment. This requires many years and may be beyond the repertoire of aid tools available.[6]

Lack of caution in dealing with this contradiction by, for example, imposing inclusive conditions for non-governmental, civic or business actors can invite a government 'backlash', explained and foreseen by Aziz Ali Mohammed (1997) and examined by Michael Bond (2000).[7] For example, government 'partnership backlash' in Africa is a reasonable interpretation of the fact that in April 2000, civic groups were not allowed to congregate in Cairo alongside the meeting between African heads of state and ministers from countries of the European Union. Despite some donor backing for a Cairo venue, NGDOs had to hold their meeting in Lisbon, seat of the country holding the EU chairmanship. This illustrates that requiring or demanding 'partnership' can, in fact, be counterproductive.

Partnership as a path to greater *complementarity* presumes an optimum division of roles, responsibilities and labour between different types of actors for economic progress and social problem solving. The legalistic 'trisectoral' view of institutional types (Brown and Korten, 1989; Salamon and Anheier, 1999; Defourny and Delvetere, 2000) posits that Northern configurations are closer to the optimum than in the South. Partnership can supposedly help move the South in the desired direction. Crudely speaking, the typical assertion from the three-sector liberal economic and democratic theory and practice is that: (1) the for-profit sector innovates and generates wealth and economic growth; (2) governments set enabling conditions for business, police the public good, regulate behaviour and maintain stability, security and the value of money; (3) the third sector deals with and makes good state and market failure experienced by different social groups. However, this implicitly denies that the third sector has intrinsic values, origins and functions that have nothing to do with the failure of states or markets. For example, religion and spiritual values are not the province of state or market, nor are identity-reinforcing ethnic or cultural associations and their sustaining norms, myths and practices. Put another way, the 'compensatory' sector is, in fact, the repository of values and norms, some of which society allows to be expressed through their historically evolved expectations about and tolerance of state and market roles and behaviour. Other non-economic or regulatory values, associations and processes remain expressed by and within the sector itself. The limitation of a three-sector view becomes even clearer if the political concept of civil society is employed instead.[8]

Civil society in its narrow Western theoretical grounding is inherently about power relations between state and citizens (van Rooy, 1998). In liberal interpretations, a fundamental task of civil society is to constrain the natural tendency of government to expand its sphere of influence, resorting to civil disobedience in extreme cases. It is stretching the point to call this complementarity a 'partnership'. The relationship is essentially adversarial, based among others on assertion of civic rights and other forms of claim-making. Hence, the aid system creates yet another contradiction by putting much effort into building civil society while expecting it to be a 'harmony model' social contract partner at the same time. A more practical approach is to recognize that there are areas and times for collaboration and for an adversarial position that depend on the historical moment, issue and trajectory of the society in question. It is simply wrong to think that 'partnership as complementarity' applies everywhere and always.

Finally, to make aid more effective, there is the intention that partnership will foster *dialogue and shared responsibility*. From the above arguments, this may or may not be true. As with so much in development, it depends. An important aspect of what it depends on are known and trusted rules of the game, institutions and places for dialogue and transmittal of alternative ideas that seek public support. Here, the media, and access to information more generally, are particularly important. From this perspective, what is needed for greater dialogue and allocating responsibility are not potentially coopting and homogenizing partnerships but greater pluralism in the sources and propagation of information and ideas. This is not to deny that many developing countries would benefit from the evolution of more places and conventions enabling different interests and groups to communicate and exchange with each other. With care, international aid can certainly help in this development. However, whether the result of better dialogue is partnership and shared responsibility or something else, like more firmly entrenched positions and better rights-based claim-making, remains open to question.

Partnership as an aid to foreign penetration

A third way of looking at the preference for partnership as the modality for pursuing the new aid agenda is as an instrument for deeper, wider and more effective penetration into a country's development choices and path. In other words, 'partnership' is a terminological Trojan Horse. There are two aspects to this perspective. One is a response to learning about the complexity of change. The other, as a way to prop up an aid system under threat in the North and the South, is to coopt or sideline potentially opposing ideas and forces that express and propagate alternative views.

Thirty years of experience in international aid has taught us just how complex and indeterminate the process of change can be. No one party can be relied on to make growth or poverty reduction a reality. Moreover, aid is just one – sometimes small (India), sometimes large (Mozambique) – component of the process. More humility, realism and reflection on inadequate performance has led the aid system to the reasonable conclusion that as many actors and forces as possible must be brought to bear on making a country more liveable for the population as a whole and viable in a rapidly evolving world order. Hence the attraction of partnership. The core problem is that the structural nature of poverty is not particularly amenable to change using what aid has mainly had to offer: time-bound programmes and projects. This reality is one reason for the current attention to policy-based assistance and comprehensive aid frame works.[9]

What such frameworks intend to do is supply and apply a common format through which aid can engage with almost every facet of change and potential development actor simultaneously at multiple levels of social organization. Partnership is a necessary rubric to make this appear both inevitable because of past experience and innocuous in its intent. But is it? The answer is probably not. Why? Because the supposed inclusiveness of the term hides the shadow side of excluding other ideas about change.[10] It is a more subtle form of external power imposition, less amenable to resistance (Lukes, 1974). By appearing to be benign, inclusive, open, all-embracing and harmonious, partnership intrinsically precludes other interpretations of reality, options and choices without overtly doing so. In sum, the selection and universal application of partnership is a mystification and distraction that not only conditions the development debate at the cost of alternatives, but legitimizes deep penetration of foreign concerns into domestic processes, inviting perverse and negative reactions. For example, one potential consequence is to:

> ... turn government accountability on its head. Governments have a duty to account to their people first and foremost through their parliaments and other mechanisms, quite independently of their obligations to external parties. Participation of external actors in this process ought to be secondary and incidental as is obviously the case in the domestic policy-making process of the donors themselves (Abugre, 1999, p18).

A secondary, but still strong, effect is to more comprehensively either bring in and coopt, or push away and negate, the agendas and concerns of other actors. Actors may have different views on how, for example, poverty can best be reduced and society made more equitable and stable, and change made sustainable over what timescale and through which path. Cooptation is a particularly important element of today's official 'partnership' strategy because aid is under threat.[11] Consequently, as many constituencies as possible must be mobilized for its continuation. This is a special concern for the Bretton Woods Institutions that, because of their governmental ownership and governance, have no direct public constituency to support their case and therefore existence.[12] Hence the active engagement with NGDOs and religious organizations in 'partnership'.

All in all, a case can be made for choosing a different way of looking at the relationships needed to make aid work better. What might they be?

Alternatives to partnership: what are they and why are they necessary?

At least two alternatives offer themselves as a guiding idea about preferred relationships in the aid system. One is cooperation, the other is solidarity. However, both must be based on the premise of interdependence.

The old way of looking at aid was in terms of *cooperation* (hence the 'C' in OECD). It has none of the normative overload of partnership. There are many, many ways of cooperating. The most appropriate way depends on the issue and interests at hand, the capacity and power of actors involved and the context. The fact that development cooperation has turned out be a condition of Northern dominance and patrimony has to do with pathologies introduced by its interpretation (Fowler, 2000a), not with the concept as such. There is every reason to retain cooperation but to make it actually work in terms of the interest of the South, which is in the interest of a globally interdependent North (Edwards, 1999). Whether the institutional reforms required will actually make this happen before it is too late is, however, open to doubt.

Another alternative is *solidarity* – in other words, a recognition of the inevitability of the need for mutual understanding, empathy and shared action in an increasingly interdependent and complicated world. While more emotive and politically loaded than 'cooperation', solidarity gets us closer to and clearer about the moral underpinning that is supposed to reflect international aid. It is a term that has motivated significant social reform and progressive relationships between people. It is less ambiguous in terms of what needs to be done relationally to bring about change (Abugre, 1999, p19).

What has been working against both of these choices is the fact that the aid system does not actually behave as an interdependent system but as a chain of dependency-inducing relationships (Sida, 1996). Each link in the chain may be connected to, but is protected from, the next by a sort of firewall, which stops the heat of inadequate performance from rising upwards and burning the real power holders. Contracting out, projects externalized from organizations that implement them, and lack of real mutuality and shared accountability protect at each link.[13] In other words, there is too little interdependency in terms of the consequences of aid built into the rules of the game and practices flowing from them. Unfortunately, the overall outcome is a loss of the credibility of aid as a solution to problems of poverty and injustice.

Consequently, a vital reason why we must seriously reconsider the use of 'partnership' is that, as the articles in this bulletin show, it can create a new stick with which the aid system will be beaten. For all the reasons given above, setting partnership and all that it implies as the relational standard will, in many instances, backfire. Non-delivery on the aspirations of partnership will create even more dissatisfaction with aid as an effective means of making the world work better for those who are losing out on 'progress'. So, let us get real and honest about what sort of relationships are desirable and possible. Business, government and organizations of civil society do not pretend to be in partnership with all those they relate to. There is no reason why the aid system should make itself even more vulnerable by doing so.

Development Partnership in Practice: NGDO Experience

To be effective, NGDOs must make and maintain a wide array of relationships and accountabilities (Edwards and Hulme, 1996). As intermediaries, three are particularly significant. The first is the relationship with those in whose name NGDOs claim legitimacy and serve: people who are poor, marginalized and suffering from injustice. The second is accountability to the public, predominantly through the government, understood as the regime in power and the bureaucracy it controls. The third are the supporters and private and public funders of the work of NGDOs.

The following features contribute to forming something akin to authentic partnership for NGDOs.

Be clear about why? Only start a relationship if you are clear about why you want it and what you realistically can and cannot put into it. Not achieving a partnership is no failure. As in any other field of life, to be effective the aid system requires a variety of relationships tailored to the actors and their interests, capabilities and purposes. Clarity means honesty about how you can relate. It prevents later accusations of failing to be a partner, with the frustration and loss of credibility that this can engender. In short, do not provide the stick with which you will be beaten.

Apply the principle of interdependence. To be authentic, partnership cannot be an 'add-on'. It must be an intrinsic feature of organizational perspective and behaviour, premised on interdependence with others in a complex, dynamic world. If, as a donor and more powerful party, you are not *really dependent* on the behaviour of your counterpart for your own credibility and viability, you have probably not moved from dependency and patronage.

Adopt a contextual, systems approach and perspective. Do not look at your relationship(s) in isolation from others that you and your counterpart have now and will need to have to be sustainable in the future. Strive for a systemic view of change and the place of your relationship within it.

Adopt an organizational not project focus. Partnership is about gaining a deep organizational relationship, which is not a 'project'. Look at a project as a vehicle to explore relationships, not as the basis of them. In doing this, the longer-term perspective is to help both parties develop the capability to analyse effectively and address unforeseen problems that will arise in the future, not just in the immediate context of a project[14] – in other words, a case where 'partnership' makes each organization more agile and adaptive.

Create a process for local validation and shared control. Work against the power asymmetry inherent in aid relationships by establishing joint processes and structures that do produce mutuality and shared control.

Invest in your own reform. Partnership is a two-way, not a one-way process. For donors, it calls for prior investment to set up the internal conditions required to share rather than retain control and to aid the weaker party to become strong enough to move from (inevitable) initial dependency through independence to self-chosen interdependence (Kaplan, 1996).

Employ the achievement of downward accountability as proxy for partnership. Increasing the amount of official or tax-based aid to NGDOs brings a relational problem in terms of gaining or retaining 'downward accountability', to those legiti-mising the organization's existence. If you cannot demonstrate the ways in which you are held accountable from below for what you do and say, then authentic part-nership is unlikely to be present. Downward accountability is a fair proxy for evaluating progress in creating partnership-type relationships.

The quest for partnership can be interpreted as part of a struggle to change the way the aid system operates in order to regain its credibility. However, this type of relationship is not always appropriate, desirable or realistically possible. Conse-quently, far more care needs to be exercised in the use of the term to prevent abuse creating greater mistrust. The primary abuse lies in 'partnership', disguising the fact that power differences exist and that the poverty and injustice this causes are un-likely to be harmoniously eradicated.

Notes

1   There is no commonly accepted definition of NGDOs. For the purpose of this chapter, they can be regarded as third-party serving, non-profit-based, legally constituted non-state organizations, directly or indirectly reliant on the system of international aid. In most cases, they function as intermediaries to promote poverty eradication, sustainable development, social justice and enduring im-provement in the circumstances of poor and excluded groups. In fewer cases, they concentrate on advocacy work for policy reform. They number in the tens of thousands worldwide. In this volume, the acronyms NGO and NGDO are equivalent and simply reflect the author's preferences.

2   The North is understood as those countries donating aid, the South as those countries receiving aid.

3   I am grateful to Dorothy Gordon for this observation.

4   The other two sectors in society sectors are government and for-profit busi-ness. As predominantly defined (Salamon and Anheier, 1997) the non-profit third sector does not equate with civil society because, among others, it does not include non-formal associational life, giving preference to bodies with a legal personality. In this chapter, the more inclusive concept of civil society is em-ployed.

5   The United States and the UK (after the fall of the Labour Party in the 1970s) have been less disposed to embrace social contracts in the form of sophisticated institutional arrangements for multistakeholder negotiation and dialogue. A speculation would be that the nature of two-party as opposed to coalition poli-tics common in continental Europe has mitigated against this type of consensual evolution.

6   Institutional development and capacity building are now significant elements of the new aid agenda. However, the system is finding it particularly difficult to achieve this, in part because it requires reforms within itself to give more power away to more competent local actors.

7   Part of the 'backlash' stems from an overstated but not completely illegitimate concern about the legitimacy, mandate and accountability of NGDO activists

who lobby for policy change (Jordan and van Tuijl, 1997). This criticism often comes from regimes whose own legitimacy can be questioned.

8 In terms of explaining the existence of a third sector, the latest contender is more historical, relying on diversity in social history (Salamon and Anheier, 1998).

9 For example, the World Bank is championing a Comprehensive Development Framework (CDF), while the United Nations System is relying on Development Assistance Frameworks (UNDAF).

10 Noam Chomsky has demonstrated how control over language controls thought and interpretation of reality This holds true in the aid system as well, to be seen, for example, in official definitions of development, needs, participation, empowerment, sustainability, etc. (Sachs, 1992).

11 The counter argument is that, in accepting engagement, NGDOs seek to coopt government. The weakness of this argument increases as NGDOs become more and more dependent on official aid. It is more difficult to alter the behaviour of those who feed you and NGDOs are not renowned for hunger strikes. In this light, non-aid related social movements might be a better bet in terms of changing the system.

12 For example, it is particularly interesting to learn that the IMF is, in fact, an anti-poverty institution, albeit full to the brim with macro-economists. I, and many others, have lived with the 'obvious' misapprehension that the IMF's role was to ensure global economic stability and efficiency! A not implausible interpretation is that the IMF is adopting anti-poverty clothing and language as a defensive response against threat from, for example, the US Congress. The Meltzer Committee recently argued for a significant reduction in the scope of IMF engagement and concentration on financial stability (*The Economist*, 18 March, 2000, p88). The Overseas Development Council (ODC, 2000) acknowledges the impact of IMF behaviour on poverty but also argues that the Fund's role be restricted and that the Poverty Reduction and Growth Facility (PRGF) be transferred to the World Bank.

13 For example, how can the World Bank make good erroneous policy 'advice' that generates enormous social costs, such as unemployment and the collapse of whole industries (Hanlon, 1997).

14 I am grateful to Jethro Pettit for this observation.

References

Abugre, C (1999) *Partners, Collaborators or Patron-clients: Defining Relationships in the Aid Industry*, Background Paper for the Canadian International Development Agency, Partnership Branch, Accra, ISODEC.

Adelman, I and Morris, C (1997) 'Editorial: development history and its implications for development theory', *World Development*, Vol 25, No 6, pp831–840.

Ayode, A (1988) 'States without citizens: an emerging African phenomenon', in D Rothchild and N Chazan, *The Precarious Balance: State and Society in Africa*, Boulder, Colorado, Lynne Rienner.

Bendell, J (ed) (2000) *Terms for Endearment: Business, NGOs and Sustainable Development*, Sheffield, Greenleaf Press.

Bond, M (2000) 'Special report: the backlash against NGOs', *Prospect*, April, pp1–5.

Brown, D and Korten, D (1989) *Voluntary Organizations: Guidelines for Donors*, Working Paper, WPS 258, Washington, DC, The World Bank.

Defourny, J and Delvetere, P (2000) *The Social Economy: The Worldwide Making of a Third Sector*, STEP Research Group, Liège, University of Liège.

Edwards, M (1999) *Future Positive: International Co-operation in the 21st Century*, London, Earthscan.

Edwards, M and Hulme, D (1996) *Beyond the Magic Bullet: NGO Performance and Accountability in the Post-Cold War World*, London, Earthscan.

Fowler, A (1998) 'Authentic partnerships in the new policy agenda for international aid: dead end or light ahead?', *Development and Change*, Vol 29, No 1, pp137–59.

Fowler, A (2000a) 'NDGO values and the fourth position: introduction to the special issue', in A Fowler (ed), *NGO Futures: Beyond Aid, Third World Quarterly Special Issue*, Vol 21, No 4, August.

Fowler, A (2000b) *Partnerships: Negotiating Relationships – A Resource for Non-governmental Development Organizations*, Occasional Paper, No 32, Oxford, International NGO Training and Research Centre.

Fowler, A (2000c) 'Degrees of separation: perspectives on the decentralization of international NGOs', in S Gibbs, *Decentralised NGO Management*, Occasional Paper, No 19, pp8–24, Oxford, International NGO Training and Research Centre.

Gidron, B, Katz, S, Meyer, M, Hesenfeld, Y, Schwartz, R and Crane, J (1999) 'Peace and conflict resolution organizations in three protracted conflicts: structures, resources and ideology', *Voluntas*, Vol 10, No 4, pp275–98.

Hanlon, J, (1997) 'Test for the Bank to make up for its mistake', *Africa Agenda*, No 14, pp32–33, Accra, Third World Network.

Jordan, L and van Tuijl, R (1997) *Political Responsibility in NGO Advocacy: Exploring Shapes of Global Democracy*, Washington, DC/The Hague, Bank Information Center/NOVIB.

Joseph, R (1983) 'Class, state and prebendel politics in Nigeria', *Journal of Commonwealth and Contemporary Politics*, Vol XXI, No 3.

Kaplan, A (1996) *The Development Practitioners' Handbook*, London, Pluto Press.

Korten, D (1995) *When Corporations Rule the World*, London, Earthscan.

Lehmann, D (1986) *Dependencia: An Ideological History*, Discussion Paper, No 219, Brighton, IDS.

Lisbon Group (1995) *Limits to Competition*, Cambridge, MA, MIT Press.

Lister, S (2000) 'Power in partnership? An analysis of an NGO's relationship with its partners', *Journal of International Development*, Vol 12, No 2, pp227–40.

Lukes, S (1974) *Power: A Radical View*, London, Macmillan.

Malhotra, K (1997) '"Something Nothing": words, lessons in partnership from Southern experience', in L Hately and K Malhotra, *Between Rhetoric and Reality: Essays on Partnership in Development*, Ottawa, North–South Institute, pp37–56.

Mathews, J (1997) 'Power shift', *Foreign Affairs*, Vol 76, No 1, pp50–66.

Mohammed, A (1997) 'Notes on MDB conditionality on governance', *International Monetary and Financial Issues for the 1990s*, Research Papers for the Group of 24, Vol III, pp139–145, New York and Geneva, United Nations.

Murphy, D and Bendall, J (1997) *In the Company of Partners: Business, Environmental Groups and Sustainable Development Post-Rio*, Bristol, Policy Press.

Nelson, P (1995) *The World Bank and Non-Governmental Organizations: The Limits of Apolitical Development*, Basingstoke, Macmillan.

ODC (2000) 'The future role of the IMF in development', Task Force Report, Washington, DC, Overseas Development Council.

OECD (1996) *Shaping the 21st Century: The Contribution of Development Co-operation*, Paris, Organisation for Economic Co-operation and Development.

Sachs, W (1992) *The Development Dictionary: A Guide to Knowledge as Power*, London, Zed Books.

Salamon, L and Anheier, H (1997) *Defining the Non-Profit Sector: A Cross-National Analysis*, Manchester, Manchester University Press.

Salamon, L and Anheier, H (1998) 'Social origins of civil society: explaining the non-profit sector cross-nationally', *Voluntas*, Vol 9, No 3, pp213–48.

Salamon, L and Anheier, H (1999) *The Emerging Sector Revisited: A Summary*, Center for Civil Society, Baltimore, John's Hopkins University.

Sida (1996) *Aid Dependency: Causes, Symptoms ana Remedies*, Stockholm, Swedish International Development Agency.

van Rooy, A (ed) (1998) *Civil Society and the Aid Industry*, London, Earthscan.

van Tuijl, P (1999) 'NGOs and human rights: sources of justice and democracy', *Journal of International Affairs*, Vol 52, No 2, pp493–512.

Wolfensohn, J (1999) 'A proposal for a comprehensive development framework', Washington, DC, World Bank (mimeo).

World Bank (1998) *Assessing Aid: What Works, What Doesn't and Why*, Washington, DC, World Bank.

Crossing the Great Divide: Building Links and Learning Between NGOs and Community-based Organizations in the North and South

John Gaventa

Introduction

Non-governmental organizations (NGOs) involved in development face a great geographical divide. On the one hand, we have those organizations which work on issues of poverty, community regeneration and the strengthening of civil society in the North. On the other hand, we find a vast range of NGOs, community-based organizations (CBOs) and others which focus on similar development issues in the South. Historically there is little sharing and learning between these groups across the hemispheres. While many larger NGOs working in the South are, in fact, based in the North, they have had little contact with issues in their own countries similar to those upon which they focus elsewhere.

Increasingly, especially in a context of globalization, this division must change. For NGOs, globalization offers a series of challenges for developing new models for linking and learning on strategies for approaching common problems in both North and South. Fortunately, we are beginning to see a number of attempts by NGOs in the North and South to forge such new ways of working.

In this chapter, I will share some concrete examples of exchanges of experience between NGOs and CBOs in poor regions of the US with their Southern counterparts. These exchanges took place, on the whole, in conjunction with the work of the Highlander Research and Education Center, based in Tennessee. Highlander has worked as an NGO for over 60 years in the poor regions of the US, especially in the rural south and the Appalachian regions. Its work in education for community empowerment and community development has contributed significantly to the strengthening of popular participation in areas of labour rights, civil rights, poverty alleviation, community regeneration and the environment. From 1976 to 1993, I worked as a staff member, and later as Director, at Highlander.

I will first of all look further at the context in which we worked – what we came to know as the 'South within the North'. Second, I will examine the context of the voluntary sector in the US, suggesting that there are very differing understandings of its nature and character. Finally, I will turn to four examples of exchange of experience between NGOs and CBOs in the North and South, with some reflections on the lessons learned in the process.

The 'South Within the North'

While we often think of poverty in the South and wealth in the North, these distinctions are increasingly misleading. While the North clearly is a place of relative wealth, it also contains within it large-scale poverty, increasing inequality and highly uneven development. In the US, we find areas within inner cities and vast rural areas where levels of poverty, unemployment, relatively poor education, illiteracy, lack of access to healthcare, and so on, provide similarities to certain parts of the South. With growing inequality in industrialized countries, the movement of jobs and industry to newly industrialized regions of the South, increasing issues of access to basic services such as healthcare for the poor in many countries, and the globalization of goods, services and information, the traditional distinctions between North and South need to be re-examined. In our work in the US, we came to recognize that there are 'Souths within the North', just as there may be 'Norths within the South' (Gaventa, 1991).

In a recent seminar series at the Institute for Development Studies on Social Exclusion in North and South, Simon Maxwell (1997) suggested that we could examine the new relationships between North and South in terms of comparisons, convergences and connections. Each is helpful in understanding issues of poverty, participation and social exclusion.

Comparisons

While poverty may not be of the same scale, nor perhaps in many places as desperate in poor areas in the North as in other parts of the world, there are parallel issues, including those of illiteracy, access to healthcare, environmental degradation, distribution of land and natural resources, and the like. While globally, for instance, the levels of inequality are known to be increasing in the South and North, it is not often realized that the level of income inequality in the US is higher than in many other countries, including those in the South. According to one study:

> The share of income among the lowest 40% of American households, in 1985, places the United States behind every one of the 25 nations with high-income economies, except for Australia and Singapore, according to the World Bank. Of the 21 low-and moderate income nations reporting income distribution, the US falls behind nine of them, including Bangladesh, Ghana, India and Pakistan. The United States' income distribution is more 'equitable' than only its client states of Central and Latin America: Guatemala, Peru, Colombia, Jamaica, Costa Rica, Venezuela, and Brazil (Couto, 1994, p22, quoting World Bank, 1991, Table 30).

In addition to these comparisons of conditions, there have also been comparative analyses and explanations for the underlying causes of these conditions. It has not been uncommon in literature on community and regional development in the US for rural areas such as Appalachia, the Black Belt south or native reservations to be analysed using colonial or developing countries analogies, or to be understood as peripheral regions in the larger world economy.

Convergences

The growth of parts of the South and the decline of parts of the North argue for a convergence of conditions in the 'low end' of the North and the 'high end' of the South. For instance, industries which used to look to low-wage rural areas for resources and labour, such as the Appalachian region of the US or the Welsh valleys in the UK, have now left for other parts of the world, leaving behind large-scale areas of deindustrialization. These convergences have led in some instances to new reversals – for instance, a South Korean plant recently came to South Wales, lured by the low-wage labour and favourable business incentives.

Connections

Beyond parallels and convergences there are also increasingly connections between poor regions of the North and South, as we are reminded by the literature on globalization. While these connections are often articulated in terms of economic connections brought on by multinationals or capital mobility, or by cultural connections encouraged by global media and information technologies, there are also social and intellectual connections involving shared development strategies and concepts; including in the voluntary sector.

The Role of NGOs and Voluntary Associations in the US – Two Views

Around the world, especially in the context of a development crisis, NGOs are increasingly being put forward as a vehicle for development, for social action and as a means of popular participation in social problem-solving. NGOs are becoming a measure of citizen's participation, and in turn, the civil society of which they are a part is seen as a critical part of democracy. As in other areas, there are important parallels between the roles that NGOs and CBOs are being called on to play as civil society actors in the South, and the role which they have played in the North. The strength of these parallels depends, though, on what kind of voluntary organization we choose to examine.

In the US, for instance, there is a long history of voluntary associations and CBOs. Although the US has lagged behind many other Western democracies (and indeed democracies in other parts of the world) in terms of voter participation or worker participation, it has long been known for its 'civic culture'. In his book *Democracy in America*, written in 1835, the French scholar Alexander de Tocqueville wrote of this American art of forming associations:

> Nothing, in my view, deserves more attention than the intellectual and moral associations in America ... In democratic countries knowledge of how to combine is the

mother of all other forms of knowledge; on its progress depends that of all the others ... (de Tocqueville, 1966, p666).

Following de Tocqueville's lead, many others have written of the importance of voluntary organizations as mediating organizations between large, bureaucratic institutions such as the state and the corporation, and the individual. Others acknowledge that voluntary organizations have been at the cutting edge of major social reforms and social movements, ranging from the temperance movement to the civil rights movement.

In modern times, the voluntary sector is composed of thousands of groups, many of which are organized and registered as non-profit organizations – that is, as private groups which exist for a public or charitable purpose. In the last 20 years, these non-profits have grown rapidly, joining the public and private sectors as key forces for social and economic action. As a generic group, these non-profits are a vast category, including churches, schools, colleges and universities, research institutions, hospitals, foundations, social action movements, welfare agencies, arts and cultural organizations, community development groups, mutual benefit societies and others.

Drawing on this rich but diverse tradition of civic association, there are those who have argued that such a model of civil society should be developed and promoted for strengthening democracy and development in other parts of the world. The number of associations or NGOs is seen as a proxy indicator for a pluralist and robust civil society. Yet perhaps we need to look more closely and critically at the nature of association in American society. While the contribution of voluntary, non-profit organizations has been great, there is nothing inherent in the status of a voluntary non-profit organization which leads it to work to remedy the inequalities or problems of society, or to strengthen the participation of the poor in dealing with development issues. In fact, within the literature on participation in the US itself, a number of critiques have been made of pluralist and open models of democracy and civil society which we often seek now to export to other parts of the world.

First, while many may participate in civic life and voluntary associations in the US, some are more able to participate than others. It is a well-known sociological fact that those who are the most privileged in socioeconomic status are also the ones most likely to participate in such civic organizations. This produces a paradox of democracy: those that are most badly affected by the pressing problems of poverty and may need to participate the most to change their conditions, are often the least able or likely to do so (see, for example, Verba and Nie, 1972). The increasing inequality between the rich and poor in the US and other countries also has profound effects on patterns of participation and organization.

Second, another body of literature has argued that the lack of participation in civil society is partly the result of barriers which have developed through power relationships that impede participation of certain actors and prevent certain issues from being raised. Rather than looking at who participates to understand civil and political life, we must examine who does not, and why (see, for instance, Bachrach and Baratz, 1970; Gaventa, 1980). From this point of view, American democracy is not necessarily as open to voluntary action as we often suggest, and the pluralism of American democracy is more a pluralism of elites than an indicator of democracy at the grassroots.

Third, recent evidence suggests that civic engagement in the US may itself be on the decline. Robert Putnam (1995, p65), for instance, writes:

> To those concerned with the weakness of civil societies in the developing or postcommunist world, the advanced Western democracies and above all the United States have typically been taken as models to be emulated. There is striking evidence, however, that the vibrancy of American civil society has notably declined over the past several decades.

Despite the declines, we often continue to present to the rest of the world an image of a healthy civil society.

A view from the grassroots

Within the US, partly in response to these arguments about shortcomings in civic participation, we have seen the growth of a new kind of organization: the grassroots community organization, or community-based group, as a vehicle for participation by the most disenfranchized. While this grassroots, community-based movement also has deep historical roots, its particular form grew out of the War on Poverty, and the civil rights and women's movements of the 1960s and 1970s. With the vacuum in social services and social policy left by the 1980s, this sector has continued to play more of a leadership role in social change. Boyte (1980; Boyte et al, 1986) and others have written about a new American populism, as communities organize to redemocratize the political system. In a recent report, Delgado (1993) argues that there are now over 6000 community organizations in operation in the US, mostly 'local, unaffiliated groups, initiated out of local residents' need to exert control over development in their communities' (p10). Among the accomplishments of community organizations has been the redress of the balance of power – by holding public servants accountable, CO has managed in many localities to put the "dispossessed at the table" with bankers, planners and politicians' (pp10–11).

These grassroots organizations are as diverse as the rest of the non-profit world. They may be organized around communities, neighbourhoods or issues. They are usually local, but increasingly are organizing into state, regional and national associations. They are supported by a vast array of intermediary organizations and NGOs which help to provide funding, training, technical assistance, research and education for their efforts. While diverse, this grassroots movement within the non-profit sector is bound together by a common set of values and characteristics, as outlined below:

- They give organization and voice to the under-represented in society, and usually are controlled by them. Grassroots organizations have played important roles in the civil rights movements, the women's movement and poor people's movements.
- They raise key issues for the rest of society, serving as a conscience for the nation, advocates for change and sources of innovation and action.
- They often work to deliver needed services – such as housing, education or child care – to groups not reached by, or failed by, the government programmes. In doing so, they seek not just to provide charity to the poor and powerless,

but to organize them and to deal with the causes of the problems rather than the symptoms.
- They serve as sources of leadership, development and empowerment, contributing to overall participation and change in the society.

In general, then, when we talk about linking NGOs from the North and the South, we must recognize this diversity within the fabric of American civic life. On the one hand, the image often given to the South of NGOs or voluntary associations in the North reflects a pluralistic and open view of American society, in which the issues of power and poverty are not clearly visible. On the other hand, there is another tradition of community-based and non-profit organizations which is focused upon remedying inequalities within the US – inequalities similar in nature to those faced by many in the South, and addressed by many Southern NGOs.

Unfortunately, many of the Northern NGOs which work in the South are themselves disconnected from grassroots organizations in their own country, many of which work on similar issues to those that they are addressing abroad. As a result, Northern NGOs may project to the South an image of society and civic life in the North which fails to acknowledge the parallels and commonalities which are potentially shared by NGOs and CBOs across the hemispheres. In so doing, they perhaps inadvertently help to perpetuate older divisions between North and South, rather than countering new trends brought on by globalization. New models of linking across borders within the NGO and voluntary sectors must be found.

Building Global Links: Case Examples

From 1976 to 1993, I worked on the staff of the Highlander Research and Education Center, a relatively small but well-known NGO located in the American South. Highlander has a history of over 60 years of carrying out education and training for grassroots communities in Appalachia and the rural south, among the poorest regions in the country. The history is a rich one, spanning work with the labour movement of the 1930s, the civil rights movement of the 1950s and 1960s, the anti-poverty and community action work of the 1970s, and environmental and community economic development in the 1980s and 1990s. As staff of this NGO, we developed the view increasingly during the 1980s that our work in the North needed to be linked to and located in the broader work for community development and empowerment conducted across the globe. There were a number of reasons for this.

First, our reading and experience suggested that, as a rural region within a wealthy nation, we shared many problems with other poor regions of the world – problems that were perhaps masked by the Northern, wealthy, urban and industrial context in which we were located. In the US, the issues of rural poor people received relatively low levels of attention compared with many other parts of the world. Yet we found parallel issues and movements in the South, especially around such problems as literacy, land reform, rural development and healthcare.

Second, we became increasingly struck by parallels in methods of working from which we could learn. Many of these grew from working in a context of relatively low literacy levels, strong cultural traditions of rural and ethnic communities, and needs for empowerment and capacity building similar to those found in the South.

Third, and perhaps most importantly, we found increasingly an interrelationship between the issues upon which we worked and those of other countries, to the extent that they simply could not be ignored. For instance, one effect of working with communities affected by the toxic poisoning of water was for the plant to close and move to Latin America, simply displacing the problem to others, rather than solving it. Increased globalization meant that communities were affected by economic blackmail which pitted poor regions and workers against one another, with threats of moving jobs elsewhere if community action became too strong.

With these issues in mind, we began to support and foster a series of exchanges attempting to make global connections between the communities with which we worked and other similar community organizations elsewhere, as well as between ourselves as an NGO and other NGOs. The connections took many forms, but mostly involved exchanges from South to North, or North to South, sharing at international workshops and occasionally joint projects.

In the following section, I will describe some of these exchanges by topic area and then turn to lessons learned from them.

Example 1: Learning about methods: strengthening grassroots voices through participatory forms of education and research

As an NGO, the Highlander Center was known particularly for its methods of using adult non-formal education as a basis for leadership development and capacity building. These methods emphasized peer learning, building on the experiences of the people themselves and linking education to action – all methods which had developed in the South as well.

In the South, many of these ideas grew from the work of Paulo Freire whose particular approach to education as a process of conscientization of the poor spread rapidly across Latin America and parts of Africa and Asia during the 1970s and 1980s. These ideas affected the work of many NGOs and CBOs in their work with poor organizations – for instance, in the ways that the methods were used in the Training for Transformation programme in southern Africa.

In the US, Highlander's work had been influenced by differing, yet somewhat similar, traditions, especially the folk school movement of Scandinavia, and the education for citizenship tradition in the US espoused by adult educators such as John Dewey and Edward Lindemann. In the American South, Highlander was perhaps best known for its work using Citizenship Schools as an approach to literacy with African Americans in a way which also contributed to awareness and organization building, much like Freire's work in north-eastern Brazil some years later.

In the late 1980s, Myles Horton, the founder of Highlander, and Paulo Freire came together to write a book about their philosophy and practice of using adult education as a force for social change in the North and South (Horton et al, 1990). In many ways, the book was an important symbol for linking two parallel yet differing traditions. (In some ways, because Freire's work was ironically often better known in the US than Horton's or that of others who represented the internal popular education work, the project helped to give attention to and legitimate a tradition already present in the North.)

In addition to this intellectual exchange, we were also involved in a number of projects during the 1980s designed to share the experiences of popular educators in the South, especially in Latin America, with those in the US and Canada. These projects included an exchange of popular educators from Latin America, the US and Canada with Nicaragua in 1983; an exchange of literacy workers with Nicaragua; and multiple visits of Southern-based educators to the US, to Highlander and to community-based groups. These exchanges were important for a number of reasons. First, concrete methods for literacy work were learned and strengthened. Second, especially given the fact that Nicaraguan literacy work was under attack by the US-supported Contras at the time, US grassroots popular educators gained a view of US foreign policy which deepened and developed their grassroots solidarity with other partners in Central America.

A similar transfer of methods from the South to the North is seen in the development and practice of participatory research. The label 'participatory research' was first used by Freire in a conference in Tanzania in the mid-1970s to refer to approaches which involved grassroots people as researchers themselves, rather than as objects of someone else's research. In 1977 in Latin America the first regional conference on participatory research (PR) was held in Cartagena. Under the auspices of the International Council of Adult Education, during the late 1970s and 1980s networks and approaches to participatory research spread rapidly, including to the North. In the US and Canada the development of PR in the South gave strength, both conceptually and practically, to the growth of similar work there. At the Highlander Center, for instance, while we were using similar approaches in our work with poor communities in the Appalachian region, we gained the name, conceptual and methodological understanding, and peer support from links with these Southern networks, through conferences, newsletters, exchanges and partnerships.

In the 1990s, a similar sharing of methods across hemispheres has occurred in the spread of participatory rural appraisal (PRA), now more commonly known as participatory learning and action (PLA), from South to North. First used as a method in India and east Africa in the mid-1980s, these tools have spread rapidly to over 70 countries, and have been used with community development workers in the North. In the UK, for instance, PRA networks have developed in Scotland and in Berkshire and the methods have been used in projects from local planning in Gloucester to assessing healthcare on housing estates in south London. In one case, PRA practitioners from the South facilitated a community-based planning exercise in Scotland (see resource materials, publications and records at IDS, University of Sussex).

The convergence and sharing of participatory methods between South and North was most recently seen in a conference in Cartagena, Colombia, in June 1997. In commemoration of the first Latin American meeting on participatory research held there 20 years before, over 1500 scholars and practitioners representing traditions of PR from both hemispheres came together for a joint congress to share their ideas and experiences.

Example 2: Linking common issues in occupational and environmental health

While the above exchanges focused on sharing methods of working, especially in participatory education and research, other exchanges have concentrated on linking groups facing common problems and responding together. At Highlander, one of the areas that became particularly important involved issues of occupational and environmental health, especially those arising from the movement of wastes and toxic produce across the globe.

Appalachia had long experience in this area. As an area with weak enforcement of laws, plenty of land and water, and a relatively (in the North) low-wage, low-literacy workforce, it was a preferred location for the development of more dangerous industries. With the globalization of markets and production, as well as increased costs and stronger environmental and occupational regulation in the North, these same industries began during the 1970s and 1980s to expand in Southern countries as well.

In 1984, Juliet Merrifield and John Gaventa from Highlander were invited by the Society for Participatory Research in Asia (PRIA) to go to India to share our work in participatory education and research with Appalachian communities on environmental and occupational health issues. Using videos made with American workers, examples were shown of workers and community groups who had organized around such issues as 'brown lung' in the textile mills, or water contamination from chemical plants. A key workshop was held in Bombay with NGOs and workers for whom this was a relatively new field.

A few months after this workshop, the Bhopal disaster occurred, in which a gas leak from United Carbide's chemical factory killed an estimated 10,000 people and maimed thousands more. Once again there were parallels – the Bhopal plant was modelled after a similar Union Carbide plant that had been built in the relatively poor, primarily black Appalachian community of Charleston, West Virginia.

Because of the links which had been built between Highlander and PRIA, they were able to respond quickly in a number of initiatives to share learning on this issue between North and South. A joint research project, *No Place to Run*, told the story of Union Carbide's record in the US, India and other communities globally. A video tape was made in the US sharing the reactions to similar (though far smaller in scope) industrial accidents in factories in the Institute plant and elsewhere; the tape was for use in India. A delegation of health and worker activists came to the US, sponsored by PRIA and Highlander, to share the story of Bhopal as well as to learn more about the experience of US NGOs in dealing with occupational and environmental health issues.

Through this effort, learning occurred at a number of levels. While the US media had attempted to portray the accident as the result of the failures of Indian management, the stories from the US helped to show that similar problems occurred there as well. While Union Carbide flew an Indian doctor from its West Virginia plant to Bhopal to assure residents that there would not be significant health problems, groups in the US were able to use freedom of information laws to obtain documents filed in West Virginia by the same doctor declaring the opposite. The visit of the Indian delegation to poor communities in the US also affected by chemical industries heightened the awareness in the North of their common vulnerabilities with communities in other parts of the world.

In India, the impact of the exchange is still being felt. Some 15 years later, Rajesh Tandon of PRIA reflected:

> These exchanges triggered off a set of activities focusing on worker awareness and occupational health. When our team visited the southern United States in the aftermath of Bhopal, we were impressed by the initiatives of local communities and workers' organizations. The timing of their visit, the sharing of experiences and the support resulted in the establishment of our Centre for Occupational and Environmental Health in PRIA, with fifteen years of experience and a lifetime of commitment (personal interview, August 1997).

Example 3: Who speaks for the North? The UN Conference on Environment and Development

Through the exchanges and work on Bhopal, as well as through other such incidents, Highlander became increasingly aware of the similarities between issues of environment and development in poor regions of the North and those of other parts of the world. In the early 1990s, with funding from the MacArthur Foundation, Highlander joined with the Institute for Development Research (IDR) and the Program in Conflict Management Alternatives (PCMA) at the University of Michigan to develop a series of exchanges around the environment and sustainable development with three Southern partners: the Kenyan Energy and Environment Organization (KENGO); the Movimiento Ambientalista Nicaraguenese (MAN); and the Indonesian Environmental Forum (WALHI).

As an initial part of the three-year exchange, the Southern delegates came to the southern US where they had a chance, in the summer of 1991, to visit rural communities also facing serious environmental issues. They expressed shock at the conditions they saw. At a concluding workshop which brought the international delegates together with representatives of local CBOs and NGOs they had visited, a delegate from Kenya posed the question: 'What will be your position at the UNCED meetings and how are people in your communities feeling about the process?' There were blank stares around the room on the faces of the US activists. 'What is UNCED?' they asked.[1]

The encounter characterized a critical problem of who speaks for the North in the international arena. While many US-based NGOs were of course working to prepare for the United Nations Conference on Environment and Development (UNCED), they were on the whole working with Southern partners, not with grass-roots communities in the North. Those speaking for the environment from the North were national governments (in this case the Bush administration) and US-based corporations. US NGOs and CBOs working on issues in the North, on the whole, have not been part of such international fora.

The encounter prompted Highlander, working with other environmental NGOs, to invite grassroots voices from the North to share in the UNCED process. Towards this end, we asked community-based groups in the North to relate their stories of environment and development as part of a report to be released at the

Rio conference, coorganized a grassroots people's forum in New York to coincide with the Fourth Preparatory Meeting leading up to the Brazil conference, and organized a delegation of grassroots community leaders to go to Brazil to interact with their counter-parts in the Southern hemisphere.

The experience was a powerful one for those involved. The grassroots report gave a very different interpretation of problems of environment and development faced in the North from that provided by the official governmental and non-governmental delegates, who attempted to downplay the problems of environmental degradation at home. Moreover, US activists saw their connections with others around the world. As one young woman from an inner city neighbourhood group dealing with a toxic waste issue wrote:

> I was surprised to find they deal with many of the same problems as the United States and more... For me it [the Earth Summit] has underscored the terrible damage we human beings have done to ourselves and our planet. It has revealed the inseparable links between the World Bank, international debt, and unchecked industrial develop-ment with poverty, hunger, serious health effects, environmental pollution and world climate change. It has shown the world that these global problems are not simply someone else's concern but a threat to everyone everywhere *(Highlander Reports,* 1993, p4).

Example 4: Speaking with new voice to the North: linking workers on jobs and trade issues

A final example involves exchanges with workers affected by job loss and by plant closings. Industries which once came to these relatively poor regions of the North looking for low-skill, low-wage labour are now moving on to newly developing parts of the South, where costs are even cheaper. The Appalachian south has been one such region which has been hard hit, as industries flee 'from the mountains to the maquiladoras' (Gaventa, 1990).

At times in such situations, the tendency of Northern workers and community members has been to blame workers elsewhere for 'stealing their jobs', not to assess the corporate and governmental policies in their own country that may have con-tributed to their job loss. Partly in response to this issue, Highlander worked with the Tennessee Industrial Renewal Network (TIRN), a coalition of unions, churches and CBOs, to organize a study tour so that women who had lost their jobs in the Appalachian region could visit their counterparts who had gained similar jobs in the Souths – in this case, the maquiladora region of Mexico.

As in other examples given above, the women workers were struck by the par-allels they found in the rapidly industrializing parts of Mexico. At the same time, they were shocked by the working and living conditions they saw, conditions pro-moted by a US corporation and government to which they felt some loyalty. The learning led to new types of action. The US workers, who themselves were prima-rily unemployed or worked in low-wage jobs, pledged to raise money for a van to be used for a new organization of women workers in Mexico. But more importantly, they began to take action in their own country on government policies which they came to see as part of the reason for their job loss, travelling throughout the state testifying on jobs and trade issues in the context of the North American Free Trade Agreement (NAFTA) debate.

Testifying before a trade policy committee, one of the women, a member of TIRN and of her local union, expressed her learning this way:

> They [the Mexican women] were glad to welcome us because they believed us when we said we would try to come back to this country and tell the American people the truth about life and work in the maquiladoras. They asked us to bring back the word to you about what is happening to those on the bottom in Mexico. Because what is happening ought to be a crime. And it is hurting not only Mexicans, it is a direct threat to the standard of living of American workers.
>
> The multi-national corporations bear much responsibility for what is happening. But it is not just the corporation I blame. I blame the government too. Our government should be insisting on corporate accountability. Instead it rewards irresponsibility. Our government should set some ground rules so companies are not pressured to compete with each other on the basis of how much they can gouge their workers. Instead, it pushes a version of free trade that encourages low wage competition.
>
> We must learn from the failures of the maquiladora program and develop a free trade agreement with Mexico that will not repeat the same patterns. We need decent jobs at decent wages for workers on both sides of the border. We need roads and sewers and schools and garbage disposal and health care and retirement plans and parks and safe workplaces and playgrounds on both sides of the border.
>
> Any trade deal we reach with Mexico should start with a commitment to a healthy development pattern for both countries (Petty, 1991, p8).

In this case, the American workers and community groups became vocal organizers, educators and activists at home regarding policy issues affecting trade, human rights and the environment in the South, as well as at home.

Conclusion: Key Lessons and Themes for North–South Learning

These are a few examples of learning that have come about through exchanges between Northern and Southern NGOs and communities. What do these examples tell us about the value of such work? Several key principles emerge.

Demythologizing North and South

First, through these exchanges we have seen that there are numerous examples of participants gaining a recognition of the commonalities between their own situations and those of others in different parts of the globe. This recognition was particularly important because of the ways in which the exchanges worked to demythologize the differences between the North and South.

For Southern activists, the image of the US as a land of relative wealth and opportunity serves as a powerful symbol, suggesting that the US model offers a more 'advanced' approach to development. Many participants talked about how important it was for them to see that the North faced similar problems as well. This deconstruction of the symbolic divisions and the recognition of commonalities, as well as differences, became a first necessary step for further learning and action.

For example, following their visit to the US, participants in the worker and occupational health exchange wrote:

> ... we did not believe the under-development we saw in the world's largest capitalist state... Though the context of that poverty is somewhat different from our situation in India, we were able to understand the growing phenomenon of third world creation within the USA. The powerless and the poor of USA face similar forces as similar groups face in India. This realisation made us keen to learn seriously from the experiences of community groups and workers' associations there (Pandey et al, 1985, p129).

A Nicaraguan participant in environmental exchanges said:

> The collaboration has provided enormous learnings for all of us... We still believed in the US discourse on democracy, on the 'perfect' US model. Through our visit to Highlander, we saw the problems and the links. Our communities and countries serve as the testing ground to see if the North can send us their waste, saying that it promoted jobs. Before the exchange, I would not have seen those relationships. This process has helped us to strengthen the relationships between communities, NGOs and communities and governments. The richness of the experience also contributed to strengthening our capacities for analysis within the diversities of our societies. By building new linkages, opportunities for reflection and communication, we are on the verge of the birth of a new methodology of participation – it's not fully cooked but it's beginning (Covey et al, 1995, p9).

Equally important for Northern participants was the debunking of received myths about the South. The US educational system and media in particular have tended to limit the understanding and images ordinary people have of the rest of the world. At one level, participants expressed amazement at the knowledge, commitment and sophistication of their Southern counterparts – a reality that did not fit with their received images of 'backward' people. Moreover, they often gained inspiration from the commitment which they saw:

> I grew up in the civil rights movement so I know about overcoming. I've had personal battles and have made it through but the day-to-day survival scenes I saw in Brazil taught me the meaning of faith, hope and forgiveness. I watched people who possess true power (quoted in *Highlander Reports*, 1993, p4).

Another Northern participant commented:

> By getting rid of our myths, we create the desire to learn more. Understanding that we have been taught wrong and then looking at the problems and consequences of that misteaching creates enormous openings. It's like turning a rock into a piece of clay that wants to be malleable by choice (quoted in Covey et al, 1995, p11).

For participants from both North and South, seeing similar problems in other parts of the world helped to highlight the universal nature of the problems they were addressing and to reinforce that they were rooted in larger patterns of development rather than in their own particular circumstance.

The value of sharing methods and approaches

The case examples have also indicated several examples of where NGOs and CBOs have learned new methods and approaches for their work across North and South – for instance, the use of popular education and PR from the South to the North, or the ways of addressing problems of industrial health from North to South. There are many other recent examples of transfer of methods in both directions – the use of community or advocacy methods have transferred from the North to the South; the adaptation of Gandhian non-violent methods to the American civil rights movement; the transfer of models of microcredit and banking from the South to organizations in the US and the UK, and so on.

At the same time, the exchanges also pointed to some differences in the types of methods of organizing and action that are possible in different contexts. Some Northern participants expressed shock at the conditions of repression and violence which they saw in other countries, while some Southern delegates learned from the relative openness which they found in the US:

> Before we went to Brazil, I knew the world was messed up. I knew about haves and have nots. I knew about the interdependence of the world's problems stemming from greed and supported by race, class, and sex division among people. I knew all this by having experienced being a Black, poor, female living in my native Kansas. What I did not know was that my experiences were similar to those of many persons from all over the world. What is worse, I was lucky not to have lived with the daily violence supporting the oppressive conditions (quoted in *Highlander Reports*, 1993, p15).

While Northern participants learned a great deal about participatory methods from the South, Southern participants reported learning about advocacy and organizing strategies from the North, as well as strategies concerned with freedom of information.

Mutual learning and horizontal relationships

The growing recognition of common issues and of the value of exchanging lessons and experiences can begin to contribute to new models of working together across hemispheres. In the past, relationships between Northern and Southern NGOs have often been somewhat vertical, with the Northern NGOs seen as donors and advisers to the South, and the Southern NGOs seen mainly as recipients and local partners. In the cases examined here, relationships were more horizontal and learning was considered a mutual process. A critical feature of the learning was the fact that people linked based *on their own experiences*. As Rajesh Tandon of PRIA put it, 'when we came together people never talked about other's realities. People talked about their own. It felt like a genuine discussion' (personal interview). The creation of mutual learning and horizontal links also allows the possibility of building the trust and social capital necessary for collaboration across borders.

Towards new organizational innovation

To deepen learning and linkages between North and South will itself require new organizational development and innovation. In the cases here, the sharing occurred mainly through isolated exchanges and workshops. A next step, but one which is equally important, is to begin to build North–South alliances and coalitions, or global civil society organizations, which can move from learning to action, and from vertical to horizontal ways of relating.

To do so is not an easy task. To develop and sustain partnerships across borders is logistically and financially difficult, and it also requires the development of new relationships of trust and social capital, new organizational forms, and new commitment to recognize and act upon issues of poverty and power in the North as well as in the South. This chapter has begun to suggest that such new approaches are possible, especially when they are built on prior learning that involves demythologizing stereotypes of North and South, sharing methods and experiences of work, and mutual, horizontal forms of exchange.

Notes

1 Drawn from Highlander Center documents and personal observation.

References

Bachrach, P and Baratz, M S (1970) Power and Poverty: Theory and Practice, Oxford University Press, New York.
Boyte, H C (1980) *The Backyard Revolution: Understanding the New Citizen Movement*, Temple University Press, Philadelphia.
Boyte, H C, Booth, H and Max, S (1986) *Citizen Action and the New American Populism*, Temple University Press, Philadelphia.
Couto, R A (1994) *An American Challenge*, Kendall/Hunt Publishing Company, Dubuque, Iowa.
Covey, J, Gaventa, J, Miller, V and Pasmore, W (1995) 'Multinational collaboration in community problem solving: a theoretical perspective', paper presented at the Conference on Organizational Dimensions of Global Change, May 1995' sponsored by the Academy of Management and Case Western Reserve University.
Delgado, G (1993) *Beyond the Politics of Place: New Directions in Community Organizing in the 1990s*, Applied Research Center, Oakland, California.
de Tocqueville, A (1966) (originally written in 1835) *Democracy in America*, Vol 2, Collins Fontana Library, London.
Gaventa, J (1980) *Power and Powerlessness: Quiescence and Rebellion in an Appalachian Valley*, University of Illinois Press, Urbana and Clarendon Press, Oxford.

Gaventa, J (1990) 'From the mountains to the maquiladoras: a case study of capital flight and its impact on workers', in J Gaventa, B Smith, and A Willingham (eds) *Communities in Economic Crisis*, Temple University Press, Philadelphia.

Gaventa, J (1991) 'Overcoming constraints to ill-health in Appalachia, community-based links with the world', in R E Morgan Jr and B Rau (eds) *Global Learning for Health*, National Council for International Health, Washington, DC.

Highlander Reports (1993) 'Making the links: the southeast and the southern hemisphere: local community leaders and the United Nations Conference on Environment and Development', Highlander Research and Education Center, Tennessee.

Horton, M, Freire, P, Bell, B, Gaventa, J and Peters, J (eds) (1990) *We Make the Road by Walking: Conversations on Education and Social Change*, Temple University Press, Philadelphia.

Maxwell, S (1997) *Comparisons, Convergence, and Connections: Development Studies in North and South*, Institute for Development Studies, Sussex.

Pandey, G, Thankappan, D, Kanhere, V and Tandon, R (1985) *Worker Activists and Educators Tour: Report of USA and UK*, Society for Participatory Research in Asia, New Delhi.

Petty, D (1991) Testimony Prepared for the Trade Staff Policy Committee, Office of the US Trade Representative, Atlanta, Georgia, 29 August, Tennessee Industrial Renewal Network, Knoxville, Tennessee.

Putnam, R D (1995) 'Bowling alone: America's declining social capital', *Journal of Democracy*, Vol 6, No 1, pp65–78.

Verba, G and Nie, N H (1972) *Participation in America: Political Democracy and Social Equality*, Harper & Row, New York.

World Bank (1991) *World Development Report 1991*, Table 30, Oxford University Press, New York.

Part 6

Measuring Achievement: Approaches and Methods

NGO Performance: What Breeds Success? New Evidence from South Asia

Michael Edwards

Introduction

What is the best way for non-governmental organizations (NGOs) to make a lasting impact on poverty? This chapter summarizes the findings of recent research into the impact, sustainability and cost-effectiveness of two NGOs in India and two projects implemented by Save the Children Fund-UK in Bangladesh. The factors determining performance are explored through the interaction of organizational decisions with the external context. Although these interactions are complex and dynamic, some clear conclusions emerge. Making a difference to livelihoods and capacities among poor people depends on NGO successes in fostering autonomous grassroots institutions and linking them with markets and political structures at higher levels. These conclusions question the current predilection among donor agencies to fund large-scale NGO service delivery.

All NGOs want to make the best possible use of their limited resources to achieve the greatest impact on poverty and powerlessness in a cost-effective manner. But how is this goal to be achieved? This question has occupied researchers and practitioners for many years, without generating a solid consensus on the answers. Some commentators advise NGOs to focus their core functions, standardize their procedures, and concentrate on maximizing 'operational performance' in the context of large-scale service delivery (Jain, 1994, 1996). Others advocate the flexibility to respond in different ways across a diverse set of activities, with an underlying emphasis on grassroots-level empowerment (Edwards and Hulme, 1992, 1995; Fowler, 1997). These differences stem from varying interpretations of NGOs and their mission, as well as from the constraints and opportunities provided by different economic and political settings. Against this background, are any generalizations valid?

This chapter reports on one study which tried to identity the factors underlying the impact, sustainability and cost-effectiveness of two intermediary NGOs in India and two projects implemented by Save the Children Fund-UK (SCF) in Bangladesh. Basic data on each of the four cases are presented in Table 17.1. Because the study aimed to promote local ownership of the findings and enhance each agency's capacity to undertake similar research for itself, the four cases were allowed to select themselves from among SCF's partners in each country. This reduced the comparability of the findings since – although each case differs from the others – these differences were not systematically controlled for in the process of case selection. Nevertheless, they do represent a useful cross-section of contexts and approaches:

- PREM (People's Rural Educational Movement) in Orissa supports the development of grassroots organizations (called 'People's Organizations' or POs) at all levels from the village to the state, to obtain, lobby for and/or manage institutions, services and programmes. It provides the appropriate mix of technical, financial and capacity-building support and works closely with POs on programme initiatives where this is necessary, but generally steers clear of direct intervention.
- Urmul Seemant in Rajasthan (which is an autonomous NGO within the wider family of the Urmul Trust) mixes support to grassroots organizations (farmers' and women's groups), with direct service delivery on contract to the state government in village-level health and education, and advocacy work related to the Indira Gandhi Canal.
- SCF's Shariatpur Project in Bangladesh is directly operational, but aims to hand over responsibility to local institutions over time. It runs a credit-and-savings programme through women's groups, and provides financial and technical support to village water-supply improvements and primary healthcare through an innovative training programme for private practitioners.
- The River Project in Bangladesh spent 20 years as an operational project of SCF, running a wide range of programmes in relief, healthcare, education, agriculture and economic development. These initiatives have been gradually wound down to refocus the work on credit-and-savings, and an 'Income Enhancement Scheme' (IES) for the very poor. SCF continues to implement the IES but has handed over the credit programme to a local NGO called 'Sinomul Mahila Samiti' (SMS), to which it has agreed to provide financial and other support for a limited period.

Hypotheses and Methods

The main hypothesis of the study was that NGO performance is the outcome of a dynamic interaction between external influences (context) and internal influences (organizational choices). In each case there is likely to be an optimal response to the opportunities and constraints provided by the external environment as it evolves, but finding it requires a certain set of organizational characteristics and a supportive relationship with resource providers. These may seem obvious points yet they are often neglected in evaluations which treat contextual factors as determinant – community characteristics, for example, or economic and political structures (Riddell and Robinson, 1996). This approach ignores the influence of the NGO itself – its strategies, culture, structure, mode of financing, and the decisions it takes over what is done, by whom and how. As other recent research has shown, these internal characteristics are equally important in determining outputs, outcomes and – as they interact with external influences – eventual impacts (Fowler et al, 1996; Zadek, 1996; Ritchey-Vance, 1996). Organizational and management theories suggest that NGOs which lack the capacity to learn and iterate or are dependent for their survival on

Table 17.1 *Basic Data for the Four Cases*

People's Rural Education Movement (PREM), Orissa, India	Urmul Seemant, Bikaner District, Rajasthan, India	Shariatpur Project (SCF), Shariatpur District, Bangladesh	River Project (SCF), Jamalpur and Gaibanda Districts, Bangladesh
Founded: 1980	**Founded:** 1984	**Founded:** 1990	**Founded:** 1975
Aims: to develop capacity among tribal people and fisherfolk to organize, make demands and address needs; to build individual and collective assets.	**Aims:** to support sustainable agriculture and income-generation among refugees and pastoralists; to improve access to health and education services,	**Aims:** to raise living standards among the very poor; to improve access to potable water; to improve the quality of healthcare provided by private practitioners,	**Aims:** originally, to improve access to basic services and hand over schools and clinics to government; now, to promote livelihood security among the very poor.
Activities: support to a federation of People's Organizations from village to state level; advice on food security, credit, health and education; research, training and advocacy on tribal rights.	**Activities:** support to farmers' and women's groups; provision of health and education services on contract to state government; training, research and advocacy related to the Indira Gandhi Canal.	**Activities** a credit-and-savings scheme for women's groups; support to village development committees, training of health practitioners; provision of tubewells under community maintenance,	**Activities:** up to 1995: relief, health, nutrition and education facilities. Since then: support to credit schemes through women's groups; targeted support to the poorest families via temporary sharecropping.
Outputs: 42 POs covering c5000 villages; 360 PO representatives elected to political office; 183 schools; 1500 seed and grain banks; a credit society with 21,000 members.	**Outputs:** 27 semi-autonomous groups with some success in collective action; 125 women in income-generation programmes earning cRs400/month; 5000 children in schools and 15,000 in ICDS, programme.	**Outputs:** 4000 members in credit groups with 90 per cent plus repayment rates and administration costs half-covered from service charges; 281 TBAs and 17 CHPs[a] trained; 208 tubewells installed (3 not functioning).	**Outputs:** to 1995: basic services provided to c.70,000 people, most now defunct. Since then: 5500 members of credit groups with 90 per cent plus repayment rates and expenses covered from service charges; 100 female sharecroppers.
External context: socially homogeneous communities; political space for grassroots organization and lobbying; the highest illiteracy and infant mortality rates in India.	**External context:** socially heterogeneous communities; government support for NGO service-provision cf grassroots organization: semi-arid ecology and low population density.	**External context:** highly unequal social structure and acute landlessness; use of force by landed elites against grassroots organization; unstable 'char' land makes cultivation difficult.	**External context:** highly unequal social structure and acute landlessness; use of force by landed elites against grassroots organization; unstable 'char' land makes cultivation difficult.

a Traditional birth attendants and community health practitioners donors who demand short-term measurable results, are unlikely to be effective in supporting the longer-term social and institutional changes that sustainable development demands (Edwards and Hulme, 1996; Fowler, 1997). The full results of the study are presented in Edwards (1996).

Three sets of methods were used in combination with each other:

1   A review of existing documents (secondary literature, project files, annual reports, evaluation and research studies, and outputs from monitoring systems); and detailed analysis of income and expenditure accounts.
2   Semi-structured interviews and guided discussions with NGO staff and participants in programmes, using a standard framework of questions (reproduced in Edwards, 1996).
3   PRA techniques during meetings and field visits (Chambers, 1994), including: direct observation by the researchers; critical incident analysis; organizational and programme timelines; diagrams of the structure, activities and linkages of the organization; time-allocation charts; flow-charts; and 'spider diagrams' (used by staff to evaluate their progress toward different objectives). Research which takes only a 'snapshot' of the current situation cannot unravel contingent and emerging interactions between contexts and organizations, but by using techniques like these it is possible to shed more light on how different influences combine over time. Examples of these diagrams, and further detail on the strengths and weaknesses of PRA techniques in organizational self-assessment, can be found in Edwards (1997).

To combat bias the same questions and exercises were used with each agency, and the results were cross-checked both against other sources of information and against the same set of answers or diagrams provided by a different level of staff, or staff in a different part of the organization. One lead researcher coordinated all four studies and the analysis of the results. Each began with a workshop to produce the timelines, structure and activity diagrams. The next three days were spent in the field and the final day took the form of another workshop to explore the preliminary findings. Feedback from this process was used by the research team to produce a draft report, which was further revised in consultation with the four agencies involved. Given that SCF's programme in Bangladesh was undergoing a major strategic review at the time of the study, some of the judgements may have been biased towards the negative. The short amount of time spent in the field may also have led to complex sociopolitical realities being underrepresented in the analysis, compared with the richness of the organizational findings. Although PRA is a good way of generating 'optimal ignorance' at the micro-level (Chambers, 1994), it is of less value in unlocking the influence of higher level forces.

The balance between these different techniques and levels of analysis was determined by the overall purpose of the study – to demonstrate that it is possible to understand what determines success in ways which are both reasonably rigorous and organizationally useful, without a huge investment of time and resources in NGOs which are already overstretched. That meant abandoning control groups, tests of statistical significance and aggregation in favour of detailed qualitative work, complemented by quantitative analysis where data were easy to find and safe to use (as in the annual accounts of each NGO). By 'layering' techniques and sources on top of each other it was possible to build up a rich picture in a short space of time.

Findings

The broad objectives of all four NGOs are the same – to achieve sustained improvements in the livelihoods of poor people and their capacity to influence the forces which shape these livelihoods. Therefore, the study explored the sustainability and cost-effectiveness of the impacts achieved, as well as the nature of the impacts themselves. Table 17.2 summarizes the scale and per capita cost of each agency's activities.

Impact

Each agency looked at impact in three ways: material living conditions (incomes and services), organizational skills and capacities (confidence and associational strength) and political empowerment (influence over decision-making). The balance between these goals, however, varied from one agency to another. The two Bangladesh cases emphasized outputs (such as improved access to credit or tubewells) and outcomes (like better health services); the two Indian NGOs made a more explicit claim to connect outcomes to impacts (on poverty, health status and political influence). At one end of the spectrum, PREM demonstrated a high impact on both material and organizational indicators across a population of over 800,000 people, at a per capita cost of £0.17. At the other extreme, the River Project showed a low impact on each dimension among a population of under 40,000 people, at a per capita cost of £4.53. These figures are a very crude measure of costs and benefits, but clearly something significant is at work. The question is, what?

The key difference lies in the multiplier effect of PREM's approach, which generates indirect benefits to many more people. In approximately the same time period, PREM has facilitated the emergence of a credit-and-savings society four times as large as those in Shariatpur or River, and a federation of POs (called FOPO) with 42 members covering around 5000 villages, compared with 27 village groups in the case of Urmul Seemant. Yet PREM's budget is only twice that of Urmul and one-third larger than the two SCF projects. PREM's approach to scaling-up does not seem to have affected the quality of work undertaken or the technical standards of the services provided. Credit-and-savings programmes initiated under PREM's guidance have repayment rates as high as those in the other case studies (90–95 per cent), and all three reach people with few assets.[1] Monitoring data show that five years in one of the 'non-formal education centres' supported by PREM has the same impact on literacy and numeracy as the same length of time spent in government schools, but under a more relevant curriculum. A recent independent evaluation of health services facilitated by PREM gave them high marks in terms of both technical standards, and coverage and sustainability (SCF, 1996). In addition, the POs have developed 1100 grain banks, 400 seed banks, 1200 land redistributions and over 150,000 acres of fruit trees in the space of only five years.

Access to loans and income-earning opportunities has increased in all four programmes as a result of credit programmes or craft production targeted explic-

Table 17.2 Costs and Beneficiaries

	Target population	Direct beneficiaries	Indirect beneficiaries	Total costs	Programme costs[a]	Administration costs	Cost per beneficiary[b]
PREM	Tribals in nine districts of Orissa	c600,000 (population of villages with fully active POs)	c240,000 (population of villages 'partially-organized' by POs)	£145,363 (1993–94)	£125,202	£20,161	£0.17
Urmul Seem ant	One half of one block in Bikaner District (c150,000)	c40,000 (women in income-generation groups, men in farmers' groups, children in 'Lok Jumbish' schools and ICDS centres	c10,000 (family members of adults in the IGA[c] and agricultural programmes)	£62,996 (1993–94)	£56,695	£6,299	£1.26
Shariatpur	Three unions of one district (c48,000)	c4000 (members of credit groups, trained TBA[d] and CHPs)	c35,000 (family members of adults in credit programme, plus population of villages with tube wells)	£109,499 (1994–95)	£76,666	£32,833	£2.74
River Project	Population of project area 70,000	c3,100 (members of credit groups, women in the IES)	c26,900 (family members of adults in credit and IES programmes)	£135,999 (1994–95)	£112,333	£26,666	£4.53

a Exchange rates at the time of the study were: £1 = 49.6 Indian Rupees or 55 Bangladesh Thaka
b Total costs divided by direct plus indirect beneficiaries
c Income-generation activities
d Traditional birth attendants and community health practitioners

itly at women, although as elsewhere control over resources is shared with men (Goetz and Sen Gupta, 1994; Hashemi, Schuler and Riley, 1996). The impact of these programmes is also seen in social terms – in the confidence which comes with access to resources, the managerial and organizational skills which develop gradually in group work, and the challenge to gender stereotypes which this form of empowerment represents. Examples of impact at this level are easier to find in the Indian cases than in Bangladesh. For example, women in credit groups in Rajasthan now take the bus to Urmul Seemant's base at Bajju (two years ago this was unheard of). Women in POs in Orissa and village groups in Rajasthan have taken legal action against men found guilty of taking more than one wife, and have reduced marriage expenses by decreasing dowry sizes and cutting the length of marriage celebrations from 15 days to two. Women's representation among the staff and trustees of the NGOs and POs in the study is not equal to that of men, but in PREM and FOPO it is close to 40 per cent in key grades – 7 out of 16 members of PREM's 'Core Team', for example, are women. It is in this area – confidence and capacities – that PREM outperforms the other cases. In Orissa, POs have increased their impact by:

- Influencing the political process. Strategic voting in the 1991 local elections ensured that 45 representatives were elected at *'panchayat'* level and 360 at ward level. Once elected, they can direct more resources to their members from government schemes for infrastructure and employment. As part of a nationwide movement of tribal groups, FOPO has successfully pressured the Indian Government to extend the provisions of the 'Panchayati Raj' Bill to 'scheduled areas' with effect from December 1996.
- Linking grassroots interests with decision-makers at the state and national levels. The 'Kalinga Fishermen's Union' is a PO with 35,000 members. It has organized demonstrations against the illegal use of large trawlers in offshore fishing grounds and – as a member of the 'All-India Fisheries Union' – succeeded in blocking a move by the giant Tata Corporation to establish a base on Lake Chilika, after questions were raised in the Indian Parliament. Three years later the Union persuaded the authorities in Delhi to revoke the licences of deep-sea trawlers operating off the coast of Orissa, and at least one trawler owner was prosecuted.
- Leveraging government resources. For example, the statewide Women's Credit and Savings Society has used its own savings to quadruple its loan capacity using a soft loan from NABARD, the State Agricultural Bank.

Contrast this with the situation in Bangladesh, where even after 20 years of working in the River Project, only two of the schools started by the project have survived and no attempt is being made by grassroots groups to pressure for change.

Sustainability

Among Bangladeshi NGOs, there is a tendency to concentrate on the sustainability of the NGO itself – the aim being for the agency to be in a position to continue serving its target group over time. This is especially true of credit providers. SMS already covers all its administrative costs from service charges on loans and the Shariatpur scheme covers half. In the two Indian cases, the definition has more to do with sustaining the *benefits* of NGO work and in particular strengthening the capacity of local people to do things for themselves into the future. In this respect PREM's strategy has been the most effective. Although it is impossible to prove whether a group is sustainable in advance of removing external support, it is possible to draw some preliminary conclusions by looking at how groups behave in the present. Urmul Seemant's staff ranked impact on community management lowest in all their spider diagrams. None of the women's groups in the Income Generation Programmes is within sight of independence; they depend on Urmul Seemant for raw materials, design, make-up of the final product and marketing, although members are more willing to travel away from their villages to take part in trade fairs in Jaipur and Delhi. The older farmers' groups show some progress towards independence and have taken on increasing responsibility for negotiations with local banks and government departments over funding and logistics. The degree of community involvement in Urmul Seemant's health and education activities varies considerably: in the Integrated Child Development Services (ICDS) programme it is low, whereas in the education work (which is seen as a shared responsibility rather than a programme of government) it is higher, with some community management via committees which can and do penalize errant teachers for poor performance. Even here, however, teachers stopped work when they heard that funding from the Swedish International Development Agencies (Sida) might be withdrawn.

In the River Project there is little evidence that any of the services developed in the 1970s and 1980s have been sustained: only two of 40+ schools remain in operation (transferred to government or to joint government/community management), and all the health facilities and workers have disappeared. After 20 years of work and almost £2 million (sterling) invested, one might expect more to have been left behind than this. Contrast this with Orissa where a failure by government to maintain 40 per cent of the 77 schools handed over in the 1990s by PREM was met with a successful campaign by POs to pressure the authorities into accepting their share of the responsibility and negotiate a joint solution (helped by the mobilization of thousands of schoolchildren). Although only 13 of the 42 members of FOPO are 'fully autonomous' in PREM's judgement, many others are well on the way, and nearly all cover their operating costs from their own funds. PREM provides financial support for programme and training costs, but the bulk comes from local banks (where savings are deposited) and government schemes (redirected via PO representation in the 'panchayat' system). In 1994, POs took legal action against representatives who failed in their duties (one 'Sarpanch' was jailed as a result), and have also suspended cooperation with PREM when dissatisfied with the performance of staff and volunteers.

Cost-effectiveness

Calculations of cost-effectiveness in all four agencies are difficult, since current costs are easier to measure than cumulative benefits. The estimates in Table 17.2 simply divide total agency budgets by the number of people receiving some form of benefit from their work, however transitory. Nevertheless, it is clear that the two Bangladesh cases (which concentrate on direct service delivery) have much higher cost-to-benefit ratios in crude terms because they have high overheads (a large number of staff and buildings at the head office and subcentres), a small number of staff-intensive activities (training and credit group promotion) and (in Shariatpur at least) higher costs associated with a foreign agency like SCF (especially salaries). Handing over the credit programme in the River Project to SMS resulted in an increase in the number of beneficiaries from 3000 to 5400 in under a year, simultaneously cutting administration costs by 75 per cent – reaching almost twice as many people for roughly a quarter of the cost incurred by SCF. It is no coincidence that local people nicknamed SCF in the River Project area 'gaab', the Bengali name for a low-priced fruit which they associated with waste. The same problem affects Urmul Seemant, which has a per capita expenditure almost five times higher than PREM for delivering similar levels of benefits to less than a quarter of the population. PREM's focus on institutional development, coupled with a low fixed cost base, makes their work exceptionally cost-effective (allowances in place of salaries, no permanent buildings in the field and no vehicles for field staff).

To summarize, there is no evidence that impact, sustainability and cost-effectiveness have to be traded-off against each other. PREM scores highly on all three counts and the River Project scores poorly across the board. PREM has facilitated improvements in access to assets and services at similar levels of quality, across a much larger population and at a fraction of the cost of the other three programmes, and has done so in a way that has strengthened local capacity to sustain these improvements into the future. The best results come where resources are directed simultaneously at organizational development and economic security, so that each supports and feeds off the other. This is a dominant theme in the rest of the chapter.

Explanations

External context

Although there are some differences between the four contexts in terms of basic indicators of poverty and human needs, they do not seem very relevant in explaining variations in NGO performance. Orissa has a lower percentage of households below the poverty line (48 per cent) than Shariatpur and River (where 71.4 per cent families are landless), but adult literacy is lower in Orissa and infant mortality rates are much higher. The Thar desert in Rajasthan and the heavily skewed land distribution of rural Bangladesh offer a less promising setting for agricultural development than Orissa, so economic development and asset-building is more difficult there. But all four agencies confront high levels of poverty and inequality.

What do seem significant are differences in social and political conditions. Where communities are more homogenous in terms of social status, or where an NGO chooses only to work with homogeneous communities, then social organization and awareness-raising is much easier. This is the case with PREM's work with tribal communities and fisherfolk in Orissa. Contrast this with the much more heterogeneous 'communities' to be found in the desert area of Rajasthan, which are made up by a range of different castes and accommodate indigenous people, refugees from Pakistan, and migrants to the Indira Gandhi Canal from other parts of the state. Gender discrimination also seems more entrenched among the caste-based villages of Rajasthan than among tribal communities in Orissa, which may account for some of the success of women in forming their own POs and in local elections. In Bangladesh, highly inegalitarian social relations based on land ownership and gender are rigidly, and sometimes violently, enforced; attempts to change them (by strengthening organizations of the poorest, as PREM has done in Orissa) are therefore resisted fiercely by local elites (Hashemi, 1995).

These influences are reinforced by variations in the amount of political space allowed for different forms of NGO activity in different contexts. In India generally, NGOs are given more leeway to become involved in grassroots organization, lobbying and advocacy, though if they go too far government will step in. The political context for NGO work is positive in both Orissa and Rajasthan, although it is more difficult in the latter where district and state officials value Urmul Seemant more for its service delivery role than for its organizational and advocacy work. In Bangladesh, the context is much more difficult. After a period during the 1970s and early 1980s when Bangladeshi NGOs experimented with conscientization strategies at village level, there has been a gradual move away from grassroots mobilization and towards service delivery as the centrepiece of NGO strategy – combined, where possible, with low-profile awareness-raising and legal education work (Hashemi, 1995; Wood, 1997). These moves have been encouraged by successive government regimes (fearful of social protest), foreign donor agencies (using NGOs to circumvent what they see as corrupt and inefficient state bureaucracies), and NGO critics among journalists and Islamic groups, who have questioned the legitimacy of NGOs in their social role and charged them with acting as a cover for external or religious interests. NGO activity outside service delivery is discouraged by a restrictive legal and regulatory framework, and direct intervention by state authorities when it is breached (Hashemi, 1995). These factors make it dangerous for Bangladeshi NGOs to adopt PREM's tactics.

External donor agencies emerge as a significant influence on NGO performance. In India, this influence has been positive but minor, with both PREM and Urmul Seemant enjoying support from a network of loyal and (for the most part) flexible international NGOs such as SCF, Oxfam and Action Aid. In Bangladesh, the picture is less positive. Here, successive SCF country directors have brought their own enthusiasms to programmes outside any strategic framework, learning from experience or clear long-term objectives. Consequently, the continuity required to attack complex and difficult development problems at grassroots level in an area like River has been lacking. The timeline for the River Project shows this clearly, with a four or five-year cycle of major programme changes coinciding with the arrival of each new director: from relief to health work, on to education, and most recently economic interventions, with each phase largely failing to build on the others.

Organizational choices

Goals and strategies
One of the strongest lessons to emerge from the research is that success is more likely when organizations identify a clear long-term goal at the outset and stick to it over time. Conversely, agencies which change their goals too often or try to follow too many goals at the same time, often lose their way. The clearest example of

this pattern is the River Project, whose timeline shows too many changes of direction and an inability to decide on core mission. The flow diagrams drawn by staff showed a *logic* to the way activities developed, but not much of a *strategy*. Relief led into health, which stimulated more of an interest in child welfare and therefore education. When parents found it difficult to meet the costs of sending their children to school, the credit programme was born, and when that failed to reach the poorest families, SCF introduced an 'Income Enhancement Scheme' which donated treadle water-pumps to women sharecroppers in the hope that they would graduate to a credit group within two to three years. But it was never clear how these activities were connected to more fundamental goals of social organization and capacity-building.

Urmul Seemant also has clear goals, but it has been more willing to take on new programmes (such as the ICDS or 'Lok Jumbish' informal schooling programmes), and terminate others (such as village-based healthcare), according to the availability of government or donor funding. This, combined with less time and resources spent on strengthening and interlinking village groups, has made it more difficult to achieve the ultimate objective of community management. Contrast this with PREM in Orissa, which identified awareness-raising and organizational development as the core goal to which everything else would be, and has been, subordinated. This has included the rejection of funding from donor agencies (including £100,000 from Action Aid): an important element in PREM's success has been the willingness to say 'no' to expansion or diversification when it considers that this might prejudice impact or sustainability.

Balancing material and social development

Securing advances in both living standards and organizational skills is crucial for sustainable change. Finding and keeping the appropriate balance between the two emerges as a key influence on NGO performance – the more equal the balance and the earlier it is established in the life of a programme, the more successful the outcome will be. This is particularly important where relief or service provision provides an entry point, as happened in both programmes in Bangladesh and with Urmul Seemant in Rajasthan. Unless attention is paid to awareness-raising and organizational development during this early phase, there is a tendency for programmes to drift into service delivery later on.

PREM was fortunate that the first drought it confronted arrived eight years after it had started work, so the first phase could be spent in developing trust and confidence, forming grassroots organizations, and providing legal education. When it arrived, the first large-scale 'material' work (fruit tree plantations, seed and grain banks) therefore had a solid foundation. At every stage in the development of the POs, material and organizational advances have gone hand-in-hand. The Fishermen's Union, for example, provides nets and practical support to improve fishing techniques and train young people in how to use them, at the same time as lobbying government to take action against illegal trawling. Advances in assets and services maintain people's interest while the process of organizational development is continuing, and provide the security which is essential for poor people to take an active role in non-economic initiatives. At the same time, advances in confidence, skills, capacities and institutions enable economic initiatives and services to be managed more effectively and equitably at community level, and/or to help people to engage more effectively in a dialogue with government to share the costs and responsibilities of operating services into the future.

In Urmul Seemant's case, the desire to fill gaps in basic health and education services and the decision to accept major government contracts (with the aim of influencing the ICDS programme) took staff time and resources away from grassroots institutional development at a crucial time. The time-allocation charts for staff in Urmul Seemant's Income-Generating Programme show, that most of the day is taken up by tasks connected to service provision or to doing things *for* village groups, leaving little time for less structured and unhurried group discussion and development. Contrast this with PREM, which spends 50 per cent of its core budget on community-level training and awareness-raising. The Shariatpur timeline shows that the first 12 months were spent in building up the project base camp and subcentres and recruiting staff. More of this early time could have been spent in building links with people in the target area, who have since criticized the subcentres as 'palaces where little work is done' and 'prisons we cannot go into' – not the best basis for a programme which ultimately depends for its success on community involvement. The 'village development committees' instigated by SCF in Shariatpur have been captured by local elites and/or fallen quickly into abeyance. As the chair of the Ghorishar Committee (which had not met for the last two years) put it, 'they are almost extinct... meaningless. [I] cannot remember anything useful that they have done at all.'

Scaling-up

There are many ways to increase the impact of NGO activities (Edwards and Hulme, 1992), but the risks associated with some are higher than others. Working with government (especially as a contractor) brings pressure to achieve short-term quantitative targets and this may destabilize other aspects of the programme. Urmul Seemant's experience with the Indian Government's ICDS programmes is a good example, with the number of preschools increasing from zero to 113 between January 1992 and December 1993 under preset targets. This led to problems with quality control (declining attendance among low-caste children) and took time away from strengthening the work with grassroots groups. But scaling-up in other ways need not have negative side effects. The number of POs in the Orissa Federation increased from 19 to 42 in the space of six years (1989–95), without any identifiable fall-off in quality. Here, the rate of graduation of autonomous grassroots organizations (approximately five years from start-up) is the key to a strategy that has achieved large-scale impact at low cost. This frees up PREM's resources to concentrate on supporting the emergence of new POs elsewhere in the state, eventually removing itself completely from the process. This is one NGO which really does 'work itself out of a job'. It is also vital to develop a representative structure (like FOPO) so that people at the grassroots can make their voices heard and articulate their demands at block, district and state levels. The absence of such a structure in Rajasthan is one of the things that undermines Urmul's attempts to scale-up the impact of their work with village groups.

Strong linkages like this are essential for sustainable impact, connecting POs with structures that can provide resources on a long-term basis (such as banks), advice and experience in the same programme areas (other NGOs) and official sanction or access to policy-makers (in local government). Strong vertical links (between village groups and state-level structures) and horizontal links (between POs) build organizational strength and social capital, and pool experience and other resources. Over time, a critical mass emerges to exert increasing pressure for change: in Orissa, FOPO has expanded its membership each year without losing its connections to grassroots POs, gaining more respect from government in the process and gradually expanding the political space available – an interesting case of a grassroots federation (and its support NGO) improving the external context over time. By contrast, the two SCF projects in Bangladesh have been isolated from other organizations locally and nationally, and even from each other.

Culture, structure, leadership and decision-making

An inspirational but not overbearing leadership is critical in providing a clear sense of direction (especially in the early days), taking difficult decisions during moments of conflict or potential threat and holding the organization together. There is clearly a great deal of respect for senior figures in PREM among tribal communities in Orissa, but it does not translate into dependence, as the examples of autonomous action cited earlier show. A strong and shared organizational culture (values, principles, philosophy), and a common analysis of the causes of poverty underwritten by long days of Frierean-style adult education among staff and volunteers, have also been important in maintaining direction in PREM's work. In particular, openness to learning, a genuine selflessness and a determination to hand over power at every opportunity, have been critical in building up the strength and success of the POs, rather than building up PREM as an intermediary.

By contrast, SCF in Bangladesh has been 'a one-man show' for considerable periods of time (to quote a senior programme manager), with the country director carrying an enormous amount of power to shape the programme as he wished (they have all been men). Until recently, Bangladeshi staff lower down the hierarchy had little authority to take decisions, even where they were better placed to do so. As their timeline showed, local staff in the River Project knew that the design of the credit scheme introduced in the late 1980s was flawed because they had been running their own informal programme for some years previously. Yet they were not even shown a copy of the new project proposal before it was approved by SCF headquarters in London. The result was a scheme with overheads that were far too high to be sustainable. Bureaucratic and highly formalized structures discourage learning, communication, initiative and risk-taking, all the things which are crucial for organizational effectiveness.

Urmul Seemant and the two SCF projects have traditional, hierarchical structures, whereas the diagrams drawn by POs in Orissa show PREM below or to the side of the Federation. Boundaries between PREM trustees and field staff – and between membership of PREM and membership of a PO – are very fluid, like threads woven through all these organizations to keep them strong collectively. The POs identify very closely with PREM, but take care to show themselves as formally separate. PREM staff are present continuously at every level of the Federation, but are not allowed to vote in elections and have no authority over decision-making. This gives them a special combination of closeness to the people they work with, and distance from formal decision-making, which seems to be very effective in promoting strong grassroots organizations. In contrast, the village groups in Rajasthan have a more dependent relationship with Urmul Seemant field-workers and, until recently, Urmul's trustees have come from local elites (such as the dairy cooperative manager and the district collector).

From the case studies there seems to be no correlation between effective performance and the use of formalized planning systems. A clear and shared sense of direction, flexibility to respond to changing needs and circumstances, and attention to learning and communication, seem to be more important. None of the four agencies in the study has a written strategic plan. There is no evidence that this has harmed PREM nor that the existence of such a plan (by itself) would have helped the others.[2] This does not mean that deliberate choices have been avoided. For example, in the late 1980s, PREM bypassed villages which they considered to be too heterogeneous or fragmented socially and economically, and selected activities with the highest potential for group organization. Informal accountability mechanisms (as long as they are applied) seem more effective than elected committees, independent audits, and so on. For example, four members of one of the POs in the Orissa decided to join the 'Janata Dal' party, contravening the rules of the Federation which state that members cannot stand for election under any of the mainstream political parties in India (to avoid cooption). The PO immediately suspended them. Informal mechanisms such as these are very powerful and, as long as they are used within a framework that gives all members a voice, can be invaluable in building a stronger and more effective organization.

All four agencies have dedicated staff working long hours in difficult conditions, but whereas PREM uses only local people, Urmul Seemant and Shariatpur have chosen to hire senior staff from outside the project area, on the assumption that this would make them less vulnerable to political patronage and other pressures. In fact (in Shariatpur) they proved to be just as susceptible and not very well accepted into the bargain. PREM has had continuity at both senior management and field-worker levels, whereas frequent changes at senior level have disrupted programme development in Shariatpur, with four programme managers in the last five years. In the River Project too, field-workers have experienced 4 or 5 changes of role over the last 20 years: from relief to feeding-centre workers, to health and education workers, to community development workers and on to credit-and-savings promoters. One had experienced 9 changes of role in 18 years. Such changes can help to build a broader range of skills, but may also make it more difficult to develop a real core competence among field staff.

Conclusions

The study

It is clear from these results that there is no such thing as a universally appropriate strategy among NGOs across such different contexts. Equally, some responses are more effective than others in the same or similar contexts (contrast Urmul Seemant with PREM); and even where the context is more difficult (as in Bangladesh), NGOs can still increase the opportunities for effective work – and improve the context in the process – by using the right strategies in the right combinations. The key factors here are the following:

- Clarity in long-term direction and a determination not to be distracted along the way.
- A balance between advances in livelihoods, and social and organizational development, right from the inception of the programme.
- Strong and active linkages vertically and horizontally to draw in resources and act as a conduit for influencing wider structures.
- The multiplier effect of strengthening local institutions to take on more responsibility for management and decision-making.

Achieving these things rests on two further sets of factors: a particular set of organizational characteristics and a supportive relationship with resource providers (donor agencies). In the former category, PREM's value base and single-mindedness in applying it have enabled them to make a reality of NGO rhetoric about empowerment – handing over control as soon as this was viable, de-emphasizing the role of the intermediary so that grassroots organizations could grow in confidence and permeating decisions with a spirit of selflessness and self-sacrifice which fed through into flat structures, low overheads, and a culture of self-enquiry. In the other three cases, the rhetoric was similar but has not been matched by the organizational characteristics required to achieve the same results. This was partly because PREM's donors were prepared to be flexible and take a long-term view, in contrast to the constant changes and heavy-handed interventions that plagued both projects in Bangladesh.

When the right organizational characteristics and a supportive relationship with donors come together, NGOs have more chance of improving the context in which they work, as PREM and other NGOs have done in Orissa. Here, success in social organization and service delivery has helped to convince a sceptical government that there is a pay-off from expanding the political space available for more radical forms of NGO activity. Over time, the process becomes self-reinforcing – NGO success breeds confidence and confidence makes more room for effective civic action. The lesson to be learned – even in more difficult contexts – is that NGO networking, constructive engagement with different levels of the state and building demand among poor people for improvements in services and governance, can improve the legal and regulatory framework, and change donor practice, in ways which are crucial for sustainable development on the ground.

The results in context

Similar findings come from other studies which have explored the performance of NGOs in different contexts, including in industrialized countries (Lewis, 1998). In their path-breaking study, Esman and Uphoff (1984, p181) concluded that 'the ability of rural residents to advance their ... interests depends substantially ... on their success in sustaining local organizations beyond the immediate tasks that precipitated them'. The same conclusion has been echoed many times since, most recently in contexts as diverse as Wignaraja's (1993) overview of lessons learned from recent social movements; women's organizations in India (Smith-Sreen, 1995); NGO – municipal collaboration throughout Latin America (Reilly, 1995); peasant federations in Ecuador and Bolivia (Bebbington, 1996); NGO credit schemes around the world (Bennett, Goldberg and Hunte, 1996); demand-driven small-scale enterprise programmes in Brazil (Tendler and Alves Amorim, 1996); Ndegwa's (1996) comparison of the Undugu Society and the Green Belt Movement in Kenya; and the OECD-wide evaluation of NGO performance which reported at the end of 1997 (Development Assistance Committee, 1997)[3]. In all these cases it was the balance between increased economic security, success in social organization and the ability to influence the political process that 'made the difference', coupled with strong and active linkages between grassroots organizations, NGOs, governments and banks (Evans, 1996; Fox, 1996; Sachikonye, 1995). We have it on no less an authority than Alexis de Tocqueville (cited in Reilly, 1995, p8) that 'if men are to remain civilized or to become so, the act of associating together must grow and improve in the same ratio in which the equality of conditions is increased'. The conclusion is clear – do not sacrifice the slow and messy process of institutional development for quick material results; the results will come – and will last – if the institutional fabric supports them.

These conclusions may appear obvious, yet it is surprising how often they are ignored by both NGOs and donor agencies, especially when there is pressure to scale-up NGO service delivery quickly, driven by a desire to retrench the state and expand the roles of non-state, actors under the aid-inspired 'New Policy Agenda' of economic liberalization and political democratization (Edwards and Hulme, 1995). Accompanied by multimillion dollar grants or subsidized loans from new facilities like the World Bank's Consultative Group to Assist the Poorest (CGAP) initiative, NGOs in South Asia and elsewhere are expanding at rates which are unknown in history (Edwards and Hulme, 1996; Hulme and Edwards, 1997). In this context it has become commonplace to hear NGOs being advised to 'professionalize' their operations, borrow management and strategic planning techniques from the corporate sector, standardize their procedures to reduce unit costs, and 'routinize the functioning of grassroots organizations' because 'too much flexibility or grassroots influence results in decisions which are sub-optimal' (Jain, 1994, 1996). This advice is offered despite mounting evidence that a lack of attention to grassroots institutional development and an overly bureaucratic, hierarchical and standardized approach to credit delivery is already harming the ability of large NGOs to reach the poorest people and to address deep-rooted problems of structural injustice (Montgomery, 1996; Rao and Kelleher, 1995).

As this chapter has shown, such prescriptions are misleading. PREM has achieved spectacular results in a little over ten years by deliberately connecting improvements in livelihoods with advances in social organization at every stage. This approach requires a favourable context, a particular set of organizational choices and characteristics (*not* standardization and hierarchy), and a set of donors who are prepared to be sensitive and flexible, allowing the balance between material and social/organizational objectives to change over time, and providing room for manoeuvre for local organizations to move at their own pace. This is difficult to do in the world of official aid where disbursement pressure and short-term accountability to donors may lead to corners being cut in the slower and more difficult areas of social and institutional change.

As the four case studies show, there is always tension between the organizational characteristics required to perform effectively as a service provider and as a catalyst for institutional development. Great care and discrimination are needed to support NGOs in finding a dynamic balance between these roles. Get this balance wrong and the result may be less, and less sustainable impact, even in material terms – as the experience of Urmul Seemant and SCF in Bangladesh demonstrates. Get it right and the results can be remarkable on both dimensions, as PREM has shown in Orissa. For donors who do want to support lasting change, the message is clear: help NGOs to find a mix of strategies appropriate to the changing context and the internal characteristics required to do so; do not push them into large-scale service delivery and short-term results.

Notes

1 Including 1500 children in Orissa and families squatting on railway sidings in River, which even the Grameen Bank has failed to do (Rutherford, 1993).
2 See Mintzberg (1994) for similar results from the corporate sector.
3 See also Uphoff et al (1997) and Riddell et al (1995).

References

Bebbington, T (1996) 'Organizations and intensifications: campesino federations, rural livelihoods and agricultural technology in the Andes and Amazonia', *World Development*, Vol 24, No 7, pp1161–1177.

Bennett, L, Goldberg, M and Hunte, P (1996) 'Ownership and sustainability: lessons on group-based financial services from South Asia', *Journal of International Development*, Vol 8, No 2, pp271–288.

Chambers, R (1994) 'The origins and practice of participatory rural appraisal', *World Development*, Vol 22, No 7, pp953–969.

Development Assistance Committee (1997) *Searching for Impact and Methods: NGO Evaluation Synthesis Study*, OECD, Paris.

Edwards, M (1996) *NGO Performance: What Breeds Success? Approaches to Work in South Asia*, Working Paper 14, Save the Children Fund, London.

Edwards, M (1997) 'Mixing PRA methods with secondary research in organizational self-assessment', *PLA Notes* Vol 29, pp10–14.

Edwards, M and Hulme, D (eds) (1992) *Making a Difference: NGOs and Development in a Changing World*, Earthscan, London.

Edwards, M and Hulme, D (eds) (1995) *Beyond the Magic Bullet: NGO Performance and Accountability in the Post-Cold War World*, Earthscan, London, and Kumarian Press, West Hartford.

Edwards, M and Hulme, D (1996) 'Too close for comfort? The impact of official aid on NGOs', *World Development*, Vol 24, No 6, pp961–974.

Esman, M and Uphoff, N (1984) *Local Organizations: Intermediaries in Rural Development*, Cornell University Press, Ithaca.

Evans, P (1996) 'Development strategies across the public–private divide: Introduction', *World Development*, Vol 24, No 6, pp1033–1037.

Fowler, A et al (1996) *Participatory Self-Assessment of NGO Capacity*, INTRAC, Oxford.

Fowler, A (1997) *Striking a Balance: A Guide to NGO Management*, Earthscan, London.

Fox, J (1996) 'How does civil society thicken? The political construction of social capital in rural Mexico', *World Development*, Vol 24, No 6, pp1089–1103.

Goetz, A and Sen Gupta, R (1994) *Who Takes the Credit? Gender, Power and Control over Loan Use in Rural Credit Programmes in Bangladesh*, Institute of Development Studies, Brighton.

Hashemi, S (1995) 'NGO accountability in Bangladesh: beneficiaries, donors and the state', in M Edwards and D Hulme (eds), *Beyond the Magic Bullet: NGO Performance and Accountability in the Post-Cold War World*, Earthscan, London, and Kumarian Press, West Hartford.

Hashemi, S, Schuler, S, and Riley, A (1996) 'Rural credit programs and women's empowerment in Bangladesh', *World Development*, Vol 24, No 4, pp635–654.

Hulme, D and Edwards, M (eds) (1997) *Too Close for Comfort? NGOs, States and Donors*, Macmillan, London and St Martin's Press, New York.

Jain, P (1994) 'Managing for success: lessons from Asian development programs', *World Development*, Vol 22, No 9, pp1363–1377.

Jain, P (1996) 'Managing credit for the rural poor: lessons from the Grameen Bank', *World Development*, Vol 24, No 1, pp79–90.

Lewis, D (ed) (1998) *Bridging the Chasm: International Perspectives on Voluntary Action*, Earthscan, London.

Mintzberg, H (1994) *The Rise and Fall of Strategic Planning*, Prentice Hall, London.

Montgomery, R (1996) 'Disciplining or protecting the poor? Avoiding the social costs of peer pressure in micro-credit schemes', *Journal of International Development*, Vol 8, No 2, pp289–305.

Ndegwa, P (1996) *The Two Faces of Civil Society: NGOs and Politics in Africa*, Kumarian Press, West Hartford, CT.

Rao, A and Kelleher, D (1995) 'Engendering organizational change: the BRAC Case', *IDS Bulletin*, Vol 26, No 3, pp69–78.

Riddell, R and Robinson, M (1996) *NGOs and Rural Poverty Alleviation*, Clarendon Press, Oxford.

Ridell, R, Bebbington, A and Peck, R (1995) *Promoting Development by Proxy: An Evaluation of the Development Impact of Government Support to Swedish NGOs*, Sida, Stockholm.

Rutherford, S (1993) *Learning to Lend*, Working Paper 5, Save the Children Fund, London.

Ritchey-Vance, M (1996) 'Social capital, sustainability and working democracy: new yardsticks for grassroots development', *Grassroots Development*, Vol 20, No 1, pp3–9.

Reilly, C (ed) (1995) *New Paths to Democratic Development in Latin America: The Rise of NGO–Municipal Collaboration*, Lynne Rienner, Boulder, Colorado.

Sachikonye, L (1995) *Democracy, Civil Society and the State: Social Movements in Southern Africa*, SAPES Books, Harare.

SCF (1996) *Evaluation of the Health Component of the People's Rural Education Movement, Orissa*, Save the Children Fund Regional Office for South Asia, Kathmandu.

Smith-Sreen, P (1995) *Accountability in Development Organizations: Experiences of Women's Organizations in India*, Sage, New Delhi.

Tendler, J and Alves Amorim, M (1996) 'Small firms and their helpers: lessons on demand', *World Development*, Vol 24, No 3, pp407–426.

Uphoff, N et al (eds) (1997) *Reasons for Hope*, Kumarian Press, West Hartford, CT.

Wignaraja, P (1993) *New Social Movements in the South: Empowering the People*, Zed Press, London.

Wood, G (1997) 'States without citizens: the problem of the franchise state', in D Hulme and M Edwards (eds), *Too Close for Comfort: NGOs, States and Donors*, Macmillan, London and St Martin's Press, New York.

Zadek, S (1996) *Value-based Organization: Organizing NGOs for Value-based Effectiveness*, New Economics Foundation, London.

Assessing NGO Performance: Difficulties, Dilemmas and a Way Ahead

Alan Fowler

Introduction

The 1990s have witnessed a significant increase in efforts to assess the performance of non-governmental, non-profit development organizations (NGOs). This trend can be traced to a number of factors. First, since the early 1980s a growing proportion of financial resources used by NGOs has derived from the official aid system, overtaking, in terms of rate of growth, their income from public giving (Fowler, 1992a). Public funds are accompanied by more stringent 'contractual' demands for financial accountability and the realization of agreed impacts (Hawley, 1993). Second, the post-Cold War rationale for official overseas development assistance (ODA) is further accelerating shifts in donor priorities towards the institutional restructuring of recipient countries, with a corresponding push on NGOs to alter their role in society. Effective management of such organizational transformations requires sound and timely information about achievement. Third, NGOs tend to argue that they are more cost-effective than governments in reaching and serving people who are poor and/or marginalized and are now being called upon to demonstrate that this is indeed the case (UNDP, 1993; van Dijk, 1994). Fourth, there is a growing realization that organizational effectiveness is positively correlated with an ability to learn from experience (Senge, 1990). This insight is argued to be of particular relevance for NGOs because, as entities dedicated to social change, they predominantly function as natural open systems (Scott, 1987, pp105–115; Fowler et al, 1992, pp17–19), where performance is very dependent on and sensitive to instability and rapid change in the external environment. Such situations are common in both the South and the North. Learning requires data about all aspects of organizational functioning, prompting greater attention to the need to gather evidence of impact and assess the capacity to adapt.

NGOs have always understood the need to assess their performance. However, the growing internal and external pressures sketched out above are bringing to light serious inadequacies in past attempts to do so; inadequacies which stem from fundamental difficulties inherent to:

1   the development approach adopted by the aid system;

2   the concept of performance when applied to non-profit organizations;
3   the way developmental NGOs need to profile themselves in order to secure and
    maintain public support and funding.

This chapter reviews the difficulties and dilemmas which accompany attempts to
determine NGO effectiveness and charts some practical ways ahead. Section 2 looks
at the basic problems of performance assessment which arise as a result of contradictions between the principles which underpin international aid and the nature of
sustainable change which aims to benefit poor people. The intrinsic difficulties of
identifying performance criteria for non-public, non-profit organizations are examined in Section 3. This analysis identifies the challenges to be overcome in
designing approaches to NGO performance assessment that are sound, practical and
cost-effective, approaches which are the subject of Section 4. The concluding section of the chapter offers some speculative observations on ongoing attempts by
NGOs to gain more insight into what they are achieving.

Factors Affecting the Assessment of Project Performance

Figure 18.1 provides an overview of the factors which condition NGOs' ability to
determine what impact they are making in terms of the people they are established
to serve. It shows the interconnections commonly found in the project flow of international development resources; the interfaces where one organization's ends
become another's means; the factors that influence the flow of resources; and the
different points at which performance can be assessed in terms of outputs, outcomes
or impacts.

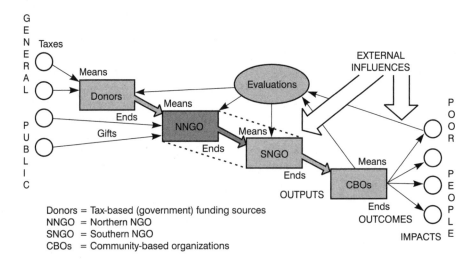

Figure 18.1 NGOs in the Aid Chain

Development as a linear process

The international aid system was initially premised on the notion of underdevelopment as a 'deficit' in capital, knowledge and technology. The transfer of such resources from richer to poorer economies, it was believed, would enable or speed up economic growth, leading to an improvement in the material circumstances and well-being of poorer strata within recipient societies. Projects – discrete packages of resources and activities – were the mechanism chosen to achieve this outcome. The project mode of development, sometimes called the 'blueprint approach', assumes that it is possible to predetermine a set of cause-and-effect relationships that will turn resources, knowledge or technology into desired and sustainable human change. In other words, that it is possible to predict and create a knowable future (Roling and de Zeeuw, 1987).

The notion of prediction and a controllable future underpins 'hard' science and its application to the physical world. It also determines what is considered to be valid knowledge and dictates the methods by which such knowledge can be gathered and validated. Most critically, knowledge must be objective in the sense that it is derived from observation in the real world, which can be demonstrated to be independent of the person(s) doing the observing. Under these assumptions it should be possible to define and plan a project as a linear process of causes and effects, using resources in a predetermined sequence of activities to produce the desired outcome. Logical framework analysis is an instrument now commonly used for designing this type of development.

Putting project development into practice requires action by a number of organizations which are tied together like a chain between the resource provider and those intended to benefit. Figure 18.1 shows this typical set-up for NGOs. From left to right in the diagram, resources move either directly (as gifts from constituents in the richer North) or indirectly (from taxes through governmental donors) to Northern NGOs (NNGOs), Southern NGOs (SNGOs) and then on to community-based organizations (CBOs) comprised of poor people and households. Each organization obtains resources (or 'means' in the figure) to fulfil its role, while its processes and capacities are tailored towards goals (or 'ends') which are set in relation to an overall mission and the specific objectives of the project. If all goes well, the result of this joint endeavour is the realization of a predefined impact on human well-being.

Despite attempts at rigorous study, there is far from unanimous evidence that project-based aid does achieve the intended effects reliably (Cassen, 1986; White and Woestman, 1994). In fact, some analysts argue that 60 per cent or more of such aid is ineffective (Korten, 1991; Hancock, 1989). If this is the case, there must be something essentially questionable about such an approach to development.

Development as complex, contingent change

Accumulated experience shows that the principle and practice described above is seriously flawed for most types of human and social change. First, the concept of a knowable future is highly questionable, as is the validity of the notion of objective knowledge (Long and Long, 1992; Wolpert, 1992). Second, the 'blueprint' approach requires an ability to control all the factors outside of the project which may influence its outcome. This degree of control is possible in a very limited number of instances, usually where technology is very dominant, as with road and bridge construction or telecommunications.

At least five other factors work against the linear approach realizing what is intended. First, as one moves along the chain in the figure, the number of actors involved increases and each has their own perspective and set of interests which are not static. Second, in their turn, each actor's behaviour is conditioned to a greater or lesser degree on external forces, with NGOs particularly dependent on the vagaries of external finance for maintenance of their core functions (Hudock, 1994). The increase of contingent factors on project progress gives rise to greater levels of uncertainty and unpredictability. Third, the timescale required for observing effects or changes tends to lengthen. For example, reducing infant mortality rates cannot be seen from the life or death of one child. Only after a longer period does this type of change become apparent. Fourth, human well-being is determined by many external elements which are integrated within an individual. Improving access to potable water, while useful in itself, won't mean much if food intake is diminishing, nor will economic investment mean much if there is no political or financial stability, nor will education mean much if it cannot be applied to anything tangible. Finally, getting returns from external flows of financial investments, knowledge or technology is determined by how people use them (their behaviour), while who benefits is determined by people's ability to organize and by the basis on which power, influence and control over resources is distributed.

An example can help to illustrate what these factors mean in terms of practical impact assessment. Assume that a particular population group suffers from poor health due to inadequate nutrition. One reason identified for this is the high percentage of harvested crops lost in storage. A project is defined and designed by an NGO to introduce improved grain stores. The *output* of the NGO's work can be measured in terms of the number of stores built and at what cost. However, the *outcome* of the project will have to be measured in terms of the reduction of crop loss during storage (which may take more than one season to determine) which, in its turn, will be critically affected by how the grain stores are used from one season to the next – that is, by people's behaviour. The nominal value of the crops saved can be set against the cost of the store to calculate a financial cost-benefit, but this will only be possible some years after their completion. Project *impact* must be sought in the improved nutritional status of the population, which is unlikely to be determined by grain alone and will require distinctive non-agricultural or economic measures, such as improvement in anthropometric status and reduced incidence of nutrition-related illnesses such as kwashiorkor. Further, the spread of impact on human well-being will be determined by the differential ability of household members to gain access to the increased food supply, experience showing that women and children tend to have the weakest entitlements.

To all of the above must be added the fact that, while varying significantly between countries, overall international aid is only a tiny proportion of the flow of resources and knowledge between countries and levels within societies. For example, the World Bank's total lending in 1993 was the equivalent of the amount transferred by international capital markets in the space of nine minutes.[1] The idea that aid can, will or does 'make the difference' to world development or the distribution of poverty is illusory; far larger forces are in play.

Together, these factors and the interplay between them reduce the validity of predictive change as an appropriate approach to socioeconomic development. Indeed, it is increasingly argued by even the most hardened physical scientists and economists that development at all levels of the natural and social order is the product of complex and contingent processes which are only partially amenable to prediction and control (Anderson et al, 1988; Waldrop, 1992; Lewin, 1994; Gell-Mann, 1994). They point out that as component systems of the world evolve, they interlock and give rise to new ('emergent') properties. For example, computerization and communication technology are creating new ways of organizing, including 'virtual organizations!'. Similarly, localized environmental degradation caused by myriad individuals struggling to survive across all continents of the world can combine to destabilize whole patterns of weather or lifestyles of the better-off. Simple rules employed by billions of people operating in parallel can lead to dramatic, unexpected outcomes.

In sum, the basic linear principles on which development aid is allocated do not correspond to the complex, contingent way that development actually occurs. This fundamental mismatch complicates performance assessment, particularly when it comes to attributing cause to effects and working out what would have happened anyway (the 'counterfactual' case). This realization has increased the call for a new sort of development professionalism not premised on linearity (Chambers, 1985, 1993). The gap between the principles of aid and the nature of poverty creation and alleviation makes life particularly difficult for NGOs who need to convince their supporters and funders that they have 'made the difference' to people's well-being. Because they cannot levy taxes, NGOs (more than official aid agencies) face a major problem of public persuasion if performance assessment cannot attribute effects to causes.

Assessing NGO Organizational Performance

NGOs must contend with the fact that they belong to a category of organization with no straightforward or uncontested measure of organizational, as distinct from project, effectiveness. In other words, unlike governments and businesses – which can be assessed respectively in terms of political support or financial returns – nonprofits have no readily acknowledged 'bottom line'.

A 'bottom line' for non-profit organizations

By nature of their (social) function, NGOs provide services to a segment of the population who are unable to meet the full cost of what they receive; if they could afford them they could go to the market as consumers (Fowler, 1989; Leat, 1993). Financial returns, therefore, cannot serve as a measure of organizational performance. Likewise, as self-established entities not owned or mandated by those they serve, feedback from political processes which are intended to legitimize governments are not appropriate. What approach can be adopted to establish the standards against which non-profit organizational performance can reasonably be assessed?

Measuring the performance of non-state, non-profit development organizations, rather than of the projects they implement, is a relative newcomer as an issue in the development arena. Its arrival is tied to the growing concern, associated with increased aid from official sources, that their organizational capacity is inadequate for the expanding role they are expected and funded to play (Campbell, 1990). For the present, therefore, analysis of the problems associated with measuring the organizational performance of developmental NGOs must draw mainly on work focusing on non-profits operating in the North.

Some 15 years ago, the well-known organizational analyst, Rosbeth Moss Kanter (1979), reviewed the wide range of conceptual dilemmas, practical difficulties, contending principles and different methods adopted in attempts to determine non-profit effectiveness, productivity and performance. She concluded:

1   That the measurement of effectiveness must be related to a particular context and life stage of the organization.
2   That rather than seeking universal measures, the need is to identify appropriate questions reflecting multiple criteria.
3   That the concept of assessment of organizational goals should be replaced with the notion of organizational uses – in other words, to recognize the fact that 'different constituencies use organizations for different purposes' (op cit, p36).

Drucker (1990) reaches essentially the same conclusions – namely, that:

1   Performance must be determined and interpreted contextually.
2   Questions should form the base of the assessment approach.
3   Standards must derive from the various constituencies that the organization serves.
4   The process of organizational assessment should be participatory.

Another approach to performance assessment of non-profits working in the North relates to the 'contract culture' which is shaping their role, position and behaviour (Smith and Lipsky, 1993) and which is rapidly permeating into the aid system (OECD, 1993). This approach focuses on the quality of service provided. Lawrie (1993, p19) identifies four types of performance indicator in this respect: (per unit) cost; take-up or 'occupancy'; impact or result; and user reaction. Each has different applications and levels of difficulty in terms of definition, the ability to obtain the needed information, and degrees of precision and tangibility. He stresses the distinction between performance indicators as unambiguous (or what he calls 'dials') and as contestable (or 'tin-openers').[2]

Lawrie notes the bias that funders have towards 'dials' and the insufficient time available to negotiate 'tin-openers'. Organizational effectiveness, in terms of quality of service, is determined by measuring gaps which exist in the expectations and perceptions of different stakeholders. What might all this mean for development NGOs?

The bottom line for development NGOs

Each of the analyses noted above highlights the difficulties involved in identifying a non-profit bottom line, even when the purpose is reasonably straightforward – for example, providing a direct welfare service such as running a home for elderly people or a shelter for the homeless. Developmental NGOs are faced with an additional obstacle because, as shown in Figure 18.1, the 'product' of their endeavours (sustainable development for poverty alleviation) is not produced by NGOs but by (poor) people themselves (Lewis et al, 1988). In other words, at best NGOs can facilitate and support the process of people's own development and need to be assessed in how well they do this, in addition to what their work realizes in terms of material change.

Yet another complication arises because the funds that Southern NGOs employ are normally derived from foreign sources. This separates the political relationship between giver and receiver, and means that there is no recognized system by which the (dis)satisfaction of those served can be fed back to the funder independent of the NGO itself.[3]

This situation does not arise in the North, where local or national political processes can serve to monitor the performance of a non-profit organization.

These problems have resulted in a situation where performance appraisal for most NGOs has remained stuck at the point of comparing outputs with intentions – that is, with (negotiated) plans such as the number of wells built, number of people attending training activities and repayment rates for credit. Crucial elements of development processes, such as people's degree of control over decisions or the capabilities of CBOs, are seldom assessed at all. There is a general consensus that this situation is neither adequate nor acceptable (Marsden, Oakley and Pratt, 1994). How can this accumulation of obstacles be overcome? Is there a way forward?

A Way Ahead in NGO Performance Assessment

The problems recounted above are not new; for a number of years both researchers and practitioners have recognized them and have been actively looking for ways to overcome them. However, more progress has been made in the area of assessing project performance than the performance of NGOs themselves. These two strands are tied together, only weakly, if at all, with the measurement of project impact separated from organizational appraisal. However, a common principle underlying both is the need to involve stakeholders more systematically.

A unifying principle: engaging multiple stakeholders structurally and systematically

Attempts to reconcile the contradictions of linear versus contingent development, as well as to assess NGO effectiveness, share a common principle – that of structured multiple stakeholder involvement.[4] In relation to project performance, a promising direction for impact assessment appears to lie in the application of frameworks and methods which allow all interested parties to have a say in defining means and ends. Causes and effects are negotiated, monitored and evaluated from the perspectives of the actors who can be reasonably assumed to have an influence on both progress and impact. One approach of this sort which has been tested in practice is the marrying together of Logical Framework Analysis (LFA) and Objective Oriented Intervention Planning (OOIP) (INTRAC/South Research, 1994). Over a period (which could extend to a year), the goals, objectives, existing context and processes to be used are discussed with the stakeholders whose involvement will be critical to a project's definition and implementation. Differences in motivation and perceptions underpinning what is to be achieved; how and who is likely to benefit, become more apparent early on, so that compromises can be negotiated. Rather than crippling a project later on, insurmountable conflicts can be identified and a decision made as to whether the preconditions exist for the initiative to be viable.

In terms of organizational appraisal, involving stakeholders in this way calls for some form of *social accounting of multiple interests* (Epstein, Flamholtz and McDonough, 1977, p76, quoted in Kanter, 1979).[5] One recent application of these principles – known as a 'social audit' and derived from a process of independent social accounting – is being tested by Traidcraft and the New Economics Foundation (Traidcraft, 1994; Zadek and Gatward, 1995). Here, performance criteria are negotiated with four key stakeholders: producers, staff, consumers and shareholders. In parallel with the financial audit, an independent person obtains feedback on stakeholders' views about the degree to which Traidcraft have fulfilled the standards agreed.[6]

More recently, OXFAM (UK and Ireland) initiated an 'assembly' of some 250 diverse stakeholders – partners, advisers, associates, volunteers, staff, senior managers, donors, 'friends' and others – to deliberate and provide advice on strategic issues facing the organization, such as whether or not to work in the UK (Oxfam, 1994). The assembly is advisory and not a formal part of Oxfam's organization. Yet the step taken by Oxfam contains a clear moral imperative to take the assembly seriously or risk being publicly derided and written off as a dishonest organization.[7] It is too early to ascertain what the influence of these initiatives will be for the overall performance of these organizations.

The importance of process

It is beyond the scope of this chapter to detail precisely how multiple stakeholder involvement is obtained in the two areas described above. However, some points are worthy of note. First, in both cases stakeholder input is not a one-off affair, but a continuous process within the organization's functioning. One option being adopted by some NGOs is to establish a permanent advisory body composed of different stakeholders whose task is to monitor organizational performance in meeting standards which have been agreed and modified by mutual consent.

Second, creating a systematic way of engaging multiple stakeholders is unlikely to be free of conflict and risk, especially where different levels of authority and power exist. In this situation, the weighting of different stakeholders is important. Additional pitfalls can arise where there is a significant disparity in understanding between donor, NGO and recipients about what development is or entails. For example, in NGOs funded by child sponsorship, a donor may wish their sponsored child to receive direct handouts, as may the child's parents. In these circumstances, how can the organization justify a non-welfare, community-based approach? Bringing parties together as stakeholders invites organizational disturbance![8]

Third, the process of stakeholder engagement should help to build the capacity of the parties involved, particularly the poor and marginalized whose ability to put forward their interests is most likely to be constrained. In sum, to be useful and meaningful, obtaining stakeholder engagement must be matched by the right processes.

NGO performance assessment as combined social judgement

Multiple stakeholder engagement allows the performance of NGOs (as organizations dedicated to social change) to be defined as the – often contested – outcome of the social judgements of the parties involved, using criteria which are important to them. The methods set out above help to temper the shortcomings of 'linear' approaches by:

- contextualizing assessment and hence taking account of contingency;
- making the interpretation of events more objective as multiple perspectives are brought to bear;
- contributing to cost-effectiveness through combining capacity-building with performance-monitoring.

In sum, the key to NGO assessment appears to lie in identifying and using as performance standards the criteria or factors which relevant people are likely to use when making a judgement. Herman and Heimovics (1994) describe and examine how this can be done in practice by constructing and employing 'vignettes'. A vignette is a picture built up from criteria and values attached to them, which relevant stakeholders would use to judge the organization. For example, as measures of effectiveness, they may include: the percentage of income spent on fund-raising, the proportion made up by contributions from volunteers, the percentage of revenue coming from government, the profile of those whom the organization actually reaches, the gender divisions within the organization, and so on. Vignettes describing what interested parties consider to be signs of effectiveness, can help to construct a bottom line.

Uniting the strands: performance as an expression of organizational capacities

A key weakness in today's practice of NGO performance assessment is the separation of project evaluations from features of the organization itself, as if each has relatively little or nothing to do with the other, which is patently not the case. For example, one recent comparative impact assessment of NGO work in credit-provision did not take organizational variables into account when explaining differences in performance (Riddell and Robinson, 1992). One way of bringing together the major facets of NGO performance is to use the concept of organizational capacity. Neither NGOs nor donors have a uniform definition of 'capacity' (James, 1994). However, current uses of the term imply that capacity can be understood as a number of core abilities, together with the means and relationships through which to express them. Analysis of the NGO sector in Africa indicates that to be effective three principal areas of ability are required.

These are:

- an ability *to be* – that is, to maintain its specific identity, values and mission;
- an ability *to do* – that is, to achieve stakeholder satisfaction; and
- an ability *to relate* – that is, to manage external interactions while retaining autonomy.

When combined, these three areas of organizational ability determine the overall performance of NGOs as well as their role and institutional position as civic actors (Fowler, 1992b; Fowler et al, 1992). Figure 18.2 is a schematic presentation of the above.

A significant amount of effort is presently being applied to the identification of appropriate indicators of capacity and effectiveness within each of these areas, although endeavours are biased towards measures of achievement in various types of poverty-reducing sectoral investments (Carvalho and White, 1993).[9] Progress in locating indicators of organizational capacity in terms of 'being' and 'relating' is less advanced, partly because of the relatively recent concern about them and partly due to the inherent difficulties described above.

The design and practical testing of organizational assessment indicators and methods currently undertaken with NGOs reconfirms that question-based approaches are likely to be the most viable.[10]

Drucker (1993) believes that there are five key questions an NGO should ask itself. These are:

1 What is our business (mission)?
2 Who is our customer?
3 What does the customer consider valuable?
4 What have been our results?
5 What is our plan?

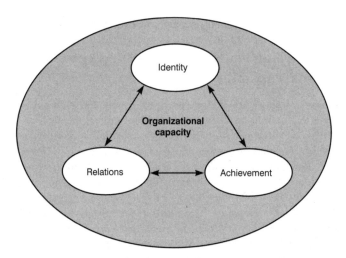

Figure 18.2 *Types of Performance as Factors in NGO Organizational Capacity*

From these derive all sorts of subquestions which must be answered by the organization in a participatory way involving all levels of staff as well as the board, facilitated by a skilled, independent outsider. However, interpreting the answers to these questions requires that users have a firm understanding of the nature of non-profit organizations. Bringing staff up to the necessary level of insight, often including the cross-cultural dimensions of organizational behaviour, requires significant investment and guided application. More often than not, it appears that time and other resource constraints present the major hurdle to Northern NGOs when carrying out a thorough organizational assessment of or with their partners. Although some Northern agencies have involved their partners in policy formulation and 'reverse evaluations' (with mixed success), there is little evidence to date to suggest that many NGOs are aware of the potential of, or are actively moving towards, a set of standards and measures for performance appraisal negotiated among their stakeholders.

Easing management tensions: linking performance and accountability

A final, and perhaps most significant feature of structured stakeholder performance assessment, is that it simultaneously resolves some of the difficulties faced by NGOs in satisfying the multiple demands for functional and strategic accountability which face them (Edwards and Hulme, 1994). NGO stakeholders are commonly characterized by contrasts in their attitude towards, power over or reliance on the organization. Typical differences include: understanding about purpose or role; perspectives on development; ability to sanction; levels of understanding about the organization itself; and diverse expectations about responsiveness, acceptable levels of service, timescales for results and impact. To some extent these differences derive from basic contradictions between the role of aid and the functioning of the global political–economic system, of which poverty and marginalization are but one product. Perspectives in North and South certainly differ considerably.

In organizational terms, these and other differences translate into more or less permanent tensions which have to be managed; most cannot be 'developed' away or resolved solely by the action of the NGO itself because their origins lie deep within the institutional structures of society. Be that as it may, although not without risks in the short term, structured engagement with stakeholders can externalize, make transparent and hence ease the tensions and associated management stresses which NGOs currently internalize. Enabling stakeholders who seldom, if ever, meet to come together and listen to the incompatibility of the demands they are placing on an NGO can be both a salutary experience and a good education for all concerned. If located within the right process, such encounters can make a significant positive difference to NGO functioning, and can help to transform North–South NGO relationships into effective partnerships.

Speculative Conclusions

There is little doubt that external pressure and internal concerns (both opportunistic and professional) will continue to push NGOs to demonstrate their effectiveness and hence their value as agents of development. Given the consistent trend to include more non-state actors in development, it is likely that the methods adopted will stretch along some form of continuum from simple participatory project-appraisal at one end to full stakeholder-determination of NGO performance criteria and judgement at the other. The factors which will determine which NGOs end up where on the spectrum are not easy to discern. A guess is that an NGO's position will be related to the profile of its funding, its ability to retain autonomy, and its particular ideology or analysis of the causes of poverty and marginalization.

The rationale and expectations associated with tax-derived finances are more likely to make NGOs relying on this type of income adopt a contracting role than those financed by the gift economy (such as Oxfam) or their own market-oriented activity (such as Traidcraft; Fowler, 1994b). In the former case, projects will probably remain the primary mode of operation linked to government agreements, treating beneficiaries as inputs rather than as actors central to the development process (World Bank, 1994). Autonomy is a more complex factor because it is determined by an NGO's ability to maintain its own policy-development and decision-making processes unimpeded by other agencies. While sources of finance play their role, the strength and unity of the constituency which 'owns' the NGO is a significant factor in helping to maintain independence of policy and action. NGOs which benefit from greater autonomy are usually better able to include a broader range of stakeholders in any or all aspects of their work.

Surprising as it may seem, relatively few development NGOs have a coherent and well-articulated understanding of why the problems they seek to address actually arise. Put differently, they lack a theory or analysis of why poverty exists as a global phenomenon. Dealing with symptoms and effects is still a sufficient justification for the existence of many NGOs. This means that they are unlikely to consider or seek to counter the structural nature of impoverishment (in the North as well as in the South) in what they choose to do. This appreciation is more likely to be found in NGOs treating poverty alleviation as a global civic endeavour requiring international solidarity and mutual responsibility. The latter type of NGO may be more inclined to recognize the interests of stakeholders outside of a project framework.

The existing literature on NGOs and development, together with the few impact studies which exist, suggest that, by the end of the century, most NGOs will be found clustering between the 'people as project-input' end of the performance assessment spectrum and a middle point pivoting around the LFA/OOIP approach, which itself may have evolved to embrace organizational as well as project performance. It is doubtful that many NGOs will be found operating on the basis of performance criteria and standards negotiated with and between their diverse stakeholders, unless this is recognized as the real bottom line for demonstrating both performance and accountability.

Notes

1 Estimate of John Clark, NGO unit of the World Bank, Washington, DC (personal communication).

2 'Dials' are supposedly unambiguous standards and measures of performance, such as the temperature shown on a thermometer. 'Tin-openers' are measures of performance which are contested, such as the minimum acceptable waiting time for an operation or for an ambulance to arrive at an emergency.

3 Independent evaluations are the normal way of providing funders with alternative feedback on the work of the NGOs they finance. There are many limitations on the utility of this instrument, among which are: 1) delay in gaining information; 2) contention on definition of terms of reference and competing paradigms used for interpretation of results; 3) critical dependence on who is selected to do the work; 4) difficulties in gaining 'objective' involvement of those served; and 5) transience of staff involved over the duration of the project and hence consistency of ideas (Marsden and Oakley, 1990; Howes, 1992; Cracknell, 1983; Carlsson et al, 1994; Marsden, Oakley and Pratt, 1994). There are now a number of initiatives, such as the Aga Khan Rural Support Programme in Pakistan, dedicated to improving on this situation using participatory and other people-centred mechanisms.

4 Stakeholders could be regarded as the groups or entities to which an NGO is accountable. For an overview of who they might be, see Edwards and Hulme (1994, pp18–24). For a discussion on the principle of stakeholders in relation to (development) organizations, see Fowler (1994a).

5 Commercial cooperations appear to be rediscovering the merits of social responsibility and social change as components of their overall goals and strategies (Smith, 1994).

6 More information can be obtained directly from Traidcraft Exchange, Kingsway, Gateshead, Tyne and Wear, Newcastle NE11 0NE, UK.

7 The (political) risk taken by Oxfam in constituting the assembly was highlighted when the gathering's advice to commence work in its home country made frontpage headlines in *The Guardian*, which argued that prevailing government policies had turned the UK into a developing country in need of Oxfam's attention (personal communication from Max Peberdy, assembly organizer).

8 I am grateful to Wendy Crane, formerly Country Director of Plan International and Action Aid, for this observation.

9 In May 1994, the World Bank hosted a meeting with NGOs to compare notes on impact assessment which focused almost exclusively on technical interventions at the project level.

10 These findings result from experience in designing and running courses on organizational assessment and organizational development with INTRAC attended by staff of over 50 Northern and Southern NGOs as well as in-house consultancy work and personal communications from Piers Campbell, Peter Baas, Rajesh Tandon, David Harding, Daudi Waithaka, Dr John Hailey and others of the growing but limited number of specialists in this area.

References

Anderson, P, Arrow, J and Pines, D (eds) (1988) *The Economy as an Evolving Complex System*, Addison-Wesley, Redwood, California.

Campbell, P (1990) 'Strengthening organizations', *NGO Management*, No 18, pp21–24.

Carlsson, J, Kohlin, G and Ekbom, A (1994) *The Political Economy of Evaluation: International Aid Agencies and the Effectiveness of Aid*, St Martin's Press, London.

Carvalho, S and White, H (1993) *Performance Indicators to Monitor Poverty Reduction*, World Bank, Washington, DC.

Cassen, R (1986) *Does Aid Work?* Oxford University Press, Oxford.

Chambers, R (1985) *Normal Professionalism, New Paradigms and Development*, paper for the seminar on Poverty Development and Food: Towards the 21st Century, Institute of Development Studies, University of Sussex, Brighton (mimeo).

Chambers, R (1993) *Challenging the Professions: Frontiers for Rural Development*, Intermediate Technology Development Group, London.

Cracknell, B (1983) *The Evaluation of Aid Projects and Programmes*, proceedings of a conference organized by the Overseas Development Administration in the Institute of Development Studies at the University of Sussex, 7–8 April, Overseas Development Administration, London.

Drucker, P (1990) *Managing the Non-Profit Organization: Principles and Practices*, Harper Collins, New York.

Drucker, P (1993) *The Five Most Important Questions You Will Ever Ask About Your Non-Profit Organization: Participant's Workbook*, Drucker Foundation/Jossey-Bass, San Francisco.

Edwards, M and Hulme, D (1994) *NGOs and Development: Performance and Accountability in the 'New World Order'*, background paper for the international conference of the same title, Save the Children/University of Manchester, 27–29 June.

Fowler, A (1989) 'Why is managing social development different?', *NGO Management Newsletter*, No 12, pp18–20.

Fowler, A (1992a) 'Distant obligations: speculations on NGO funding and the global market', *Review of African Political Economy*, No 55, pp9–29.

Fowler, A (1992b) *Prioritizing Institutional Development: A New Role for NGO Centres for Study and Development*, Gate Keeper Series, No 35, International Institute for Environment and Development, London.

Fowler, A, Campbell, P and Pratt, B (1992) *Institutional Development and NGOs in Africa: Policy Perspectives for European Development Agencies*, International NGO Training and Research Centre, and Novib, Oxford and The Hague.

Fowler, A (1994a) *The World Bank and its Stakeholders: Who are They and Why?*, discussion paper, Human Resources Vice Presidency, World Bank, Washington, DC.

Fowler, A (1994b) 'Capacity building and NGOs: a case of strengthening ladles for the global soup kitchen?', *Institutional Development*, Vol 1, No 1.

Gell-Mann, M (1994) *The Quark and the Jaguar*, Freeman, New York.

Hancock, G (1989) *The Lords of Poverty*, Atlantic Monthly Press, New York.

Hawley, K (1993) *From Grants to Contracts: A Practical Guide for Voluntary Organizations*, National Council of Voluntary Organizations/Directory of Social Change, London.

Herman, R and Heimovics, R (1994) 'A cross-national study of a method for researching nonprofit organizational effectiveness', *Voluntas*, Vol 5, No 1, pp86–100.

Howes, M (1992) 'Linking paradigms and practice: key issues in the appraisal, monitoring and evaluation of British NGO projects' *Journal of International Development*, Vol 4, No 4, pp375–396.

Hudock, A (1994) *Sustaining Southern NGOs in Resource-Dependent Environments*, paper presented at the Development Studies Association Annual Conference, University of Lancaster, September.

INTRAC/South Research (1994) *A Tool for Project Management and People Driven Development*, reports of a workshop on LFA/OIP, Leuven, International NGO Training and Research Centre/South Research, Oxford/Brussels.

James, R (1994) 'Strengthening the capacity of Southern NGO partners', Occasional Papers Series, Vol 1, No 5, International NGO Training and Research Centre, Oxford.

Kanter, R M (1979) *The Measurement of Organizational Effectiveness. Productivity, Performance and Success: Issues and Dilemmas in Service and Non-Profit Organizations*, PONPO Working Paper, No 8, Institution for Social and Policy Studies, Yale University, CT.

Korten, D (1991) 'International assistance: a problem posing as a solution', *Development: Seeds of Change*, No 2/3, Society for International Development, Rome.

Lawrie, A (1993) *Quality of Service: Measuring Performance for Voluntary Organizations*, National Council of Voluntary Organizations/Director of Social Change, London.

Leat, D (1993) *Managing Across Sectors: Similarities and Differences Between For-Profit and Voluntary Non-Profit Organizations*, VOLPROF, City University Business School, London, March

Lewin, P (1994) *Complexity*, Phoenix, London.

Lewis, J et al (1988) *Strengthening the Poor: What Have We Learned?* Overseas Development Council, US–Third World Policy Perspectives, No 10, Washington, DC.

Long, N and Long, A (eds) (1992) *Battlefields of Knowledge: The Interlocking of Theory and Practice in Social Research and Development*, Routledge, London.

Marsden, D and Oakley, P (eds) (1990) *Evaluating Social Development Projects*, Development Guidelines, No 5, Oxfam, Oxford.

Marsden, D, Oakley, P and Pratt, B (eds) (1994) *Measuring the Process: Guidelines for Evaluating Social Development*, International NGO Training and Research Centre, Oxford.

OECD (1993) *Non-Governmental Organizations and Governments: Stakeholders for Development*, Paris.

Oxfam Assembly (1994) *Talking, Listening, Sharing*, Oxfam Assembly Office, Oxfam, Oxford.

Riddell, R and Robinson, M (1992) *The Impact of NGO Poverty Alleviation Projects: Results of the Case Study Evaluations*, Working Paper, No 68, Overseas Development Institute, London.

Roling, N and de Zeeuw, H (1987) *Improving the Quality of Rural Poverty Alleviation*, final report of the working party on The Small Farmer and Development Co-operation, International Agricultural Centre, Wageningen.

Scott, W (1987) *Organizations: Rational, Natural and Open Systems*, Prentice Hall, Englewood Cliffs.

Senge, P (1990) *The Fifth Discipline: The Art and Practice of the Learning Organization*, Doubleday, New York.

Smith, S and Lipsky, M (1993) *Non-Profits for Hire: The Welfare State in the Age of Contracting*, Harvard University Press, Cambridge, Massachusetts.

Smith, C (1994) 'The new corporate philanthropy', *Harvard Business Bureau*, pp105–116, May–June.

Traidcraft (1994) *Social Audit Report 1993*, Traidcraft Exchange, Newcastle upon Tyne.

UNDP (1993) *Human Development Report*, Oxford University Press, Oxford.

Van Dijk, M (1994) 'The effectiveness of NGOs: insights from Danish, British and Dutch impact studies', *Schriften des Deutschen Ubersee-Instituts Hamburg*, No 28, pp27–42.

Waldrop, M (1992) *Complexity: The Emerging Science at the Edge of Order and Chaos*, Simon & Schuster, New York.

White, H and Woestman, L (1994) 'The quality of aid: measuring trends in donor performance', *Development and Change*, Vol 25, No 3, pp527–554.

Wolpert, L (1992) *The Unnatural Nature of Science*, Faber & Faber, London.

World Bank (1994) *The World Bank and Participation*, Operations Policy Department, World Bank, Washington, DC.

Zadek, S and Gatward, M (1995) 'Transforming the transnational NGOs: social auditing or bust?', in M Edwards and D Hulme (eds) *NGOs – Performance and Accountability: Beyond the Magic Bullet*, Earthscan, London.

Social Capital, Sustainability and Working Democracy: New Yardsticks for Grassroots Development

Marion Ritchey-Vance

'The historical record strongly suggests that the successful communities became rich because they were civic, not the other way around.' With this conclusion Robert Putnam[1] gives legitimacy to a powerful phenomenon that educators and grassroots development folk have known intuitively for years. Putnam demonstrates in Making Democracy Work: Civic Traditions in Modern Italy that neighborhood associations, choral societies and sports clubs are not just a nice by-product of social and economic prosperity; they are essential underpinnings of it.

That he struck a chord is evident in the unlikely popularity of a tome that details methodical research on ten centuries of civic traditions in Italy. Putnam studied the performance of 20 regional governments from the initiation of Italy's decentralization process in 1970 through the early 1990s. His conclusions regarding the relationship among democracy, development and civicism resound far beyond Italy's borders to countries in both the developed and developing world that are struggling to understand how social, political and economic variables interact. Not surprisingly, the findings that Putnam brings centre stage have profound implications for grassroots development projects, particularly the way in which the development community gauges its impact:

> Similar to the notions of physical and human capital, the term 'social capital' refers to features of social organizations – such as networks, norms, and trust – that increase a society's productive potential. Though largely neglected in discussions of public policy, social capital substantially enhances returns to investments in physical and human capital… The implications for social and economic policy are far-reaching.

If fostering civics and social capital is important for development, then the yardstick for measuring developmental success needs to be recalibrated to take this into account.

Reflections on a Quarter Century

Twenty-five years' experience at the grassroots has brought the Inter-American Foundation (IAF) to similar conclusions. Since 1971, the crux of the IAF's work has been strengthening the myriad forms of community action in Latin America – from neighborhood and peasant associations to sophisticated credit networks. Yet little of that effort was routinely reflected in project reporting, which tended to focus on the implementation of project activities (such as training courses) rather than on more complex project results in personal and organizational capacity or increased voice in decision-making.

In our bottom-line society, 'results' tend to be equated with an immediate, tangible product – something that can be captured with a dollar sign or a snapshot. However, as veteran field-workers know, today's successful product often turns into tomorrow's white elephant (in the form of empty community centres and abandoned public housing) if it is not the fruit of a broader, participatory process.

This is not to say that the emphasis on results is misplaced. It is particularly vital today in a world of growing demand and dwindling resources. The question is, What constitutes 'results'? What do we really want to achieve and how can we tell whether we are achieving it? What measures of community-based development take into account both success in the short run and sustainability over time?

In 1992, IAF staff began a systematic effort to address those questions and to widen the lens through which the IAF looks at and documents results (see *Grassroots Development*, Vol 17, No 1). The conceptual tool that evolved is the Grassroots Development Framework. It is intended to help the Foundation answer difficult questions: Did grants in fact strengthen civic organizations? Are the organizations achieving a measure of self-sufficiency? Have they made a difference in the quality of life of their beneficiaries? And have the recipient organizations contributed to any change in policies, practices or attitudes in the surrounding community that transcend the immediate project and improve the climate for local initiative?

From the Drawing Board to the Field

Once the basic concepts of the Grassroots Development Framework had been debated and largely accepted in-house, the IAF sponsored pilot tests in Uruguay, Ecuador, the Dominican Republic and Costa Rica. These four In-Country Support teams (ICSs) joined subsequently by others, became the principal architects of the indicators, the data collection methodologies and the instruments that took the framework from the drawing board to the field.

Consultations between the IAF and ICS staff produced the categories, variables, and definitions that became the embryo of a 'common language' that would help to facilitate the exchange of experience between programmes and across sectoral lines. Only when the concepts and definitions were clear and there was a broad consensus about what was important to measure did IAF shift attention to specific indicators of progress or accomplishment. The current challenge is to test, hone and revise the indicators.

Pilot Application

One of the earliest pilot tests was carried out in 1994 by the Ecuador ICS, COMUNIDEC. The profile that emerged from applying the framework to 24 or-

Box 19.1 The Grassroots Development Framework

Tangible   Intangible
Broader Impact

**Strengthening
Organizations**

**Direct
Benefits**

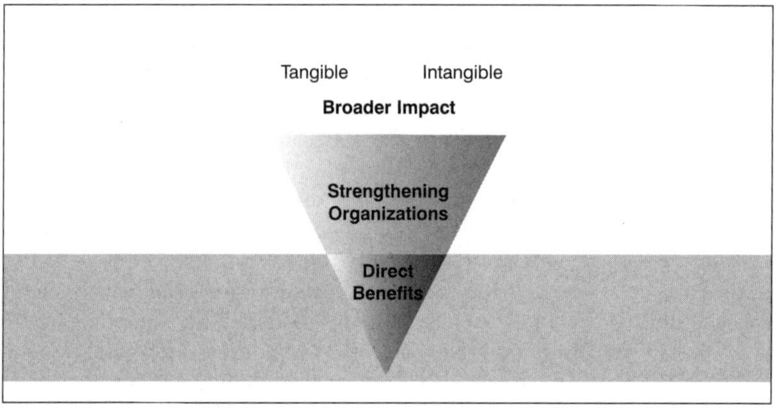

Figure 19.1 *The Grassroots Development Framework*

The premise of the framework is that grassroots development produces results on three levels, and that there are important intangible, as well as tangible, results that need to be taken into account (Figure 19.1).

The six resulting windows or 'categories' in the graphic illustration arose not from theory but from the life stories of hundreds of organizations (Figure 19.2a).

Each category in turn is defined by a set of concepts or 'variables' that attempt to capture its essence. At the heart of the framework are the 22 variables identified through a long and rich dialogue between Foundation staff and In-Country Support teams.[2] Variables track results, not activities. The conical shape that gives the framework its nick-name 'the Cone' represents the widening impact of grassroots development from the individual through the organization to the community or society at large (Figure 19.2b).

All the facets of the framework are interconnected and there is a constant flow among them (Figure 19.2c).

The balance among the variables is key. Strategic planning capability, for example, is an important achievement at the organizational level. But if it is not accompanied by a clear vision of where the organization is going, planning becomes a sterile exercise. Mobilization of resources is key, but if the organization compromises its autonomy in the process, it may become ineffective in the long run.

Participation, empowerment and sustainability are basic tenets of the Foundation. Although they form the conceptual undergirding of the framework, they do not appear explicitly. The framework intentionally breaks down these abstract concepts into more concrete and measurable components.

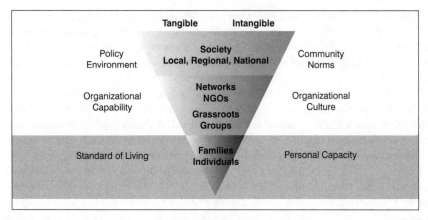

Figure 19.2a

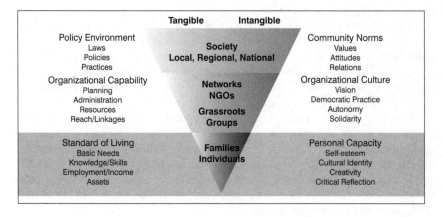

Figure 19.2b

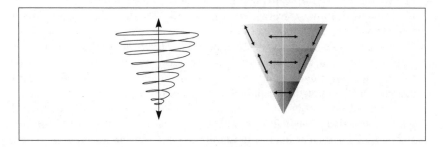

Figure 19.2c

ganizations in Ecuador would not surprise Robert Putnam. Although the results fell into all six 'windows' of the framework, the category that stands out is Organizational Culture. Three variables that ranked among the top five 'results' are in fact the building-blocks of social capital: democratic practices, accountability and autonomy.

Some interesting patterns emerge from the Ecuador pilot study (see text box for greater detail). The results documented are distributed relatively evenly through the six categories of the framework and are divided almost equally between tangible and intangible (47 per cent and 53 per cent, respectively). ICS staff found that the framework helped to visualize the various strategies employed by different types of grantees. Non-governmental organizations (NGOs) appear to concentrate on organizational strengthening as a means for delivering benefits at the grassroots and/ or for influencing the policy environment and changing norms. Grassroots community organizations begin with the basic building-block of personal capacity as a means to encourage a more democratic culture and ultimately affect values and attitudes. Other types of grantees target the policy environment and work for change that will be felt on a regional or national scale.

Statistics from the study show that 80 per cent of the beneficiaries contributed voluntary time or labour to a project; 72 per cent had acquired new knowledge of civic rights and responsibilities; and 74 per cent were linked into some larger network. Nearly 80 per cent cited (positive) change in behaviors and attitudes in their environs, including greater tolerance for ethnic diversity, easing of racial and religious tensions, and better coordination among development agencies.

Reaching out for a broader sample, the Foundation asked ICSs to conduct a one-month survey of Grants active between October 1993 and April 1995. Various methods of data collection were used, including a review of grantee and monitoring reports, grantee interviews and grantee responses to questionnaires. Data was collected on a limited number of variables: practices, relations, resources, democratic activities, basic needs, income and employment. This quick survey of results produced some interesting statistics:

- *Mobilization of Resources.* Over the years, the Foundation has reported its leverage capacity at $1.50 generated for each dollar invested. Data collected with the framework show an average return of US$3.25 to the dollar, with figures as high as $4.30 in the Southern Cone.
- *Practices.* Combined figures for the four geographic regions show that methodologies pioneered by IAF grantees have been replicated, adapted by, or disseminated to 6029 non-governmental organizations (NGOs) and 1186 public sector organizations. The 'best practices' reported were in work with youth and women and in the fields of preventive health, environment and training. Collectively, IAF grantees have shared methodologies with international organization in 209 instances.
- *Relations.* Of particular interest in this era of democratization and decentralization is the degree to which the organizations supported by the Foundation are interacting with and influencing governments and other organizations in civil society, at the municipal and national level. Over 80 per cent of the organizations reported increase in their capacity to negotiate with the public and private sectors.

BOX 19.2 RESULTS OF A PILOT APPLICATION

The Ecuador pilot study included 24 organizations that had received Foundation funding over a period or eight years or more. In all, they cover 803,650 direct or potential beneficiaries, representing 7.6 per cent of the country's population. The sample, chosen to be representative of the ethnic and geographic distribution of the IAF's grant portfolio in Ecuador, includes 14 grassroots organizations, nine support institutions, and one quasi-governmental agency.

The results registered in Ecuador are distilled from a variety of sources. They include existing files and reports, key observers and third parties, individual interviews and workshops. The principal instrument was the 'taller participativo' or group discussion technique pioneered by COMUNIDEC to elicit input from all segments or the community and encourage reflection and analysis as a basis for ongoing self-evaluation. In preparation, the ICS team conducting the study in Ecuador 'translated' the framework into a set of open-ended questions to stimulate discussion. They then entered the results into a database, and devised a set of parameters that enabled them to analyse the data by category, variable, indicator and development approach to discern patterns and trends.

The common good

Unlike conventional capital, social capital is a public good in that it is not the private property of those who benefit from it. Most often the ties, norms, and trust that constitute social capital are created as a by-product of other social activities and then transferred from one social setting to another. – Putnam

The idea of fostering a sense of civic responsibility and of safeguarding things (such as air quality) that belong neither to the state nor to private individuals, but that are vital to everyone's well-being, is gaining currency among Latin American NGOs.

Fundación Natura, one of the nine NGOs or support institutions covered in the Ecuador results study, serves as a good illustration of the role of NGOs in 'the common good'. Natura was founded by Ecuadorian professionals concerned with the deterioration of the nation's natural resources. Its main thrust is to raise public awareness of deforestation and erosion. Natura operates with a small salaried staff supported by an active board of directors and a fleet of volunteers. Funding comes from its local membership of 800, from the Ecuadorian private sector, and from international agencies.

Direct benefits. Fundación Natura has reached 50 per cent of its potential audience of 20,000 with its environmental awareness campaign. Technical assistance has resulted in controlling the use of pesticides and diagnosing and treating cases of toxic poisoning. In addition to specific agricultural techniques, 50 per cent of the beneficiaries learned management and dissemination skills. The search for non-toxic farming methods has sparked a revival of traditional peasant lore and stimulated creativity among small farmers. Thirty-four per cent of the beneficiary population is using alternative methods of farming and measuring yields.

Organization. Fundación Natura's well-trained staff conducts strategic planning on a regular basis. The organization's leadership style – with emphasis on teamwork, shared decision-making and respect for minority points of view – sets an

---

BOX 19.2 CONTINUED

example for the organizations with which it works. Natura maintains close ties with numerous other Ecuadorian organizations and is a member of ten world-wide networks. Although a large portion of its funding still comes from international donors, Natura has been more successful than most in establishing a local membership base and raising funds from the private sector.

Broader impact. Through national and international fora and a series of publications, Fundación Natura has succeeded in drawing the nation's attention to the problems of pesticides, deforestation and erosion. The Fundación drafted and helped pass laws regulating the production, importation, marketing and use of pesticides and other chemical products. These will have significant long-term impact nationwide.

By marshaling citizens, businessmen and government officials to cooperate on environmental problems that affect them all, Natura has helped to bridge cultural barriers and break down stereotypes.

The Lens You See Through

When the framework was applied to assess the effectiveness of the Mexican grantee PAIR (Program for Integrated Use of Natural Resources), it became clear just how different a project can look when the lens for viewing results is widened. Traditional monitoring of this non-timber forest products grant shows that, as provided in its grant agreement, PAIR worked with two municipalities in the state of Oaxaca to improve coffee production, introduce vanilla and cacao crops, protect hardwood forests and begin a reforestation project. 'Results' included upgrading 20 hectares of coffee, planting 20 hectares of cacao and establishing nine experimental plots of vanilla as well as a nursery that provided 5000 seedlings of cedar and aguatillo (an indigenous tree), which were transplanted into the cacao and vanilla fields.

Notwithstanding the importance of these results, asking a different set of questions produced a whole new perspective on the scope of PAIR's effect. With the framework, the IAF learned that PAIR has collaborated with half a dozen other major NGOs in the area, and worked closely with local and regional producer organizations such as the Asociacion Agricola Local Morada de Colibries y Fondos Regionales de la Chinantla. Coverage has expanded from the two pilot municipalities to an additional ten municipalities, involving local government, NGOs and peasant organizations. On the strength of PAIR's track record in natural resource planning and use in Oaxaca and other states, several of its founders were named to national posts. Biologist Julia Carabia Lillo joined the cabinet as Secretary of Environment, Natural Resources and Fishing (SEMARNAP). Enrique Provencio serves as Undersecretary for Planning of SEMARNAP and Biologist Carlos Toledo Manzur is Director of Regional Development, promoting on a national scale the approaches to natural resource use and conservation successfully demonstrated by PAIR. All of these are important consequences that are not detected with traditional results analysis.

Feedback from the Field

The 18-month pilot phase alternated field tests with workshops and feedback sessions. The richness of project profiles that emerged from applying the framework dispelled much initial scepticism. 'We discovered,' said the Colombian ICS learning coordinator, 'that the Cone is a prism. Before, we were seeing only the white light. Now we see a full spectrum of colour.'

But the field tests also pointed to a number of concerns and operational problems. Virtually everyone underscored the importance of *context* as a backdrop and basis for interpreting results, and of understanding the strategy employed or the process developed. Also, timeframe continues to be a major question as results often become manifest well after a grant has ended. In a similar vein, trying to determine the degree of causality between results and a given grant is neither practical nor germane. More relevant is an understanding of the relationships among results, strategy and context that will help to identify which development approaches work under which circumstances.

The framework also has specific shortcomings when applied to certain types of projects. For instance, more work is needed (and is under way) to develop adequate indicators for productive enterprises and to ensure that issues of gender are taken into account.

Because some of the measures necessarily rely on informed opinion, ICSs verify data provided by grantees by consulting a variety of sources including 'outsiders' and knowledgeable third parties; cross-checking data over time; and contracting fully-fledged evaluations where warranted. Several ICSs report that data become more reliable as grantees participate in framing indicators and take the framework to heart to help them to improve their own performance.

These reports are encouraging since grantees' attitudes towards the framework are a key to its potential success or failure. As one ICS in the Andean Regional Workshop articulated the challenge. 'There are two ways of applying the Cone. One is to get the boxes checked and the forms filled in, and the other is to make sure that grantees have the opportunity to really appropriate this tool so that it becomes a genuine part of their own planning and evaluation.'

Consequently, the most heartening feedback was the response from grantees. The degree of interest was a striking departure from the weary resignation that tends to greet new demands for information. One reason is identification with the integral nature of the framework.

'This is what we've been wanting from funders for a long time,' remarked a Dominican NGO leader. 'It's the first time the intangible things are taken into account. That's what most of the effort goes into, but we've never known how to record the results.'

Perhaps the most encouraging sign of the potential of the framework is its spillover in several countries to projects beyond the IAF orbit. FORO JUVENIL, a respected grantee group in Uruguay, has worked actively with the ICS to integrate the framework as a basis for identifying and analysing the results of their job training programme.

'Once we really master the Cone as a framework and as a tool, it will give us the means to set up and manage our own information system... tailored if need be to our own particular vision.' After a year's trial, staff opted to extend the framework to the other three major programmes of FORO, although none is funded by IAF.

Shared Experience

Other development assistance organizations are also tackling the results problem. Several have consulted with the IAF about the Grassroots Development Framework: United States Agency for International Development (USAID), the Peace Corps, the African Development Foundation, the International Youth Foundation, the Bernard Van Leer Foundation, the World Wildlife Federation and the newly formed Inter-American Corporation for Grassroots Development.

In conjunction with its matching fund agreement with the IAF, the Venezuelan oil company PDVSA is introducing the framework as the basis for monitoring and reporting on its affiliates' contributions to grassroots development. Collectively they will contribute US$2.5 million dollars to community projects throughout Venezuela in Fiscal Year 1996.

In Colombia, a consortium of 11 foundations and NGOs has opted to use the Grassroots Development Framework as the common tool for documenting the impact on families, organizations and communities of the jointly sponsored projects known as OCDs, or community development organizations.

Through an agreement with the recently created AIDS-prevention organization Alianza Internacional, the Ecuador ICS (COMUNIDEC) is working with Alianza's local affiliate FIFSIDA, the Foundation for Initiatives Against AIDS. Seeking an alternative to 'evaluations that count the number of condoms distributed', Alianza has engaged COMUNIDEC to adapt the framework to its needs and provide training for staff of the 14 projects now under way in Quito. Using the basic structure – the three levels and the tangible and intangible sides – COMUNIDEC has adjusted the framework by tailoring the titles of the categories and some of the variables to match specific goals. With this tweaked version of the framework, an Alianza official commented that evaluation in the health field, which 'tends to be ultratechnical, sophisticated, expensive' and the province of specialists is being conducted by frontline workers who are finding a 'tool that is accessible, that they themselves can use, that demystifies this business of evaluation'.

Within the IAF: Beauty and the (Potential) Beast

At the Foundation itself, the framework is slowly being woven into the cycle of programme planning, project analysis, monitoring and reporting of results – which in turn feeds back into programme planning. It helps to situate and give perspective to individual case histories. The intent is to broaden the horizons and the analytical framework at all stages.

As with any attempt to systematize project monitoring and evaluation, there are caveats. Care must be taken not to:

• use the framework as a prescriptive device rather than an organizing principle;

- check the boxes, rather than seek to broaden understanding;
- overcomplicate, by proliferating the number of variables and indicators;
- lose sight of the forest (understanding process) for the trees (only reporting numbers); and
- let the tail wag the dog, skewing projects and programmes to accommodate 'the system'.

Pitfalls notwithstanding, the framework *has* captured the imagination of many who understand very well that, as Putnam described, 'the social capital embodied in norms and networks of civic engagement seems to be a precondition for economic development as well as for effective government'. The attractions of the framework are:

- conceptual clarity;
- simplicity (as described by the Brazil ICS 'it is a 'simple' concept that allows NGOs and grassroots groups – and even beneficiaries – to adopt it as part of their institutional life');
- visual, graphic presentation;
- flexibility, to adjust for context and adapt methodologies;
- versatility, to apply in broad brushstrokes to an entire grant portfolio or in detail to a given project; and
- vitality, which springs from broad participation and a two-year dialogue among staff and ICSs to build the system.

Do Measures Really Matter?

Measures matter, critically, because what the development assistance community chooses to measure is what we ultimately get from grassroots development. If the international and multilateral funders that are now turning to NGOs as channels for development assistance value and reward only the 'tangible, quantifiable results', that is what NGOs (consciously or unconsciously) will emphasize. Cost/efficiency measures will produce bricks and mortar, but at the expense of less visible, less marketable efforts to build human capacity and social capital. 'Those concerned with democracy and development ... should lift their sights beyond instant results. Building social capital will not be easy, but it is the key to making democracy work' (Putnam).

The experience distilled from decades in Latin America sheds light on issues that increasingly face the United States as well. Poverty isn't just the lack of material goods. It is also distance from decision-making and a sense of being devalued that manifests itself as apathy, anger and a weakening of the civic culture. The kind of short-term, tangible results that satisfy planners and funders may mask the symptoms of underdevelopment. Recognizing and measuring progress towards real solutions calls for imagination, creativity and a willingness to take the long view.

The Foundation is clearly not alone in the quest to assess the real impact of grassroots funding and to articulate that impact to decision-makers who seek quantifiable, visible results. As a Venezuelan who works with international funding agencies put it, 'people are thirsty' for ways to evaluate and communicate the effects of their work. Among both funders and NGOs, a new yardstick, with new units of measure is in the making to help quench this thirst. Robert Putnam's work in Italy gives historical weight and legitimacy to the emerging yardstick and the importance of the social capital it measures.

Notes

1 Robert Putnam is Peter and Isabel Malkin Professor of Public Policy at Harvard University. His publications, in addition to *Making Democracy Work: Civic Traditions in Modern Italy*, include the popular essay 'Bowling Alone: America's Declining Social Capital' and 'The Prosperous Community: Social Capital and Public Affairs'.

2 In-Country Support teams (ICS) are local organizations contracted by the Foundation to monitor IAF-supported projects, identify potential grantees, and provide technical assistance to IAF grantee organizations.

20

Accounting for Change: The Practice of Social Auditing

Simon Zadek and Peter Raynard

Introduction

Major changes throughout the 1980s has meant a delegation by the state to commercial and private, non-profit organizations, in key social and economic spheres. This shift has created a need for accounting practices that assess the social impact and ethical behaviour of such organizations, as well as their financial and environmental performance. This chapter, by examining three contemporary social and ethical accounting systems, explains how far down the road we are in acounting for change. It concludes that 'social auditing' techniques are currently the most theoretically well rooted, comprehensive and practical, in that they give voice to those affected by the organization, strengthens the organization's strategic management procedures, and makes the organization both more transparent and accountable.

A New Moral Mandate

Of the many changes that took place in the 1980's, the most important has arguably been the systematic transfer of the moral mandate that for decades had been almost the sole preserve of the state, to commercial and private, non-profit organizations. This transfer happened in many shapes and guises, including the privatization of previously nationalized industries, the dismantling of legislation that had historically preserved labour rights, the relentless process of international trade liberalization and the retreat of many aspects of the welfare state. These patterns of change have all allowed greater freedom for commercial organizations to determine their own moral or social stances and for the non-profits to take up the moral mantle in advocacy and service provision.

It did not take long for this new situation to generate a complex and problematic relationship between institutional survival and success, and moral rhetoric and aims. The corporate sector discovered that their social activities could underpin effective advertising, as well as often providing staff with productive insights into other parts of the economy (Goyder, 1987). The non-profits discovered increasingly graphic ways of depicting social misery as a route to fund-raising (Hancock, 1989).

Both sectors, albeit in different ways, found themselves balanced on a publicly declared moral tightrope.

The Verification Problem

This mixture of socially responsible activities and public relations hype created, in short, a verification problem. Financial performance could be reasonably well verified within established statutory frameworks. Verification of environmental performance was rapidly becoming an established procedure, albeit through best practice and benchmarking rather than through statutory force. Some aspects of social performance assessment were reasonably well understood and accepted, such as in relation to equal opportunities legislation, corporate gift-giving, secondments and customer service.

The broader dimensions of social performance remain, however, outside of the statutory realm. Indeed, not only do most of the many claims of social performance remain unverified, they are often quite unverifiable given the types of information that the organizations concerned are generating regarding their own activities. The recent experience of the fierce debate about the ethics of the international body care company, Body Shop International, illustrated the problem very clearly. Because all parties to the debate presented little more than anecdotes, there was no real clarity as to what the Body Shop's activities actually were.

The recent Body Shop experience highlights two key issues. The first is that it should be expected that there will be an increasing number of challenges to the moral rhetoric of those organizations claiming to have aims and practices that go beyond the struggle for profit or institutional survival: 'The high moral tone taken by the Body Shop has exposed it as a target for scrutiny' (The *Independent*, 23 July 1994, p3).

The double-edge of reacknowledging the moral responsibilities of all institutions – including business – is that these responsibilities will become entangled in the cut and thrust of survival. The second therefore, is that there is a paramount need for clear verification procedures. The work of organizations such as the New Consumer (in the UK) and the Council for Economic Priorities (in the USA), has contributed to the evolution of such procedures (Adams et al, 1991). However, verification of practices in relation to social aims remains underdeveloped, particularly for larger organizations with extended, complex patterns of activities and influences.

Social and Ethical Accounting:
A Comparative Overview

Social and ethical accounting can be, and has been in practice, undertaken in many different ways. Comparison is not straightforward, since the circumstances of different accounting processes are often critical in determining both the design and the practice. It can be problematic to compare two approaches that have evolved through application to very different types of organization, whether in terms of size, ownership and control, pattern of aims or activities. At a very simple level, the matter of equal opportunties for staff may involve radically different issues for organizations of different sizes, at different stages of their life-cycles, with different levels of financial and time surpluses, and in different cultures. In an organization where social accounting has been carried out, the relationship, for example, between its core Christian values and the secular societal norms of equal opportunities has raised many issues which cannot be resolved easily or compared with the situation of other organizations (Traidcraft, 1994).

With this qualification in mind, we have constructed a cautious comparison of three approaches to social and ethical accounting. The three have been chosen on the grounds that they all:

*   have been thrown against the litmus test of practical application;
*   represent (to the authors) broadly sound approaches;
*   are likely to be at the core of approaches adopted in the future.

With the limits to comparison in mind and the rationale for selection, the three approaches compared below are:

*   *Social auditing*: broadly the system developed by the New Economics Foundation and Traidcraft plc, and now being used in adapted form by Body Shop plc, Happy Computers, Shared Earth, several non-governmental organizations (NGOs) and the New Economics Foundation itself (New Economics Foundation, 1994; Pearce, 1993; Shared Earth, 1994; Traidcraft, 1994).
*   *Ethical accounting statement:* system developed at the Copenhagen Business School, adopted first by SBN Bank and now in use in a range of companies and socially oriented organizations in Denmark and Norway (Pruzan and Tyssen, 1990; SBN Bank, 1993).
*   *Social statement:* system developed in the USA with the company Ben and Jerry's.

Table 20.1 offers an outline comparison of the approach taken by each of these three methods to nine critical features of social and ethical accounting. The table suggests a number of strong similarities between the three methods. First, they all start from a position that the key to the process is to give voice to a wide range of stakeholders. None of the approaches in this sense restrict the scope of stakeholder consultation through design, although operational differences can create variations in the practical scope of consultation. Second, they all involve a commitment to a regular accounting cycle, which has in practice meant an annual cycle. There is nothing within the accounting process that makes an annual cycle particularly significant. Rather, the annual cycle has tended to arise through a deliberate sychronization with financial and environmental reporting cycles, as well as annual reports (in the case of Ben & Jerry's) and Annual General Shareholder Meetings (in the case of Traidcraft plc). Third, all three approaches involve the publication of the accounts and thus its availability to the stakeholders themselves.

Table 20.1 *Outline Comparison Between Different Approaches to Social and Ethical Accounting*

Principle	Social audit	Ethical accounting statement	Social statement
Multiple stakeholder perspective	Yes	Yes	Yes
Comprehensive[1]	Yes	Yes	No
Regular	Yes	Yes	Yes
External benchmarking	Yes[2]	No	No
Target-setting	Yes	Yes	No
Systematic bookkeeping	Yes	Yes	No[3]
External verification	Yes	No	Yes
Audit group	Yes	No	No
Publication of accounts	Yes	Yes	Yes

The above table also shows a number of important differences between the three approaches. First, the social audit and ethical accounting statement approaches are notably different from the social statement approach in being comprehensive and systematic. Also, the construction of a social statement does not, as the opening comments in their 1993 social assessment stressed (as part of their Annual Report), involve a systematic accounting process: 'the company (Ben & Jerry's) does not as yet maintain or have available the complete records that would allow a social audit to be accomplished on a timely basis' (Ben & Jerry's Annual Report, 1993). A distinguished person is invited to investigate any aspect of the company's activities, and to report on them in a manner that he or she might wish. This relatively ad hoc approach does limit the process in that it is impossible for a systematic account of the organization's activities to be constructed, particularly when the organization is large and geographically dispersed. It follows from this that the social statement does not lead the organization to establishing a systematic approach to social book-keeping, which is an evolving but important feature of the other two approaches.

A second significant difference between the three methods concerns their approach to benchmarking. The ethical accounting statement approach rejects any external benchmarking, arguing that this form of comparability is largely meaningless. A rigorous approach to assessing the changing pattern of different stakeholder group perspectives *over time* is instead the focus of this benchmarking process.[4] The social statement similarly does not involve any systematic external benchmarking, although (unlike the ethical accounting statement) there is nothing inherent within the approach that prevents external comparisons to be made. The social audit approach both allows for and encourages external benchmarking. However, the external benchmarking is in general restricted to the third level of value-constructs, 'societal aims', as discussed below. This allows for external benchmarking against aims for which there are generally accepted indicators.

The third significant difference concerns the matter of target-setting. The social statement approach does not in general lead to explicit, publically declared, target-setting. This reflects a view of it primarily as a reporting tool, 'accounting' in its most basic sense. The social audit and ethical accounting statement approaches, on the other hand, both involve target-setting. Target-setting under social auditing takes place outside of the formal accounting and auditing process. The organization itself sets targets that subsequently appear in the proceeding social audit. These targets often arise in practice from dialogue that takes place with stakeholders within the social auditing process. The ethical accounting statement approach, on the other hand, involves target-setting as a formally integrated part of the accounting cycle. Once the formal accounting for the previous year has been completed, the organization brings together 'dialogue circles' comprising members and representatives of each stakeholder group. The dialogue circles are reponsible for making recommendations for the adoption of targets to the senior managers of the organization concerned.

In this sense, then, the social auditing and ethical accounting statement approaches are not only accounting tools in the traditional sense of reporting past behaviour. Nor are they only an accountability tool, in the sense of giving practical leverage to stakeholder groups through the provision of information. They are in addition practical strategic planning and management tools. In this latter role, the two approaches are particularly relevant to those organizations which have explicit non-financial objectives, and can be of critical use for those organizations which can only survive in the long run if these objectives are addressed adequately.

The final significant difference considered here concerns the matter of external verification. In this critical area, it is necessary to distinguish a number of differences and their possible reasons. First, the social statement and the social audit both involve external verification, whereas the ethical accounting statement does not. Interestingly, when this difference was discussed at a meeting of some of the principle architects of the various approaches, it came as some surprise to most that the veracity of the main example of ethical accounting, the annual statement produced (without external verification) by SBN Bank, had never been challenged.[5] To those working elsewhere in Europe, this seemed quite inconceivable. The view expressed by those involved in its production argued that the relative smallness, homogeneity and strong sense of 'moral economy' in Denmark and Scandanavia as a whole was central in explaining why unverified accounts could go unchallenged in this manner.

The social statement and social audit approaches are both externally verified, but in very different ways. The social audit approach to verification is discussed in more detail below, but in brief, places considerable stress on ensuring multiple levels of verification, each involving both an auditor and stakeholders themselves. The social statement, on the other hand, has a far more individualistic approach to external verification. It is the responsibility of the one 'distinguished person' to investigate the organization, write the social statement and in this sense validate it as an objective statement about the organization's social impact.

Focus on Social Auditing

The more recent history of social and ethical accounting has seen rapid developments in both methods and applications. This section explores in more detail the method underlying one of the three approaches outlined in the comparative section above, 'social auditing'.

Social auditing is 'a means of assessing the social impact and ethical behaviour of an organization or set of activities in relation to its aims and those of its stakeholders... Stakeholders are individuals and groups who are affected by, or can affect, the activities under review' (Zadek, 1994, pp632–633). Social auditing has a number of particular characteristics, some of which have been outlined above. The following description, however, offers both more detail on key features of social auditing and highlights its underlying principles.

Polyvocal. The approach is based on the views and accounts of all stakeholders, as well as the mission statement and wider interests of the organization concerned. Furthermore, social auditing does not seek to judge the relative relevance of these different views, many of which in practice can offer very different accounts and judgements of the same set of events. Rather, it seeks to report these different viewpoints and where possible to contextualize them with other information in a manner that allows the audience to come to a view as to how to deal with the various perspectives. In the Traidcraft social audit for 1993, for example, it was reported that a significant number of staff considered that the lower paid levels were receiving too little in relation to the organization's 'fair trade' declarations. At the same time, the quantitative data showed that these staff were being paid roughly the same as people working in other trading organizations doing similar work. These two views were conflicting, but not incompatible. Traidcraft's staff considered that comparability was an inadequate basis for setting wages for an organization with a declared social policy such as Traidcraft's. The role of the social audit was not to decide on this matter, or even judge whether one or other of the views should be omitted from the published audit. The role of the social audit, rather, was to show the different viewpoints in as clear a manner as possible to enable all of the stakeholders, particularly the staff (including management) and the board, to understand the issues being raised and the root of the different existing perspectives.

Social auditing in this sense follows a broadly constructionist approach to accounting, as, for example, set out in Guba and Lincoln's *Fourth Generation Evaluation* (1989). To avoid this approach to 'accounting receptivity' degenerating into an unmanageable soup of values, aims and measures of performance, social auditing practice has been moving towards a three-tier categorization of values (see Figure 20.1):[6]

- *Core aims* of the organization, generally reflected in its mission statements. These would include, for example, trading relationships, attitudes towards staff, forms of corporate involvement in community activities and, of course, the need for financial viability and in some cases surpluses and dividends.
- *Specific stakeholder aims*, which are those that are identified during the consultation process with identified stakeholder groups. This would generally include staff and for commercial organizations often some combination of suppliers, customers and the wider community in which the organizations are active. For non-governmental organizations (NGOs), stakeholder groups can include funders, policy-makers, collaborators and beneficiaries, as well as staff and volunteers.
- *Societal aims*, which are those 'benchmark' concerns established in the societies in which the organization is active. This might include, for example, social

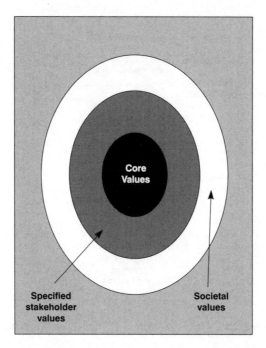

Figure 20.1 *Polyvocal a Three-tier Approach*

norms made explicit through statutory means, such as in equal opportunities legislation. However, important social norms are often not made explicit or statutory. In these situations, these norms are often in practice voiced through specific stakeholder perspectives.

Multi-directional accounting. The three-tier approach outlined in Figure 20.1 requires a complex consultation process. In particular, accounting needs to take place in several directions at the same time. Staff of an organization, for example, would be consulted as stakeholders (see Figure 20.2). From this perspective, they would be able to highlight their own values and interests and to construct indicators to measure the organization's performance on that basis. The same staff, on the other hand, would be subject to a performance assessment themselves in order to judge the organization's performance against its core values or the values declared by other stakeholders. This complexity, it should be stressed, is not simply a 'feature' of the accounting procedure. Rather, it is a formalization of the very complexity of values, aims and two-way accountability that in practice exist within organizations (and indeed societies in general).

Comprehensive. The approach supports and encourages comprehensive assessments of an organization's social impact and ethical behaviour. It is critical that this principle is upheld to avoid any exclusion (deliberate or otherwise) of reporting of one or other aspect of the organization's activities. There has been interest shown by some organizations, for example, in applying social auditing to one part of their

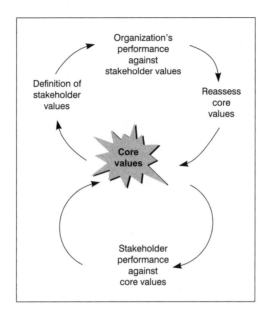

Figure 20.2 *Multi-directional Stakeholder Consultation*

activities, such as their 'community work'. While there certainly would be value in understanding the impact of such activities in themselves, such an approach would endanger the integrity of the social audit approach more generally, and therefore has been resisted to date.

It is recognized, however, that practical considerations make it impossible for every aspect to be dealt with during each accounting cycle. It would be impossible or certainly prohibitively costly, for example, for Body Shop to consult fully with every one of its suppliers, franchisees and staff every single year. For this reason, the auditor's report (see below) each year makes recommendations as to what areas the organization should focus its accounting in the coming cycles.

Comparative. The issue of comparability has been one of the most contentious issues with which the social auditing method has had to grapple (as well as other social and ethical accounting approaches). On the one hand is the difficulty of comparing social and ethical effects across different situations, as the previous section highlighted. On the other hand was a recognition of the need to provide some basis for contextualizing social accounts for them to have any meaning. The need for meaning ultimately meant comparison of one kind or another. Thus, the issue is *how* rather than *whether* to maximize the level of meaning through enabling comparison. This is a very different standpoint than that taken by, for example, the proponents of the ethical accounting statement and social statement approaches, which explicitly reject comparison with other organizations.

Externally validated. The principle of external verification is central to social auditing, as it is with classical evaluation. However, the classical approach to external validation is fraught with difficulties. The 'evaluator', for example, typically has an impositional role. In the case of NGOs, for example, the evalutor often acts on behalf of donors and therefore tends to restrict the scope of the assessment to the interests of these parties. A further difficulty is how the external assessor can retain her or his 'objectivity'. The more they invest in understanding what is going on, the less objective they become, and yet to remain outside of the process involves the maintenance of a high level of ignorance.

The social audit process has attempted to deal with these issues through a two-stage approach to external validation. In the first instance, an external person – the auditor – develops and agrees a methodology with the organization and stakeholders, and monitors the preparation of the social accounts. The social accounts are prepared by the organization, however, rather than the auditor. During this process, the auditor is expected to become compromised to some degree in order to get close enough to the organization to understand what is going on. This is acknowledged and accepted rather than hidden from view. Thus, as an additional cross-check, the auditor establishes an audit group which considers the social accounts by interrogating the auditor and the organization during a single session once the draft accounts have been prepared. The audit group includes people who can represent the interests of the key stakeholder groups involved and have expertise in issues related to the particular organization's activities. For example, the New Economics Foundation's audit group, consisted of people from different areas of the NGO community, such as Intermediate Technology, the Environment Council and the World Development Movement. It is through this latter dialogue that the values and concerns of the stakeholders are once again secured within the accounting process. It is centrally these values that create meaning for the accounts, rather than a professionalized (in the sense of 'devalued') accounting process.

Disclosure. The results must be disclosed to the stakeholders, as well as other possible groups. Thus, unlike traditional evaluations, the social audit is in the public domain. This is critical, since it is largely through public disclosure that the interests of diverse stakeholders are made effective.

The significance of this stage of the social audit process cannot be overestimated. With financial audits, it is the fact of full disclosure that allows shareholders and other interested parties to assess the performance of the organization and to decide whether to pressurize the organization to change its practices, to purchase or to sell shares. The publication of social audits fulfils a similar purpose in the social domain. The revelation, for example, that a company has not traded according to its declared ethical principles or has acted against the values and interests of other stakeholders offers the opportunity for stakeholders to bring pressure on the organization to change its practices, or at least to amend its declared principles in line with its practice.

Conclusion

Social auditing is an approach, not a solution. It allows organizations to move towards new forms of accountability without major shifts in ownership and organization form. It allows for an evolutionary process of taking stakeholder interests more directly into account and having to report on activities according to their interests. Finally, through the information thrown up by social auditing and its open publication, it can be effective in reorienting the organization's activities towards stakeholder interests.

Notes

1   None of the approaches are comprehensive during any one cycle, since the costs of such an approach would be prohibitive. The difference is that the Ben & Jerry's approach adopts a sampling approach and only reports on that basis, whereas the other two approaches seek to be comprehensive over a number of cycles.

2   Partial external benchmarking seems to be possible, although the Ethical Accounting Statement approach views this not to be the case.

3   Ben & Jerry's does not aspire to be systematic, whereas the NEF/Traidcraft approach is moving towards a greater systematization of social bookkeeping.

4   A piece of computer software has been developed by the Copenhagen Business School to support the Ethical Accounting Statement process which allows for scaled questionnaire responses to be compared across years.

5   Comments by Peter Pruzan at a meeting of social and ethical accounting practitioners in Dessau, Germany, in July 1994.

6   Particular thanks to David Wheeler and Maria Sillanpaa of Body Shop plc for helping to clarify these different levels.

References

Adams A, Carruthers, J and Hamil, S (1991) *Changing Corporate Culture: a Guide to Social and Environmental Policy and Practice in Britain's Top Companies*, Kogan Page, London.

Ben & Jerry's (1993), *Annual Report*, Ben & Jerry's, Vermont.

Goyder, M (1961) *The Responsible Company*, Blackwell, Oxford.

Goyder, G (1987) *The Just Enterprise*, André Deutsch, London.

Gray, R (1993) *Accounting for the Environment*, Paul Chapman, London.

Guba, E G and Lincoln, Y S (1989) *Fourth Generation Evaluation*, Sage, London.

Hancock, G (1989) *Lords of Poverty: The Power, Prestige, and Corruption of the International Aid Business*, Atlantic Monthly Press, New York.

New Economics Foundation (1994) *New Economics Foundation Social Audit 1993/94*, New Economics Foundation, London.

Pearce, J (1993) *At the Heart of the Community Enterprise*, Calouste Gulbenkian Foundation, London.

Pruzan, P and Thyssen, O (1990) 'Conflict and consensus: ethics as a shared value horizon for strategic planning', *Human Systems Development*, No 9, pp134–152.

SBN Bank (1993) *Ethical Accounting Statement 1993*, SBN Bank, Denmark.

Shared Earth (1994) *Shared Earth Social Audit 1993/94*, Shared Earth, York.

Traidcraft plc (1994) *Traidcraft plc Social Audit 1993/94*, Traidcraft plc, Gateshead.

Zadek, S (1994) 'Trading ethics: auditing the market', *Journal of Economic Issues*, Vol XXVIII, No 2, June, pp631–645.

Part 7

Becoming a Learning Organization

21

Organizational Learning in Non-governmental Organizations: What Have We Learned?

Michael Edwards

Introduction

Learning is considered to be an essential component of organizational effectiveness in all sectors – private, public and non-governmental. All non-governmental organizations (NGOs) aspire to be 'learning organizations', yet few have reflected systematically on the success in this regard. This chapter summarizes the experience to date of international NGOs that have prioritized learning as an objective, drawing out areas of both success and failure, and reflecting on whether there are any features that distinguish learning in NGOs from learning in other types of organization. A simple typology and set of tests of NGO-learning are presented, along with a series of challenges for the future.

The chapter examines organizational or 'institutional' learning in development NGOs based in the industrialized world but working internationally, such as Oxfam and Save the Children. (Most NGOs use the term 'institutional learning' loosely, without necessarily being 'institutions' themselves in the formal sense of the term. 'Organizational learning' is the preferred term throughout this chapter.) This is not to detract from the central importance of learning in Southern NGOs, but reflects the biases of my own experiences working for a range of NGOs in the North. Although management 'gurus' come and go, effective learning as a key to performance and results remains a constant theme in management writings (Senge, 1990; Drucker, 1990; Handy, 1993; Peters, 1994). The same conclusion surfaces constantly in the NGO literature (Edwards and Hulme, 1992, 1995), where there is a small but growing body of critical work which looks specifically at learning processes and outcomes (Edwards, 1994b; Roche, 1995; Fowler, 1997). Learning about NGO work on the ground is essential to identify what works and what does not, more or less, cost-effectively: learning about the impact of wider forces (such as macroeconomic policy) is crucial if NGOs are to advocate for change successfully at national and international levels; learning is the foundation for accountability, dissemination and influence, all things that are increasingly important to NGOs as they move away from a reliance on small-scale project interventions and engage in the broader processes of development; learning about changes in the external environment (donor

policy and development ideology, for example) is necessary if NGOs are to anticipate threats and opportunities, and prepare for them; learning is a key component
of staff development and effectiveness; and learning from the ideas and experiences
of others is vital if NGOs are to keep themselves alive to innovation and challenge.
In the past, NGOs have been insulated from the costs of not learning by a loyal but
relatively uninformed donor base and by their ideological popularity with government funding agencies. But in a future dominated by increasing competition, demands
from donors for 'results', closer scrutiny of the NGO world from its critics, more
transparency and greater accountability, this is unlikely to continue (Hulme and
Edwards, 1996). Both development effectiveness and institutional survival demand
that NGOs learn much more, and more effectively. This chapter a general overview
of learning experiences to date in international NGOs and offers some pointers for
the future.

Learning in NGOS

There are at least four things which (although they affect all organizations to some
degree) are especially important in shaping NGO learning.

The nature of development

Gleick (1987, p24) likens living in the world to walking through a maze in which
the walls rearrange themselves with each step one takes. NGOs know from their
experience (especially in participatory development work) that this is a true description of the world they inhabit. Development situations are inherently unstable,
uncertain, contingent, complex and diverse (Roche, 1995; Uphoff, 1992; Angelides
and Caiden, 1994). Problems are caused by a multitude of interrelated factors that
change as they interact with the problem and with each other; communities and
institutions are fractured by different interest groups and perceptions of the same
problem, so there is no single 'reality' to be had; unintended consequences and
'second- or third-order effects' are highly influential, yet rarely intentional, predictable or measurable (Uphoff, 1995); connections are often more important than
static facts (Hills, 1994). Development processes are non-linear 'open' systems that
are extremely fluid, in which continuous learning is the sine qua non of being able
to respond and intervene effectively. Even if an NGO understands what led to sustainable change in one location, it cannot assume that the same course of action
would lead to the same outcome in another. Knowledge advances through the
observation and analysis of unexpected phenomena, as well as reflection on what is
already familiar.

    This means that 'double-loop' learning, in which connections are made con-
tinuously between learning and decision-making throughout the organization, takes
precedence over simple error-correction (Argyris and Schon, 1978). Problem-
solving gives way to the task of anticipating or preventing problems from shifting
or spreading, and living with diversity and non-standardization (Angelides and Caiden,
1994). Building people's capacity to learn and make connections becomes more

important than accumulating information about lessons learned in the past. Interesting (positive or negative) experiences are targeted for learning instead of 'averaging' experience across the board. Patterns and generalizations may still be made, but are made not by aggregating diverse experiences but by identifying common elements, deviations from what is expected (Roche, 1995), or the 'edges of experience' (Davies, 1995). In the messy, complex and unpredictable world that NGOs inhabit, it is the *process* of learning that really matters. Of course, the world is not completely messy nor entirely unpredictable, so NGOs need not abandon their search for static lessons learned (guidelines or models of good practice, repositories of knowledge and experience, and so on).

Information, knowledge and wisdom

NGOs often confuse information (the raw material that enters the learning system), knowledge (systematizing information by filtering, testing, comparing, analysing and generalizing) and wisdom (the ability to utilize knowledge and experience in action; Edwards, 1996a). For NGOs especially, wisdom is the most important because learning that is not utilized effectively in practice is of little value (Edwards, 1989; 1994). The goal is not to store up information about the world, but to change it (or to help others to do so); information and knowledge are important in this task, but 'there is so much written and written so well that another effort always seems redundant. We quote from each other and generally say the same things. *When we act it is different, because it is a discovery*' (Roy et al, 1994, pi). Learning requires action because many of the mechanisms that are responsible for poverty and violence are invisible until they are activated by attempts at change.

NGO learning is therefore 'reflection-in-action' or 'learning-by-doing' (Schon, 1987); coaching is more important than training, dialogue replaces teaching and technical problem-solving is placed in a wider context of reflective enquiry. 'Knowhow' is more important than 'know-what' (Edwards, 1996a). This requires NGOs to support staff in a process of structured learning from experience so that learning skills and abilities are developed continuously and lessons are genuinely learned and used. It also requires strong feedback mechanisms to connect information, knowledge and action. Because NGOs are embedded simultaneously in the worlds of action and understanding, have a presence that crosses national boundaries and possess a value system which (in theory) promotes learning and communication, they have a strong set of comparative advantages in learning terms.

Accommodating error and failure

Real learning is never easy or comfortable because it implies change and challenge. Superficial learning is common, with lessons learned stored away, lost on the shelves or accepted with managerial rhetoric which 'supports these conclusions completely' and then quietly ignores them in practice. Selective learning is also frequent – lessons that are acceptable to power-brokers obviously have much more chance of being actioned; a challenge to the agency's 'sacred cows' is much less likely. In such circumstances, identifying the lessons of experience is not sufficient to induce change; there must also be a strategy to address these blockages (see 'Learning in NGOs, below). No organization likes to admit failure or ignorance, or risk personal dis-comfort and organizational destabilization by facing up to the need to change. Yet development is inherently about failure as well as success – what was once thought a failure may have unanticipated beneficial effects, whereas what appeared successful at one point in time may turn out to be unsustainable. Learning from failure is essential if the same problems are going to be avoided in future. To see NGOs acknowledging their failures is a good thing; it only becomes a bad thing if the same failures are repeated (Smillie, 1995).

Belief versus knowledge

It is, perhaps, a truism that only people learn, not institutions. Organizational sys-tems and structures can help or hinder, but the bottom line concerns individuals. This is particularly important for NGOs to recognize because by and large NGOs are populated by people who have strong beliefs, values and commitments to the work they are doing. They may be driven, therefore, more by what they believe in than what they learn; or they may confuse the two, given that beliefs often stem from knowledge derived many years ago during formal education and training. NGOs need to differentiate between things that they learn (implying some sort of rigorous methodology and analysis), things that they believe they have learned (without such rigour), and things they believe in regardless of learning (their basic values and principles). All three categories are valid and valuable, but for different ends. Save the Children-UK (SCF), for example, insists on taking a 'child-centred' approach to development (Save the Children Fund, 1995). The case for this approach can be made on both normative grounds (children's rights) and practical grounds (society will benefit) but the evidence to prove the practical case does not yet exist. As value-led organizations, NGOs will inevitably confront dilemmas like this, where the interpretation of lessons learned will be contested. Is it the case that 'seeing is believing' or that 'believing is seeing'? Whose reality counts? (Chambers, 1993).

Problems and Solutions

In practice, there is nothing magical about NGOs as organizations that enables them to resolve these complex learning dilemmas, whatever their comparative advantages in theory (Edwards, 1994b). Empirical studies of NGO learning reveal a common pattern and suggest some clear avenues for improvement (Edwards, 1994b; Slim, 1993; Roche, 1995; Smillie, 1995; Kelleher and McLaren, 1996).

Culture

Activist cultures often see learning as a luxury, separate from and secondary to 'real work', so time and space for learning is difficult to protect. Differences in learning styles and languages are also a feature of a large, dispersed, multicultural staff.

Changing NGO cultures is always difficult, but by introducing the right incen-tives and structures it is possible to encourage staff to favour enquiry, experimentation and risk-taking. Cultural change is an amalgam of changes in other areas and occurs when members of the organization see themselves, and judge each other, in different ways. What is important is to start the process off, however imperfectly, so that others can follow.

Attitudes and incentives

Learning requires self-criticism, humility, honesty and openness, the ability to welcome error as an opportunity to move forward rather than as a mistake to be concealed. There are no easy ways to develop these attitudes in people, but certain things (hierarchy, disbursement pressures, fear of failure) can be addressed to make the organizational environment more conducive. But often in NGOs, incentives and rewards for learning are weak and diffuse; failures are disguised or punished; inertia, defensiveness, complacency and territoriality may override openness; 'risk-aversion' is commonplace; and job insecurity and short-term contracts make staff less likely to invest time in learning because they lack a stake in the long-term future of the agency or feel that they cannot influence the outcome of events. The bottom line here is reassuring staff (especially in the field) that their opinions and experience are valued. Is surprising how often this basic advice is ignored, especially in centralized management structures. More widely, staff need to feel secure that in making time and space for reflection and learning they are not going to be punished; learning has to be legitimized by senior managers and the necessary resources protected, within a clear and shared vision that prioritizes learning goals (Senge, 1990). Oxfam-UK has recently initiated a 'Cross-Programme Learning Fund' to create more space for learning with relatively few resources (Roche, 1995). Learning has to be built into job descriptions (for senior managers as well as for frontline staff), and rewards for experimentation and inquiry should be built into staff appraisal systems. Donors can help here by including additional resources for learning in grants and holding NGOs accountable for what they learn. In NGOs that exist to transfer financial resources to projects or partners, there must be an explicit link between learning and resources received if incentives for learning are to be made concrete.

Structures

Hierarchical, centralized, control-oriented structures are inimical to learning; the 'tunnel vision of the project system' (Smillie, 1995) compresses timescales and discourages experimentation; departmental barriers reinforce a tendency to guard information jealously rather than exchange it freely. Hierarchy and centralization distance decision-makers from the sharp end, so compromising the link between learning and action, and the ability to adapt quickly to a dynamic and uncertain world. They encourage distrust and stagnation because 'rationality' in such systems requires that staff compete with each other and disguise their mistakes (Brown, 1994). In contrast, in flatter and more democratic structures it becomes rational to cooperate. Buchanan-Smith et al (1994) show how the highly decentralized early-warning system in Turkana (Kenya) enabled decisions to be taken quickly in 1990–1991 because information and lessons learned could be transmitted very quickly into the right response. So strong feedback loops between learning, action and decisions over resources are essential. Learning organizations are decentralized, organically structured and task-oriented, with flexible units and teams built around pieces of work for which they are jointly accountable (Wierdsma and Swieringha, 1992). Boundaries are pragmatic, often temporary, and designed to facilitate cooperation through mutual interdependence. Horizontal linkages are deliberately fostered and professional distinctions blurred (for example, between programme and research staff). Planning is 'hypothesis-led' (Dudley, 1996, p190) so that projects are designed to be experimental. Different views and approaches are allowed to coexist until proved to be deficient.

Systems and priorities

In most NGOs systems for accessing, storing, transferring and disseminating learning are underdeveloped, underresourced and inefficient. Information overload is common – there is a huge amount of information around, but too little a structure to ensure that the right people get what they need at the right time. There must be a balance between different kinds of learning (or learning for different purposes) and particularly between internal and external learning, formal and informal learning processes, and the need to achieve coherence while respecting diversity (see What Kinds of Learning Should NGOs Invest In?, below). The learning process can be likened to an iceberg, with a huge underwater mass representing all the learning that goes on in the field, and a small tip emerging above the surface representing the formalization of lessons learned in policy statements, good practice manuals, and so on. If the balance shifts too far towards the formal, local initiative may be stifled and the process can become academic; if it moves too far in the other direction mistakes might be repeated and opportunities for wider learning lost because people are only learning from their own, limited experience. A preoccupation with documented knowledge and information-storage is common in NGOs (a throwback to conventional 'banking' concepts of education in which the purpose of learning is to accumulate facts). But such knowledge may quickly become obsolete and may block the entry of new knowledge into the system – learning is a continuous process in which information and knowledge appear, disappear and reappear. Building learning capacities should take precedence over building costly structures for information storage and retrieval.

Public relations

A perceived need to provide a continuous stream of uncomplicated success stories to lever funds from the public detracts from the depth of self-criticism and analysis required if NGOs are to be serious about learning; rising competition for funds leads NGOs to prioritize public relations over genuine learning (that is, highlighting the good and burying the bad: Hulme and Edwards, 1996); and the pressure to demonstrate 'low overheads' to donors detracts from the investments required to learn effectively, even though it is clear that learning is essential to achieve leverage and impact (and ought therefore not to be classified as an overhead at all – Fowler, 1997). Many NGO staff worry that learning is too expensive, until they, or their organization, have to pay for their mistakes. NGOs are not very good at dealing with 'discordant information' – that is, learning which challenges the organizational consensus or threatens short-term institutional interests, particularly about roles and responsibilities, and especially if (as an NGO based in the North) it is wedded to an operational role in the South (see Learning in NGOs, below).

All this is not to say that NGOs currently do not learn; only that they face considerable barriers in doing so, so that learning tends to be concentrated in particular parts of the organization (especially at field level) and in particular areas of work (usually those which are less contentious).

Learning in NGOs: What Have We Learned?

At a general level, it is incontrovertible that NGOs are significantly more thoughtful, analytical and mature in their self-criticism than they were 20 years ago. The output of materials on and about NGOs and their work has risen considerably, especially over the past five years and much of this has come from within the NGO community itself (Edwards and Hulme, 1992, 1995; Smillie, 1995; Fowler, 1997). Learning has taken place both at the broad level of NGO roles, identities, effectiveness and accountabilities, at the detailed level of sectoral interventions and innovations, and, in terms of methodologies of development work such as participatory rural appraisal (PRA). There is an acknowledged 'reverse flow' of ideas and influence from NGOs to official agencies in areas such as participation and the 'process approach' to development work, gender and sustainable development.

But there are three more fundamental tests of learning among NGOs: first, are such changes related to learning or to other influences? It is impossible to disaggregate internal and external influences in any scientific way, but at least some of the changes in NGO activity over the past decade do seem to be related to external pressures, influences and fashions. For example, nearly all NGOs are still preoccupied with formalistic strategic planning models which were abandoned some years ago by those in the corporate sector from whom NGOs have borrowed. The current interest of many organizations in micro-finance may have started as a response to poverty and the lessons of previous NGO programmes, but now threatens to displace other, equally important aspects of NGO work such as institutional development (Hulme and Edwards, 1996). The easy availability of donor funding for some activities rather than others is obviously an important factor here, but learning organizations do not simply go where the money is; they are driven by, and remain loyal to, the lessons of their experience in the field. A similar point could be made about the prominence of certain forms of project appraisal and monitoring methodologies such as the Logical Framework and its derivatives. Are increasing numbers of NGOs adopting these models because their experience demonstrates that they are superior, or because they are fashionable and/or are a requirement of certain bilateral donors (Edwards and Hulme, 1995)?

Second, is it the case that NGOs do not learn or that they do not put into practice what they do learn? Do we really need more research or just more action to implement what we already know? NGOs know how to facilitate effective grassroots development work: take your time, understand the situations, build on local knowledge and understandings, combat discrimination, develop strong local institutions, let things develop organically, and so on. Often, however, what is known is difficult to persevere with, for all sorts of reasons, including funding constraints, supporter attitudes and pressures of time. But unless NGOs have the courage to apply the lessons they learn and mechanisms to link action with accountability, learning from experience can simply mean the freedom to repeat the same mistakes. This is particularly so with 'discordant information'. In SCF-UK, for example, there has been an ongoing debate over many years on the issue of approaches to work – should the agency be operational in the field, a funder of Southern partners, an advocacy and campaigning organization, a think-tank, or all four? This debate proved very difficult to move forward because different individuals held strongly divergent views that no amount of 'learning' seemed to influence. In 1995, there were staff changes in key positions that resulted in a strategic review of SCF's work, and a study in India and Bangladesh that seemed to show that more impact could be achieved if Save the Children supported partners in the process of local institutional development (Edwards, 1996b). The coincidence of new learning and a more receptive environment for the lessons learned meant that the debate moved much more quickly. One can read this story, of course, in two ways: as a success story, with the feedback loop between learning and action taking less than ten years to operate, or as a sign that SCF moves too slowly to adapt to a rapidly changing environment. The point is that learning by itself is insufficient to deal with discordant information.

Third, are NGOs better prepared to anticipate and respond to the changes that are occurring around them? Are they more secure and sustainable than a decade ago? Can they overcome constraints that might formerly have crippled them? Are they clear about their future roles and are they positioning themselves in good time to play them effectively? Is morale inside NGOs improving (often one of the best signs of a learning organization)? At first sight the answers to such questions are not encouraging: the 'New Policy Agenda' that is sweeping through development agencies was largely unanticipated by most NGOs and, consequently, NGOs are still struggling to come to terms with it (Edwards and Hulme, 1995). Levels of financial dependence on government grants are increasing and public support in many countries seems to have reached a plateau. Northern NGOs are experiencing an unprecedented period of self-questioning which manifests itself in more or less continuous strategic reviews, restructurings and new mission statements. Criticisms of NGO performance and accountability are mounting, although official support for NGOs remains strong thus far (Smillie, 1995; Sogge, 1996; Edwards and Hulme, 1995). Although welcomed on the surface, the rise of Southern NGOs has thrown many Northern NGOs into a defensive mode. Weak learning in many NGOs has contributed to a basic lack of clarity about future form and function.

What Kinds of Learning Should NGOs Invest In?

In large, multilayered, complex, diffuse systems (which is what international NGOs are), the learning process must be carefully structured it is going to be successful. It is not possible for everyone to learn everything, all the time; this leads to learning which is aimless, amorphous and fragmented, in which information and knowledge disappear into organizational black holes or remain lodged in the head of one or two individuals. There needs to be a balance between different types of learning, between learning in different parts of the organization, and between learning for different purposes. But this must be achieved without sacrificing the freedom and flexibility emphasized earlier (see Introduction) as the hallmark of successful learning in open systems. Additionally, different types of learning carry different implications for the NGO in terms of skills, structures, systems and resources, and there may be trade-offs and choices to be made. For example, an NGO that prioritizes participatory learning in the field may look very different from one that is primarily concerned with campaigning in the North. The balance between participatory, field-based learning and learning which feeds into wider policy and advocacy-related work is probably the most difficult for NGOs to strike.

Participatory learning in the field

'The things we need to learn because, *for our own reasons*, we really need to know them, we don't forget' (J Holt in Dudley, 1993, p67). Direct, experiential learning among fieldworkers is the foundation for other forms of learning linked to good practice, policy and advocacy work. If learning is not taking place at grassroots level, then other layers in the learning system will be defective. Encouraging action-reflection and learning from experience on a continuous basis among field staff, partners and people in projects must, therefore, take top priority. Experience shows that people are unlikely to use or value learning if they see learning as someone else's responsibility (as is traditional in organizations that divide those who 'think' from those who 'do'). So NGOs need to pay special attention to encouraging learning among those who traditionally have not been encouraged to see themselves in this light. Additionally, staff are not going to use information that they consider to be irrelevant to the immediate needs, whether by virtue of language, jargon, accessibility, length, format or timeliness. NGOs tend to be excessively dependent on the (often badly) written word, but converting information into knowledge and knowledge into learning in a multicultural environment requires a much more imaginative approach, using visual communications (such as video), face-to-face encounters and informal dialogue. The prime purpose of learning at grassroots level must be to promote self-development and social and economic change at that level, not to unearth interesting insights for consumption in the headquarters. Learning is a process of personal growth and discovery, not just the accumulation of knowledge. This does not mean that information from the grassroots cannot be used by NGOs to lobby for change (though it almost certainly means that more attention should be given to supporting research, policy and advocacy work undertaken directly by communities, partners and field teams); such information is fundamental if NGOs are to operate as an effective 'reality check' on the impact of official policy or propaganda from governments (or NGOs themselves!).

Facilitating learning at this level is a matter of adjusting the project development process so that there is enough time, space and flexibility for those involved to learn; introducing incentives and rewards for learning along the lines spelled out earlier; and changing agency culture. Experience suggests that there is no substitute for strong leadership in encouraging learning of this sort; where senior field managers encourage their staff and protect the necessary space and resources, learning can be successfully prioritized. Conversely, blueprint approaches to planning, rushing and the imposition of external agendas mean that there is no space to reflect, let alone to learn.

Project-based learning

NGOs obviously need to learn about their performance, cost-effectiveness and practice. They need to monitor and evaluate their work and develop stronger accountability systems both downwards (to the grassroots) and upwards (to trustees and donors). 'Always ask how we can do what we already do better', is Drucker's (1990) advice, to which one might add 'always ask whether we could be doing other things instead'. Encouraging project workers to do these things for themselves is essential and requires the same changes as outlined above in relation to participatory learning. As an NGO worker in Palestine put it, 'we need to tell our own stories' – to have the opportunity to stand back, reflect on experience, analyse it from the local perspective (which may differ from that of the outsider) and document it. There is a copious literature on project-level research, monitoring and evaluation among NGOs, but perhaps a few points from SCF's experience may be useful in considering how to build the results of project-level learning into the wider institutional context. SCF has developed a wide range of good practice guides and manuals; a computerized global information system that provides access to grey material on all projects (retrieved through subject and geographical keywords); incentives for exchange visits, workshops, contract extensions and short sabbaticals to write up project experiences; more systematic induction procedures linked to the outputs of the project monitoring and evaluation system; and revised job descriptions that emphasize learning as well as doing (Slim, 1993; Edwards, 1994b). One of the most important conclusions of reviewing these innovations is that SCF overestimated the degree to which busy project staff would access written information, and more generally would put time and effort into using sophisticated systems that store lessons learned on electronic media. A second lesson is that the depth of analysis required to pull together the lessons of project experience and synthesize them into a usable form is significantly greater than most field staff possess, without considerable investments in further training and support. Lighter, more decentralized systems are required, based less on the written word and more on supporting people *in the field* to 'tell their own stories'.

Policy and advocacy-related learning

Project experience and the lessons of practice are the building-blocks of NGO operational policy, but they must be generalized if policy is to have any meaning. It is only at the level of policy that findings achieve a sufficient level of generality to be of interest and relevance to wider audiences. Senge (1990, p94) calls the search for these patterns the key to learning and action. Yet herein lies a dilemma. As pointed out earlier, the reality of the situations in which NGOs intervene is complex, diverse, uncertain and contingent. If every situation is different and every experience unique, how is generalization possible? Additionally, if development is such a dynamic process, how can generalizations made at one moment in time be useful in another? This is a challenging dilemma and one to which NGOs need to give a lot more consideration. In addressing it a number of avenues suggest themselves: first, it is better to generalize by identifying key, common elements in patterns of experience rather than trying to aggregate the experiences themselves (as in 'the average community in Africa is … '). Second, focus on experiences that seem especially interesting or different: Davies (1995) calls this the 'principle of sampling the edges of experience'; Roche (1995) 'learning by deviation'. Third, look for differences in interpretation of the same experience among stakeholders, and explore them because such differences indicate that something important is happening. Fourth, experiment with purposive sampling or strategic selection of project-level experiences to try to reduce bias. Fifth, build on long-term project experience and local research to give a richer picture of trends and pool the resulting information between different projects (or NGOs) in the same area (SAF, 1996).

These are all ways of distilling lessons of experience into policy without over-generalizing. Another way is to gather information about a predetermined subject through more rigorous research. SCF has a great deal of experience in this area of learning (Edwards and Hulme, 1992, 1995; LaFond, 1995; Tolfree, 1995). Although credible intellectually and influential in policy terms, this research was too disconnected from field realities to elicit much of a sense of interest or ownership from inside the organization. This has meant that the results of the research have been used outside SCF, but not inside – the feedback loop to internal action was not strong enough, and a large part of the reason for this was the way in which the research was carried out by separate teams based in SCF's headquarters with weak links to the field.

These dilemmas are even more acute when NGOs wish to use lessons from their experience in advocacy and campaigning work where information can be distorted or used selectively in order to support a predetermined position. In advocacy work it is particularly important that NGOs learn from sources outside the agency as well as internal contacts and experience, as this helps to challenge what can become too cosy a consensus when judgements are being made about ambiguous information. What originates as learning specific to a particular context (for example, the impact of user fees on access to a hospital) may be transposed into a general statement for lobbying the World Bank ('user fees are bad' – Edwards, 1994b). The general statement may still be true or at least may be an accurate description of what the NGO believes to be true, but unless the method by which it has been arrived at is made transparent, the result can be both flawed and misleading.

Visionary thinking

A final area of NGO learning concerns 'possibility-creating' or 'envisioning' the future (Kelleher and McLaren, 1996) – dreaming of new worlds, thinking the unthinkable, and learning outside of the normal parameters of NGO roles, interests and agendas. Is this a luxury in an era when hundreds of millions of people still live in absolute poverty? Although it can only be a minor component of NGO learning as a whole, this sort of thinking might actually be extremely important to NGO effectiveness in the future because it keeps NGOs alive to new possibilities in a rapidly changing world. Conventional development assistance may well form only a small part of efforts to promote development in the years to come because there are other areas for action that are going to be as or more influential – 'values of interconnectedness, humility and service; relationships of respect and equality; and lifestyles which promote sustainable development over short-term gain', to use Hulme and Edwards's words (1996), not to mention alternative trading, international alliances for advocacy and 'development' work in the North. Shifting patterns of poverty and exclusion and the changing nature of development assistance will foster new roles for NGOs in both the North and the South, and as they change NGOs will need to prioritize different forms of learning and learning in new areas. This will require NGOs to spend more time and resources in unfamiliar territory: learning about alternatives to current economic orthodoxies and value systems; making links with churches, spiritual movements and other non-development networks; and being open to influence from unexpected directions. The characteristics of the learning organization will serve NGOs well in this respect, but the lessons learned may well be surprising ones.

There are, then, many different types of learning and each has its own requirements. It is certainly advisable for NGOs to make a conscious decision about which forms of learning they wish to prioritize, so that they can ensure that they learn effectively in key areas. Particularly, NGOs need to strike the right balance between participatory learning among staff, partners and others at grassroots and project levels; and learning which is intended to feed into wider policy, advocacy and campaigning activities at national and international levels. There will always be a tension between local ownership of learning and information (the need to respect diversity and flexibility), and the need for NGOs to achieve some degree of coherence, quality control and methodological standardization if they are to carry on a sensible dialogue above the project level with anyone else. Questions of legitimacy (who speaks for whom?) are likely to be especially acute whenever NGOs based in the North advocate on behalf of people and 'partners' in the South. As Korten (1987) and Avina (1993) have pointed out, the place and pattern of organizational learning also changes as NGOs evolve through their 'lifecycles' (although not all in the same way or at the same speed). Agencies that prioritize advocacy and international linkages – with the goal of becoming a 'movement' for change – will present a very different learning profile to organizations that maintain a focus on operational work and internal management information requirements.

Linkages for Learning

NGOs have a clear comparative advantage over formal research institutions in fostering participatory learning and action research (Hulme, 1994). However, as the need to generalize increases, different skills are required: a knowledge of formal research methods, analytical rigour, an overview of the literature and independence from internal (institutional) agendas that may ignore discordant information. Information must be transformed into knowledge that is systematized, synthesized, analysed and interpreted. A knowledge of theory is important, however much practitioners may distrust it because theory is what underlies policy: 'practical men in authority who believe themselves to be quite exempt from any intellectual influences, are usually the slaves of some defunct economist', as Keynes reminds us. Most NGO personnel lack these skills, so collaboration with those who do have them (in universities, other research institutions and among consultants) is important. One of the lessons SCF has learned from five years of policy-related research is that forging alliances with others is a better way of moving forward than creating large research departments inside an NGO. Such collaborative partnerships produce benefits for all parties: a better understanding of field-level realities, more informed practice, better generalization and theory-building, stronger feedback loops, and the promotion of a real learning culture in both NGOs and universities. Independent researchers can provide a source of challenge and foundational thinking which few NGOs can match, whereas NGOs can and should make some of their own resources available for such work in the light of declining government budgets for development-related research. Otherwise, 'research', which should be a process of searching for the truth, may be used to validate what NGOs already think they know. Indeed, this is an area in which NGOs have much more of a role than they have realized: Brown (1994) has made a convincing case that NGOs are 'bridging organizations' par excellence. As a result of their position as intermediaries between grassroots communities and other institutions, NGOs are ideally placed to foster the cooperative relationships among diverse groups that are essential for sustained progress. Taking this point further, Edwards and Hulme (1995) and Riddell (1996) paint a future for NGOs as actors in multi-layered alliances and coalitions made up of all sorts of different groups working synergistically towards broad but common goals. If this is true, then the skills of the bridging organization (as of the learning organization) become paramount.

However, fostering collaboration carries risks as well as opportunities. It takes a great deal of time to foster trust, overcome preconceived suspicions and hostilities, allow joint working to evolve organically and preserve space for independent action when appropriate. NGOs and academics are rarely natural partners because of their different traditions. Close and continuous contact over an extended period of time is required to cement collaborative relationships, with long-term 'partnership frameworks' allowing mutual trust and confidence to develop within a constantly shifting pattern of tasks and responsibilities (Development Studies Association, 1994). Researchers can 'accompany' NGO programmes or areas of work; also useful are staff exchanges (secondments and sabbaticals, internships, reciprocal representation on boards) and incentives from research funders to join NGO academic research efforts. NGOs need to move beyond using researchers as short-term consultants because (although obviously useful in certain circumstances) this does little to foster longer-term collaboration. Links between like-minded individuals in both NGO and research institutions are likely to prove crucial, and clearly stated goals and outputs are essential. Roles, responsibilities and obligations must be agreed in advance, and there must be clear guidelines on the ownership and use of any information generated. Cooperation must be seen to generate outputs which are useful for both sides: more academic publications for researchers and more accessible and action-oriented outputs for the NGO. This means that partnerships must be extremely flexible (Development Studies Association, 1994).

There is another reason for collaborating with the formal research community in NGO policy and advocacy work – credibility. Often, a degree of 'academic respectability' is needed to persuade others to take conclusions seriously. This will continue to be the case until NGOs become much more adept in their learning role, able to convince the sceptics that their conclusions are arrived at rigorously and are not simply the reflection of predetermined agendas. By allying themselves with research institutions, NGOs can combine the power of grassroots testimony and clearly articulated normative positions (which are their strengths), with detailed narratives and rigorous enquiry. This is a very powerful combination, although one whose potential for influencing change remains largely untapped at present. This is partly because it is a very difficult combination to achieve. The dilemma of rigour and relevance may be dissolved if we can develop an epistemology of practice which places technical problem-solving within a broader context of reflective equiry, shows how reflection-in-action may be rigorous in its own right, and 'links the art of practice in its uncertainty and uniqueness to the scientist's art of research'. (Schon, 1983, p69). But how is this to be achieved? This chapter offers some insights, and others come from a small group of researchers who are pioneering new methodologies to link 'micro-' and 'macro-level' processes together (Booth, 1996; Bevan, 1996; SAF, 1996). But there is no doubt that this remains a very challenging area for NGO learning, no less for social science as a whole.

Conclusions

Amid the sheer complexity and diversity of NGO learning experiences, styles, themes and priorities, one message stands out: what matters most is that NGOs *do* learn, that they always try to learn more effectively, and that they do not stop learning even when they think they have found the answers. There will always be tensions between participatory learning and respect for diversity on the one hand, and the disciplines imposed by the need to link learning with policy, advocacy, campaigning and public engagement on the other. Undoubtedly, NGOs need to develop their ability to manage these tensions more effectively. In this task, openness, humility, service, enquiry, sharing and solidarity – as well as strategy and resources – are crucial. These are the qualities that underlie genuine learning in any organization, but if NGOs still retain their claim to a distinctive identity as value-based organizations, then they ought to be particularly well equipped to develop themselves in this respect. NGOs have learned much about themselves and about development over the past two decades, but their real potential as learning organizations has yet to be unlocked.

References

Angelides, C and Caiden, G (1994) 'Adjusting policy-thinking to global pragmatics and future problematics', *Public Administration and Development*, Vol 14, pp223–241.

Avina, J (1993) 'The evolutionary life cycle of non-governmental development organizations', *Public Administration and Development*, Vol 13, pp453–474.

Argyris, C and Schon, D (1978) *Organizational Learning: A Theory of Action Perspective*, Addison-Wesley, Menlo Park.

Bevan, P (1996) *Understanding Poverty in Uganda: Adding a Sociological Dimension*, Centre for the Study of African Economies, Oxford University, Working Paper, No 10.

Booth, D (ed) (1994) *Rethinking Social Development: Theory, Research and Practice*, Longman, London and New York.

Booth, D (1996) 'Bridging the micro–macro divide in policy-oriented research', *Development in Practice*, Vol 5, pp294–304.

Brown, L D (1994) 'Creating social capital: nongovernmental development organizations and intersectoral problem-solving', Institute for Development Research, Boston, Mass.

Buchanan-Smith, M, Davies, S and Petty, C (1994) 'Food security: let them eat information', *IDS Bulletin*, Vol 25, pp69–80.

Chambers, R (1993) 'All power deceives', *IDS Bulletin*, Vol 25, pp14–26.

Davies, R (1995) *The Management of Diversity in NGO Development Programmes*, Centre for Development Studies, University College, Swansea.

Development Studies Association (1994) *Report of a Workshop on the Academic–Practitioner Interface*, Development Studies Association, Manchester.

Drucker, P (1990) *Managing the Non-Profit Organization*, Harper Collins, New York.

Dudley, E (1993) *The Critical Villager: Beyond Community Participation*, Routledge, London.

Dudley, E (1996) 'Educating fieldworkers', in N Hamdi (ed) *Educating for Real: the Training of Professionals for Development Practice*, IT Publications, London.

Edwards, M (1989) 'The irrelevance of development studies', *Third World Quarterly*, Vol 11, pp116–135.

Edwards, M (1994a) 'New directions in social development research: the search for relevance', in D Booth (ed) *Redefining Social Development: Theory, Research and Practice*, Longman, London and New York.

Edwards, M (1994b) 'NGOs in the age of information', *IDS Bulletin*, Vol 25, pp117–124.

Edwards, M (1996a) 'The getting of wisdom: educating the reflective practitioner', in N Hamdi (ed) *Educating For Real: the Training of Professionals for Development Practice*, IT Publications, London.

Edwards, M (1996b) *NGOs in South Asia: What Breeds Success?*, Save the Children Fund Overseas Department, Working Paper, No 14, London.

Edwards, M and Hulme, D (eds) (1992) *Making a Difference: NGOs and Development in a Changing World*, Earthscan, London.

Edwards, M and Hulme, D (eds) (1995) *Beyond the Magic Bullet: NGO Performance and Accountability in the Post-Cold War World*, Earthscan, London, and Kumarian Press, West Hartford.

Fowler, A (1997) *Striking a Balance: a Guide to NGO Management*, Earthscan, London.

Gleick, J (1987) *Chaos: An Emerging Science*, Pan, London.

Handy, C (1993) *Understanding Organizations*, Penguin, Harmondsworth.

Hills, G (1994) 'The knowledge disease', *Resurgence*, Vol 164, p48.

Hulme, D (1994) 'Social development research and the third sector: NGOs as users and subjects of social enquiry', in D Booth (ed) *Redefining Social Development: Theory, Research and Practice*, Longman, London and New York.

Hulme, D and Edwards, M (eds) (1996) *Too Close for Comfort? NGOs, States and Donors*, Macmillan, London and St Martin's Press, New York.

Kelleher, D and McLaren, K (1996) *Grabbing the Tiger by the Tail: NGOs Learning for Organizational Change*, Canadian Council for International Cooperation, Ottawa.

Korten, D (1987) 'Third generation NGO strategies: a key to people-centred development', *World Development*, Vol 15 (supplement), pp145–159.

LaFond, A (1995) *Sustaining Primary Health Care*, Earthscan, London.

Peters, T (1994) *The Pursuit of WOW!*, Macmillan, London.

Riddell, R (1996) *Trends in International Cooperation*, paper prepared for the Round Table on 'Promoting Public Support for Canadian Development Cooperation', Aga Khan Foundation, Ottawa, July.

Roche, C (1994) 'Operationality in turbulence: the need for change', *Development in Practice*, Vol 4, pp160–171.

Roche, C (1995) *Institutional Learning in Oxfam: Some Thoughts*, Oxfam, Oxford.

Roy, A, Dey, N and Singh, S (1994) *Living with Dignity and Social Justice: Rural Workers' Rights to Creative Development*, Social Work Research Centre, Tilonia, India.

Save the Children Fund (1995) *Towards a Children's Agenda: New Challenges for Social Development*, Save the Children Fund, London.

Schon, D (1983) *The Reflective Practitioner*, Temple Smith, London.

Schon, D (1987) *Educating the Reflective Practitioner: Toward a New Design for Teaching and Learning in the Professions*, Jossey-Bass, San Francisco.

Senge, P (1990) *The Fifth Discipline: the Art and Practice of the Learning Organization*, Random House, London.

Slim, H (1993) *Institutional Learning Review and Future Priorities*, Save the Children Fund, London.

Smillie, I (1995) 'Painting Canadian roses red', in M Edwards and D Hulme (eds), *Beyond the Magic Bullet: NGO Performance and Accountability in the Post-Cold War World*, Earthscan, London, and Kumarian Press, West Hartford.

Smillie, I (1995) *The Alms Bazaar*, IT Publications, London.

Sogge, D (ed) (1996) *Compassion or Calculation? The Politics of Private Foreign Aid*, Pluto Press, London.

Structural Adjustment Forum (1996) 'Uniting grassroots experience with macro-policy research', *Structural Adjustment Forum*, Vol 6.

Tolfree, D (1995) *Roofs and Roots: The Care of Separated Children in the Third World*, Arena, Aldershot.

Uphoff, N (1992) *Learning from Gal Oya: Possibilities for Participatory Development and Post-Newtonian Social Science*, Cornell University Press, Ithaca, New York.

Uphoff, N (1995) 'Why NGOs are not a third sector: a sectoral analysis with some thoughts on evaluation and sustainability', in M Edwards and D Hulme (eds), *Beyond the Magic Bullet: NGO Performance and Accountability in the Post-Cold War World*, Earthscan, London, and Kumarian Press, West Hartford.

Wierdsma, A and Swieringha, J (1992) *Becoming a Learning Organization*, Addison-Wesley, London.

22

On the Road to Becoming a Learning Organization

James Taylor

The concept of the 'learning organization' was popularized by Peter Senge in his book entitled *The Fifth Discipline: The Art & Practice of The Learning Organization* (1990). Senge's book focuses on the need for companies to:

*   understand the threats they are constantly faced with;
*   recognize new opportunities; and
*   maintain a competitive edge.

This article will not critique or draw on Senge's conclusions but will simply make use of the concept of the learning organization to share some insights that we have gained from sharing in non-government organizations' (NGOs) and community-based organizations' (CBOs) attempts to become more effective and efficient.

What is a Learning Organization?

I would define the learning organization as: 'The organization which builds and improves its own practice consciously and continually devising and developing the means to draw learning from its own (and others') experience.'

Although a simple definition, it contains four critical elements that require some elaboration. First, a learning organization is not defined as an organization which learns, but as one which learns consciously. It introduces a level of *conscious* intent and commitment to the process of learning. The importance of this point is to note that all organizations, and all the people within them, are learning all the time. They are learning from a variety of sources and in a variety of ways. Very often the learning is taking place at an unconscious level and is therefore not being effectively captured and maximally used to change and improve future practice.

The concept of 'the learning organization' is potentially undermining if it is interpreted as implying that organizations and individuals have not been learning in the past, and therefore require 'imported' models and techniques in order to start the learning process. The concept is used most effectively as a reminder that the process of learning is inherent in everyone and in all organizations. The first challenge is not to start learning, but to become more conscious of how learning already takes place, in order to use and further develop this innate ability.

The second challenge is to understand why the learning that is taking place is not being used more effectively to improve practice.

The second condition to qualify as a learning organization in terms of the definition is to achieve *'improved practice'*. This simply means that the test for whether learning has, in fact, taken place lies in the extent to which the practice of the organization has actually improved. There are other forms or learning which are not measured in changed practice. In fact, much of what is valued in our society is the type of learning which need not necessarily have any impact on what we 'do' at all. Learning is very often measured in what we 'know' or what we can 'remember'. It is often displayed as the ability to access information and build it into convincing argument or debate. While knowledge, information and the ability to think critically and analytically can play an important role in the type of learning which results in changed action, knowing or understanding does not guarantee changed practice. In most organizations we have known and worked with (including our own) there are many examples of this block between 'knowing' and 'doing'. All too often we 'know' (at the rational or understanding level) what our major problems and challenges are – but are unable to implement the 'action' required to address them. The definition implies that we qualify as learning organizations only to the extent to which we are improving our practice, which is a step beyond having great insights and understanding.

The third aspect of the learning organization highlighted by the definition is the *ongoing nature of learning* that is required of the learning organization. In the learning organization the process not only becomes more conscious, but also continuous – continuous not in the sense of becoming a totally reflective, inward-looking, 'navel-gazing' type of organization, but in achieving an appropriate balance between reflection, learning and action. The learning organization recognizes that learning is not a 'one-off' activity where you find the ultimate answer and then forget about it and move on to other things. It is understood that learning is a cumulative process which needs to start where you are, and constantly progress at a pace dictated by a combination of your organizational needs and the needs of those who you serve. Learning builds on itself through improved action, which in turn opens new opportunities for understanding and further learning. Ideally, the process of learning is an ongoing upward spiral through which the implementation of improved practice, when measured against expected outcomes, continually provides opportunity for new learning.

Finally, the definition highlights *'experience' as a source of learning*. The learning organization will draw on a variety of sources for its learning, but places specific emphasis on developing the means and ability to exploit its own actions and experiences fully as a primary source of learning.

NGOs as 'Learning Organizations'

The concept of the learning organization has specific relevance to NGOs in the development sector, in part because they have so much in common with all organizations across all sectors, and in part because there are aspects of their need for learning that are unique.

What development NGOs have in common with all other organizations is that they utilize both human and material resources in order to meet some societal need. When the resources consumed can no longer be justified in relation to the needs that are being met, the future existence of the organization is called into question. The ability to achieve the fundamental balance between inputs and outputs at this level is dependent on the organization's ability to identify, understand and adapt its responses to changing needs. These responses must not only be effective in meeting the specific need but also be efficient in its use of the resources – otherwise the societal resources should be made available to others who can achieve more with them. Along with all other organizations, the NGO's ability to remain essentially viable over time depends on its ability to learn and adapt.

But in significant respects NGOs differ from other organizations in ways that make it all the more important for them to take their own ability to learn extremely seriously. Perhaps the primary difference lies in the fundamental role and purpose that the development sector expects itself to fulfil in society. The ultimate societal need that the development sector concerns itself with is the need for social cohesion and integration; it works against the forces that increasingly marginalize, exclude and impoverish more and more of its members. Despite their stated good intentions (and best efforts) to create and distribute wealth, the economic and state sectors have proven to be ineffectual in reversing these trends. The development sector is charged with the primary responsibility for learning about these destructive forces and seeking ways of reversing them.

The private and public sectors effectively control the vast majority of society's material and production resources and consequently its formal learning institutions. But despite this advantage they have not generated a body of theory or practice which has been effective in redressing the vast imbalances in society. The NGO development sector is therefore challenged to maximize its learning as a means of improving its impact. There are no blueprints to follow, there is no benefit of having 'simple bottom lines', there are no guaranteed recipes for success. The development sector has to use its very limited resources highly efficiently to generate truly creative and innovative learning which can address the societal problems that those much closer to the resources and power are incapable of addressing. Its own store of past experience, its often monumental failures and many and meaningful successes, must be recognized as its libraries of knowledge and materials for learning.

At a micro-level we perpetually encounter the frustrations of individuals and organizations searching for answers to their questions and needs from outside their own organizations, their own sectors and very often their own continents and realities. While not implying that knowledge and experience cannot be transferred over great distances and from different situations, we do know that organizations are all too often disappointed in their attempts to 'import' learning. There are now many specialist trainers, consultants and donor organizations identifying what NGOs need, and packaging responses to these needs. There are courses, models and packaged responses to an increasing, array of NGO needs: from planning tools and methodologies to management courses, from computer-based monitoring systems to fieldwork intervention methodologies – but they are often not being experienced as a great help. They are, in fact, often being experienced as undermining and distracting when 'pushed' by those in positions of power over resources. Organizations are starting to recognize that the most effective training is that over which they have substantial control or influence, and which is directly related to their own learning processes and needs. A learning organization is one which accepts responsibility for its own learning and does not abdicate it to others.

Another significant difference between NGOs and organizations in other sectors is the fact that they do not get their funds directly from those to whom they provide services. There is very often no meaningful relationship, or ability to exert influence, between the recipient of NGO services and the funder of the NGO. This separation of accountability has significant consequences. Among them is the fact that long periods of time can lapse between a service becoming irrelevant, inadequate or inefficient and the threat of funds being withdrawn. This can remove a critical pressure for learning and provides further motivation for keeping learning in NGOs conscious and intentional.

Where and How to Start

The point at which to start is to recognize that you are already a learning organization. Look at how and where learning takes place in your systems and procedures and become more conscious of it. For a start, any time that planning takes place, an opportunity is created for learning. When any form of monitoring or evaluation is added, the chance that learning will take place is vastly improved. Planning is essentially a process of looking towards some point in the future and imagining, or dreaming, of an ideal situation, then identifying the steps that need to be taken to get from the present (which is known) to the unknown future. When progress and achievement are measured against a plan, learning should be the product. Increasingly, NGOs are planning, monitoring and evaluating with more rigour. In so doing they are creating opportunities for learning.

To give a simple example, a budget is no more than a plan – it looks to the future and imagines how much you will spend. After the spending has taken place it is important to compare actual expenditure to planned expenditure. No matter whether you have overspent, underspent or are exactly on target, questions immediately spring to mind. Questions like: 'What went wrong? What did I overlook in drawing up the budget?' or 'What went right this month? How did I manage to remain within budget?' The answers to these questions must be seen for what they are and consciously captured as important learnings – learnings that can contribute enormously to improving future budgeting. So out of the tension between planned and actual outcomes arise questions.

Finding the right questions and exploring them leads to the type of learning which forms the foundation of learning organizations. Using existing planning and evaluation opportunities in organizations is an obvious place to start. In fact, any situation where work is being reviewed is an opportunity for learning. Writing reports about field activity or organizational achievements (either for internal use or for other interested parties such as funders) should be viewed as opportunities for learning. Once you start looking there are limitless opportunities where learning from your own experience can improve your future practice dramatically. Imagine how those dreaded never-ending meetings could improve over time if the last item on every agenda was 'evaluation and learnings from meeting'.

Ideally, all activity or action should be part of a plan, reflected upon, learned from, and the learning built into improved future plans. The following learning cycle incorporates these steps:

Figure 22.1 *Action Learning Cycle*

Another obvious and vital opportunity for learning in organizations is with individuals, in relation to their own practice. Again, there are many organizational processes and procedures through which the work of individuals are monitored, reviewed or evaluated. In learning organizations all of these will be used consciously to learn from.

Enormous creative energy is released in organizations when these 'supervision' type sessions can be experienced as opportunities for learning as opposed to opportunities for policing (or 'snoopervision'). When performance appraisals are looked forward to as opportunities for affirmation and learning, the organization is well on its way to earning the title of 'learning organization'. Remember that organizations themselves cannot learn – it is ultimately the individuals within them who have to do the learning.

Why is it So Difficult?

If action learning is so common sense and all organizations and individuals learn anyway, why is it necessary to put so much emphasis on the learning organization? The fact of the matter is that very few of these ostensibly obvious and straightforward opportunities for learning are ever utilized. The same mistakes are made over and over again. We continue implementing programmes long after we actually (secretly) know that they are not working, or are having the opposite effect to what was intended. For years we attend meetings that frustrate us, are inefficient in the extreme and leave us feeling disempowered.

The primary reason for it not being as easy as it sounds is that the type of learning that goes beyond remembering and understanding to improve action, involves behavioural change. The moment actual changes in behaviour are expected as an outcome, all the forces that always work against change are unleashed. At the heart of it is the expectation that individuals will let go of their old, tried and tested ways of doing things. The habits and techniques that have become second nature and can be carried out without thinking, need to be abandoned for new ways of doing things that we are not good at or familiar with. Even when rationally we 'know' that there are alternative ways of doing things that are far superior to those being used at present, the knowledge is often insufficient to get us to let go of our old ways.

In addition to the personal difficulty in taking new learnings on board, there are organizational dynamics that also mitigate against learning. Two of the most obvious are both found at the level of organizational culture. As part of their unconscious identity, organizations differ in the balance they display between planning, acting (or implementing) and reflecting. Some organizations seem frenetically driven to do, do, do. They view any reflection as indulgent and inefficient. Other organizations seem to be trapped in deep soul-searching, navel-gazing reflection which seldom delivers sufficient clarity on which practical, implementable action plans can be built. Each learning organization needs to find the balance between action and reflection which is right for them and produces learning which continually improves their practice.

The other organizational dynamic which seriously limits learning is the tendency to undermine and threaten rather than provide challenging, supportive and trusting environments in which individuals can risk and learn. All too often organizations, despite their best intentions, end up as fairly threatening places in which to work. They reflect a broader culture in which getting things wrong is directly related to failure. A culture in which it is better to avoid and evade things that are not going too well for as long as you can, as there is the danger that they will reflect badly on your performance. To learn one needs to have a safe space in which you are challenged to deliver to the maximum of your potential, can risk making mistakes, be supported in drawing learning from both successes and failures, and in which you are joined in celebrating achievements. Remember that learning is a cumulative process. There is no need to start with the most difficult and challenging aspect of organizational life. The challenge is to start simply by becoming conscious of what you are already doing and enter the ongoing cycle. You are already learning, but you could be benefiting much more from each experience by learning more consciously.

References

Senge, P (1990) *The Fifth Discipline: The Art and Practice of the Learning Organization*, Doubleday, New York.

Taylor, J, Marais, D and Kaplan, A (1997) *Action Learning for Development – Use Your Experience to Improve your Effectiveness*, Cape Town, Juta Press.

23

An NGDO Strategy: Learning for Leverage

Alan Fowler

At first, non-governmental development organization (NGDO) competence was built up from local action – from doing things with and for people who are poor and marginalized. Realizing the limitations of this effort, the past ten years or so have seen local action complemented by NGDO attempts to scale up their impact by getting bigger and doing more – through diffusion of experience and by gaining influence on macro-policy.[1] NGDOs need to prioritize this last strategy because, as global poverty and aid trends show, they will never have anywhere near the resources required to address the scale of the problem. They need to get to the heart of causes. Aside from local limitations in physical resources and adverse natural conditions, these causes are due to human choices leading to exploitation at all social and geo-political levels, usually accompanied by a denial of basic rights.

NGDOs need to push forward on leverage so that their primary goal eventually becomes one of influencing the larger forces which cause deprivation, using local development action and service delivery as their tools. In other words, the immediate shift needed in NGDO thinking is to learn in order to apply leverage on others – the shift in Figure 23.1. Today, NGDO activity is concentrated towards the left of the figure. Moreover, as social budgets are cut, funding to fill in the gaps left by governments is creating pressure to move even further left. However, strategically, from the perspectives of enhanced effectiveness, value for money and greater scale of impact, this is the wrong direction in which to go. The NGDO strategic challenge is to use service delivery and other development activities as sources of experimentation, innovation, demonstration and learning for leverage. The comprehensive studies led by John Farrington (1993) show, for example, how this is being done in extending agricultural innovation.[2] As Figure 23.1 suggests, it is unrealistic to expect all NGDOs to work purely on the basis of learning for leverage. Nevertheless, while many NGDOs still concentrate their efforts on direct development action to solve problems, satisfy needs and build capacities – singly or in alliance with others – they must pay more attention to exerting leverage than is currently the case. This section looks at how to introduce such an emphasis in terms of methods and tactics.

Learning for Leverage in Practice

Moving towards a learning-for-leverage strategy raises a number of questions, such as who should be learning, about what, to apply leverage to whom, in what way?[3] Table 23.1 represents this information.

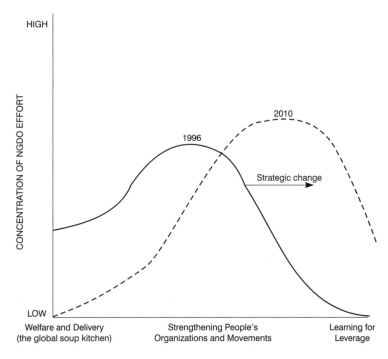

Figure 23.1 *Shift in NGDO strategies and roles*

There is no reason why an NGDO should bring in-house all the expertise it needs to learn in these areas. Collaboration with sensitive academics, institutes for applied social studies and other NGDOs with suitable expertise can all be tried. Increasingly, some types of leverage will require a strong mix of NGDO operational learning and grassroots testimony, combined with sound macro-analysis which professional researchers can provide. In forging the necessary productive relationships, cultural differences between practitioners and researchers will be a crucial obstacle to overcome.[4] Irrespective of who does what, the items listed in Table 23.1 can be grouped into eight areas:

- Functional, participatory, learning about operations in the field – what works for who, what does not and why.
- Intervention/project-based learning about why negotiations do or do not happen and how development approaches can be improved.
- Organization-oriented learning about how the whole NGDO functions and how it can be made more effective.
- Civic learning about how NGDO activities work their way into, and influence, the ability of civil society to interact with government and market.
- Policy-linked learning which looks for patterns in experience and generic features which shape the overall development process and the aid system.
- Advocacy-linked learning which searches for examples and 'peoples stories' and can underpin pressure for change.

Table 23.1 *Learning within NGDOs*

Who should be learning?	*What should they be learning about?*
Field staff	<ul><li>participation in practice;</li><li>effective empowerment;</li><li>local level collaboration with government and other NGDOs;</li><li>gender dimensions of local development.</li></ul>
Technical specialists	<ul><li>best practice in their area of expertise;</li><li>ways of integrating with other disciplines;</li><li>how to improve cost-effectiveness;</li><li>how existing internal and external policies affect performance.</li></ul>
Operational managers	<ul><li>what factors make interventions/ projects work well or badly – for example, funding conditions;</li><li>how to be more cost-effective;</li><li>how to coordinate internally and externally.</li></ul>
Fund-raisers/development educationalists	<ul><li>principles and insights to be used in negotiation with professional donors;</li><li>new messages to get across to private contributors;</li><li>examples of impact and what made things work or fail.</li></ul>
Leaders	<ul><li>how policy choices and strategies work out in practice;</li><li>how to make external relationships more effective;</li><li>how best to exert influence;</li><li>what environmental factors have had unforeseen effects and which must be taken into account;</li><li>the quality and costs of donors.</li></ul>
Governors	<ul><li>the degree of stakeholder satisfaction;</li><li>consistency between mission, strategy and impact;</li><li>improving social standing and credibility of the organization.</li></ul>

- Scientific learning about the relation between trends, actions and context which can contribute to renewal of vision, mission and strategies as well as the propagation of new ideas or understandings about development.
- Learning about learning by critically reviewing the internal processes being used when compared with their leverage effects.

Leveraging Who with What?

Assuming that an NGDO has got its learning act together, the next question is what sort of leverage should be applied to whom? Direct leverage for an NGDO typically involves engaging with more powerful actors to change how they behave. Indirect leverage involves informing and supporting others, such as people's organizations and social movements. Here, we focus on direct leverage.

At its most basic, direct leverage involves finding the sensitive spot in another organization and applying the right sort of pressure – in other words, the most appropriate type of input that will cause change. At this stage only broad generalizations can be made about the probable best fit between the target of leverage and the best instrument to apply. There are at least six instruments NGDOs can apply when trying to influence others: demonstration; public-policy advocacy; political lobbying; monitoring of compliance with public policies and laws; propagating new ideas and findings from studies; and research and public education. Table 23.2 sets out the probable fit between types of leverage and development actors.

Table 23.2 *Probable Fit Between Who to Lever with What*

Who to lever *Instruments for leverage*	*Other NGDOs*	*Aid agencies*	*Govern-ment[5]*	*NGDO supporters*	*General public*	*Business*
Demonstration of practical development alternatives	High	High	Medium	High	Medium	Medium
Policy advocacy based on field testimony and validated 'stories':						
• alternatives to existing policies	Medium	High	High	High	Medium	Medium
• lessons on better implementation	Medium	High	High	Low	Low	Low
Lobbying in political arenas, events and via constituencies	Low	High	High	High	Medium	Medium
Monitoring reports on legal and policy compliance and impact	Low	Medium	High	Low	Low	High
Findings of applied research with new insights, ideas, frameworks or policy options	High	High	Medium	Low	Low	Medium
Development education	Low	Medium	Low	High	Medium	?

Demonstration is most likely to impact those doing similar activities and supporters who gain greater confidence in the NGDO's competence. However, unless the approach adopted by the NGDO corresponds with the organizational structure of government – for example, by focusing on an administrative area as the CONVERGENCE network is doing in the Philippines, it may be more difficult to convince those responsible of the merits of the NGDO alternative. Increasingly, NGDOs will need to exert leverage on local as well as national governments and will have to tailor their way of working accordingly. If the setting is right, demonstrations can also influence business – for example, energy-saving devices have developed into commercially viable products and industries.

Both policy advocacy and lobbying can be aimed directly at governments and politicians and can be pursued indirectly through constituencies and mobilization of the wider public. Only when the issue has strong resonance is the general public likely to act in support of an NGDO. Consequently, greatest leverage is most likely through direct interaction with governments and aid agencies.[6] Policy which affects businesses often results in galvanizing the opposition, as is the case of rain forest preservation in Brazil, promotion of generic rather than brand mark drugs and advancing the merits of small-scale rather than giant dams.

Monitoring and reporting on the extent to which a public body fulfils the intentions of its policy commitment or applies the law as it should, can be very effective depending on the political context, in relation to modifying government behaviour, especially when there are opportunities to publicize details in international fora. However, this may be a high risk approach where the regime in power is autocratic or worse. Impact on business can also be significant when, for example, adherence to environmental or safety standards is in question.

For the reasons detailed above, development education has not been very successful in gaining leverage through broad public action. New strategies are needed which will lead to less ambivalent, positive public judgement on international cooperation. To sum up, gaining leverage means choosing the right sort of learning to influence the most significant actor(s) with the most effective instruments. This strategy is illustrated in Figure 23.2 and is followed by a look at important tactics.

From Barricades to Martial Arts: Complementing a Leverage Strategy with Appropriate Tactics

To be effective, new strategies must be supported by appropriate tactics. In the case of learning for leverage, the key tactical change is to move away from the notion of manning the barricades against political imperialism and market exploitation, be it local or international. Instead, what is needed are tactics which draw on the principles of martial arts – such as judo and jujitsu – using the momentum and energy of the opponent to knock them off-balance and throw them in the direction wanted. The parallel in international aid is to identify and exploit contradictions and weaknesses in the aid and economic system, its agents, and in the political system with its power holders.

Martial arts is a more subtle approach, demanding greater insight into how systems operate. For example, capital accumulation by poor people can be used as a bargaining chip in policy negotiations, while parallel markets and barter trade

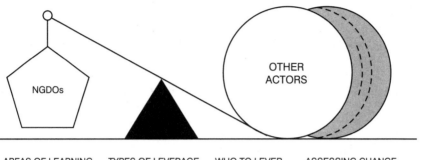

AREAS OF LEARNING	TYPES OF LEVERAGE	WHO TO LEVER	ASSESSING CHANGE
• Functional	• Demonstration	• NGDOs	• Aid policy and practice
• Project	• Policy advocacy	• Aid agencies	• Public policy and legal reform
• Organization	• Political lobbying	• Government	• Corporate and market reform
• Civic	• Monitoring	• Business	• Better governance
• Policy	• New ideas	• Politicians	• More civic strength
• Advocacy	• Development education	• Supporters	
• Scientific		• General public	
• Learning			

Figure 23.2 *Learning for Leverage*

can alter how local markets function. The fair trade movement has shown that, when presented with alternative choices, people are prepared to pay more, threatening the market share of commercial competitors. Barter economies are another example and these are springing up in localities within London and internationally. Exploiting market imperatives may call for temporary tactical alliances with strange bedfellows. For example, Greenpeace has found that its campaigns for stricter pollution controls are being actively supported by businesses which aim to clean up the environment. Combining their efforts strengthens pressure and leverage on governments who, whatever other functions they give up, will retain a monopoly role in enforcing public policy.

In politics, one martial arts tactic is to make use of the 'reverse hold' which clients have on patrons who have to deliver in order to hold on to their position. For example, by playing one patron off against another, clients can gain leverage on political decisions and public resource flows, which is how 'pork barrel' constituency-based politics works anyway. The general point is that while there is a time and place for confrontation with power holders, this cannot be the premise. Indeed, a long-term aim for NGDOs and other civic organizations is to reach a position where governments and businesses acknowledge and respect citizen power as the complementary 'third force'.

The tactics and strategies described will probably see NGDOs through the next 15 years or so.

Notes

1   Edwards and Hulme, 1992, pp15.
2   Farrington, et al, 1993.
3   This section draws on work done by Mike Edwards, 1996b.

4   In June 1994, the Development Studies Association of UK and Ireland held a workshop to look at improving the interface between development practitioners and academics (DSA, 1994).
5   This column assumes that the regime in power has some popular legitimacy, is interested in development and not just staying in control by any means.
6   Philippine NGDOs, for example, came together to agree on issues in the field of land and housing, leading to a concentration of effort on reforming the government's housing programme and specific laws regulating access and title to land (PHILSSA, 1995).

References

DSA (1994) 'The academic–practitioner interface', report of a workshop held in Manchester on 30 June, Development Studies Association, London.

Edwards, M (1996) 'Becoming a learning organization, or the search for the Holy Grail?', paper presented at the Aga Khan Foundation Round Table on Systematic Learning: Promoting Support for Canadian Development Cooperation, Ottawa.

Edwards, M and Hulme, D (eds) (1992) *Making a Difference: NGOs and Development in a Changing World*, Earthscan, London.

Farrington, J and Bebbington, A (1993) *Reluctant Partners? Non-Governmental Organizations, the State and Agricultural Development*, Routledge, London.

Fierlbeck, K (1997) 'Civil Society', in S Rai and W Grant (eds) *Globalizing Democracy: Power, Legitimacy, and the Interpretation of Democratic Ideas*, Manchester University Press.

Fowler, A (1982) 'Temperatures in development funding: the hot money model', *Development: Seeds of Change*, Vol 2, pp81–82, Society of International Development, Rome.

Fowler, A (1992) 'Decentralization for international NGOs', *Development in Practice*, Vol 2, No 2, pp121–124, Oxfam, Oxford.

Galtung, J (1975) 'The centre–periphery model in development', *Development*, Society for International Development, Rome.

Huntington, S (1993) 'The clash of cultures', *Foreign Affairs*, Vol 72, No 3.

Kennedy, P (1993) *Preparing for the Twenty-First Century*, Harper Collins, New York.

Korten, D (1995) *When Corporations Rule the World*, Earthscan, London.

Lehmann, D (1986) *Dependencia: An Ideological History*, Discussion Paper, No 219, Institute of Development Studies, University of Sussex, Brighton.

Lessem, R (1989) *Global Management Principles*, Prentice Hall, London.

Lipshutz, R (1992) 'Reconstructing world politics: the emergence of global civil society', *Millennium*, Vol 21, pp39–420.

Mosley, P and Hudson, J (1995) *Aid Effectiveness: A Study of the Effectiveness of Overseas Aid in the Main Countries Receiving ODA Assistance*, Overseas Development Administration, London.

Okada, T (1994) *The Global Information Infrastructure and the Work of Private Voluntary Organizations*, Food for the Hungry, Washington, DC.

PHILSSA (1995) *What Should We Lobby For? The Laws, Programs and Policies People's Groups and NGOs Should Work for the Field of Land and Housing*, Partnership of Philippine Support Service Agencies and Urban Poor Associates, Manila.

Ronfeldt, D and Thorup, C (1993) *North America in the Era of Citizen Networks: State, Society and Security*, Rand Corporation, Santa Monica, California.

Smillie, I (1995) *The Alms Bazaar: Altruism Under Fire – Non-Profit Organizations and International Development IT*, Publications, London.
Sogge, D (ed) (1996) *Compassion and Calculation*, Pluto Press, London.
Thurow, L (1996) *The Future of Capitalism*, William Morrow, New York.

Part 8

Mobilizing Resources and Sustaining the Organization

24

Defining Sustainability

Lisa Cannon

Types of Sustainability

One literature review on sustainability (Jordan, 1996, D2–D4) says that definitions of sustainability can be categorized into three different types: benefit, organizational and financial.

Benefit sustainability

This refers to a continuation of the benefits that result from an activity, with or without the programmes or organizations that stimulated that benefit in the first place. The source of those benefits may change (that is, a health non-governmental organization (NGO) may close, but the services it provided are offered by a government clinic in the same area), but the benefit is still available because the demand for it is strong (Jordan, 1996, citing Van Sant).

Organizational sustainability

Organizational or institutional sustainability places importance on 'building sustainable organizations to achieve sustainable development benefits' (Jordan, 1996, citing Kean 1987).

Financial sustainability

This is 'a component of organizational sustainability, [although] the two are often confused' (Jordan, 1996, D2–D6). Most definitions of financial sustainability have to do with an organization's ability to raise resources from a variety of sources (local, national and international, private and public). Also, that this mix of resources should include increasing amounts of local funding and earned income, to move the organization away from dependency on foreign donors.

A fourth type is community sustainability. Many NGOs aim to contribute (either directly or indirectly) to the building of sustainable communities. This means that communities will not become dependent on NGOs in the long term for the provision of services, but will be empowered to:

* create community-based organizations (CBOs) to provide services;

- effectively lobby government to provide services;
- create services within the private sector.

It is necessary to understand the various ways of defining sustainability because different stakeholders may be using different definitions depending on their perspective and priorities. For example, some donors are concerned mainly about the sustainability of benefits because this is largely how their own success as donors will be measured. They will see institutional sustainability of the organizations they support as a means to deliver sustainable benefits. If and when an NGO or CBO is no longer making a significant contribution to providing and sustaining benefits, donors may lose interest. Other donors may place more emphasis on NGO organizational sustainability, not only for its contribution to creating sustainable benefits, but also for its broader value in building civil society. Community members could have a different perspective. They may be committed to helping to sustain the NGO as long as it contributes towards the sustainability of their community by delivering sustainable benefits. When these benefits can no longer be seen, the community is likely to lose interest in sustaining the NGO.

NGOs often start out with a narrow understanding of sustainability as being just about money. However, they usually end up realizing that getting the money side of things right has implications for many other aspects of the organization, including the services it provides and how it interacts with communities. Even if an organization is financially sustainable, it will not survive unless other fundamental sustainability issues are sorted out.

Ideally, each NGO needs to develop its own definition of sustainability which takes into account the various aspects of sustainability, the links between these, and the organization's own context, focus and circumstances. The goal should be to come up with a definition that is broad and flexible enough to take into account the many different factors which affect sustainability, yet focused enough to provide a sense of common direction and purpose.

Key Questions to Think About in Drafting Your Organization's Own Definition of Sustainability

- What are we trying to sustain? Our organization? The benefits provided? Or are we trying to create conditions for building sustainable communities? If the answer is more than one of the above, how are these different elements linked?
- Who are we trying to sustain? Our staff? Communities? Who within communities? Are we taking gender, age, race and other differences into account?
- Who needs to be involved? What are the roles and responsibilities of each of the following in helping to sustain our organization? Staff? Board? Community? Other stakeholders?
- How long will we need to sustain our organization to accomplish our objectives?
- Are we focusing on financial sustainability? Or are we thinking about financial sustainability within the broader context of organizational sustainability?

What South African NGOs Say

In workshops conducted with South African NGOs, a number of key learnings emerged about what sustainability is:

- Sustainability is a process of moving from less to more, not necessarily equal to complete financial self-reliance.
- A mix of local, national and international funding is desirable for increased financial sustainability.
- The best strategic mix of number and types of funders will vary for each organization. While it is generally good to have more than just one or two funders, this is not always so. For example, one CBO had many funders who all gave small amounts but still required high inputs of time to maintain. In this case, having many funders made them less sustainable than if they had fewer funders who gave more money.
- Financial sustainability strategies must take into account the very different needs and realities of NGOs and CBOs and of rural versus urban organizations.

References

Fowler, Alan (1997) *Striking a Balance: A Guide to Enhancing the Effectiveness of Non-Governmental Organizations in International Development*, London, Earthscan.

Fox, L M and Bruce Shearer, S (eds) (1997) *Sustaining Civil Society: Strategies for Resource Mobilization*, Washington, DC, CIVICUS.

Jordan, P L (1996) *Strengthening the Public–Private Partner: An Assessment of USAID's Management of PVO and NGO Activities*, Appendix, Washington, DC, Centre for Development Information and Evaluation, USAID.

PACT 'Civil society toolbox': *www.pactworld.org*.

25

Options, Strategies and Trade-offs in Resource Mobilization

Alan Fowler

> ... many CSOs can benefit by stepping back from their day-to-day demands ... to take a strategic view of resource enhancement possibilities (Schearer, de Oliveira and Tandon, 1997).

Resources steer organizations.[1] How you raise the resources you need, and from which source, has a strong influence on what an organization is and what it can be. This chapter examines how resources impact on non-governmental development organizations (NGDOs). It provides a framework of 14 resource options and characteristics against which different options can be assessed for their likely effects.

The chapter starts with a cautionary note about equating money with sustainability. Finance is a necessary, but not sufficient, condition. The subsequent section takes a broad view of what is going on in terms of resource supply and demand that is likely to affect NGDO strategies. Then, using insights from theories of resource dependency, the chapter identifies the strategic choices available, together with the major trade-offs they imply.

Fixing the Financial Fixation

There is an old American school of thought arguing that the final measure of non-profit performance is continuity in raising money.[2] If the organization is not doing something right for someone, it will eventually wither away and die.[3] As the saying goes, you can fool some people all of the time and all of the people some of the time, but you can't fool all of the people all of the time. This holds particularly true for NGDOs that, in many countries, are the object of government mistrust and public suspicion. They face a tough test in ensuring resource continuity.

The underlying point is that success at resource mobilization is the standard by which NGDOs should be judged. This is the ultimate 'bottom line'. No resources means no organization. Consequently, a perceived threat to resource supply leads to a natural tendency to concentrate on finding new sources as if this is what solely matters. As described below, such a threatening perception exists, leading to a concerted effort to look for alternatives.

A concern to secure an NGDO's resource base – away from international aid – started in the late 1980s. The book *Towards Greater Financial Autonomy*, was probably a seminal start to what has followed.[4] The approach adopted by the writers was for NGDOs to become completely self-financing. This goal is no longer seen to be realistic or necessarily desirable. It has been displaced by a number of trends. For a start, this book was written before the 'discovery' of civil society in relation to development. This new concept provided both a framework for and impetus to investment in studies, training courses and specialist organizations, such as the International Fund Raising Group and the World Alliance for Citizen Participation (CIVICUS).[5] Another change has been the adoption of partnership by all and sundry in the official aid industry. Collaboration and cross-financing between sectors of government, business and civil society is now a common part of a financing agenda. Further, there is a growing assertiveness and increase in claim-making by NGDOs on government for subsidies to help provide public goods and services. If governments are prepared to provide tax and other concessions to attract businesses – a foregone income – why shouldn't NGDOs have a right to support for the added value of social provisions?

But the last point leads to one reason why resource mobilization is not the sole answer to organizational sustainability. The case to be made rests on demonstrated NGDO performance. In its turn, maintaining performance requires an organization that can learn and adapt to environmental changes and to stay its civic self in the process – the topic of this chapter. In short, organizational sustainability is more than just a question of money.[6] Sustainability pivots in the interplay between resources, impact and organizational regeneration. With this fact in mind, we turn to the issue of resource mobilization.

NGDOs and Resource Supply and Demand

All organizations are both shaped by and shape their environments. The degree to which both occur varies enormously. For example, transnational corporations resulting from recent mergers in the banking, oil, transport and communications industries can and do wield enormous economic clout, as well as producing far-reaching social effects in terms, for example, of employment.[7] Nevertheless, they have to continue to raise and retain capital by generating value for shareholders, and maintain a positive reputation with present and future consumers. Apparent arrogance about the merits of genetic engineering and the benefits of 'terminator genes' tarnished the Monsanto brand name, for example, causing loss of consumer trust, market valuation and share price. The damage to public image was so severe that the name Monsanto was dropped in a merger with another corporation.

Despite a perception that Northern governments are all-powerful, their behaviour is increasingly bounded by the demands of globalization, particularly the free movement of capital and elimination of trade barriers. Unless they make conditions for domestic and inward investment attractive, capital will go elsewhere. In addition, in an increasingly democratic world, the regimes elected to control the bureaucratic machines and public resources must satisfy enough citizens if they wish to remain in power. Hence, governments must behave in ways that recognize international competition for resource and produce policies and outputs that ensure public acceptance of domestic taxation.

The contribution of non-profit organizations to a country's economy may be more than people realize.[8] Nevertheless, they remain modest economic actors overall. However, through public pressure and interest groups, size is not necessarily the determinant of impact. Non-profits can have significant effects in terms of politics and policy if their agendas resonate with, and are sufficiently sustained by, civil society. The impact of civic institutions depends on public trust and support, even if this is expressed through public finance.

These generalizations indicate that no matter the type, or how big or how small, organizations are continually challenged to adjust and optimize their exchanges with the world outside their boundaries. The current flurry of studies, proposals and initiatives aimed at improving the sustainability of NGDO resources, especially money, can be seen as an accelerated adjustment to both perceived and real changes to their environment. The major contextual changes influencing NGDOs can be looked at in terms of alterations in supply and demand.

Supply-side dynamics

On the supply side, the rapid growth of Southern and Eastern NGDOs has been fed by and resulted in a heavy dependence on foreign aid.[9] Aid resources reach them both directly from official donors and Northern NGDOs and indirectly via loans and grants to their governments.[10] There is an overall trend of official aid to finance Southern NGDOs directly in-country and to bring them into projects and programmes to be implemented by governments. Southern NGDO experience of these modalities is mixed, summed up in the question: are we partners or contractors?[11] This question is a strategic issue for NGDOs. The fact that it matters so much relates to the substantial degree that NGDOs rely on official aid.

The past decade has seen a decline by 21 per cent in the real levels of finance allocated to overseas development assistance. After steady reduction in real terms, a recent increase in official aid, the first since 1994, added US$3.2 billion to the 1997 level of $48.3 billion. This amounts to a growth of 8.9 per cent. At 0.23 per cent of donor gross national product (GNP), this level still falls far short of the agreed target of 0.7 per cent.[12] However, even these improving figures should be read with caution. Detailed study suggests that official figures suffer from conscious, elevating distortions:

> Recently, aid flows have tended increasingly to benefit activities that do not fit the Organization for Economic Co-operation's (OECD) strict definition of aid. Changes in OECD conditionality and in donor ideology after the Cold War also appear to weight the scale against recipient countries.
>
> Official data from the OECD support the view that there was no resource shift to the East and that official aid was additional. Closer examination, however, suggests that changes in reporting and recording have artificially boosted ODA figures, thus hiding both indications of a geographical shift and a decline in ODA in the strict sense of a proportion of Gross National Domestic Product. Further findings of the study suggest that:
>
> • Changes in the OECD's interpretation of ODA have increased officially declared aid in the 1990s.

- The inclusion of expenditures directed at 'solving global common problems' – not development aid according to OECD definitions – has boosted.
- A new ideology of donors and new forms of conditionality could be used to justify giving less aid.
- New conditionalities have shifted the balance against recipient countries. State-led development appears at times to have been substituted by state-subsidised private sector activity, often favouring investors from donor countries.[13]

In sum, aid as originally understood is probably still decreasing, while policy conditions are changing the parameters by which it can be accessed and by whom.

For NGDOs, the effect of this supply-side trend has been very mixed. On the one hand, donor policies that develop civil society and concentrate on poverty are opening NGDO access to official funds, some previously assigned to government.[14] Consequently, the total finance available to NGDOs has increased from about US$6 billion at the beginning of the decade to about $13 billion today. Private funding has remained more or less static while other, previously very limited sources – such as for-profit activity or business support – are increasing minimally. Consequently, the proportion of official, tax-derived, funds in the NGDO total has increased from about 20 to about 50 per cent.[15] In other words, NGDOs have become more tied to official aid and hence more exposed to changes in its policies and priorities.

However, a growth in official aid to and through NGDOs is very unevenly distributed geographically and between NGDO types[16] Latin American NGDOs continue to experience a rapid drop in the foreign aid available to them. A similar reduction is being felt in the East Asian 'tiger economies'.[17] At the same time, poverty focus and political considerations are starting to concentrate official assistance. A poverty focus is moving foreign aid towards countries in South Asia and sub-Saharan Africa with a high number or high proportion of people who are poor. Politics directs aid to countries, either emerging from civil war, as for example in Cambodia, or a Communist history, such as Vietnam and Laos, that would benefit from private enterprise, voluntary association, civic growth and finance for social compensation programmes during a period of transition.[18]

The bureaucratic threshold for gaining access to official aid is high. It requires 'spare' resources for pre-investments in participatory investigation and writing proposals. It also requires a high degree of 'development literacy' and professional competence. For many Southern NGDOs both of these commodities are in short supply, and this therefore benefits their Northern counterparts. In addition, there is still a tendency for foreign donors to prefer, or in the case of Canada require, a domestic NGDO in funding to Southern NGDOs. Therefore, again, the South is relatively disadvantaged in terms of access.[19]

An additional feature feeding the supply of resources to NGDOs is the global instability caused by climatic and man-made disasters. What this means for the demand side is explained below. On the supply-side it means a growing proportion of aid allocated to humanitarian action – currently amounting to some 7 per cent of the total in 1997, up from 2.6 per cent in 1990.[20] Again, Northern NGDOs tend to have more capacity to respond and deliver than their Southern counterparts, which is one reason why the United Nations High Commission for Refugees (UNHCR) is intent on local capacity-building in the South.[21]

NGDO access to domestic funds is dependent on the political economy of a country, its historical and cultural circumstances and legal conditions. Together, they create an environment that determines the extent to which NGDO resources can be mobilized locally and with what types of strategies and degrees of difficulty. Where there is a tradition of NGDO-type intermediary organizations, government support, civic awareness and propensity to give are likely to be already established. However, at risk of gross generalization, the purpose of such support is likely to be the provision of institutional welfare rather than development as currently understood.[22]

Conversely, there are countries where informal relations and reciprocal networks – the 'economy of affection' common to sub-Saharan Africa[23] – are the foundation for social support. The notion of funding an intermediary runs counter to the needs of sustaining social capital and a system of mutual obligation. An emerging and enlightened middle class may be prepared to finance NGDOs, but mass support is less probable. And even middle-class support is more likely to be premised on social welfare rather than activism.

Where NGDOs have been active in establishing a new, democratic political order, as in much of Latin America and in South Africa, relations with the new regimes could be expected to result in policies that open government funding to NGDOs. The question arising is: on what terms does this occur? Can and will such support be accessible in ways that respect the autonomy that was an essential feature of the NGDO contribution to political reform? Alternatively, will the new regime expect NGDOs to continue as 'brothers and sisters in arms', by playing an uncritical supportive role?[24]

For countries now adopting a market economy while retaining single-party, Communist-inspired political systems, as in China, the whole notion of autonomy is questioned. In China, despite an unclear legal status and ambiguous regulations, that are not uncommon elsewhere,[25] both domestic and foreign NGDOs are required to have a 'partnering' governmental or party institution.[26] Government resources – salary maintenance and subsidies, for example – are consequently a common foundation of domestic NGDO operations and sustainability, albeit with some modest progress in fund-raising from Chinese citizens.[27]

Finally, recent developments in China reflect a common problem faced by many NGDOs when trying to gain access to domestic resources; this is the problem of political and social legitimacy.[28] Where NGDOs are perceived to be a product of external interventions, colonial history or extensions and instruments of foreign aid and its masters, the foundation for domestic support is inevitably weak. In countries newly independent from the Soviet Union and in Russia itself, a new breed of non-profit organization is already perceived as a cover for organized crime or simply to provide employment generation for those establishing them.[29] The basic ethics of voluntarism and trust in philanthropic intentions are insufficiently present or, if present, are more likely to be expressed through long-standing, informal and intimate relationships – not through support to intermediary NGDOs.

From these broad generalizations, it is apparent that the present supply-side picture is both positive and negative for NGDOs. Crudely put, an NGDO's ability to capitalize on supply-side shifts depends on where it is on the globe and if it is

Northern or Southern with already good capacity for development and/or emergency work.

The demand-side

The demand-side for NGDO development work is dominated by policy shifts associated with aid conditions and particular aspects of globalization. On the policy front there is consistent pressure for governments to do less and to do better at what they should do well. Typical tasks are sound economic management; creation and maintenance of an enabling environment for business and citizen initiatives; a fair and just application of the law; protection of human rights; provision of social safety nets as a last resort; and ensuring physical security for the population. Correspondingly, people should carry a bigger responsibility for their own welfare and costs of social service. They must learn to expect less from government services and hopefully, in much of sub-Saharan Africa, less state predation as well. In parallel, public ownership of productive enterprises should be reduced, if not eliminated, as should barriers to trade and capital flows under rules and agreements of the World Trade Organization (WTO).

Within this global policy framework, it is assumed that the social costs of adapting to the economic demands of globalization – such as unemployment or impoverishment – will only be short-term. The eventual acceleration in national economic growth because of more efficient market operation and investment, together with lowering prices – as international comparative advantages of factor inputs 'kick in' – will produce benefits for everyone in the end. In sum, there are transition costs of globalizing adjustment that temporarily overlay and add to the social impact of structural reform in state society relations.

Aside from the realism of the assumptions underlying the growth model being employed,[30] the demand-side question for NGDOs is: who wins and who loses from the additive effects of adjusting and structural changes? A crude answer is those – the poor and marginalized – already least able to cope before and while these two transitions were underway. The nature and breadth of this category are situationally dependent. But the general scenario is one of growing disparities between an emerging group of a few super-rich, a growing but insecure middle class and a perpetual category of the poor, relying for survival on subsistence, mutual support and public subsidy.

But whoever are identified as most likely to lose in this process, the structural nature of the anticipated shift in state functions will inevitably create a public service demand on Southern NGDOs. The demand is akin to that already manifested in the majority of their domestic counterparts in the North. Domestic non-profit organizations, predominantly in the North, fulfil a 'Third Way' welfare substitution and social service role based on a social compact or contract financed by a mix of government subsidy, contracts and user fees for service[31] – the developmental dimension of NGDOs will be under pressure unless their response offers an adequate counterweight. This is an important dimension of the strategic choices that NGDOs face in selecting how they want to mobilize domestic resources.

Combined, the forces sketched above are poverty inducing, and not just in the short term, for the capitalist free-market economic model has no intrinsic redistribution method or intention. Equity remains in the realm of politics and public choice. Consequently, the demand for policy advocacy should remain high on an NGDO agenda. However, as previously alluded to, will this be possible if there is greater dependency on public funds? Compromise in policy assertiveness is therefore another strategic issue and choice to be made in selecting a resource mobilization path.[32]

Southern governments have mixed views about the real agenda of aid conditions and its lessening of their role – not to mention a reduction in the potential for patronage on which much of their politics is based.[33] Nothing as clear-cut as a state–NGDO compact yet exists in most Southern countries where overt or covert mistrust on both sides is attended by increasing exploratory engagement.[34] Nevertheless, for heavily aid-dependent countries it is reasonable to anticipate that aid conditions reflecting donor domestic policies will push their way down the aid chain into the state-society arena, creating expectations of, and funds for, an NGDO service role. Spill-over of funders' domestic policies have usually had this effect in the past. For example, the Thatcher–Reagan era of supposed state retrenchment corresponded with the introduction of the cruder forms of structural adjustment conditions on recipients of aid. Subsequent refinements to adjustment and the drive for partnership with everyone for development corresponds to the Clinton–Major era, now reinforced by 'Third Way' harmony of the Clinton–Blair–Schröder and guarded Jospin quartet in their ode to 'social-liberalism'.[35]

However, governments are also under pressure to be more efficient so that taxes can be kept low, competitive and attractive for international business and knowledgeable manpower. This requirement can increase an interest in learning from NGDOs about how more can be done with less. Hence innovation and experimentation may be an NGDO niche role that is better appreciated and called upon, but probably in domains selected by government and not by NGDOs themselves, unless they make it happen. Southern NGDOs and their governments can also be allies – for example, in setting out positions in terms of the rules and practices of the WTO. Through their international contacts, NGDOs are sometimes better placed to gather information and help to develop government capacity for negotiation, as happened prior to and during the WTO Seattle debacle. However, to expand this type of demand would require a change of the typical government perception that NGDOs are 'the opposition' and insufficiently professional or internationally connected enough to have anything valuable to offer.[36]

Another potential source of demand on NGDOs will not come from government, but will be directed against it. Greater and less inhibited flows of information across borders and a more educated public are forces for greater assertiveness towards state policies and actions. In other words, NGDOs can be at the forefront of increased popular activism for pro-poor structural reforms and trading conditions. One example is the month-long tour, in June 1999, of a caravan of Southern people's organizations through G8 industrialized countries as a symbolic protest highlighting the negative impact of the global trading system on their lives and livelihoods.

Alongside structural and transitional demands on NGDOs are the natural and man-made disasters that help them to gain a public profile and substantial resources that, on occasion, can cross-subsidize development work or at least secure a better cash flow. Hurricane Mitch devastated parts of Central America in 1999; a cyclone hit and killed 8000 people in Orissa in India in November, 1999; Turkey and Taiwan sustained major damage and loss of life through earthquakes in 1999. Conflicts in Kosovo, Africa's Great Lakes region, Sierra Leone, southern Sudan and atrocities in other locations, like East Timor, all conspire to maintain local and global instability and human tragedy. These instabilities and the humanitarian demands they cause – in 1997 some 14 million refugees and asylum seekers and 19 million internally displaced people – create opportunities for NGDO humanitarian action. Much of this support is provided by official sources and channelled through Northern NGDOs.[37] The question currently being asked is whether or not this work can move beyond UN–NGDO subcontracting to a more equitable arrangement of pre-agreed 'task-sharing'.[38]

Overall, there is every reason to expect a continuation in the escalation of demand for certain types of NGDO activity. The biggest source is state unburdening through substitution for government welfare and social services – health, education, water and sanitation, for example. It would be burying one's head in the sand to suggest that – faced with government cutbacks – this role is not what poor people would want NGDOs to play. Non-service roles, such as advocacy for reform, innovation and government reinforcement, are also possibilities, but are unlikely to be of a comparable size or as prevalent. For the foreseeable future, humanitarian demands will continue to arise.

Setting supply possibilities against the profile of demand in a given context – and making the right choices – is an important part of creating a resource mobilization strategy. Another element is examining and dealing with trade-offs in terms of the implications for the organization itself associated with different courses of action. The concept of resource dependency can, and without them knowing it, does, help NGDOs in making trade-offs.

Moving from Dependency – Criteria for Resource Mobilization

Within changes in supply and demand, NGDOs have to make decisions about where to invest their energies in terms of mobilizing local resources. From a sustainability perspective, one task is to reduce resource vulnerability. But an NGDO is vulnerable in another way as well. Strategic choices in terms of resources have a ramification beyond their reliability. Why? Because the choices made can also affect what the organization stands for, which equates to a second task of protecting its mission and identity. In more technical terms, the profile of resources employed codetermines organizational identity. Using ideas generated by theories of contingency and resource dependency, this section explores various aspects of this dual vulnerability as a foundation for understanding the trade-offs that NGDOs employ when choosing which resources to mobilize and how.[39]

Resource dependency

A contingent view pays central attention to the transactions and exchanges between an organization and its environment. On the input side, an organization is dependent on what the environment has to offer in terms of resources. On the output side, organizations can act to alter the environment in ways that increase, secure or stabilize the resources it requires. Typically, this is through providing goods and services that society wants and values, as well as pursuing interests in the political arena. NGDOs do both. For example, they draft proposals for funding and submit them to donors, while simultaneously seeking to change the conditions donors use to allocate their resources in order to make them more accessible. Their ability to do the latter depends on being seen to produce something of social value. In terms of organizational types, 'pure' non-profit organizations are particularly susceptible to change in the characteristics of their resources. This is because they do not control their generation as profits, like business; nor do they control their extraction as taxes from citizens, the resource base of government. Consequently, those providing resources to NGDOs can, and do, exert a significant element of control or power, even if this is not their intention, it is a common, almost inevitable effect, paralleling the problem of CBO dependency described in Chapter 2. The consequences of resource instability, therefore, fall more heavily on NGDOs than on those funding them. The relations between NGDOs and typical resource providers, donors and governments, are heavily unbalanced: funders typically exercise more control over NGDOs than NGDOs do over their funders.

As a result, NGDOs are particularly sensitive to the stability of resources they rely on. In unstable periods, as sketched above, they have to adjust their external relationship to try to restore continuity and stability. A vital issue is how to do this in ways that are not at the cost of mission and identity. The phenomenon of an NGDO's client group or activities altering because of changes in resource conditions has been called 'mission creep' or 'goal displacement'. One result is an inconsistency between mission and action on the ground. Another result is internal confusion as the gap between rhetoric and reality increases – not an uncommon feature of NGDO behaviour.

Sensitivity also depends on how critical the resource is for organizational functioning and outputs. Typically, because the project-mode of development funding is averse to paying general overheads, resources that cover an NGDO's core costs are usually the most critical. As we will see, this translates into a compelling desire to set up endowments that generate untied funds.

In appraising alternative resources, NGDOs face the issue of maintaining autonomy in their own decision-making. Being able to negotiate fair terms without compromising on freedom of internal decision-making is important, as is the ability to say 'no' when it is necessary. Such ability can be eroded to different degrees by different sources of resources. This raises the issue of proportionality. Excessive reliance on a single source of funding not controlled by the organization is a normal sign of high vulnerability, high sensitivity, high criticality and low autonomy. It is not necessarily indicative of low consistency if the mission of both parties is sufficiently similar, but this problem comes readily into play if the provider shifts policy or perspective.

Finally, an NGDO must assess the organizational implications of taking on a new type of financial resource. How much internal adjustment will need to be made?

What management and human resource demands will arise? How compatible will new resources be with existing processes, values and culture? Low compatibility brings significant organizational demands; high compatibility few if any.

The concepts used above help in understanding the factors involved in NGDOs' strategic choices for resource mobilization:

- *Vulnerability:* an NGDO's ability to suffer costs imposed by external events. Highly vulnerable NGOs are unable to cope, invulnerable NGDOs are unaffected.
- *Sensitivity:* the degree and speed at which changes in a resource impact on the NGDO. Low sensitivity means that external changes do not cause immediate severe disruption, high sensitivity means that they do.
- *Criticality:* the probability that an existing resource can be replaced by another for the same function. Highly critical resources – such as core support – cannot be replaced easily; resources with low criticality can.
- *Consistency:* an ability to alter a resource profile without compromising mission and identity. High consistency resources mean that an NGDO is less forced to compromise than it must do if it is to gain access to low consistency resources. Typically, swapping donors creates a consistency challenge as each has its own conditions and preferences.[40]
- *Autonomy:* the degree to which the resource affects the ability to say 'no' when it is needed. Turning away or not pursuing available resources – when the demand-side is essentially infinite – is not easy but it should always be possible. If it is not possible, NGDO decision-making is effectively enslaved to the dictates of others. It is not autonomous. Hence autonomy is reflected in an NGDO's freedom in decision-making about resources it wishes to access and the outputs and social value it will provide.
- *Compatibility:* the degree of similarity between new and existing resources that call for minor to major modification to the organization's processes, structure and functioning – for example, creating a new department or recruiting staff with different professional cultures, values and aspirations.

An NGDO with a resource profile characterized by low vulnerability, low sensitivity, low criticality, high consistency, substantial autonomy and high compatibility is likely to be more agile and adaptive than an NGDO with the opposite profile. Common sense would suggest that an NGDO that achieves the preferred profile is not only more insightful but also has its strategic house in order – it is capacitated. Achieving this condition has a lot to do with reputation, learning, leadership, a secure identity and self-awareness.

All the foregoing feeds into two features that dominate thinking behind the many efforts currently being put into NGDO resource mobilization. They can be summed up in two words: 'dependency' and 'diversification'. Given the high degree of NGDO reliance on foreign funds and the perceived unreliability of this source, the basic goal of resource mobilization is to reduce dependency on foreign aid by diversifying the resource base.[41] For example, studies in the US confirm that '... diversified revenue sources are more likely to be associated with a strong financial position than concentrated revenue sources'.[42] The question arising is how do NGDOs go about this task in relation to the six aspects of resource dependency summarized above?

Strategic Options, Trade-offs and Dilemmas

What strategic options do NGDOs have as they seek to reduce vulnerability and dependency? What trade-offs and dilemmas do they face in making the best choices?

Strategic options

The major options available to NGDOs in terms of diversifying and localizing their resource base are summarized in Figure 25.1. The first major strategic choice is between human and material resources and finance. Given that NGDO dependency is essentially monetary, the latter tends to dominate over the former. But the former option is most likely to avoid the dilemma of mission creep and introducing inconsistency. Mobilizing volunteer and community resources is also a strategy that keeps an NGDO closest to the real commitment of community-based organizations (CBOs) and, hence, to sustained impact.

Within the financial option, NGDOs face two immediate decision paths. One is whether to generate financial resources itself. This keeps the NGDO in greater control. The threat to autonomy is likely to be minimal. Own control also means that vulnerability to outsiders is not necessarily increased, that sensitivity can be decreased and that critical resources can be replaced because the NGDO decides where to put the surplus it produces.

An alternative option is to access a surplus created by others. This choice brings with it issues of reduced autonomy, heightened sensitivity and vulnerability, a threat to consistency, but the possibility of reducing high dependency on foreign aid. The

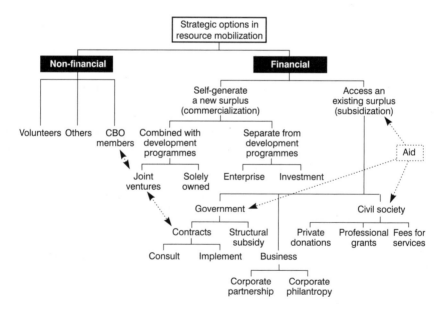

Figure 25.1 *NGDO Options in Resource Mobilization*

BOX 25.1 THE SOCIAL CAPITAL FIDUCIARY FUND OF ARGENTINA (FONCAP)

In July 1997 the executive branch of the Argentine government signed the decree creating FONCAP. The initiative was generated in the Argentine Secretariat of Social Development and its main purpose is to get community organizations to become the leading players in the creation of a structure to provide financial services to the huge quantity of small economic units. It is hoped that this would make it possible to build a consolidated and independent social sector. From this perspective, it is the intent of FONCAP that access to credit should improve the economic conditions of the most needy families and help to generate bonds of trust and links between social and public sector organizations and the national private sector and international cooperation sector. The fund is designed to last 30 years and has been started with US$40 million in capital from the national budget.

Source: Valderrama, M (1999) 'Latin American NGOs in an Age of Scarcity: When Quality Matters', paper presented at a conference on NGOs in a Global Future, 8–11 January, Birmingham

---

probability of such negative aspects actually occurring depends, in turn, on the source generating the financial surplus: government, business or civil society.

For NGDOs, the potential drawbacks of opting to gain access to a surplus produced by others must be set against the benefits of diversification. This is where proportionality comes into play. Simply shifting from a heavy dependency on foreign aid to a heavy dependency on domestic government revenues may make things worse, rather than better. The effect will depend on state–society relations and the willingness of government to negotiate rather than impose conditions. There is no straightforward answer. It is a question of judgement.

Figure 25.1 is a simplified version of a much more complex reality. All sorts of linkages and combinations are not shown. For example, it is quite possible that joint ventures with CBOs are made possible by the CBOs' own access to government funds as well as from their own resources. In turn, government finance to CBOs may be from its own resources, such as from the Social Capital Fiduciary Fund of Argentina (FONCAP) described in Box 25.1 or from aid grants or loans. World Bank social funds are a typical example of the latter.[43] In fact, in the period 1993–1997 some 40 per cent of World Bank funded projects made some provision for NGDO/CBO involvement. Within these projects, about 80 per cent of funds were designated for supporting CBOs.[44] In addition, NGDOs may raise capital to start up self-generating enterprises from voluntary and in-kind contributions. Nevertheless, the framework corresponds reasonably well with the division of options that NGDOs face in practice.

Moreover, these options are not a question of either/or. Sensible NGDOs look to all three major strategic possibilities as they seek to diversify and reduce aid dependency. For example, in its 25-year history, the Bangladesh Rural Advancement Committee (BRAC) has used all of them. The latest additions being the establishment

Table 25.1 *Probable Effects of Different Resource Options*

Resource factor likely impact	Non-financial option	Finance option Self-generating a surplus	Finance option Gaining access to an existing surplus
Vulnerability	Reduced	Reduced	Increased
Sensitivity	Reduced	Reduced	Increased
Criticality	Unchanged	Reduced	Unchanged
Consistency	Reinforced	Retained	Reduced
Autonomy	Unchanged	Reinforced	Reduced
Compatibility	High	Moderate	Source dependent

of a bank (transforming the credit-based rural development programme) and a fee-paying university. Few NGDOs become as complex as BRAC in terms of its strategic mix. But NGDOs should be able to explore all possibilities, while bearing in mind that the organizational and management difficulties they pose multiply as the mix expands.

In terms of overall strategic choice, Table 25.1 summarizes the likely effects on the six factors described in the previous section for each of the three major resource options discussed so far. It can be seen that the non-financial and self-financing options are more likely to alter beneficially an NGDO's resource profile as it moves away from aid dependency than the third alternative – gaining access to a financial surplus generated by someone else. Shifting from aid dependency to dependency on local sources other than your own generated internally is the less advantageous choice.

Entries in the third column are the least certain: the outcome of tapping a surplus generated by others is so highly dependent on the specific source. However, like donor agencies, whoever it is will have an agenda and interests that will need to be satisfied if agreement is to be reached. Some compromise will be inevitable. Hence, dependency on the stability and reliability of resources generated by others will at least remain, but is more likely to increase, particularly where the source is not 'developmental' in its nature, for example businesses.[45]

Resource trade-offs and NGDO positioning

Finally, we need to pay attention to two major organizational concerns. This is the effect that resource diversification can have on:

1 an NGDO's contribution to society; and
2 its ability to act in its own terms.

In short, what role does an NGDO play and produce that is of social value? In addition, how autonomous is the organization from governments that also have social responsibilities and agendas or corporations that want to be more citizen-like in their behaviour? These two factors critically affect an NGDO's position and identity in society and are shown as the axes of strategic choice in Figure 25.2.

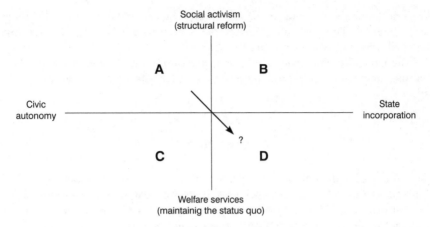

Figure 25.2 *Important Trade-offs in NGDO Strategic Positioning*

The nature of the resource base constructed by NGDOs determines both what they do and their distance from the state. In terms of contribution to society, their impact lies along a vertical axis with, at its base, welfare provision that responds to state and market failure without attempting to change the structure of each: their work essentially maintains the status quo. The other extreme is where NGDOs are solely concerned about reforming how state, market and society work in favour of the poor and marginalized. Their agenda is activism and structural change.

The horizontal axis signals NGDO distance from state or corporate influence or control over their internal affairs, particularly decision-making about what role to play in society.[46] In the case of China, domestic NGDOs are closely allied with state and party. At the other extreme are NGDOs not affiliated to the state in any way at all. Within whatever the law allows, they enjoy complete freedom of decision-making that may or may not correspond to government agendas and priorities. Foundations deriving income from market investments may enjoy this degree of autonomy. This horizontal axis is therefore a very rough guide to an NGDO's 'civicness'.

The combination of role and autonomy locates NGDOs somewhere in this graphic framework. If recent data on non-profit organizations in industrialized countries are anything to go by, most organizations appear to inhabit quadrants 'C' and 'D'. In terms of services, the ratio between welfare and recreation and advocacy is about 70:30. While in terms of revenues, the split between government finance, fees for service and private giving is in the order of 40:50:10.[47]

Not surprisingly, quadrant 'B' is relatively uninhabited. Public finance for 'autonomous' non-profits to pursue reform agendas 'against' those providing the finance is almost a contradiction in terms. The bulk of resources in this quadrant come from private giving, especially from philanthropic foundations.

Many NGDOs would consider themselves – or would like to be – somewhere in quadrant 'A'.[48] However, the summary of forces shaping supply and demand, suggests a pressure from NGDOs to move towards quadrant 'C'. In political terms, such a move would imply that NGDO legitimacy is altering from civic to public with direct accountability to citizens being replaced by accountability to and through public bodies.[49] The trade-offs NGDOs make in terms of changing their resource base will influence whether or not this happens.

The issue of staying true to 'civic' position and role underlies much of NGDO self-questioning and soul-searching as they consider what to do in a 'future beyond aid'.

Summary

Using a resource dependency perspective, this chapter covers strategic options, choices and trade-offs associated with resource mobilization towards sustainability. Generally speaking, the goal in changing the resource profile is to reduce dependency on foreign aid by diversifying towards domestic sources.

There are major shifts in resource supply and demand that shape the NGDO operating environment. The overall picture is of an uneven change in availability of aid resources for NGDOs that is often not being made good by domestic sources, especially from government. Hence, there is the fear that some NGDOs will not survive.

Environmental changes are to the disadvantage of some types of NGDOs and to the gain of others that are already better resourced and more capable. There is a squeeze on weaker, middle-sized NGDOs, and those that do not have a clear 'niche', to the benefit of larger, often Northern, organizations. Increasing humanitarian demands are reinforcing this differential impact of changes in resource levels and conditions for NGDO access.

Six concepts assist in understanding the factors NGDOs take into account when assessing options. They are:

- Vulnerability: an NGDO's ability to suffer costs imposed by external events affecting the resource.
- Sensitivity: the degree and speed at which changes in a resource will impact on the NGDO.
- Criticality: the probability that an existing resource can be replaced by another for the same function.
- Consistency: an ability to alter a resource profile without compromising mission and identity.
- Autonomy: the degree to which the resource affects free decision-making and ability to negotiate terms and say 'no' when necessary.
- Compatibility: the degree of similarity in organizational demands between new and existing resources.

NGDOs face a primary division in the types of resources they can mobilize. They can choose between non-financial and financial sources and, within the latter, between generating funds themselves or tapping into finance generated by others. A comparative table suggests that the first two options are most likely to bring positive change in the above six factors. The latter option is more prone to creating contrary effects and to introduce organizational stress. However, the extent to which this occurs depends on which sub-source is accessed.

An important trade-off for NGDOs is one which links the profile of resources to its position in society in terms of its role and 'civicness', or distance from government. The external environment is tending to push NGDOs to more welfare roles and closer proximity to government and business. Countering or accommodating this trend is an important feature of strategic decision-making.

Notes

1   For example, see Smillie and Helmich, 1993 and 1999.
2   This does not necessarily hold true for self-financing foundations whose endowments generate revenue irrespective of whether or not they bring any benefit to society.
3   Kanter, 1979.
4   Vincent and Campbell, 1989.
5   Following on from Vincent and Campbell are a number of important studies that are required reading for anyone interested in the resource dimension of sustainability. See Bennett and Gibbs, 1996; Norton, 1996; Fox and Schearer, 1997; Cannon, 1999; and Holloway, 1999.
6   Brown, 1998.
7   For a critical analysis of corporate power, see Korten, 1995.
8   Salamon and Anheier, 1999.
9   Informed observers suggest that international aid accounts for some 95 per cent of the funds employed by Southern NGDOs.
10 For a detailed analysis of paths for aid flows, see Fowler, 1997, pp135–148.
11 This question is also being posed by Northern NGDOs. See Smillie, Douxchamps, Sholes and Covey, 1996; INTRAC, 1998.
12 *Development Information Update*, no 1, Development Initiatives, Evercreech, July 1999.
13 Raffer, 1999, abstracted in <http:/www.ids.ac.uk/id21/static/9ckrl.html> 23 October.
14 For official aid and civil society, see van Rooy. 1998. For examples of poverty focus see DFID, 1997, a White Paper produced by the UK Department for International Development, London.
15 Firm figures on NGDO funding levels and distribution of sources are notoriously difficult to find. For attempts, see Fowler, 1992a, 1999; OECD, 1999.
16 For details of trends in aid allocations, see *Geographical Distribution of Financial Flows to Aid Recipients*, OECD, 1999 <http:www.oecd.org>
17 Valderrama, 1999; Aldaba, 1999.
18 For the situation of non-profit-making organizations in Vietnam, see Sidel, 1997. The Netherlands has just gone through a review designed to reduce aid concentration countries from about 60 to 20.
19 INTRAC, 1998.
20 Data supplied by Development Initiatives, derived from DAC data sheets. With thanks to Judith Randell.

21 UNHCR, 1994.
22 Public support to religious institutions and orders is typical, as are contributions to funds established by a royal family, as in Thailand. Development per se is seldom the intention.
23 Hyden, 1980, 1983.
24 This debate has been a significant feature of NGO–ANC relations pre- and post-apartheid.
25 Ge Yunsong, 1999. The issue of legislative frameworks is receiving significant attention. See, for example, ICNPL, 1996; CIVICUS; 1997.
26 Zhu Youhong, 1999; Young and Woo, 1999.
27 One example is the Chinese Youth Development Foundation (CYDF) – with roots in the Communist Youth League – that has successfully mobilized non-governmental resources from affluent Chinese in Hong Kong, to improve access to primary schools.
28 Gao Bingzhong, 1999.
29 To counter this public image, the Charities Aid Foundation (CAF) will be training journalists on the work of NGOs so that '... they may overcome their instinctive distrust of charities as covers for organised crime' *CAF Bulletin*, September 1999.
30 Bretton Woods Project, 1999.
31 Fowler, 1994; Kendall, 1999; Salamon et al, 1999.
32 Such a compromise has been characterized as 'creeping self-censorship': Edwards, 1993.
33 Kapur, 1997.
34 In some countries, the situation is said to be deteriorating, exemplified by more stringent and disempowering laws for non-profit-making organizations: van Tuijl, 1999.
35 Bourdieu, 1999.
36 There is also the tactical issue of overcoming government 'ego' and an historically conditioned view in many developing countries that government always knows best about everything all the time.
37 International Federation of Red Cross and Red Crescent Societies, 1998.
38 Weiss, 1998.
39 See Pfeffer and Salancik, 1978. For an application to NGDOs, see Hudock, 1995.
40 For a case study, see Holloway, 1997; Sobhan, 1997.
41 There are ways of establishing a diversification index to assess present conditions and compare future options; Chang and Tuckman, 1994.
42 Ibid, p273.
43 Schmidt and Marc, 1994.
44 Gibbs, Fumo and Kuby, 1999, pxii.
45 This does not mean that businesses do not have a developmental impact. They do and it is quite profound. The point is that the perspective of their support is not social development or equity as such.
46 A common proxy for autonomy is the proportion of tax money in an NGDO's budget. However, this is too simplistic because the degree of influence a state exerts through its funds depends on the nature of the political system. Unlike two-party majority rule, proportional representation seems to exert a temper-

ing influence on the propensity of states to interfere with the non-profit-making organizations they fund. The development foundations in Germany and the Netherlands enjoy substantial autonomy despite significant government funding that can amount to 95 per cent of their total. Transitions in political regime, unlike in Britain and the USA, do not lead to significant directionality being exerted by the incoming party. For example, in the case of Britain, the Labour government treats NGDOs as a particular type of development contractor, rather than civic entities with autonomous agendas. Reform to donor funding 'windows' for NGDOs – the Civil Society Challenge Fund and Participatory Partnership Agreements – are premised on applicants having a sufficiently similar agenda to the Department for International Development (DFID) itself.

47 Salamon, et al, 1999.
48 This self-perception is not as applicable as many would imagine. In terms of money volume, NGDOs are providers of social services, increasingly drawing on a subsidy provided by international aid.
49 Fowler, 1999, p5.

References

Aldaba, F (1999) 'The future of Philippine NGOs: no escape from the market in a world with declining aid', paper presented at a conference on NGOs in a Global Future, 8–11 January, Birmingham.

Bennett, J and Gibbs, S (1996) *NGO Funding Strategies: An Introduction for Southern and Eastern NGOs*, International NGO Training and Research Centre, Oxford.

Bourdieu, P (ed) (1999) *The Weight of the World: Social Suffering in Contemporary Society*, Pluto Press, London.

Bretton Woods Project (1999) *Questioning the IMF, World Bank Growth Model*, The Bretton Woods Project, London.

Brown, D R (1998) 'Evaluating institutional sustainability in development programmes: beyond the dollars and cents', *Journal of International Development*, Vol 10, No 1, pp55–70.

Cannon, L (1999) 'Defining sustainability', *OD Debate*, Vol 6, No 1, pp12–13, Glenwood, SA, February.

Chang, C and Tuckman, H (1994) 'Revenue diversification among non-profits', *Voluntas*, Vol 5, No 3, pp273–290.

CIVICUS (1997) *Legal Principles for Citizen Participation: Towards a Legal Framework for Civil Society Organizations*, CIVICUS, Washington, DC.

DFID (1997) *Eliminating World Poverty: A Challenge for the 21st Century*, White Paper on International Development, Department for International Development, London.

Edwards, M (1993) 'Does the doormat influence the boot? Critical thoughts on UK NGOs and international advocacy', *Development In Practice*, Vol 3, No 3, pp163–175, Oxfam, Oxford.

Fowler, A (1992) 'Distant obligations: speculations on NGO funding and the global market', *Review of African Political Economy*, Vol 55, pp9–29, Sheffield, November.

Fowler, A (1994) 'Capacity building and NGOs: a case of strengthening ladles for the global soup kitchen?', *Institutional Development*, Vol 1, No 1, pp18–24, PRIA, Delhi.

Fowler, A (1997) *Striking a Balance: A Guide to Enhancing the Effectiveness of Non-Governmental Organizations in International Development*, Earthscan, London.

Fowler, A (1999) 'NGDOs as a moment in history: beyond aid to civic entrepreneurship?' paper presented at a conference on NGOs in a Global Future, 8–11 January, Birmingham.

Fox, L and Schearer, B (eds) (1997) *Sustaining Civil Society: Strategies for Resource Mobilization*, CIVICUS, Washington, DC.

Gao Bingzhong (1999) 'The rise of associations and their legitimation problems', paper presented at an International Conference of the Development of Non-profit Organizations and the China Project Hope, Beijing, November.

Ge Yunsong (1999) 'On the establishment of social organizations under Chinese law', paper presented at an International Conference of the Development of Non-profit Organizations and the China Project Hope, Beijing, November.

Gibbs, C, Fumo, C and Kuby, T (1999) *Nongovernmental Organizations in Bank-Supported Projects: A Review*, Evaluation Department, World Bank, Washington, DC.

Holloway, R (1997) *Exit Strategies: Transitioning from International to Local NGO Leadership*, PACT, New York.

Holloway, R (1999) *Towards Financial Self-Reliance: A Handbook of Approaches to Resource Mobilization for Citizens' Organizations in the South – Trainer's Manual*, Beta Edition, Aga Khan Foundation, Geneva.

Hudock, A (1995) 'Sustaining Southern NGOs in Resource-Dependent Environments', *Journal of International Development*, Vol 7, No 4, pp653–668.

Hyden, G (1980) *Beyond Ujamaa in Tanzania: Underdevelopment and an Uncaptured Peasantry*, Heinemann, London.

Hyden, G (1983) *No-Short Cuts to Progress: African Development Management in Perspective*, University of California Press, Berkeley.

ICNPL (1996) *Global Standards and Best Practices for Laws Governing Non-Governmental Organizations*, study commisioned by the World Bank, International Center for Non-profit Law, Washington.

IFRCRCS (1997) *World Disasters Report 1997*, International Federation of Red Cross and Red Crescent Societies, Geneva, Oxford University Press, Oxford.

INTRAC (1998) *Direct Funding from a Southern Perspective – Strengthening Civil Society?* International NGO Training and Research Centre, Oxford.

Kanter, R (1979) *The Measurement of Organizational Effectiveness, Productivity, Performance and Success: Issues and Dilemmas in Service and Non-Profit Organizations*, PONPO Working Paper, No 8, Yale University, Institution for Social and Policy Studies, Institute of Development Research, Boston.

Kapur, D (1997) 'New conditionalities of the international financial institutions', *International Monetary and Financial Issues for the 1990s*, pp127–138, Research Papers for the Group of 24, Vol III, United Nations, New York and Geneva.

Korten, D (1995) *When Corporations Rule the World*, Earthscan, London.

Norton, M (1996) *The WorldWide Fundraiser's Handbook: A Guide to Fundraising for Southern NGOs and Voluntary Organizations*, Directory of Social Change, London.

OECD (1999) *The Facts About European NGOs Active in International Development*, Organisation for Economic Co-operation and Development, Paris.

Pfeffer, J and Salancik, G (1978) *The External Control of Organizations: A Resource Dependence Perspective*, Harper & Row, New York.

Raffer, K (1999) 'More conditions and less money: shifts in aid policies during the 1990s', paper presented at the Development Studies Association Conference, University of Bath, 11 September.

Salamon, L and Anheier, H (1999) *The Emerging Sector Revisited: A Summary*, Center for Civil Society Studies, Johns Hopkins University, Baltimore.

Salamon, L et al (1999) *Global Civil Society: Dimensions of the Nonprofit Sector*, Institute for Policy Studies, Center for Civil Society Studies, Johns Hopkins University, Baltimore.

Schearer, B, de Oliveira, M and Tandon, R (1997) 'A strategic guide to resource enhancement', in L Fox and B Schearer (eds) *Sustaining Civil Society: Strategies for Resource Mobilization*, CIVICUS, Washington, DC.

Schmidt, M and Marc, A (1994) 'Participation in social funds', *Environment Department Papers*, No 004, The World Bank, Washington, DC.

Sidel, M (1997) 'The emergence of the voluntary sector and philanthropy in Vietnam: functions, legal regulation and prospects for the future', *Voluntas*, Vol 8, No 3, pp283–302.

Smillie, I and Helmich, H (eds) (1993) *Non-Governmental Organizations and Governments: Stakeholders for Development*, OECD, Paris.

Smillie, I and Helmich H (eds) (1999) *Stakeholders: Government – NGO Partnerships for Development*, Earthscan, London.

Smillie, I, Douxchamps, F, Sholes, R and Covey, J (1996) *Partners or Contractors? Official Donor Agencies and Direct Funding Mechanisms: Three Northern Case Studies – CIDA, EU and USAID*, Occasional Paper Series, No 11, International NGO Training and Research Centre, Oxford.

Sobhan, B (1997) 'Partners or contractors? The relationship between official aid agencies and NGOs in Bangladesh', *Occasional Paper Series*, No 14, International NGO Training and Research Centre, Oxford.

UNCHR (1994) *Partnership in Action (PARINAC): Oslo Declaration and Plan of Action*, UNCHR, Geneva.

Valderrama, M (1999) 'Latin American NGOs in an age of scarcity: when quality matters', paper presented at a conference on NGOs in a Global Future, 8–11 January, Birmingham.

van Rooy, A (ed) (1998) *Civil Society and the Aid Industry: The Politics and Promise*, Earthscan, London.

van Tuijl, P (1999) 'NGOs and human rights: sources of justice and democracy', *Journal of International Affairs*, Vol 52, No 2, pp493–512.

Vincent, F and Campbell, P (1989) *Towards Greater Financial Autonomy – A Guide for Voluntary Organisations and Community Groups*, IRED, Geneva.

Weiss, T (ed) (1998) *Beyond UN Subcontracting: Task-sharing with Regional Security Arrangements and Service-providing NGOs*, Macmillan, Basingstoke.

Young, N and Woo, A (1999) *An Introduction to the Non-Profit Sector in China*, Charities Aid Foundation, London (draft).

Zhu Youhong (1999) 'Social innovation of China's third sector: views on the birth and development of non-profit organizations', paper presented at an International Conference of the Development of Non-profit Organizations and the China Project Hope, Beijing, November.

Part 9

Dealing with Gender

26

Getting Institutions Right for Women in Development

Anne Marie Goetz

'Getting institutions right' has today become as central to development discourse and practice as getting prices right was in the 1980s. The focus has shifted from changing supply signals to understanding the politics of how institutions regulate and coordinate societies, how people's needs are interpreted by policy-makers, and how resources are allocated. The purpose of the focus on understanding institutions, at least in most contemporary 'good governance' debates, has been to promote institution-building, to encourage the efficient use of public resources and to encourage private investment (Moore et al, 1994, p8) – getting institutions 'right' for market efficiency. What might be involved in getting institutions right *for women* is a question not often asked. It should be. In developing countries, Gender and Development policy objectives have been accepted at least in by principle, the development establishment for some time now, yet the fact that social institutions and development organizations continue to produce gendered outcomes which can be constraining or disadvantageous for women means that we must investigate these institutions and organizations from a feminist perspective.

It is important to stress that institutions have not necessarily been 'right' for men either, shaping choices for them in limiting ways according to gender, class and race in a variety of contexts. The focus in this chapter on getting institutions right *for women*, however, is meant to signal that a concern with gender justice should be a core value when analyzing institutions and organizations and making proposals for change.

This chapter examines the project of institutionalizing gender equity in the development context. This is sometimes known as 'mainstreaming' gender equity concerns in development institutions. This chapter introduces the theoretical and empirical discussion of the gendered nature of a range of development organizations, from non-governmental organizations (NGOs) to state bureaucracies. It considers the relationship between gendered aspects of organization and gender-discriminatory outcomes in the development process. Ultimately, the goal of gender-sensitive institutional change is to routinize gender-equitable forms of social interaction and to challenge the legitimacy of forms of social organization which discriminate against women. The chapter also outlines strategies to make gender equity routine in development organizations. The objective is to promote accountability to women in development institutions by identifying the organizational and political conditions under which economic and political gains for women in developing states might be achieved and sustained.

Institutional Contexts of Development Organizations

This chapter sets out to investigate gendered features of development organizations and their institutional environments, and yet these are not normally considered to be highly gendered arenas. With regard to gender, the family is most commonly identified as the primary institution in which women's entitlements and capabilities are so distorted as to undermine their capacity to manage transactions to their advantage in other institutions. Other institutions tend to be seen as relatively gender-neutral territory. Institutions such as the market mechanism are assumed to manage transactions efficiently on the basis of voluntary contracts. Public-sector institutions are assumed to have nothing to do with the structural and systemic nature of women's disadvantage, which is seen to be the outcome of transactions in other institutions like the market and household. Recently, however, a much stronger appreciation has developed of a gendered dynamic shaping institutions beyond the household, where gender relations are understood to constitute institutions such that these institutions reproduce gendered inequities to varying degrees. In other words, we can now talk of specifically gendered market failures and gendered public-sector institutional failures: markets fail to invest in and reward women's productive and reproductive work; public institutions fail to include women equitably among the 'public' that they serve. These gendered preference systems are more than discriminatory attitudes or irrational choices on the part of individuals, or unintended oversights in policy. Nor are they deliberate policy outcomes. They are embedded in the norms, structures and practices of institutions.

It is helpful at this stage to make a conceptual distinction between institutions and organizations. In English, unfortunately, 'institution' can mean anything from an organization to the vague sociological notion of recurrent patterns of human behaviour. While this range of meanings is too broad to be analytically useful, it is difficult to settle on a definition of institutions which is much more precise. Following the economist Douglas North, institutions are best understood as frameworks for socially constructed rules and norms which function to limit choice. They are 'humanly devised constraints' (1990, p3) which reduce uncertainty and provide structure to everyday life, making certain forms of behaviour predictable and routine, institutionalizing them. The project for gender-sensitive institutional change is therefore to routinize gender-equitable forms of social interaction and to challenge the legitimacy of forms of social organization which discriminate against women. Recognizing the human dimension in the construction of institutions alerts us to the fact that they are not immutable or 'natural' approaches to organizing human relationships, and also to the fact that all institutions embody a history of social choices by particular groups. A critical analysis of institutions can show how these choices are sometimes socially suboptimal, not made with either equity or efficiency in mind, but rather made to preserve the power of particular groups.

Other definitions of institutions emphasize their role in generating experience. The sociologists Anthony Giddens and RW Connell suggest that by setting limits to, or boundaries around, social practice, including thought, institutions shape human experience and personal identity (Giddens, 1986; Connell, 1987). The experience of gender difference, therefore, can be seen to be a product of institutions, where it is the outcome of institutionalized patterns of distributing resources and social value, public and private power.

Understanding institutions as historically constructed frameworks for behavioural rules and as generators of experience contributes to understanding why it is that when new agents (such as women) and orientations (such as concerns with gender equity) are introduced to institutions, outcomes can seem so little changed. Institutional rules, structures, practices and the identities of the agents which animate them may continue primarily to serve the political and social interests which institutions were designed to promote in the first place.

Gender redistributive policies have characteristics which tend to create resistance and opposition within the organizational and broader institutional environment. Policies to mainstream women in development activities previously reserved for men – such as those which enhance women's rate of market engagement – involve participants in activities designed to change people's most unquestioned behaviours and deeply cherished beliefs. The business of expanding women's access to and control over resources and of revaluing their roles in the rural economy, disrupts traditional interpretations of gendered need and worth upon which patterns of female exclusion and denial are based. Unsurprisingly, given the importance of systems of gender inequality for individual, kin and community identity, such policies can attract significant hostility from target communities.

This hostility which stems from cultural norms exists, of course, within bureaucracies as well. Among bureaucrats, it may be expressed in the circumspection and equivocation which can fracture gender policy rhetoric; in the insistence, for example, on gender-role complementarity and the denial of conflicting gender interests, or in the use of gender policy to service other objectives, such as family planning or efficiency goals. Diffidence towards the gender-transformatory aspects of policy can also be reflected in the tendency to downplay the empowerment-related objectives of such programmes and to focus instead on the 'technical' matters of quantifiable input provision, in a process which turns a blind eye to issues of women's actual control over these inputs. Or it can be expressed structurally through resource allocation patterns which leave gender-related programmes stranded on the peripheries of regular government development budgets, as short-lived, foreign-funded pilot initiatives.

The familiar analogy between institutions and the 'rules of the game' in competitive sport (cf Schiavo-Campo, 1994; Evans, 1993) is helpful in expanding on this problem. 'Rules of the game' are adapted to the capabilities of the players; they challenge players and allow for fair and manageable competition between particular categories of players. However, there may be completely new contestants entering the game at a much later stage whose capabilities are not reflected in the parameters of the game. Like pygmies competing with the Harlem Globetrotters on a conventionally designed basketball court, they will be unable to win because they cannot change some of the basic 'rules' – like the height of the net or the size of the court. Most often, new participants have to adapt their behaviour to the existing rules. They may learn to win, but often at the cost of bringing their 'different' needs and interests to play, as when overachieving managerial women become 'sociological males' (Kanter, 1977). After all the trouble of 'breaking in' to institutions, new participants find it surprisingly hard to 'speak out' in their own voice.

An alternative, of course, is to opt out entirely – to create new forms of institutions and organizations. Women's organizations represent this kind of response. They are oriented to developing new structures and organizational cultures which reflect women's needs, interests and behavioural preferences. It is no accident that women's organizations the world over often concern themselves with gender-specific problems, which find unsatisfactory response from public or private institutions – problems such as sexual violence and personal physical security in the home.

Organizations are formed within the environmental constraint represented by institutions they create the concrete mechanisms through which formal and informal rules are applied, societies are regulated and coordinated, resources are distributed, and cultural systems are validated and reproduced. Over time, however, they can have a transformative impact on the institutional arena, changing underlying rules, systems and incentive structures. Douglas North suggests that there are three main institutional arenas which provide a general normative 'environmental constraint' for organizations. These, and the organizations they embrace, are:

- *The state* This is the larger institutional environment for the public service administration, the legal system and organizations which manage coercion such as the military and the police. Public service bureaucracies of particular importance in impinging on people's capacities to realize their endowments include: the educational and health system, marketing boards, agricultural research and extension systems, infrastructure, energy, irrigation and water supply. Also important is the nature of political institutions which shape patterns of representation and accountability (single versus multi-party systems, the organization of local government, and so on).
- *The market* The framework for organizations such as firms, producers' cooperatives and financial intermediaries.
- *The community* The context for the organization of families or households, kin and lineage systems, local patron–client relationships, village tribunals or other organizations presiding over customary law. Organizations or associations of 'civil society' exist in this arena: NGOs, women's organizations, civic organizations.

Different institutional arenas each structure social transactions and maintain social order through different dominant dynamics or norms. According to Moore, the state and its bureaucracies respect the principles of hierarchy, the market is structured around notions of competition and community-level transactions often respond to notions of solidarity (Moore, 1992, p66). The public sector will have a normative environment shaped by bureaucratic values and methods stressing impartiality and accountability; market organizations will be based on principles of exchange on the basis of voluntary contracts; and the community may be shaped by ideologies of intrafamilial altruism, shared identities on the basis of religion, gender, region, ethnicity, lineage or generational groups, or shared problems and concerns over matters such as community welfare, environmental protection, labour rights, and so on.

For policy purposes, the organizations in each institutional arena pose different challenges for gender-sensitive change. The public sector is usually seen as the easiest to penetrate, given the much more obviously humanly constructed (as opposed to seemingly ascribed, 'natural', or 'God-given') nature of its rules and norms. The formal impartiality of bureaucratic norms based on merit and the inclusiveness of democratic principles (if and when they are positively espoused by states) seem to offer women a chance to participate as part of the 'public' served by the public sector. The market, on the other hand, is perceived as a notoriously hostile arena in which to achieve gender-equitable outcomes, given the disadvantages that women entrants face with their lower human and capital resource endowments. Some organizations based on the principles of solidarity, such as NGOs, are regarded as particularly promising sites for gender-sensitive change strategies, out of faith in the responsiveness of egalitarian value-driven cultures to women's needs and interests.

Frustration with the pathologies associated with state bureaucracies, including their susceptibility to capture by elite interests, asymmetrical principal–agent relationships allowing for little participation by clients, and a notorious indifference to equity issues in status-conscious civil service cultures, has led aid donors to prefer working through NGOs whose decentralized command and communication structures, and investment in participatory decision-making processes, are promoted as models for the public administration (Korten, 1987; Fowler, 1990; Buvinic, 1989). There is a largely unexamined assumption that these organizations are also more receptive than state bureaucracies to the problems of the poor in general and to poor women. This seems to be based on the assumption that collective as opposed to corporate management approaches should admit of greater involvement of subaltern groups, as should other structural features which reverse information flows from the top down to the bottom up, expand on fieldworkers' decision-making power, and enhance the participation of local groups in decision-making. Some recent studies challenge this presumed comparative advantage of NGOs with regard to their gender sensitivity. NGOs can be as deeply structured by male privilege and preference as other organizations, and indeed, can be as bureaucratic and hierarchical as public-sector institutions. NGOs which appeal to notions of a 'moral economy' and community solidarity often reproduce deeply gendered aspects of community institutions.

Gendered Outcomes

The persistence of gendered outcomes of everyday decision-making in both state and NGOs, often in spite of policy rhetoric promoting gender-sensitive changes, has led to the conclusion that institutions themselves are gendered; that relations of administration in the public sector, or exchange in the private sector, are gendered. In deconstructing institutions by gender, it is easiest to begin by identifying their gendered effects or their 'gendering' outcomes, and move from there to understanding how they are actually constituted by gender difference. It helps to work through an example, so here we take the case of rural development. In most countries, striking gender differentials persist in efforts to integrate women to development programmes in the productive sectors, particularly agricultural production. Analysis of implementation patterns show that women's identity for policy is often limited to those features of their lives which centre on their contribution to family welfare and on their needs as dependants of men, rather than their needs as agricultural producers. Table 26.1 schematizes gender-dichotomous patterns in rural development

Table 26.1 *Policy Benefits and Delivery Practices Compared for Men and Women's Rural Development Programmes*

Differences in:	'Mainstream' economic development system	Subsidiary community welfare subsystem
Central orientation	To address the production needs of 'farmers', of 'primary' workers, or 'household heads', and 'breadwinners'	To improve household and community management, addressed to 'subsistence', voluntary, or 'secondary' labour; geared to 'mothers' and their dysfunctional families
Justifications appealed to for policy legitimacy	Macro-economic planning considerations in national priority policies	'Basic needs' considerations in projects
Monitoring and implementing agencies	Ministries of Agriculture, of Local Government or of Rural Infrastructure	Separate women's bureaux within line Ministries, NGOs and women's organizations
Significance of benefits	Individual access to modern agricultural technology, to the modern banking system, etc	Group-based access to appropriate small-scale technology and micro-enterprise training
Degree of autonomy accorded beneficiaries	Active subjects participating in policy-making	Passive objects on whom change is visited
Funding base	Permanent government budgets for national development priorities	Foreign-funded pilot projects

programmes. It is an adaptation of a method used by Nancy Fraser (1989) to deconstruct public policy from a gender perspective and it has the institutional environment of government rural development programmes in South Asia in mind.

The table, obviously, is a very abstract representation of dichotomous patterns in policy interpretation and implementation, and it makes generalizations which obscure great complexities in policy interpretation. Nevertheless, the general point can be made that there are often gendered subtexts and dichotomies in institutional practices and outcomes. There can be an implicitly 'masculine' mainstream system of development programmes addressing the needs of primary producers, while an implicitly 'feminine' sub-system is tied to household and community management, and is geared to mothers and their dysfunctional (that is, malnourished, poorly educated, sometimes female-headed, or simply too large) families, and sometimes their degraded environments. 'Producers' such as 'farmers' are implicitly men. Agricultural development policies rarely involve training and recruiting women extension agents, research in crops which women grow, and ensuring that market information and new production inputs reach women farmers. Instead, there are projects to enhance women's kitchen gardening or homestead-based income-generating efforts. Policies for women differ markedly in the justifications appealed to for policy legitimacy (community development problems instead of national production targets), in monitoring and implementing agencies, and in their funding base. They differ, too, in the degree of autonomy and rights they accord beneficiaries, with male producers' associations more likely than women's associations to be consulted in public decision-making.[1]

These differences send unambiguous messages to policy clients about their social identity, their relative importance and social worth. Such programmes can enhance women's survival chances within the traditional family. But in doing so, they can help to reinforce the traditional assumptions about women's roles which contribute to their lower entitlements and capacities for self-development, although this will depend on the ways that women themselves receive and react to policy messages. Such policies hardly provide women with an institutional alternative to dependence on the family, which employment rights or equitable participation in the market might do. They institutionalize a profound gender division in public policy clientship which reinforces notions that women's and children's needs are rightly matters for private, male, provision.

It is important to note that gender differences in policy delivery approaches should not be seen as necessarily discriminatory. For example, group-based approaches to delivering credit, training or appropriate technology to women may be much more appropriate than a more individualized approach. A group approach may allow women to build a sense of solidarity for mutual support, something which men may not need as badly because of their greater social power individually, or which they may have already developed through class-based mobilizing. *Sameness* is not required in policy delivery approaches but, rather, sensitivity to difference, respect for equal rights and a commitment to outcomes which are empowering for women. Thus, a group-based framework for delivering resources to women is not a problem if one objective is its contribution to women's collective empowerment. It is, however, a problem if it is merely an instrument for more efficient development practice; a means of managing controlled and uniform resource delivery.[2] It is also a problem if organizations assume women's identity for public policy as being conditioned by their social relationships as dependants of men, and construct their interpretation of women's needs and interests accordingly.

The Gendered Constitution of Institutions

The general example of gender-differential outcomes in the organization of rural development suggests that institutions do not just passively mirror gender differences in social organization; they also produce gender differences through their structures and in their everyday practices. With the exception of the organization of families and kinship systems, it is not always obvious how institutional norms and the organizational structures and relationships which enact them are constituted by gender, particularly since norms embedded in bureaucratic impartiality or voluntary exchange appear, on the surface, to be gender-neutral. In the family, by contrast, the foundational institutional contract – marriage – is clearly gender-ascriptive. The conjugal contract is made between a woman and a man, and the language of kinship (such as sister, brother, uncle, aunt) is explicitly gendered. But there is an ideological and conceptual split between 'public' and 'domestic' or 'private' institutions, where a foundational principle is that public relations of production, exchange and administration are indifferent to gender difference. A classic tenet of the Weberian view of bureaucratic organization, for example, is that public bureaucracies are insulated from the social and political relations in which they are embedded, and in particular, abstracted from patrimonial, and by implication, patriarchal relations. The absence of explicitly gendered organizing principles disguises the salience of gender divisions of labour, power and desire as organizing principles in these contexts (Connell, 1987). As Kabeer notes:

> Despite the separation of domestic institutions from the public domains of production and exchange, familial norms and values are constantly drawn on to construct the terms on which women and men enter, and participate, in public life and in the market place... Both within and across institutions, gender operates as a pervasive allocational principle, linking production with reproduction, domestic with public domains, and the macroeconomy with the [local]-level institutions within which development processes are played out (1994, p62).

Each major institutional arena is gendered in its male bias – its failure to value, recognize or accommodate reproductive work, defining it as 'unproductive' or basing effective participation on a capacity to attain freedom from the reproductive sphere. Institutions are gendered in their active male preference; they exclude women as members or clients/recipients; or alternatively, they actively 'feminize' women's participation to entrench their secondary, nurturing, supportive roles or dependence on men, in institutions outside the household.

All institutions beyond the household or domestic sphere are gendered to the degree that they are located in a 'public' and 'productive' economy, while neglecting the human resource subsidy which the 'domestic' and 'reproductive' economy provides to the 'productive' economy (Elson, 1994, p39). Because the sexual division of labour relegates reproductive functions primarily to women, men are better able to pursue their interests in the 'productive' economy, while women's participation is always conditioned by the way their roles in the reproductive economy have shaped their endowments. This socially constructed and gendered split between 'public' and 'private' is then deeply reinforced – institutionalized – through the formation of social networks or shared understandings and conventions of exclusion and inclusion, justified ideologically, which privilege the participation of the particular social group that has freed itself from reproductive work (ibid, p37). In the market, for example, while conventional economics explains social norms in producer relationships as mechanisms to monopolize sources of labour or capital for efficiency purposes, critical social scientists have demonstrated that contractual arrangements for social exclusion and inclusion actually function as techniques of social control, maintaining the social and political standing of one gender or a particular class (Evans, 1993; Bardhan, 1983; Hart, 1991). These social norms are often not explicit, but rather are embedded in the structures and hierarchies of institutions, in the conditions and requirements for access and participation, in their incentive and accountability structures.

A good example of embedded gendered exclusion in institutional structures and practices is the way that financial intermediaries have excluded women (and the poor in general). The successes of special credit institutions in challenging this demonstrates directions for positive institutional change to include women. High barriers to equitable participation by the poor and especially women, in financial markets are maintained through basic rules of participation which favour proper-tied male producers. The collateral requirement in borrowing excludes women who often do not own land; the transaction costs involved in loan processing and man-agement procedures means that small loans, especially consumption loans, which women may prefer, are not favoured by banks. The physical location of banks re-quires travel away from home, which may be difficult for women and basic application procedures may require a degree of literacy not attained by many women producers.

Innovations in financial intermediation pioneered by organizations like the Grameen Bank in Bangladesh have demonstrated the enormously positive gender-sensitive impact which changes to these structures and practices can have. Replacing collateral requirements with peer monitoring of loan use and repayment and on-the-spot loan approval, has cut loan access transaction costs to the woman borrower and loan management costs to the lender, while also making it possible to lend smaller amounts. Bringing banking to the village eliminates the social and economic costs of mobility to women. The elimination of complex application procedures requir-ing literate borrowers and the waiving of requirements for male guarantors for women's loans, allows women access to the financial system in their own right.

Structures and Agents

From this point on in this chapter, the discussion focuses mainly on organizations, rather than on institutions more generally. The key to devising strategies to change organizations to enhance their receptivity and accountability to women whether as citizens of the state, participants in development programmes or staff members in organizations, is to understand the gendered dynamics of decision-making and organizational functioning. Norms, legitimating ideologies and disciplinary foundations are imprinted on organizational structures such as management hierarchies. These produce everyday procedures and practices which inform incentive systems, formal performance standards and informal organizational cultures which direct the be-haviour of individual agents. Human agents, participants in organizations, do not simply respond passively to incentive systems or policy directives, however. They bring their individual ideologies and behavioural patterns to their work in ways which can eventually change practices and structures.

The role of individual agents in affecting institutional functioning is often neglected, partly because of structuralist assumptions which overdetermine the impact of power relations and resource endowments on individuals. Whether within the family or in a state bureaucracy, individuals have agency affecting their response to institutional incentives. In development service institutions, individual agents have important roles in affecting the impact of policy, nowhere more so than at the implementation level. This partly explains how progressive gender policy goals can be subverted in implementation processes, as the critical arena for the realization of the spirit of policy commitments is at the interface between development workers and the organization's membership.

Individual agents in organizations may or may not share in a general institutional ambivalence to gender-redistributive policy, but given the precariousness of their career positions within their organizations, their options are limited to compliance with dominant attitudes or a very risky commitment to more 'counter-cultural' policy goals such as gender equity. At the lower levels of development bureaucracies, organizational agents constantly interact with beneficiaries and because of this are in a position to retain an awareness of the real needs and capabilities of their beneficiaries. Organizational agents receive authoritative interpretations of the needs of women beneficiaries from their superiors (who have themselves 'translated' the interpretations of policy elites), interpretations embedded in the programme inputs which they are expected to dispense, and in the delivery practices which they are expected to pursue. But their own perspectives on legitimate needs and programme practices may vary according to their own interactions with beneficiaries, their notions of their own identities, and their individual positions within class, organizational and gender hierarchies.

A Gendered Archaeology of Organizations[3]

The process of understanding the gendered nature of organizations engages researchers in an 'archaeological' investigation; it involves disinterring and reinterpreting histories and scrutinizing artefacts such as favoured concepts, terms of inclusion or exclusion, symbols of success or failure. It involves investigating the traces which gendered patterns of privilege leave in the organization and architecture of space and time, and in behavioural patterns which are tolerated or punished. Here, eight elements of a 'gendered archaeology' are outlined.

Institutional and organizational history

A starting-point in analysing organizations by gender is to identify the gender interests which over time, have shaped their broader institutional frameworks. This is not a particularly easy task. Take the case of the state, which is the broader institutional framework for individual development bureaucracies in the public administration. In the West, studies of the history of the definition of the modern 'public' sphere by Carole Pateman and others, have shown that women were excluded from public citizenship in the sense that its definitional criterion was some form of 'independence' defined in terms of the male experience, including property ownership, bearing arms and 'employment' (Pateman, 1988; Okin, 1991; Gordon, 1990, p20). The resulting gendered split between public and private came to institutionalize women's exclusion from the concerns and practices of public institutions.

Understanding the history of how a particular group has established an institution can illuminate how patterns of exclusion became institutionalized, and this helps in identifying critical points for change. But feminist analysts run into the same difficulties as Marxist functionalists if they substitute gender for class and assume a conspiracy of male interests monopolizing certain institutions. For example, Mies' argument that the state is a 'general patriarch' (Mies, 1986), an executive of men as a group, suggests a homogeneous and passive tool for a monolithic larger interest. It underestimates the complexity of the state, with its many different organizations with sometimes conflicting interests, offering differing prospects for feminist incursions. It obscures histories of women's struggles and makes it hard to explain genuine victories achieved in women's interests.

Also, 'men's interests' are presumably just as difficult to identify 'objectively' as women's,[4] nor is the category of 'men' any more valid as a universal than is the category of 'women'. The historical record, however, does show that men tend to act, across divisions like class or race, more cohesively than women do in defence of certain gender interests, and they do so in ways which mean that public institutions help to forge connections between men's public and private power. In part, this is due to their longer occupation of public office and to their literal dominance of decision-making and decision-enforcing. It is also due to the historical embedding of their needs and interests in the structures and practices of public institutions. Attention to the historical processes through which certain institutions come to promote male dominance and female dependence should help to illuminate the mutability of dominant interests through politics and contestation.[5]

Attention to gendered institutional histories also illuminates the gendered subtexts of apparently neutral organizing structures, practices and ideologies, to help explain why these prove so resistant to women and their interests. The past cannot be changed, but new interpretations of established histories can be empowering for change processes when the historical construction of contemporary 'givens' or 'facts' is understood. Taking the history of the Western state again, we know that women's voice was initially explicitly excluded from institutional procedures for ensuring participation, such as the vote, and processes underlining political legitimacy, such as securing popular consent. This gives grand concepts like democracy a gendered subtext, defining women out of equal and effective public participation (Phillips, 1991). In the labour market, investigations into the history of agricultural labour processes or trade-union formation, illuminate points at which the active exclusion of women was part of the negotiation of men's economic security vis-à-vis employers (Hart, 1991; Cockburn, 1983). These examples point to the need to redefine the meaning of concepts such as citizenship and 'production' in order to give women's civil rights an equal foundation.

The gendered cognitive context

The ideologies and disciplines that animate organizations can institutionalize strong gender biases. Conventional economics, for example, which guides thinking in many development organizations, has been identified as 'fundamentally disabled' in its

capacity to understand women's inequality as a function of gendered power relations because of its choice-theoretic analytical framework (Elson, 1994, p39).
Organizations oriented to social and human development have been more open to
the inclusion of gender perspectives, but until recently women have tended to be
included in 'feminized' ways, as objects of family welfare policy. Feminist critiques
of disciplinary frameworks from economics to anthropology have contributed conceptual and theoretical revisions to allow for the inclusion of gendered perspectives.
These critiques have been important in efforts to valorize and legitimate women's
perspectives on the ways that institutions conceptualize their environments and roles.

Gendered organizational culture

Some feminist analysts of bureaucracies, such as Kathy Ferguson, argue that literal
male dominance is embedded in distinctive features of bureaucratic culture such as
the valorization of instrumental rationality, top-down command and communication
systems, specialization, as well as aggressive, goal-oriented styles of management. The
suggestion that these represent innate sexual characteriztics is highly contentious, as
indeed is its corollary: the suggestion that these features of administration necessarily exclude positive outcomes for women. Stewart and Taylor (1997) give an example
of this in their description of working with the police in Zimbabwe – a strongly
masculinized and hierarchical institution – to promote better responses to problems of domestic violence. In spite of serious problems with the male culture of the
police, the centralized structure and discipline of the police force, along with its
strong logistical capability and extensive network of outposts – all aspects of rigid
hierarchy and strict command relationships – were a positive advantage in expanding the coverage of the project and ensuring a uniformity in the application of new
gender-sensitive procedures.

Gendered participants

All institutions have privileged participants, included and excluded groups, superiors and subordinates. Identification of the gender of 'winners' and 'losers' in the
market, or of decision-makers versus decision-takers in organizations, is important
in determining which group's interests are served by a particular institution. Men
tend to dominate most formal public-sector institutions and most private-sector
market institutions, as well as most socially significant civil society associations.
Whether more women in decision-making positions would reorient institutions
towards responsiveness to women's gender interests remains a hypothetical question, as there are few empirical cases of women dominating public institutions.
Conversely, the mere fact of male dominance does not necessarily preclude men
from representing women and acting in their interests. In actuality, however, men
as a group do appear to act to defend their interests as a gender, even across class
divisions, particularly in terms of defending male employment security and privileged market access. The tantalizing possibility that a greater physical presence and
more tangible participation of women in public institutions might change the character of these institutions, however, is behind the focus on women bureaucrats,
fieldstaff and politicians in the literature. Most case studies cannot reach a conclu-

sion about the capacity of women 'insiders' to promote women's interests because they are investigating contexts in which women are in a dramatic minority and lack structured external support such as might come from women's organizations. However, Ackerly's (1997) study of credit programmes in Bangladesh, and the chapters on women's organizations by Stewart and Taylor (1997) strongly imply that investing in the confidence and security of women staff has been a key to successful efforts to promote women's empowerment in development programmes.

Gendered space and time

The physical and social capabilities of those who dominate institutions will be reflected in performance or success criteria, and in the physical and social – or spatial and temporal – structure of an organization's work. Men's social capacity to achieve relative liberation from child care and domestic responsibilities allows them more time for work or institutional interactions beyond the home, while their social independence gives them cultural rights to mobility and autonomy outside the home. Institutional time management of working hours and life-cycle/career trajectories, will reflect these capabilities, as will the physical location of the institution. Thus institutions from markets to schools can be particularly inaccessible to women if they are distant from home, open only during hours when women are doing work for which there are few labour substitutes and if they fail to provide space for children. An example of gender-friendly changes to institutional space and time is China's post-1986 approach to community-managed primary education in which measures such as flexible schooling hours, sibling care facilities at school and special schools for girls, accommodated girls' space and time constraints (World Bank, 1994, p60).

Yasmin (1997) gives a detail account of organizational approaches to structuring space and time. Comparing a women's development NGO to mixed NGOs in Bangladesh, she demonstrates how it is possible to overcome seemingly intractable constraints on women staff's capacity to travel and live away from home through gender-sensitive provisions for women's accommodation and mobility. These efforts have transformed the public space of the office into a comfortable quasi-domestic space, with provision for child care, for eating and sleeping; bringing the private into the public, the home into the office. Other NGOs in Bangladesh, such as the Bangladesh Rural Advancement Committee (BRAC) also have offices-cum-living quarters in rural areas. There is a marked difference in their character, however, with many aspects of the 'domestic' – particularly children – excluded or concealed; the public space remains relatively 'unpolluted' by the domestic. Although the women's organization's approach makes the public arena much more accommodating of women, it tends to be derided by outside observers such as donors who regard its offices as 'dowdy', with the implication that there are efficiency costs to this domestic informality.

For changes to space management to contribute to women's empowerment, rather than being experienced as paternalistic forms of control or protection, considerable time must be invested in raising women's self-confidence and capacities to defend their rights. Yasmin (1997) shows that this time investment is usually considered wasteful and inefficient by 'mainstream' organizations. Just as a substantial time investment is critical for embracing new staff, so too is it an important element of working for women's empowerment on the level of programme implementation, where work to unseat internalized feelings of inferiority and to build up solidarities and resource bases as alternatives to dependence on men, takes tremendous amounts of time. These, too, are activities that mainstream organizations prefer to sacrifice in favour of easily measurable, quantifiable achievements such as quantities of credit disbursed and recovered and numbers of new members registered and numbers of people trained in particular skills.

The sexuality of organizations

One aspect of the gendering of public space is the way that the sexed body is perceived in that space. Although ostensibly absent from non-'domestic' spaces, sexuality is inevitably an element of human interaction in any location and the way that various 'permitted' forms of sexuality are managed, as in the military, or ignored, as often the case in school settings, will have implications for women's physical security or ability to gain respect as equal participants, rather than as sex objects (Hearn et al, 1989). Rao and Kelleher (1997) address this issue explicitly in raising problems of the harassment or 'teasing' of women staff by men in BRAC, and in discussing management efforts to accommodate certain expressions of female sexuality such as maternity and menstruation, as well as efforts to control (hetero)sexuality by discouraging liaisons between staff.

The contribution of women both individually and as a group can be devalued by invoking the symbolic significance of the public–private divide to associate their presence and affectivity in the organization with their private identities. Sex-typed tasks signal this, but its most insidious expression is the problem of sexual harassment, which deeply undercuts the identity and effectiveness of women as autonomous and equal public agents.

Gendered authority structures

On the one hand, gendered ideologies and disciplinary structures can leave little space for women to validate their perspectives, and on the other, gendered ways of organizing space, time and sexuality can make it difficult for women to compete effectively with men or to thrive and succeed in certain institutional environments. Gendered authority structures can further undermine efforts to establish direction and vision in women's gender interests because of the lack of cultural association between women and 'public' power, and because of the ways that male authority is entrenched in hierarchies and command-and-control systems. The greater significance assigned to male achievements and forms of expression as a consequence of their near-monopoly of control in organizations, is reflected in organizational value systems, the gendering of particular skills, and in particular in the gendering of authority symbols. This makes it difficult for women to command authority for their approaches and views in organizations, and results in the familiar phenomenon of women having to take on sociologically male attributes (such as 'male' authoritative behaviour, power dressing, minimizing the demands of home and family) in order to gain recognition in male-dominated power systems. Gendered authority systems affect the nature of relationships between male fieldstaff and beneficiaries, not just producing greater deference on the part of women beneficiaries, but also institutionalizing a pattern in which male staff first seek women's husbands' permission before working with women, making men the mediators between the project and village women.

Gendered incentive and accountability systems

Together, the above gendered dimensions of organizational practice within institutions add up to the creation of gendered incentive and accountability systems. Incentives may be tied more to quantitatively measurable performance targets than to qualitative matters such as promoting empowerment processes. Accountability may be oriented towards more vociferously demanding constituencies (such as funders or well-organized clients such as producers' associations) rather than downwards or horizontally towards women's groups. The near-global mood of neo-liberalism in the management of public institutions, with the imposition of commercial contracts for services which may be hard to measure in monetary terms (such as counselling victims of domestic violence, consciousness-raising work, community care or academic reflection) has meant the introduction of new principles, relationships and incentives which can marginalize many concerns and projects associated with women's empowerment.

Notes

1   A similarly dichotomous map could be developed to trace the institutionalization of poverty-alleviation measures, with many poverty programmes funded on a pilot basis by outside donors, differing dramatically in the resources and rights accorded to participants.

2   Increasing concern is being expressed about the problem of instrumentalism in efforts to promote gender and development policy – where, for example, resource provision to women or girls is justified on the grounds of positive externalities such as women's apparently greater propensity to invest in household well-being or fertility control (Jackson, 1996; Baden and Goetz, 1997). It is important not to be too doctrinaire about this problem, however, as to do so denies women's agency and capacity to take advantage of new resources for their own needs, whatever the objectives of policy-makers.

3   I am grateful to Maxine Molyneux for suggesting that this is an 'archaeological' approach to exploring organizations.

4   For discussions of women's gender interests, and in particular whether 'objective' or 'strategic' interests can be identified for women as a gender, see Molyneux (1985), Jonasdottir (1988) and Fierlbeck (1997).

5   This suggests a model of the state such as that proposed in 'state-centred' approaches, cf Skocpol and Amenta (1986), Evans et al (1985) or Block's conflict model of the state (1987).

References

Ackerly, B (1997) 'What's in a design? The effects of NGO programme delivery choices on women's empowerment in Bangladesh', A M Goetz (ed) *Getting Institutions Right for Women in Development*, Zed Press, London.

Baden, S and Goetz, A M (1997) 'Who needs [sex] when you can have [gender]? Conflicting discourses on gender at Beijing', *Feminist Review*.

Bardhan, K (1983) 'Economic growth, poverty, and rural labour markets in India: a survey of research', *Working Paper 54*, Rural Employment Policy Research Programme, ILO.

Block, F (ed) (1987) *Revising State Theory: Essays in Politics and Postindustrialism*, Temple, Philadelphia.

Buvinic, M (1989) 'Investing in poor women: the psychology of donor support', *World Development*, Vol 17, No 7, pp1045–1057.

Cockburn, Cynthia (1983) *Brothers. Male Dominance and Technological Change*, Pluto Press, London.

Connell, R W (1987) *Gender and Power*, Polity Press, Cambridge.

Elson, Diane (1994) 'Micro, meso, macro: gender and economic analysis in the context of policy reform', in I Bakker (ed) *The Strategic Silence Gender and Economic Policy*, Zed Books, London.

Evans, Alison (1993) '"Contracted-out": some reflections on gender, power, and agrarian institutions', *IDS Bulletin*, Vol 24, July.

Evans, P, Rueschemeyer, D and Skocpol, T (1985) *Bringing the State Back In*, Cambridge University Press, Cambridge.

Fierlbeck K (1997) 'Getting representation right for women in development: accountability, consent and the articulation of women's interests', in A M Goetz, op cit.

Fowler, A (1990) 'Doing it better? Where and how NGOs have a comparative advantage in facilitating development', *AERDD Bulletin*, Vol 28.

Fraser, Nancy (1989) *Unruly Practices: Power, Discourse, and Gender in Contemporary Social Theory*, Polity Press, Cambridge.

Giddens, A (1986) *Sociology: A Brief but Critical Introduction*, Macmillan, London.

Goetz, Anne-Marie (1991) 'Feminism and the claim to know: contradictions in feminist approaches to women in development', in Rebecca Grant and Kathleen Newland (eds) *Gender and International Relations*, Indiana University Press, Bloomington.

Gordon, Linda (ed) (1994) *Women, the State, and Welfare*, University of Wisconsin Press, Wisconsin.

Hart, Gillian (1991) 'Engendering everyday resistance: gender, patronage, and production politics in rural Malaysia', *Journal of Peasant Studies*, Vol 19, No 1.

Hearn, Jeff, Sheppard, D, Tancred-Sheriff, P and Burrell, G (eds) (1989) *The Sexuality of Organization*, Sage, London.

Jackson, C (1996) 'Rescuing gender from the poverty trap', *World Development*, Vol 24, No 3.

Jonasdottir, A K (1988) 'On the concept of interest, women's interests, and the limitations of interest theory', in K B Jones and A K Jonasdottir (eds) *The Political Interests of Gender*, Sage, London.

Kabeer, N (1994) *Reversed Realities: Gender Hierarchies in Development Thought*, Verso, London.

Kanter, Rosabeth Moss (1977) *Men and Women of the Corporation*, Basic Books, New York.

Korten, David (1987) 'Third generation NGO strategies: a key to people centered development', *World Development*, Vol 15, Autumn.

Mies, Maria (1986) *Patriarchy and Accumulation on a World Scale*, Zed Books, London.

Molyneux, M (1985) 'Mobilization without emancipation? Women's interests, state and revolution in Nicaragua', *Feminist Studies*, Vol 11, No 2, pp227–54.

Moore, H and Vaughan, M (1994) *Cutting Down Trees: Gender, Nutrition and Agricultural Change in the Northern Province of Zambia, 1890–1990*, James Currey, London.

Moore, Mick (1992) 'Competition and pluralism in public bureaucracies', *IDS Bulletin*, Vol 23, No 4.

North, D C (1990) *Institutions, Institutional Change, and Economic Performance*, Cambridge University Press, Cambridge.

Okin, Susan Moller (1991) 'Gender, the public and the private', in D Held (ed) *Political Theory Today*, Polity Press, Cambridge.

Pateman, C (1988) *The Sexual Contract*, Polity Press, Cambridge; Stanford University Press, Stanford, CT.

Phillips, A (1991) *Engendering Democracy*, Polity Press, Cambridge.

Rao, A and Kelleher, D (1997) 'Engendering organizational change: the BRAC Case', in A M Goetz (ed) op cit.

Razavi, S and Miller, C (1995) *From WID to GAD: Conceptual Shifts in the Women and Development Discourse*, UNRISD Occasional Paper, No 1, Geneva.

Schiavo-Campo, Salvatore (ed) (1994) *Institutional Change and the Public Sector in Economies in Transition*, World Bank, Discussion Paper, Washington, DC.

Skocpol, T and Amenta, E (1986) 'States and social policies', *Annual Review of Sociology*, No 12, pp131–57.

Stewart, S and Taylor, J (1997) 'Women organizing women: "doing it backwards and in high heels"', in A M Goetz (ed), op cit.

World Bank (1994) *Governance: The World Bank's Experience*, World Bank, Washington, DC.

Yasmin, T (1997) 'What is different about women's organizations', in A M Goetz, op cit.

27

The Role of Gender in NGDOs[1]

Alan Fowler

As in any community, gender is a dimension of non-government development organizations (NGDOs). First, it can be found in the way that roles and power are divided along gender lines. Second, it is expressed in the degree to which male and female principles are reflected and valued in organizational culture. The two are related, but are not the same and hence are frequently confused. A third aspect of gender is in an NGDO's development approach. Gender awareness within NGDOs affects their sensitivity to work relationships and there is a link between the ways in which gender expresses itself and how NGDOs ultimately perform in development.

Gender as an NGDO Issue

Gender dimensions of development have been around a long time, originally framed as WID – women in development. However, the growth of gender awareness is out of step with its translation into practice, which lags a long way behind. One reason for this gap is to do with organization. Our task, therefore, is to focus on the organizational obstacles to gender-sensitive development, which means looking at how they are being overcome within NGDOs.

Recognizing gender as an organizational issue within NGDOs has been best documented by Northern agencies; this has introduced an element of bias. Moreover, in addition to pressures from local women, Southern and Eastern NGDOs' appreciation of gender has been influenced by Northern demands and sometimes negative reactions to them. Put another way, whatever their merits, Northern initatives towards better gender relations have provoked the feeling that this type of sensitivity is a Northern cultural imposition, especially among men. Whatever the justification for this response, putting gender-sensitive rhetoric into practice is tough because it requires getting into the 'deep structure' of organizational psychology and stereotyping, which are culturally determined.

The journey we make in this section begins with a restatement of why gender is a crucial issue in NGDO development work. Then, to see the historical trajectory, we look briefly at how the appreciation of gender has evolved in the aid system, leading to today's concern with gender in organizations as well as in development initiatives. Altering gender aspects of NGDOs usually meets with resistance. Why and what can be done about it, are therefore the next topics to address. Finally, we look at the way gender issues shape North–South relationships between NGDOs and how this aspect of their interaction can be made more constructive.

Why is gender an issue for NGDOs?

Why should gender be at the forefront of NGDO concerns? First, social justice as a moral imperative calls for direct attention to who wins and who loses in society. While varying by degree, place and time, women systematically lose out to men in terms of access to society's resources and power over decisions. Further, as producers, women are usually responsible for providing the subsistence foodstuffs and informal 'off-farm' incomes which determine family survival. Consequently, their efforts, abilities and incentives are vital factors in determining the profile and scale of poverty. An additional developmental reason is that investments in women have a greater tendency to translate into increased household well-being than into consumption. Socially, women are central in maintaining cohesion, stability and local organizational capacity. All are important conditions for ensuring the sustainability of benefits which result from development interventions. Women's fertility determines long-term population growth rates. Their control over reproduction translates into the threshold above which economic growth can mean per capita improvements. In short, for an NGDO to be blind to the position and concerns of women is to choose ineffectiveness. Some observers would say that it is an inexcusable sign of deep-lying organizational prejudice.

The trajectory: from WID to GAD

For most of the 1970s and 1980s, the appreciation of gender was framed in terms of the position and development needs of women. In keeping with its standard mode of operation, the aid system and NGDOs defined projects specifically for women and established women's units to promote their interests. Generally speaking, WID became an add-on, something parallel to what was already being done out there or set up as an entity with responsibility for women, the rest of the organization carrying on as before. Women's issues became a ghetto.[2]

While WID is still around, a more recent trend is gender in development (GAD). This takes as its starting point the definition of gender: sexual specificity in culturally determined perspectives on the roles and relationships between men and women, rather than the position of women per se. GAD acknowledges gender differences and disaggregates development work and impacts in terms of men and women as complementary actors. While the GAD approach aims to improve quality of life for all, gender analysis concentrates on how existing patterns and structures in gender relations can be modified in favour of greater balance and equity.[3]

The shift to GAD from WID stemmed, among others, from the way in which governments had taken women's concerns on board. In the South, the response was initially due to donor pressure. Establishing specialist women's units, which is what governments and NGDOs did, may have provided a focal point but also marginalized their impact. In response to this experience, greater attention is now being paid not just to GAD, as opposed to WID thinking, but also to mainstreaming gender awareness throughout organizations. In other words, there is now a realization that a major impediment to applying gender principles in development work is within organizations themselves – the problem is not just out there with projects. But, to be effective, strategies need to be underpinned by an analysis of obstacles which stand in the way of gender awareness. What does this mean for NGDOs?

Box 27.1 Obstacles to a Gender-fair NGDO Culture

A gender-fair organizational culture is one which recognizes and draws on the complementary potential of men and women's life experiences and competencies in all aspects of organizational life.

Covert obstacles
Covert obstacles arise from deep-lying but dimly understood attitudes of the organization's power holders, usually imported from patriarchal cultural surroundings. Typical attitudes are:

- assuming that women are best suited to support roles;
- applying male norms to everyone's behaviour;
- repressed anxiety about female rejection which translates into keeping women in their place, including overt disrespect, control, violence and sexual harassment;
- treating female authority as something to be countered, contained or marginalized;
- disrespect for femininity and hence feminine principles in organizational behaviour, often signalled by sexist humour;
- inability to accommodate different communication styles: non-assertive women are ignored, while forcefulness is criticized as unfeminine.

Overt obstacles
Overt obstacles result from covert feelings and prevent women from making their full contribution to organizational functioning. They include:

- too few women in positions of authority;
- tokenism, which allocates professional women to stereotyped functions, such as secretaries and personnel officers, rather than line managers;
- assessments which are used to subvert change;
- defensive action which argues that biases against women are an inviolable part of existing culture rather than a failure to be remedied;
- an over-proportion of women in non-professional positions, creating low expectations for and about women's value;
- working hours and lack of facilities which act as barriers to women who are mothers;
- downplaying the importance of gender as a legitimate organization-wide issue.

Source: Adapted from a contribution by Nicky May

The gender of NGDOs

As organizations, NGDOs are not gender neutral.[4] By and large, NGDO organizations reflect rather than contradict wider society with its stereotypical views of women; here, women act as servers of men; seldom function as decision- or policy-

makers; and are seen as women first and workers second.[5] Judgement on performance differs, with women having to prove themselves by being twice as good as men.
Norms of behaviour, rules, physical structures, organizational divisions of power
and tasks, and functional categories naturally tend to reflect and favour men rather
than women. And, importantly, informal communication, decision-making and
negotiation take place in male preserves.[6]

Patriarchal bias in organizational culture does not mean that NGDOs are not
feminine in their development work – far from it. NGDOs are essentially caring
institutions, concerned enough about an aspect of society to do something about it.
This difference implies either a discontinuity or tension between a feminine development approach and masculine organizational culture – an inconsistency which
contributes to frustration, reduced effectiveness and, on occasion, wholesale questioning of the sincerity of leaders/managers. Reaching effective gender-fair development
work would, therefore, be aided by gender, fair NGDO culture and practice. What
commonly stands in the way of this happening is summarized in Box 27.1.

Making NGDO Culture More Gender-balanced and Fair

What do you do if your NGDO believes that gender must feature more strongly in
its culture? Existing experience suggests the following items for NGDOs interested
in becoming more gender-sensitive and fair.

First, have a holistic view of what needs to be changed organizationally. This
would include:

Identity:
• ensure gender features in belief and value statements;
• establish policies about gender in the organization and in development;
• ensure the governance system is gender-fair.

Structure and systems:
• set targets for women at different staffing levels;
• create job structures which recognize gender features and their relative contributions, such as female communications officers for issues affecting women's
  rights;
• arrange provision for child care;
• have gender specialists with systems which clarify their contribution and degree
  of influence;
• build alliances to learn about and promote gender-sensitive approaches;
• collect gender disaggregated data for all planning activities and for assessment
  of organizational performance.

People:
• provide gender training for managers;
• include gender awareness in recruitment and selection;
• include gender as an item in staff development;
• have gender training scheduled for all employees, including women;

- create mixed gender teams whenever appropriate.

Second, specialist gender skills (in a unit) should be complimented with mainstreaming – both are necessary. Avoid compartmentalizing or tokenism. Third, avoid deflection through endless studies or dilution of policy to a lowest common denominator.

If these are things which need to be done, how can they be implemented? Experience from Northern agencies provides the pointers and strategies to be found in Box 27.2.

Box 27.2 Strategies for Creating a Gender-balanced NGDO Culture

Altering organizational culture is the most difficult and time-consuming type of organizational change. It is a long-term process which requires commitment and perseverance. People are loath to address, let alone give up, ingrained, subconscious beliefs and attitudes in which they are secure. This must be respected. To change culture, go carefully, but with conviction.

Preconditions
A number of preconditions must be in place if change strategies are to be meaningful. The following are important:

- The leadership, even if not convinced, should not be actively opposed to gender fairness (forcing it on partners is counter-productive).
- Resources for change, including time, should be overtly allocated; activities must not be treated as an add-on to business as usual.
- Change management should be a recognized responsibility with agreed progress indicators.

Strategies and steps
Strategies:
- Change should be incremental, comprehensive and iterative – that is, continually returning to check on responses, problems and achievements.
- Getting and keeping people on board is vital.
- Deal with people's reservations; do not disregard the value of resistance.

Steps:
- Start a process of diagnosis analysis.
- Introduce frameworks and tools for gender analysis, linking external cultural dimensions to what is happening internally.
- Identify the myths and prejudices existing within and between men and women in the organization.
- Place organizational culture in the context of life-cycle; identify where forces for and against change are likely to lie.

BOX 27.2 CONTINUED

- Build consensus on what sort of change is needed over what timescale. Do not give up. Cultural change is an iterative and incremental process, especially when management is not ready.
- Diagnose the personal reorientation needs in terms of individual knowledge, attitude and working relations with others.
- Introduce training, counselling and team-building.
- Identify outside allies, such as women's organizations, who can support the direction of change by providing information, experience and advice.
- Periodically monitor progress and provide organization-wide feedback on what is being achieved.
- Gradually reduce the intensity of change activities, but do not stop because organizational change is a constant process.

Source: Adapted from a contribution by Nick May

Gender fairness is also a common subject of dialogue between partner NGDOs who may be at different stages in appreciating its importance. How can this, often cross-cultural, dialogue be made effective?

Gender in NGDO Partnerships

Initially, acknowledgement of the gender dimensions of development was not equally shared or valued between NGDOs. An old complaint from the South was that gender issues were an imposition and conditionality. However, the women's movement in the South and the Beijing NGDO Conference have shown that gender issues are not simply Northern priorities pushed along the aid chain, but exist within the lives of women everywhere. But while the hurdle of imposition has been pushed aside, there are still differences in perception between North, South and East in how gender issues can best be understood and addressed within organizations. In striving for partnership, how can such differences be addressed between NGDOs from different cultures?

Difficulties arising from dialogues about gender in NGDO partnerships are related to other issues as well. However, because gender gets to the heart of social relations, there is little doubt that this topic is one of the most difficult to deal with; doing so calls for gender to be an integral part of a human resource strategy. A seminar organized by a confederation of European NGDOs came to the following advice when placing gender within the context of partnership.[7] As with all approaches to the dimensions of culture, the first step is to be aware of cultural history and organizational values.

Changes should be identified and summarized in order to encourage gender fairness. Dialogue should be used to:

- explore and prioritize respective positions;
- create a consensus wherever possible and acknowledge differences where they occur;
- look for likely internal and external resistance to proposed changes.

It is helpful, furthermore, to do a disaggregated stakeholder analysis in order to look for those actors who are likely to accept or reject change. Clarify the required personal attitudes of those who may function as change agents.

- Be clear about how organizationally deep change should go and then sort out differences according to time frames.
- Make an assessment of the other forces and factors in play, arriving at a reasoned guess of the chances of success.
- Agree on an ongoing participative process for monitoring.
- Encourage donor sensitivity about the links between gender and funding conditions.

Recipients should also be clear about limits to change and use this as a reference point for dialogue, to ensure that their own identity is not compromised.

Notes

1   This chapter draws on input and advice from Nicky May. I am very grateful for her guidance and education on gender in development and in NGDOs.
2   Moser, 1993; Oestergaaard, 1993.
3   See *The Oxfam Handbook of Development and Relief*, 1993, pp200–211.
4   Goetz, 1992.
5   My own observations suggest that a comparison between non-profits and commercial companies would show a higher proportion of women further up in the organization, but I do not know of any study which would confirm or refute this.
6   Golf courses, clubs and male toilets are not unusual locations.
7   MacDonald, 1994b.

References

Goetz, Anne-Marie (1992) 'Gender and administration', *Bulletin*, Vol 23, No 4, Institute of Development Studies, University of Sussex, Brighton.
MacDonald, M (1994) 'Gender in partnership: Eurostep gender workshop 2', Eurostep, Brussels.
Moser, C (1993) *Gender Planning and Development: Theory, Practice and Training*, Routledge, London.
Oestergaard, L (ed) (1993) *Gender and Development: A Practical Guide*, Routledge, London.
Oxfam (1996) *Handbook of Development and Relief*, Oxfam, Oxford.

28

Organizational Gender Diagnosis

Ellen Sprenger

This framework was developed by Ellen Sprenger[1], who is the senior policy adviser on Gender and Development for Novib. It is based on Tichy[2] and is further adapted from ETC, the Netherlands. We invite you to do-it-yourself and rate your organization. The purpose is to examine the level of gender balance within an organization, identify areas of weakness and to develop strategies and action plans for improvement.

At a recent staff workshop, some Olive staff applied this to their organization.[3] Despite initial scepticism regarding 'rating' themselves, they found it an immensely illuminating and graphic way of looking at their organization. They also found the framework to be applicable to areas outside of gender. The questions asked are very useful for any diagnosis.

For an organization to function, three crucial elements are needed:

- a mission or mandate
- an organizational structure
- human resources.

To get insight into the functioning of an organization we need to ask questions about:

- the technical
- political, and
- cultural points of view of an organization.

Each of these six areas is placed in a framework and elaborated below.

When putting these three crucial elements together with the three viewpoints in the form of a framework, *nine building blocks of an organization* can be identified.

Framework for Quick Organizational Gender Scanning

Each of the nine blocks has questions attached to it (given in diagrammatic form on p417):

Block 1: Policies and Action
- Are the mission and mandate of the organization based on a thorough analysis of the context, including gender relations?

With this we mean goals and strategies, including all the managerial processes to realize those goals.

With this we mean clarity on tasks, responsibilities, and authorities within the organization, ways of working, flow of information and communication, and learning within the organization; includes external stakeholders.

With this we mean staff recruitment, staff development, performance appraisal and non-financial reward and incentive systems, and attitudinal issues.

How are social, technical and financial resources organized in order to produce the desired output in the most efficient manner?

Who influences whom and about what? This question relates to power and resource allocation and to who reaps the benefits.

Who talks to whom about what? This question relates to the relations network, values, standards, beliefs and interpretations shared by staff.

	Mission or mandate	Organizational structure	Human resources
Technical point of view	Block 1	Block 4	Block 7
Political point of view	Block 2	Block 5	Block 8
Cultural point of view	Block 3	Block 6	Block 9

- Does the organization have a clear policy which includes a gender policy?
- Does the gender policy include an activity plan with time frames (for example, moments for monitoring and evaluation) and allocation of responsibilities?
- Are adequate financial resources allocated for the implementation of the gender policy?
- Does the organization conduct its monitoring and evaluation and strategic planning in a gender disaggregated manner?
- Does the product of the organization contribute to the empowerment of women and changing unequal gender relations at target group level?

Block 2: Policy Influence

- Do management and board take responsibility for policy development and implementation in the field of gender?
- Does management promote internal consultations on issues related to policy development and implementation?
- Are there many interactions with external stakeholders such as beneficiaries (women and men), pressure or interest groups, researchers, consultants, gender networks and institutes, politicians, donor agencies, and so on?
- Are opinions of external stakeholders valued and taken seriously by management?

Block 3: Organizational Culture

- Does gender fit into the image of the organization according to staff?
- Does everyone feel ownership over the gender policy?
- Do women within the organization and among beneficiaries, perceive the organization to be woman friendly?
- Does the organization comply with gender – sensitive behaviour, for example, the language used, jokes and comments made, images and materials displayed and procedures on sexual harassment?
- Does the organization have a reputation of integrity and competence on gender issues, for example, among women's organizations and (outside) individuals with commitment to gender issues?

Block 4: Tasks and Responsibilities

- Are tasks and responsibilities in the field of gender clearly demarcated?
- Are effective mechanisms in place for coordination, consultation and organizational gender learning between various parts of the organization, both horizontally and vertically?
- Are there sufficient information to do the job well?
- Are staff with specific gender expertise and responsibilities, located at key positions in the organization?
- Is the existing gender structure (for example, a women's or gender unit versus one or more individuals at decentralized locations; or one full-time staff member versus several part-time staff members) the most appropriate one?

Block 5: Decision-making

- Are decisions being made on the basis of monitoring and evaluation exercises, among others, in the field of gender?

- Are staff, including gender specialists, participating in decision-making processes?
- Are decisions (in the field of gender) dealt with in a timely manner?
- Are conflicts in the workplace dealt with adequately – for example, around issues of sexual harassment, dealing with resistance to gender or side effects of affirmative action?

Block 6: Cooperation and learning

- Does the organization promote teamwork, involving both women and men and including gender focal persons?
- Do staff members support each other in problem-solving and identification of new challenges in the field of gender?
- Does the organization promote exchange, collaboration and other forms of inter-action with women's organizations and organizations, institutions or individuals active in the field of gender?
- Are new innovative ideas and practices welcomed, reflected upon and incorporated into existing practices?

Block 7: Staff and Expertise

- Is management committed to promoting female representation at all levels of the organization, including the board?
- Is this commitment translated into concrete targets and time frames?
- Is new staff selected on the basis of gender sensitivity and capacity to deal with gender issues in very practical terms?
- Do men and women receive equal pay for equal work? Are job descriptions clearly defined (as far as gender is concerned)?
- Are gender issues discussed during performance appraisal interviews?
- Is there a gradual increase of gender expertise among all staff members – for example, as a result of training?

Block 8: Room for Manoeuvre

- Does the organization allow space for staff who wish to organize around parts of their identity (for example, sex, religion, ethnicity, age, sexual preference, physical ability)?
- Does the organization have an adequate infrastructure to enable female staff to carry out their work (for example, in relation to safe working environment, toilet facilities, transport arrangements, working hours)?
- Is good performance being rewarded, including in the field of gender – for example, by making good practices available to others, both inside and outside the organization, or by congratulating individual staff members?
- Do staff value different styles of working – for example, men and women in non-traditional fields of work, more formal or less formal working environments, leadership styles, ways of chairing meetings, and so on?
- Are interesting career opportunities offered to both women and men?

	Mission or mandate	Organizational structure	Human resources
Technical point of view	**1 Policies and Action** • analysis • policy • activity plan • budget • monitoring and evaluation • impact	**4 Tasks and Responsibilities** • coordination and consultation • information system • gender infrastructure	**7 Expertise** • quantity • quality; recruitment • wages • job description • appraisal • training
Political point of view	**2 Policy Influence** • role of management • people influencing the organization from within • people who influence the organization from the outside	**5 Decision-making** • adequate information • participation in discussion and decision-making • conflict management	**8 Room for Manoeuvre** • space for organizing • physical infrastructure • reward or incentive systems • diversity of styles • career opportunities
Cultural point of view	**3 Organizational Culture** • image • ownership • woman friendliness • reputation	**6 Cooperation and Learning** • teamwork • support • networking outside of organization • reflection and innovation	**9 Attitude** • enthusiasm • commitment • willingness to change • stereotyping

Block 9: Attitude

• Are staff enthusiastic about the work they do?
• Are staff committed to the implementation of the gender policy?
• Are staff open to new ideas and innovation and is there a willingness to change practices?
• Is gender taken seriously and discussed openly by men and women?
• Is stereotyping (for example, 'those gender-blind men' or 'those feminists') addressed and countered by individual staff members?

The actual diagnosis consists of four steps:

1 Scanning –taking a picture
Answer the different questions per block and grade them:

1 – high score
2 – medium score
3 – low score

Calculate the average per block. You can now see which blocks are stronger and which are weaker, by identifying the high-, medium- or low-scoring blocks.

It is important to keep in mind the external context of the organization so that the appraisal is contextualized. What could be high performance in one situation could very well be low performance in another. It is also recommended to do this scanning exercise with different people from the same organization or people who know the organization well.

2 Dynamic analysis
The objective of the dynamic analysis is to analyse the functioning of the organiza-tion. On the basis of the scan we need to ask the following questions:

*   Why is it the way it is?
*   What changes are currently taking place?
*   How can strengths and weaknesses be explained?

In answering the questions three types of dynamics should be addressed:

History – present (for example, has something changed over time? How has the organization responded to the changing external environment?)

Internal – External (for example, what external factors are influencing the organi-zation? Are there specific external expectations or demands?)

Top – Bottom (for example, how are decisions being made? Who introduces change or innovation? What are the energy points in the organization?)

*   What are the main strengths and weaknesses the dynamic helps you to identify?
*   Go back to the nine building-blocks and identify which blocks correspond with the now identified strengths and weaknesses. The dynamic analysis adds an extra dimension to your earlier quick scan. Consequently, the outcome could be different.

3 Diagnosing
The objective of diagnosing is to identify strategies for change. For a strategy to be successful a number of requirements need to be met:

*   It needs to be explanatory.
*   It should be based on an understanding of the organization.
*   It should be acceptable to the organization.
*   It should be realistic.

What strategies for change can be identified? In which building-block do you want to start (entry point)? Which building-block refers to the objective you want to attain (exit point)?

Write 'entry point' in the building-block you want to start with and indicate with arrows how you want to reach your exit point (i.e. objective). Including other building blocks could be an option. This is your strategy or route through the organization.

4 Activity plan – identifying what to do
On the basis of the dynamic analysis and diagnosis you can now identify activities that will help you to follow your route and attain the objective. Write down key activities per identified building-block.

Notes

1   Ellen's areas of special focus include organization development, monitoring and evaluation, and feminist leadership development. She is co-author of the recently published *Gender and Organizational Change – bridging the gap between policy and practice* (Macdonald, Sprenger, Dubel (1997), KIT Press). Currently, Ellen is the coordinator of the Oxfam International Gender and Diversity Working group. She welcomes feedback on this approach at ellen.sprenger@novib.nl

2   Tichy, N (1983) *Managing Strategic Change – technical, political and cultural dynamics.* University of Michigan, John Wyley & Sons Publications

3   This chapter initially appeard as an article in *OD Debate* in February 1998. *OD Debate* is produced and published by Olive (Organization Development and Training) in South Africa (http:// www.epages.net/olive).

Part 10

Human Resources:
Their Management, Development
and Leadership

29

Leadership and Management

Allan Kaplan

Leadership: Art and Discipline

'To become a centre of influence holding people together is a grave matter and fraught with great responsibility. It requires greatness of spirit, consistency, and strength. Therefore let him who wishes to gather others about him ask himself whether he is equal to the undertaking ...' *I Ching*

Allow the questions implied by the quotation to enter into you. Are you a leader? Do you wish to lead? If leadership is required of you, do you have the will to develop yourself such that you can assume the gravity with sufficient responsibility? Are you willing to learn? For as the words above attest, leadership is no light matter.

Leadership is about responsibility. It requires acceptance of the importance of one's self, coupled with appreciation for the greater importance of others over oneself; leadership entails liability for those whom one leads. Leadership thereby becomes a discipline in its own right. It is not something 'added-on' to one's other responsibilities, professional expertise or sundry duties. Leadership must be learned – studied and exercised – as a discipline in its own right – indeed, as the most taxing discipline of all. Taxing not least because leadership is an art rather than a science. There is no set of rules. Guidelines yes, to attune oneself to the process and dynamics of the people and lives one is given responsibility for; and techniques to aid one's facilitation. But life remains beyond one's control, inherently unpredictable and forever responding to one's interventions. The consequences of the leader's decisions and actions are not given to the leader at the time of making them. One is always adapting as consequences reveal themselves, yet always accepting responsibility, in spite of the unpredictability.

The inherent contradiction contained in having to take responsibility for a reality which is unpredictable and therefore beyond one's ultimate control is but one of the many tensions which form the context within which leadership is exercised. Exerting authority in a way which allows others freedom to develop their own creativity is another. The need for immediate yet inclusive decision-making and the importance of encouraging participation to ensure collective ownership of organizational strategy while having to demonstrate strong visionary capability oneself is yet another. The list is endless; this is the very stuff of leadership. Holding these contradictions in creative tension demands a maturity of a very high order; the kind of maturity we associate with wisdom rather than simply with knowledge or skill. Such is the challenge and such is the reward. For leadership is more than responsibility; it is also a privilege.

Privilege, of course, is a double-edged sword. It is a gift which is bestowed, but it is also power to be wielded. Privilege brings power, and leadership is about nothing if it is not about power. Intrinsic to the nature of power is its potential abuse; power does have the ability to corrupt, hence the importance of recognizing the necessity for cultivating wisdom rather than relying merely on skill and knowledge. It is equally necessary, however, not to deny or avoid the attribute of power. Without the element of power we lose a defining characteristic of leadership, not in the negative but in the positive sense.

Either through position or personality, the leader has the power to impact on the world, to change the world. This, in fact, is the essence of leadership: the leader is one who does not accept the limitations of a given situation or set of circumstances, but acts to transform such constraints into new realities and takes responsibility for the privilege. Leadership, then, is more than a job; it is a calling. What, therefore, do we need to know in order to practise leadership with dignity?

Ambiguity and contradiction

The tensions that arise out of contradictions are the very stuff of leadership. Ambiguity and uncertainty, those corollaries of contradiction, are the terrain within which, and upon which, leadership is exercised. Leadership is about being able to act decisively given ambiguity and uncertainty, rather than in the absence of these things. Bad leadership often results from a denial of this reality. To act decisively and to take responsibility for one's actions while knowing and acknowledging that one may be proved wrong through no 'fault' of one's own, and that there is no final way of knowing, is the mark of the great leader, the leader who shows 'greatness of spirit'.

A major form of ambiguity and contradiction that the leader needs to embrace as a primary responsibility, is that between 'holding the whole' and 'breaking boundaries'. The leader is responsible for the 'collectivity', for the 'communal whole'. Communication, transparency and consultation, and the understanding that 'a convoy only moves as fast as the slowest ship' (Lievegoed, 1978, p5), inform the activities aimed at protecting the boundaries of the community for which one is responsible. Yet the downside of these activities is that they can lead to isolation of the community and loss of relevance.

The leader is also responsible for maintaining the community or organization at the cutting edge, for ensuring that it has a cutting edge. Thus the leader is responsible for breaking the boundaries of received knowledge, of 'common sense', of patterns of thinking and behaving which have built themselves into routines over the years, routines which lull people to sleep. The leader has to maintain continuity while simultaneously promoting change. The intersection between letting go of the old and taking on the new, is most often a place of uncertainty where rules are broken, and habit and routine are replaced with periods of chaos.

Managing chaos

The leader is thus often called upon to act and to maintain a stable, though not fixed, centre, in the midst of swirling chaos. Peter Vaill, in Managing as a Performing Art, uses the metaphor of white-water rafting to describe the kind of chaos to which the leader is subjected, and maintains that the myth of leadership assumes that there are periods of calm in between the rapids, where the river is placid and slow, and one can relax. This is a myth, says Vaill (1991, p30); in reality chaos is a permanent part of the terrain, not an aberration or particularity.

Vaill decries the tendency to isolate 'leadership competencies' from the person practising leadership and then to assume that such 'competencies' exist independently as lists of functions, tasks and skills that can be learned on short courses. The leadership role, he says, calls for 'individuality, it calls for the whole person' (Vaill, 1991, p19). It calls for a developmental approach to assuming a leadership capacity within oneself, rather than a 'quick fix' approach.

Lievegoed (1981) contrasts what he calls the 'philosophy of efficiency' with the 'philosophy of surplus'. The philosophy of efficiency is the lazy approach; the attempt to do more with less. In these terms, the shortest courses of 'add-on competencies' are the way to train leadership. The philosophy of surplus, however, is the wellspring of creativity; rather than being content with superficiality one deepens oneself, one's self-knowledge, the concepts with which one works, so that one does not simply repeat techniques and skills that may have been appropriate in previous situations, but adapts out of a reservoir within oneself, to respond with creativity to new situations.

Self-development

Self-development is the path required of the person who would be leader. There is no substitute for working on oneself, for knowing oneself. There is no substitute for questioning everything, for taking nothing for granted, for looking beneath and behind the skills and techniques one is taught, at the underlying paradigms, so that one obtains mastery over them, freedom to challenge and adapt and refashion.

Self-development is important too, because leadership needs to be versatile in order to respond to different situations differently, rather than narrow, responding to all situations in the same way. Organizations and communities develop, grow and change; people differ, circumstances vary. The leader should be able to tap different parts of him/herself appropriate to the time and place. According to Elaine Yarborough (1985, pp55–63), we have an orchestra inside ourselves. We need to learn to play all of the instruments rather than just a few; and we need to be able to conduct, to allow all the different parts of oneself to play as one whole.

Many parts of ourselves have never been used, or lie hidden, unable to be tapped. But other parts are denied, avoided, pushed deep down into the unconscious and repressed. It is these denied aspects of ourselves that pose the greatest danger to the development of leadership capacity within oneself.

The shadow

Depth psychology uses the concept of the shadow to denote those parts of oneself which one denies. Robert Johnson (1991) describes it as follows:

> The shadow is that part of us we fail to see or know... We all are born whole and, let us hope, will die whole. But somewhere early on our way, we eat one of the wonderful fruits of the tree of knowledge, things separate into good and evil, and we begin the shadow-making process; we divide our lives. In the cultural process we sort out our God-given characteristics into those that are acceptable to society and those that have to be put away. This is wonderful and necessary, and there would be no civilised behaviour without this sorting out of good and evil. But the refused and unacceptable characteristics do not go away; they only collect in the dark corners of our personality. When they have been hidden long enough, they take on a life of their own – the shadow life. The shadow is that which has not entered adequately into consciousness. It is the despised quarter of our being. It often has an energy potential nearly as great as our ego.

Second, and simultaneously, the shadow takes on a life of its own. That which is repressed ends up by being unconsciously projected on to things, and particularly people, in the outside world. So the leader denies promotional opportunities for those he calls 'soft' people, or will not listen to their advice; at the extreme, he denies the accountant's advice because the accountant is conciliatory and self-effacing, and the organization begins to fail financially. Such a person is not fit to lead.

Yet such people do lead. Such situations occur all the time. It is not that one needs to be perfect, nor that one should have mastered and understood oneself before taking up the mantle of leadership. However, leaders do need to commit themselves to such a process, and the problem is that people often rise to leadership by a tendency towards extraversion, which can mean a tendency to ignore what is going on inside themselves. The link between leadership and self-knowledge calls us to re-examine that denial of the inner life.

Authority

Effective leadership, ultimately, does not depend on position; it depends on the respect that one can command. It depends on real authority, rather than on ambition or manipulation or contrived structuring. Such things will work for a time, but will eventually fail. It is worthwhile to note that the root of the word 'authority' is 'author'. One develops authentic authority by becoming the author of one's circumstances, instead of the subject. And to be the author of one's life requires self-mastery, sure-footedness and the ability to adapt one's story where necessary.

These things may read theoretically, but their verification lies in your own reflections. Think only of the leaders you have known whom you respect, whom you would follow, whom you would regard as authentic. There is no substitute for authenticity, for honesty or for transparency. It may be that the real leader is recognized by his or her ability to ask the right questions, rather than through being able to come up with ready answers.

Asking the right questions reveals reality, lays it bare, so to speak, in a way that ready answers never can. The faculty of questioning enables something more to happen. It opens the leadership function up to allow other members of the group to participate, to question and attempt answers. It encourages creativity and insight in others, as well as ownership. And the ultimate test of leadership, the ultimate privilege of power, is the ability, given power, to hold that power in check so that others can begin to lead, to gain power themselves. Facilitating the growth of leadership in others is perhaps the highest form of the art of leadership, and its greatest triumph.

Leadership: Function and Stance

' ... style is no substitute for substance ... ' *John Heider*

What are the major areas of focus for the leader of an organization; and how should the leader mediate his or her primary functions? I should like to start with two broad statements.

First, leaders are responsible for ensuring that their organization performs effectively with respect to its aims and objectives. The organization needs to have impact, and it needs to be relevant and appropriate impact. Simultaneously, the leader is responsible for maintaining the organization such that it remains capable of accomplishing its tasks. Put another way – to use Covey's (1989) phraseology – one of the failures of leadership is that it often concentrates on organizational production to the virtual exclusion of maintaining the production capacity of the organization.

Second, the essence of leadership lies in ensuring that both 'production' and 'production capacity' have their place simultaneously, and that creativity arises out of the tension between the two. The quest is for balance rather than compromise. Different organizations will call for different emphases at different times; different people will require different approaches from leadership in order to facilitate development. The leader should be in control therefore of both polarities and the continuum between them, rather than at the mercy of conflicting possibilities and personal biases.

A model for organizational leadership

In organizational life, which areas does the leader need to concentrate on most? Which areas stand out as demanding the leader's attention? How does the leader 'read' these areas, recognize where the strengths and weaknesses lie, and identify what form of intervention will increase organizational excellence?

The model discussed in the following pages to answer these questions consists of three sets of polarities. Each set concerns one element of organizational life, while the polarities themselves are diametrically opposed ways of dealing with these elements.

First set
Organizations consist of people; they are nothing without them. People are, indeed, the very reason for organizational formation. The richness of an organization, the quality of its work, the value of its output – all these are dependent, above all, on the people who staff it.

First Element – People

People are notoriously different. As a leader it is your responsibility to aim for the ideal, in order actually to achieve a moderately productive environment. And the ideal is a community of souls wherein each is able to participate and find meaning, in which people respect each other as well as the rules that arise to regulate their behaviour, and where individual creativity is able to flower.

There are a number of aspects of organizational life which relate directly to the development of a community of people, and where the leader should therefore have an overview: staff recruitment and induction, the legal and economic conditions of employment, and human resource development (staff training, monitoring and evaluation and supervision, the reflective practices of the organization, counselling and development). Team-building and conflict resolution also fall within this element, as does communication. Direct involvement is not demanded; delegation is an important leadership capacity that should be used intelligently. But a direct grasp of the strategy and efficacy of each of these areas is essential.

First Polarity – Confronting/Supporting

The leader is responsible for the development of his or her colleagues such that they are able to build their own capacity and thus become ever greater assets to the organization and its work. Assisting people with their own development processes requires the ability to work in two opposing modalities. One is the modality of confrontation; the other that of support.

Yarborough (1983) refers to these two modalities as 'hard' and 'soft' interventions. Hard intervention skills involve confrontation; suggestions or advocacy for change; teaching a specific skill; indicating that you as leader will not tolerate certain specific behaviours. Hard interventions are often necessary but always dangerous. They may signal a projection of the leader's shadow, rather than an objective response to events. A special awareness is called for. Even if hard interventions succeed brilliantly, there is often little cause for celebration. There has been an injury. Someone's process has been violated.

Soft interventions do not break into other people's processes. They are an attempt to provide support, and as such they assume trust in the ability and integrity of the other. Soft interventions are nurturing and collaborative. They involve forming tentative guesses about the meaning of behaviour, reflecting behaviours that are observed without interpretation, indicating to people the consequences of their behaviour, or simply changing a response to a person or group without giving direct feedback. Soft interventions involve waiting longer than usual to intervene; trusting that people can and will reach their own conclusions about productive behaviour, and providing a structure for them to do this.

Both hard and soft interventions, and thought-through responses to people and situations should be considered. At different times one needs to be directive or facilitative. Leaders need to cultivate the ability to do to both.

Second set

Organizations are known by what they do, although sometimes more by what they purport to do than by what they actually do, a problem closer to the heart of development and human service organizations than to commercial organizations, which at least produce a quantifiable product. For NGOs, the quality of the work they do, or the external effect of this work, is more important, yet less easy to evaluate. Hence the potential for deluding both self and others is that much greater. Establishing and sustaining a 'true' identity is thus of major importance for NGOs and a primary concern for leadership.

Second Element – Identity

It is the leader's job to keep the organization at the cutting edge of its particular field, to ensure that the organization is doing the right thing, is relevant, effective and in demand. It is also important that individual staff members partake in the organizational identity, draw meaning and motivation from it and feel that it is theirs, that they can own it and develop it and give their all. Organizational identity comes not simply from organizational aims and objectives, but also from the efficacy of these aims and objectives; how well the organization performs and how much impact they have on the user or client.

There are, then, two areas of organizational identity that the leader must concentrate on: forward direction and the assessment of achievements to date – and, of course, the interaction between the two.

Forward direction involves clarifying the organizational mission, which is dependent on both the context in which the organization finds itself and the particular set of creative visions incorporated in its staff. Mission needs to be operationalized. We need to move beyond broad vision to strategy, the 'how' of accomplishing aims with a scarcity of resources and in the midst of environmental constraints. The leader, therefore, is responsible for maintaining a constant watch on the environment and context; to ensure that vision is held collectively and not simply in the hands of a few people; to strategize around it, to do detailed planning, to be aware of timing, deadlines, logistics and the interaction of people and departments or programmes. There is a need for individual planning and accountability as well as for group synergy.

At the same time, work on forward direction needs to be balanced and informed by the assessment of achievements. Evaluation and monitoring are important areas for leadership. Individuals, programmes, the organizational vision or mission itself, should be monitored and evaluated constantly, not simply in terms of whether we have done what we said we would do, but how well we have done it and where we can improve. This is the arena for organizational learning, for the development of a learning organization, of an organizational culture which is open to critique and challenge, which asks itself the hard questions and is able to respond appropriately.

Second Polarity – Focusing/Grounding

The leader should be able to focus and prioritize. In order to do so the leader needs two faculties. The first is the capacity to envision, to project him- or herself and his or her organization into an unknown future, to imagine that which is yet to come, to see opportunities where others see threats, and to see the gift and challenge brought by crisis and danger.

The second is the ability to choose a course of action, which is easily said, but in fact one of the toughest leadership tasks of all, for all choice involves sacrifice. The leader is not simply a visionary; neither is the leader simply the one who can cut to the heart of the matter and make the hard choices quickly. Focusing involves both.

Moving from focusing to grounding, we see a similar interweaving of opposing forms. Grounding is an activity related more to analytical than to conceptual thinking. Grounding is concentrating not on what could be but on what is, not on what we should be achieving but on what we are, or have, achieved. Grounding is moving away from the future to look squarely at the constraints of the present. Grounding is also the attempt to build institutional memory, to establish precedents on which to base our focusing activities.

Third set

Organizations require form; they are not anarchic collectives of free-floating activity. They require rules, procedures, conditions of service. Neither democracy, nor equality, nor productive fellowship can be achieved without them. Rules, procedures and structures can, however, paralyse an organization and inhibit creativity. Organizations need to keep structures and rules to a minimum.

Third Element – Structure

Structures and procedures should be designed to enhance rather than inhibit communication. They should be transparent so that all staff can understand them and operate freely within them. All structures will entail some degree of hierarchy, for hierarchy is an intrinsic attribute of complex structure.

Structures include the division of work into manageable units and procedures for integrating them into the organization as a whole. Structures include decision-making procedures and communication channels. Structures also articulate lines of accountability and procedures for ensuring that accountability enhances rather than inhibits productivity and creativity. Leaders should ensure that structures and procedures match the needs of the organization as it evolves.

Third Polarity – Mobilizing/Giving Meaning

This third element translates into two opposing modalities with respect to leadership. These modalities relate to 'giving meaning' (holding the organization together) and 'mobilizing' (or breaking boundaries). Giving meaning refers to the leader's role in providing a sense of security and familiarity to staff so that they are able to work within a recognizable and coherent framework. People have recourse to a structure that exists in and of itself, rather than at the whim of the leader. The leader embodies a feeling of stability and maturity.

On the other hand, the organization runs the danger of becoming inflexible and getting stuck. It is up to the leader to act as a mobilizing force. The method is one of subversion, of operating from outside the bounds set by the framework and by the norms that have built up in the organization. Rather than a father or mother figure, the leader here is youth – questioning, rebelling, taking nothing for granted. No structures or procedures should be strong enough to hold the leader captive if their time has passed.

Of course, the application of these elements changes as the organization grows, ages and develops. In the early phases of birth and growth, structure is the least important element, and people are swept up in the enthusiasm of the impulse.

Figure 29.1 *A Composite Model for Organizational Leadership*

Organizational mission and strategy are paramount. Later, structure assumes more importance.

Style is no substitute for substance. 'When one has no character one has to apply a method' (Camus, 1983). The point is the same. The development of leadership capacity is the development of substance and character, not merely the assumption of particular skills and techniques appropriate to certain styles of leadership. One must develop the ability to observe what is needed, the faculties to respond with what is needed, and the fluidity to change one's responses with a minimum of inner resistance. One must develop sufficient inner authority to allow the situation to lead one to the correct response.

Leadership: Practice and Development

> On the streets of New York, a man asks directions of two long-haired freaks lounging on the sidewalk. The man is hesitant and shy, dressed in bow-tie and suit, a violin case in his hand. 'What is the best way to get to Carnegie Hall?' he enquires. 'Practise, man, practise' comes the reply.

None of us are born leaders. We all have to develop leadership capacity as we grow. The previous sections describe what we should be striving for as leaders, not what we should expect to be before we become one. Much of what the leader needs to know cannot be learned theoretically, before the job has begun. Experience, and reflection on that experience, is the true guru from whom to learn.

Many who design training courses for leadership will not find this position satisfactory. Yet leadership courses, provided they are conducted in-service can constitute important areas of learning. So too can the reading of books and articles, seminars and talks, and conversations with other leaders – all these things are ways of learning from others and as such are immensely valuable. Nonetheless, there is no substitute for working on oneself, getting to know oneself, and learning through reflection on one's own action. What follows are a number of avenues for working on oneself in the pursuit of leadership excellence.

Observation

The previous sections are predicated on the ability to observe what is going on in order to choose the appropriate response. Accurate observation lies at the heart of successful leadership. There are many ways to improve one's observation skills. Learning to draw or attending art classes, can assist immeasurably in learning to see. Seeing cannot be taken for granted; as with any other skill, it is a learned activity.

One can also engage in listening exercises with colleagues. Some of these might include: holding back from responding to a statement until you have ascertained whether you have heard it correctly; repeating what you have heard in your own words before responding; and attempting to listen on a number of levels at once, thus the content level, the feeling or emotional level, and the level of intentionality (trying to hear beneath the words to the underlying will, or intention, of the speaker).

Intentionally observing what is going on in a meeting in terms of group dynamics and having the space to feed back to the group as a check on accuracy, is another excellent observation exercise. Simply making a pact with colleagues to report to each other on what each has observed on their way to work in the morning is another.

The use of metaphor – imaginatively characterizing what you are seeing through the use of an alternative perspective from another area of life – is often a great aid to insightful observation. For leaders, the metaphor of the hawk is appropriate. The hawk glides high in the sky, calm, relaxed; everything is seen from its high vantage point; the overview is all-encompassing and diffuse. But within the overall, generalized picture the tiny individual mouse is suddenly seen. The ability to focus becomes keen and the hawk will swoop down, accurately and efficiently, to isolate one tiny element within a vast panorama.

Therapy

Many people regard psychotherapy as an indication that a person is sick, or at least has problems that cannot be solved without radical assistance. This is an unfortunate perspective, as we have already seen that there are vast areas of ourselves that are hidden, suppressed or unconscious, that affect the way we respond to the world. Therapy can be an important way of getting to know ourselves better and thus becoming better leaders. There are many forms of therapy to choose from. We should not forget also that there are therapies which do not require the intervention of a therapist, such as taking time out alone, away from the confusions of everyday life, to take stock and centre oneself.

Action-reflection

Observation of one's own action, reflection on that action, and the drawing out of lessons and principles for future action, is perhaps the most important tool of all. There is a standard procedure for action-reflection, depicted in Figure 29.2 below, which can be used as an aid in this process.

Begin with the experiences themselves, observe yourself while you are acting, jot down notes to jog the memory later when you have the chance. Reflect on your experiences, review the things that happened and the way you acted, note foreseen and unforeseen consequences, where plans went awry and where intentions surprised you with success. See if you can find patterns in what you observe, try to draw principles for future behaviour out of these patterns, develop your own learnings and principles (perhaps even your own theory of leadership).

Use these principles to change your behaviour, to plan different and innovative ways of approaching your future leadership tasks.

Figure 29.2 *The Standard Procedure for Action-reflection*

Mentorship and developmental counselling

Action-reflection, performed alone, will only take one so far. The danger is that one's observations are predetermined by how one sees the world, so that one's reflections never break out of the mode of thinking that has already been developed. It helps, then, to have a mentor with whom one can reflect, who can challenge and confront and provide alternative perspectives (and also advice). Coupled with developmental counselling, this can be a powerful tool.

Developmental counselling is a structured form of action-reflection using a mentor, or partner, as counsellor. Structured meetings, held monthly or bi-monthly or even every third month, set the framework for this process. The practitioner writes a report detailing experiences for the period, noting questions which have arisen, reflecting on successes and failures, strengths and weaknesses, omissions in terms of the plan one had set oneself, recurring doubts and problem areas. This report is worked through together with the counsellor in a lengthy session, isolated from interruptions. The counsellor helps the practitioner to reflect objectively, to identify the relevant patterns, and to set new plans and goals for the coming period.

Experience indicates that there is no greater method for developing leadership than the combination of action-reflection and developmental counselling.

Evaluation

Finally, there is no substitute for good, old-fashioned, honest evaluation. This can be a particularly terrifying experience for a leader, particularly one who is insecure. But it is an essential method for learning and improving. It does not need to be viewed as a vote of confidence or no-confidence, nor as a judgement which, if negative, should lead to abdication.

But if the leader is genuinely interested in improving, there are few places where more valuable feedback can be attained than through those whom one is leading. One does not have to take every bit of advice or criticism; people are dealing with their own issues in their feedback. But an evaluation honestly conducted will lead to an underlying picture of the leader which will prove an invaluable tool for self-development.

For this kind of evaluation to work, it is important that the leader does not conduct the evaluation him or herself; that utter confidentiality is assured and maintained; and that leadership feeds back learning to those who participated in the evaluation. In the final analysis this is simple decency, and simple decency will probably take the leader further than technique or skill.

Leadership to Management: Form and Substance

'Trust God, but tie your camel ... ' *Rumi*

The preceding sections have been written as much for managers as for leaders, and indeed these two functions are inseparable. Except perhaps in the early days of organizational creation, no leader will be effective without taking management seriously, without learning the necessities of management, without becoming a good manager. At the same time, no manager will be able to cope with his or her responsibilities without incorporating the kind of leadership capacity described in previous sections.

Vaill (1991, p16) puts it this way: '... today's executives (managers) must be leaders. The precedence of leadership over management has never been more imperative than it is today. One can't simply "manage an existing system", for the unstable environment continually threatens to render any given structure and set of policies out of sync with its demands and opportunities. Under these conditions, a leadership model is far more appropriate than a managerial model. The leader constantly invents strategies that are intended to improve the systems adaptation to its present and future environment.'

Management is about controlling an existing system, while leadership is about invention and adaptation. Leadership is fluid, flexible, responsive, innovative; the image that arises is one of movement and change. Management, on the other hand, is about controlling movement through systems and procedures. It is slower, less mercurial, both static and continuous, more set in its ways. The image is one of stationary structure, a supportive framework.

Leadership is process; it is continually in motion. Management is the product of that process, as well as its saviour. Left to itself, movement would travel on into infinity and there would be no boundary, no brakes. Structure provides movement with a framework within which it can move without overreaching itself. Management grounds leadership by setting up and maintaining the systems that provide the organization with coherence, continuity and sense, with the weight required to prevent it from drifting off. Management is the organization's way of coping with the fact that leadership's head is always in the clouds.

Covey (1989) refers to the idea that all things are created twice. The first creation is a mental one, the second physical. He provides as an example the construction of a house. The first creation is the mental one, the design itself. The second is the putting together of the bricks and mortar, the construction itself. Leadership, in this sense, is the design, while management is the building. Leadership is the formative force, management the physical substance. Leadership is water; management is earth. Leadership is process, management is product.

It is incumbent on leadership to ensure that the organization is effective in what it does; that its strategies, and the way in which it gives effect to these, are appropriate and have impact. It is incumbent on management to ensure that the organization is efficient in what it does; that its internal systems function logically and smoothly. To put it simplistically, while leadership ensures that the organization does the right thing, management ensures that things are done right (see Table 29.1).

Management then, is about giving substance to organizational direction, and form to organizational needs. It is about setting up systems and procedures, controlling these systems and procedures so that they function optimally and are adhered to, and ensuring that the various systems and structures are articulated coherently.

Systems and procedures facilitate the smooth running of the organization. They provide a structure within which people can operate, and provide a measure of

Table 29.1 *The Major Differences Between Management and Leadership.*

Management	Leadership
Administers	Innovates
Focuses on systems	Focuses on people
Relies on control	Inspires trust
Short-range view	Long-range perspective
Asks how and when	Asks what and why
Eye on bottom-line	Eye on horizon
Imitates	Originates
Accepts status quo	Challenges status quo
Does things right	Does the right thing

equality in the sense that 'everyone is equal before the law'. The attempt of many organizations to develop a democratic organizational form is often interpreted as the need to allow each person full freedom, without accountability. But experience has shown that freedom without accountability leads to the 'law of the jungle' where the most powerful dominate all others. At the same time, excessive structure can lead to extreme forms of bureaucratic absurdity where people's creativity and motivation are stifled under the weight of inexorable and relentless systems and procedures. Balance is vital.

One of the main areas where the quest for balance is so important is the question of discipline and accountability. Here, management entails the establishment of performance standards and the measurement, evaluation and correction of performance. Systems and procedures need to be designed in order to ensure accountability and compliance. At the same time, such systems, once in place, should not be applied by rote. There is always a need to balance organizational and individual needs. When this is ignored, conflict and tension result. The setting up and monitoring of systems can be regarded as pure management. But adjustments of the system to respond to the ebb and flow of organizational and individual fluctuations demand leadership skills on the part of the manager.

Similarly, detailed organizational planning is a function that lies squarely in the hands of management. It includes the setting of objectives and schedules, and the development and control of budgets. It is absurd, however, to imagine that these plans and budgets will ever run like clockwork. Environments and people change, successful plans alter the conditions that lead to their success, and failed plans need to be evaluated and recast. The ability to look, from the outside, at the plans one has developed, rather than simply operating within them, is one of the leadership components of management, while the detailed creation and monitoring of those plans is one of the management components of leadership.

Some general principles that the manager may want to take note of are the following:

- People who are charged with the responsibility of accomplishing a given task must be given the necessary authority to carry it out.
- The number of people a manager carries responsibility for should be limited to the fewest possible under given circumstances to do the job effectively.
- Managers should attempt to delegate as many routine matters as possible, and in general decisions should be made at as low an organizational level as possible.
- Beware of dual accountability, where personnel are responsible to more than one person. In most modern organizations this is inevitable as strategies differentiate and programmes multiply, but one should be conscious of the dangers and try to ensure that multiple accountabilities are as coherent and transparent as possible, and that systems are set in place for their management.

It is also important to mention the special difficulties of management in a development or human service organization. First, production is not carried out on the shop floor, where it can be seen and monitored. Neither can production be quantified easily, as it can in many a commercial operation. On the contrary, production usually takes place outside of the organization itself, with communities, individuals and other organizations. Production is not easily quantified when the required outcome is the development of the client. And production is not under the control of staff or the organization when production means the facilitation of others' development. Results are as dependent on the client as the organizational practitioner.

In these conditions, managerial control needs to be exercised especially sensitively. Systems and procedures need to be set up which do not simply measure quantifiable results but which bring in – and facilitate discussion of – relevant information which will keep the organization conscious of the nuances of 'success' and 'failure', unanticipated consequences and early warning signals concerning the need to adapt strategies or skills. Where quantifiable results are only one part of the story it is particularly easy for management to fudge the issue or to lose control (and then sometimes to become dictatorial in compensation for doubt).

Second, supply and demand are separated. In commercial ventures, productivity and effectiveness are directly related to income. Not so with development or non-profit organizations, where the supply of financial resources is often not linked to effectiveness or impact. In other words, supply does not come from clients but from donors, and is therefore not (directly) linked to demand. This can lead to internal tension as different parts of the organization hold themselves accountable to different constituencies. It can also lead to despondency when effort goes unrewarded or to 'flabbiness' if the organization has more resources than it can utilize effectively.

Management often finds itself caught between the maintenance of systems and demands for system adaptation. This is not a problem that will disappear with time or with the well-managed organization. As with leadership, the need to keep on one's toes goes with the territory.

Self-Management: Exercise and Improvement

'Nothing can be done without solitude... It's very difficult nowadays to be alone because we all own watches. Have you ever seen a saint with a watch?' *Picasso*

Self-management is the basis for management, leadership and good organization. Good organization is unobtainable without competent leadership and management, and the ability to manage oneself is at the heart of competent leadership. In a way, if one can manage oneself, the rest of management follows as common sense.

The trick to learning self-management is often touted as the need to learn time-management. Time-management courses have become the ubiquitous quick-fix solution to the problems of self-management. And there is indeed much to learn from understanding the techniques in managing time as a useful adjunct to other efforts at self-mastery. But in and of themselves courses are inadequate and confuse the trainee by missing the point. It is, after all, not time which has to be managed, but oneself.

Having techniques at one's disposal does not imply that they will actually be adopted and used to one's own advantage, for the adoption of techniques implies a prior level of self-management expertise. Many people who have heard that the use of a diary is a basic prerequisite for adequate time management fail to use the diary precisely because they are lacking in the self-discipline required for self-management.

Self-management is not a technique, neither is it a set of techniques. While techniques will aid immeasurably, the essence of self-management is inner discipline, the honing of oneself so that one becomes an effective instrument in one's own hands.

Covey (1989) talks of three essential principles that form the basis of self-mastery:

Be proactive

The first principle is the basis for all others and reads simply 'Be proactive'. You will find the word 'proactive' sprinkled through most books and courses on organization, management and leadership. In order to be effective, you must take charge, exert your will, act preemptively, anticipate and work ahead of events.

To be proactive means more than simply taking the initiative. It means that we are responsible for our own lives. It means that we do not regard ourselves as determined by outer conditions; rather that our behaviour is a function of our decisions, not our conditions. You may recall that this was, in fact, the way in which this chapter started. I stated at the outset that the leader is one who does not accept the limitations of a 'given' situation or set of circumstances, but acts to transform such constraints into new realities. The principles of self-management begin, appropriately enough, in the same way.

There is an old adage that says 'For he (sic) who thinks the problem is out there, that thinking is the problem'. The point is that unless you take responsibility you cannot change anything. Ultimately, the only person over whom you have any kind of control is yourself. Change yourself. Recognize your responsibility (meaning that you have the ability to choose your response). Do not blame circumstances, conditions or conditioning for your behaviour.

Begin with the end in mind

Beginning with the end in mind is a direct corollary of this first principle. Once you have accepted the need to act on the basis of your own responsibility and to take charge of your future, the second task is to visualize that future. In other words, you need an 'end' to move towards, a goal to guide your planning, a star to navigate by. And this star or goal or end is not given to you; you need to create it yourself.

Beginning with the end in mind implies imagination, the ability to conceive a future 'state' which does not yet exist. You need to project yourself out there, into the future; to take it in hand, to look backwards from that vantage point to where you are now so that you can see what needs to be done to get there. Beginning with the end in mind is the first step in planning; it is the goal towards which planning is directed.

The precise 'end' with which you will begin will differ from person to person and situation to situation. Some people, at certain stages of their life, may want to visualize what they would like to have achieved by the time they die, and thereby begin to plan their life-circumstances around this end. This may imply major life changes. One can also visualize a goal that is much closer and part of one's current life-circumstances. For example, if you have just taken over leadership of a problematic organization, it will help to get beyond current reactive attempts at crisis management if you visualize what the organization will look like when you have succeeded in transforming it. You can then work backwards from this vision into the steps needed to achieve it, and thus into concrete planning.

Take an interim period ahead of you; one or two or five years, depending on how far ahead you feel you can see. Visualize what you would like to have achieved by then – as leader and manager, and perhaps also, if you wish, on a more personal level. Write this down as a personal mission statement, your guiding light. Then, look at all the major areas in which something would have to be achieved in order to realize the overall mission. Write a goal statement for each of these areas. Once you have done this, you will feel as you are in control, that you are being responsible and proactive, and that you are able to plan constructively.

Put first things first

This principle takes up where the other two finish. Once we have accepted that we are responsible and have visualized the end to which we will work, we then need to plan. Putting first things first is a means of prioritising and sequencing activities and objectives, and lies at the heart of planning. 'Plan tomorrow today; plan next week this week; plan next month this month and next year this year.' What this practice implies is the prioritization of the planning process itself. Planning takes time, and so is often shelved. Yet we do so at our peril or at least at the peril of self-management.

With the two principles outlined previously we have the belief that we can choose a future, as well as a picture of what that future is. The current principle takes it one step further and demands that you plan for that future, for that choice, in detail. Planning is an integral part of self-management, one of its cornerstones. Planning involves taking a goal towards which one is aiming and inquiring as to the individual steps that are necessary to achieve this goal. And then sequencing these steps in terms of time and consequence – putting first things first.

Nevertheless, as much as you may plan, it helps to plan in time for the unexpected demand, the suddenly changed situation. It is when confronted with these uncertainties that many managers crumble and go back to reactive management, continually fighting fires and complaining that nothing stands still long enough to take it in hand.

Putting first things first means that, in spite of what is coming towards us, we will choose how and to what we will respond. We will not simply react, losing our heads and doing whatever seems most urgent. This is crisis management and is supremely ineffectual. We need to choose what is most important, and prioritize and sequence accordingly. This needs a cool head, but it also needs understanding of the underlying principle and commitment to it.

References

Camus, A (1983) *The Fall*, Harmondsworth, Penguin.
Covey, S (1989) *The Seven Habits of Highly Effective People*, New York, Simon & Schuster.
De Pree, M (1989) *Leadership is an Art*, New York, Doubleday.
Heider, J (1988) *Tao of Leadership*, London, Bantam Books.

I Ching (trans Richard Wilhelm) (1971) London, Routledge & Kegan Paul.

Johnson, R (1991) *Owning Your Own Shadow*, San Francisco, Harper.

Kaplan, A (1994) *NGOs, Civil Society and Capacity Building: Towards the Development of Strategy*, Durban, Olive Information Service, AVOCADO Series, May.

Lievegoed, B (1978) *Forming Curative Communities*, London, Rudolf Steiner Press.

Lievegoed, B (1981) Informal lecture.

Msoki, M (1994) '"Organizational revitalisation": toward a greater understanding of strategy formulation and the complexities that underly the process', Cape Town, Community Development Resource Association, Working Paper (unpublished).

Palmer, P (1990) Paper delivered by Parker Palmer at the annual celebration dinner of the Indiana office for campus ministeries (unpublished).

Vaill, P (1991) *Managing as a Performing Art*, San Francisco, Jossey-Bass Publishers.

Yarborough, E (1985) 'Making peace with yourself' in N Wollman (ed) *Working for Peace*, San Luis Obispo, Impact.

30

Human Resource Management

Alan Fowler

Human resource management (HRM) is an important function of non-government development organizations (NGDOs). It should not be located in one place – the personnel department – but instead be part and parcel of recognizing and utilizing people's competencies: a task of managers everywhere.[1] HRM is not just about the technical functions of personnel management. It is an approach that sees people as a key resource rather than as a unit of production.[2] Our first concern is to set a framework linking personnel management with NGDOs' overall aims, and to look at some of the key things the HRM has to get right in order for people to be effective. This focuses on: motivation and incentives; the competencies and formation of front-line staff who provide the interface to primary stakeholders; the role of expatriate technical assistance and processes of bringing the right people into the organization and helping to build their personal capabilities.

Linking Human Resource Management to NGDO Work

The requirements for HRM flow out of an NGDO's overall mission. Figure 30.1 is the 'flow' used by an international NGDO to work out what human resources it needs to implement in a new country strategy, recognizing that the existing situation already provides a foundation for human resources.

Human resource needs are defined in terms of competencies – that is, the skills, knowledge, attitudes and values needed to do the various tasks of translating vision into action. It is the gap between what is available and what is required. While strategic planning assesses longer-term needs, any learning organization is constantly making this assessment and investing in individual improvements. Human resource management is fed by and responds to this ongoing identification of needs, and the performance and potential of existing staff and volunteers. While leaders/managers are involved in this process and can set the motivational tone, they face particular problems in getting the mix of incentives right. Why is this so?

Managing the Mix of Motivation and Incentives

In NGDOs, the leaders/managers have tasks to fulfil beyond those of internal routines – sometimes called the bureaucratic hygiene – and project management.[3] In terms of motivation, it is most important to satisfy the psychological needs of staff, helping them to constructively relate to others inside and outside the organization. NGDOs predominantly 'relate' to communities rather than produce products, and the abiding stress on partnerships, and now on alliances, coalitions and networks, signals the deep-lying significance of relationships to NGDOs' subconscious life and needs.[4]

The style that leaders/managers employ in going about maintaining their own relationships – through consultation, dialogue, listening, and joint reflection – are an important source of motivation for others. However, psychological motivation does not put bread on the table – material incentives and working conditions also play their part in people's attitudes to doing what is expected of them. In the early years of NGDO activity, financial incentives were supposed to be offset by the moral reward of contributing to social change. The extent to which this really reflected the situation throughout the world is open to question, especially in the resource-poor South where cultural norms express service to others in different ways. Whatever the case, things are different today.

Becoming more businesslike and market-oriented in the 1990s affects NGDO incentives by making financial rewards more significant for retaining and motivating staff. In addition, the predatory behaviour of official aid agencies is also altering the incentive pattern of NGDOs.

The pro-NGDO policies of the intergovernmental aid system are leading to an escalation in the market value of experienced NGDO staff. The situation is especially acute in heavily aid-dependent countries with a small NGDO community, such as Tanzania and Nepal.[5] With political pressure to disburse more funds through the second and third sectors, official aid agencies offering relatively high salaries and sometimes hard-currency, tax-free payments, are absorbing some of the most capable NGDO people.[6] In this way the thinking and implementation capacity of the sector may be weakened; as a result, a serious imbalance may emerge when it comes to civic-policy influencing, interfacing with government in general, and in collaborative undertakings where NGDOs end up the weakest partner.

In addition to contracting their services, donor absorption of NGDO personnel tilts the NGDO ethos away from moral commitment towards material reward, which may in the long run throw the developmental child away with the aid bath-water. Leaders/managers face serious dilemmas in striking the appropriate balance between tangible and intangible incentives in their organizations. While trends are similar across the world, I have not come across any rules-of-thumb to help with solutions; the choices being made are situation-specific. It is worthwhile highlighting, however, the requirements of community change agents (CAs), as this is a central issue in human resource management for NGDOs.

Human Resource Management and the Crucial Role of Change Agents

NGDO leaders/managers have little effect without followers. In operational NGDOs, the most important followers are those furthest away, who are out on the organizational periphery and working as community change agents. What can leaders/managers

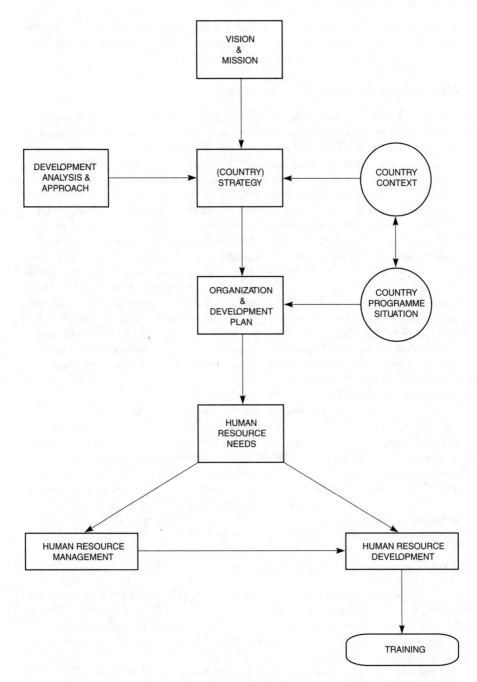

Figure 30.1 *Human Resource Management in the Context of NGDO Work*

do so that these followers become the centre of the organization rather than remain on its edge? The answers are: select properly; 'form' appropriately; and then empower organizationally. What does this mean in practice?

Recruiting insiders or outsiders?

CAs are catalysts of people's development action; this often requires comparative experience. But an effective catalyst also requires deep insight into the community in question, as well as trust and acceptance by them. Do you recruit therefore from within the community or bring someone from outside? Opinions differ. Outsiders must climb steep learning curves and go through a usually long process of gaining local acceptance, which can be helped or hindered by existing cultural prejudices. In addition, working away from home ties external CAs more to the NGDO and its intentions than to the community. Insiders obviously have local insight but may find local credibility difficult if they take on a new role, especially if linked to external resources where personal commitment to the common good may be overridden by personal reward.[7] Furthermore, because insiders remain within their group, sharing the NGDO vision, mission and identity is likely to be weaker. On balance, it seems that CAs coming from outside the community are probably more appropriate.[8] Though not without its dangers, community members who are potential CAs have more to contribute through their actions in community-based organizations (CBOs) than on the NGDO payroll. As Umtali[9] points out: 'We need a new breed of change agents who, first and foremost, care for people as human beings, who treat them as subjects and not objects or recipients of change, who steep themselves in the aspirations, problems and wisdom of the people.'

If a CA's stance towards poor people is wrong, their technical skill and knowledge will seldom be sufficient compensation. Key personality traits which make up the needed stance include: patience, a habit of listening rather than talking, interpersonal sensitivity, teamwork, self-confidence without arrogance, empathy, commitment, respectfulness, diplomacy and perseverance. Skills in communication are vital, as is an ability to analyse and diagnose events. Gender, age and socioeconomic standing are additional criteria to be applied, all directed at gaining community trust and fulfilling two roles, initially as facilitator of group awareness and then as adviser or consultant on the changes people want for themselves.

The 'forming' of change agents

A crucial task of human resource development (HRD) is to form CAs. The word 'forming' is used instead of training in order to stress that CAs become effective by learning through experience – that is, reflecting on what they have been through, rather than by classroom instruction. Too often, NGDOs place CAs on courses which do not engage them in real-life situations. How this can be done differently is covered in detail in a book by Stan Burkey.[10] Transactional analysis (TA), DELTA Training[11] and participatory rural appraisal (PRA), are types of orientation for CAs which lend themselves to action-based learning. The preferred approach, however, is not to treat these simply as techniques, but to sequence them as different practical engagements which, together, cover the whole process of sustainable development.

Each exposure should be followed by opportunities for dialogue, reflection and self-criticism. It is important that after initial forming, or after learning new skills, the organization matches up to what has been acquired.

Depending on individual motivation, mismatches between participatory methods and non-participatory organizational culture can lead to frustration, cynicism or apathy, which undermine commitment and reduce the moral reward. A feeling of voicelessness in NGDOs will become apparent in a CA's work with communities. In the words of one CA, 'If you are not being heard, why listen?'. The life of a CA then becomes one of earning a living first. Effective NGDOs take steps to stop this happening. One step is organizational empowerment, described below. In addition, time is created for CAs, staff and volunteers to discuss their situation and concerns within a team setting; new ideas are sought or introduced through a bottom-up approach; staff are systematically included in organizational consultations and invited to come up with proposals; income differentials between authority levels are modest, reflecting a CA's comparative value to the organization; and there is a system which gives everyone a formal input – though not necessarily formal control – over organizational policy and practice. Committees are one frequent approach; representation in the governance structure which to common in Latin America, is another.

The third step: organizational empowerment

The crux of empowerment for change agents is having the authority to make decisions with communities. This should not be in a strategic vacuum, of course, and not without negotiated performance criteria, but the necessary power and trust must be present.[12] In any case, systems for achieving this are a necessary but not sufficient condition. A more important, subtle element of empowerment lies in a leader's/manager's conviction that the NGDO values social justice, not just for its primary stakeholders but also for its staff. The more confidence that CAs have in the way management reaches and implements decisions affecting them, the less likely they are to misuse the trust they are given, which in turn strengthens management confidence in sharing authority. This is where internal transparency is vital. Promises made are seen to be kept, consultation is treated seriously and moral principles are consistently applied.

The element of staff confidence in management is, in fact, important for all staff and takes on added dimensions when expatriates are involved. HRM must therefore be sensitive to this dimension too.

HRM and NGDO Expatriates: Yes or No? Where and When?

The official aid system has reached the conclusion that expatriate technical cooperation has been a very expensive failure; however, it seems unable to kick the habit.[13] Are NGDO expatriates appropriate? Expatriates are still commonly recruited to work in foreign countries for Northern NGDOs, or for local NGDOs who request expertise they cannot find or afford. The circumstances under which this happens are often far from straightforward, with implicit as well as explicit agendas in play. This section looks at expatriates as a human resource and the dilemmas this poses for the giver, the recipient and expatriates themselves.

When to use expatriates

> The justification for employing expatriates in [supporting] operational work is mostly unconvincing. Northerners' skills, knowledge, and ability to represent the poor have been over-rated, while Southerners' incompetence, vulnerability to corruption, and lack of concern for the poor are usually exaggerated.[14]

This is the first paragraph in Emma Crewe's analysis of factors associated with NGDO expatriates. Her conclusion is to choose insiders – that is, country nationals, whenever possible. This principle is consistent with development goals of building and using local capacity, and reduces time and costs associated with gaining local knowledge and local acceptance. Given the short-term contract nature of expatriate appointments, local people can also provide greater continuity and greater investment in the South as their remuneration is not repatriated. What situations, therefore, can justify an expatriate from the North or from the South?

- Skills are not available and a gap needs to be filled while training is provided by a local person.
- There is a need for confidence-building and communication with the donor in the short term.
- An exchange of mutual learning and breaking down of stereotypical views between North, South and East are required.
- If comparative experience is needed, expatriates may contribute to reduced learning time and capitalization on investments in outside knowledge.
- There is a recognized, valid need for the challenging inputs that expatriates can bring.

To these reasons can be added less justifiable, but nevertheless more common, justifications for expatriates being chosen, especially for management positions. These are to:

- act as 'impartial' gatekeepers for resources;
- ensure that organizational concerns are fully respected and taken care of;
- ensure cross-country consistency with interpretations of organizational mission and policies;
- promote the organization's national identity (fulfilling a tacit expectation, if not formal condition, of bilateral donors).

Underlying the first three of these justifications is the notion that because expatriates are in a foreign setting and externally dependent, their primary allegiance will be to the international NGDO, and thereafter to the country of work and its people. In other words, it boils down to a higher probability that in unpredictable situations the individual can be trusted to act consistently with the NGDO's best interests.

A number of international NGDOs are fully conscious of the inconsistency in development principles which this belief introduces. HRM strategies have therefore been adopted by some NGDOs to reduce this often unspoken, but nonetheless common, preference for expatriates in the South and East. Their laudable objective is to reach a situation where degree of trust has nothing to do with country of origin. This is, however, a tall order given that trust is culturally preconditioned; differences are usually trusted less.

While certainly no panacea for establishing trust, acknowledging the importance of building personal affinity with the organizational culture is a step in the right direction.

Personal allegiance: expatriate moral dilemmas

Expatriates are not always imposed on an NGDO. Often Southern and Eastern NGDOs see the merits of an outsider who will bring useful skills, insights on how the North works, contacts for fund-raising, and who, importantly, are free – someone else pays. This is usually the case with volunteers. But even though the expatriate is requested, problems can still arise. Typical of such problems are: dual allegiance to the NGDO and to the sending organization, especially if financial resources are involved as well; and value differences which may be of an unconscious racial nature.

In North Tanzania, a local NGDO had been struggling to raise funds for work with poor urban communities. Every dialogue with donors led to adjustments away from what was originally intended and closer to donor priorities. To assist in fund-raising, the NGDO applied for and obtained a Danish volunteer. So successful were her efforts in helping to draft and send out proposals that eventually two donors approved assistance for the same project. For the NGDO's management, this was a windfall which could be used for what it saw to be really necessary, the 'donor' project being implemented as well. For the volunteer, this stance was dishonest and after repeatedly asking the NGDO's director to be open about dual funding, which he refused to do, she informed donors of the duplication, and was promptly sacked. What went wrong?

The past ten years have seen a growing trend to couple funds to volunteers and other NGDO expatriates, which can only increase the moral dilemmas they face. The expatriates' induction process can partly address this problem by analysing typical situations which call for moral choices.

Yet again, these steps do not guarantee that no friction will occur, only that the 'rules of the game' are established from the outset.

Expatriate appointments in local NGDOs are usually accompanied by a plan to build local 'counterpart' capacity. There are other ways of doing so, and this is where HRM moves to HRD – that is, specific initiatives to improve the competencies of staff and volunteers.

The existing strategies to best utilize and trust expatriates are:

- make a clear distinction between national and international posts;
- employ conditions of service which are equitable for Northern and Southern expatriates and which do not penalize a national who applies for an international post in his own country;

- pay significant attention to selection on the basis of personal values and beliefs, as well as professional competencies, including an assessment of ability to deal with moral dilemmas;
- put much effort into induction, not simply concentrating on operational procedures and manuals, but also exposing and exploring organizational culture.

This is done by:

- integrating strategies with internal policy discussions, where dilemmas are laid on the table and critical trade-offs made;
- interacting with Northern constituencies in order to understand their socio-economic profile and expectations;
- meeting with some board members to understand their perspectives and thinking;
- talking through likely practical issues that require on-the-spot personal judgement, such as dealing with political pressures and irresponsible staff behaviour;
- mapping and comparing individual and organizational cultural norms and mores.[15]

In addition, agencies can and are doing the following:

- Before recruitment, be up front with the collaborating organization about whether or not the volunteer is under an obligation to report to the agency; in other words, are they expected to have a direct line of communication? The preferred situation is one of primary allegiance to the host organization.
- Agree from the outset how any irreconcilable differences will be signalled and arbitrated, preferably bringing in a mutually respected third party.
- Indicate the degree to which financial resources are or are not coupled to the presence of an expatriate.

Human Resource Development

HRD is a label covering a wide range of activities which should lead to better capabilities and hence effectiveness of staff.[16] This section summarizes the types of HRD which leaders/managers can chose from, then relates them to different types of staff commonly found in operational NGDOs.

Types of HRD

There are eight distinctive types of HRD available to NGDOs. They can all be considered as forms of training understood as a time-bound process which results in individuals acquiring the appropriate values, attitudes, skills and knowledge required to improve their performance in relation to the organization's mission. The eight include the following:

- *Internally designed courses:* training events designed specifically for the NGDO and therefore tailored to its needs. They are cost-effective when a large number of people need to learn the same things.

- *Pre-packaged courses* (local and foreign): pre-packaged events whose content is sufficiently similar to the needs of the individual, though per capita costs remain high.
- *Workshops:* 'output-oriented' gatherings, which are useful for solving a particular problem, especially where joint ownership is needed.
- *Seminars/conferences:* provide an exposure to issues or people, network information, create relationships and facilitate individual broadening or insights.
- *On-the job training:* a method of practically exchanging expertise between one person and another. It is suitable where it is difficult to release staff, the tasks involved are technical or routine, or where detailed observation is needed to ensure that competence has been gained.
- *Exchanges:* tend to be short-term visits to gain an understanding of other ways of doing things, to see innovations, to gain new ideas and horizons, and to introduce new staff.
- *Secondment:* normally involves someone taking on a known role in a different setting, with training in mind. Secondments can help people to do old things in new ways as they adapt to other circumstances.
- *Self-study/correspondence courses:* systematic ways of gathering knowledge for an individual, sometimes accompanied by group work with others doing the same study. They are often chosen where access is difficult, the topic specialized, there is no urgency and where a recognized qualification is required but course attendance is not an option.

Each of these methods has different costs and benefits and are more suited to some types of staff than others, depending on their personal career trajectory.

Categories of NGDO staff

There are no standardized job types or cadres in NGDOs to use as a point of reference. Therefore, the following five types of staff are used (see Table 30.1); they would need to be translated into categories which make sense to each organization.

Table 30.2 brings together the eight types of HRD and the five cadres of NGDO staff, and assesses the relative merits of the relationship between each in relation to costs and benefits and strengths and weaknesses. Where internal HRD is not an option, HRM needs to competently deal with the process of finding and bringing new personnel into the organization. What this involves comprises our concluding topic.

Recruiting New Staff

There are four stages to bringing new staff on board so that they find their place and function effectively. The stages of new recruitment are: specifying the job, notifying the pool of people available, selecting an individual, and induction into the NGDO's processes.

Table 30.1 *Types of NGDO staff*

Category	Sample description
Change agent: (community development worker, community organizer, extension officer)	Task is to work directly with the primary stakeholders as catalyst, facilitator, information source, adviser.
Technical specialist: (sector specialist, technical officer, communications/ information officer, fund-raiser; HRM, HRD staff)	Provide technical support to change agents, learning from field operations; problem-solver, trouble-shooter; technical liaison to similar people in other agencies; lobby and advocacy work in area of expertise.
Administrative/support staff: (accounting, purchasing, transport, audit, documentation)	Provide non-programme/project services to CAs, specialist staff and all management levels.
First-line manager: (field supervisor, field coordinator)	Provide direct functional support and guidance to the work of CAs, dealing with daily problems.
Middle manager: (branch manager, zone manager, area manager)	Carry direct responsibility and authority for staff and costs in all programme operations and performance.
Senior managers: (chief executive, executive director programme, finance, research, marketing directors)	Carry authority and responsibility for strategy, performance and learning in programmes and across the organization as a whole, with accountability to the governing body.

Person specifications

In order to begin a recruitment process a specification needs to be checked to see if it is consistent with the requirements of the organizational plan. The specification sets out the primary tasks, authority and responsibility associated with the job; the minimum specifications in terms of skill, knowledge, attitude and values; the position in the organization; cultural requirements; religious requirements; any trends/growth/changes envisaged in the future; the expected duration of contract; formal education; budget/salary scales and applicable limits; the location of work; and, any salient points to be borne in mind during advertising and selection – for example, if a particular gender, nationality, age or experience is sought. The specification is the basis for the advertisement and recruitment exercise.

Notification and identification

The conditions affecting recruitment vary from country to country as does the (NGO) pool in which recruitment is to take place. The first assessment to be made is whether the person specification is likely to be satisfied locally. If this is thought unlikely, advertising abroad can be considered. If both local and foreign advertising takes place, it is important to ensure consistency and not, for example, demand more years of experience in local than in international advertisements, which does occur.

Advertisements can also test the arena, to determine if local recruitment is likely or if the specification is realistic. Comparisons can also be made with other similar organizations to check on the appropriateness of salary levels versus qualifications. Identification of potential candidates is also frequently done by informal networking, poaching and direct head-hunting. Personnel recruitment bureaux can also be used if the NGDO wishes to avoid some of the pressures normally associated with recruiting in politicized environments where there is mass unemployment.

Selection

The selection process is likely to vary with the cadre concerned. Only some general pointers can be given therefore. These are:

- the selection process should identify a candidate's *potential* as well as their ability to satisfy the specification;
- fairness is more apparent if the process is transparent, requiring good public communication;
- interviewing should be both structured and open-ended and can involve both group and individual encounters;
- testing should be both job-specific and generic – for example, to assess judgement, discretion, decision-making capability, values and attitudes;
- references, when sought, should be both verbal and written;
- (early) life histories can be important sources for indicating potential;
- independent assessors can offer a beneficial comparative view of candidates.

Induction into the organization

Like selection, the induction process will usually differ between cadres. When designing induction, background information should be provided, such as:

- documentation on the NGDO as a whole;
- details on the strategy and programme being run;
- personnel policies and conditions of service;
- a collation of any policies that have been approved by the board;
- a document explaining the NGDO's development approach.

For international NGDOs, some of the documents can best be produced to serve the whole organization; others need to be tailor-made by each country. In addition, induction could involve:

Table 30.2 Applying HRD Methods to NGO Cadres

Cadre \\ Method	Internal courses	Packaged courses	Workshops	Seminars/ conferences	On-the-job training	Exchanges (visits)	Secondment	Self-study
Change agents (CAs)	cost effective; relevant; highly recommended	suited for specialist technical areas; proven utility; relevance may be a problem	team building; for experienced staff; skilled facilitator vital; good to generate knowledge from experience	good for local level interagency sharing	practical orientation; suited to induction and orientation; good for special skill development	suited to local level interagency		requires motivation and commitment; may help identify high performer; requires an agency policy
Junior and intermediate managers	good for specific organizational systems; high cost if numbers low or irregular; adaptation of external courses recommended	ditto	good for problem-solving; good to develop horizontal linkages; good for cadre strengthening	provides exposure and broadening; less suited for junior management except local-level interagency		usually relevant and useful; recommended	use only very selectively	ditto
Senior/top managers	ditto	ditto	ditto; highly recommended	builds networking; provides exposure and broadening; important for policy development and conceptual issues	limited application	useful for policy exchange and strategic development	recommended where suitable opportunities exist	

Cadre	*Method* *Internal courses*	*Packaged courses*	*Workshops*	*Seminars/ conferences*	*On-the-job training*	*Exchanges (visits)*	*Secondment*	*Self-study*
Technical specialists	suited for specialist team development	ditto	as for junior and intermediate managers	ditto; highly recommended	ditto	useful and relevant; recommended	ditto	ditto; helps keep abreast with specialist knowledge
Administration and programme support	relevant but normally of limited application	relevant to professional development	useful within departments	important for internal information sharing	ditto	useful within country programmes	limited application	as for CAs
All cadres	good for addressing specific issues	suited to specialist technical areas	encourages reflection and participation; good for organization-building; skilled facilitator vital	information sharing	suited to orientation and induction	good for developing ideas and learning techniques	case-by-case decision	requires individual motivation; needs a country policy on support

- a meeting with key staff;
- training in participatory planning and resource-appraisal methods;
- assigning a mentor for two to three months;
- visiting selected programmes or development initiatives;
- specific upgrading in specialized skills or procedures.

An important outcome of the induction period is that the new staff member understands the NGDO as a development agency, identifies with what the organization stands for and is trying to achieve, and can explain this when relating to the outside world.

Notes

1 A new field in HRM for some NGDOs emerges from their work on complex humanitarian emergencies (CHE). Increasingly, NGDOs must deal with trauma and psychological stress experienced by staff working in CHEs where their 'neutrality' rests on a knife edge. Providing an adequate psychosocial support system must now be added to the HRM repertoire.
2 For an introduction to HRM, see McKenna and Beach, 1995.
3 Bureaucratic hygiene is the boring but necessary routine tasks which keep the organization 'clean' and healthy. Typically, these include filing documents, timely response to correspondence, regular staff appraisals, the discipline of accounting and donor reporting, and so on.
4 Organizational psychology applies psychological insights to understand how groups behave. Basic psychological features, such as the need for respect, avoidance of fear and anxiety, aggression, dependency and so on, steer people towards or away from particular types of organizations. NGOs, governments and business offer different sorts of solutions to psychological predispositions and needs. The state sector provides authority and strong leadership which may satisfy a person's need for security and dependency. Business and the market can satisfy needs for aggression towards, or flight from, enemies. The third sector offers association and 'pairing', satisfying the need for an ideal relationship, human solidarity and oneness.
5 The mechanism of buying competent people out of NGDOs into the official aid system is creating an unhealthy upward spiral in NGDO costs because they have to compete to retain or attract people who can do the work that donors expect with the necessary quality. In turn, donors must pay more to attract NGDO people, and so it goes on.
6 Where economies are collapsing, who can take issue with an individual choosing for the means to educate children and build up reserves?
7 Constantino-David, 1995, p156. This article is a good examination of the trade-offs between internal-external community organizers.
8 Burkey, 1993, p73–83.
9 Umtali, quoted in Burkey, op cit, p76.

10 For a survey of training in participatory development approaches, see IIED, 1994b.
11 DELTA is Development Education and Leadership Training for Action, which uses a neo-Freirian approach to community mobilization. See Hope and Timmel, 1984.
12 Empowerment of staff is a prevailing concern, or fashion, with the Western business world. The trust which this involves is, however, difficult to cultivate when career guarantees turn out to be worthless because of down-sizing. Too much trust can also lead to bankruptcy as it did with Tim Leason and Barings Bank.
13 See Berg, 1994, and further readings. The widely acknowledged failure of technical assistance has still not led to necessary changes in donor behaviour. Under the headline 'Reliance on overseas experts decried', it was pointed out by the World Bank representative in Nairobi that spending on technical cooperation in some African countries has exceeded wage bills of the entire civil service. It was questioned whether such spending had produced commensurate returns. The conference at which this took place agreed that it had not. Reported in *The Daily Nation*, 19 January 1996. Technical cooperation is probably one of the most lamentable shortcomings and wastes in international aid.
14 Crewe, 1994, p1.
15 Organizational induction to NGDOs is usually a sorry, hurried affair. Culture, ritual and language are all to be learnt by exposure to the job, hopefully before the project ends or the contract is over.
16 This section draws on a study commissioned by ActionAid UK.

References

Berg, E (1994) *Improving Technical Cooperation: Some Key Issues*, OECD, Paris.
Burkey, S (1993) *People First: A Guide to Self-Reliant, Particatory Development*, Zed Press, London.
Constantino-David, K (1995) 'Community Organizing in the Philippines: The Experience of Development NGOs', in G Craig and M Mayo (eds) *Community Empowerment: A Reader in Participation and Development*, Sage, London.
Crewe, E (1994) *Expatriates Working for Sustainability*, School of African and Asian Studies, University of Sussex.
Darlington, T (1989) 'Management learning and voluntary organizations', Discussion Document, No 1, The Management Unit, National Council for Voluntary Organizations, London.
Hope, A and Timmel, S (1984) *Training for Transformation*, Vol 1–3, Mambo Press, Gweru.
IIED (1994) Special Issue on Training, *RRA Notes*, No 19, International Institute for Environment and Development, London.
McKenna, E and Beech, N (1995) *The Essence of Human Resource Management*, Prentice Hall, London.

Index